Eighth Edition

CULTURAL ANTHROPOLOGY

*Spanish - parago
english - read*

Carol R. Ember ▼ *Melvin Ember*

Hunter College of the City of New York
Human Relations Area Files

Human Relations Area Files

Prentice Hall, Upper Saddle River, New Jersey 07458

Library of Congress Cataloging–in–Publication Data

Ember, Carol R.
   Cultural anthropology / Carol R. Ember and Melvin Ember. — 8th ed.
      p.   cm.
   Includes bibliographical references and index.
   ISBN 0-13-346552-7 (pbk.)
   1. Ethnology.   I. Ember, Melvin.   II. Title.
GN316.E45   1996
   306—dc20   95–4831
                                                            CIP

Editorial/production supervisor: Joan E. Foley
Acquisitions editor: Nancy Roberts
Editorial assistant: Pat Naturale
Marketing manager: Kris Kleinsmith
Copy editor: Margo Quinto
Permissions specialist: Mary Helen Fitzgerald
Creative design director: Leslie Osher
Art director: Anne Bonanno Nieglos
Interior and cover designer: Donna Wickes
Illustrator: Mirella Signoretto
Cover art: Diego Rivera, "Tarascan Civilization: Dying of Fabrics," 1942.
   National Palace, Mexico City, Mexico. Giraudon/Art Resource.
Photo editor: Lorinda Morris-Nantz
Photo researcher: Suzanne Skloot
Buyer: Mary Ann Gloriande

© 1996, 1993, 1990, 1988, 1985, 1981, 1977, 1973 by Prentice-Hall, Inc.
Simon & Schuster/A Viacom Company
Upper Saddle River, New Jersey 07458

Printed in the United States of America

10   9   8   7   6   5   4   3   2   1

ISBN 0-13-346552-7

Prentice-Hall International (UK) Limited, *London*
Prentice-Hall of Australia Pty. Limited, *Sydney*
Prentice-Hall Canada Inc., *Toronto*
Prentice-Hall Hispanoamericana, S.A., *Mexico*
Prentice-Hall of India Private Limited, *New Delhi*
Prentice-Hall of Japan, Inc., *Tokyo*
Simon & Schuster Asia Pte. Ltd., *Singapore*
Editora Prentice-Hall do Brasil, Ltda., *Rio de Janeiro*

Contents

Boxes

Current Issues

New Perspectives on Gender

Research Frontiers

Preface

This edition is our biggest revision to date. In addition to updating all the chapters and responding to suggestions from reviewers, we have added new features to each chapter. The most significant one is that each chapter now has two featured boxes highlighting recent developments in the news as well as in anthropology and related disciplines. The boxes deal with three kinds of topic: current issues, research frontiers, and new perspectives on gender. We discuss the new boxes in some detail below. Then we list many of the other things that are new in each chapter. Many of the graphics in the book are new also.

As always, the book goes beyond description. We are interested not only in *what* humans were and are like; we are also interested in *why* humans are the way they are, why they got to be that way, and why they vary. When there are alternative explanations, we try to communicate the necessity to evaluate them both on logical grounds and on the basis of the available evidence. The chapter titled "Explanation and Evidence" is designed to help students distinguish between theory and evidence and to see how explanations can be and have been tested. Throughout the book, we note when the available evidence is not clear or is still lacking. We will be pleased if we succeed in helping students understand that no idea, including ideas put forward in textbooks, should be accepted simply as authority.

NEW FEATURES

Boxes in Each Chapter

"Current Issues" deal with topics students may have heard about in the news (examples: the increase in single-parent families, deforestation of the Amazon) or topics that are currently the subject of debate in the profession (examples: science versus humanism, human rights and cultural relativity).

"Research Frontiers" include a look at researchers at work or an in-depth look at new research or a research controversy (examples: love, intimacy, and sexual jealousy; the universality of emotions expressed in masks).

"New Perspectives on Gender" involve issues pertaining to sex and gender, both in anthropology and everyday life (examples: sexism in language, separate women's associations and women's status and power, morality in women versus men).

Glossary Terms at the End of Each Chapter

At the end of each chapter we list the new terms that have been introduced. (These terms were identified by boldface type and defined in the text.) We deliberately do not repeat the definitions at the end of the chapter to allow students to test themselves against the definitions provided in the glossary at the end of the book.

Critical Questions at the End of Each Chapter

We also provide three or four questions at the end of each chapter that may stimulate thinking about the implications of the chapter. The questions do not ask for repetition of what is in the text; we want students to extrapolate, to imagine, beyond what we know or think we know.

HIGHLIGHTS OF WHAT IS NEW IN THIS EDITION

▼

Chapter 1 (What Is Anthropology?). We have added a new section on applied anthropology as a subfield and revised our Figure 1-1 to indicate that applied anthropology draws on people from all areas of anthropology. We have also added a new section on specialization within ethnology by region, subject matter, and theoretical orientation. Using medical anthropology as an example, we show how new specialties in ethnology are related to other subfields of anthropology as well as to other disciplines. The boxes in this chapter focus on two researchers at work, an archaeologist and an ethnologist.

Chapter 2 (The Concept of Culture). A box on human rights asks whether the Western countries are ethnocentric with regard to ideas about human rights. Our second box discusses the idea that "good" anthropology makes "the familiar strange, and the strange familiar."

Chapter 3 (Schools of Thought). Our first box discusses how the prominence of a few women in the early years of anthropology in the U.S. probably encouraged women to enter the field in large numbers. The second box uses a research question about the Abelam of New Guinea to illustrate how different theoretical orientations suggest different types of answers.

Chapter 4 (Explanation and Evidence). The first box in this chapter explores the differences between scientific and humanistic understanding and points out that the different approaches are not really incompatible. In the second box, we have two purposes. One is to give a feeling for the experience of fieldwork; the second is to use the Mead-Freeman controversy to explore the issue of how we can know that an ethnographer was accurate. We have considerably expanded our discussion of fieldwork and participant observation in the section on ethnography. We have also added a section on within-culture comparisons.

Chapter 5 (Communication and Language). The first box deals with the problem of language extinction and what some anthropologists are doing about it. To stimulate thinking about the possible impact of language on thought, we ask in the second box whether the English language promotes sexist

thinking and we refer to new research on the subject. We have expanded and revised the sections on social status and speech and on gender differences in speech. An entirely new section is devoted to multilingualism and code-switching.

Chapter 6 (Getting Food). Many of our examples now refer to recent ethnography. For instance, we refer to recent work on the Inupiaq of Northern Alaska and the Yanomamö. And instead of describing a society as of the ethnographic present, we have added newer material where possible to show how the culture has changed. We were able to do this with the Australian aborigines, the Inupiaq, and the Lapps. We have added a section on "Market Foragers" to emphasize that most people in a modern market economy are not in fact producers of food. Our first box deals with the change in view from "Man the Hunter" to "Woman the Gatherer" and we raise the question of whether either view is accurate. Although it is commonly thought that industrialization is mainly to blame for negative developments in the environment, our second box deals with the negative effects (in preindustrial times) of irrigation, animal grazing, and overhunting.

Chapter 7 (Economic Systems). In discussing customs of land ownership we now include material about the effects of particular political and social systems (e.g., feudal and manor systems; collectives in Bulgaria), and we have added a new subsection on colonialism and natives' control over land. In our first box we address the controversy over whether communal ownership leads to economic disaster. In the section on the conversion of resources, we have added a new subsection on types of production—domestic, elite and aristocratic, industrial, postindustrial. In discussing the distribution of resources we have expanded the section on balanced reciprocity and indicated that balances cannot be evaluated simply in economic terms, that there are other reasons to value things. In this context we have added a discussion of the distinction between gift and commodity exchanges. After we discuss commercialization, we use a box to illustrate the impact of the world-system on local economies, with special reference to the deforestation of the Amazon.

Chapter 8 (Social Stratification). In the first of the boxes in this chapter, we discuss recent changes in the United States, particularly the widening of the gap between rich and poor, and how people feel about the changes. In our second box, we now discuss social stratification on the global level—how the gap between rich and poor countries has been widening too and what may account for that trend. In discussing caste and "race" in the United States, we now discuss how discrimination still limits social mobility among African Americans, even though many have joined the elite. Our discussion of the emergence of stratification now deals with how leaders may be able to aggrandize themselves.

Chapter 9 (Sex, Gender, and Culture). We now discuss how the concepts of gender do not always involve just two genders. We have revised our section on gender contributions to work, emphasizing all of the ways women contribute, and how conclusions about contributions by gender depend on how you measure "work." In the section on gender differences in personality, we now discuss a recent reanalysis of Mead's work on Mundugumor. In our first box, we discuss research on why women's political participation may be increasing in some Coast Salish communities (of western Washington State and British Columbia) now that they have elected councils. A second box examines cross-cultural research about why some societies allow women to participate in combat. Finally, we have incorporated new survey results on the United States in the section on variation in sexual attitudes and practices.

Chapter 10 (Marriage and the Family). We have revised our discussion of the Nayar, adding new material about recent changes. We have updated our discussion of female-female marriages. With regard to the incest taboo and its extensions beyond the family, we now present evidence that marriage between groups does not necessarily increase cooperation between them, and we include a discussion of incest between commoner brothers and sisters in ancient Egypt. To introduce additional topics regarding the husband-wife relationship that are only beginning to be investigated, we have added a box on variation in love, intimacy, and sexual jealousy. We now discuss the advantages of polygyny as perceived by people in Kenya. The box in the section on family organization discusses why one-parent families are on the increase in countries like ours. We also now discuss the business advantages of nonlocalized extended families in China.

Chapter 11 (Marital Residence and Kinship). One of the boxes discusses the possible relationship between neolocality and adolescent rebellion. The second box is on how variation in residence and kinship affects the lives of women. We also now discuss the effect of long-distance trade and wage labor on matrilocal residence, using the example of the Miskito in Central America.

Chapter 12 (Associations and Interest Groups). We now discuss changes in the functions of associations, as in Lakota military associations after contact, Filipino associations in Hawaii after many Filipinos came there, and the incorporation of regional and family associations into powerful ethnic associations in Chinatowns. We have added a section on multiethnic associations such as the women's Wok Meri in Papua New Guinea and the Alaska Federation of Natives. We now discuss a society (Norway) in which participation in clubs is remarkably extensive, and why that may be. Our first box addresses the question of whether separate women's associations increase women's status and power; our second box discusses why street gangs develop and why they often become violent.

Chapter 13 (Political Life). We have added material on how colonialization has transformed legal systems and ways of making decisions. Our first box deals with how new local courts among the Abelam of New Guinea are allowing women to address sexual grievances. We have expanded our discussion of political process, particularly how people get to be leaders. We have added a section on "big women" on Vanatinai island, off the southeast coast of New Guinea. Our second box deals with the cross-national and cross-cultural relationship between economic development and democracy. We have added a discussion of avoidance as a peaceful mechanism of conflict resolution (in addition to negotiation and mediation). We have added a discussion of cultural patterns of violence and the use of violence as a way to resolve conflict.

Chapter 14 (Psychology and Culture). We have included a new discussion of probable human universals in the psychological realm. As a way of explaining cultural variation in child rearing, we now examine differences in "indulgence" of infants—how quickly parents and others feed or hold or otherwise respond to crying. In the section on explaining variation in psychological characteristics, we have added a discussion of general cultural themes, exploring different cultural concepts of the self and whether the individual or the collective is emphasized. The first box in this chapter discusses the idea that women have a different sense of themselves than men have and therefore a different sense of morality. In our second box, which refers to a recent comparison of preschools in Japan, China, and the United States, we discuss how schools may consciously and unconsciously teach values. We now deal with the effects of school, literacy, and malnutrition on cognitive performance. Our discussion of socialization has added material on parental acceptance/rejection and the possible effects of prolonged mother-infant holding. Finally, we have updated our discussion of cross-cultural variation in mental illness.

Chapter 15 (Religion and Magic). One box discusses research on New England fishermen that suggests how their taboos, or "rituals of avoidance," may be anxiety-reducing. Our second box discusses the emergence of new religions (or "cults") and points out that nearly all of the major churches or religions in the world began as minority sects or cults. We have expanded our treatment of revitalization movements, which used to be in the chapter on culture change.

Chapter 16 (The Arts). In regard to how the arts change over time, we now discuss the myth that the art of "simpler" peoples is timeless, and we have added a section on changes in art as a result of European contact. We now discuss some innovative and emergent aspects of folklore, such as urban legends. We address the role of ethnocentrism in studies of art with a new section on how Western museums and art critics look at the visual art of less complex cultures. There is a box on how art varies with different kinds of political systems. In our second box, dealing with universal symbolism in art, we review recent research on the emotions displayed in masks.

Chapter 17 (Culture Change). To convey that much of culture change in the modern world is generated internally, one of the new boxes examines what has happened in Communist China—what has changed because of goverment intervention and what has persisted nevertheless. Because cultures all over the world are converging in many ways, but still exhibit many differences, another box addresses the issue of whether cultural diversity will disappear in a computerized, rapid-transit world.

Chapter 18 (Applied Anthropology and Social Problems). We have increased our coverage of applied anthropology in this edition. We discuss the history and types of applied anthropology in the United

States, the ethical issues involved in trying to improve people's lives, the difficulties in evaluating whether a program is beneficial, and ways of implementing planned changes. There is a box on how anthropological work can be useful to business. To convey the process of research in applied work, our second box focuses on how researchers tried to find out why people were not availing themselves of a free antimalaria drug in Guatemala. We discuss how research may suggest possible solutions to various global social problems, including AIDS, disasters, homelessness, crime, family violence, and war.

OTHER FEATURES OF THE BOOK

Readability

We derive a lot of pleasure from trying to describe research findings, especially complicated ones, in ways that introductory students can understand. Thus, we try to minimize technical jargon, using only those terms students must know to appreciate the achievements of anthropology and to take advanced courses. We think readability is important not only because it may enhance the reader's understanding of what we write, but also because it should make learning about anthropology more enjoyable! When new terms are introduced, which of course must happen sometimes, they are set off in boldface type and defined right away.

A Complete Glossary at the End of the Book

As we noted above, the important glossary terms to study for each chapter are highlighted (without definitions) right after the summary, so students can readily check their understanding after they have read the chapter. A complete glossary is provided at the back of the book to serve as a convenient reference for the student.

References

Because we believe firmly in the importance of evidence, we think it essential to tell our readers, both professional and student, what our conclusions are based on. Usually the basis is published research. References to the relevant studies are provided in complete notes at the end of the chapter, and a complete bibliography is also provided at the end of the book.

Summaries and Suggested Readings

In addition to the outline provided at the beginning of each chapter, there is a detailed summary at the end of the chapter that will help the student review the major concepts and findings discussed. Suggested readings are included to provide general or more extensive references on the subject matter of the chapter.

Supplements

The supplements package for this textbook is of exceptional quality. From the *Instructor's Manual* to the *Themes of the Times,* each component has been meticulously crafted to amplify and illuminate materials in the text itself.

Instructor's Resource Manual. This manual offers learning objectives, chapter outlines, teaching tips, suggestions for classroom activities, and topics for class discussion and written assignments.

Test Item File. This test bank contains over 1500 multiple-choice, true-false, and essay questions that are page-referenced to the text.

Prentice Hall Custom Test. Prentice Hall's new testing software program permits instructors to edit any or all items in the *Test Item File* and add their own questions. Other special features of this program, which is available for DOS, Windows, and Macintosh computers, include random generation of an item set, creation of alternate versions of the same test, scrambling question sequence, and test preview before printing.

Videos. A selection of high-quality award-winning videos from the Filmmakers Library collection is available upon adoption. Please see your Prentice Hall sales representative for more information.

The New York Times Supplement. *The New York Times* and Prentice Hall are sponsoring *Themes of the Times,* a program designed to enhance student access to current information relevant to the classroom. Through this program, the core subject matter provided in the text is supplemented by a collection of timely articles from one of the world's most distinguished newspapers, *The New York Times.* These articles demonstrate the vital, ongoing connection between what is learned in the classroom and what is happening in the world around us.

To enjoy the wealth of information of *The New York Times* daily, a reduced subscription rate is available. For information, call toll-free: 1–800–631–1222.

Prentice Hall and *The New York Times* are proud to co-sponsor *Themes of the Times.* We hope it will make the reading of both textbooks and newspapers a more dynamic, involving process.

Transparency Acetates. Taken from graphs, diagrams, and tables in this text and other sources, over 50 full-color transparencies offer an effective means of amplifying lecture topics.

Study Guide. This supplement for students offers chapter outlines and summaries, definitions of key concepts, self tests, and applied exercises for each chapter of the book.

JUST IN TIME: CUSTOMIZED ORIGINAL CHAPTERS FOR YOUR STUDENTS

The authors have commissioned three new series of original chapters from which instructors can choose supplemental readings to accompany this text. These new series are titled *Portraits of Culture: Ethnographic Originals, Research Frontiers in Anthropology,* and *Cross-Cultural Research for Social Science.* The instructor can mix and match chapters from one or more of these series. (Many of these chapters are referred to in this edition.) Please see your local Prentice Hall representative or telephone 1–800–77SOURC to receive more information about these series.

ACKNOWLEDGMENTS

We thank the people at Prentice Hall for various kinds of help, especially Nancy Roberts, editor-in-chief for the social sciences, Kris Kleinsmith for marketing, Joan Foley for seeing the manuscript through the production process, and Suzanne Skloot for photo research.

We are grateful to a number of people, including a few who wish to remain anonymous, for agreeing to review our chapters and make suggestions. These reviewers include: Richard Anderson, Kansas City Art Institute; C. Loring Brace, University of Michigan; Jill Brody, Louisiana State University; Daniel Brown, University of Hawaii at Hilo; Allan Burns, University of Florida, Gainesville; James G. Chadney, University of Northern Iowa; Elizabeth Chapman; John W. Cole, University of Massachusetts, Amherst; Rebecca Cramer, Johnson County Community College; Dona Davis, University of South Dakota; Linda E. Duchin, Tacoma Community College; Carol M. Eastman, University of Washington; Luther P. Gerlach, University of Minnesota; Norval Glenn, University of Texas, Austin; W. Penn Handwerker, Humboldt State University; Karen M. Hjerpe; Kevin Hunt, Indiana University; Lorena Madrigal, University of South Florida; Nancy P. McKee, Washington State University; Jon L. Olson, California State University, Los Angeles; Dennis E. Shaw, Miami-Dade Community College; Joel Sherzer, University of Texas; John Townsend, Syracuse University; Susan S. Wadley, Syracuse University; Linda Wolfe, East Carolina University.

We thank all of you, named and unnamed, who gave us advice.

Carol R. Ember and Melvin Ember

About the Authors

Carol R. Ember started at Antioch College as a chemistry major. She began taking social science courses because some were required, but she soon found herself intrigued. There were lots of questions without answers and she became excited about the possibility of a research career in social science. She spent a year in graduate school at Cornell studying sociology before continuing on to Harvard where she studied anthropology primarily with John and Beatrice Whiting.

For her Ph.D. dissertation she worked among the Luo of Kenya. While there she noticed that many boys were assigned "girls work," such as babysitting and household chores, because their mothers (who did most of the agriculture) did not have enough girls to help out. She decided to study the possible effects of task assignment on the social behavior of boys. Using systematic behavior observations, she compared girls, boys who did a great deal of girls' work, and boys who did little such work. She found that boys assigned girls' work were intermediate in many social behaviors, compared with the other boys and girls. Later, she did cross-cultural research on variation in marriage, family, descent groups, and war and peace, mainly in collaboration with Melvin Ember, whom she married in 1970. All of these cross-cultural studies tested theories on data for worldwide samples of societies.

From 1970 to the present, she has taught at Hunter College of the City University of New York. She has also served as President of the Society of Cross-Cultural Research and is one of the Directors of the Summer Institutes in Comparative Anthro-

pological Research which are funded by the National Science Foundation.

After graduating from Columbia College, Melvin Ember went to Yale for his Ph.D. His mentor at Yale was George Peter Murdock, an anthropologist who was instrumental in promoting cross-cultural research and building a full-text database on the cultures of the world to facilitate cross-cultural hypothesis-testing. This database came to be known as the Human Relations Area Files (it was called that because it was originally sponsored by the Institute of Human Relations at Yale). Growing in annual installments, and now distributed in electronic format, the HRAF database currently covers more than 355 cultures, past and present, all over the world.

Melvin Ember did fieldwork for his dissertation in American Samoa, where he conducted a comparison of three villages to study the effects of commercialization on political life. In addition, he did research on descent groups and how they changed with the increase of buying and selling. His cross-cultural studies focused originally on variation in marital residence and descent groups. He has also done cross-cultural research on the relationship between economic and political development, the origin and extension of the incest taboo, the causes of polygyny, and how archaeological correlates of social customs can help us draw inferences about the past.

After four years of research at the National Institute of Mental Health, he taught at Antioch College and then Hunter College of the City University of New York. He has served as President of the Society for Cross-Cultural Research and has been President since 1987 of the Human Relations Area Files, Inc., a nonprofit research agency of Yale University.

1

What Is Anthropology?

Anthropology, by definition, is a discipline of infinite curiosity about human beings. The term comes from the Greek *anthropos* for "man, human" and *logos* for "study." Anthropologists seek answers to an enormous variety of questions about humans. They are interested in discovering when, where, and why humans appeared on the earth, how and why they have changed since then, and how and why modern human populations vary in certain physical features. Anthropologists are also interested in how and why societies in the past and present have varied in their customary ideas and practices.

But a definition of anthropology as the study of human beings is not complete, for according to such a definition anthropology would appear to incorporate a whole catalog of disciplines: sociology, psychology, political science, economics, history, human biology, and perhaps even the humanistic disciplines of philosophy and literature. Needless to say, practitioners of the many other disciplines concerned with humans would not be happy to be regarded as being in subbranches of anthropology. After all, most of those disciplines have existed longer than anthropology, and each is somewhat distinctive. There must, then, be something unique about anthropology—a reason for

its having developed as a separate discipline and for its having retained a separate identity over the last 100 years.

THE SCOPE OF ANTHROPOLOGY

Anthropologists are generally thought of as individuals who travel to little-known corners of the world to study exotic peoples or who dig deep into the earth to uncover the fossil remains or the tools and pots of people who lived long ago. These views, though clearly stereotyped, do indicate how anthropology differs from other disciplines concerned with humans: anthropology is broader in scope (both geographically and historically.) Anthropology is concerned explicitly and directly with all varieties of people throughout the world, not only those close at hand or within a limited area. It is also interested in people of all periods. Beginning with the immediate ancestors of humans, who lived a few million years ago, anthropology traces the development of humans until the present. Every part of the world that has ever contained a human population is of interest to anthropologists.

FIGURE 1–1

The four major subdisciplines of anthropology (in bold letters) may be classified according to subject matter (physical or cultural) and according to the period with which each is concerned (distant past versus recent past and present). There are applications of anthropology in all four subdisciplines.

Anthropologists have not always been as broad and comprehensive in their concerns as they are today. Traditionally, they concentrated on non-Western cultures and left the study of Western civilization and similarly complex societies, with their recorded histories, to other disciplines. In recent years, however, this general division of labor among the disciplines has begun to disappear. Now anthropologists can be found at work in cities of the industrial world as well as in remote villages of the non-Western world.

What induces anthropologists to choose so broad a subject for study? In part, they are motivated by the belief that any suggested generalization about human beings, any possible explanation of some characteristic of human culture or biology, should be shown to apply to many times and places of human existence. If a generalization or explanation does not prove to apply widely, we are entitled or even obliged to be skeptical about it. The skeptical attitude, in the absence of persuasive evidence, is our best protection against accepting invalid ideas about humans.

For example, when American educators discovered in the 1960s that black schoolchildren rarely drank milk, they assumed that lack of money or education was the cause. But evidence from anthropology suggested a different explanation. Anthropologists had known for years that in many parts of the world where milking animals are kept, people do not drink fresh milk; rather, they sour it before they drink it, or they make it into cheese. Why they do so is now clear. Many people lack an enzyme, lactase, that is necessary for breaking down lactose, the sugar in milk. When such people drink regular milk it actually interferes with digestion—not only is the lactose in milk not digested, but other nutrients are less likely to be digested as well. In many cases, drinking milk will cause cramps, stomach gas, diarrhea, and nausea. Studies indicate that milk intolerance is found in many parts of the world.[1] The condition is common in adulthood among Asians, southern Europeans, Arabs and Jews, West Africans, Inuit (Eskimos), and North and South American Indians, as well as American blacks! Because anthropologists are acquainted with human life in an enormous variety of geographical and historical settings, they are often able to correct mistaken beliefs about different groups of people.

THE HOLISTIC APPROACH

In addition to the worldwide as well as historical scope of anthropology, another distinguishing fea-

ture of the discipline is its **holistic,** or multifaceted, approach to the study of human beings. Anthropologists study not only all varieties of people but many aspects of human experience as well. For example, when describing a group of people, an anthropologist might discuss the history of the area in which the people live, the physical environment, the organization of family life, the general features of their language, the group's settlement patterns, political and economic systems, religion, and styles of art and dress.

In the past, individual anthropologists tried to be holistic and cover all aspects of a subject. Today, as in many other disciplines, so much information has been accumulated that anthropologists tend to specialize in one topic or area. Thus, one anthropologist may investigate the physical characteristics of some of our prehistoric ancestors. Another may study the biological effect of the environment on a human population over time. Still another will concentrate on the customs of a particular group of people. Despite this specialization, however, the discipline of anthropology retains its holistic orientation in that its many different specialties, taken together, describe many aspects of human existence, both past and present, on all levels of complexity.

THE ANTHROPOLOGICAL CURIOSITY

Thus far we have described anthropology as being broader in scope, both historically and geographically, and more holistic in approach than other disciplines concerned with human beings. But this statement again implies that anthropology is the all-inclusive human science. How, then, is anthropology really different from those other disciplines? We suggest that anthropology's distinctiveness lies principally in the kind of curiosity it arouses.

Anthropologists are concerned with many types of questions: Where, when, and why did people first begin living in cities? Why do some peoples have darker skin than others? Why do some languages contain more color terms than other languages? Why, in some societies, are men allowed to be married to several women simultaneously? Although these questions deal with very different aspects of human existence, they have at least one thing in common: they all deal with *typical characteristics* of particular populations. The typical characteristic of a people might be relatively dark skin, a language having many color terms, or the practice of having several wives. This concern with typical characteristics (traits, customs) of populations is perhaps the most distinguishing feature of anthropology. For example, whereas economists take our monetary system for granted and study how it operates, anthropologists ask why *only some* societies during the last few thousand years used money. In short, anthropologists are curious about the typical characteristics of human populations—how and why such populations and their characteristics have varied—throughout the ages.

FIELDS OF ANTHROPOLOGY

Different anthropologists concentrate on different typical characteristics of societies. Some are concerned primarily with *biological* or *physical characteristics* of human populations; others are interested principally in what we call *cultural characteristics.* Hence, there are two broad classifications of subject matter in anthropology: **physical (biological) anthropology** and **cultural anthropology.** Physical anthropology is one major field of anthropology. Cultural anthropology is divided into three major subfields—archeology, linguistics, and ethnology. Ethnology, the study of recent cultures, is often referred to by the parent name, cultural anthropology.

Physical Anthropology

Physical anthropology seeks to answer two distinct sets of questions. The first set includes questions about the emergence of humans and their later evolution (this is the focus called **human paleontology**

Paleontologist Richard Leakey holding fossilized skull of early human

or **paleoanthropology**). The second set includes questions about how and why contemporary human populations vary biologically (the focus referred to as **human variation**).

In order to reconstruct human evolution, human paleontologists search for and study the buried, hardened remains or impressions—known as **fossils**—of humans, prehumans, and related animals. Paleontologists working in East Africa, for instance, have excavated the fossil remains of humanlike beings who lived more than 3 million years ago. These findings have suggested the approximate dates when our ancestors began to develop two-legged walking, very flexible hands, and a larger brain.

In attempting to clarify evolutionary relationships, human paleontologists may use not only the fossil record but also geological information on the succession of climates, environments, and plant and animal populations. Moreover, when reconstructing the past of humans, paleontologists are also interested in the behavior and evolution of our closest relatives among the mammals—the prosimians, monkeys, and apes, which, like ourselves, are members of the order of **Primates.** (Anthropologists, psychologists, and biologists who specialize in the study of primates are called **primatologists.**) Species of primates are observed in the wild and in the laboratory. One especially popular subject of study is the chimpanzee, which bears a close resemblance to humans in behavior and physical appearance, has a similar blood chemistry, and is susceptible to many of the same diseases.

From primate studies, physical anthropologists try to discover characteristics that are distinctly human, as opposed to those that might be part of the primate heritage. With this information, they may be able to infer what our prehistoric ancestors were like. The inferences from primate studies are checked against the fossil record. The evidence from the earth, collected in bits and pieces, is correlated with scientific observations of our closest living relatives.

In short, physical anthropologists piece together bits of information obtained from different sources. They construct theories that explain the changes observed in the fossil record and then attempt to evaluate their theories by checking one kind of evidence against another. Human paleontology thus overlaps a great deal with disciplines such as geology, general vertebrate (and particularly primate) paleontology, comparative anatomy, and the study of comparative primate behavior.

The second major focus of physical anthropology—the study of human variation—investigates how and why contemporary human populations differ in physical or biological characteristics. All living people belong to one species, ***Homo sapiens,*** for all can successfully interbreed. Yet there is much that varies among human populations. The investigators of human variation ask such questions as these: Why are some peoples taller than others? How have human populations adapted physically to their environmental conditions? Are some peoples, such as Inuit (Eskimos), better equipped than other peoples to endure cold? Does darker skin pigmentation offer special protection against the tropical sun?

To better understand the biological variations observable among contemporary human populations, physical anthropologists use the principles, concepts, and techniques of (at least) three other disciplines: human genetics (the study of human traits that are inherited), population biology (the study of environmental effects on, and interaction with, population characteristics), and epidemiology (the study of how and why diseases affect different populations in different ways). Research on human variation, therefore, overlaps with research in other fields. Persons who consider themselves physical anthropologists, however, are concerned most with human populations and how they vary biologically.

Cultural Anthropology

To an anthropologist, the term **culture** generally refers to the customary ways of thinking and behaving of a particular population or society. The culture of a social group, therefore, is composed of its language, general knowledge, religious beliefs, food preferences, music, work habits, taboos, and so forth. **Archaeology** (the study of past cultures through their material remains), **anthropological linguistics** (the anthropological study of languages), and **ethnology** (the study of existing and recent cultures), the subdisciplines we consider next, are all directly concerned with human culture. Thus, they can be grouped under the broad classification of cultural anthropology.

Archaeology. The archaeologist seeks not only to reconstruct the daily life and customs of peoples who lived in the past but also to trace cultural changes and to offer possible explanations of those changes. This concern is similar to that of the historian, but the archaeologist reaches much farther back in time. The historian deals only with societies that left written records and is therefore limited to the last 5,000 years of human history. Human societies, however, have existed for more than a million years, and only a small proportion in the last 5,000 years did not have writing. For all those past societies lacking a written record, the archaeologist serves as historian. Lacking written records for study, archaeologists must try to reconstruct history from the remains of human cultures. Some of these remains are as grand as the Mayan temples discovered at Chichén Itzá in Yucatán, Mexico. More often they are as ordinary as bits of broken pottery, stone tools, and garbage heaps.

Nadine Peacock, a biological anthropologist, studying reproduction and health among the Efe-Ituri Pygmies of Zaire

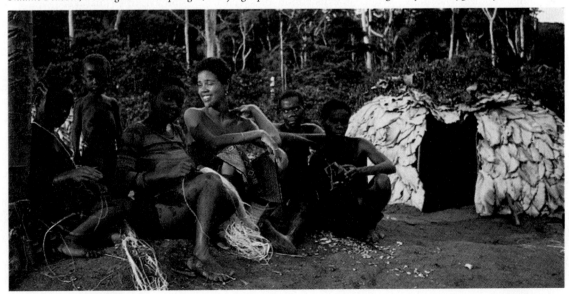

Most archaeologists deal with **prehistory,** the time before written records. But there is a specialty within archaeology, called **historical archaeology,** that studies the remains of recent peoples who left written records. This specialty, as its name implies, employs the methods of archaeologists *and* the methods of historians to study recent societies for which we have both archaeological and historical information.

In trying to understand how and why ways of life have changed through time in different parts of the world, archaeologists collect materials from sites of human occupation. Usually, these sites must be unearthed. On the basis of materials they have excavated and otherwise collected, they then ask various questions: Where, when, and why did the distinctive human characteristic of toolmaking first emerge? Where, when, and why did agriculture first

Research Frontiers

RESEARCHER AT WORK: ELIZABETH M. BRUMFIEL

Now professor of anthropology at Albion College, Elizabeth Brumfiel became interested in the origins of social inequality when she was just an undergraduate. Archaeologists had known for some time that substantial wealth differences between families developed only recently (archaeologically speaking), that is, only after about 6,000 years ago. The archaeological indicators of inequality are fairly clear—elaborate burials with valuable goods for some families and large differences in houses and possessions. But *why* the transformation occurred was not so clear. When she was in graduate school at the University of Michigan, Brumfiel says, she didn't accept the then-current explanation—that inequality provided benefits to the society (for example, the standard of living of most people improved as the leaders got richer). So, for her Ph.D. research in central Mexico, she began to test the "benefit" explanation in an area that had been independent politically at first and then became part of the

Elizabeth Brumfiel

Aztec empire. She studied the surface material remains in the area and historical documents written by Europeans and Aztec nobility. Her findings contradicted the benefit explanation of social inequality; she found little improvement in the standard of living of the local people after the Aztec empire had absorbed them.

Another important part of her research agenda is understanding the lives of women. How were they affected by the expansion of the Aztec empire? Did their work change? How were women portrayed in art? In the Aztec capital of Tenochtitlan, images of militarism and masculinity became increasingly important with the growth of the empire, and sculptures showed

women in subordinate positions (for example, kneeling). But the images of women in the area of Brumfiel's fieldwork did not change. For example, most of the sculptures after the Aztecs had taken over still showed women standing, not kneeling.

Like many anthropologists, Brumfiel asked herself how she could contribute to the community in which she did her fieldwork. She decided to design an exhibit to display the successes of the people who had lived in the area for 1,200 years. That exhibit is now finished and open.

As she continues to explore issues about the origins of inequality and the position of women, she is quite comfortable with knowing that someone will think that she has "gotten it wrong, and will set out on a lifetime of archaeological research to find her own answers."

Source: *Elizabeth M. Brumfiel, "Origins of Social Inequality," in Carol R. Ember, Melvin Ember, and Peter N. Peregrine, eds.,* Research Frontiers in Anthropology *(Englewood Cliffs, NJ: Prentice Hall, 1995). Prentice Hall/Simon & Schuster Custom Publishing.*

develop? Where, when, and why did people first begin to live in cities?

To collect the data they need in order to suggest answers to these and other questions, archaeologists use techniques and findings borrowed from other disciplines as well as what they can infer from anthropological studies of recent and contemporary cultures. For example, to guess where to dig for evidence of early toolmaking, archaeologists rely on geology to tell them where sites of early human occupation are likely (because of erosion and uplifting) to be found near the existing surface of the earth. (The evidence available today indicates that the earliest toolmakers lived in East Africa.) To infer when agriculture first developed, archaeologists date the relevant excavated materials by a process originally developed by chemists. And to try to understand why cities first emerged, archaeologists may need information from historians, geographers, and others about how recent and contemporary cities are related economically and politically to their hinterlands. If we can discover what recent and contemporary cities have in common, perhaps we can speculate on why cities developed originally. Archaeologists can then test those speculations. Thus, archaeologists may use information from the present and recent past in trying to understand the distant past.

Anthropological Linguistics. A second branch of cultural anthropology is linguistics, the study of languages. As a science, the study of languages is somewhat older than anthropology. The two disciplines became closely associated in the early days of anthropological fieldwork, when anthropologists enlisted the help of linguists to study unwritten languages. In contrast with other linguists, then, anthropological linguists are interested primarily in the history and structure of formerly unwritten languages.

Like physical anthropologists, linguists study changes that have taken place over time and contemporary variation. Some anthropological linguists are concerned with the emergence of language and also with the divergence of languages over thousands of years. The study of how languages change over time and how they may be related is known as **historical linguistics.** Anthropological linguists are also interested in how contemporary languages differ—especially in the way they differ in construction. This focus of linguistics is generally called **structural** (or **descriptive**) **linguistics.** The study of how language is used in social contexts is called **sociolinguistics.**

In contrast with the human paleontologist and archaeologist, who have physical remains to help them reconstruct change over time, the historical linguist is dealing only with languages—and usually unwritten ones at that. (Remember that writing is only about 5,000 years old, and most languages since then have not been written.) Because an unwritten language must be heard in order to be studied, it does not leave any traces once its speakers have died. Linguists interested in reconstructing the history of unwritten languages must begin in the present, with comparisons of contemporary languages. On the basis of these comparisons, they draw inferences about the kinds of change in language that may have occurred in the past and that may account for similarities and differences observed in the present. The historical linguist typically asks such questions as these: Did two or more contemporary languages diverge from a common ancestral language? If they are related, how far back in time did they begin to differ?

Unlike the historical linguist, the descriptive (or structural) linguist is typically concerned with discovering and recording the principles that determine how sounds and words are put together in speech. For example, a structural description of a particular language might tell us that the sounds *t* and *k* are interchangeable in a word without causing a difference in meaning. In the islands of American Samoa, one could say *Tutuila* or *Kukuila* as the name of the largest island and everyone, except perhaps the visiting anthropologist, would understand that the same island was being mentioned.

The sociolinguist is interested in the social aspects of language, including what people speak about and how they interact conversationally, their attitudes toward speakers of other dialects or languages, and how people speak differently in different social contexts. In English, for example, we do not address everyone we meet in the same way. "Hi, Sandy" may be the customary way a person greets a friend. But we would probably feel uncomfortable addressing a doctor by first name; instead we would probably say, "Good morning, Dr. Brown." Such variations in language use, which are determined by the social status of the persons being addressed, are significant for the sociolinguist.

Ethnology. Ethnologists seek to understand how and why peoples today and in the recent past differ in their customary ways of thinking and acting. Ethnology, then, is concerned with patterns of thought and behavior, such as marriage customs, kinship organization, political and economic systems, religion, folk art, and music, and with the ways in which these patterns differ in contemporary societies. Ethnologists

RESEARCHER AT WORK: TERENCE E. HAYS

Books and articles often report research in a straightforward manner. Here's the problem; here's the answer—that kind of thing. But many researchers know from experience that knowledge does not always come in a straightforward manner. Now a professor at Rhode Island College, Terence Hays has reflected on the twists and turns in his fieldwork among the Ndumba in the Eastern Highlands Province of Papua New Guinea. He first started out studying whether different types of people (for example, women and men) had different types of plant knowledge and whether they classified plants differently.

Terence Hays (right)

also study the dynamics of culture—that is, how various cultures develop and change. In addition, they are interested in the relationship between beliefs and practices within a culture. Thus, the aim of ethnologists is largely the same as that of archaeologists. Ethnologists, however, generally use data collected through observation and interviewing of living peoples. Archaeologists, on the other hand, must work with fragmentary remains of past cultures, on the basis of which they can only make inferences about the customs of prehistoric peoples.

One type of ethnologist, the **ethnographer,** usually spends a year or so living with, talking to, and observing the people whose customs he or she is studying. This fieldwork provides the data for a detailed description (an **ethnography**) of many aspects of the customary behavior and thought of those people. The ethnographer not only tries to describe the general patterns of their life but also may suggest answers to such questions as: How are economic and political behavior related? How may the customs of people be adapted to environ-

mental conditions? Is there any relationship between beliefs about the supernatural and beliefs or practices about the natural world? In other words, the ethnographer depicts the way of life of a particular group of people and may also suggest explanations for some of the customs observed.

Because so many cultures have undergone extensive change in the recent past, it is fortunate that another type of ethnologist, the **ethnohistorian,** is prepared to study how the ways of life of a particular group of people have changed over time. Ethnohistorians investigate written documents (which may or may not have been produced by anthropologists). They may spend many years going through documents, such as missionary accounts, reports by traders and explorers, and government records, to try to establish the cultural changes that have occurred. Unlike ethnographers, who rely mostly on their own observations, ethnohistorians rely on the reports of others. Often, they must attempt to piece together and make sense of widely scattered, and even apparently contradictory, infor-

(The interest in plant and animal classification, ethnobiology, is closely connected with linguistic research.) In the course of his first fieldwork in 1972, he witnessed an initiation ceremony for ten- to twelve-year-old males—a dramatic and traumatic rite-of-passage ceremony that included the physical trauma of nose-bleeding as well as the social traumas of "attacks" by women and seclusion in the forest. The ceremony was full of symbolism of why the sexes needed to avoid each other. And, while he collected stories and myths about plants for his research on ethnobiology, he kept uncovering themes in the stories about the danger of men's associating with women.

His curiosity was aroused about these ceremonies and myths. How important are myths in perpetuating cultural themes? Do other societies that have separate men's houses have similar myths?

He realized when he returned home from the field that many societies have similar stories. Are these generally linked to initiation rites and to physical segregation of the sexes? Answering these questions required comparison, so he embarked on collecting myths and folktales from colleagues who worked in other New Guinea highland societies. In the course of collecting these comparative materials, he realized he didn't have all the ethnographic information he needed. So he went back to the field to get it. As Hays remarked, "As an ethnographer I was continually faced with the question, . . . How do you know it's true? But even when I could reach a (hard-won) conviction that something was true for the Ndumba, the second question awaited: How do you know it's generally true, which you can't know without comparison?"

Source: Terence E. Hays, "From Ethnographer to Comparativist and Back Again," in Carol R. Ember, Melvin Ember, and Peter N. Peregrine, eds., Research Frontiers in Anthropology (Englewood Cliffs, NJ: Prentice Hall, 1995). Prentice Hall/Simon & Schuster Custom Publishing.

mation. Thus, the ethnohistorian's research is very much like that of the historian, except that the ethnohistorian is usually concerned with the history of a people who did not themselves leave written records. The ethnohistorian tries to reconstruct the recent history of a people and may also suggest why certain changes in their way of life took place.

With the data collected and analyzed by the ethnographer and ethnohistorian, the work of a third type of ethnologist, the **cross-cultural researcher,** can be done. The cross-cultural researcher is interested in discovering why certain cultural characteristics may be found in some societies but not in others. Why, for example, do some societies have plural marriages (one spouse of one sex and two or more spouses of the other sex), circumcision of adolescent boys, or belief in a high god or supreme being? In testing possible answers to such questions, cross-cultural researchers use data from samples of cultures to try to arrive at general explanations of cultural variation.

Because ethnologists may be interested in many aspects of customary behavior and thought, from economic behavior to political behavior to styles of art, music, and religion, ethnology overlaps with disciplines that concentrate on some particular aspect of human existence, such as sociology, psychology, economics, political science, art, music, and comparative religion. But the distinctive feature of cultural anthropology is its interest in how all these aspects of human existence vary from society to society, in all historical periods and in all parts of the world.

Specialization

As disciplines grow, they tend to develop more and more specialities. This trend is probably inevitable because as knowledge accumulates and methods become more advanced there is a limit to what any one person can reasonably keep track of. So, in addition to the general divisions we have outlined already, particular anthropologists tend to identify themselves with a variety of specializations. It is common for anthropologists to have a geographical specialty, which may be as broad as Old World or New World or as narrow as the southwestern United States. And those who study the past (archaeologists or human paleontologists) may also specialize in different time periods. Ethnologists often specialize in more specific subject matters in addition to one or two cultural areas. Just as most of the chapters in this book refer to broad subject specialties, so are there ethnologists who identify themselves as *economic anthropologists*, or *political anthropologists*, or *psychological anthropologists*. Others may identify themselves by theoretical orientations (which we discuss more fully in the chapter on schools of thought), such as *cultural ecologists*, who are concerned with the relationship between culture and the physical and social environment. These specialities are not mutually exclusive. A cultural ecologist, for example, might be interested in effects of the environment on economic behavior, or political behavior, or how people bring up their children.

Does specialization isolate an anthropologist from other kinds of research? Not necessarily. Some specialties have to draw on information from several fields, inside and outside anthropology. For example, *medical anthropologists* study human health and illness, so they need to understand the cultural context in which people spend their lives (especially their economy, diet, patterns of social interaction) and their attitudes and beliefs regarding illness and health as well as the biological aspects of the situation (which may require understanding human variation and the genetics of the population). There are many anthropologists who believe that important insights come from other fields and who regularly seek out possible connections with them.

Applied Anthropology

As we will discuss more fully in the chapter on applied anthropology and social problems, there are people from each of the four major subdisciplines of anthropology who apply anthropological knowledge to achieve practical goals, usually in the service of an agency outside the traditional academic setting. Physical anthropologists may be called upon to give forensic evidence in court, or they may work in public health or in the design of clothes and equipment to fit human anatomy. Archaeologists may be involved in preserving and exhibiting artifacts for museums and in doing contract work to find and preserve cultural sites that might be damaged by construction or excavation. Linguists may

work in educational (bilingual or multilingual) training programs. Ethnologists work in a wide variety of applied projects ranging from community development, health care, and agricultural improvement to personnel and organizational management and assessment of the impact of change programs on people's lives.[2] Because applied anthropology puts anthropological knowledge to use, basic understanding of humans and their cultures is essential to the enterprise.

THE USEFULNESS OF ANTHROPOLOGY

For many centuries, the idea of traveling to the moon was only a dream. Yet in 1969 the dream became a reality when a U.S. Air Force officer gingerly planted his space boot in the moon dust. As the moon shot demonstrates, we know a great deal about the laws of nature in the physical world. If we did not understand so much, the technological achievements we are so proud of would not be possible.

In comparison, we know little about people, about how and why they behave as they do. When we consider the great number of social problems facing us, the importance and relevance of continuing research in cultural anthropology and the other social sciences become evident. Because social problems such as violence in the streets and wars between nations are products of human behavior, we need to find out what conditions produce those problems. Once we gain such understanding, we may be able to change the conditions and so reduce or even solve the problems.

That anthropology and other sciences dealing with humans began to develop only relatively recently is not in itself a sufficient reason for our knowing so little. Why, in our quest for knowledge of all kinds, did we wait so long to study ourselves? Leslie White suggested that in the history of science those phenomena most remote from us and least significant as determinants of human behavior were the first to be studied. The reason, he thought, is that humans like to think of themselves as citadels of free will, subject to no laws of nature. Hence there is no need to see ourselves as objects to be explained.[3]

The belief that it is impossible to account for human behavior scientifically, either because our actions and beliefs are too individualistic and complex or because human beings are understandable only in otherworldly terms, is a self-fulfilling idea.

We cannot discover principles explaining human behavior if we neither believe there are such principles nor bother to look for them. The result is assured from the beginning: persons who do not believe in principles of human behavior will be reinforced by their finding none. If we are to increase our understanding of human beings, we first have to believe it is possible to do so.

Anthropology is useful, then, to the degree that it contributes to our understanding of human beings. In addition, it is useful because it helps us avoid misunderstandings between peoples. If we can understand why other groups are different from ourselves, we might have less reason to condemn them for behavior that appears strange to us. We may then come to realize that many differences among peoples are products of physical and cultural adaptations to different environments.

For example, someone who first finds out about the !Kung[4] as they lived in the Kalahari Desert of southern Africa in the 1950s might think that the !Kung were savages. The !Kung wore little clothing, had few possessions, lived in meager shelters, and enjoyed none of our technological niceties. But let us reflect on how a typical North American community might react if it awoke to find itself in an environment similar to that in which the !Kung lived. The people would find that the arid land makes both agriculture and animal husbandry impossible, and they might have to think about adopting a nomadic existence. They might then discard many of their material possessions so that they could travel easily, in order to take advantage of changing water and wild food supplies. Because of the extreme heat and the lack of extra water for laundry, they might find it more practical to be almost naked than to wear clothes. They would undoubtedly find it impossible to build elaborate homes. For social security, they might start to share the food brought into the group. Thus, if they survived at all, they might end up looking and acting far more like the !Kung looked than like typical North Americans.

Physical differences, too, may be seen as results of adaptations to the environment. For example, in our society we admire people who are tall and slim. If these same individuals were forced to live above the Arctic Circle, however, they might wish they could trade their tall, slim bodies for short, compact ones, because stocky physiques appear to conserve body heat more effectively and may therefore be more adaptive in cold climates.

Exposure to anthropology might help to alleviate some of the misunderstandings that arise between people of different cultural groups from subtle causes operating below the level of consciousness. For example, different cultures have different conceptions of the gestures and interpersonal distances that are appropriate under various circumstances. Arabs consider it proper to stand close

Foragers such as the !Kung pictured here have to change their campsites to collect wild resources through the year. They cannot carry much with them, and the short time they spend in a particular site does not encourage the building of permanent housing.

Tourism is one way to learn about other cultures, as here in Asmat country of western New Guinea. But anthropology is a better way. It tells us not just how cultures are different, but helps us to understand why.

enough to other people to smell them.[5] On the basis of the popularity of deodorants in our culture, we can deduce that Americans prefer to keep the olfactory dimension out of interpersonal relations. We may feel that a person who comes too close is being too intimate. We should remember, however, that this person may only be acting according to a culturally conditioned conception of what is proper in a given situation. If our intolerance for others results in part from a lack of understanding of why peoples vary, then the knowledge accumulated by anthropologists may help lessen that intolerance.

Knowledge of our past may also bring both a feeling of humility and a sense of accomplishment. If we are to attempt to deal with the problems of our world, we must be aware of our vulnerability so that we do not think that the problems will solve themselves. But we also have to think enough of our accomplishments to believe that we can find solutions to our problems.

Much of the trouble people get themselves into may be a result of their feelings of self-importance and invulnerability—in short, their lack of humility. Knowing something about our evolutionary past may help us to understand and accept our place in the biological world. Just as for any other form of life, there is no guarantee that any particular human pop-

ulation, or even the entire human species, will perpetuate itself indefinitely. The earth changes, the environment changes, and humanity itself changes; what survives and flourishes in the present might not do so in the future.

Yet our vulnerability should not make us feel powerless. There are many reasons to feel confident about the future. Consider what we have accomplished so far. By means of tools and weapons fashioned from sticks and stones, we were able to hunt animals larger and more powerful than ourselves. We discovered how to make fire, and we learned to use it to keep ourselves warm and to cook our food. As we domesticated plants and animals, we gained greater control over our food supply and were able to establish more permanent settlements. We mined and smelted ores to fashion more durable tools. We built cities and irrigation systems, monuments and ships. We made it possible to travel from one continent to another in a single day. We conquered various illnesses and prolonged human life.

In short, human beings and their cultures have changed considerably over the course of history. Human populations have often been able to adapt to changing circumstances. Let us hope that humans continue to adapt to the challenges of the present and the future.

▼ SUMMARY

1. Anthropology is literally the study of human beings. It differs from other disciplines concerned with people in that it is broader in scope. It is concerned with humans in all places of the world (not simply those places close to us), and it traces human evolution and cultural development from millions of years ago to the present day.

2. Another distinguishing feature of anthropology is its holistic approach to the study of human beings. Anthropologists study not only all varieties of people but also all aspects of those peoples' experiences.

3. Anthropologists are concerned with identifying and explaining typical characteristics (traits, customs) of particular human populations.

4. Physical anthropology is one of the major fields of the discipline. Physical anthropology studies the emergence of humans and their later physical evolution (the focus called human paleontology). It also studies how and why contemporary human populations vary biologically (the focus called human variation).

5. The second broad area of concern to anthropology is cultural anthropology. Its three subfields—archaeology, anthropological linguistics, and ethnology—all deal with aspects of human culture—that is, with the customary ways of thinking and behaving of a particular society.

6. Archaeologists seek not only to reconstruct the daily life and customs of prehistoric peoples but also to trace cultural changes and offer possible explanations of those changes. Therefore, archaeologists try to reconstruct history from the remains of human cultures.

7. Anthropological linguists are concerned with the emergence of language and with the divergence of languages over time (a subject known as historical linguistics). They also study how contemporary languages differ, both in construction (structural or descriptive linguistics) and in use in actual speech (sociolinguistics).

8. The ethnologist seeks to understand how and why peoples of today and the recent past differ in their customary ways of thinking and acting. One type of ethnologist, the ethnographer, usually spends a year or so living with and talking to a particular population and observing their customs. Later, she or he may prepare a detailed report of the group's behavior, which is called an ethnography. Another type of ethnologist, the ethnohistorian, investigates written documents to determine how the ways of life of a particular group of people have changed over time. A third type of ethnologist—the cross-cultural researcher—studies data collected by ethnographers and ethnohistorians for a sample of cultures and attempts to discover which explanations of particular customs may be generally applicable.

9. In all four major subdisciplines of anthropology, there are applied anthropologists, people who apply anthropological knowledge to achieve more practical goals, usually in the service of an agency outside the traditional academic setting.

10. Anthropology may help people to be more tolerant. Anthropological studies can show us why other people are the way they are, both culturally and physically. Customs or actions that appear improper or offensive to us may be adaptations to particular environmental and social conditions.

11. Anthropology is also valuable in that knowledge of our past may bring us both a feeling of humility and a sense of accomplishment. Like any other form of life, we have no guarantee that any particular human population will perpetuate itself indefinitely. Yet knowledge of our achievements in the past may give us confidence in our ability to solve the problems of the future.

▼ GLOSSARY TERMS

anthropological linguistics	archaeology	ethnographer	historical archaeology
anthropology	cross-cultural researcher	ethnography	historical linguistics
applied (practicing) anthropology	cultural anthropology	ethnohistorian	holistic
	culture	ethnology	
		fossils	

Homo sapiens	physical (biological)	Primates	structural (or
human paleontology	anthropology	primatologists	descriptive)
human variation	prehistory	sociolinguistics	linguistics
paleoanthropology			

▼ CRITICAL QUESTIONS

1. Why study anthropology?
2. How does anthropology differ from other fields of study you've encountered?
3. What do you think about the suggestion that anthropology is the fundamental discipline concerned with humans?

▼ SUGGESTED READING

AKMAJIAN, A., DEMERS, R. A., AND HARNISH, R. M. *Linguistics: An Introduction to Language and Communication*, 3rd ed. Cambridge, MA: M.I.T. Press, 1990. A survey of many of the kinds of research on language and communication.

EMBER, C. R., EMBER, M., AND PEREGRINE P. N. EDS. *Research Frontiers in Anthropology*. Englewood Cliffs, NJ: Prentice Hall, 1995. Prentice Hall/Simon & Schuster Custom Publishing. Particularly appropriate to this chapter are pieces written by ten researchers from different subfields of anthropology about their careers and personal research experiences ("Researchers at Work"). They are: physical anthropologists Timothy Bromage and Katharine Milton, archaeologists Richard Blanton and Elizabeth Brumfiel, linguists Benjamin Blount and Susan Philips, ethnologists Carol Ember and Terence Hays, and applied anthropologists Andrew Miracle and Susan Weller.

FAGAN, B. M. *People of the Earth: An Introduction to World Prehistory*, 7th ed. New York: Harper Collins, 1992.

A survey of world prehistory, describing what we know from archaeology about hunters and gatherers, farmers, and cities and civilizations in all areas of the world.

HARRISON, G. A., TANNER, J. M., PILBEAM, D. R., AND BAKER, P. T. *Human Biology: An Introduction to Human Evolution, Variation, Growth, and Adaptability*, 3rd ed. Oxford: Oxford University Press, 1988. A survey of research and recent developments in the study of human evolution, human genetics and variation, human growth and constitution, and human adaptability.

HOWELLS, W. *Getting Here: The Story of Human Evolution*. Washington, D.C.: Compass Press, 1993. An accessible introduction to the study of human evolution.

KONNER, M. *The Tangled Wing: Biological Constraints on the Human Spirit*. New York: Harper & Row, 1987. A biological anthropologist discusses the biological and cultural roots of human behavior and emotions.

▼ NOTES

[1]Gail G. Harrison, "Primary Adult Lactase Deficiency: A Problem in Anthropological Genetics," *American Anthropologist*, 77 (1975): 812–35; William H. Durham, *Coevolution: Genes, Culture and Human Diversity* (Stanford, CA: Stanford University Press, 1991), pp. 228-37.

[2]Andrew W. Miracle, "A Shaman to Organizations," in Carol R. Ember, Melvin Ember, and Peter N. Peregrine, eds., *Research Frontiers in Anthropology* (Englewood Cliffs, NJ: Prentice Hall, 1995), Prentice Hall/Simon & Schuster Custom Publishing; Gilbert Kushner, "Applied Anthropology," in William G. Emener and Mar-

garet Darrow, eds., *Career Explorations in Human Services* (Springfield, IL: Charles C. Thomas, 1991).

[3]Leslie A. White, "The Expansion of the Scope of Science," in Morton H. Fried, ed., *Readings in Anthropology*, 2nd ed., vol. 1 (New York: Thomas Y. Crowell, 1968), pp. 15–24.

[4]The exclamation point in the word *!Kung* signifies one of the clicking sounds made with the tongue by speakers of the !Kung language.

[5]Edward T. Hall, *The Hidden Dimension* (Garden City, NY: Doubleday, 1966), pp. 144–53.

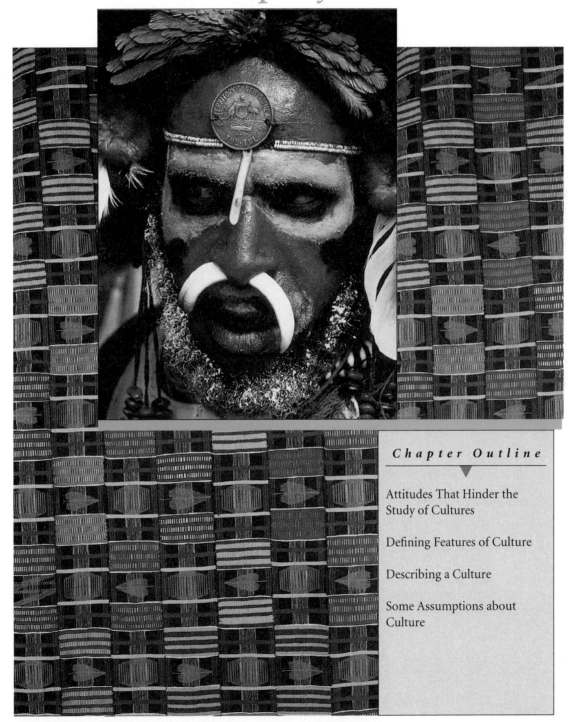

2

The Concept of Culture

We all consider ourselves to be unique individuals with a set of personal opinions, preferences, habits, and quirks. Indeed, all of us *are* unique individuals, and yet most of us share the feeling that it is wrong to eat dogs, the belief that bacteria or viruses cause illness, the habit of sleeping on a bed. There are many such feelings, beliefs, and habits that we share with most of the people who live in our society. We hardly ever think about the ideas and customs we share, but they constitute what anthropologists refer to as North American "culture."

We tend not to think about our culture because it is so much a part of us that we take it for granted. If and when we become aware that other peoples have different feelings from ours, different beliefs, and different habits, we begin to think of how we share certain ideas and customs. We would never even think of the possibility of eating dog meat if we were not aware that people in some other societies commonly do so. We would not realize that our belief in germs was cultural if we were not aware that people in some societies think that illness is caused by witchcraft or evil spirits. We could not become aware that it is our custom to sleep on beds if we were not aware that people in many societies sleep on the floor or ground. It is only when we compare ourselves with people in other societies that we become aware of cultural differences and similarities. This is, in fact, the way that anthropology as a profession began; when Europeans began to explore and move to faraway places, they were forced to confront the sometimes striking facts of cultural variation.

ATTITUDES THAT HINDER THE STUDY OF CULTURES

Many of the Europeans who first came to those faraway places were revolted or shocked by customs they observed. Such reactions are not surprising. People commonly feel that their own customary behaviors and attitudes are the correct ones, that people who do not share those patterns are immoral or inferior. But our own customs and ideas may appear bizarre or barbaric to an observer from another society. Hindus in India, for example, would consider our custom of eating beef both primitive and disgusting. In their culture, the cow is a sacred animal and may not be slaughtered for food. In many societies a baby is almost constantly carried by someone, in someone's lap, or asleep next to others.[1] People in such societies may think it is cruel

of us to leave babies alone for long periods of time, often in devices that resemble cages (cribs and playpens). Even our most ordinary customs—the daily rituals we take for granted—might seem thoroughly absurd when viewed from an objective perspective. An observer of our society might justifiably take notes on certain strange behaviors that seem quite ordinary to us, as the following extract shows:

> The daily body ritual performed by everyone includes a mouth-rite. Despite the fact that these people are so punctilious about the care of the mouth, this rite involves a practice which strikes the uninitiated stranger as revolting. It was reported to me that the ritual consists of inserting a small bundle of hog hairs into the mouth, along with certain magical powders, and then moving the bundle in a highly formalized series of gestures. In addition to the private mouth-rite, the people seek out a holy-mouth man once or twice a year. These practitioners have an impressive set of paraphernalia, consisting of a variety of augers, awls, probes, and prods. The use of these objects in the exorcism of the evils of the mouth involves almost unbelievable ritual torture of the client. The holy-mouth man opens the client's mouth and, using the above mentioned tools, enlarges any holes which decay may have created in teeth. Magical materials are put into these holes. If there are no naturally occurring holes in the teeth, large sections of one or more teeth are gouged out so that the supernatural substance can be applied. In the client's view, the purpose of these ministrations is to arrest decay and to draw friends. The extremely sacred and traditional character of the rite is evident in the fact that the natives return to the holy-mouth man year after year, despite the fact that their teeth continue to decay.[2]

We are likely to protest that to understand the behaviors of a particular society—in this case our own—the observer must try to find out more about why the people in that society say they do things. For example, the observer might find out that periodic visits to the "holy-mouth man" are for medical, not magical, purposes. Indeed, the observer, after some questioning, might discover that the "mouth-rite" has no sacred or religious connotations whatsoever. The anthropological attitude that a society's customs and ideas should be described objectively and understood in the context of that society's problems and opportunities is called **cultural relativism.** Because this attitude fosters empathy and understanding, it is humanistic; because it requires impartial observation and involves attempts to test possible explanations of customs, the attitude of cultural relativism is also scientific.

In general, cultural relativism is impeded by two different but commonly held attitudes. The first is the tendency toward negative evaluation, which usually results from ethnocentrism; the second is the tendency toward positive evaluation, which often takes the form of a naive yearning for the simple life of the "noble savage."

Ethnocentrism

The person whose vision is limited strictly to her or his own needs and desires is generally ineffective in dealing with other people. We call such an individual egocentric, and we would be sorry to have such a person for a psychiatrist. The person who judges other cultures solely in terms of his or her own culture is **ethnocentric.** (This attitude is called **ethnocentrism.**) Such people are not only ill equipped to do anthropological work, but they also may be unable to recognize and deal with social problems in their own society.

For example, an ethnocentric North American would view as barbaric the ceremonies that initiate adolescent boys into manhood in many societies. These ceremonies often involve hazing, difficult tests of courage and endurance, and painful circumcision. The ethnocentric North American would be unable to understand why anyone would willingly endure such hardships merely to be publicly accepted as an adult. The same type of ethno-

HUMAN RIGHTS AND CULTURAL RELATIVITY

The news increasingly reports violations of human rights the world over—examples range from jailing individuals for expressing political ideas to ethnic massacre. But faced with criticism from the West, people in other countries are increasingly saying that the West should not dictate ideas about human rights to the rest of the world. Indeed, many countries say they have different codes of ethics. Are the Western countries taking their own cultural ideas and applying them to the rest of the world, thereby being ethnocentric? Should we instead employ the concept of cultural relativism, considering each culture on its own terms? If we do that, then it may not be possible to have a universal standard of human rights. Many would say that there are no easy answers to these questions, but

ignoring cultural differences does not help.

What we do know is that *all* cultures have ethical standards, but they do not always emphasize the same things. So, for example, some cultures emphasize individual political rights; others may emphasize political order. Some cultures emphasize protection of individual property; others emphasize the sharing or equitable distribution of resources. The United States may have freedom to dissent and the right not to have property taken away, but people can be deprived of health insurance or of food if they lack the money to buy it.

Can the concept of cultural relativism be reconciled with the concept of an international code of human rights? Probably not completely. Paul Rosenblatt recognizes the dilemma but nonetheless thinks that something has

to be done to stop torture and "ethnic cleansing," among other things. He makes the case that "to the extent that it is easier to persuade people whose viewpoints and values one understands, relativism can be a tool for change . . . a relativist's awareness of the values and understanding of the elite makes it easier to know what arguments would be persuasive. (For example, in a society in which the group rather than the individual has great primacy, it might be persuasive to try to show how respect for individual rights benefits the group.)" What do you think?

Source: *Paul C. Rosenblatt, "Human Rights Violations Across Cultures,"* in Carol R. Ember, Melvin Ember, and Peter N. Peregrine, eds., Research Frontiers in Anthropology *(Englewood Cliffs, NJ: Prentice Hall, 1995). Prentice Hall/ Simon & Schuster Custom Publishing.*

centric thinking, however, would make it difficult for such a person to ask whether our treatment of adolescents, which generally lacks clear markers of attainment of adult status, makes adolescence in North America an even more difficult time than it need be. Ethnocentrism, then, hinders our understanding of the customs of other people and, at the same time, keeps us from understanding our own customs. If we think that everything we do is best, we are not likely to ask why we do what we do or why "they" do what "they" do.

The "Noble Savage"

Whenever we are weary of the complexities of civilization, we may long for a way of life that is "closer to nature" or "simpler" than our own. For instance, a young North American whose parent is holding two or three jobs just to provide the family with bare necessities might briefly be attracted to the lifestyle of the !Kung of the Kalahari Desert as of the 1950s. The !Kung shared their food and therefore were often free to engage in leisure activities during the greater part of the day. They obtained all their food by hunting animals and gathering wild plants.

They had no facilities for refrigeration, so sharing a freshly killed animal was clearly more sensible than hoarding rotten meat. Moreover, the sharing provided a kind of social security system for the !Kung. If a hunter was unable to catch an animal on a certain day, he could obtain food for himself and his family from someone else in his band. Conversely, at some later date the game he caught would provide food for the family of some other unsuccessful hunter. This system of sharing also ensured that persons too young or too old to help with the collecting of food would still be fed.

The food-sharing system of the !Kung, however, was a solution to the problems posed by their special environment and is not necessarily a practical solution to problems in our own society. Moreover, other aspects of !Kung life would not appeal to many North Americans. For example, when the nomadic !Kung decided to move their camps, they had to carry all the family possessions, substantial amounts of food and water, and all young children below age 4 or 5. This is a sizable burden to carry for any distance. The !Kung traveled about 1500 miles in a single year.[3] Thus, for them being nomadic meant that families could not have many possessions. It is un-

Because we are ethnocentric about many things, it is often difficult to criticize our own customs—some of which might be shocking to a member of another society. A grandfather in China regularly cares for his grandchild. In contrast, an elderly American man generally spends his days alone.

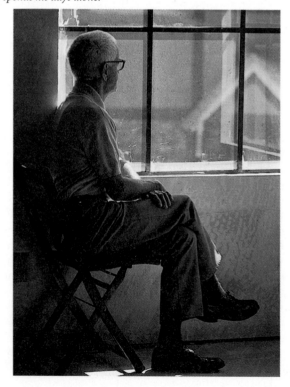

likely then that most North Americans would find the !Kung way of life enviable in all respects.

The point here is not that we should avoid comparing our culture with others, but that we should not romanticize other cultures. Most of the customs of other societies probably are, or were, appropriate to their physical and social environments, just as most of our customs probably are, or were, appropriate to our own environment. Cultural relativism asks that all customs of a society be viewed objectively, not ethnocentrically or romantically.

Does cultural relativism mean that the actions of another society, or of our own, should not be judged? Does our insistence on objectivity mean that anthropologists should not make moral judgments about the cultural phenomena they observe and try to explain? Not really. Anthropologists do make judgments, and some try to change behavior they think is harmful. But judgments need not and should not preclude objectivity. Our goal in research is to strive for accurate description and explanation in spite of any judgments we might have. In the chapter on explanation and evidence, we discuss some procedures that scientists, including anthropologists, use to minimize the possibility that their own expectations will affect their observations and tests of explanations.

We have tried so far in this chapter to convey intuitively what culture is, and we have discussed attitudes that hinder or bias the study of cultures. Now let us turn to what seem to be the defining features of culture for most anthropologists.

DEFINING FEATURES OF CULTURE

In everyday usage, the word *culture* refers to a desirable quality we can acquire by attending a sufficient number of plays and concerts and trudging through several miles of art galleries. The anthropologist, however, has a different definition, as Ralph Linton explained:

Culture refers to the total way of life of any society, not simply to those parts of this way which the society regards as higher or more desirable. Thus culture, when applied to our own way of life, has nothing to do with playing the piano or reading Browning. For the social scientist such activities are simply elements within the totality of our culture. This totality also includes such mundane activities as washing dishes or driving an automobile, and for the purposes of cultural studies these stand quite on a par with "the finer things of life." It follows that for the social scientist there are no uncultured societies or even individuals. Every society has a culture, no matter how simple this culture may be, and every human being is cultured, in the sense of participating in some culture or other.[4]

Culture, then, refers to innumerable aspects of life. Some anthropologists think of culture as the rules or ideas behind behavior.[5] Most anthropologists think of culture as including the learned behaviors as well as the beliefs, attitudes, values, and ideals that are characteristic of a particular society or population.

Culture Is Commonly Shared

If only one person thinks or does a certain thing, that thought or action represents a personal habit, not a pattern of culture. For a thought or action to be considered cultural, it must be commonly shared by some population or group of individuals. Even if some behavior is not commonly practiced, it is cultural if most people think it is appropriate. The idea that marriage should involve only one man and only one woman is cultural in our society. Most North Americans share this idea and act accordingly when they marry. The role of president or prime minister is not widely shared—after all, there is only one such person at a time—but the role is cultural because most inhabitants of a country with such a position agree that it should exist, and its occupant is generally expected to exhibit certain behaviors. We usually share many values, beliefs, and behaviors with our families and friends (although anthropologists are not particularly concerned with this type of cultural group). We commonly share cultural characteristics with segments of our population whose ethnic or regional origins, religious affiliations, and occupations are the same as or similar to our own. We have certain practices, beliefs, and feelings in common with most North Americans. And we share certain characteristics with people beyond our society who have similar interests (such as rules for international sporting events) or similar roots (as do the various English-speaking nations).

When we talk about the commonly shared customs of a society, which constitute the central concern of cultural anthropology, we are referring to a *culture*. When we talk about the commonly shared customs of a group within a society, which are a central concern of sociology, we are referring to a **subculture.** And when we study the commonly shared customs of some group that includes different societies, we are talking about a phenome-

culture is:

non for which we do not have a single word (only compound phrases including the word *culture*). So, for example, we refer to *Western culture* (the cultural characteristics of societies in or derived from western Europe) and the *culture of poverty* (the presumed cultural characteristics of poor people the world over).

We must remember that even when anthropologists refer to something as cultural, there is always individual variation, which means that not everyone in a society shares a particular cultural characteristic of the society. For example, it is cultural in our society for adults to live apart from parents. But not all adults in our society do so, nor do all adults wish to do so. The custom of living apart from parents is considered cultural because most adults practice that custom. As Edward Sapir noted in the late 1930s, in every society studied by anthropologists—in the simplest as well as the most complex—individuals do not *all* think and act the same.[6] As we discuss below, individual variation is the source of new culture.[7]

Culture Is Learned

Not all things shared generally by a population are cultural. The typical hair color of a population is not cultural. Nor is eating. For something to be considered cultural, it must be learned as well as shared. A typical hair color (unless dyed) is not cultural because it is genetically determined. Humans eat because they must, but what and when and how they eat are learned and vary from culture to culture. North Americans do not think dogs are edible, and indeed the idea of eating dogs horrifies us. But in China, as in some other societies, dog meat is considered delicious. In our society, many people consider a baked ham to be a holiday dish. In several societies of the Middle East, however, including those of Egypt and Israel, eating the meat of a pig is forbidden by sacred writings.

To some extent, all animals exhibit learned behaviors, some of which may be shared by most individuals in a population and may therefore be considered cultural. But different animal species vary in the degree to which their shared behaviors are learned or are instinctive. The sociable ants, for instance, despite all their patterned social behavior, do not appear to have much, if any, culture. They divide their labor, construct their nests, form their raiding columns, and carry off their dead, all without having been taught to do so and without imitating the behavior of other ants. In contrast, much of the behavior of humans appears to be culturally patterned.

We are increasingly discovering that our closest biological relatives—the monkeys and the apes—learn a wide variety of behaviors. Some of their learned responses are as basic as those involved in maternal care; others are as frivolous as the taste for candy. Some of these learned behaviors when shared could be described as cultural. For example, as we discuss in more detail in the chapter on communication and language, vervet monkeys learn to use a certain call in the presence of circling eagles, who prey on the monkeys. The call seems to mean "Watch out—there are eagles around!" Its meaning seems to be shared or understood by the group, because they all respond similarly (they look up) when one individual sounds the call.

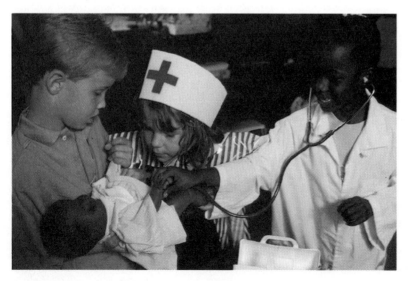

When children play at adult roles, they are often imitating what the culture allows or prefers.

portion of an animal's life span occu-
...hood seems to reflect the degree to
...al depends on learned behavior for
...eys and apes have relatively long
...ared with other animals. Humans
...ngest childhood of any animal, re-
...dependence on learned behavior.
...may acquire much learned behav-
...r and imitation, as do monkeys
...an learned behavior is probably
...of spoken, symbolic language.

...known to anthropologists,
...of society, have had a com-
...symbolic communication,
...nguage is *symbolic* in that a
...resent what it stands for
...*present*.

...of language has tremen-
...nsmission of culture. It
...can tell a child that a
...erous and should be
...describe the snake in
...eter, color, texture,
...on. The parent can
...where the child is
...lain how the child
...ncounter a snake,
...all the symbolic
...well the related
...f symbolic lan-
...d have to wait
...ke and then,
...such a crea-
...we probably
...ion so effi-
...e heir to so
rich an...

T... ...ething is cul-
tural if ...ehavior, belief, attitude,
value, or ...generally shared by the members of a
group. Traditionally, anthropologists have usually
been concerned with the cultural characteristics of a
society, by which they mean a group of people who
occupy a particular territory and speak a common
language not generally understood by neighboring
peoples. By this definition, societies do not necessarily correspond to nations. There are many nations, particularly the "new" ones, that have within
their boundaries different peoples speaking mutually unintelligible languages. By our definition of
society, such nations are composed of many different societies and cultures. Also, by our definition of
society, some societies may even include more than

one nation. For example, we would have to say that
Canada and the United States form a single society
because the two groups generally speak English, live
next to each other, and share many common beliefs,
values, and practices. That is why we refer to "North
American culture" in this chapter. Not everyone
would agree that Canada and the United States
form a single society; some would prefer to consider
the United States and Canada two different societies
because they are separate political entities.

Given that a society refers to a group of people who occupy a particular territory and speak
a common language not generally understood
by neighboring peoples, when an anthropologist
speaks about *a* **culture,** she or he is usually referring to that set of learned and shared beliefs,
values, and behaviors generally characteristic of a
particular society. But now that we have defined
what is cultural, we must ask a further question:
How does an anthropologist go about deciding
which particular behaviors, values, and beliefs of individuals are cultural?

DESCRIBING A CULTURE

Individual Variation

Describing a particular culture might seem relatively uncomplicated at first: you simply observe
what the people in that society do and then record
their behavior. But consider the substantial difficulties you might encounter. How would you decide
which people to observe? And what would you conclude if each of the first dozen people you observed
or talked to behaved quite differently in the same
situation? Admittedly, you would be unlikely to encounter such extreme divergence of behaviors. Yet
there would tend to be significant individual variation in the actual behaviors observed, even when individuals were responding to the same generalized
situation and conforming to cultural expectations.

To better understand how an anthropologist
might make sense of diverse behaviors, let us
examine this diversity as it exists at a professional
football game in the United States. When people
attend a football game, various members of the
crowd behave differently while "The Star-Spangled
Banner" is being played. As they stand and listen,
some people remove their hats; a child munches
popcorn; a former soldier stands at attention; a
teenager searches the crowd for a friend; and the two
head coaches take a final opportunity to intone secret
chants and spells designed to sap the strength of the

opposing team. Yet, despite these individual variations, most of the people at the game respond in a basically similar manner: nearly everyone stands silently, facing the flag. Moreover, if you go to several football games, you will observe that many aspects of the event are notably similar. Although the plays used will vary from game to game, the rules of the game are never different, and, although the colors of the uniforms of the teams are different, the players never appear on the field dressed in swimsuits.

Although the variations in individual reactions to a given stimulus are theoretically limitless, in fact they tend to fall within easily recognizable limits. The child listening to the anthem may continue to eat popcorn, but will probably not do a rain dance. Similarly, it is unlikely that the coaches will react to that same stimulus by running onto the field and embracing the singer. Variations in behavior, then, are confined within socially acceptable limits, and it is part of the anthropologist's goal to find out what those limits are. He or she may note, for example, that some limitations on behavior have a practical purpose: a spectator who disrupts the game by wandering onto the field would be required to leave. Other limitations are purely traditional. In our society it is

In deciding what is cultural behavior, anthropologists look for commonalities, but there is always individual variation. Here, just before a game most of the crowd, but not all, are facing forward and placing a hand over the heart during the playing of the national anthem.

considered proper for a man to remove his overcoat if he becomes overheated, but others would undoubtedly frown upon his removing his trousers even if the weather was quite warm. Using such observations, the anthropologist attempts to discover the customs and the ranges of acceptable behavior that characterize the society under study.

By focusing on the range of customary behavior, discovered by observing or asking about individual variation, the anthropologist is able to describe cultural characteristics of a group. For example, an anthropologist interested in describing courtship and marriage in our society would initially encounter a variety of behaviors. The anthropologist may note that one couple prefers to go to a concert on a first date, whereas another couple chooses to go bowling; some couples have very long engagements and others never become engaged at all; some couples emphasize religious rituals in the marriage ceremony, but others are married by civil authorities; and so on. Despite this variability, the anthropologist, after further observation and interviewing, might begin to detect certain regularities in courting practices. Although couples may do many different things on their first and subsequent dates, they nearly always arrange the dates by themselves, they try to avoid their parents when on dates, they often manage to find themselves alone at the end of a date, they put their lips together frequently, and so forth. After a series of more and more closely spaced encounters, a man and woman may decide to declare themselves publicly as a couple, either by announcing that they are engaged or by revealing that they are living together or intend to do so. Finally, if the two of them decide to marry, they must in some way have their union recorded by the civil authorities.

In our society a person who wishes to marry cannot completely disregard the customary patterns of courtship. If a man saw a woman on the street and decided he wanted to marry her, he could conceivably choose a quicker and more direct form of action than the usual dating procedure. He could get on a horse, ride to the woman's home, snatch her up in his arms, and gallop away with her. In Sicily, until recently such a couple would have been considered legally married, even if the woman had never met the man before or had no intention of marrying. But in our society, any man who acted in such a fashion would be arrested and jailed for kidnapping and would probably have his sanity challenged. Such behavior would not be acceptable in our society. Although individual behaviors may vary, most social behavior falls within culturally acceptable limits.

Cultural Constraints

A primary limit on the range of the individual behavior variations is the culture itself. The noted French sociologist Emile Durkheim stressed that culture is something *outside* us exerting a strong coercive power on us. We do not always feel the constraints of our culture because we generally conform to the types of conduct and thought it requires. Standards or rules about what is acceptable behavior are referred to by social scientists as **norms.** The importance of a norm usually can be judged by how members of a society respond when the norm is violated.

Cultural constraints are of two basic types, *direct* and *indirect*. Naturally, the direct constraints are the more obvious. For example, if you choose to wear a casual shorts outfit to a wedding, you will probably be subject to some ridicule and a certain amount of social isolation. But if you choose to wear nothing, you may be exposed to a stronger, more direct cultural constraint—arrest for indecent exposure.

Although indirect forms of cultural constraint are less obvious than direct ones, they are no less effective. Durkheim illustrated this point when he wrote, "I am not obliged to speak French with my fellow-countrymen, nor to use the legal currency, but I cannot possibly do otherwise. If I tried to escape this necessity, my attempt would fail miserably."[8] In other words, if Durkheim had decided he would rather speak Serbo-Croatian than French, nobody would have tried to stop him. But no one would have

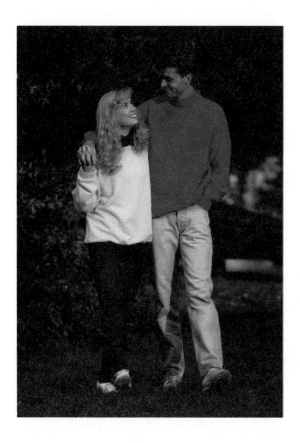

Couples in our society vary in how they date or go out, but they often spend time by themselves and express some affection in public. In contrast, couples in some societies are rarely seen by themselves and never display affection in public.

understood him either. And, although he would not have been put into prison for trying to buy groceries with Icelandic money, he would have had difficulty convincing the local merchants to sell him food.

In a series of classic experiments on conformity, Solomon Asch revealed how strong cultural constraints can be. Asch coached the majority of a group of college students to give deliberately incorrect answers to questions involving visual stimuli. A "critical subject," the one student in the room who was not so coached, had no idea that the other participants would purposely misinterpret the evidence presented to them. Asch found that in one-third of the experiments, the critical subjects *consistently* allowed their own correct perceptions to be distorted by the obviously incorrect statements of the others. And in another 40 percent of the experiments, the critical subject yielded to the opinion of the group some of the time.[9]

The existence of social or cultural constraints, however, is not necessarily incompatible with individuality. Cultural constraints are usually exercised most forcefully around the limits of acceptable behavior. Thus, there is often a broad range of behavior within which individuals can exercise their uniqueness. And individuals do not always give in to the wishes of the majority. In the Asch experiments, many individuals (one-fourth of the critical subjects) consistently retained their independent opinions in the face of complete disagreement with the majority.

Ideal versus Actual Cultural Patterns

Every society has ideas (values and norms) about how people in particular situations ought to feel and behave. In everyday terms we speak of these ideas as *ideals;* in anthropology we refer to them as *ideal cultural patterns.* These patterns tend to be reinforced through cultural constraints. But we all know that people do not always behave according to the standards they express. If they did, there would be no need for direct or indirect constraints. Some of our ideal patterns differ from actual behavior because the ideal is outmoded—that is, it is based on the way a society used to be. (Consider the ideal of "free enterprise"—that industry should be totally free of governmental regulation.) Other ideal patterns may never have been actual patterns and may represent merely what people would like to see as correct behavior.

To illustrate the difference between ideal and actual culture, consider the idealized belief, long cherished in North America, that everybody is "equal before the law," that everybody should be treated in the same way by the police and courts. Of course, we know that this is not always true. The rich, for example, may receive less jail time and be sent to nicer prisons. Nevertheless, the ideal is still part of our culture—most of us continue to believe that the law *should* be applied equally to all.

How to Discover Cultural Patterns

There are two basic ways in which an anthropologist can discover cultural patterns. When dealing with customs that are overt or highly visible within a society—for example, our custom of sending children to school—the investigator can determine the existence of such practices and study them with the aid of a few knowledgeable persons. When dealing with a particular sphere of behavior that encompasses many individual variations, or when the people studied are unaware of their pattern of behavior, the anthropologist should collect information from a sample of individuals in order to establish what the cultural pattern is.

One example of a cultural pattern that most people in a society are not aware of is how far apart people stand when they are having a conversation. Yet there is considerable reason to believe that unconscious cultural rules govern such behavior. These rules become obvious when we interact with people who have different rules. We may experience considerable discomfort when another person stands too close (indicating too much intimacy) or too far (indicating unfriendliness). Edward Hall reported that Arabs customarily stand quite close to others—close enough, in fact, to be able to smell the other person. In interactions between Arabs and North Americans, then, the Arabs will move closer at the same time that the North Americans back away.[10]

If we wanted to arrive at the cultural rule for conversational distance between casual acquaintances, let us say, we could study a sample of individuals from a society and determine the *modal response,* or *mode.* The mode is a statistical term that refers to the most frequently encountered response in a given series of responses. So, for the North American pattern of casual conversational distance, we would plot the actual distance for many observed pairs of people. Some pairs may be 2 feet apart, some 2.5, and some 4 feet apart. If the observer counts the number of times every particular distance is observed, these counts provide what we call a *frequency distribution.* The distance with the highest frequency is the modal pattern. Very often the frequency distribution takes the form of a *bell-shaped curve,* as shown in Figure 2–1. There the characteristic measured is plotted on the horizontal axis (in this case, the distance between conversational pairs) and the number of times each distance is observed (its frequency) is plotted on the vertical axis. If we were to plot how a sample of North American casual conversational pairs is distributed, we would probably get a bell-shaped curve that peaks at around 3 feet.[11] Is it any wonder, then, that we sometimes speak of keeping others "at arm's length"?

Frequency distributions may be calculated on the basis of behaviors exhibited or responses given by all the members of a particular population. But studying everybody is rarely necessary. Instead, most social scientists rely on a subset, or *sample,* that is believed to be representative of the larger population. The best way to ensure that a sample is representative is to choose a **random sample**—that is, give all individuals an equal chance of being chosen. If a sample is random, it probably will include examples of all frequent variations of behavior or response exhibited in the society or community in roughly the proportions in which they actually occur.

Because it is relatively easy to make generalizations about public aspects of a culture, such as the existence of an executive, legislative, and judicial branch in the United States government, or about widely shared norms or behaviors, which almost anyone can identify correctly, random sampling often is not necessary. But in dealing with aspects of culture that are more private, difficult to put into words, or unconscious, the investigator may have to observe or interview a random sample of people in order to generalize correctly about whether or not there are cultural patterns. The reason is that most people may not be aware of others' private behavior and thoughts (such as sexual attitudes and behavior), nor are they aware of unconscious cultural patterns (such as conversational distance). The fact that something is less readily observed publically or harder to put into words does not imply that it is less likely to be shared. However, it is harder to discover those aspects of culture.

Although we may be able to discover by interviews and observation that a behavior, thought, or feeling is widely shared within a society, how do we establish that something commonly shared is learned, so that we can call it cultural? Establishing that something is or is not learned may be difficult. Because children are not reared apart from adult caretakers, the behaviors they exhibit as part of their genetic inheritance are not clearly separated from those they learn from others around them. We suspect that particular behaviors and ideas are learned if they vary from society to society. And we suspect purely genetic determinism when particular behaviors or ideas are found in all societies. For example, as we will see in the chapter on language, children the world over seem to acquire language at about the same time, and the structure of their early utterances seems to be similar. These facts suggest that human children are born with an innate grammar. However, although early-childhood language seems similar the world over, the particular languages spoken by adults in different societies show considerable variability. This variability suggests that particular languages have to be learned. Similarly, if the courtship patterns of one society differ markedly from those of another, we can be fairly certain that those courtship patterns are learned and therefore cultural. Of course, anthropologists may sometimes err in their presumption that a particular behavior, thought, or feeling is purely cultural.

SOME ASSUMPTIONS ABOUT CULTURE

Culture Is Generally Adaptive

There are some cultural behaviors that, if carried to an extreme, would decrease the chances of survival of a particular society. For example, certain tribes in New Guinea view women as essentially unclean and dangerous individuals with whom physical contact should be as limited as possible. Suppose the men in one such tribe decided to avoid contact, including sexual contact, with women completely. Clearly, we

FIGURE 2–1
Frequency Distribution Curve

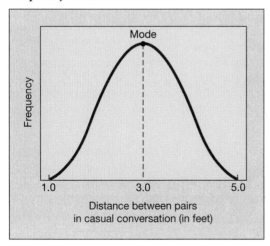

"ON THE STRANGE AND THE FAMILIAR IN RECENT ANTHROPOLOGICAL THOUGHT"

Melford Spiro was struck by a remark by T. S. Eliot that the hallmark of good poetry was "the making of the familiar strange, and the strange familiar," for it seemed to Spiro that this too was the hallmark of "good" anthropology.

Just how do anthropologists do that? Spiro says they do it primarily by translating what other people do (other cultures—which at first seem strange) *and* what we do (the anthropologist's own culture—the familiar) into a third set of concepts—anthropological concepts. By doing so, anthropologists avoid ethnocentrism—seeing others in terms of our own culture—and at the same time avoid seeing our culture as it might be evaluated by others. Referring to both the strange and the familiar in terms of a third set of concepts makes both the strange and the familiar easier to discuss and contrast.

Let's apply this principle to what we discussed about how far apart strangers typically stand when they have a conversation. If we just used the point of view of our own (North American culture) we might end up saying that Arabs stand too close. If we took the Arab point of view, we might say Arabs stand where it is comfortable, and North Americans stand too far. If we continued to switch to the point of view of other societies, we might end up saying that both Arabs and North Americans stand too close or both too far. But, if we apply concepts *outside* of both, such as a measure of distance in feet or meters, then we are able to describe typical conversational distances in all groups, not just in the world today, but in the world tomorrow too. Such an outside or objective point of view makes it possible to ask: Why is conversational distance closer in some cultures than in others? If we ask that question, then cultures can be ordered from less to more distance, without saying what feels "close" or "far" or what distance feels right.

Spiro tells us that for the last few decades some anthropologists have rejected the view that we could or should make "the strange familiar." They think that cultures are so diverse, so fundamentally different, so incomparable, that no translation is possible. But, Spiro points out, "The proponents of this view . . . do precisely that—they themselves describe and interpret strange cultures—those strange cultures cannot be so strange after all."

We would point out that anthropologists have not completely succeeded in banishing the biases that come from their own culture, their gender, their training, or their personality when they do fieldwork in other cultures. But biases themselves can be studied and compared. So, for example, if we think that women and men anthropologists observe different things, we can compare their observations. If we want to find out whether North American anthropologists observe differently than anthropologists from elsewhere, we can compare their observations too. And think how much more we might know when we have people from different perspectives looking at the same thing and sharing their responses. If they can share their responses, what they are observing cannot be so strange.

Source: *Melford Spiro, "On the Strange and the Familiar in Recent Anthropological Thought," in Carol R. Ember, Melvin Ember, and Peter N. Peregrine, eds.,* Research Frontiers in Anthropology *(Englewood Cliffs, NJ: Prentice Hall, 1995). Prentice Hall/Simon & Schuster Custom Publishing.*

would not expect such a society to survive for long. Although this example may appear extreme, it indicates that customs that diminish the survival chances of a society are not likely to persist. Either the people clinging to those customs will become extinct, taking the customs with them, or the customs will be replaced, thereby possibly helping the people to survive. By either process, **maladaptive** customs (those that diminish the chances of survival and reproduction) are likely to disappear. The customs of a society that enhance survival and reproductive success are **adaptive** and are likely to persist. Hence, we assume that if a society has survived to be described in the annals of anthropology (the "ethnographic record"), much if not most of its cultural repertoire is adaptive, or was at one time.

When we say that a custom is adaptive, however, we mean it is adaptive only with respect to a specific physical and social environment. What may be adaptive in one environment may not be adaptive in another. Therefore, when we ask why a society may have a particular custom, we really are asking if that custom makes sense as an adaptation to that society's particular environmental conditions.

Many cultural behaviors that would otherwise appear incomprehensible to us may be understandable as a society's response to its environment. For example, we might express surprise at certain societies' postpartum sex taboos that prohibit women from engaging in sexual intercourse until their two-year-olds are ready to be weaned. But in the tropical areas where such taboos exist, they may represent a people's means of adjusting to their physical environment. If there were no such taboo and a mother had another baby soon, she could no longer continue to nurse the older baby. Without its mother's milk, the older child might succumb to *kwashiorkor,* a severe protein-deficiency disease that is common in those tropical areas. The taboo, then, may serve to give infants a better chance to survive.[12] Thus, a long postpartum sex taboo may be an adaptive custom in certain tropical countries. In nontropical areas where kwashiorkor is not a problem, the same taboo may not be advantageous.

Just as culture represents an adjustment to the physical environment and to biological demands, it may also represent an adjustment to the social environment—that is, to neighboring peoples. For example, we do not know for sure why the Hopi Indians of what is now the state of Arizona began building their settlements on the tops of mesas. They must have had strong reasons for doing so, because there were many difficulties in building on such sites—the problem of hauling water long distances to the settlements, for instance. It is possible that the Hopi chose to locate their villages on mesa tops for defensive reasons when Athapaskan-speaking groups of Indians (the Navaho and Apache) moved into the Hopi area. In other words, the Hopi may have adjusted their living habits to their social environment.

A given custom represents one society's adaptation to its environment; it does not represent all possible adaptations. Different societies may choose different means of adjusting to the same situation. Thus, among some Native South American Indian societies where people's diets are low in protein, there is no long postpartum sex taboo, but induced abortion is reported to be a common practice. This practice may serve the same function of spacing out live births and thereby preventing too early weaning of children. The Hopi Indians, when suddenly confronted by the Navaho and Apache, clearly had to take some action to protect themselves. But instead of deciding to build their settlements on easily defended mesa tops, they could conceivably have developed a standing army.

Why a society develops a particular response to a problem, rather than some other possible response, always requires explanation. The choice may depend largely on whether a particular response is possible, given the existing cultural repertoire. For example, in the Hopi case a standing army would not have been a likely response to the problem of invaders because the Hopi economy probably could not have supported any large group of full-time specialists such as soldiers. As we shall see later in the chapter on food-getting, full-time specialists have to be fed by the regular production of more food than the people involved in food production generally need, and such a level of food production did not exist among the Hopi. The strategy of moving their villages to easily defended mesa tops may have been the easiest option, given the Hopi economy.

Although we may assume that societies surviving long enough to be described have had many more adaptive culture traits than maladaptive traits, that does not mean that *all* culture traits are adaptive. Some, if not many, traits may be neutral in terms of adaptation. That is, they may have no direct relationship to reproductive success. Consider, for example, rules about what to wear at weddings and funerals, how to set the table, and how far to stand from someone. Perhaps someone will uncover survival and reproductive consequences of these shared behaviors, but probably they are neutral in terms of survival. Such neutral traits may once have had adaptive consequences, or they may never have had any.

We must remember that a society is not forced to adapt its culture to changing environmental circumstances. First, even in the face of changed circumstances, people may choose not to change their customs. For example, the Tapirapé of central Brazil did not alter their customs limiting the number of births, even though they suffered severe population losses after contact with Europeans and their diseases. The Tapirapé population fell to fewer than 100 people from over 1,000. Clearly they were on the way to extinction, yet they continued to value small families. Not only did they believe that a woman should have no more than three children, but they took specific steps to achieve this limitation. They practiced infanticide if twins were born, if the third child was of the same sex as the first two children, and if the possible fathers broke certain taboos during pregnancy or in the child's infancy.[13]

Of course, it is also possible that a people will behave maladaptively even if they try to alter their behavior. After all, although people may alter their behavior according to what they perceive will be helpful to them, what they perceive to be helpful may not prove to be adaptive.

The Indians who lived hundreds of years ago at Mesa Verde, Colorado, built their villages in inaccessible places, presumably as an adaptation to the need to defend themselves against attack.

Culture Is Mostly Integrated

When we hear of an unfamiliar cultural pattern, our natural response is to try to imagine how that pattern would work in our own society. We might wonder, for example, what would happen if North American women adopted a long postpartum sex taboo—say, one year of abstinence after the birth of a baby. Such a question is purely whimsical, for the customs of one culture cannot easily be grafted onto another culture. A long postpartum sex taboo presupposes a lack of effective birth-control methods, but our society already has many such methods. Moreover, a long postpartum sex taboo could conceivably affect important aspects of our culture, such as the idea that a happy marriage is a sexy one. The point is that with such a taboo imposed on it, our culture would no longer be the same. Too many aspects of the culture would have to be changed to accommodate the new behavior. This is so because our culture is mostly integrated.

In saying that a culture is mostly *integrated*, we mean that the elements or traits that make up that culture are not just a random assortment of customs but are mostly adjusted to or consistent with one another. One reason anthropologists believe that culture tends to be integrated is that culture is generally adaptive. If certain customs are more adaptive in particular settings, then those "bundles" of traits will generally be found together under similar conditions. For example, the !Kung, as we have mentioned, subsisted by hunting wild animals and gathering wild plants. They were also nomadic, had very small communities, had few material possessions, and shared food within their bands. As we will see later, these cultural traits usually occur together when people depend on hunting and gathering for their food.

A culture may also tend to be integrated for psychological reasons. The traits of a culture—attitudes, values, ideals, and rules for behavior—are stored, after all, in the brains of individuals. Research in social psychology has suggested that people tend to modify beliefs or behaviors that are not cognitively or conceptually consistent with other information.[14] We do not expect cultures to be completely integrated, just as we do not expect individuals to be completely consistent. But if a tendency toward cognitive consistency is found in humans, we might expect that at least some aspects of a culture would tend to be integrated for that reason.

How this pressure for consistency works is not hard to imagine. Children, for example, seem to be very good at remembering *all* the things their parents say. If they ask for something and the parents say no, they may say, "But you said I could yesterday." This pressure for consistency may even make parents change their minds! Of course, not everything one wants to do is consistent with the rest of one's desires, but there surely is pressure from within and without to make it so.

Humans are also capable of rational decision making: they can often, if not usually, figure out that certain things are not easy to do because of other things they do. For example, if society has a long postpartum sex taboo, we might expect that most people in the society could figure out that it would be easier to observe the taboo if husband and wife did not sleep in the same bed. Or, if people drive on the left side of the road (as in England), it is easier and less dangerous to drive a car whose steering wheel is on the right, because that placement allows you to judge more accurately how close you are to cars coming at you from the opposite direction.

Consistency or integration of culture traits may also be produced by less conscious psychological processes. As we discuss in the chapters on psychology and culture, religion and magic, and the arts, people may generalize (transfer) their experiences from one realm of life to another. For example, where children are taught that it is wrong to express anger toward family and friends, it turns out that folktales parallel the child rearing: anger and aggression in the folktales tend to be directed only toward strangers, not toward family and friends. It seems as if the expression of anger is too frightening (or maladaptive) to be expressed close to home, even in folktales.

The tendency for a culture to be integrated, then, may be cognitively and emotionally, as well as adaptively, induced.

Culture Is Always Changing

When you examine the history of a society, it is obvious that its culture has changed over time. Some of the shared behaviors, beliefs, and values that were common at one time are modified or replaced at another time. In North American society, we only have to consider our attitudes toward sex and marriage to realize that a lot of our culture has changed recently. The impetus for change may come from within the society or from without. From within, the uncon-

scious or conscious pressure for consistency will produce culture change if enough people adjust old behavior and thinking to new. Change can also occur if people try to invent better ways of doing things. Michael Chibnik suggests that people who confront a new problem conduct mental or small "experiments" to decide how to behave. These experiments may give rise to new cultural traits.[15]

A good deal of culture change may be stimulated by changes in the external environment. For example, if people move into an arid area, they will have to either give up farming or develop a system of irrigation. In the modern world, changes in the social environment are probably more frequent stimuli for culture change than changes in the physical environment. Many North Americans, for example, started to think seriously about conserving energy, and about using sources of energy other than oil, only after oil supplies from the Near East were curtailed in 1973 and 1974. Different societies have often affected each other, and a significant amount of drastic and rapid culture change that has occurred in the last few hundred years has been due to the colonial expansion of Western societies into other areas of the world. Native Americans, for instance, were forced to alter their life-styles drastically when they were driven off their lands and confined to reservations. In the chapter on culture change toward the end of the book, we discuss the major patterns of culture change in the modern world, much of it affected by the expansion of the West.

If we assume that cultures are more than random collections of behaviors, beliefs, and values—that they tend to be adaptive, integrated, and changing—then the similarities and differences between them should be understandable. That is, we can expect that similar circumstances within or outside the culture will give rise to, or favor, similar cultural responses. Although we may assume that cultural variation is understandable, the task of discovering which particular circumstances favor which particular patterns is a large and difficult one. In the chapters that follow, we hope to convey the main points of what anthropologists think they know about aspects of cultural variation, and what they do not know. We frequently describe particular cultures to illustrate aspects of cultural variation. When we do so, the reader should understand that the culture described is probably not the same now, since the sources of our material always refer to some previous time.[16] For example, the !Kung of the 1990s are not necessarily like the !Kung of the 1950s.

▼ SUMMARY

1. Despite very strong individual differences, the members of a particular society closely agree in their responses to certain phenomena because they share common beliefs, attitudes, values, ideals, and behaviors, which constitute their culture.

2. The anthropological attitude that a society's customs and ideas should be studied objectively and understood in the context of that society's culture is called cultural relativism. In general, cultural relativism is impeded by two different but commonly held attitudes: first, the tendency toward negative evaluation, or ethnocentrism; second, the tendency toward positive evaluation, which often takes the form of a naive yearning for the simple life of the "noble savage."

3. Culture may be defined as the learned behaviors, beliefs, attitudes, values, and ideals generally shared by the members of a group.

4. The size of the group within which cultural traits are shared can vary from a particular society or a segment of that society to a group that transcends national boundaries. When anthropologists refer to a culture, they usually are referring to the cultural patterns of a particular society—that is, a particular territorial population speaking a language not generally understood by neighboring territorial populations.

5. A defining feature of culture is that it is learned. Although other animals exhibit some cultural behavior, humans are unusual in the number and complexity of the learned patterns they transmit to their young. And they have a unique way of transmitting their culture: through spoken, symbolic language.

6. Anthropologists seek to discover the customs and ranges of acceptable behavior that constitute the culture of a society under study. In doing so, they focus on general or shared patterns of behavior rather than on individual variations. When dealing with practices that are highly visible, or with beliefs that are almost unanimous, the investigator can rely on observation or on a few knowledgeable persons. With less obvious behaviors or attitudes, the anthropologist must collect information from a sample of individuals. The mode of a frequency distribution can then be used to express the cultural pattern.

7. Every society develops a series of ideal cultural patterns that represent what most members of the society believe to be the correct behavior in particular situations. A society's ideal cultural patterns, however, do not always agree with its actual cultural patterns.

8. One important factor that limits the range of individual variation is the culture itself, which acts directly or indirectly as a constraint on behavior. The existence of cultural constraints, however, is not necessarily incompatible with individuality.

9. Several assumptions are frequently made about culture. First, culture is generally adaptive to the particular conditions of its physical and social environment. What may be adaptive in one environment may not be adaptive in another. Some cultural traits may be neutral in terms of adaptation, some may merely have been adaptive in the past, and still others may be maladaptive. Second, culture is mostly integrated, in that the elements or traits that make up the culture are mostly adjusted to or consistent with one another. Third, culture is always changing.

▼ GLOSSARY TERMS

adaptive

cultural relativism

culture

ethnocentric

ethnocentrism

maladaptive

norms

random sample

society

subculture

▼ CRITICAL QUESTIONS

1. Would it be adaptive for a society to have everyone adhere to the cultural norms?
2. Why does culture change more rapidly in some societies than in others?
3. Does the concept of cultural relativism promote international understanding, or does it hinder attempts to have international agreement on acceptable behavior, such as human rights?

▼ SUGGESTED READING

DE VITA, P., AND ARMSTRONG, D. *Distant Mirrors: America as a Foreign Culture.* Belmont, CA.: Wadsworth Publishing, 1993. Several foreign scholars look at the culture of the United States. Their perceptions challenge persons who were born in the United States to look at their culture from a new perspective.

EMBER, M., EMBER, C. R., AND LEVINSON, D. *Portraits of Culture: Ethnographic Originals.* Englewood Cliffs, NJ: Prentice Hall, 1995. Prentice Hall/Simon & Schuster Custom Publishing. A series of original mini-ethnographies, each describing a different culture and written by someone with firsthand experience in that culture. Each piece provides a portrait of the culture, including how it has recently changed.

FREILICH, M., ed. *The Meaning of Culture.* Lexington, MA: Xerox, 1972. Several views of culture are presented. See especially chapters 7–21.

HALL, E. T., AND HALL, M. R. *Hidden Differences: Doing Business with the Japanese.* Garden City, NY: Anchor (Doubleday), 1987. When people from different cultures interact, their difficulties often stem from hidden, unstated cultural rules of how to behave. On the basis of extensive interviews in the United States and Japan, the authors analyze these hidden communications.

KROEBER, A. L. *The Nature of Culture.* Chicago: University of Chicago Press, 1952. A collection of papers on the nature of culture by a distinguished pioneer in North American anthropology.

SPIRO, M. "On the Strange and the Familiar in Recent Anthropological Thought," in C. R. Ember, M. Ember, and P. N. Peregrine, eds., *Research Frontiers in Anthropology* (Englewood Cliffs, NJ: Prentice Hall, 1995), Prentice Hall/Simon & Schuster Custom Publishing. The author discusses the controversy about whether it is possible in anthropology to make "the strange familiar." Are cultures so diverse and so fundamentally different that it is not really possible for an outsider to understand or describe them?

WERNER, O., AND SCHOEPFLE, G. M. *Systematic Fieldwork. Volume 1: Foundations of Ethnography and Interviewing.* Newbury Park, CA: Sage Publications, 1987. A detailed presentation and discussion of the methods used to discover patterns of culture on the basis of fieldwork.

▼ NOTES

[1]Barry Hewlett, "Diverse Contexts of Human Infancy," in Carol R. Ember and Melvin Ember, eds., *Cross-Cultural Research for Social Science* (Englewood Cliffs, NJ: Prentice Hall, 1995). Prentice Hall/Simon & Schuster Custom Publishing.

[2]Horace Miner, "Body Rituals among the Nacirema," *American Anthropologist,* 58 (1956): 504–5 (reproduced by permission of the American Anthropological Association from *American Anthropologist,* 58: 504–5, 1956). Although Miner is not a foreign visitor, he wrote this description in a way that shows how these behaviors might be seen from an outside perspective.

[3]Richard B. Lee, "Population Growth and the Beginnings of Sedentary Life among the !Kung Bushmen," in Brian Spooner, ed., *Population Growth: Anthropological Implications* (Cambridge, MA: M.I.T. Press, 1972), pp. 329–42.

[4]Ralph Linton, *The Cultural Background of Personality* (New York: Appleton-Century-Crofts, 1945), p. 30.

[5]See, for example, Dorothy Holland and Naomi Quinn, eds., *Cultural Models in Language and Thought* (Cambridge: Cambridge University Press, 1987), p. 4.

[6]Edward Sapir, "Why Cultural Anthropology Needs the Psychiatrist," *Psychiatry,* 1 (1938): 7–12; cited by Pertti J. Pelto and Gretel H. Pelto, "Intra-Cultural Diversity: Some Theoretical Issues," *American Ethnologist,* 2 (1975): 1.

[7]Pelto and Pelto, "Intra-Cultural Diversity," pp. 14–15.

[8]Emile Durkheim, *The Rules of Sociological Method,* 8th ed., trans. Sarah A. Soloway and John H. Mueller, ed. George E. Catlin (New York: Free Press, 1938 [originally published 1895]), p. 3.

[9]Solomon Asch, "Studies of Independence and Conformity: A Minority of One against a Unanimous Majority," *Psychological Monographs,* 70 (1956): 1–70.

[10]Edward T. Hall, *The Hidden Dimension,* (Garden City, NY: Doubleday, 1966), pp. 159–60.

[11]Ibid., p. 120.

[12]John W. M. Whiting, "Effects of Climate on Certain Cultural Practices," in Ward H. Goodenough, ed., *Explorations in Cultural Anthropology: Essays in Honor of George Peter Murdock.* (New York: McGraw-Hill, 1964), pp. 511–44.

[13]Charles Wagley, "Cultural Influences on Population: A Comparison of Two Tupi Tribes," in Patricia J. Lyon, ed., *Native South Americans: Ethnology of the Least Known Continent* (Boston: Little, Brown, 1974), pp. 377–84.

[14]Roger Brown, *Social Psychology* (New York: Free Press, 1965), pp. 549–609.

[15]Michael Chibnik, "The Evolution of Cultural Rules," *Journal of Anthropological Research,* 37 (1981): 256–68.

[16]Indeed, some of the cultures we refer to may have been quite different before as well as after the time referred to. For example, the !Kung hunter-gatherers of southern Africa probably were not only hunter-gatherers in the past. There is evidence that the !Kung of the Kalahari Desert have switched from hunting and gathering to herding animals, and back again, many times in the past. See Carmel Schrire, "An Inquiry into the Evolutionary Status and Apparent Identity of San Hunter-Gatherers," *Human Ecology,* 8 (1980): 9–32.

3

Schools of Thought in Cultural Anthropology

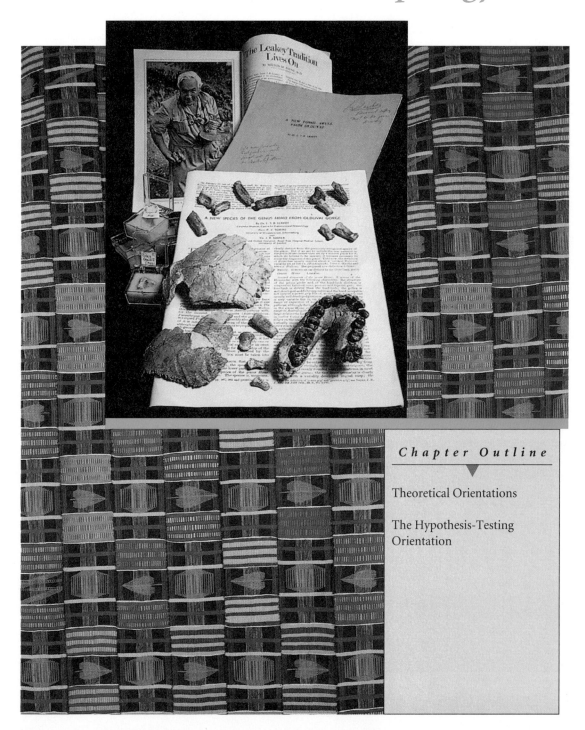

Anthropologists have been going to live in other societies for nearly a hundred years. At first, there were only a few such hardy (some would say foolhardy) souls. But their number slowly increased over the years as more and more individuals became interested in the challenge of spending a year or so in some usually distant place, without the comforts of home, to learn how some other people lived and thought. The idea was to add to our knowledge so that we might someday come to understand how human cultural behavior could vary so much and yet be so much the same at different times and in different places.

Close to 2,000 societies have now been described to some extent in the literature of anthropology. This enormous wealth of information constitutes our data bank of cultural variation. If we are to understand how and why cultures differ and are similar, we must do more than simply inspect this mass of information. We must have ideas about what we should look for. Just as a photographer must aim and focus a camera in order to capture a scene, so an anthropologist must focus on what she or he considers important in order to describe, and possibly explain, some particular aspect of culture. Even the most thorough observer must concentrate on certain aspects of life and neglect others.

Which aspects of life an individual anthropologist concentrates on usually reflects his or her theoretical orientation, subject interest, or preferred method of research. A *theoretical orientation* is a general attitude about how cultural phenomena are to be explained. In this chapter we describe some of the major theoretical orientations that have existed in cultural anthropology. We also describe some recent schools of thought that identify themselves in terms of subject interests or methods of research.

The members of our profession do not always fit neatly into one of the categories we identify here. Nevertheless, such general labels as *interpretive anthropologist, functionalist, cultural ecologist,* and *psychological anthropologist* do provide us with a way to discuss the different styles of explanation exhibited by cultural anthropologists.

THEORETICAL ORIENTATIONS

In anthropology, as in any discipline, there is a continual ebb and flow of ideas. One theoretical orientation will arise and may grow in popularity until another is proposed in opposition to it. Often, one orientation will capitalize on those aspects of a problem that a previous orientation ignored or played down. In our survey of the orientations that have developed since the emergence of cultural anthropology as a professional discipline, we will use an approximate historical sequence. As we discuss each school of thought, we will indicate what kinds of information or phenomena it emphasizes (if it does) as explanatory factors. Some of these orientations have passed into history by now; others continue to attract adherents.

Early Evolutionism

In the early years of anthropology, the prevailing view was that culture generally develops (or evolves) in a uniform and progressive manner. It was thought that most societies pass through the same series of stages, to arrive ultimately at a common end. The sources of culture change were generally assumed to be embedded within the culture from the beginning, and therefore the ultimate course of

Simplicity of technology should not be taken to imply backwardness. The Inuit have very ingenious ways of dealing with their extremely difficult environment. Constructing an igloo out of specially shaped blocks of ice, as shown here in the Canadian Arctic, is not easy.

development was thought to be internally determined. Two nineteenth-century anthropologists whose writings exemplified the theory that culture generally evolves uniformly and progressively were Edward B. Tylor (1832–1917) and Lewis Henry Morgan (1818–1889). *Anthropologists.*

Tylor maintained that culture evolved from the simple to the complex and that all societies passed through three basic stages of development: from savagery through barbarism to civilization.[1] "Progress" was therefore possible for all. To account for cultural variation, Tylor and other early evolutionists postulated that different contemporary societies were at different stages of evolution. According to this view, the "simpler" peoples of the day had not yet reached "higher" stages. Thus, simpler contemporary societies were thought to resemble ancient societies. The more advanced societies, on the other hand, testified to cultural evolution by exhibiting what Tylor called *survivals*—traces of earlier customs that survive in present-day cultures. The making of pottery is an example of a survival in the sense used by Tylor. Earlier peoples made their cooking pots out of clay; today we generally make them out of metal because it is more durable. But we still prefer dishes made out of clay.

Tylor believed there was a kind of psychic unity among all peoples that explained parallel evolutionary sequences in different cultural traditions. In other words, because of the basic similarities common to all peoples, different societies often find the same solutions to the same problems independently. But Tylor also noted that cultural traits may spread from one society to another by simple **diffusion**—the borrowing by one culture of a trait belonging to another as the result of contact between the two.

Another nineteenth-century proponent of uniform and progressive cultural evolution was Lewis Henry Morgan. A lawyer in upstate New York, Morgan became interested in the local Iroquois Indians and defended their reservation in a land-grant case. In gratitude, the Iroquois "adopted" Morgan.

In his best-known work, *Ancient Society,* Morgan postulated several sequences in the evolution of human culture. For example, he speculated that the family evolved through six stages. Human society began as a "horde living in promiscuity," with no sexual prohibitions and no real family structure. Next was a stage in which a group of brothers was married to a group of sisters and brother-sister matings were permitted. In the third stage, group marriage was practiced, but brothers and sisters were not allowed to mate. The fourth stage, which sup-

posedly evolved during barbarism, was characterized by a loosely paired male and female who still lived with other people. Then came the husband-dominant family, in which the husband could have more than one wife simultaneously. Finally, the stage of civilization was distinguished by the monogamous family, with just one wife and one husband who were relatively equal in status.[2]

Morgan believed that family units became progressively smaller and more self-contained as human society developed. But his postulated sequence for the evolution of the family is not supported by the enormous amount of ethnographic data that has been collected since his time. For example, no recent society that Morgan would call savage indulges in group marriage or allows brother-sister mating. (In the chapter on marriage and the family, we discuss how recent cultures have varied in regard to marriage customs.)

Karl Marx was struck by the parallels between Morgan's evolutionism and his own theory of history. Marx and his co-worker, Friedrich Engels, devised a theory in which the institutions of monogamy, private property, and the state were assumed to be chiefly responsible for the exploitation of the working classes in modern industrialized societies. Marx and Engels extended Morgan's evolutionary scheme to include a future stage of cultural evolution in which monogamy, private property, and the state would cease to exist and the "communism" of primitive society would once more come into being.

The evolutionism of Tylor, Morgan, and others of the nineteenth century is largely rejected today. For one thing, their theories cannot satisfactorily account for cultural variation—why, for instance, some societies today are in "upper savagery" and others in "civilization." The "psychic unity of mankind" or "germs of thought" that were postulated to account for parallel evolution cannot also account for cultural differences. Another weakness in the early evolutionist theories is that they cannot explain why some societies have regressed or even become extinct. And finally, although other societies may have progressed to "civilization," some of them have not passed through all the stages. Thus, early evolutionist theory cannot explain the details of cultural evolution and variation as anthropology now knows them.

Historical Particularism

The beginning of the twentieth century brought the end of evolutionism's reign in cultural anthropology. Its leading opponent was Franz Boas

(1858–1942), whose main disagreement with the evolutionists involved their assumption that universal laws governed all human culture. Boas pointed out that these nineteenth-century individuals lacked sufficient data (as did Boas himself) to formulate many useful generalizations. Boas almost single-handedly trained the first generation of American anthropologists, including (among others) Alfred Kroeber, Robert Lowie, Edward Sapir, Melville Herskovits, Ruth Benedict, Clark Wissler, E. Adamson Hoebel, and Margaret Mead.[3]

Boas stressed the apparently enormous complexity of cultural variation, and perhaps because of this complexity he believed it was premature to formulate universal laws. He felt that single cultural traits had to be studied in the context of the society in which they appeared. In 1896, Boas published an article entitled "The Limitation of the Comparative Method of Anthropology,"[4] which dealt with his objections to the evolutionist approach. In it, he stated that anthropologists should spend less time developing theories based on insufficient data. Rather, they should devote their energies to collecting as much data as possible, as quickly as possible, before cultures disappeared (as so many already had, after contact with foreign societies). He asserted that only after this body of data was gathered could valid interpretations be made and theories proposed.

Boas expected that if a tremendous quantity of data was collected, the laws governing cultural variation would emerge from the mass of information by themselves. According to the method he advocated, the essence of science is to mistrust all expectations and to rely only on facts. But, the "facts" that are recorded, even by the most diligent observer, will necessarily reflect what that individual considers important. Collecting done without some preliminary theorizing, without ideas about what to expect, is meaningless, for the facts that are most important may be ignored while irrelevant ones may be recorded. Although it was appropriate for Boas to criticize previous "armchair theorizing," his concern with innumerable local details did not encourage a belief that it might be possible to explain the major variations in culture that anthropologists observe.

Diffusionism

In the late nineteenth and early twentieth centuries, while the cultural evolutionism of Tylor and Morgan was still popular, diffusionism began to take hold among anthropologists in several parts of the world. The two main schools with a diffusionist viewpoint were the British and the German-Austrian.

The main spokesmen for the British school of diffusionism were G. Elliot Smith, William J. Perry, and W. H. R. Rivers. Smith and Perry stated that most aspects of higher civilization were developed in Egypt (which was relatively advanced culturally because of its early development of agriculture) and were then diffused throughout the world as other peoples came into contact with the Egyptians.[5] The British diffusionists thought that the independent parallel evolution of a particular cultural trait in two widely removed areas of the world was extremely rare. People, they believed, are inherently uninventive and invariably prefer to borrow the inventions of another culture rather than develop ideas for themselves. This viewpoint was never widely accepted, and it has now been abandoned completely.

Inspired by Fredrick Ratzel, Fritz Graebner and Father Wilhelm Schmidt led the early twentieth-century German-Austrian diffusionist school. This school also held that people borrow from other cultures because they are basically uninventive themselves. Graebner and Schmidt suggested that cultural traits can diffuse as a group, as well as singly, over great distances.[6] In contrast to Smith and Perry of the British school, who assumed that all cultural traits originated in one place (Egypt) and filtered out to cultures throughout the world, the German-Austrian school suggested the existence and diffusion of several different cultural complexes (plural in German, *Kulturkreise*).[7] Like the British diffusionists, however, the *Kulturkreis* (singular)

Franz Boas

PROMINENCE OF WOMEN IN ANTHROPOLOGY

Compared with other social sciences, anthropology (particularly ethnology) is unusual in having had a considerable number of prominent women in the early development of the discipline. In the 1920s the women included Ruth Benedict, Ruth Bunzel, Esther Goldfrank, Margaret Mead, Elsie Clews Parsons, and Hortense Powdermaker. Women's writing in anthropology is referred to at a higher rate than in other fields, and women are prominent in anthropology in another way—since 1983–1984 women were granted at least 50 percent of the doctoral degrees in the field and the percentage is climbing. In recent years women have been elected more often than men to the presidency of the American Anthropological Association. Were the early women (and the women they trained) important role models for later women? Was anthropology seen as a field where women can and do make a difference? We don't yet have more than intuitive answers to those questions, but perhaps we will get definitive answers from studying women who are considering different careers. What are their perceptions, and do

those perceptions influence their choices? Is there something about anthropology that especially appeals to women?

Given the male dominance of many fields, at least in their beginnings, what accounted for the prominence of these early women in the first place? Was it partly historical accident? Franz Boas, at Columbia, was responsible for training most of the first generation of American anthropologists, including some of the early women (Benedict, Mead, Bunzel, and Goldfrank); Powdermaker received training in England, primarily with Bronislaw Malinowski. Was Boas more receptive than other professors in the United States to mentoring women? We know that Ruth Benedict became quite close to Boas, referring to him in a letter as "Papa Franz."

Some of these early women anthropologists published books that were popular successes: Ruth Benedict's *Patterns of Culture;* Margaret Mead's *Coming of Age in Samoa* and *Growing Up in New Guinea.* Popular writing undoubtedly helped them become widely known to the public.

Gender equality is not the same as numerical equality. For

example, there are still many more male full professors than female in anthropology. There are signs, however, that gender inequality is disappearing. In the last few years, women have received half the positions in academia, with no indications of a salary differential; as they are promoted (it is hoped, equitably), the gap at the top should disappear.

It may be that the presence of prominent women anthropologists was important in encouraging women to enter the field. It would be nice to know whether there is a general relationship between the number of female role models and the subsequent entry of women into a profession. Perhaps future comparative studies of various professions will tell us.

Sources: *Marvin Harris,* The Rise of Anthropological Theory: A History of Theories of Culture *(New York: Thomas Y. Crowell, 1968); Lewis L. Langness,* The Study of Culture *(Novato, CA: Chandler and Sharp, 1974); Catherine Lutz, "The Erasure of Women's Writing in Sociocultural Anthropology,"* American Ethnologist, *17 (1990): 611–27; Candice Bradley and Ulrika Dahl, "The Committee on the Status of Women in Anthropology/American Anthropological Association 1992 Vita Dataset: A Report to the Committee to Study the Academic Employment of Women in Anthropology and the Committee on the Status of Women in Anthropology," November 1993; Candice Bradley (personal communication, 1994).*

school provided little documentation for the historical relationships it assumed.

A separate American diffusionist school of thought, led by Clark Wissler and Alfred Kroeber (both students of Boas), also arose in the first few decades of the twentieth century. It was similar in method to the German-Austrian school but more modest in its claims. The American diffusionists attributed the characteristic features of a culture area to a geographical *culture center,* where the traits were first developed and from which they then diffused outward. This theory led Wissler to formulate his age-area principle: if a given trait diffuses outward from a single culture center, it follows that the most widely distributed traits found to exist around such a center must be the oldest traits.[8]

Although most anthropologists today acknowledge the spread of traits by diffusion, few try to account for most aspects of cultural development and variation in terms of diffusion. For one thing, the diffusionists dealt only in a very superficial way with the question of how cultural traits are transferred from one society to another. The failing was a serious one, because one of the things we want to explain is why a culture accepts or rejects or modifies a trait that one of its neighbors has. Also, even if it could be demonstrated how and why a trait diffused outward from a cultural center, we would still be no closer to an explanation of how or why the trait developed within that center in the first place.

Functionalism

In biology, different parts of an organism may be described by their functions, the parts they play in maintaining the life of the whole organism. **Functionalism** in social science similarly looks for the part (function) some aspect of culture or social life plays in maintaining a system. Two quite different schools of functionalism arose in conjunction with two British anthropologists—Bronislaw Malinowski (1884–1942) and Arthur Reginald Radcliffe-Brown (1881–1955).

Malinowski's version of functionalism assumes that all cultural traits serve the needs of *individuals* in a society. That is, the function of a culture trait is its ability to satisfy some *basic* or *derived need* of the members of the group. The basic needs include nutrition, reproduction, bodily comfort, safety, relaxation, movement, and growth. Some aspects of the culture satisfy these basic needs. In doing so, they give rise to derived needs that must also be satisfied. For example, culture traits that satisfy the basic need for food give rise to the secondary, or derived, need for cooperation in food collection or production. Societies will in turn develop forms of political organization and social control that guarantee the required cooperation. How did Malinowski explain such things as religion and magic? He suggested that since humans always live with a certain amount of uncertainty and anxiety, they need stability and continuity. Religion and magic are functional in that they serve those needs.[9]

Unlike Malinowski, Radcliffe-Brown felt that the various aspects of social behavior *maintain a society's social structure* rather than satisfying individual needs. By social structure, he meant the total network of existing social relationships in a society.[10] Since Radcliffe-Brown's version of functionalism emphasized the social structure as the system to be maintained, the phrase *structural-functionalism* is often used to describe his approach.

An example of Radcliffe-Brown's structural-functionalist approach is his analysis of the ways in which different societies deal with the tensions that are likely to develop among people related through marriage. To reduce potential tension between in-laws, he suggested, societies do one of two things. They may develop strict rules forbidding the persons involved ever to interact face to face (as do the Navahos, for example, in requiring a man to avoid his mother-in-law). Or they may allow mutual disrespect and teasing between the in-laws. Radcliffe-Brown suggested that avoidance is likely to occur between in-laws of different generations, whereas disrespectful teasing is likely between in-laws of the same generation.[11] Both avoidance and teasing, he suggested, are ways to avoid real conflict and help maintain the social structure. (American mother-in-law jokes may also help relieve tension.)

The major objection to Malinowski's functionalism is that it cannot readily account for cultural variation. Most of the needs he identified—such as the need for food—are universal: all societies must deal with them if they are to survive. Thus, while the functionalist approach may tell us why all societies engage in food-getting, it cannot tell why different societies have different food-getting practices. In other words, functionalism does not explain why certain specific cultural patterns arise to fulfill a need that might be fulfilled just as easily by any of a number of alternative possibilities.

A major problem of the structural-functionalist approach is that it is difficult to determine whether a particular custom is in fact functional in the sense of contributing to the maintenance of the social system. In biology, the contribution an organ makes to the health or life of an animal can be assessed by removing it. But we cannot subtract a cultural trait from a society to see if the trait really does contribute to the maintenance of that group. It is conceivable that certain customs within the society may be neutral or even detrimental to its maintenance.

We cannot assume that all of a society's customs are functional merely because the society is functioning at the moment. And even if we are able to assess whether a particular custom is functional, this theoretical orientation fails to deal with the question of why a particular society chooses to meet its structural needs in a particular way. A given problem does not necessarily have only one solution. We still must explain why one of several possible solutions is chosen.

Psychological Approaches

In the 1920s, some American anthropologists began to study the relationship between culture and personality. While there are varying opinions about how the culture-and-personality school got started, the writings of Sigmund Freud and other psychoanalysts were undoubtedly influential. Edward Sapir, one of Boas's earliest students, reviewed psychoanalytical books and seems to have influenced two other students of Boas—Ruth Benedict and Margaret Mead—who became early proponents of a psychological orientation.[12]

In *Patterns of Culture,* Benedict argued not only that cultures are patterned but also that different cultures could be characterized in terms of different personality types. In contrast to Benedict, Mead did not attempt to describe cultures in terms of personality types. But for Mead as well as Benedict, culture and personality were strongly linked. After studying three societies in New Guinea, Mead suggested that each of those societies had a different pattern of sex differences in personality. In other words, men and women were different psychologically in the three societies, and the differences were not the same across the three societies. If the women in one could act like the men in another, Mead concluded that culture, not biology, was mainly responsible for personality differences between the sexes. Although many of Benedict's and Mead's assertions were later challenged, the research of these two women aroused a great deal of interest in personality and culture and in anthropology in general.

In seminars at Columbia University in the 1930s and 1940s, Ralph Linton, an anthropologist, and Abram Kardiner, a psychoanalyst, developed

important ideas for culture-and-personality studies. Kardiner suggested that in every culture there is a *basic personality* that is produced by certain shared cultural experiences. In other words, just as a child's later personality may be shaped by his or her earlier experiences, so the personality of adults in a society should be shaped by common cultural experiences. These shared experiences derive from the society's **primary institutions,** which have to do with the customary ways of making a living, the customary composition of the family, and the customs of child rearing. The basic personality structure, in turn, gives rise to the aspects of culture, called **secondary institutions,** that are created to satisfy and reconcile the needs and conflicts that constitute the basic personality structure. These institutions—which include ritual, religion, and folklore—are considered secondary because they presumably stem from the basic personality structure.[13]

Not all psychological anthropologists use Kardiner's entire scheme. But most assume that there is a set of typical personality characteristics in a society, whether they call it "basic personality," "national character," or "modal personality." And most accept Kardiner's assumption that the typical personality is produced by certain aspects of cultural experience, particularly the customs of child rearing.

During World War II and shortly thereafter, the culture-and-personality orientation was applied to complex societies. Most of these studies of national character attributed the apparent personality traits of different nations to aspects of child rearing. For example, three studies suggested that adult Japanese were compulsive because of the strict toilet training they received as children.[14] Similarly, the manic-depressive swings in emotion believed to be common among Russians were attributed by Geoffrey Gorer and John Rickman to the practice in Soviet nurseries of swaddling infants from birth.[15] (Swaddling involves wrapping cloth strips around an infant's body to keep arms and legs immobile.) This practice was thought to cause anger and frustration in the infant that were later expressed in the adult as manic-depressive behavior.

Unfortunately, because it was wartime, the investigators working on Japanese compulsiveness were unable to do any fieldwork. The anthropologists studying Russian character were also forced to use indirect research methods. Later, when researchers were able to obtain firsthand data from more representative samples of subjects, they discovered that the conclusions of the earlier studies were not always reliable. For example, it was found that the toilet-training practices of the Japanese

Margaret Mead in Bali

were not particularly strict. In other words, the early studies of national character had been crude attempts of analysis from a distance and were not always accurate about personality differences between complex societies.

As time went on, the focus of the psychological approach changed. While retaining their interest in Freudian theories and the relation between child training and adult personality, some anthropologists began to investigate the possible determinants of variation in child-training practices. For example, in a comparative study, Herbert Barry, Irvin Child, and Margaret Bacon suggested that the future food supply in herding and agricultural societies is best ensured by adherence to an established routine, because mistakes may jeopardize a year's food supply. In most hunting and fishing societies, however, mistakes will affect only the daily food supply. Therefore, adherence to routine is not so essential, and individual initiative may be encouraged. As the investigators predicted, the cross-cultural evidence indicates that agricultural societies are apt to stress obedience and responsibility in their child training, whereas hunting and fishing societies tend to emphasize independence and self-reliance.[16]

In addition to exploring the determinants of different patterns of child training, some studies have elaborated on Kardiner's suggestion that

personality traits and processes may account for cross-cultural associations between one cultural pattern and another. The argument in these studies is that certain culture traits produce certain psychological characteristics, which in turn give rise to other culture traits. Such a mediating influence of personality is suggested, for example, by the work of John Whiting and Irvin Child on cultural explanations of illness.[17] They suggest that severe punishment for aggression in childhood (a cultural characteristic) may lead to an exaggerated preoccupation with aggression in adulthood (a psychological characteristic), which may in turn predispose adults to believe that aggressive behavior causes illness (a cultural characteristic).

To generalize about the psychological approach to cultural anthropology, then, we may say that it tries to understand how psychological factors and processes may help to explain cultural practices.

Later Evolutionism

The evolutionary approach to cultural variation did not die with the nineteenth century. In the 1930s, Leslie A. White attacked the Boasian emphasis on historical particularism and championed the evolutionist orientation.

Though quickly labeled a neo-evolutionist, White rejected the term, insisting that his approach did not depart significantly from the theories adopted in the nineteenth century. What White did add to the classical evolutionist approach was a conception of culture as an energy-capturing system. According to his "basic law" of cultural evolution, "other factors remaining constant, *culture evolves as the amount of energy harnessed per capita per year is increased or as the efficiency of the instrumental means of putting the energy to work is increased.*"[18] In other words, a more advanced technology gives humans control over more energy (human, animal, solar, and so on), and cultures expand and change as a result.

White's orientation has been criticized for the same reasons that the ideas of Tylor and Morgan were. In describing what has happened in the evolution of human culture, he assumed that cultural evolution is determined strictly by conditions (preeminently technological ones) inside the culture. That is, he explicitly denied the possibility of environmental, historical, or psychological influences on cultural evolution. The main problem with such an orientation is that it cannot explain why some cultures evolve while others either do not evolve or become extinct. Thus, White's theory of energy capture as the mechanism of cultural evolution side-steps the question of why only some cultures are able to increase their energy capture.

Julian H. Steward, another later evolutionist, divided evolutionary thought into three schools: unilinear, universal, and multilinear.[19] Steward believed that Morgan and Tylor's theories exemplified the unilinear approach to cultural evolution—the classical nineteenth-century orientation that attempted to place particular cultures on the rungs of a sort of evolutionary ladder. Universal evolutionists such as Leslie White, on the other hand, were concerned with culture in the broad sense, rather than with individual cultures. Steward classified himself as a multilinear evolutionist—one who deals with the evolution of particular cultures and only with demonstrated sequences of parallel culture change in different areas.

Steward was concerned with explaining specific cultural differences and similarities. Consequently, he was critical of White's vague generalities and his disregard of environmental influences. White, on the other hand, asserted that Steward fell into the historical-particularist trap of paying too much attention to particular cases.

Marshall Sahlins and Elman Service, who were students and colleagues of both White and Steward, combined the views of those two individuals by recognizing two kinds of evolution—specific and general.[20] **Specific evolution** refers to the particular sequence of change and adaptation of a particular society in a given environment. **General evolution** refers to a general progress of human society, in which higher forms (having higher energy capture) arise from and surpass lower forms. Thus, specific evolution is similar to Steward's multilinear evolution, and general evolution resembles White's universal evolution. Although this synthesis does serve to integrate the two points of view, it does not give us a way of explaining why general evolutionary progress has occurred. But, unlike the early evolutionists, some of the later evolutionists did suggest a mechanism to account for the evolution of particular cultures—namely, adaptation to particular environments.

STRUCTURALISM

Claude Lévi-Strauss (born 1908) has been the leading proponent of an approach to cultural analysis called **structuralism.** Lévi-Strauss's structuralism differs from that of Radcliffe-Brown. Whereas Radcliffe-Brown concentrated on how the elements of a society function as a system, Lévi-Strauss concentrates more on the origins of the systems themselves. He sees culture, as expressed in art, ritual, and the patterns of daily life, as a surface representation of the underlying structure of the human mind. Consider, for example, how he tries to account for what anthropologists call a *moiety system*. Such a system is said to exist if a society is divided into two large intermarrying kin groups (each called a *moiety*—probably derived from the French word *moitié*, meaning "half"). Lévi-Strauss says that moiety systems reflect the human mind's predisposition to think and behave in terms of *binary oppositions* (contrasts between one thing and another).[21] Clearly, a moiety system involves a binary opposition: You are born into one of two groups and you marry someone in the other. The problem with Lévi-Strauss's explanation of moieties is that he is postulating a constant—the human mind's supposed dualism—to account for a cultural feature that is not universal. Moiety systems are found in only a relatively small number of societies, so how could something that is universal explain something else that is not?

Lévi-Strauss's interpretations of cultural phenomena (which tend to be far more involved and difficult to follow than the example just described) have concentrated on the presumed cognitive processes of people—that is, the ways in which people supposedly perceive and classify things in the world around them. In studies such as *The Savage Mind* and *The Raw and the Cooked*, he suggested that even technologically simple groups often construct elaborate systems of classification of plants and animals, not only for practical purposes but also out of a need for such intellectual activity.[22]

Structuralism has influenced thinking not only in France; Britain too has been receptive. But the British structuralists, such as Edmund Leach, Rodney Needham, and Mary Douglas, do not follow Lévi-Strauss in looking for panhuman or universal principles in the human mind. Rather, they concentrate on applying structural analysis to particular societies and particular social institutions.[23] For example, Mary Douglas discusses an argument that took place in her home over whether soup is an "appropriate" supper. She suggests that meals (in her household and in culturally similar households) have certain structural principles. They have contrasts—hot and cold, bland and spiced, liquid and semiliquid—and various textures. They must incorporate cereals, vegetables, and animal protein. Douglas concludes that if the food served does not follow these principles, it cannot be considered a meal![24]

Some structuralist writings have been criticized for their concentration on abstruse, theoretical analysis at the expense of solid, ethnological observation and evidence. For example, it is not always clear how Lévi-Strauss derived a particular structuralist interpretation, and in the absence of any systematically collected supporting evidence, the reader must decide whether the interpretation seems plausible. Thus, Lévi-Strauss's studies have come to be regarded by many as vague and untestable, as self-contained intellectual constructs with little explanatory value. Moreover, even if there are some universal patterns that underlie cultural phenomena, universals or constants cannot explain cultural differences.

Ethnoscience

Lévi-Strauss's structuralist approach involves intuitively grasping the rules of thought that may underlie a given culture. An ethnographic approach known as **ethnoscience** attempts to derive these rules from a logical analysis of ethnographic data that are kept as free as possible from contamination by the observer's own cultural biases.

The approach of ethnoscience is similar to that of Lévi-Strauss insofar as both are influenced by the methodology of descriptive linguistics, but there the similarity ends. Rather than collecting data according to a predetermined set of anthropological categories, the ethnoscientist seeks to understand a people's world from their point of view. Utilizing what she or he has discovered about them through studying their language, and particularly the words they use to describe what they do, the ethnoscientist tries to formulate the rules that generate acceptable behavior in the culture. The rules in question are believed to be comparable to the grammatical rules that generate the correct use of language.

Many ethnoscientists think that if we can discover the rules that generate correct cultural behavior, we can explain much of what people do and why they do it. Probably individuals do generally act according to the conscious and unconscious rules they have internalized. But we still need to understand why a particular society has developed the particular cultural rules it has. Just as a grammar does not explain how a language came to be what it is, so the ethnoscientific discovery of a culture's rules does not explain why those rules developed.

Cultural Ecology

Some anthropologists are mostly concerned with the influence of environment on culture. Julian Steward was one of the first to advocate the study of **cultural ecology**—the analysis of the relationship between a culture and its environment. Steward felt that the explanation for some aspects of cultural variation could be found in the adaptation of societies to their particular environments. But rather than merely hypothesize that the environment did or did not determine cultural variation, Steward wished to resolve the question empirically—that is, he wanted to carry out investigations to substantiate his viewpoint.[25]

Steward felt, however, that cultural ecology must be separated from biological ecology (the study of the relationships between organisms and their environment). Later cultural ecologists such as Andrew Vayda and Roy Rappaport wish to incorporate principles of biological ecology into the study of cultural ecology in order to make a single science of ecology.[26] In their view, cultural traits, just like biological traits, can be considered adaptive or maladaptive. Cultural ecologists assume that cultural adaptation involves the mechanism of natural selection—the more frequent survival and reproduction of the better-adapted. Environment, including the physical and social environment, affects the development of culture traits in that "individuals or populations behaving in certain different ways have different degrees of success in survival and reproduction and, consequently, in the transmission of their ways of behaving from generation to generation."[27]

Consider how culture and environment may interact among the Tsembaga, who live in the interior of New Guinea.[28] The Tsembaga are horticulturists, living mainly on the root crops and greens they grow in home gardens. They also raise pigs. The pigs are seldom eaten; instead, they serve other useful functions. They keep residential areas clean by consuming garbage, and they help prepare the soil for planting by rooting in it. Small numbers of pigs are easy to keep; they run free all day, returning at night to eat whatever substandard tubers are found in the course of their owners' harvesting of their daily rations. Thus pigs, which require a minimum of maintenance, serve the Tsembaga both as janitors and as cultivating machines.

But problems arise when the pig herd grows large. Often there are not enough substandard tubers, and then the pigs must be fed human rations. Also, although a small number of pigs will clean up yards and soften the soil in the gardens, a large herd is likely to intrude upon garden crops. Pigs can even break up communities. If one person's pig invades a neighbor's garden, the garden owner often retaliates by killing the offending pig. In turn, the dead animal's owner may kill the garden owner, the garden owner's wife, or one of his pigs. As the number of such feuds increases, people begin to put as much distance as possible between their pigs and other people's gardens.

solution

Rappaport suggests that to cope with the problem of pig overpopulation, the Tsembaga have developed an elaborate cycle of rituals that involves the slaughter of large numbers of surplus pigs. The pigs can then be distributed in the form of pork—a valuable commodity—to friends and to ancestors (who, the Tsembaga believe, will grant them strength and courage in return). Thus, this cultural practice of ritual pig feasts can be viewed as a possible adaptation to environmental factors that produce a surplus pig population.

The cultural ecologist tries to explain cultural variation by suggesting how a particular trait is adaptive in a particular physical or social environment. In applying this orientation to a specific society, the ecologist may be subject to the same kind of criticism that has been directed at the structural-functionalist. Just as the structural-functionalist may not be able to show that a particular custom is functional, so the ecologist who is analyzing a specific society may not be able to show that a particular custom is adaptive. With regard to the Tsembaga, for example, it is hard to know whether their ritual pig feasts are more adaptive than other possible solutions to the problem of pig overpopulation. Might it be more adaptive to slaughter and eat pigs regularly so that pig herds never get too large?

Without being able to contrast the effects of alternative solutions, a cultural ecologist studying a single society may find it difficult to obtain evidence that a custom already in place is more adaptive than other possible solutions to the problem.

Political Economy

Like cultural ecology, the school of thought known as political economy assumes that external forces explain the way a society changes and adapts. But it is not the natural environment, or social environment in general, that is central to the approach of political economy. What is central is the social and political impact of those powerful state societies (principally Spain, Portugal, Britain, and France) that transformed the world by colonialism and imperialism and fostered the development of a worldwide economy or world-system.[29]

Some of the earliest figures associated with the political economy approach (in anthropology) were trained at Columbia University when Julian Steward was a professor there. For those students, Steward's cultural ecology was insufficiently attentive to recent world history. For example, Eric Wolf and Sidney Mintz argued that the communities they studied in Puerto Rico developed as they did because of colonialism and the establishment of plantations to supply sugar and coffee to Europe and North America.[30] And Eleanor Leacock, who studied the Montagnais-Naskapi Indians of Labrador, suggested that their system of family hunting territories was not an old characteristic, present before European contact, but developed instead out of the Indians' early involvement in the European-introduced fur trade.[31]

Central to the later and continuing intellectual development of political economy in anthropology are the writings (published in the 1960s and 1970s) of two political sociologists, André Frank and Immanuel Wallerstein. Frank suggested that the development of a region (Europe, for example) depended on the suppression of development or underdevelopment of other regions (the New World, Africa). He argued that if we want to understand why a country remains underdeveloped, we must understand how it is exploited by developed nations.[32] Frank is concerned with what happened in the underdeveloped world. Wallerstein is more concerned with how capitalism developed in the privileged countries and how the expansionist requirements of the capitalist countries led to the emergence of the world-system.[33]

YES

The political economy or world-system view has inspired many anthropologists to study history more explicitly and to explore the impact of external political and economic processes on local events and cultures in the underdeveloped world. In the past, when anthropologists first started doing fieldwork in the far corners of the world, they could imagine that the cultures they were studying (or reconstructing) could be investigated as if those cultures were more or less isolated from external influences and forces. In the modern world, such isolation hardly exists. The political economy approach has reminded us that the world, every part of it, is interconnected for better or worse.

Sociobiology and Behavioral Ecology

The idea that natural selection can operate on the behavioral or social characteristics of populations (and not just on their physical traits) is shared by cultural ecology and another, more recent, theoretical orientation called **behavioral ecology** (or earlier, **sociobiology**). Developed mainly by biologists, particularly those who have concentrated on the social insects, the behavioral ecology or sociobiological orientation involves the application of biological evolutionary principles to the social behavior of animals, including humans. Some cultural anthropologists have employed theory in behavioral ecology to explain some aspects of cultural variation.[34]

How is behavioral ecology different from cultural ecology? Although both orientations assume the importance of natural selection in cultural evolution, they differ in important ways. Cultural ecology focuses mostly on what biologists would call **group selection:** cultural ecologists talk mostly about how a certain behavioral or social characteristic may be adaptive for a group or society in a given environment. (A newly emergent behavioral or social trait that is adaptive is likely to be passed on to future generations by cultural transmission.) In contrast, behavioral ecology focuses mostly on what biologists call **individual selection:** behavioral ecologists talk mostly about how a certain characteristic may be adaptive for an individual in a given environment.[35] By *adaptive* is meant the ability of an individual to get her or his genes into future generations. Does this viewpoint imply that behavior is transmitted only through genes? No, say behavioral ecologists—what matters is that behavior is heritable—transmitted in some way (by genes or learning) to persons who share your genes (usually offspring).[36] If a certain behavior is adaptive for individuals in a particular environment, it should become more widespread in future generations as the individuals with those traits increase in number.

Whereas a cultural ecologist such as Rappaport might consider how ritual pig feasts were adaptive for the Tsembaga as a whole, behavioral ecologists would insist that to speak of adaptation it must be shown how the pig feasts benefited individuals and their closest kin. Behavioral ecologists might raise the following possibilities regarding pig feasts. Do the people who organize pig feasts have more children? If so, then pig feasts may benefit an individual reproductively. Are people who have excess pigs more likely to be killed because their pigs destroy

Sometimes you can have too many pigs. A pig feast solves this problem and maintains or creates close ties between groups. Here we see preparations for a pig feast on the island of Tanna in the New Hebrides.

others' gardens? If so, then finding a way to cut down on pigs benefits the survival chances and hence the reproductive chances of individuals. We do not know of a direct comparison of the predictions of cultural ecology and behavioral ecology, but these questions may convey how the behavioral ecology approach is different.

In general, behavioral ecological theory does not expect that "social good" will prevail unless "individual good" underlies it. Take the idea of conserving the earth's resources for the long-term benefit of others. If individuals and families are seeking to maximize their own benefits, behavioral ecology would not expect conservation practices unless an individual or family saw short-term negative effects of their not conserving. Indeed, Bobbi Low finds cross-culturally that conservation ideas (reasons to leave resources untouched) are very rare, occurring in only 5 percent of the societies surveyed.[37]

This is not to say that behavioral ecology cannot explain some kinds of altruism—when a person does something apparently for the good of another person. Adopting or caring for a child of a relative may help perpetuate your own genes. Sharing food with others today may increase your own food intake in the future.

But behavioral ecology has difficulty explaining human behaviors that appear to be completely altruistic with no apparent gain for the altruist. How can we explain why so many people in the United States and other countries believe in the value of conservation? And why did some people in Nazi Germany, at risk to their own safety, hide people from the Nazis?

Interpretive Approaches

Since about the 1960s, writers in the field of literary criticism have influenced the development of a variety of "interpretive" approaches in cultural anthropology, particularly with respect to ethnography.[38] Clifford Geertz popularized the idea that a culture is like a literary text that can be analyzed for meaning, as the ethnographer interprets it. According to Geertz, ethnographers choose to interpret the meaning of things in their field cultures that are of interest to themselves. Then they try to convey their interpretations of cultural meaning to people of their own culture. Thus, according to Geertz, the ethnographer is a kind of selective intercultural translator.[39]

Some anthropologists think that interpretation is the only achievable goal in cultural anthropology, because they do not believe it is possible to describe or measure cultural phenomena (and other things involving humans) in objective or unbiased ways.[40] Scientific anthropologists do not agree. To be sure, interpretive ethnographies might provide insights. But we do not have to believe what an interpretation suggests, no matter how eloquently it is stated. (We are rarely given objective evidence to support an interpretation.) Scientific researchers

The Abelam display their decorated giant yams shown here hanging from inclined poles. For possible explanations, see box on next page.

EVALUATING ALTERNATIVE THEORIES

In working among the Abelam of New Guinea, Richard Scaglion was puzzled why they invest so much energy in growing giant ceremonial yams, sometimes more than 10 feet long. And why do they abstain from sex for six months while they grow them? Of course, to try to understand, we need to know much more about the Abelam way of life. Scaglion had read about them, lived among them, and talked to them, but, as many ethnographers have discovered, the answers to why questions don't just leap out at you. Answers, at least tentative ones, often come from theoretical orientations that suggest how or where to look for answers. Richard Scaglion considers several possibilities. As Donald Tuzin had suggested for a nearby group, the Plains Arapesh, yams may be *symbols* of or stand for shared cultural understandings. (Looking for the meanings of symbols is a kind of interpretative approach to eth-

nographic data.) The Abelam think of yams as having souls who appreciate tranquility. Yams also have family lines; at marriage, the joining of family lines is symbolized by planting different yam lines in the same garden. During the yam-growing cycle (remember that yams appreciate tranquility), lethal warfare and conflict become channeled mostly into competitive but nonlethal yam-growing contests. So yam growing may be *functional* in the sense that it helps to foster harmony. Then again, ceremonial yam growing may have adaptive *ecological* consequences. Just as the Tsembaga pig feasts seemed to keep human population in line with resources, Scaglion thinks that ceremonial yam growing did too. Growing pig populations damage gardens and create conflicts, but during competitive yam ceremonies pigs are also given away, so the pig population declines. Wild animals that are hunted also have a

chance to replenish themselves because hunting is frowned upon during the yam-growing cycle.

As Scaglion's discussion illustrates, theoretical orientations help researchers derive explanations. They do not have to be "rival" explanations, in the sense that one has to be right and others wrong; more than one theory may help explain some phenomenon. But we can't assume that just because a theory sounds good, it *is* correct and helps us to understand. The important point is that we need something more to evaluate theory. As we discuss in the next chapter, we have to find ways to *test* a theory against evidence. Until we do that, we really don't know how many, or if indeed *any,* of the theories available are helpful.

Source: *Richard Scaglion, "Abelam: Giant Yams and Cycles of Sex, Warfare and Ritual," in Melvin Ember, Carol R. Ember, and David Levinson, eds.,* Portraits of Culture: Ethnographic Originals. *(Englewood Cliffs, NJ: Prentice Hall, 1995). Prentice Hall/Simon & Schuster Custom Publishing.*

---

have developed many techniques for minimizing bias and increasing the objectivity of measurement. Thus, interpretive anthropologists who deny the possibility of scientific understanding of human behavior and thinking may not know how much has been achieved so far by scientific studies of cultural phenomena, which we try to convey in the chapters that follow.

As Dan Sperber has suggested, the task of interpretation in cultural anthropology is clearly different from the task of explanation.[41] The goal of intepretation is to convey intuitive understanding

of human experience in a *particular* culture (intuitive in the sense of not requiring conscious reasoning or systematic methods of inquiry). Thus the interpretive ethnographer is like a novelist (or literary critic). In contrast, the goal of explanation is to provide causal and general understanding of cultural phenomena (causal in the sense of mechanisms that account for why something comes to be shared in a population, and general in the sense of applying to a number of similar cases).

Does one goal (interpretation versus explanation) preclude or invalidate the other? We don't think so. We share Sperber's view that interpretation and explanation are not opposed goals: they just are different kinds of understanding. Indeed, an intuitive interpretation described in causal and general terms might turn out, when scientifically tested, to be a powerful explanation!

THE HYPOTHESIS-TESTING ORIENTATION

▼

An increasing number of contemporary cultural anthropologists would explicitly deny that they prefer any particular theoretical orientation, subject interest, or method of research. Rather, they think of themselves as having a *hypothesis-testing* orientation. Any type of theory might be considered and a variety of research methods might be employed by such anthropologists. Their major goal is to test possible explanations because they believe that any explanation should be exposed to the possibility of being falsified by some set of systematically collected data. In the absence of such a test, these anthropologists would say that we are entitled or even obliged to be skeptical about the validity of any suggested explanation.

To those with a hypothesis-testing orientation, the plausibility or persuasiveness of an explanation cannot be considered a sufficient reason to accept it; the explanation must be tested and supported. And even if it is supported, there still may be grounds for skepticism. According to this orientation, then, all knowledge is uncertain and therefore subject to increasing or decreasing confirmation as new tests are made. If this is true—and it may be uncomfortable to acknowledge—it means that we will never arrive at absolute truth. On the other hand—and this is encouraging—we should be able to achieve a more and more reliable understanding if we keep testing our theories.

▼ SUMMARY

1. Which aspects of life an individual anthropologist concentrates on usually reflects his or her theoretical orientation, subject interest, or preferred method of research.

2. A theoretical orientation is usually a general attitude about how cultural phenomena are to be explained.

3. The prevailing theoretical orientation in anthropology during the nineteenth century was based on a belief that culture generally evolves in a uniform and progressive manner; that is, most societies were believed to pass through the same series of stages, to arrive ultimately at a common end. Two proponents of this early theory of cultural evolution were Edward B. Tylor and Lewis Henry Morgan.

4. During the early twentieth century the leading opponent of evolutionism was Franz Boas, who rejected the way in which early evolutionists had assumed that universal laws governed all human culture. Boas stressed the importance of collecting as much anthropological data as possible, from which the laws governing cultural variation would supposedly emerge by themselves.

5. The diffusionist approach, popular in the late nineteenth and early twentieth centuries, was developed by two main schools—the British and the German-Austrian. In general, diffusionists believed that most aspects of high civilization had emerged in culture centers from which they then diffused outward.

6. Functionalism looks for the part (function) some aspect of culture or social life plays in maintaining a system. There are two quite different schools of functionalism. Malinowski's version of functionalism assumes that all cultural traits serve the needs of *individuals* in a society. Radcliffe-Brown felt that the various aspects of social behavior *maintain a society's social structure* rather than satisfying individual needs.

7. The psychological orientation in anthropology, which began in the 1920s, seeks to understand how psychological factors and processes may help us explain cultural practices.

8. In the 1930s, the evolutionary approach to cultural development was revived by Leslie A. White, who proposed that "culture evolves . . . as the efficiency of the instrumental means of putting . . . energy to work is increased." Anthropologists such as Julian H. Steward, Marshall Sahlins, and El-

man Service have also presented evolutionary viewpoints in recent times.

9. Claude Lévi-Strauss has been the leading proponent of structuralism. Essentially, Lévi-Strauss sees culture, as it is expressed in art, ritual, and the patterns of daily life, as a surface representation of the underlying patterns of the human mind.

10. Whereas Lévi-Strauss's approach involves intuitively grasping the rules of thought that may underlie a given culture, an ethnographic approach known as ethnoscience attempts to derive these rules from a logical analysis of data—particularly the words people use to describe their activities. In this way, the ethnoscientist tries to formulate the rules that generate acceptable behavior in a given culture.

11. Cultural ecology seeks to understand the relationships between cultures and their physical and social environments. Cultural ecologists ask how a particular culture trait may be adaptive in its environment.

12. The theoretical orientation called political economy focuses on the impact of external political and economic processes, particularly as connected to colonialism and imperialism, on local events and cultures in the underdeveloped world. The political economy approach has reminded us that all parts of the world are interconnected for better or worse.

13. Sociobiology (more recently called behavioral ecology) is a theoretical orientation that involves the application of biological evolutionary principles to the social behavior of animals, including humans.

14. Interpretive approaches consider cultures as texts to be analyzed for their meaning. The ethnographer is thus like a novelist or literary critic.

15. Finally, there are cultural anthropologists who do not follow any particular theoretical orientation or prefer any particular subject matter or method of research. These anthropologists think of themselves as having a hypothesis-testing orientation.

▼ GLOSSARY TERMS

behavioral ecology	general evolution	sociobiology
cultural ecology	group selection	specific evolution
diffusion	individual selection	structuralism
ethnoscience	primary institutions	
functionalism	secondary institutions	

▼ CRITICAL QUESTIONS

1. In anthropology as in many other fields, one theoretical orientation will arise and may grow in popularity until another is proposed in opposition to it. Is this kind of rejection healthy for a discipline?

2. Does a theoretical orientation enhance one's way of looking at the world, or does it blind oneself to other possibilities?

3. Although anthropology is holistic in including the study of humans as both biological organisms and as cultural or social organisms, cultural and biological theories are rarely considered together. Why? Does this divergence help or hinder cultural anthropology?

▼ SUGGESTED READING

HARRIS, M. *The Rise of Anthropological Theory: A History of Theories of Culture.* New York: Thomas Y. Crowell, 1968. A critical review of the history of anthropological theory from 1750 to the 1960s. The author discusses the social context of, and the personalities involved in, the different theoretical orientations.

LANGNESS, L. L. *The Study of Culture,* rev. ed. Novato, CA: Chandler and Sharp, 1987. A survey of the history of theory in the study of culture. Significant theorists and their concepts and concerns are the main focus. The book also describes how the development of culture theory has been linked to developments in other disciplines.

LETT, J. *The Human Enterprise: A Critical Introduction to Anthropological Theory.* Boulder, CO: Westview Press, 1987. This book about anthropological theory begins with fundamental questions: What is knowledge? What do we mean by explanation? What is science? The author then considers anthropological approaches to these questions and critically reviews major anthropological theoretical orientations or paradigms.

MANNERS, R. A., AND KAPLAN, D., eds. *Theory in Anthropology: A Sourcebook.* Chicago: Aldine, 1968. A massive compilation of readings representing the leading theoretical orientations of the past.

STOCKING, G. W., JR., ed. *History of Anthropology,* vols. 1–6. Madison, WI: University of Wisconsin, 1983–1989. A series of edited volumes on various topics in the history of anthropology, including the beginnings of fieldwork in anthropology (vol. 1, *Observers Observed: Essays on Ethnographic Fieldwork*) and romantic motives that may have driven people to become anthropologists (vol. 6, *Romantic Motives: Essays on Anthropological Sensibility*).

▼ NOTES

[1] Edward B. Tylor, *Primitive Culture* (New York: Harper Torchbooks, 1958 [originally published 1871]).

[2] Lewis Henry Morgan, *Ancient Society* (Cambridge, MA: Harvard University Press, Belknap Press, 1964 [originally published 1877]).

[3] L. L. Langness, *The Study of Culture* (San Francisco: Chandler and Sharp, 1974), p. 50.

[4] Reprinted in Franz Boas, *Race, Language, and Culture* (New York: Macmillan, 1940), pp. 270–80.

[5] Marvin Harris, *The Rise of Anthropological Theory: A History of Theories of Culture* (New York: Thomas Y. Crowell, 1968), pp. 380–84; Langness, *The Study of Culture,* pp. 50–53.

[6] Ibid.

[7] Ibid.

[8] Langness, *The Study of Culture,* pp. 53–58; Harris, *The Rise of Anthropological Theory,* pp. 304–77.

[9] Bronislaw Malinowski, "The Group and the Individual in Functional Analysis," *American Journal of Sociology,* 44 (1939): 938–64.

[10] A. R. Radcliffe-Brown, *Structure and Function in Primitive Society* (London: Cohen & West, 1952).

[11] Ibid., pp. 92–93.

[12] Langness, *The Study of Culture,* pp. 85–93; Philip K. Bock, *Continuities in Psychological Anthropology: A Historical Introduction* (San Francisco: W. H. Freeman and Company, 1980), pp. 57–82.

[13] Abram Kardiner, with Ralph Linton, *The Individual and His Society* (New York: Columbia University Press, 1939), pp. 471–87.

[14] Ruth Benedict, *The Chrysanthemum and the Sword* (Boston: Houghton Mifflin, 1946); Geoffrey Gorer, "Themes in Japanese Culture," *Transactions of the New York Academy of Sciences,* 5 (1943): 106–24; and Weston LaBarre, "Some Observations on Character Structure in the Orient: The Japanese," *Psychiatry,* 8 (1945): 326–42.

[15] Geoffrey Gorer and John Rickman, *The People of Great Russia: A Psychological Study* (New York: Chanticleer, 1950).

[16] Herbert Barry III, Irvin L. Child, and Margaret K. Bacon, "Relation of Child Training to Subsistence Economy," *American Anthropologist,* 61 (1959): 51–63.

[17] John W. M. Whiting and Irvin L. Child, *Child Training and Personality: A Cross-Cultural Study* (New Haven: Yale University Press, 1953).

[18] Leslie A. White, *The Science of Culture: A Study of Man and Civilization* (New York: Farrar, Straus & Cudahy, 1949), pp. 368–69.

[19] Julian H. Steward, *Theory of Culture Change,* (Urbana: University of Illinois Press, 1955).

[20] Marshall D. Sahlins and Elman R. Service, *Evolution and Culture* (Ann Arbor: University of Michigan Press, 1960).

[21] Claude Lévi-Strauss, *The Elementary Structures of Kinship,* rev. ed., trans. James H. Bell and J. R. von Sturmer, ed. Rodney Needham (Boston: Beacon Press, 1969), p. 75.

[22] Claude Lévi-Strauss. *The Savage Mind,* trans. George Weidenfeld and Nicolson, Ltd. (Chicago: University of Chicago Press, 1966 [first published in French, 1962]); and Lévi-Strauss, *The Raw and the Cooked,* trans.

John Weightman and Doreen Weightman (New York: Harper & Row, 1969 [first published in French, 1964]).

[23]Sherry B. Ortner, "Theory in Anthropology since the Sixties," *Comparative Studies in Society and History,* 26 (1984): 126–66.

[24]Mary Douglas, *Implicit Meanings: Essays in Anthropology,* (London: Routledge and Kegan Paul, 1975).

[25]Julian H. Steward, "The Concept and Method of Cultural Ecology," in Steward, *Theory of Culture Change,* pp. 30–42.

[26]Andrew P. Vayda and Roy A. Rappaport, "Ecology: Cultural and Noncultural," in James H. Clifton, ed., *Introduction to Cultural Anthropology* (Boston: Houghton Mifflin, 1968), pp. 477–97.

[27]Ibid., p. 493.

[28]See Roy A. Rappaport, "Ritual Regulation of Environmental Relations among a New Guinea People," *Ethnology,* 6 (1967): 17–30.

[29]Ortner, "Theory in Anthropology since the Sixties," pp. 141–42.

[30]William Roseberry, "Political Economy," *Annual Review of Anthropology,* 17 (1988): 163; see also Eric R. Wolf, "San José: Subcultures of a 'Traditional' Coffee Municipality," and Sidney W. Mintz, "Canamelar: The Subculture of a Rural Sugar Plantation Proletariat," in Julian H. Steward, Robert A. Manners, Eric R. Wolf, Elena Padilla Seda, Sidney W. Mintz, and Raymond L. Scheele, *The People of Puerto Rico* (Urbana: University of Illinois Press, 1956), pp. 171–264.

[31]Roseberry, "Political Economy," p. 164; see also Eleanor Leacock, "The Montagnais 'Hunting Territory' and the Fur Trade," *American Anthropological Association,* Memoir 78 (1954): 1–59.

[32]Roseberry, "Political Economy," p. 166; see also André Gunder Frank, *Capitalism and Underdevelopment in Latin America: Historical Studies of Chile and Brazil* (New York: Monthly Review Press, 1967).

[33]Roseberry, "Political Economy," pp. 166–67; see also Immanuel Wallerstein, *The Modern World-System* (New York: Academic Press, 1974).

[34]William Irons, "Natural Selection, Adaptation, and Human Social Behavior," in Napoleon A. Chagnon and William Irons, eds., *Evolutionary Biology and Human Social Behavior: An Anthropological Perspective* (North Scituate, MA: Duxbury, 1979), pp. 10–12. For a mathematical model and a computer simulation suggesting that group selection is likely in cultural evolution, see Robert Boyd and Peter J. Richerson, "Group Selection among Alternative Evolutionarily Stable Strategies," *Journal of Theoretical Biology,* 145 (1990): 331–42.

[35]Irons, "Natural Selection, Adaptation, and Human Social Behavior."

[36]Bobbi S. Low, "Behavioral Ecology, 'Sociobiology' and Human Behavior," in Carol R. Ember, Melvin Ember, and Peter N. Peregrine, eds., *Research Frontiers in Anthropology* (Englewood Cliffs, NJ: Prentice Hall, 1995). Prentice Hall/Simon & Schuster Custom Publishing.

[37]Ibid.

[38]James Clifford, "Introduction: Partial Truths," in James Clifford and George E. Marcus, eds., *Writing Culture: The Poetics and Politics of Ethnography* (Berkeley: University of California Press, 1986), p. 3.

[39]Clifford Geertz, "Thick Description: Toward an Interpretive Theory of Culture," and "Deep Play: Notes on the Balinese Cockfight," in Clifford Geertz, *The Interpretation of Cultures: Selected Essays* (New York: Basic Books, 1973), pp. 3–30, 412–53; see also discussion of Geertz in George E. Marcus and Michael M. J. Fischer, *Anthropology as Cultural Critique: An Experimental Moment in the Human Sciences* (Chicago: University of Chicago Press, 1986), pp. 26–29.

[40]For discussion of this position, see Marcus and Fischer, *Anthropology as Cultural Critique,* pp. x, 180–81.

[41]Dan Sperber, *On Anthropological Knowledge: Three Essays* (Cambridge: Cambridge University Press, 1985), p. 34.

4

Explanation and Evidence

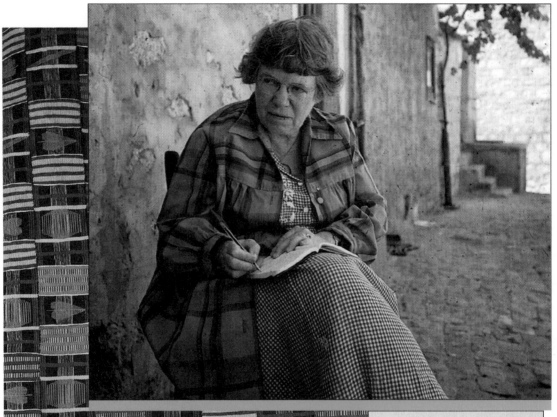

Chapter Outline

Explanations

Why Theories Cannot Be
Proved

Generating Theories

Evidence: Testing Explanations

Types of Research in Cultural
Anthropology

An important part of any discipline is description. A cultural anthropologist who goes to study a group of people tries to describe how the people live. How do they get food? How do they organize labor? How do they marry? The traditional goal of fieldwork is to arrive at accurate answers to such descriptive questions. But as important as accurate description is, it is not the ultimate goal of anthropology. Anthropologists want to understand—to know *why* people have certain traits or customs, not just that they *do* have them. As difficult as the *how* and *what* questions are to answer, the *why* questions are even harder. *Why* questions deal with explanations, which are harder to generate and harder to evaluate. In science, to understand is to explain, and so the major goal of science is to arrive at trustworthy explanations.[1]

This chapter is concerned largely with scientific understanding—what it means to explain and what kinds of evidence are needed to evaluate an explanation. We also discuss the various types of research that are conducted in cultural anthropology, from ethnography and ethnohistory to cross-cultural comparisons.

EXPLANATIONS

An **explanation** is an answer to a why question. But there are many types of explanation, some more satisfying than others. For example, suppose we ask why a society has a long postpartum sex taboo.

SCIENCE AND HUMANISM

This chapter deals largely with the scientific view of understanding, but there are anthropologists who question whether the scientific approach is desirable or possible. They often describe themselves as humanists who use the human capacity to intuit, empathize, evoke, interpret, and illuminate as ways to understand. This orientation offers a very different kind of understanding because compared with that offered by science it does not insist on objectivity, nor does it insist on putting insights to empirical test as science does. This is not to say that scientists do not intuit or interpret—they often do in the process of deriving theories, which involves creative leaps of imagination. And scientists, like anyone else, may empathize with the plight or problems of the people they study. But the crucial difference between the humanistic and scientific orientations lies in the end result; for humanists interpretation or evocation is the goal, for scientists the goal is testing interpretations to see if they may be wrong.

Is objectivity possible? Or, because we are humans observing other humans, can we only be subjective? Objectivity requires trying to get at the truth despite the observer's subjective desires or needs. Is that possible? Can any human be unbiased? In an absolute sense, no one can be completely free of bias. But science has ways to strive for objectivity; it does not need to assume that every human is completely unbiased. Remember that even when humans do physical science they are often the observers, or the creators of the instruments that do the observation. When an instrument points to a number, two humans may get slightly different readings because they look at the instrument from different angles. But neither person will be far off the mark, and the average of readings of two or more individuals will be very close to the "true" score. But do we see other people objectively? Undoubtedly, some things are harder to "see" than others. It is easier to know objectively that wives and husbands usually sit down to dinner together, harder to "see" how they feel about one another. Suppose you are in a society where you

We could guess that the people in that society *want* to abstain from sex for a year or so after the birth of a baby. Is this an explanation? Yes, because it does suggest that people have a *purpose* in practicing the custom; it therefore partly answers the why question. But such an explanation would not be very satisfying because it does not specify what the purpose of the custom might be. How about the idea that people have a long postpartum sex taboo because it is their tradition? Yes, that too is an explanation, but it is not satisfactory for a different reason. It is a *tautology;* that is, the thing to be explained (the taboo) is being explained by itself, by its prior existence. To explain something in terms of tradition is to say that people do it because they already do it, which is not very informative. What kinds of explanations are more satisfactory, then? In science, there are two kinds of explanation that researchers try to achieve—associations and theories.

Associations

One way of explaining something (an observation, an action, a habit, a custom) is to say how it conforms to a general principle or relationship. So to explain why the water left out in the basin froze last night, we say that it was quite cold last night and that water freezes at 32° F. The statement that water solidifies (becomes ice) at 32° is a statement of a relationship or association between two **variables**—things or quantities that vary. In this case, variation in the state of water (liquid versus solid) is related to variation in the temperature of the air (above versus

never see any obvious expression of affection between husbands and wives. At first, your own cultural bias might lead you to think that such couples don't care for each other much. Such an observation might indeed be biased (and not objective) if it turned out that couples privately expressed affection to each other but avoided public expressions. Or, it might be that couples communicated their affection for each other in ways you didn't notice. But that doesn't mean that you wouldn't be able to figure this out eventually. In trying to understand the meaning of female-male relationships, you might very well try to establish close, personal relationships with some families. You might then ask people to tell you stories to try to see how they portrayed relations between husband and wife. In short, a humanistic approach might help you understand how couples "really" feel about each other. But a scientist might go through the same procedure too in order to come to a tentative understanding.

As this example illustrates, humanistic understanding and science are not really incompatible. Both the scientist and the humanist would agree on the need to convey what a culture is like (for example, with regard to how couples feel about each other). But the scientist would insist on more. First, you would try to verify, perhaps by systematic interviewing, how commonly a feeling is shared in the culture. Second, you would want to explain why this feeling is common in some cultures but not in others. Therefore, you would have to create a theory to explain the variation. Then you would have to collect evidence to test the theory to see if it might be wrong.

If humans are always biased observers, how can humanists convey the meaning behind other cultures? Aren't humanists trying to get close to the "truth" too? The poet Marianne Moore wrote that poetry gives us "imaginary gardens with real toads in them." Can imagination, humanistic or scientific, be meaningful without at least some real toads?

Sources: *James Lett, "Scientific Anthropology," in David Levinson and Melvin Ember, eds.,* Encyclopedia of Cultural Anthropology, *4 vols. (New York: Henry Holt, 1995). The quote from Marianne Moore is from John Timpane, "Essay: The Poetry of Science,"* Scientific American, *July 1991, 128.*

below 32° F). The truth of the relationship is suggested by repeated observations. In the physical sciences, such relationships are called **laws** when they are accepted by almost all scientists. We find such explanations satisfactory because they allow us to predict what will happen in the future or to understand something that has happened regularly in the past. In the social sciences, associations are usually stated probabilistically: we say that two or more variables *tend* to be related in a predictable way, which means that there are usually some exceptions. For example, to explain why a society has a long postpartum sex taboo, we can point to the association (or correlation) that John Whiting found in a worldwide sample of societies: societies with apparently low-protein diets tend to have long postpartum sex taboos.[2] We call the relationship between low protein and the sex taboo a **statistical association,** which means that the observed relationship is unlikely to be due to chance.

Even though laws and statistical associations explain by relating what is to be explained to other things, we want to know more—why those laws or associations exist. Why does water freeze at 32° F? Why do societies with low-protein diets tend to have long postpartum sex taboos? Therefore, scientists try to formulate theories that will explain the observed relationships (laws and statistical associations).[3]

Theories

Theories—explanations of laws and statistical associations—are more complicated than the observed relationships they are intended to explain. It is difficult to be precise about what a theory is. By way of example, let us return to the question of why some societies have long postpartum sex taboos. We have already seen that a known statistical association can be used to help explain it: in general (but not always), if a society has a low-protein diet, it will have a long postpartum sex taboo. But most people would ask additional questions. Why does a low-protein diet explain the taboo? What is the mechanism by which a society with such a diet develops the custom of a long postpartum sex taboo? A theory is intended to answer such questions. In the chapter on the concept of culture, we briefly discussed John Whiting's theory that a long postpartum sex taboo may be an adaptation to certain conditions. Particularly in tropical areas, where the major food staples are low in protein, babies are vulnerable to the protein-deficiency disease called kwashiorkor. But if a baby could continue to nurse for a long time, it might have more of a chance to survive. The postpartum sex taboo might be adaptive, Whiting's theory suggests, because it increases the likelihood of a baby's survival. That is, if a mother puts off having another baby for a while, the first baby might have a better chance to survive because it can be fed mother's milk for a longer time. Whiting suggests that parents may be unconsciously or consciously aware that having another baby too soon might jeopardize the survival of the first baby, and so they might decide that it would be a good idea to abstain from intercourse for more than a year after the birth of the first baby.

As this example of a theory illustrates, there are differences between a theory and an association. A theory is more complicated, containing a series of statements. An association usually states quite simply that there is a relationship between two or a few measured variables. Another difference is that, although a theory may mention some things that are observable (such as the presence of a long postpartum sex taboo), parts of it are difficult or impossible to observe directly. For example, with regard to Whiting's theory, it would be difficult to find out if people had deliberately or unconsciously decided to practice a long postpartum sex taboo because they recognized that babies would thereby have a better chance to survive. Then too, the concept of adaptation—that some characteristic promotes greater reproductive success—is difficult to verify because it is difficult to find out whether different individuals or groups have different rates of reproduction because they do or do not practice the supposedly adaptive custom. So, some concepts or implications in a theory are unobservable (at least at the present time) and only some aspects may be observable. In contrast, statistical associations or laws are based entirely on observations.[4]

WHY THEORIES CANNOT BE PROVED

Many people think that the theories they learned in physics or chemistry classes have been proved. Unfortunately, many students get that impression because their teachers may present "lessons" in an authoritative manner. It is now generally agreed by scientists and philosophers of science that theories may have considerable evidence supporting them, but no theory can be said to be proved or unquestionably true. This is because many of the concepts and ideas in theories are not directly observable and therefore not directly verifiable. For example, scientists may try to explain how light behaves by postulating that it consists of particles called photons. But we cannot observe photons even with the most powerful microscope. So, exactly what a photon looks like and exactly how it works remain in the realm of the unprovable. The photon is a **theoretical construct,** something that cannot be observed or verified directly. Because all theories contain such ideas, theories cannot be proved entirely or with absolute certainty.[5]

Why should we bother with theories, then, if we cannot prove that they are true? Perhaps the main advantage of a theory as a kind of explanation is that it may lead to new understanding or knowledge. A theory can suggest new relationships or imply new predictions that might be supported or confirmed by new research. For example, Whiting's theory about long postpartum sex taboos has implications that could be investigated by researchers. Because the theory discusses how a long postpartum sex taboo might be adaptive, we would expect that certain changes will result in the taboo's disappearance. For example, suppose people adopted either mechanical birth-control devices or began to give supplementary high-protein foods to babies. With birth control, a family could space births without abstaining from sex, so we would expect the custom of postpartum abstinence to disappear. So too, we would expect it to disappear with protein supplements for babies, because kwashiorkor would then be less likely to afflict the babies. Whiting's ideas might also prompt investigators to try to find out whether parents are consciously or unconsciously aware of the problem of close birth spacing in areas with low supplies of protein.

Although theories cannot be proved, they are rejectable. The method of **falsification** (which shows that a theory seems to be wrong) is the main way that theories are judged.[6] Scientists derive implications or predictions that should be true *if* the theory is correct. So, for example, Whiting predicted from his theory that societies with long postpartum sex taboos would be found more often in the tropics than in temperate regions and that they would be likely to have low protein supplies. Such predictions of what might be found are called **hypotheses.** If the predictions turn out *not* to be correct, the researcher is obliged to conclude that there may be something wrong with the theory (or something wrong with the test of the theory). Theories that are not falsified are accepted for the time being because the available evidence seems to be consistent with them. But remember that no matter how much the available evidence seems to support a theory, we can never be certain it is true. There is always the possibility that some implication of it, some hypothesis derivable from it, will not be confirmed in the future.

GENERATING THEORIES

In the previous chapter we discussed many of the theoretical orientations that have existed in cultural anthropology. Most of these orientations merely suggest where to look for answers to questions; they do not by themselves suggest particular explanations for particular phenomena. You cannot directly deduce a theory from a theoretical orientation. For example, an anthropologist with an ecological theoretical orientation is likely to say that some particular custom exists because it is or used to be adaptive. But exactly how a particular custom may be adaptive must still be specified; the mechanism of its adaptiveness is not automatically suggested by the theoretical orientation. Whiting's theory suggests specific conditions under which the long postpartum sex taboo might be adaptive. The theory does not just say that the taboo is adaptive. How, then, does an anthropologist develop an explanation or theory for some particular phenomenon?

It is difficult to specify any one procedure that is guaranteed to produce a theory, because developing a theory requires creative imagination, and no

An atom, like a photon, cannot be observed. But there are theories about atoms and what they look like. This traditional model of a beryllium atom is now thought to be somewhat inaccurate: the electrons are probably more eccentric in their orbits and further from the nucleus.

discovery procedure by itself necessarily generates creativity. Too much dependence on a particular theoretical orientation may, in fact, be detrimental, because it may blind the investigator to other possibilities. A more important factor in generating a theory may be the investigator's belief that it is possible to do so. A person who believes that something is explainable will be more apt to notice possibly connected facts, as well as to recall possibly relevant considerations, and to put them all together in some explanatory way.

We *can* point to some procedures that have helped anthropologists produce explanations of cultural phenomena. These procedures seem to consist of two types; anthropologists may be helped by analysis of a particular society (we refer to this as *single-case analysis*), or they may try to come up with a theory by a *comparative study* of more than one society.

In analyzing a single case, the anthropologist may be interested in explaining a particular custom. While in the field, one may ask informants why they practice (or think they practice) the custom. Sometimes such inquiries will elicit a plausible explanation. But more often than not, the informants may merely answer, "We have always done it that way." The investigator may then make a kind of mental search through other features of the society or its environment that may be connected with the custom. If possible, the anthropologist may try to view the situation historically, to see if the custom appeared rather recently. If it did, what possible explanatory conditions appeared just before the custom?

An anthropologist may also generate an explanation by comparing different societies that share this characteristic, in order to determine what other characteristics regularly occur along with it. Societies in which the characteristic is lacking would also be considered, because a possible cause of that characteristic should be absent in those societies. If the anthropologist discovers that a characteristic occurs regularly in different cultures along with certain other features, we may be reasonably certain that the possible causes of that characteristic have been narrowed down.

It must be remembered, however, that the investigator is not a computer. It is not necessary to search through all the characteristics that might be shared by different cultures. The investigator usually looks only at those traits that can plausibly be connected. Here is where an individual's theoretical orientation generally comes into play, since that orientation usually points to the possible importance of one particular set of factors over others.

EVIDENCE: TESTING EXPLANATIONS

In any field of investigation, theories are generally the most plentiful commodity, apparently because of the human predisposition to try to make sense of the world. It is necessary, then, for us to have procedures that enable us to select from among the many available theories those that are more likely to be correct. "Just as mutations arise naturally but are not all beneficial, so hypotheses [theories] emerge naturally but are not all correct. If progress is to occur, therefore, we require a superfluity of hypotheses and also a mechanism of selection."[7] In other words, generating a theory or interpretation is not enough. We need some reliable method of testing whether or not that interpretation is likely to be correct. If an interpretation is not correct, it may detract from our efforts to achieve understanding by misleading us into thinking the problem is already solved.

The strategy of all kinds of testing in science is to predict what one would expect to find if a particular interpretation were correct and then to conduct an investigation to see if the prediction is borne out. If the prediction is not borne out, the investigator is obliged to accept the possibility that the interpretation is wrong. If, however, the prediction holds true, then the investigator is entitled to say that there is evidence to support the theory. Thus, conducting research designed to test expectations derived from theory allows us to eliminate some interpretations and to accept others, at least tentatively.

Operationalization and Measurement

We test predictions derived from a theory to see if the theory may be correct, to see if it is consistent with observable events or conditions in the real world. A theory and the predictions derived from it are not useful if there is no way to measure the events or conditions mentioned in the predictions. If there is no way of relating the theory to observable events, it does not matter how good the theory sounds—it is still not a useful scientific theory.[8] To transform theoretical predictions into statements that might be verified, a researcher provides an **operational definition** of each of the concepts or variables mentioned in the prediction. An operational definition is a description of the procedure that is followed to measure the variable.[9]

Whiting predicted that societies with a low-protein diet would have a long postpartum sex

The Yanomamö Indians of Brazil depend mostly on root crops. The Masai pastoralists of Kenya depend largely on milk and other products of cattle.

taboo. Amount of protein in the diet is a variable; some societies have more, others have less. Length of the postpartum sex taboo is a variable; a society may have a short taboo or a long taboo. Whiting operationally defined the first variable, *amount of protein,* in terms of staple foods.[10] For example, if a society depended mostly on root and tree crops (such as cassava and bananas), Whiting rated the society as having low protein. If the society depended mostly on cereal crops (wheat, barley, corn, oats, and so on), he rated it as having moderate protein, because cereal crops have more protein by weight than root and tree crops. If the society depended mostly on hunting, fishing, or herding for food, he rated it as having high protein. The other variable in Whiting's prediction, *length of postpartum sex taboo,* was operationalized as follows: a society was rated as having a long taboo if couples customarily abstained from sex for more than a year after the birth of a baby; abstention for a year or less was considered a short taboo.

Specifying an operational definition for each variable is extremely important because it allows other investigators to check on a researcher's results.[11] Science depends on *replication,* or the repetition of results. Only when many researchers observe a particular association can we call that association or relationship a law. Providing operational definitions is extremely important also because it allows others to evaluate whether a measure is appropriate. Only when we are told exactly how something was measured can we judge whether the measure reflects what it is supposed to reflect. Specifying measures publically is so important in science that we are obliged to be skeptical of any conclusions offered by a researcher who fails to say how variables were measured.

To **measure** something is to say how it compares with other things on some scale of variation.[12]

People often assume that a measuring device is always a physical instrument (such as a scale or a ruler), but physical devices are not necessary to measure something. Classification is also a form of measurement. When we classify persons as male or female, or employed versus unemployed, we are dividing them into sets. Deciding which set they belong to is a kind of measure because doing so allows us to compare them. We can also measure things by deciding which cases or examples have more or less of something (for instance, more or less protein in the diet). The measures employed in physical science are usually based on scales that allow us to assign numbers to each case: we may measure height in meters and weight in grams, for example. However we measure our variables, the fact that we *can* measure them means that we can test our hypotheses to see if the predicted relationships actually exist, at least most of the time.

Sampling

After an investigator decides how to measure the variables in some predicted relationship, she or he must decide how to select which cases to investigate to see if the predicted relationship holds. If the prediction is about the behavior of people, the sampling decision involves which people to observe. If the prediction is about an association between societal customs, the sampling decision involves which societies should be studied. Investigators must decide not only which cases to choose but also how many to choose. No researcher can investigate all the possible cases, so choices must be made. Some choices are better than others. In the chapter on the concept of culture, we talked about the advantages of random sampling. A random sample is one in which all cases selected had an equal chance to be included in the sample. Almost all statistical tests used to evaluate the results of research require random sampling, because only results based on a random sample can be assumed to be probably true for some larger set or universe of cases.

Before a researcher can sample randomly, he or she must specify the **sampling universe**—that is, the list of cases to be sampled from. Suppose an anthropologist is doing fieldwork in a society. Unless the society is very small, it is usually not practical to use the whole society as the sampling universe. Because most fieldworkers want to remain in a community for a considerable length of time, the community usually becomes the sampling universe. If a cross-cultural researcher wants to test an explanation, she or he needs to sample the world's societies. But we do not have descriptions of all the societies, past and present, that have existed in the world. So samples are usually drawn from published lists of described societies that have been classified or coded according to standard cultural variables,[13] or they are drawn from the Human Relations Area Files (HRAF), an indexed, annually growing collection of original ethnographic books and articles on more than 350 societies past and present around the world.[14]

Random sampling is still not employed that often in anthropology, but a nonrandom sample might still be fairly representative if the investigator has not personally chosen the cases for study. We should be particularly suspicious of any sample that may reflect the investigator's own biases or interests. For example, if an investigator picks only the people with whom she or he is friendly, the sample is suspicious. If cross-cultural researchers select sample societies because ethnographies on them happen to be on their own bookshelves, such samples are also suspicious. A sampling procedure should be designed to get a fair representation of the sampling universe, not a biased selection. If we want to increase our chances of getting a representative sample, we have to use a random-sampling procedure. To do so, we conventionally number the cases in the statistical universe and then use a table of random numbers to draw our sample cases.

Statistical Evaluation

When the researcher has measured the variables of interest for all the sample cases, he or she is ready to see if the predicted relationship actually exists in the data. Remember, the results may not turn out to be what the theory predicts. Sometimes the researcher constructs a *contingency table*, like that shown in Table 4–1, to see if the variables are associated as predicted. In Whiting's sample of 172 societies, each case is assigned to a box, or *cell*, in the table, depending on how the society is measured on the two variables of interest. For example, a society that has a long postpartum sex taboo and low protein is placed in the lowest right-hand cell of the Duration columns. (In Whiting's sample—see Table 4–1—there are 27 such societies.) A society that has a short postpartum sex taboo and low protein is placed in the lowest left-hand cell. (There are 20 such societies in the sample.) The statistical question is: Does the way the cases are distributed in the six cells of the table support Whiting's prediction? If we looked just at the table, we might not know what to say. Many cases appear to be in the expected places. For example, most of the high-protein cases, 47 of 62, have short taboos, and most of the low-protein cases, 27 of 47, have long taboos. But there are also many exceptions (for example, 20 cases have low protein and a short taboo). So, although many cases appear to be in the expected places, there are also many exceptions. Do the exceptions invalidate the prediction? How many exceptions

▼▼▼▼▼▼
TABLE 4–1
Association between Availability of Protein and Duration of Postpartum Sex Taboo

AVAILABILITY OF PROTEIN	DURATION OF POSTPARTUM SEX TABOO		TOTAL
	Short (0–1 Year)	*Long (More Than 1 Year)*	
High	47	15	62
Medium	38	25	63
Low	20	27	47
Total	105	67	172

Source: *Adapted from chapter by John W. M. Whiting in Ward H. Goodenough, ed.,* Explorations in Cultural Anthropology *(New York: McGraw-Hill, 1964), p. 520.*

would compel us to reject the hypothesis? Here is where we resort to statistical *tests of significance.*

Statisticians have devised various tests that tell us how "perfect" a result has to be for us to believe that there is probably an association between the variables of interest, that one variable generally predicts the other. Essentially, every statistical result is evaluated in the same objective way. We ask: What is the chance that this result is purely accidental, that there is really no association at all between the two variables? Although some of the mathematical ways of answering this question are rather complicated, the answer always involves a **probability value** (or **p-value**)—the likelihood that the observed result or a stronger one could have occurred by chance. The statistical test used by Whiting gives a p-value of less than .01 ($p < .01$) for the observed result. In other words, there is less than 1 chance out of 100 that the relationship observed is purely accidental. A p-value of less than .01 is a fairly low probability; most social scientists conventionally agree to call any result with a p-value of .05 or less (5 or fewer chances out of 100) a **statistically significant** or probably true result. *When we describe relationships or associations in the rest of this book, we are almost always referring to results that have been found to be statistically significant.*

But why should a probably true relationship have any exceptions? If a theory is really correct, shouldn't *all* the cases fit? There are many reasons why we cannot ever expect a perfect result. First, even if a theory is correct (for example, if a low-protein diet really does favor the adoption of a long postpartum sex taboo), there may still be other causes that we have not investigated. Some of the societies could have a long taboo even though they have high protein. For example, societies that depend mostly on hunting for their food (and that would therefore be classified as having a high-protein diet) may have a problem carrying infants from one campsite to another and may practice a long postpartum sex taboo so that two infants will not have to be carried at the same time. Exceptions to the predicted relationship might also occur because of *cultural lag.*[15] Suppose that a society recently changed crops and is now no longer a low-protein society but still practices the taboo. This society would be an exception to the predicted relationship, but it might fit the theory if it stopped practicing the taboo in a few years. Measurement inaccuracy is another source of exceptions. Whiting's measure of protein, which is based on the major sources of food, is not a very precise measure of protein in the diet. It does not take into account the possibility that a "tree-crop" society might get a lot of protein from fishing or raising pigs. So it might turn out that some supposedly low-protein societies have been misclassified, which may be one reason there are 20 cases in the lowest cell in the left-hand column of Table 4–1. Measurement error usually produces exceptions.

Significant statistical associations that are predictable from a theory offer tentative support for the theory. But much more is needed before we can be fairly confident about the theory. Replication is needed to confirm whether the predictions can be reproduced by other researchers using other samples. Other predictions should be derived from the theory to see if they too are supported. The theory should be pitted against alternative explanations to see which theory works better. We may have to combine theories if the alternative explanations also predict the relationship in question. The research process in science thus requires time and patience. Perhaps most important, it requires that researchers be humble. No matter how wonderful one's own theory seems, it is important to acknowledge that it may be wrong. If we don't acknowledge that possibility, we can't be motivated to test our theories. If we don't test our theories, we can never tell the difference between a better or worse theory, and we will be saddled forever with our present ignorance. In science, knowledge or understanding is explained variation. And so, if we want to understand more, we have to keep testing our beliefs against sets of objective evidence that could falsify our beliefs.

TYPES OF RESEARCH IN CULTURAL ANTHROPOLOGY

Cultural anthropologists use several different methods to conduct research. Each has certain advantages and disadvantages in generating and testing explanations. The types of research in cultural anthropology can be classified according to two criteria. One is the *spatial* scope of the study (analysis of a single society, analysis of several societies in a region, or analysis of a worldwide sample of societies). The other criterion is the *temporal* scope of the study (historical versus nonhistorical). The combination of these criteria is shown in Table 4–2, which identifies each of the major types of research in cultural anthropology.

Ethnography

Around the beginning of the twentieth century, anthropologists realized that if they were to produce anything of scientific value, they would have

▼▼▼▼▼▼

TABLE 4–2 *Types of Research in Cultural Anthropology*

	NONHISTORICAL	HISTORICAL
Single society	• Ethnography • Within-culture comparison	• Ethnohistory • Within-culture comparison
Region	Controlled comparison	Controlled comparison
Worldwide sample	Cross-cultural research	Cross-historical research

to study their subject in depth. To describe cultures more accurately, they started to live among the people they were studying. They observed, and even took part in, the important events of those societies and carefully questioned the people about their native customs. This method is known as **participant-observation.** Participant-observation always involves **fieldwork,** which is first-hand experience with the people you are studying, but fieldwork may also involve other methods, such as conducting a census or a survey.[16]

Fieldwork, the cornerstone of modern anthropology, is the means by which most anthropological information is obtained. Regardless of other methods that anthropologists may use, participant-observation, usually for a year or more, is regarded

Current Issues

FIELDWORK: HOW CAN WE KNOW WHAT IS TRUE?

Hardly any cultural anthropologist disputes the value of fieldwork in another culture, both for what it contributes to understanding others and for what it contributes to understanding yourself and your own culture. Probably it is the immersion that does it: living with other people (which we call participant-observation) allows you to see things you would not otherwise notice. At the same time, you cannot help but realize how the smallest habitual things you do, which you may have thought were just natural, are just wrong in your field site. At the beginning, there is culture shock because there is so much you don't comprehend. And, at the end, there is culture shock when you

return home: all of a sudden, many things in your own society now feel strange. Indeed, the experience is so profound that most cultural anthropologists feel that fieldwork provides them with the "deepest" kind of knowledge. Not just deep, but real.

Although few people doubt the value of fieldwork, challenges have come about veracity. Consider the controversy over the fieldwork of Margaret Mead, who lived on a small island in American Samoa in the 1920s and wrote about the sexual freedom of adolescents in *Coming of Age in Samoa*. Derek Freeman, who worked in Western Samoa largely in the 1960s, wrote a scathing critique of Mead's fieldwork in his *Margaret Mead and*

Samoa: The Making and Unmaking of an Anthropological Myth. Essentially, Freeman said that Mead got most things wrong: for example, he stated that the Samoans are puritanical in their sexuality. If both did fieldwork, and fieldwork gives us real, deep knowledge, then they should both be right. But how can they be? Was one a good fieldworker and the other not? How can we know what is true?

Paul Shankman suggests that both might be partly right if we recognize several things. First, he points out that we can speak of sexual permissiveness and sexual restrictiveness only in comparative terms. We need to understand that Mead did her fieldwork at a time when preas fundamental. In contrast to the casual descriptions of travelers and adventurers, anthropologists' descriptions must record, describe, analyze, and eventually formulate a picture of the culture, or at least part of it.[17] After doing fieldwork, an anthropologist may prepare an *ethnography*—a description and analysis of a single society.

How one goes about doing long-term participant-observation in another culture, and more important, doing it well, is not so straightforward. Much of it depends on the person, the culture, and the interaction between the two. Without doubt, the experience is physically and psychologically demanding, comparable often to a rite of passage. Although it helps enormously to learn the local language before one goes, it is often not possible to do so, and so most anthropologists find themselves struggling to communicate in addition to trying to figure out how to behave properly. Participant-observation itself carries its own dilemma. For participating implies living like the people you have come to study, trying to subjectively understand what they think and feel by doing what they do, whereas observation implies a certain amount of objectivity and detachment.[18] Because participant-observation is such a personal experience, it is not surprising that anthropologists have begun to realize that *reflecting* on their experiences and their personal interaction with the people they live with is an important part of understanding the enterprise.

An essential part of participant-observation process is taking notes, jotting down things observed, questions you asked and answers obtained, and things to check out later. Often these notes cannot be extensive or may not be legible later, so it is important to set aside time each day to go over and elaborate on your information, and classify it somehow, so you can find it later.[19]

marital sex was uncommon in the United States (sex patterns changed subsequently). So, in contrast with American girls during Mead's time, Samoan girls may have seemed more sexually free. Second, Samoa changed a great deal over time with missionization, colonialization, World War II, and commercialization. And, third, Samoa was variable—American Samoa versus Western Samoa, rural versus urban. So, what the two fieldworkers experienced may have been quite different, and therefore they could both be right. But in fact, Shankman suggests that if we ignore Mead's and Freeman's conclusions about permissive or restrictive sexuality, if we separate *ideal* from *actual* behavior, and if we look at actual data on individual sexual behavior as collected by both Mead and Freeman, the two fieldworkers are not all that different—Samoans are in the middle of the worldwide range of cultures in regard to the occurrence of premarital sex.

What do we conclude from this controversy? As many anthropologists are now pointing out, it is important to reflect on the possible influences of the context of the fieldwork, the qualities of the person doing it, how that person interacts with the people she or he lives with, and the kinds of methods used to try to verify conclusions. Others point out that reflection, although important, is not enough. If we want to be more sure that we are understanding correctly, it is not sufficient to assume that the traditional style of fieldwork (participant-observation and interviewing of a few selected informants) can always discover the truth in a field situation. Particularly for those behaviors that are private, or more variable, or not easily verbalized, anthropological fieldworkers should consider interviewing a representative sample of people and using tests of informant accuracy.

Sources: *Paul Shankman, "Sex, Lies, and Anthropologists: Margaret Mead, Derek Freeman, and Samoa," in Carol R. Ember, Melvin Ember, and Peter N. Peregrine, eds.,* Research Frontiers in Anthropology *(Englewood Cliffs, NJ: Prentice Hall 1995). Prentice Hall/Simon & Schuster Custom Publishing. Melvin Ember, "Evidence and Science in Ethnography: Reflections on the Freeman-Mead Controversy,"* American Anthropologist, *87 (1985): 906–9.*

Participant-observation is quite valuable for understanding some aspects of culture, particularly the things that are the most public, readily talked about, and most widely agreed upon. But more systematic methods are important too: mapping, house-to-house censuses, behavior observations (for example, to determine how people spend their time), as well as focused interviews with a sample of informants.

Ethnographies and ethnographic articles on particular topics provide much of the essential data for all kinds of studies in cultural anthropology. To make a comparison of societies in a given region, or worldwide, an anthropologist would require ethnographic data on many societies.

With regard to the goal of generating theory, ethnography, with its in-depth, firsthand, long-term observation, provides an investigator with a wealth of descriptive material covering a wide range of phenomena. Thus, it may stimulate interpretations about the way different aspects of the culture are related to each other and to features of the environment. The ethnographer in the field has the opportunity to get to know the context of a society's customs by directly asking the people about those customs and by observing the phenomena that appear to be associated with those practices. In addition, the ethnographer who develops a possible explanation for some custom can test that hunch by collecting new information related to it. In this sense, the ethnographer is similar to a physician who is trying to understand why a patient has certain symptoms of illness.

Although ethnography is extremely useful for generating explanations, a field study of a single site does not generally provide sufficient data to test a hypothesis. For example, an ethnographer may think that a particular society practices *polygyny* (one man married to two or more women simultaneously) because it has more women than men. But the ethnographer could not be reasonably sure that this explanation was correct unless the results of a comparative study of a sample of societies showed that most polygynous societies have more women than men. After all, the fact that one society has both these conditions could be a historical accident rather than a result of some necessary connection between the two conditions.

Within-Culture Comparisons

An ethnographer could test a theory within one society if she or he decides to compare individuals, families, households, communities, or districts.

The natural variability that exists can be used to create a comparison. Suppose we want to verify Whiting's assumption that in a society with low-protein diets, longer postpartum taboos enhance the survival of babies. Although almost all couples might practice a long postpartum sex taboo because it was customary, some couples might not adhere to the taboo consistently and some couples might not conceive quickly after the taboo was lifted. So we would expect some variation in spacing between births. If we collected information on the births of each mother and the survival outcome of each birth, we would be able to compare the survival rates of children born a short time after the mother's last pregnancy with those of children born after longer intervals. A significantly higher survival rate for the births after longer intervals would support Whiting's theory. What if some communities within the society had access to more protein than others? If Whiting's theory is correct, those communities with more protein should also have a higher survival rate for babies. If there were variation in the length of the postpartum sex taboo, the communities with more protein should have shorter taboos.

Whether or not we can design intracultural tests of hypotheses depends on whether we have sufficient variability in the variables of our hypothesis. More often than not we do, and we can make use of that variation to test hypotheses within a culture.

Nonhistorical Controlled Comparison

In a nonhistorical controlled comparison, the anthropologist compares ethnographic information obtained from societies found in a particular region—societies that presumably have similar histories and occupy similar environments. The anthropologist who conducts a regional comparison is apt to be familiar with the complex of cultural features associated with that region. These features may provide a good understanding of the context of the phenomenon that is to be explained. An anthropologist's knowledge of the region under study, however, is probably not as great as the ethnographer's knowledge of a single society. Still, the anthropologist's understanding of local details is greater in a regional comparison than in a worldwide comparison. The worldwide comparison is necessarily so broad that the investigator is unlikely to know a great deal about any of the societies being compared.

The regional controlled comparison is useful not only for generating explanations but also for testing them. Because some of the societies being compared will have the characteristic that is to be explained and some will not, the anthropologist can determine whether the conditions hypothesized to be related are in fact related, at least in that region. We must remember, however, that two or more conditions may be related in one region for reasons peculiar to that region. Therefore, an explanation supported in one region may not pertain in others.

Cross-Cultural Research

Anthropologists can generate interpretations on the basis of worldwide comparisons by looking for differences between those societies having, and those lacking, a particular characteristic. But the most common use of worldwide comparisons has probably been to test explanations. The cross-cultural researcher first identifies conditions that should generally be associated if a particular theory is correct. Then she or he looks at a worldwide sample of societies to see if the expected association generally holds true. The advantage of cross-cultural research is that the conclusion drawn from it is probably applicable to most societies, *if* the sample used for testing has been more or less randomly selected. In other words, in contrast with the results of a regional comparison, which may or may not be applicable to other regions, the results of a cross-

Cross-cultural researchers are not the only anthropologists who use computers for statistical analysis. Physical anthropologists Randall White and Jean de Rousseau (here examining a Neandertal jawbone) also use computers in their research.

cultural study are presumably applicable to most societies and most regions.

As we have noted, the greater the number of societies examined in a study, the less likely it is that the investigator will have detailed knowledge of the societies involved. So if a cross-cultural test does not support a particular explanation, the investigator may not know enough about the sample societies to know how to modify the interpretation or come up with a new one. In this situation, the anthropologist may reexamine the details of one or more particular societies in order to stimulate fresh thinking on the subject. Another limitation of cross-cultural research, as a means both of generating and of testing explanations, is that only those explanations for which the required information is generally available in ethnographies can be tested. An investigator interested in explaining something that has not been generally described must resort to some other research strategy to collect data.

Historical Research

Ethnohistory is the study of descriptive materials about a single society at more than one point in time. It provides the essential data for historical studies of all types, just as ethnography provides the essential data for all nonhistorical types of research. Ethnohistorical data may consist of sources other than the ethnographic reports prepared by anthropologists—accounts by explorers, missionaries, traders, and government officials. Ethnohistorians, like historians, cannot simply assume that all the documents used are simply descriptions of fact; they were written by very different kinds of people with very different goals and purposes. So it is necessary to separate what may be fact from what may be speculative interpretation. In terms of generating and testing hypotheses, studies of single societies over time tend to be subject to the same limitations as studies of single societies confined to a single period. Like their nonhistorical counterparts, studies that concentrate on a single society observed through time are likely to generate more than one hypothesis, but they do not generally provide the opportunity to establish with reasonable certainty which of those hypotheses is correct. Cross-cultural historical studies (of which we have only a few examples thus far) suffer from the opposite limitation. They provide ample means of testing hypotheses through comparison, but they are severely constrained (because of the necessity of working with secondhand data) in their ability to generate hypotheses derived from the available data.

There is, however, one advantage to historical studies of any type. The goal of theory in cultural anthropology is to explain variation in cultural patterns: that is, to specify what conditions will favor one cultural pattern rather than another. Such specification requires us to assume that the supposed causal, or favoring, conditions antedated the pattern to be explained. Theories or explanations, then, imply a *sequence* of changes over time, which are the stuff of history. Therefore, if we want to come closer to an understanding of the reasons for the cultural variations we are investigating, we should examine historical sequences. These will help us determine whether the conditions we think caused various phenomena truly antedated those phenomena and thus might more reliably be said to have caused them. If we can examine historical sequences, we may be able to make sure that we do not put the cart before the horse.

The major impediment to historical research is that collecting and analyzing historical data—particularly when they come from the scattered accounts of explorers, missionaries, and traders—is a tedious and exasperating task. It may be more efficient to test explanations nonhistorically first, in order to eliminate some interpretations. Only when an interpretation survives a nonhistorical test should we look to historical data to test the presumed sequence.

In the chapters that follow, we discuss not only what we strongly suspect about the determinants of cultural variation but also what we do not know or only dimly suspect. We devote a lot of our discussion to what we do not know—what has not yet been the subject of research that tests hypotheses and theories—because we want to convey a sense of what cultural anthropology might learn in the future.

▼ SUMMARY

1. As important as accurate description is, it is not the ultimate goal of anthropology. Anthropologists want to understand—to know *why* people have certain traits or customs, not just that they *do* have them.

2. In science, to understand is to explain. Scientists try to achieve two kinds of explanation—associations (observed relationships between two or more variables) and theories (explanations of associations).

3. A theory is more complicated than an association. Some concepts or implications in a theory are unobservable; an association is based entirely on observations.

4. Theories can never be proved with absolute certainty. There is always the possibility that some implication, some derivable hypothesis, will not be confirmed by future research.

5. A theory is rejectable through the method of falsification. Scientists derive predictions that should be true *if* the theory is correct. If the predictions turn out to be incorrect, scientists are obliged to conclude that there may be something wrong with the theory.

6. To make a satisfactory test, we have to specify operationally how we measure the variables involved in the relationships we expect to exist, so that other researchers can try to replicate, or repeat, our results.

7. Tests of predictions should employ samples that are representative. The most objective way to obtain a representative sample is to select the sample cases randomly.

8. The results of tests are evaluated by statistical methods that assign probability values to the results. These values allow us to distinguish between probably true and probably accidental results.

9. Cultural anthropologists use several different methods to conduct research. Each has certain advantages and disadvantages in generating and testing explanations. The types of research in cultural anthropology can be classified according to two criteria: the spatial scope of the study (analysis of a single society, analysis of several or more societies in a region, or analysis of a worldwide sample of societies) and the temporal scope of the study (historical versus nonhistorical). The basic research methods, then, are ethnography and ethnohistory, historical and nonhistorical controlled comparisons, and historical and nonhistorical cross-cultural research.

▼ GLOSSARY TERMS

explanation

measure

statistical association

falsification

operational definition

statistically significant

fieldwork

participant-observation

theoretical construct

hypotheses

probability value (p-value)

theories

laws

sampling universe

variable

▼ CRITICAL QUESTIONS

1. Can a unique event be explained?
2. How does measurement go beyond observation?
3. Why is scientific understanding always uncertain?
4. Under what conditions would you trust someone's observation?
5. If two ethnographers describing the same culture disagree, how do we decide who's right?

▼ SUGGESTED READING

BERNARD, H. R. *Research Methods in Cultural Anthropology: Qualitative and Quantitative Approaches,* 2nd ed. Newbury Park, CA: Sage Publications, 1994. Proceeding step by step through the research process, this book surveys how to prepare for a field study and how to collect and analyze the data produced.

"Cross-Cultural and Comparative Research: Theory and Method." *Behavior Science Research,* 25 (1991): 1–270. This special issue provides an extensive "state-of-the-art" coverage of the goals, achievements, and problems in cross-cultural and comparative research.

EMBER, C. R., EMBER, M., AND PEREGRINE, P. N., eds. *Research Frontiers in Anthropology.* Englewood Cliffs, NJ: Prentice Hall, 1995. Prentice Hall/Simon & Schuster Custom Publishing. This series contains four types of articles about ongoing and future research: (1) anthropologists at work, (2) the state of current understanding of classic research questions and controversies, (3) the newest research methods, (4) research on social problems.

McCAIN, G., AND SEGAL, E. M. *The Game of Science,* 5th ed. Monterey, CA: Brooks/Cole, 1987. A very readable book about how scientists do research. The authors emphasize that science is a game we play against our own ignorance.

POGGIE, JOHN J., JR., DEWALT, BILLIE R., AND DRESSLER, WILLIAM W., eds. *Anthropological Research: Process and Application.* Albany, NY: State University of New York Press, 1992. The chapters in this volume illustrate how a research question is translated into operational research. Also stressed is the importance of blending qualitative and quantitative methods, variability within cultures, and the practical application of answers to research questions.

THOMAS, D. H. *Refiguring Anthropology: First Principles of Probability and Statistics.* Prospect Heights, IL: Waveland Press, 1986. The first textbook on statistical methods for anthropology. Other introductory texts on statistics cover many of the same topics, but this textbook is the first one that refers mainly to anthropological studies for examples.

WERNER, O., AND SCHOEPFLE, G. M. *Systematic Fieldwork. Volume 1: Foundations of Ethnography and Interviewing.* Newbury Park, CA: Sage Publications, 1987. A detailed presentation and discussion of the methods used to discover patterns of culture on the basis of fieldwork.

▼ NOTES

[1]Carl G. Hempel, *Aspects of Scientific Explanation* (New York: Free Press, 1965), p. 139.

[2]John W. M. Whiting, "Effects of Climate on Certain Cultural Practices," in Ward H. Goodenough, ed., *Explorations in Cultural Anthropology* (New York: McGraw-Hill, 1964), pp. 511–44.

[3]Ernest Nagel, *The Structure of Science: Problems in the Logic of Scientific Explanation* (New York: Harcourt, Brace & World, 1961), pp. 88–89.

[4]Ibid., pp. 83–90.

[5]Ibid., p. 85. See also Garvin McCain and Erwin M. Segal, *The Game of Science,* 5th ed. (Monterey, CA: Brooks/Cole, 1982), pp. 75–79.

[6]McCain and Segal, *The Game of Science,* pp. 62–64.

[7]Peter Caws, "The Structure of Discovery," *Science,* December 12, 1969, 1378.

[8]McCain and Segal, *The Game of Science,* p. 114.

[9]Ibid., pp. 56–57, 131–32.

[10]Whiting, "Effects of Climate on Certain Cultural Practices," pp. 519–20.

[11]McCain and Segal, *The Game of Science,* pp. 67–69.

[12]Hubert M. Blalock, Jr., *Social Statistics,* 2nd ed. (New York: McGraw-Hill, 1972), pp. 15–20; and David H. Thomas, *Refiguring Anthropology: First Principles of Probability and Statistics* (Prospect Heights, IL: Waveland Press, 1986), pp. 18–28. See also Melvin Ember, "Taxonomy in Comparative Studies," in Raoul Naroll and Ronald Cohen, eds., *A Handbook of Method in Cultural Anthropology* (Garden City, NY: Natural History Press, 1970), pp. 701–3.

[13]For examples, see George P. Murdock, "Ethnographic Atlas: A Summary," *Ethnology,* 6 (1967): 109–236; and George P. Murdock and Douglas R. White, "Standard Cross-Cultural Sample," *Ethnology,* 8 (1969): 329–69.

[14]Sets of the HRAF in paper or microfiche format, and now in electronic format, are found in almost 300 universities and research institutions around the world. For guides, see David Levinson, *Instructor's and Librarian's Guide to the HRAF Archive* (New Haven, CT: Human Relations Area Files, 1988); and Carol R. Ember and Melvin Ember, *Guide to Cross-Cultural Research Using the HRAF Archive* (New Haven, CT: Human Relations Area Files, 1988).

[15]Cultural lag occurs when change in one aspect of culture takes time to produce change in another aspect. For the original definition of this concept, see William F. Ogburn, *Social Change* (New York: Huebsch, 1922), pp. 200–80.

[16]H. Russell Bernard, *Research Methods in Cultural Anthropology* (Newbury Park, CA.: Sage Publications, 1988), p. 148.

[17]James L. Peacock, *The Anthropological Lens: Harsh Light, Soft Focus* (Cambridge: Cambridge University Press, 1986), p. 54.

[18]Robert Lawless, Vinson H. Sutlive, Jr., and Mario D. Zamora, eds., *Fieldwork: The Human Experience* (New York: Gordon and Breach Science Publishers, 1983), pp. xi–xxi; Peacock, *The Anthropological Lens,* pp. 54-65.

[19]Bernard, *Research Methods,* pp. 180-202.

Communication and Language

Few of us can remember the moment when we first became aware that words signified something. Yet that moment was a milestone for us, not just in the acquisition of language but in becoming acquainted with all the complex, elaborate behavior that constitutes our culture. Without language, the transmission of complex traditions would be virtually impossible, and each person would be trapped within his or her own world of private sensations.

Helen Keller, left deaf and blind by illness at the age of nineteen months, gives a moving account of the afternoon she first established contact with another human being through words.

> [My teacher] brought me my hat, and I knew I was going out into the warm sunshine. This thought, if a wordless sensation may be called a thought, made me hop and skip with pleasure.
>
> We walked down the path to the well house, attracted by the fragrance of the honeysuckle with which it was covered. Someone was drawing water and my teacher placed my hand under the spout. As the cool stream gushed over one hand she spelled into the other the word *water,* first slowly, then rapidly. Suddenly I felt a misty consciousness as of something forgotten—a thrill of returning thought; and somehow the mystery of language was revealed to me. I knew then that w-a-t-e-r meant the wonderful cool something that was flowing over my hand. That living word awakened my soul, gave it light, hope, joy, set it free! There were barriers still, it is true, barriers that could in time be swept away.
>
> I left the well house eager to learn. Everything had a name, and each name gave birth to a new thought. As we returned to the house every object which I touched seemed to quiver with life. That was because I saw everything with the strange, new sight that had come to me.[1]

COMMUNICATION

Against all odds, Helen Keller had come to understand the essential function language plays in all societies—namely, that of communication. The word *communicate* comes from the Latin verb *communicare,* "to share," "to impart that which is *common.*" We communicate by agreeing, consciously or unconsciously, to call an object, a movement, or an abstract concept by a common name. For example, speakers of English have agreed to call the color of grass green, even though we have no way of comparing precisely how two persons actually experience this color. What we share is the agreement to call similar sensations *green.* Any system of language consists of publicly accepted symbols by which individuals try to share private experiences.

Our communication obviously is not limited to spoken language. We communicate directly through body stance, gesture, and tone of voice and indirectly through systems of signs and symbols, such as writing, algebraic equations, musical scores, painting, code flags, and road signs. But despite all the competing systems of communication available to us, we must recognize the overriding importance of spoken language. It is probably the major transmitter of culture, allowing us to share and pass on our complex configuration of attitudes, beliefs, and patterns of behavior.

Animal Communication

Systems of communication are not unique to human beings. Other animal species communicate in a variety of ways. One way is by sound: a bird may communicate by a call that "this is my territory"; a squirrel may utter a cry that leads other squirrels to flee from danger. Another means of animal communication is odor. An ant releases a chemical when it dies, and its fellows then carry it away to the compost heap. Apparently the communication is highly effective; a healthy ant painted with the death chemical will be dragged to the funeral heap again and again.

Another means of communication, body movement, is used by bees to convey the location of food sources. Karl von Frisch discovered that the black Austrian honey bee—by choosing a round dance, a wagging dance, or a short, straight run—could communicate not only the precise direction of the source of food but also its distance from the hive.[2]

Although primates use all three methods of communication—sound, odor, and body movement—sound is the method that most concerns us in this chapter because spoken language is our own major means of communication. Nonhuman primates communicate vocally too, making various kinds of calls (but not very many of them). In the past, only human communication was thought to be symbolic. Recent research suggests that some monkey and ape calls in the wild are also symbolic.

When we say that a communication (call, word, sentence) is *symbolic,* we mean at least two things. First, the communication has meaning even when its referent (whatever is referred to) is not present. Second, the meaning is arbitrary: the receiver of the message could not guess its meaning just from the sound(s) and does not know the

We have known for some time that parrots can mimic human speech. But the fact that Irene Pepperberg's parrot named Alex has learned to understand spoken sentences and to reply appropriately to questions about quantities and colors suggests that even a bird-brain is not too small to be capable of symbolic communication. How else can we explain Alex's mostly correct counts (80 percent of the time) of "two," "three," "four," "five," and "sih" (six) for new objects that he is asked to give the number of?

meaning instinctively. In other words, symbols have to be learned. There is no compelling or "natural" reason that the word *dog* in English should refer to a smallish four-legged carnivore that is the bane of letter carriers.

Vervet monkeys in Africa are not as closely related to humans as are African apes. Nevertheless, scientists who have observed vervet monkeys in their natural environment consider at least three of their alarm calls to be symbolic because each of them *means* (refers to) a different kind of predator—eagles, pythons, leopards—and monkeys react differently to each call. For example, they look up when they hear the "eagle" call. Experimentally, in the absence of the referent, investigators have been able to evoke the normal reaction to a call by playing it back electronically. Another indication that the vervet alarm calls are symbolic is that infant vervets appear to need some time to learn the referent for each. When they are very young, infants apply a particular call to more animals than adult vervets apply the call to. So, for example, infant vervets will often make the eagle warning call when they see any flying bird. The infants learn the appropriate referent apparently through adult vervets' repetition of infants' "correct" calls; in any case, the infants gradually learn to restrict the call to eagles. This process is probably not too different from the way a North American

infant in an English-speaking family first applies the "word" *dada* to all adult males and gradually learns to restrict it to one person.[3]

All of the nonhuman vocalizations we have described so far enable individual animals to convey messages. The sender gives a signal that is received and "decoded" by the receiver, who usually responds with a specific action or reply. How is human vocalization different? Since monkeys and apes appear to use symbols at least some of the time, it is not appropriate to emphasize symbolism as the distinctive feature of human language. However, there is a significant quantitative difference between human language and other primates' systems of vocal communication—all human languages employ a much larger set of symbols. Another and perhaps more important difference is that the other primates' vocal systems tend to be *closed*: different calls are not often combined to produce new, meaningful utterances. In contrast, as we shall see, human languages are *open* systems, governed by complex rules about how sounds and sequences of sounds can be combined to produce an infinite variety of new meanings.[4]

The idea that humans can transmit many more complex messages than any other animal does not begin to convey how different human language is from other communication systems. No chimpanzee could say the equivalent of "I'm going to the ball game next Wednesday with my friend Jim if it's not raining." Humans can not only talk (and think) with language about things completely out of context; they also can be deliberately or unconsciously ambiguous in their messages. If a person asks you for help, you could say, "Sure, I'll do it when I have time," leaving the other person uncertain about whether your help is ever going to materialize.

Primates in the wild do not exhibit anything close to human language. But recent successful attempts to teach apes to communicate with humans and with each other using human-created signs have led some scholars to question the traditional assumption that the gap between human and other animal communication is enormous. Chimpanzees Washoe and Nim and the gorilla Koko were taught hand signs based on American Sign Language (ASL; used by the deaf in the United States). The chimpanzee Sarah was trained with plastic symbols, but more recently Lana, Sherman, Austin, and a pygmy chimpanzee, Kanzi, have been trained on symbol keyboards connected to computers. Sherman and Austin began to communicate with each other about actions they were intending to do, such as the types of tools they needed to solve a problem. And they were able to classify items into categories, such as "food" and "tools." In contrast to other apes, Kanzi learned symbols just by seeing humans point to them when they spoke to him. He did not need rewards or to have his hands put in the right position. And he understood a great deal of what was spoken to him. For example, when he was five years old, Kanzi heard someone talk about throwing a ball in the river, and he turned around and did so. Kanzi has come closest of all the "students" to having a primitive English grammar when he strings symbols together.[5] If chimpanzees and other primates have the capacity to *use* nonspoken language and even to understand spoken language, then the difference between humans and nonhumans may not be as great as people used to think.

Are these apes really using language? There is a lot of agreement among investigators that nonhuman primates have the ability to "symbol"—to refer to something (or a class of things) with an arbitrary "label" (gesture or sequence of sounds).[6] For example, the gorilla Koko (with a repertoire of about 375 signs) extended the sign for *drinking straw* to plastic tubing, hoses, cigarettes, and radio antennae. Washoe originally learned the sign *dirty* to refer to feces and other soil and then began to use it insultingly, as in "dirty Roger," when her trainer Roger Fouts refused to give her things she wanted. Even the mistakes made by the apes suggest that they are using signs symbolically, just as words are used in spoken language. For example, the sign *cat* may be used for dog if the animal learned *cat* first (just as our daughter Kathy said "dog" to all pictures of four-footed animals, including elephants, when she was eighteen months old).

In spite of the new evidence, Jane Hill believes that the answer about whether apes use language is still quite controversial because language is not one unitary thing. For instance, when we get to the structure of sounds (phonology) later in this chapter, we will see that every human language has certain ways of combining sounds and ways of *not* combining those sounds. Although apes do not use sounds, the combination of symbols can be thought of as analogous to the combining of sound elements. Yet there does not appear to be anything comparable to linguistic rules for allowed and not allowed combinations. Another major difference is that humans have many kinds of discourse. Humans may make lists and speeches, tell stories, argue, and recite poetry. Apes do none of those things. But apes do have some of the capacities for some of the elements of human language. Therefore under-standing their capacities may help us better understand the evolution of human language.[7]

THE ORIGINS OF LANGUAGE

How long humans have had spoken language is not known. Recently, Philip Lieberman and Jeffrey Laitman have argued that language as we know it developed only with the emergence of modern-looking humans (before or about 100,000 years ago) who had the mouth and throat anatomy we have.[8] According to Lieberman and Laitman, premodern humans (including the Neandertals) did not have the vocal anatomy required for language. Their argument is based on controversial reconstructions of the mouths and throats of earlier humans, and so their conclusions are not widely accepted.[9]

Most speculation about the origins of language has centered on the question of how natural selection may have favored the open quality of language. All known human languages are open in the sense that utterances can be combined in various ways to produce new meanings.[10] Somehow a call system of communication was eventually changed to a system based on small units of sound that could be put together in many different ways to form meaningful utterances. For example, an English speaker can combine *care* and *full (careful)* to mean one thing, then use each of the two elements in other combinations to mean different things. *Care* can be used to make *carefree, careless,* or *caretaker; full* can be used to make *powerful* or *wonderful.* And, because language is a system of shared symbols, it can be reformed into an infinite variety of expressions and be understood by all who share these symbols. In this way, for example, T. S. Eliot could form a sentence never before formed—"In the room the women come and go / talking of Michelangelo,"[11]—and the sense of his sentence, though not necessarily his private meaning, could be understood by all speakers of English.

One set of theoreticians of grammar suggests that there may be a *language-acquisition device* in the brain, as innate to humans as call systems are to the other animals.[12] As the forebrain evolved, this device may have become part of our biological inheritance. Whether the device in fact exists is not yet clear. But we do know that the actual development of individual language is not completely biologically determined; if it were, all human beings would speak the same brain-generated language. Instead, about 4,000 to 5,000 mutually unintelligible languages have been identified. More than 2,000 of them were still spoken as of recently, most by peoples who did not traditionally have a system of writing. Indeed, the earliest writing systems are not that old; they appeared only about 5,000 years ago.[13]

Can we learn anything about the origins of language by studying the languages of nonliterate and technologically simpler societies? The answer is no, because such languages are not simpler or less developed than ours. The sound systems, vocabularies, and grammars of technologically simpler peoples are in no way inferior to those of peoples with more complex technology.[14]

Of course, Australian aborigines will not be able to name the sophisticated machines used in our society. Their language, however, has the potential for doing so. As we will see later in this chapter, all languages possess the amount of vocabulary their speakers need, and languages expand in response to cultural changes. A language that lacks terminology for some of our conveniences may have a rich vocabulary for events or natural phenomena that are of particular importance to the people in that society.

If there are no primitive languages, and if the earliest languages have left no traces that would allow us to reconstruct them, does that mean we cannot investigate the origins of language? Some linguists think that understanding the way children acquire language, which we discuss shortly, can help us understand the origins of language. Recently, other linguists have suggested that an understanding of how *creole* languages develop will also tell us something about the origins of language.

Creole Languages

Some languages have developed quite recently in various places around the world where European colonial powers established commercial enterprises that relied on imported labor, generally slaves. The laborers in one place often came from several different societies and in the beginning would speak with their masters and with each other in some kind of *pidgin* (simplified) version of the masters' language. Pidgin languages lack many of the building blocks found in the languages of whole societies, building blocks such as prepositions (*to, on,* and so forth) and auxiliary verbs (designating future and other tenses). Many pidgin languages developed into and were replaced by so-called creole languages, which incorporate much of the vocabulary

of the masters' language but also have a grammar that differs from it and from the grammars of the laborers' native languages.[15]

Derek Bickerton argues that there are striking grammatical similarities in creole languages all over the world. This similarity, he thinks, is consistent with the idea that there is a universal grammar inherited by all humans. Creole languages, therefore, may resemble early human languages. All creoles use intonation instead of a change in word order to ask a question. The creole equivalent of the question "Can you fix this?" would be to say, "You can fix this?" The creole version puts a rising inflection at the end; in contrast, the English version reverses the subject and verb without much inflection at the end. Creoles all express the future and the past in the same grammatical way, by the use of particles (such as the English *shall*) between subject and verb, and they all employ double negatives, as in the Guyana English creole "Nobody no like me."[16]

Children's Acquisition of Language

Apparently a child is equipped from birth with the capacity to reproduce all the sounds used by the world's languages and to learn any system of grammar. The language the child learns is the one spoken by the parents or caretakers.

Children's acquisition of the structure and meaning of language has been called the most difficult intellectual achievement in life. If that is so, it is pleasing to note that they accomplish it with relative ease and vast enjoyment. This "difficult intellectual achievement" may in reality be a natural response to the capacity for language that is one of humans' genetic characteristics. All over the world children begin to learn language at about the same age—and in no culture do children wait until they are seven or ten years old. By twelve or thirteen months children are able to name a few objects and actions and by eighteen to twenty months they seem to be able to make one key word stand for a whole sentence: "Out!" for "Take me out for a walk right now"; "Juice!" for "I want some juice now." Evidence now suggests that children acquire the concept of a word as a whole, learning sequences of sounds that are stressed or at the ends of words (for example, "raffe" for giraffe). Even deaf children learning signs in ASL tend to acquire and use signs in a similar fashion.[17]

Children the world over tend to progress to two-word sentences at the age of about eighteen to twenty-four months. In those sentences they ex-

CAN LANGUAGES BE KEPT FROM EXTINCTION?

Not only animal and plant species are endangered; many peoples and their languages are too. In the last few hundred years (and continuing in some places today), Western expansion and colonization have led to the depopulation and extinction of many native societies, mainly as a result of introduced disease and campaigns of extermination. Thus, many languages disappeared with the peoples that spoke them. More than fifty aboriginal languages in Australia (of approximately 200) disappeared relatively quickly as a result of massacre and disease. Nowadays native languages are endangered more by the fact that they are not being passed on to children. Political and economic dominance by speakers of Western languages undoubtedly play an enormous role in this process. First, schooling is usually conducted in the dominant language. Second, when another culture is dominant, the children themselves may prefer to speak in the language perceived to have higher prestige; indeed, parents sometimes encourage this ten-

dency. It is estimated that by the year 2000 almost all the languages of aboriginal Australia will be gone. This is a worldwide trend. Michael Krauss, a linguist who tracks disappearing languages, estimates that 90 percent of the world's languages are endangered. Here is another example: only two of the twenty native Alaskan languages are currently being taught to children, who therefore speak English only.

What can be done? Krauss, who is particularly interested in native Alaskan languages, is trying to do something. With help from the state government of Alaska, Krauss is developing materials on native languages to help teachers promote bilingual education as a way of preserving native languages. A very different approach has been taken by H. Russell Bernard, who believes that "to keep a language truly alive we must produce authors." With the help of computer technology, which allows reconfiguring a keyboard to produce special characters for sounds, Bernard has taught native speakers to write their na-

tive languages directly on computers. These texts then become the basis for dictionaries. So far, more than eighty people, speaking twelve endangered languages, have become authors in Mexico and South America. Although these authors may not be using the standardized characters used by linguists to represent sounds, they are producing "written" materials that might otherwise be lost forever. These texts provide more than just information about language—in their works the authors convey ideas about curing illness, acquiring food, raising children, and settling disputes.

We are not sure when humans first developed spoken language. But the enormous linguistic diversity on this planet took a long time to develop. Unfortunately, it may take only a short time for that diversity to become a thing of the past.

Source: *Seth Shulman, "Nurturing Native Tongues,"* Technology Review, *May/June 1993, 16; Janet Holmes,* An Introduction to Sociolinguistics *(London: Longman, 1992), pp. 61–62.*

press themselves in "telegraph" form—using noun-like words and verblike or function words but leaving out the seemingly less important words. So a two-word sentence such as "Shoes off" may stand for "Take my shoes off" or "More milk" may stand for "Give me more milk please."[18] They do not utter their two words in random order, sometimes

saying "off" first, other times saying "shoes" first. If a child says "shoes off" then he or she will also say "clothes off" and "hat off." They seem to select an order that fits the conventions of adult language, so they are likely to say "Daddy eat," not "Eat Daddy." In other words, they tend to put the subject first, as adults do. And they tend to say

Toward the end of their first year, babies begin to name a few objects and actions.

"Mommy coat" rather than "Coat Mommy" to indicate "Mommy's coat."[19] Parents do not utter sentences such as "Daddy eat," so children seem to know a lot about how to put words together with little or no direct teaching from their parents. Consider the five-year-old who, confronted with the unfamiliar "Gloria in Excelsis," sang quite happily, "Gloria eats eggshells." To make the words fit the structure of English grammar was more important than to make the words fit the meaning of the Christmas pageant.

If there is a basic grammar imprinted in the human mind, we should not be surprised that children's early and later speech patterns seem to be similar in different languages. We might also expect children's later speech to be similar to the structure of creole languages. And it is, according to Derek Bickerton.[20] The "errors" children make in speaking are consistent with the grammar of creoles. For example, English-speaking children three to four years old tend to ask questions by intonation alone, and they tend to use double negatives such as "I don't see no dog," even though the adults around them do not speak that way and consider the children's speech "wrong."

Future research on children's acquisition of language and on the structure of creole languages may bring us closer to understanding the origins of human language. But even if there is a universal grammar, we still need to understand how and why the thousands of languages in the world vary—which brings us to the conceptual tools linguists have had to invent in order to study languages.

STRUCTURAL LINGUISTICS

In every society children do not need to be taught "grammar" to learn how to speak. They begin to grasp the essential structure of their language at a very early age, without direct instruction. If you show English-speaking children a picture of one "gork" and then a picture of two of these creatures, they will say there are two "gorks." They somehow know that adding an *s* to a noun means more than one. But they do not know this consciously, and adults may not either. One of the most surprising features of human language is that meaningful sounds and sound sequences are combined according to rules that often are not consciously known by the speakers.

These rules should not be equated with the "rules of grammar" you may have been taught in school (so that you would speak "correctly"). Rather, when linguists talk about rules they are referring to the patterns of speaking that are discoverable in actual speech. Needless to say, there is some overlap between the actual rules of speaking and the "rules" taught in school. But there are rules that children never hear about in school, because their teachers are not linguists and are not aware of them. So when linguists use the term *grammar,* they are *not* referring to the prescriptive rules that people are supposed to follow in speaking. Rather, *grammar* to the linguist consists of the actual, often unconscious principles that predict how most people talk. As we have noted, young children may speak two-word sentences that conform to a linguistic rule, but their speech is hardly considered "correct"!

Discovering the mostly unconscious rules operating in a language is a very difficult task. Linguists have had to invent special concepts and methods of transcription (writing) to permit them to describe: (1) what the rules or principles are that predict how sounds are made and how they are used (often, slightly varying sounds are used interchangeably in words without creating a difference in meaning); (2) how sound sequences (and sometimes even individual sounds) convey meaning and how meaningful sound sequences are strung together to form words; and (3) how words are strung together to form phrases and sentences. Thus, **structural** (or **descriptive**) **linguistics** tries to discover the rules of **phonology** (the patterning of sounds), **morphology** (the patterning of sound sequences and words), and **syntax** (the patterning of phrases and sentences) that predict how most speakers of a language talk.

Understanding the language of another people is an essential part of understanding the culture of that people. Although sometimes what people say is contradicted by their observed behavior, there is little doubt that it is hard to understand the beliefs, attitudes, values, and worldview of a people without understanding their language and the nuances of how that language is used. Even behavior, which theoretically one can observe without understanding language, usually cannot be readily understood without interpretation. Imagine that you see people go by a certain rock and seemingly walk out of their way to avoid it. Suppose they believe that an evil spirit resides there. How could you possibly know that without being able to ask and to understand their answer?

Phonology

Most of us have had the experience of trying to learn another language and finding out that some sounds are exceedingly difficult to make. Although the human vocal tract can theoretically make a very large number of different sounds (**phones** to linguists), each language uses only some of them. It is not that we cannot make the sounds that are strange to us; we just have not acquired the habits of making those sounds. And until the sounds become habitual for us, they continue to be difficult to make.

Finding it difficult to make certain sounds is only one of the reasons we have trouble learning a "foreign" language. Another problem is that we may not be used to combining certain sounds or making a certain sound in a particular position in a word. So English speakers find it difficult to combine *z* and *d*, as Russian speakers often do (because we never do so in English), or to pronounce words in Samoan (a South Pacific language) that begin with the sound English speakers write as *ng*, even though we have no trouble putting that sound at the end of words, as in the English *sing* and *hitting*.

In order to study the patterning of sounds, linguists who are interested in phonology have to write down speech utterances as sequences of sound. This task would be almost impossible if linguists were restricted to using their own alphabet (say the one we use to write English), because other languages use sounds that are difficult to represent with the English alphabet or because the alphabet

we use in English can represent a particular sound in different ways. (English writing represents the sound *f* by *f* as in *food*, but also as *gh* in *tough* and *ph* in *phone*.) To overcome these difficulties in writing sounds with the letters of existing writing systems, linguists have developed systems of transcription in which each "letter" or sound symbol is meant to represent one particular sound.

Once linguists have identified the sounds or phones used in a language, they try to identify how those sounds are classified unconsciously (by the speakers of the language) into **phonemes.** A phoneme is a set of varying sounds that do not make any difference in meaning. In other words, when one phone of a phoneme class is substituted for another phone of the same class, speakers will say that the utterances are the same.

The ways in which sounds are grouped together into phonemes vary from language to language. In English the sound of *l* in *lake* is considered quite different from the sound of *r* in *rake;* the two sounds belong to different phonemes because they make a difference in meaning to English speakers. But in Samoan, *l* and *r* can be used interchangeably in a word without making a difference in meaning; in Samoan, these two sounds belong to the same phoneme. So, Samoan speakers may say "Leupena" sometimes and "Reupena" at other times when they are referring to someone who in English would be called "Reuben." English speakers may joke about languages that confuse *l* and *r*, but they are not usually aware that we do the same thing with other pairs of sounds. For example, consider how we pronounce the word we spell as "butter." Some people say this word with a *t* in the middle; others say it with a *d*. We recognize "butter" and "budder" as the same word; the interchangeability of *t* and *d* in the middle of the word referring to a dairy spread does not make a difference in meaning. Speakers of some other languages would hear "butter" and "budder" as different words and make fun of us for confusing *t* and *d*! None of this means that a speaker of a language cannot learn to hear or identify the slight difference in sounds in the same phoneme, but the differences do not matter in ordinary circumstances.

After discovering which sounds are grouped into phonemes (that is, which sounds can be substituted for each other without making a difference in meaning), linguists can begin to discover the sound sequences that are allowed in a language and the usually unconscious rules that predict those sequences. For example, words in English rarely start with three nonvowel sounds. But when they do, the first sound or phone is always an *s,* as in *strike* and *scratch.*[21] (Some other words in English may start with three consonants but only two sounds are involved, as in *chrome* where the *ch* stands for the sound in *k.*) Linguists' descriptions of the patterning of sounds (phonology) in different languages may allow them to investigate why languages vary in their sound rules. For example, why are two or more consonants strung together in some languages, whereas in other languages vowels are always put between consonants? The Samoan language now has a word for "Christmas" borrowed from English. But the borrowed word has been changed to fit the rules of Samoan. In the English word, two consonants come first (*k* and *r,* which we spell as *ch* and *r*). The Samoan word is *Kerisimasi:* a vowel has been inserted between each pair of consonants and the word ends with a vowel, which is exactly how all Samoan words are constructed.

Some recent research on infants suggests that they may be neurologically "primed" to ignore meaningless variations of sound (those that are part of the same phoneme) in the language they hear at home. After rewarding infants for turning their heads when a sound changes, experimenters began to vary sounds within phomenes to see if Swedish and American infants would respond to those changes. It turns out that as early as six months of age, infants "ignore" sound shifts within the same phoneme of their own language, but they "hear" the sound shift within the phoneme of the other language. Researchers are not sure *how* babies learn to make this distinction, but they seem to acquire much of the phonology of their language very early indeed.[22]

Morphology

Morphology is the study of a variety of questions about words, in particular, what words are and how they are formed. We take our words so much for granted that we do not realize how complicated it is to say what words are. People do not usually pause between words when they speak; if we did not know our language, a sentence would seem like a continuous stream of sounds. This is how we first hear a foreign language. It is only when we understand the language and write down what we say that we separate (by spaces) what we call *words.* But a word is really only an arbitrary sequence of sounds that has a meaning; we would not "hear" words as separate units if we did not understand the language to which they belong.

Because anthropological linguists traditionally investigated unwritten languages, sometimes without the aid of interpreters, they had to figure out which sequences of sounds conveyed meaning. And because words in many languages can often be broken down into smaller meaningful units, linguists had to invent special words to refer to those units. The smallest unit of language that has a meaning is a **morph.** One or more morphs with the same meaning make up a **morpheme.** For example, the prefix *in-,* as in *indefinite,* and the prefix *un-,* as in *unclear,* are morphs that belong to the morpheme meaning *not.* A morph or morpheme should not be confused with a word. Although some words are single morphs or morphemes (for example, *for* and *giraffe* in English), many words are built on a combination of morphs, generally prefixes, roots, and suffixes. Thus *cow* is one word, but the word *cows* contains two meaningful units—a root *(cow)* and a suffix (pronounced like *z*) meaning more than one. The **lexicon** of a language, which a dictionary approximates, consists of words and morphs and their meanings.

It seems likely that the intuitive grasp children have of the structure of their language includes a recognition of morphology, the patterning of sound sequences and words. Once they learn that the morph /-z/ added to a noun-type word indicates more than one, they plow ahead with *mans,* and *childs;* once they grasp that the morpheme class pronounced /-t/ or /-d/ or /-ed/ added to the end of a verb indicates that the action took place in the past, they apply that concept generally and invent *runned, drinked, costed.* They see a ball roll near*er* and near*er,* and they transfer that concept to a kite, which goes upp*er* and upp*er.* From their mistakes as well as their successes, we can see that they understand the regular uses of morphemes. By the age of seven, they have mastered many of the irregular forms as well—that is, they learn which morphs of a morpheme are used when.

The child's intuitive grasp of the dependence of some morphemes on others corresponds to the linguist's recognition of free morphemes and bound morphemes. A *free* morpheme has meaning standing alone—that is, it can be a separate word. A *bound* morpheme displays its meaning only when attached to another morpheme. The morph pronounced /-t/ of the bound morpheme meaning *past tense* is attached to the root *walk* to produce *walked;* but the /-t/ cannot stand alone or have meaning by itself.

In English, the meaning of an utterance (containing a subject, verb, object, and so forth) usually depends on the order of the words. "The dog bit the child" is different in meaning from "The child bit the dog." But in many other languages, the grammatical meaning of an utterance does not depend much, if at all, on the order of the words. Rather, meaning may be determined by how the morphs in a word are ordered. For example, in Luo (a language of East Africa) the same bound morpheme may mean the subject or object of an action. If the morpheme is the prefix to a verb, it means the subject; if it is the suffix to a verb, it means the object. Another way that grammatical meaning may be conveyed is by altering or adding a bound morpheme to a word to indicate what part of speech it is. For example, in Russian, the word for "mail" when it is the subject of a sentence is pronounced something like "pawchtah." When "mail" is used as the object of a verb, as in "I gave her the mail," the ending of the word changes to "pawchtoo." And if I say "What was in the mail?" the word becomes "pawchtyeh."

Some languages have so many bound morphemes that they might express as a complex but single word what is considered a sentence in English. For example, the English sentence "He will give it to you" can be expressed in Wishram, a Chinookan dialect that was spoken along the Columbia River in the Pacific Northwest, as *acimluda* (a-c-i-m-l-ud-a, literally "will-he-him-thee-to-give-will"). Note that the pronoun *it* in English is gender-neutral; Wishram requires that *it* be given a gender, in this case "him."[23]

Syntax

Because language is an open system, we can make up meaningful utterances that we have never heard before. We are constantly creating new phrases and sentences. Just as they do for morphology, the speakers of a language seem to have an intuitive grasp of syntax—the rules that predict how phrases and sentences are generally formed. These "rules" may be partly learned in school, but children know many of them even before they get to school. In adulthood, our understanding of morphology and syntax is so intuitive that we can even understand a nonsense sentence, such as the following famous one from Lewis Carroll's *Through the Looking Glass:*

> 'Twas brillig, and the slithy toves
> Did gyre and gimble in the wabe

Simply from the ordering of the words in the sentence, we can surmise which part of speech a word is, as well as its function in the sentence. *Brillig* is an adjective; *slithy* an adjective; *toves* a noun and the subject of the sentence; *gyre* and *gimble* verbs; and *wabe* a noun and the object of a prepositional phrase. Of course, an understanding of morphology helps too. The *-y* ending in *slithy* is an indication that the latter is an adjective, and the *-s* ending in *toves* tells us that we most probably have more than one of these creatures.

In addition to producing and understanding an infinite variety of sentences, speakers of a language can tell when a sentence is not "correct" without consulting grammar books. For example, an English speaker can tell that "Child the dog the hit" is not an acceptable sentence but "The child hit the dog" is fine. There must then be a set of rules underlying how phrases and sentences are constructed in a language.[24] Speakers of a language know these implicit rules of syntax but are not usually consciously aware of them. The linguist's description of the syntax of a language tries to make these rules explicit.

HISTORICAL LINGUISTICS

The field of **historical linguistics** focuses on how languages change over time. Written works provide the best data for establishing such changes. For example, the following passage from Chaucer's *Canterbury Tales,* written in the English of the fourteenth century, has recognizable elements but is different enough from modern English to require a translation.

> *A Frere ther was, a wantowne and a merye,*
> *A lymytour, a ful solempne man.*
> *In alle the ordres foure is noon that kan*
> *So muche of daliaunce and fair language.*
> *He hadde maad ful many a mariage*
> *Of yonge wommen at his owene cost.*
> *Unto his ordre he was a noble post.*
> *Ful wel biloued and famulier was he*
> *With frankeleyns ouer al in his contree,*
> *And with worthy wommen of the toun;*
> *For he hadde power of confessioun,*
> *As seyde hymself, moore than a curat,*
> *For of his ordre he was licenciat.*

> *A Friar there was, wanton and merry,*
> *A limiter [a friar limited to certain districts], a full solemn [very important] man.*
> *In all the orders four there is none that knows*
> *So much of dalliance [flirting] and fair [engaging] language.*
> *He had made [arranged] many a marriage*

Of young women at his own cost.
Unto his order he was a noble post [pillar].
Full well beloved and familiar was he
With franklins [wealthy landowners] all over his
country
And also with worthy women of the town;
For he had power of confession,
As he said himself, more than a curate,
For of his order, he was a licentiate [licensed by the
Pope].[25]

In this passage we can recognize several changes. Many words are spelled differently today. In some cases, meaning has changed; *full,* for example, would be translated today as *very.* What is less evident is that changes in pronunciation have occurred. For example, the *g* in *mariage* (marriage) was pronounced *zh,* as in the French from which it was borrowed, whereas now it is pronounced like either *g* in *George.*

Because languages spoken in the past leave no traces unless they were written, and most of the languages known to anthropology were not written by their speakers, you might guess that historical linguists can study linguistic change only by studying written languages such as English. But that is not the case. Linguists can reconstruct changes that have occurred by comparing contemporary languages that are very similar. Such languages show phonological, morphological, and syntactical similarities because they usually derive from a common ancestral language. For example, Romanian, Italian, French, Spanish, and Portuguese have many similarities. On the basis of these similarities, linguists can reconstruct what the ancestral language was like and how it changed into what we call the Romance languages. Of course, these reconstructions can easily be tested and confirmed because we know from many surviving writings what the ancestral language (Latin) was like; and we know from documents how Latin diversified as the Roman Empire expanded. Thus, common ancestry is frequently the reason why neighboring (and sometimes even separated) languages show patterns of similarity.

But languages can be similar for other reasons too. Contact between speech communities, often with one group dominant over another, may lead one language to borrow from the other. For example, English borrowed a lot of vocabulary from French after England was conquered by the French-speaking Normans in A.D. 1066. Languages may also show similarities even though they do not derive from a common ancestral language and even though there has been no contact or borrowing between them; such similarities may reflect common or universal features of human cultures or human brains or both. (As we noted earlier in this chapter, the grammatical similarities exhibited by creole languages may reflect how the human brain is "wired.") Finally, even unrelated and separated languages may show some similarities because of the phenomenon of convergence; similarities can develop because some processes of linguistic change may have only a few possible outcomes.

Language Families and Culture History

Latin is the ancestral language of the Romance languages. We know this from documentary (written) records. But if the ancestral language of a set of similar languages is not known from written records, linguists still can reconstruct many features of that language by comparing the derived languages. (Such a reconstructed language is called a **protolanguage.**) That is, by comparing presumably related languages, linguists can become aware of the features that many of them have in common, features that were probably found in the common ancestral language. The languages that derive from the same protolanguage are called a *language family.* Most languages spoken in the world today can be grouped into fewer than thirty families. The language family English belongs to is called *Indo-European,* because it includes most of the languages of Europe and some of the languages of India. About 50 percent of the world's more than 4 billion people speak Indo-European languages.[26] Another very large language family, now spoken by more than a billion people, is Sino-Tibetan, which includes the languages of northern and southern China as well as those of Tibet and Myanmar (or Burma, as it was formerly named).

The field of historical linguistics got its start in 1786 when a British scholar living in India, Sir William Jones, noticed similarities between Sanskrit (the language spoken and written in ancient India) and classical Greek, Latin, and more recent European languages.[27] In 1822, Jakob Grimm, one of the brothers Grimm of fairy-tale fame, formulated rules to describe the sound shifts that had occurred when the various Indo-European languages diverged from each other. So, for example, in English and the other languages in the Germanic branch of the Indo-European family, *d* regularly shifted to *t* (compare the English *two* and *ten* with the Latin *duo* and *decem*) and *p* regularly shifted to *f* (English *father* and *foot,* Latin *pater* and *pes*). Scholars generally agree that the Indo-European languages derive from a language spoken 5,000 to 6,000 years ago.[28] The ancestral Indo-European language, many of whose features have now been reconstructed, is called *proto-Indo-European,* or *PIE* for short. Table 5–1 shows the branches and existing languages of the family.

Where did PIE originate? Some linguists believe that the approximate location of a protolanguage is suggested by the words for plants and animals in the derived languages. More specifically, among these different languages, the words that are **cognates** (that are similar in sound and meaning) presumably refer to plants and animals that were present in the original homeland. So if we know where those animals and plants were located 5,000 to 6,000 years ago, we can guess where PIE people lived. Among all the cognates for trees in the Indo-European languages, Paul Friedrich has identified eighteen that he believes were present

in the eastern Ukraine in 3000 B.C.; on this basis he suggests that the eastern Ukraine was the PIE homeland.[29] Also consistent with this hypothesis is the fact that the Balto-Slavic subfamily of Indo-European (which includes most of the languages in and around the former Soviet Union) has the most tree names (compared with other subfamilies) that are similar to the reconstructed form in proto-Indo-European.[30]

Marija Gimbutas thinks we can even identify the proto-Indo-Europeans archaeologically. She believes that the PIE people were probably the people associated with what is known as the Kurgan culture (5000–2000 B.C.), which spread out of the Ukraine around 3000 B.C. The Kurgan people were herders, keeping and raising horses, cattle, sheep, and pigs. They also relied on hunting and grain cultivation. Burials suggest differences in wealth and special status for men.[31] Why the Kurgan and linguistically similar people were able to expand to many places in Europe and the Near East is not yet clear (some have

▼▼▼▼▼▼
TABLE 5-1
Branches and Existing Languages of the Indo-European Language Family

LANGUAGE	BRANCH	LANGUAGE	BRANCH
Albanian	Albanian	Greek	Greek
Armenian	Armenian	Balachi	Indo-Iranian
Bulgarian	Balto-Slavic	Bengali	
Czech		Farsi (Persian)	
Latvian		Gujarati	
Lithuanian		Hindi	
Polish		Kati	
Russian		Kurdish	
Serbo-Croatian		Marathi	
Ukrainian		Pashta	
		Punjabi	
Breton	Celtic	Romany	
Irish (Gaelic)		Sinhalese	
Welsh		Shina	
		Urdu	
Africaans	Germanic		
Danish		Catalan	Italic
Dutch		French	
English		Italian	
German		Portuguese	
Icelandic		Provençal	
Norwegian		Romanian	
Swedish		Sardinian	
Yiddish		Spanish	

Source: *Adapted from Merritt Ruhlen,* A Guide to the World's Languages, Volume I: Classification *(Stanford, CA: Stanford University Press, 1987), pp. 293–94.*

suggested that horses and horse-drawn wagons, and perhaps horseback riding, provided important military advantages).[32] In any case, it *is* clear that many Kurgan cultural elements were distributed after 3000 B.C. over a wide area of the Old World.

Colin Renfrew disagrees with the notion that the Ukraine was the homeland of PIE. He thinks that PIE is 2,000–3,000 years older than Kurgan culture and that the PIE people lived in a different place. Renfrew locates the PIE homeland in eastern Anatolia (Turkey) in 6000–7000 B.C., and he suggests (on the basis of archaeological evidence) that the spread of Indo-European to Europe and what is now Iran, Afghanistan, and India accompanied the spread of farming to those areas.[33]

Just as some historical linguists and archaeologists have suggested when and where the PIE people may have lived originally and how they may have spread, other linguists and archaeologists have suggested culture histories for other language families. For example, the Bantu languages in Africa (spoken by perhaps 100 million people) form a subfamily of the larger Niger-Congo family of languages. Bantu speakers currently live in a wide band across the center of Africa and down the eastern and western sides of southern Africa. All of the Bantu languages presumably derive from people who spoke proto-Bantu. But where was their homeland?

As in the case of proto-Indo-European, different theories have been proposed. But most historical linguists now agree with Joseph Greenberg's suggestion that the origin of Bantu was in what is now the Middle Benue area of eastern Nigeria.[34] The point of origin is presumably where there is the greatest diversity of related languages and **dialects** (varying forms of a language); it is assumed that the place of origin has had the most time for linguistic diversity to develop, compared with an area only recently occupied by a related language. For example, England (the homeland of English) has more dialect diversity than New Zealand or Australia.

Why were the Bantu able to spread so widely over the last few thousand years? Anthropologists have only begun to guess.[35] Initially, the Bantu probably kept goats and practiced some form of agriculture and thereby were able to spread, displacing hunter-gatherers in the area. As the Bantu speakers expanded, they began to cultivate certain cereal crops and herd sheep and cattle. Around this time, after 1000 B.C., they also began to use and make iron tools, which may have given them significant advantages. In any case, by 1,500 to 2,000 years ago Bantu speakers had spread throughout central Africa and into the northern reaches of southern Africa. But speakers of non-Bantu languages still live in eastern, southern, and southwestern Africa.

THE PROCESSES OF LINGUISTIC DIVERGENCE

The historical or comparative linguist hopes to do more than record and date linguistic divergence. Just as the physical anthropologist may attempt to develop explanations for human variation, so the linguist investigates the possible causes of linguistic variation.

Some of the divergence undoubtedly comes about gradually. When groups of people speaking the same language lose communication with one another because they become separated either physically or socially, they begin to accumulate small changes in phonology, morphology, and syntax (which occur continuously in any language). Eventually, if the separation continues, the former dialects of the same language will become separate languages; that is, they will become mutually unintelligible, as German and English now are.

Geographical barriers such as large bodies of water, deserts, and mountains may separate speakers of what was once the same language, but distance by itself can also produce divergence. For example, if we compare dialects of English in the British Isles, it is clear that the regions farthest away from each other are the most different linguistically (compare the northeast of Scotland and London).[36] In northern India, hundreds of semi-isolated villages and regions developed hundreds of local dialects. Today, the inhabitants of each village understand the dialects of the surrounding villages and, with a little more difficulty, the dialects of the next circle of villages. But slight dialect shifts accumulate village by village, and it seems as if different languages are being spoken at the opposite ends of the region, which are separated by over a thousand miles.[37]

Even where there is little geographical separation there may still be a great deal of dialect differentiation because of social distance. So, for example, the spread of a linguistic feature may be halted by racial, religious, or social-class differences that inhibit communication.[38] In the village of Khalapur in North India, John Gumperz found substantial differences in speech between the "untouchable" groups and other groups. Members of the untouchable groups have work contacts with members of other groups, but no friendships.[39] Without friendships and the easy communication between friends, dialect differentiation can readily develop.

Whereas isolation brings gradual divergence between speech communities, contact results in greater resemblance. This effect is particularly evident when contact between mutually unintelligible languages introduces *borrowed* words, which usually name some new item borrowed from the other culture—*tomato, canoe, sushi,* and so on. Bilingual groups within a culture may also introduce foreign words, especially when the mainstream language has no real equivalent. Thus, *salsa* has come into English, and *le weekend* into French.

Conquest and colonization often result in extensive and rapid borrowing, if not linguistic replacement. The Norman conquest of England introduced French as the language of the new aristocracy. It was 300 years before the educated classes began to write in English. During this time the English borrowed words from French and Latin, and the two languages—English and French—became more alike than they would otherwise have been. About 50 percent of the English general vocabulary originated in French. As this example suggests, different social classes may react to language contact differentially. For example, English aristocrats eventually called their meat "pork" and "beef" (derived from the French words), but the people who raised the animals and prepared them for eating continued (at least for a while) to refer to the meat as "pig" and "bull," the original Anglo-Saxon words.

In those 300 years of extensive contact, the grammar of English remained relatively stable. English lost most of its inflections or case endings, but it adopted little of the French grammar. In general, the borrowing of words (particularly free morphemes[40]) is much more common than the borrowing of grammar.[41] As we might expect, borrowing by one language from another can make the borrowing language more different from its *sibling languages* (those derived from a common ancestral language) than it would otherwise be. Partly as a result of the French influence, the English vocabulary looks quite different from the languages to which it is actually most similar in terms of phonology and grammar—German, Dutch, and the Scandinavian languages.

If languages simply diverged gradually we would expect to find many language families and many languages in small areas. Such appears to be the case among the aboriginal languages of northern Australia. But in some areas of the world there are very widespread language families. How, for example, did Indo-European languages become so widespread? Although we cannot be sure what happened in the Indo-European case, it is possible that the ancestral population (and descendants of that population) expanded by military means.[42] Military expansion and conquest can have profound linguistic consequences, much more than simply borrowing some vocabulary as English did from French. For one population may replace another, effectively killing off a language. Conquest can also result in enormous pressure on the conquered to learn and use the language of the superiors. Once children stop being taught their native language, that language cannot survive for long (see Box, page 72).

RELATIONSHIPS BETWEEN LANGUAGE AND CULTURE

Some attempts to explain the diversity of languages have focused on the possible interactions between language and other aspects of culture. On the one hand, if it can be shown that a culture can affect the structure and content of its language, then it would follow that linguistic diversity derives at least in part from cultural diversity. On the other hand, the direction of influence between culture and language might work in reverse: linguistic features and structures might affect other aspects of the culture.

Cultural Influences on Language

One way a society's language may reflect its corresponding culture is in **lexical content,** or vocabulary. Which experiences, events, or objects are singled out and given words may be a result of cultural characteristics.

Basic Words for Colors, Plants, and Animals. Early in this century many linguists pointed to the lexical domain (vocabulary) of color words to illustrate the supposed truth that languages vary arbitrarily or without apparent reason. Different languages had not only different numbers of basic or fundamental color words (from two to twelve or so—for example, the words *red, green,* and *blue* in English), but they also, it was thought, had no consistency in the way they classified or divided the colors of the spectrum. But findings from a comparative (cross-linguistic) study contradicted these traditional presumptions about variation in the number and meaning of basic color words. On the basis of their study of at first 20 and later over 100 languages, Brent Berlin and Paul

Kay found that languages did not encode color in completely arbitrary ways.[43]

Although different languages do have different numbers of basic color words, most speakers of any language are very likely to point to the same color chips as the best representatives of particular colors. (For example, people the world over mean more or less the same color when they are asked to select the *best* "red.") Moreover, there appears to be a nearly universal sequence by which basic color words are added to a language.[44] If a language has just two basic color words, they will always refer to "black" (or dark) hues and "white" (or light) hues. If a language has three basic color words, the third word will nearly always be "red." The next category to appear is either "yellow" or "grue" (green/blue); then different words for green and blue; and so on. To be sure, we usually do not see the process by which basic color words are added to a language. But we can infer the usual sequence because, for example, if a language has a word for "yellow" it will almost always have a word for "red," whereas having a word for "red" does not mean that the language will have a word for "yellow."

What exactly is a *basic* color word? All languages (even the ones with only two basic color terms) have many different ways of expressing how color varies. For example, in English we have words such as turquoise, blue-green, scarlet, crimson, and sky blue. Linguists do not consider these to be basic color words. In English the basic color words are *white, black, red, green, yellow, blue, brown, pink, purple, orange,* and *gray*. One feature of a basic color word is that it consists of a single morph; it cannot include two or more units of meaning. This feature eliminates combinations such as *blue-green* and *sky blue*. A second feature of a basic color word is that the color it represents is not generally included in a higher-order color term. For example, scarlet and crimson are usually considered variants of red, turquoise a variant of blue. A third feature is that basic terms tend to be the first-named words when people are asked for color words. Finally, for a word to be considered a basic color word, many individual speakers of the language have to agree on the central meaning (in the color spectrum) of the word.[45]

Why do different societies (languages) vary in number of basic color terms? Berlin and Kay suggest that the number of basic color terms in a language increases with technological specialization as color is used to decorate and distinguish objects.[46] Cross-linguistic variation in number of basic color terms does not mean that some languages make more color distinctions than others. Every language could make a particular distinction by combining words (for example, "fresh leaf" for green); a language need not have a separate basic term for that color.

A relatively large number of basic color terms are related also to a biological factor.[47] Peoples with darker (more pigmented) eyes seem to have more trouble distinguishing colors at the dark (blue-green) end of the spectrum than do people with lighter eyes. It might be expected, then, that peoples who live nearer the equator (who tend to have darker eyes, presumably for protection against damaging ultraviolet radiation) would tend to have fewer basic color terms. And they do.[48] Moreover, it seems that the cultural and biological factors are both required to account for cross-linguistic variation in the number of basic color terms. Societies tend to have six or more such terms (with separate terms for blue and green) only when they are relatively far from the equator and only when their cultures are more technologically specialized.[49] As we will see in later chapters, technological specialization tends to go with larger communities, more centralized governments, occupational specialization, and more social inequality. Societies with such traits are often referred to in a shorthand way as more "complex," which should not be taken to mean "better."

Echoing Berlin and Kay's finding that basic color terms seem to be added in a more or less universal sequence, other researchers have found what seem to be developmental sequences in other lexical domains. Two such domains are general, or *life-form,* terms for plants and for animals. Life-form terms are higher-order classifications. All languages have lower-order terms for specific plants and animals. For example, English has words such as *oak* and *pine, sparrow* and *salmon*. English speakers make finer distinctions too—*pin oak* and *white pine, white-throated sparrow* and *red salmon*. But why in some languages do people have a larger number of general terms such as *tree, bird,* and *fish*? It seems that these general terms show a universal developmental sequence too. That is, terms seem to be added in a somewhat consistent order. After "plant" comes a term for "tree"; then one for "grerb" (small, green, leafy, nonwoody plant); then "bush" (for plants between tree and grerb in size); then "grass"; then "vine."[50] The life-form terms for animals seem also to be added in sequence; after "animal," comes a term for "fish," then "bird," then "snake," then "wug" (for small creatures other than fish, birds, and snakes—for example, worms and bugs), then "mammal."[51]

More complex societies tend to have a larger number of general, or life-form, terms for plants and animals than do simpler societies, just as they tend to have a larger number of basic color terms. Why? And do all realms or domains of vocabulary increase in size as social complexity increases? If we look at the total vocabulary of a language (as can be counted in a dictionary), more complex societies do have larger vocabularies.[52] But we have to remember that complex societies have many kinds of specialists, and dictionaries will include the terms used by such specialists. If we look instead at the **core** (nonspecialist) **vocabulary** of languages, it seems that all languages have a core vocabulary of about the same size.[53] Indeed, although some domains increase in size with social complexity, some remain the same and still others decrease. An example of a smaller vocabulary domain in complex societies is that of specific names for plants. Urban North Americans may know general terms for plants, but they know relatively few names for specific plants. The typical individual in a small-scale society can commonly name 400 to 800 plant species; a typical person in our own and similar societies may be able to name only 40 to 80.[54] The number of life-form terms is larger in societies in which ordinary people know less about particular plants and animals.[55]

The evidence now available strongly supports the idea that the vocabulary of a language reflects the everyday distinctions that are important in the society. Those aspects of environment or culture that are of special importance will receive greater attention in the language.

Grammar. Most of the examples we could accumulate would show that a culture influences the names of things visible in its environment. Evidence for cultural influence on the grammatical structure of a language is less extensive. Harry Hoijer draws attention to the verb categories in the language of the Navaho, a traditionally nomadic people. These categories center mainly in the reporting of events, or *eventings,* as he calls them. Hoijer notes that in "the reporting of actions and events, and the framing of substantive concepts, Navaho emphasizes movement and specifies the nature, direction, and status of such movement in considerable detail."[56] For example, Navaho has one category for eventings that are in motion and another for eventings that have ceased moving. Hoijer concludes that the emphasis on events in the process of occurring reflects the Navaho's nomadic experience over the

centuries, an experience also reflected in their myths and folklore.

A linguistic emphasis on events may or may not be generally characteristic of nomadic peoples. No one has as yet investigated the matter cross-culturally or comparatively. But there are indications that systematic comparative research would turn up other grammatical features that are related to cultural characteristics. For example, many languages lack the possessive transitive verb we write as "have," as in "I have." Instead, the language may say something such as "it is to me." A cross-cultural study has suggested that a language may develop the verb "have" after the speakers of that language have developed a system of private property, or personal ownership of resources.[57]As we shall see later in the chapter on economic systems, the concept of private property is far from universal and tends to occur only in complex societies with social inequality. In contrast, many societies have some kind of communal ownership (by kin groups or communities). How people talk about owning seems to reflect how they own: societies that lack a concept of private property also lack the verb *have.*

Linguistic Influences on Culture: The Sapir-Whorf Hypothesis

There is general agreement that culture influences language. But there is less agreement about the opposite possibility—that language influences (other aspects of) culture. Edward Sapir and Benjamin Lee Whorf suggested that language is a force in its own right—that it affects how individuals in a society per-

Urban North Americans tend to use general or life-form terms for plants and animals; very few urban North Americans could name the many specific plants in this garden. People in less complex societies know many specific names for plants and animals.

ceive and conceive reality. This suggestion is known as the Sapir-Whorf hypothesis.[58] In comparing the English language with Hopi, Whorf pointed out that English-language categories convey discreteness with regard to time and space, but Hopi does not. English has a discrete past, present, and future and things occur at a definite time. Hopi expresses things with more of an idea of on-going processes without time being apportioned into fixed segments. According to Richard Wardhaugh, Whorf believed that these language differences lead Hopi and English speakers to see the world differently.[59]

As intriguing as that idea is, the relevant evidence is mixed. Linguists today do not generally accept the view that language coerces thought, but some suspect that particular features of language may facilitate certain patterns of thought.[60] The influences may be clearest in poetry and metaphors (words and phrases applied to other than their ordinary subjects, as in "all the world's a stage").[61] One of the serious problems in testing the Sapir-Whorf hypothesis is that researchers need to figure out how to separate the effects of other aspects of culture from the effects of language.

One approach that may reveal the direction of influence between language and culture is to study how children in different cultures (speaking different languages) develop concepts as they grow up. If language influences the formation of a particular concept, we might expect that children will acquire that concept earlier in societies where the languages emphasize that concept. For example, some languages make more of gender differences than others. Do children develop gender identity earlier when their language emphasizes gender? (Very young girls and boys seem to believe they can switch genders by dressing in opposite-sex clothes, suggesting that they have not yet developed a stable sense that they are unchangeably girls or boys.) Alexander Guiora and his colleagues have studied children growing up in Hebrew-speaking homes (Israel), English-speaking homes (the United States), and Finnish-speaking homes (Finland). Hebrew has the most gender emphasis of the three languages; all nouns are either masculine or feminine and even second-person and plural pronouns are differentiated by gender. English emphasizes gender less, differentiating by gender only in the third-person singular (she or her or hers, he or him or his). Finnish emphasizes gender the least; although some words, such as *man* and *woman,* convey gender, differentiation by gender is otherwise lacking in the language. Consistent with the idea that language may influence thought, He-brew-speaking children acquire the concept of stable gender identity the earliest on the average, Finnish-speaking children the latest.[62]

Recently some researchers have suggested that Chinese kindergarten students are better in math than kindergarten students in the United States because the Chinese words for numbers are shorter and easier to remember, and therefore the Chinese students don't have to rely as much on finger counting as do their American counterparts.[63] But just as with the concept of gender and when it is acquired, it is hard to know whether language or something else about the society is creating the difference observed.

THE ETHNOGRAPHY OF SPEAKING

Traditionally, linguists concentrated on trying to understand the structure of a language, the usually unconscious rules that predict how the people of a given society typically speak. In recent years, many linguists have begun to study how people in a society vary in how they speak. This type of linguistic study, sociolinguistics, is concerned with the *ethnography of speaking*—that is, with cultural and subcultural patterns of speech variation in different social contexts.[64]

The sociolinguist might ask, for example, what kinds of things one talks about in casual conversation with a stranger. A foreigner may know English vocabulary and grammar well but may not know that one typically chats with a stranger about the weather or where one comes from, and not about what one ate that day or how much money one earns. A foreigner may be familiar with much of the culture of a North American city, but if that person divulges the real state of his or her health and feelings to the first person who says "How are you?" she or he has much to learn about "small talk" in North American English.

Similarly, North Americans tend to get confused in societies where greetings are quite different from ours. People in some other societies may ask as a greeting, "Where are you going?" or "What are you cooking?" Some Americans may think such questions are rude; others may try to answer in excruciating detail, not realizing that only vague answers are expected, just as we don't really expect a detailed answer when we ask people how they are.

Strangers shake hands when they meet; friends touch each other more. How we speak to others also differs according to degree of friendship.

Social Status and Speech

That a foreign speaker of a language may know little about the small talk of that language is but one example of the sociolinguistic principle that what we say and how we say it are not wholly predictable by the rules of our language. Who we are socially and whom we are talking to may greatly affect what we say and how we say it.

In a study interviewing children in a New England town, John Fischer noted that in formal interviews, children were likely to pronounce the ending in words such as *singing* and *fishing,* but in informal conversations they said "singin'" and "fishin'." Moreover, he noted that the phenomenon also appeared to be related to social class—children from higher-status families were less likely to drop the ending than were children from lower-status families. Subsequent studies in English-speaking areas tend to support Fischer's observations with regard to this speech pattern. Other patterns are observed as well. For example, in Norwich, England, lower classes tend to drop the *h* in words such as *hammer,* but in all classes the pattern of dropping the *h* increases in casual situations.[65]

Research has shown that English people from higher-class backgrounds tend to have more homogeneous speech, conforming more to what is considered standard English (the type of speech heard on television or radio), whereas people from lower-class backgrounds have very heterogeneous speech, varying in their speaking according to the local or dialect area they come from.[66]

In some societies, social status differences may be associated with more marked differentiation of words. Clifford Geertz, in his study of Javanese, showed that the vocabularies of the three rather sharply divided groups in Javanese society—peasants, townspeople, and aristocrats—reflect their separate positions. For example, the concept *now* will be expressed differently in these three groups: a peasant will use *saiki* (considered the lowest and roughest form of the word); a townsman will use *saniki* (considered somewhat more elegant); and an aristocrat will use *samenika* (the most elegant form).[67]

Status relationships between people can also influence the way they speak to each other. Terms of address are a good example. In English, forms of address are relatively simple. One is called either by a first name or by a title (such as *Doctor,* or *Professor, Ms., Mister*) followed by a last name. A study by Roger Brown and Marguerite Ford indicates that terms of address in English vary with the nature of the relationship between the speakers.[68] The reciprocal use of first names generally signifies an informal or intimate relationship between two persons. A title and last name used reciprocally usually indicates a more formal or businesslike relationship between individuals who are roughly equal in status. Nonreciprocal use of first names and titles in English is reserved for speakers who recognize a marked difference in status between them. This status difference can be a function of age (as when a child refers to her mother's friend as Mrs. Miller and is in turn addressed as Sally), or the status difference can be due to occupational hierarchy (as when a person refers to his boss as Ms. Ramirez and is in turn addressed as Joe). In some cases, generally between boys and between men, the use of the last name alone represents a middle ground between the intimate and the formal usages.

In some societies, terms of address do not reflect equality or inequality of social status as much as they reflect other kinds of social relationships. Among the Nuer of the Sudan, kin and age relationships (in addition to the formality of the occasion) influence how you address someone. Soon after birth every Nuer child is given a personal name, which is used by the child's paternal relatives and by close friends in the paternal village. The maternal grandparents give the child another personal name, which the mother's family and friends of her family use. Children also have inherited clan names, but these are used only at formal ceremonies. When they are older, children get ox-names. A girl may choose an ox-name from the bull calf of a cow she milks; the name is used by her female age-group friends. A boy is given an ox during his initiation ceremony and he acquires that ox-name; his male age-group friends may use his ox-name instead of his personal name.[69]

Gender Differences in Speech

In many societies the speech of men differs from the speech of women. The variation can be slight, as in our own society, or more extreme, as with the Carib Indians (in the Lesser Antilles of the West Indies), among whom women and men use different words for the same concepts.[70] In Japan, males and females use entirely different words for numerous concepts (for example, the male word for water is *mizu,* the female version is *ohiya*), and females often add the polite prefix *o-* (females will tend to say *ohasi* for chopsticks; males will tend to say *hasi*).[71] In the United States and in other Western societies, there are differences in the speech of females and males, but they are not as dramatic as in the Carib and Japanese cases. For example, in the preceding section we noted the tendency for the *g* to be dropped in words such as *singing* when the situation is informal and when the social class background is lower. But there is also a gender difference—women are more likely than men to keep the *g* sound and less likely than men to drop the *h* in words such as *happy*. In Montreal, women are less likely than men to drop the *l* in phrases such as *il fait* ("he does") or in the idiom *il y a* ("there is/are").

Gender differences occur in intonation and in phrasing of sentences as well. Robin Lakoff found that in English women tend to answer questions with sentences that have rising inflections at the end instead of a falling intonation associated with a firm answer. Women also tend to add questions to statements, such as "They caught the robber last week, didn't they?"[72]

"Davis, you're fired—are you O.K. with that? (Reprinted courtesy of Mankoff/The Cartoon Bank.)

One explanation for the gender differences, particularly with regard to pronunciation, is that women in many societies may be more concerned than men with being "correct."[73] (Not in the linguist's sense; it is important to remember that linguists do not consider one form of speech more correct than another, just as they do not consider one dialect superior to another—all are equally capable of expressing a complex variety of thoughts and ideas.) In societies with social classes, what is considered more correct by the average person may be what is associated with the upper class. In other societies, what is older may be considered more correct. For example, in the Native American language of Koasati (which used to be spoken in Louisiana), males and females used different endings in certain verbs. The differences seemed to be disappearing in the 1930s, when the research on Koasati was done: young girls used the male forms and only older women used the female forms. Koasati men said that the women's speech was a "better" form of speech.[74] Gender differences in speech may parallel some of the gender differences noted in other social behavior (as we will see in the chapter on sex, gender, and culture): girls are more likely than boys to behave in ways that are acceptable to adults.

There are not enough studies to know just how common it is for women to exhibit more linguistic "correctness." We do know of some instances where it is not the case. For example, in a community in Madagascar where people speak Merina, a dialect of Malagasy, it is considered socially correct to avoid explicit directives. So instead of directly ordering an action, a Merina-speaker will try to say it indirectly. Also, it is polite to avoid negative remarks, such as expressing anger toward someone else. In this community, however, it is *women,* not men, who often break the rules; women speak more directly and express anger more often.[75] This differ-

DOES THE ENGLISH LANGUAGE PROMOTE SEXIST THINKING?

Does English promote sexist thinking? Or does the language merely reflect the gender inequalities that already exist? For those who wish to promote gender equality, the answers to these questions are important because if language influences thoughts (along the lines put forward by Edward Sapir and Benjamin Whorf), then linguistic change will be necessary in order to bring about change in the culture of gender. If it is the other way around, that is, if language reflects inequality, then social, economic, and political changes have to come before we can expect substantial linguistic change to occur.

Leaving aside for the moment which changes first, how does English represent gender inequity? Consider the following written by Benjamin Lee Whorf: "Speech is the best show man puts on. . . . Language helps man in his thinking." While *man*

in English technically refers to humans and *his* technically refers to a single person's thinking (of either gender), the frequent use of such words plausibly could convey that males are more important. Similarly, do the words *chairman, policeman, businessman, salesman* convey that males are supposed to have those jobs? What is conveyed when there are two words for the two genders? *Actor* and *actress. Hero* and *heroine.* Usually the base word is male and the suffix is added for the female form. Does the suffix convey that the female form is an afterthought or less important?

It is not just the structure of the language that may convey gender inequity. There are also differences in usage and metaphor. Although there is a female and male form for someone who has lost a spouse (*widow* and *widower*), many people will say "Sally is Henry's widow" but

hardly anyone would say "Henry is Sally's widower." Why? Is it considered more important that a woman was formerly attached to a man than that a man was formerly attached to a woman? Given this usage, it is not surprising that *widow* (the female form) is the basic term in this case, *widower* (the male form) the derived term. And how come in the pairs *sir/madam, master/mistress, wizard/witch,* the female version has acquired negative connotations? Why are so many animal images applied to women? They may be described as *chicks, hen-peckers, cows, dogs, bitches, kittens,* and *birds.*

Coming back to the original questions, how would we know whether language promotes sexism or sexism influences language? One way to find out is to do experimental studies, such as the one conducted by Fatemeh Khosroshashi. Some individuals were asked to read texts written

ence may be related to the fact that women are more involved in buying and selling in the marketplace.

Some researchers have questioned whether it is correctness that is at issue. Rather, we may be dealing in these examples with unequal prestige and power. Women may try to raise their status by conforming more to standard speech. When they answer a question with a rising inflection, they may be expressing uncertainty and a lack of power. Alternatively, perhaps women want to be more cooperative conversationalists. Speaking in a more "standard" fashion is consistent with being more likely to be un-

derstood by others. Answering a question with another question leads to continued conversation.[76]

Multilingualism and Codeswitching

For many people in the world the ability to speak more than one language is a normal part of life. One language may be spoken at home, another in school, the marketplace, or in government. Or more than one language may be spoken at home if family members come from different cultures and still other languages are spoken outside. Some countries with *man* and *he* and *his* referring to people; others were asked to read texts with more gender-neutral phrasing. Individuals were subsequently asked to draw pictures to go with the texts—the ones who read the texts with more "male" terminology drew more accompanying pictures of men, strongly suggesting that the use of the terms *man, he,* and *his* conveyed the thought that the people in the text were men, not women, *because* of the vocabulary used. We need many more such studies to help address the intellectual question of which comes first, linguistic or nonlinguistic culture.

It would be important to know whether societies with more "male-oriented" language *are* more male-dominated than are societies without such distinctions. We don't have that kind of comparative research yet. But one study by Robert and Ruth Munroe looked at the *proportion* of female and male nouns in ten languages (six

Indo-European; four non-European) in which nouns have "gender." Although none of those societies could be described as having "female-bias," the Munroes were able to ask whether those societies with less male-bias in social customs (for example, all children are equally likely to inherit property) have a higher proportion of *female* nouns than *male* nouns (more *female* than *male* nouns). The answer appears to be yes. While this study does not reveal what came first, studies like it are important if we want to discover how language differences may be related to other aspects of culture. If male-oriented languages are not related to male dominance, then it is not likely that *sexist* thinking is a consequence of language.

On the assumption that language may influence thought, many are pushing for changes in the way English is used, if not structured. It is hard to get English speakers to adopt a gender-neutral singular pronoun

to replace *he*. Attempts to do so go back to the eighteenth century and include suggestions of *tey, thon, per,* and *s/he*. Although these attempts have not succeeded, the way English is written and spoken has begun to change. Words or phrases such as *chair* (or *chairperson*), *police officer, sales assistant (salesperson)* have begun to replace their former-*man* versions. If Whorf were writing his sentence now it probably would be written "Speech is the best show humans put on. . . . Language helps people think."

Sources: *Janet Holmes,* An Introduction to Sociolinguistics *(London, Longman, 1992), pp. 336–43; Suzanne Romaine,* Language in Society: An Introduction to Sociolinguistics *(Oxford: Oxford University Press, 1994), pp. 105–16; Richard Wardhaugh,* An Introduction to Sociolinguistics, *2nd ed. (Oxford: Blackwell, 1992), pp. 315–17; Robin Lakoff, "Language and Woman's Place,"* Language in Society, *2(1973): 45–80; Fatemeh Khosroshashi, "Penguins Don't Care, But Women Do: A Social Identity Analysis of a Whorfian Problem,"* Language in Society, *18 (1989): 505–25; Robert L. Munroe and Ruth H. Munroe, "A Cross-Cultural Study of Sex Gender and Social Structure,"* Ethnology, *8 (1969): 206–11.*

explicitly promote multilingualism. For example, Singapore has four official languages—English, Mandarin (one of the Chinese languages), Tamil, and Malay. English is stressed for trade, Mandarin as the language of communication with most of China, Malay as the language of the general region, and Tamil as the language of an important ethnic group. Moreover, most of the population speak Hokkien, another Chinese language. Education is likely to be in English and Mandarin.[77]

What happens when people who know two or more languages communicate with each other?

Very often you find them **codeswitching,** using more than one language in the course of conversing.[78] Switching can occur in the middle of a Spanish-English bilingual sentence, as in "*No van a* bring it up in the meeting" ("They are not going to bring it up in the meeting").[79] Or switching can occur when the topic or situation changes, such as from social talk to schoolwork. Why do speakers of more than one language sometimes switch? Although speakers switch for a lot of different reasons, what is clear is that the switching is not a haphazard mix that comes from laziness or ignorance—

codeswitching involves a great deal of knowledge of two or more languages and an awareness of what is considered appropriate or inappropriate in the community. For example, in the Puerto Rican community in New York City, codeswitching within the same sentence seems to be common in speech among friends, but if a stranger who looks like a Spanish speaker approaches, the language will shift entirely to Spanish.[80]

Although each community may have its own "rules" for codeswitching, variations in practice may need to be understood in terms of the broader political and historical context. For example, German speakers in Transylvania, where Romanian is the national language, hardly ever codeswitch to Romanian. Perhaps the reason is that, before the end of World War II, German speakers were a privileged economic group who looked down upon landless Romanians and their language. During socialism the German speakers lost their economic privilege, but they continued to speak German among themselves. In the rare cases that Romanian is used among German speakers it tends to be associated with "low-status" speech, such as singing bawdy songs. The opposite situation occurred in a Hungarian region of German-speaking Austria. The people of this agricultural region annexed to Austria in 1921 were fairly poor peasant farmers. After World War II, business expansion began to attract labor from rural areas, so many Hungarians eagerly moved into jobs in industry. German was seen by the younger generations as a symbol of higher status and upward mobility; not surprisingly, codeswitching between Hungarian and German became part of their conversations. Indeed in the third generation, German has become the language of choice, except when speaking to the oldest Hungarians. The Hungarian-Austrian situation is fairly common in many parts of the world, where the language of the politically dominant group ends up being "linguistically dominant."[81]

Interethnic Communication

Even when they speak the same language, people from different ethnic groups may have some misunderstandings in communication because of the different unconscious rules they have about *how* to have a conversation. For example, English-speaking Athapaskan Indians in Canada seem to think that conversation with a white Canadian should be avoided except when they think they know the point of view of the white (who is generally more powerful politically). On the other hand, white English speakers think they should use conversation to get to know others (as at a cocktail party). So they pause a certain amount of time to let the other person talk, but they pause a much shorter time than an Athapaskan English speaker would. If the other person doesn't respond, the white English speaker, feeling awkward, will say something else. By the time an Athapaskan Indian is ready to talk, the white is already talking and the Athapaskan Indian considers it impolite to interrupt. It is easy to see how whites and Athapaskan Indians can misunderstand each other. Athapaskan Indians think white English speakers talk too much and don't let Indians express their views, and whites think Athapaskan Indians do not want to talk or get to know whites.[82]

The field of sociolinguistics is a relatively new specialty in linguistics. At present, sociolinguists seem to be interested primarily in describing variation in the use of language. Eventually, however, sociolinguistic research may enable us to understand why such variation exists. Why, for example, do some societies use many different status terms in address? Why do some societies use modes of speaking that vary with the sex of the speaker? An understanding of why language varies in different contexts might also suggest why structural aspects of language change over time. For as social contexts in a society change, the structure of the language might also tend to change.

▼ SUMMARY

1. The essential function language plays in all societies is that of communication. Although human communication is not limited to spoken language, such language is of overriding importance because it is the primary vehicle through which culture is shared and transmitted.

2. Systems of communication are not unique to humans. Other animal species communicate in a variety of ways—by sound, odor, body movement, and so forth. The ability of chimpanzees and gorillas to learn and use sign language suggests that symbolic communication is not unique to hu-

mans. Still, human language is distinctive as a communication system in that its spoken and symbolic nature permits an infinite number of combinations and recombinations of meaning.

3. Structural (or descriptive) linguists try to discover the rules of phonology (the patterning of sounds), morphology (the patterning of sound sequences and words), and syntax (the patterning of phrases and sentences) that predict how most speakers of a language talk.

4. By comparative analysis of cognates and grammar, historical linguists test the notion that certain languages derive from a common ancestral language, or protolanguage. The goals are to reconstruct the features of the protolanguage, to hypothesize how the offspring languages separated from the protolanguage or from each other, and to establish the approximate dates of such separations.

5. When two groups of people speaking the same language lose communication with each other because they become separated either physically or socially, they begin to accumulate small changes in phonology, morphology, and syntax. If the separation continues, the two former dialects of the same language will eventually become separate languages—that is, they will become mutually unintelligible.

6. Whereas isolation brings about divergence between speech communities, contact results in greater resemblance. This effect is particularly evident when contact between mutually unintelligible languages introduces borrowed words, most of which name some new item borrowed from the other culture.

7. Some attempts to explain the diversity of languages have focused on the possible interaction between language and other aspects of culture. On the one hand, if it can be shown that a culture can affect the structure and content of its language, then it would follow that linguistic diversity derives at least in part from cultural diversity. On the other hand, the direction of influence between culture and language might work in reverse; the linguistic structures might affect other aspects of the culture.

8. In recent years, linguists have begun to study variations in how people actually use language when speaking. This type of linguistic study, called sociolinguistics, is concerned with the ethnography of speaking—that is, with cultural and subcultural patterns of speaking in different social contexts.

▼ GLOSSARY TERMS

codeswitching	lexical content	morphology	protolanguage
cognates	lexicon	phonemes	structural (or descriptive)
core vocabulary	morph	phones	linguistics
dialects	morpheme	phonology	syntax
historical linguistics			

▼ CRITICAL QUESTIONS

1. Why might natural selection have favored the development of true language in humans but not in apes?
2. Would the world be better off with many different languages spoken or with just one universal language?
3. Can you think of some new behavior or way of thinking that led people to adopt or invent new vocabulary or some new pattern of speech?

▼ SUGGESTED READING

AKMAJIAN, A., DEMERS, R. A., AND HARNISH, R. M. *Linguistics: An Introduction to Language and Communication,* 3rd ed. Cambridge, MA: M.I.T. Press, 1990. A survey of many varieties of research in linguistics.

BROWN, C. H., AND WITKOWSKI, S. R. "Language Universals," Appendix B in D. Levinson and M. J. Malone, eds., *Toward Explaining Human Culture: A Critical Review of the Findings of Worldwide Cross-Cultural Research.* New Haven, CT: HRAF Press, 1980. A review of studies of universals in human languages, including universals in phonology and grammar. Focuses especially on developmental sequences in the lexicon or vocabulary.

HILL, J. "Do Apes Have Language?" in C. R. Ember, M. Ember, and P. N. Peregrine, eds. *Research Frontiers in Anthropology* (Englewood Cliffs, NJ: Prentice Hall, 1995). Prentice Hall/Simon & Schuster Custom Publishing. A discussion of the differences and similarities between human and ape language.

HOLMES, J. *An Introduction to Sociolinguistics* (London: Longman, 1992). The author surveys a variety of topics on the ways people use language in different contexts.

SAPIR, E. *Language: An Introduction to the Study of Speech.* New York: Harcourt Brace Jovanovich, 1949 [originally published 1921]. A classic nontechnical introduction to the study of human languages and how they vary. Also discusses the relations between language and thought.

WARDHAUGH, R. *An Introduction to Sociolinguistics,* 2nd ed. Oxford: Blackwell, 1992. This introduction to sociolinguistics covers, among other topics, language change, multilingualism, regional and social variation, and language and gender.

▼ NOTES

[1]Helen Keller, *The Story of My Life* (New York: Dell, 1974 [originally published 1902]), p. 34.

[2]Karl von Frisch, "Dialects in the Language of the Bees," *Scientific American,* August 1962, 78–87.

[3]Robert M. Seyfarth and Dorothy L. Cheney, "How Monkeys See the World: A Review of Recent Research on East African Vervet Monkeys," in Charles T. Snowdon, Charles H. Brown, and Michael R. Petersen, eds., *Primate Communication* (New York: Cambridge University Press, 1982), pp. 242, 246.

[4]C. F. Hockett and R. Ascher, "The Human Revolution," *Current Anthropology,* 5 (1964): 135–68.

[5]S. Savage-Rumbaugh, "Language Training of Apes," in Steve Jones, Robert Martin, and David Pilbeam, eds., *The Cambridge Encyclopedia of Human Evolution* (Cambridge: Cambridge University Press, 1992), pp. 138–41.

[6]Jane H. Hill, "Apes and Language," *Annual Review of Anthropology,* 7 (1978): 94.

[7]Jane H. Hill, "Do Apes Have Language?" in Carol R. Ember, Melvin Ember, and Peter N. Peregrine, eds., *Research Frontiers in Anthropology* (Englewood Cliffs, NJ: Prentice Hall, 1995). Prentice Hall/Simon & Schuster Custom Publishing.

[8]Philip Lieberman, *Uniquely Human: The Evolution of Speech, Thought, and Selfless Behavior* (Cambridge, MA: Harvard University Press, 1991), pp. 109–10, and Jeffrey Laitman, "The Anatomy of Human Speech," *Natural History,* August 1984, 20–27.

[9]Ronald C. Carlisle and Michael I. Siegel, "Additional Comments on Problems in the Interpretation of Neanderthal Speech Capabilities," *American Anthropologist,* 80 (1978): 367–72.

[10]C. F. Hockett and R. Ascher, "The Human Revolution," pp. 135–68.

[11]T. S. Eliot, "The Love Song of J. Alfred Prufrock," in *Collected Poems, 1909–1962* (New York: Harcourt, Brace & World, 1963).

[12]See Noam Chomsky, *Reflections on Language* (New York: Pantheon, 1975).

[13]Wayne M. Senner, "Theories and Myths on the Origins of Writing: A Historical Overview," in Wayne M. Senner, ed., *The Origins of Writing* (Lincoln: University of Nebraska Press, 1989), pp. 1–26.

[14]Franklin C. Southworth and Chandler J. Daswani, *Foundations of Linguistics* (New York: Free Press, 1974), p. 312. See also Franz Boas, "On Grammatical Categories," in Dell Hymes, ed., *Language in Culture and Society: A Reader in Linguistics and Anthropology* (New York: Harper & Row, 1964 [originally published 1911]), pp. 121–23.

[15]Derek Bickerton, "Creole Languages," *Scientific American,* July 1983, 116–22.

[16]Ibid., p. 122.

[17]Lila R. Gleitman and Eric Wanner, "Language Acquisition: The State of the State of the Art," in Eric Wanner and Lila R. Gleitman, eds., *Language Acquisition: The State of the Art* (Cambridge: Cambridge University Press, 1982), pp. 3–48; Ben G. Blount, "The Development of Language in Children," in Ruth H. Munroe, Robert L. Munroe, and Beatrice B. Whiting, eds., *Handbook of Cross-Cultural Human Development* (New York: Garland, 1981), pp. 379–402.

[18]Roger Brown, "The First Sentence of Child and Chimpanzee," in Thomas A. Sebeok and Jean Umiker-

Sebeok, eds., *Speaking of Apes,* (New York: Plenum), pp. 93–94.

[19]Peter A. de Villiers and Jill G. de Villiers, *Early Language* (Cambridge, MA: Harvard University Press, 1979), p. 48; see also Wanner and Gleitman, eds., *Language Acquisition.*

[20]Bickerton, "Creole Languages," p. 122.

[21]Adrian Akmajian, Richard A. Demers, and Robert M. Harnish, *Linguistics: An Introduction to Language and Communication,* 2nd ed. (Cambridge, MA: M.I.T. Press, 1984), p. 136.

[22]Maria Barinaga, "Priming the Brain's Language Pump," *Science,* January 31, 1992, 535.

[23]E. Sapir and M. Swadesh, "American Indian Grammatical Categories," in Hymes, ed., *Language in Culture and Society,* p. 103.

[24]Akmajian, Demers, and Harnish, *Linguistics,* pp. 164–66.

[25]Chaucer, *The Prologue to the Canterbury Tales, the Knightes Tale, the Nonnes Prestes Tale,* ed. Mark H. Liddell (New York: Macmillan, 1926), p. 8. Our modern English translation is based on the glossary in this book.

[26]Akmajian, Demers, and Harnish, *Linguistics,* p. 356.

[27]Philip Baldi, *An Introduction to the Indo-European Languages* (Carbondale: Southern Illinois University Press, 1983), p. 3.

[28]Ibid., p. 12.

[29]Paul Friedrich, *Proto-Indo-European Trees: The Arboreal System of a Prehistoric People* (Chicago: University of Chicago Press, 1970), p. 168.

[30]Ibid., p. 166.

[31]Marija Gimbutas, "An Archaeologist's View of PIE* in 1975," *Journal of Indo-European Studies,* 2 (1974): 293–95. See also Susan N. Skomal and Edgar C. Polomé, eds., *Proto-Indo-European: The Archaeology of a Linguistic Problem* (Washington, D.C.: Washington Institute for the Study of Man, 1987).

[32]David Anthony, Dimitri Y. Telegin, and Dorcas Brown, "The Origin of Horseback Riding," *Scientific American,* December 1991, pp. 94–100.

[33]Colin Renfrew, *Archaeology and Language: The Puzzle of Indo-European Origins* (London: Jonathan Cape, 1987).

[34]Joseph H. Greenberg, "Linguistic Evidence Regarding Bantu Origins," *Journal of African History,* 13 (1972): 189–216; see also D. W. Phillipson, "Archaeology and Bantu Linguistics," *World Archaeology,* 8 (1976): 71.

[35]Phillipson, "Archaeology and Bantu Linguistics," p. 79.

[36]Peter Trudgill, *Sociolinguistics: An Introduction to Language and Society,* rev. ed. (New York: Penguin, 1983), p. 34.

[37]John J. Gumperz, "Speech Variation and the Study of Indian Civilization," *American Anthropologist,* 63 (1961): 976–88.

[38]Trudgill, *Sociolinguistics,* p. 35.

[39]John J. Gumperz, "Dialect Differences and Social Stratification in a North Indian Village," in *Language in Social Groups: Essays by John J. Gumperz,* selected and introduced by Anwar S. Dil (Stanford, CA: Stanford University Press, 1971), p. 45.

[40]Uriel Weinreich, *Languages in Contact* (The Hague: Mouton, 1968), p. 31.

[41]But see Sarah Grey Thomason and Terrence Kaufman, *Language Contact, Creolization, and Genetic Linguistics* (Berkeley: University of California Press, 1988), for a discussion of how grammatical changes due to contact may be more important than was previously assumed.

[42]Colin Renfrew, "World Linguistic Diversity," *Scientific American,* January 1994, pp. 116–23.

[43]Brent Berlin and Paul Kay, *Basic Color Terms: Their Universality and Evolution* (Berkeley: University of California Press, 1969).

[44]Ibid.

[45]Ibid., pp. 5–6.

[46]Ibid., p. 104; Stanley R. Witkowski and Cecil H. Brown, "Lexical Universals," *Annual Review of Anthropology,* 7 (1978): 427–51.

[47]Marc H. Bornstein, "The Psychophysiological Component of Cultural Difference in Color Naming and Illusion Susceptibility," *Behavior Science Notes,* 8 (1973):41-101

[48]Melvin Ember, "Size of Color Lexicon: Interaction of Cultural and Biological Factors," *American Anthropologist,* 80 (1978):364-67.

[49]Ibid.

[50]Cecil H. Brown, "Folk Botanical Life-Forms: Their Universality and Growth," *American Anthropologist,* 79 (1977): 317–42.

[51]Cecil H. Brown, "Folk Zoological Life-Forms: Their Universality and Growth," *American Anthropologist,* 81 (1979): 791–817.

[52]Stanley R. Witkowski and Harold W. Burris, "Societal Complexity and Lexical Growth," *Behavior Science Research,* 16 (1981): 143–59.

[53]Ibid.

[54]Cecil H. Brown and Stanley R. Witkowski, "Language Universals," Appendix B in David Levinson and Martin J. Malone, eds., *Toward Explaining Human Culture: A Critical Review of the Findings of Worldwide Cross-Cultural Research* (New Haven, CT: HRAF Press, 1980), p. 379.

[55]Cecil H. Brown, "World View and Lexical Uniformities," *Reviews in Anthropology,* 11 (1984): 106.

[56]Harry Hoijer, "Cultural Implications of Some Navaho Linguistic Categories," in Hymes, ed., *Language in Culture and Society,* p. 146 [originally published 1951].

[57]Karen E. Webb, "An Evolutionary Aspect of Social Structure and a Verb 'Have'," *American Anthropologist,* 79 (1977): 42–49; see also Floyd Webster Rudmin, "Dominance, Social Control, and Ownership: A His-

tory and a Cross-Cultural Study of Motivations for Private Property," *Behavior Science Research,* 22 (1988): 130–60.

[58]Edward Sapir, "Conceptual Categories in Primitive Languages," paper presented at the autumn meeting of the National Academy of Sciences, New Haven, CT, 1931, published in *Science,* 74 (1931): 578; see also John B. Carroll, ed., *Language, Thought, and Reality: Selected Writings of Benjamin Lee Whorf* (New York: John Wiley, 1956), pp. 65–86.

[59]Richard Wardhaugh, *An Introduction to Sociolinguistics,* 2nd ed. (Oxford: Blackwell, 1992), p. 221.

[60]J. Peter Denny, "The 'Extendedness' Variable in Classifier Semantics: Universal Features and Cultural Variation," in Madeleine Mathiot, ed., *Ethnolinguistics: Boas, Sapir and Whorf Revisited* (The Hague: Mouton, 1979), p. 97.

[61]Paul Friedrich, *The Language Parallax* (Austin: University of Texas Press, 1986).

[62]Alexander Z. Guiora, Benjamin Beit-Hallahmi, Risto Fried, and Cecelia Yoder, "Language Environment and Gender Identity Attainment," *Language Learning,* 32 (1982): 289–304.

[63]"Language May Give Chinese an Edge in Math," *Science,* October 29, 1993, 651.

[64]Dell Hymes, *Foundations in Sociolinguistics: An Ethnographic Approach* (Philadelphia: University of Pennsylvania Press, 1974), pp. 83–117.

[65]Wardhaugh, *An Introduction to Sociolinguistics,* research summarized in chapter 7, pp. 160–91.

[66]Trudgill, *Sociolinguistics,* pp. 41–42.

[67]Clifford Geertz, *The Religion of Java* (New York: Free Press, 1960), pp. 248–60; see also J. Joseph Errington, "On the Nature of the Sociolinguistic Sign: Describing the Javanese Speech Levels," in Elizabeth Mertz and Richard J. Parmentier, eds., *Semiotic Mediation: Sociocultural and Psychological Perspectives* (Orlando, FL: Academic Press, 1985), pp. 287–310.

[68]Roger Brown and Marguerite Ford, "Address in American English," *Journal of Abnormal and Social Psychology,* 62 (1961) 375–85.

[69]E. E. Evans-Pritchard, "Nuer Modes of Address," *Uganda Journal,* 12 (1948): 166–71.

[70]Wardhaugh, *An Introduction to Sociolinguistics,* pp. 313–14.

[71]Janet S. Shibamoto, "The Womanly Woman: Japanese Female Speech," in Susan U. Philips, Susan Steele, and Christine Tanz, eds., *Language, Gender, and Sex in Comparative Perspective* (Cambridge: Cambridge University Press, 1987), p. 28.

[72]Robin Lakoff, "Language and Woman's Place," *Language in Society,* 2(1973): 45–80; Robin Tolmach Lakoff, "Why Can't a Woman Be Less Like a Man?" in Robin Tolmach Lakoff, ed., *Talking Power: The Politics of Language in Our Lives* (New York: Basic Books, 1990), pp. 198–214.

[73]Wardhaugh, *An Introduction to Sociolinguistics,* pp. 322–23; Janet Holmes, *An Introduction to Sociolinguistics* (London: Longman, 1992), pp. 172–73; Trudgill, *Sociolinguistics,* pp. 87–88.

[74]Mary R. Haas, "Men's and Women's Speech in Koasati," *Language,* 20 (1944): 142–49.

[75]Elinor Keenan, "Norm-makers, Norm-Breakers: Uses of Speech by Men and Women in a Malagasy Community," in Richard Bauman and Joel Sherzer, eds., *Explorations in the Ethnography of Speaking,* 2nd ed. (New York: Cambridge University Press, 1989), pp. 125–43.

[76]Holmes, *An Introduction to Sociolinguistics,* pp. 176–81.

[77]Wardhaugh, *An Introduction to Sociolinguistics,* pp. 98–104.

[78]Monica Heller, "Introduction," in Monica Heller, ed., *Codeswitching: Anthropological and Sociolinguistic Perspectives* (Berlin: Mouton de Gruyter, 1988), p. 1.

[79]Wardhaugh, *An Introduction to Sociolinguistics,* p. 107, citing an example from C. Pfaff, "Constraints on Language Mixing," *Language,* 55 (1979): 291–318.

[80]Ibid., p. 108.

[81]Susan Gal, "The Political Economy of Code Choice," in Heller, *Codeswitching,* pp. 249–55.

[82]Ron Scollon and Suzanne B. K. Scollon, *Narrative, Literacy and Face in Interethnic Communication* (Norwood, NJ: ABLEX Publishing, 1981), pp. 11–36.

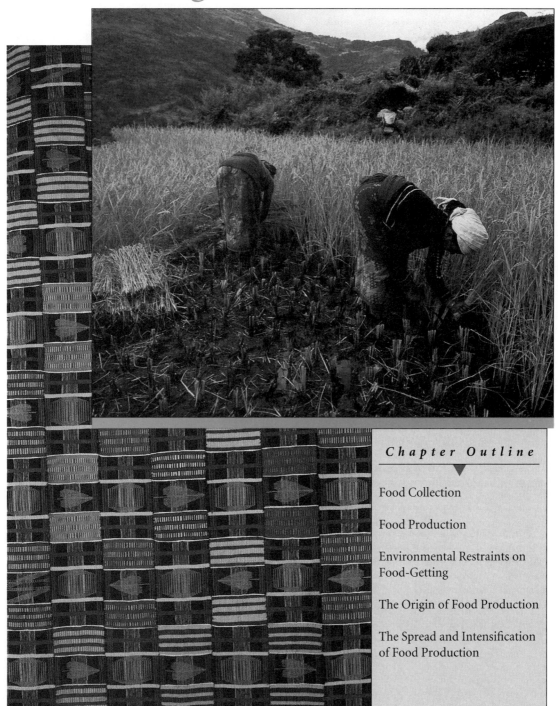

6

Getting Food

For most people in our society, getting food consists of a trip to the supermarket. Within an hour, we can gather enough food from the shelves to last us a week. Seasons don't daunt us. Week after week, we know food will be there. But we do not think of what would happen if the food were not delivered to the supermarket. We wouldn't be able to eat—and without eating for a while, we would die. Despite the old adage "Man [or woman] does not live by bread alone," without bread or the equivalent we could not live at all. Food-getting activities, then, take precedence over other activities important to survival. Reproduction, social control (the maintenance of peace and order within a group), defense against external threat, and the transmission of knowledge and skills to future generations—none could take place without energy derived from food. But it is not merely energy that is required for survival and long-term reproduction. Food-getting strategies need to provide the appropriate combination of nutrients throughout varying seasons and changing environmental conditions. Food-getting activities are also important because, as we will see in this and other chapters, the way a society gets its food strongly predicts other aspects of culture—from community size and permanence of settlement to type of economy and degree of inequality and type of political system, and even art styles and religious beliefs and practices.

In contrast with our own and similar societies, most societies have not had food-getting specialists. Rather, almost all able-bodied adults were engaged in getting food. During the 2 to 5 million years that humans have been on earth, 99 percent of the time they have obtained food by gathering wild plants, hunting wild animals, and fishing. Agriculture is a relatively recent phenomenon, dating back only about 10,000 years. And industrial or mechanized agriculture is hardly more than a century old! Harvesting machines have been used a little bit longer, but self-propelled machines had to wait for the internal combustion engine and the rise of the oil industry.

In this chapter we look at the ways different societies get food and we discuss some of the features associated with the different patterns. We ask why societies vary in their food-getting strategies. We shall see that the physical environment by itself has only a limited or restraining effect on how a society gets most of its food. To explain the variation more fully, we need to ask why societies in the prehistoric past switched from collecting wild food resources to cultivating plants and raising animals.

FOOD COLLECTION

Food collection may be generally defined as all forms of **subsistence technology** in which food-getting is dependent on naturally occurring resources—that is, wild plants and animals. Although this was the way humans got their food for most of human history, the few remaining food collectors in the world today (also referred to as **foragers**) live in what have been called the *marginal* areas of the earth—deserts, the Arctic, and dense tropical forests—habitats that do not allow easy exploitation by modern agricultural technologies.

Anthropologists are interested in studying the relatively few food-collecting societies still available for observation. These groups may help us understand some aspects of human life in the past, when all people were foragers. But we must be cautious in drawing inferences about the past from our observations of contemporary food collectors for three reasons. First, earlier foragers lived in almost all types of environments, including some very bountiful ones. Therefore, what we observe among recent and contemporary food collectors, who generally live in deserts, the Arctic, and tropical forests, may not be comparable to what would have been observable in more favorable environments in the past.[1] Second, contemporary foragers are not relics of the past: Like all contemporary societies, they have evolved and are still evolving. This means that the adaptations we observe in contemporary groups may be different from the adaptations made by foragers in the past. (For example, few if any contemporary hunters use stone arrowheads.) Third, recent and contemporary foragers have been interacting with kinds of societies that did not exist until after 10,000 years ago—agriculturalists, pastoralists, and intrusive powerful state societies.[2] Let us now examine two areas of the world with very different environments where recent food collectors lived—Australia and the North American Arctic.

Australian Aborigines

Before Europeans came to the Australian continent, all the aboriginal people who lived there depended on food collection. Although the way of life of Australian aborigines is now considerably altered, we consider the life of the Ngatatjara as described by Richard Gould in the 1960s, when they still lived by gathering wild plants and hunting wild animals in the Gibson Desert of western Australia.[3] We mostly use the present tense in our discussion because that is the custom in ethnographic writing; but the reader should understand that we are referring to aboriginal life in the 1960s.

The Ngatatjara desert environment averages less than 8 inches of rain per year, and the temperature in summer may rise to 118° F. The few permanent water holes are separated by hundreds of square miles of sand, scrub, and rock. Even before Europeans arrived in Australia, the area was sparsely populated—fewer than one person per 35 to 40 square miles. Now there are even fewer people, because the aboriginal population was decimated by introduced diseases and mistreatment after the Europeans arrived.

On a typical day, the camp begins to stir just before sunrise, while it is still dark. Children are sent to fetch water, and the people breakfast on water and food left over from the night before. In the cool of the early morning, the adults talk and make plans for the day. The talking goes on for a while. Where should they go for food—to places they have been to recently or to new places? Sometimes there are other considerations. For example, one woman may want to search for plants whose bark she needs to make new sandals. When the women decide which plants they want to collect and where they think those plants are most likely to be found, they take up their digging sticks and set out with large wooden bowls of drinking water on their heads. Their children ride on their hips or walk alongside. Meanwhile, the men may have decided to hunt emus, 6-foot-tall ostrichlike birds that do not fly. The men go to a creek bed where they will wait to ambush any game that may come along. They lie patiently behind a screen of brush they have set up, hoping for a chance to throw a spear at an emu or even a kangaroo. They can throw only once, because if they miss, the game will run away.

By noon the men and women are usually back at camp, the women with their wooden bowls each filled with up to 15 pounds of fruit or other plant foods, the men more often than not with only some small game such as lizards and rabbits. The men's food-getting is less certain of success than the women's, so most of the Ngatatjara aborigines' diet is plant food. The daily cooked meal is eaten toward evening, after an afternoon spent resting, gossiping, and making or repairing tools.

The aborigines traditionally were nomadic, moving their campsites fairly frequently. The campsites were isolated and inhabited by only a small number of people, or they were clusters of groups including as many as eighty persons. The aborigines never established a campsite right next to a place with water. If they were too close, their presence would frighten game away and might cause tension with neighboring bands, who also would wait for game to come to the scarce watering spots.

Nowadays, many aborigines live in small settled villages. For example, in the 1980s Victoria Burbank worked in a village she calls "Mangrove" in the Northern Territory of Australia. The once nomadic aborigines now live in a village of about 600, which was founded in the 1950s around a Protestant mission. Their houses have stoves, refrigerators, toilets, washing machines, and even television. Their children attend school full-time, and there is a health clinic for their medical needs. They still do some foraging, but most of their food comes from the store. Some earn wages, but many subsist on government welfare checks.[4]

The Inuit (Eskimo)

The diet of the Australian aborigines mainly included gathered wild plant foods. But for the Inuit (Eskimo) peoples, who live all year round in the North American Arctic, plants are too scarce to be the most important part of the diet. From Greenland and Labrador in the east to Alaska in the west, the Inuit used to depend almost entirely on sea and land mammals and fish. (The term *Eskimo* is used widely in the West, but it is not a word in any of the native languages in that area. Many of the native Arctic groups, particularly those now living in Canada, prefer to be called Inuit.)

We shall focus here on the traditional life of the north Alaskan Inupiaq as described by Ernest Burch for the beginning of the nineteenth century (the "ethnographic present" in the following discussion).[5] Northern Alaska is relatively "warm" for its latitude but not for most of us farther south; little sun and below-zero temperatures for a month or so in the winter are hardly warm. Rivers and lakes freeze in October and do not thaw until May. Even the ocean freezes for part of the winter.

What the Inupiaq collect for food depends mostly on the season, but the critical resources are sea mammals (ranging in size from whales to seals), fish, and caribou or wild reindeer. The usual technique for hunting sea mammals is to hurl a toggle harpoon into a sea mammal from a kayak. It is very difficult to kill a moving sea mammal, so hunters attach a line to the animal with the harpoon; on the other end of the line is a sealskin float that indicates where the harpooned sea mammal can be located.

A modern Inuit hunter, wearing a Caribou parka and seal-skin boots, aims a rifle while sitting behind the camouflage of an umbrella off Ellesmere Island.

The sea mammal gets more and more tired pulling the float until the hunter is able to kill it with a lance. One man can manage alone to hunt smaller sea mammals, but groups of men are needed to hunt whales. In the winter, when the sea ice is frozen, a different hunting technique is used. A hunter must locate a breathing hole and then wait, immobile and attentive, for hours or sometimes days until a seal comes up for air. The instant the seal surfaces, the hunter must aim perfectly with the harpoon. The women butcher the animal, prepare it for eating or storage, and process the skin. All of the skin clothing is sewn by women. They also hunt small animals, such as hares, and do much of the fishing. A variety of techniques are used for fishing—hook and line, spearing, and ambushing with nets and dams. Women make the fishing nets, and it takes the better part of a year to make one. Although there are not many plants to gather, the women do that too.

Related families usually live together and move camp by boat or sled to be in the best place to intercept the migratory animals and fish. For instance, caribou migrate, so the Inupiaq try to catch them by building a corral in a place through which they are expected to pass. A network of interrelated families lives and moves in a territory of thousands of square miles, moving outside it only when they have made arrangements with other groups to do so.

Much has changed since the time described above. Now the Inupiaq live in villages or towns with many modern conveniences. In the village of Kivalina there are permanent houses with electricity, telephones, and televisions. Dog teams have been replaced by all-terrain vehicles and snowmobiles. There are powerful outboard motors rather than skin-boats. Many men and women have full-time wage-paying jobs. But, even though the people may buy most of their food, there is still a preference for traditional foods. So the Inupiaq still hunt and fish on the weekends.

General Features of Food Collectors

Despite the differences in terrain and climate under which they live and the different food-collecting technologies they use, Australian aborigines, Inuit, and most other recent foragers traditionally have certain cultural patterns in common (see Table 6-1 on page 98). Most live in small communities in sparsely populated territories and follow a nomadic lifestyle, forming no permanent settlements. As a rule, they do not recognize individual land rights. Their communities do not generally have different classes of people and tend to have no specialized or full-time political officials.[6] But food collectors who depend heavily on fishing are more likely to have bigger and more permanent communities and somewhat more social inequality than do those who forage for game and plants.[7] Division of labor in food-collecting societies is based largely on age and gender. Men exclusively hunt large marine and land animals, men usually do most of the fishing, and women usually gather wild plant foods.[8]

Is there a typical pattern of food-getting among food collectors? Many anthropologists have assumed for some years that foragers typically get their food more from gathering than from hunting and that women contribute more than men to subsistence (because women generally do the gathering).[9] Although gathering is the most important food-getting activity for some food collectors (for example, the Ngatatjara aborigines and the !Kung of southern Africa), this is not true for most recent food-collecting societies. A survey of 180 such societies indicates that there is a lot of variation with regard to which food-getting activity is most important to the society: gathering is the most important activity for 30 percent of the surveyed societies, hunting for 25 percent, and fishing for 38 percent. (Perhaps, then, we should call most recent food collectors fisher-gatherer-hunters!) In any case, because men generally do the fishing as well as the hunting, the men usually contribute more to food-getting than do the women among recent food collectors.[10]

Because food collectors move their camps often and walk great distances, it may seem that the food-collecting way of life is difficult. Although we do not have enough quantitative studies to tell us what is typical of most food collectors, studies

FROM MAN THE HUNTER,
TO WOMAN THE GATHERER, TO . . .?

Anthropologists know it is important to understand the food-collecting way of life, for all humans were food collectors until 10,000 years ago. An important conference was held in 1966 to bring together anthropologists of all types to discuss what was known about food collectors. Organized by Richard B. Lee and Irven DeVore, the conference and the resulting book were called *Man the Hunter*. At the time, the word *man* was used widely in anthropology as a way of referring to humans in general. But referring to man the hunter appeared to ignore women, since women rarely do the hunting among recent foragers. It was not that women's contribution was entirely ignored by the contributors to *Man the Hunter*. Indeed, Richard Lee pointed out that some food collectors such as the !Kung of southwest Africa depended mostly on gathering, which was mainly women's work. Even so, the title of the conference and of the resulting book conveyed that hunting, and the work of men, was most important among food collectors.

With the growing women's movement in the United States, thinking in anthropology subsequently began to change. New questions began to be asked. What were women doing? How much did they contribute to subsistence and to other essential economic activities? How much time did they work? What were their views of the world? What kinds of mate choices did women have? What kinds of decisions did they make? How much influence did women have?

In 1981, a book edited by Francis Dahlberg appeared. It was titled *Woman the Gatherer*. The editor was well aware that gathering is *not* usually the most important subsistence activity among food collectors. It may be more important among contemporary foragers such as the !Kung and Australian aborigines who live in warmer climates. But gathering is less important in colder climates, where most recent foragers have lived. Indeed, if we look at a large sample of recent foragers, we discover that fishing is more often the most important subsistence activity, more important (providing more calories) than either gathering or hunting! Why the title *Woman the Gatherer* then? Although the editor did not say so explicitly, we suggest that the title was intended to raise consciousness about the importance of women.

We now know that food-collecting societies show considerable variability in how they get their food, so neither "Man the Hunter" nor "Woman the Gatherer" describes most foragers accurately. A book title such as *Food Collectors* or *Foraging Humans* may not as be as catchy as *Man the Hunter* or *Woman the Gatherer*, but it would be more gender-fair.

Sources: *Richard B. Lee and Irven DeVore, eds.,* Man the Hunter *(Chicago: Aldine, 1968); Frances Dahlberg, ed.,* Woman the Gatherer *(New Haven, CT: Yale University Press, 1981); Carol R. Ember, "Myths about Hunter-Gatherers,"* Ethnology, *18 (1978): 439–48 (reprinted in Melvin Ember and Carol R. Ember,* Marriage, Family, and Kinship: Comparative Studies of Social Organization *[New Haven, CT: HRAF Press, 1983], pp. 313–31).*

of two Australian aborigine groups[11] and of one !Kung group[12] indicate that those food collectors do not spend many hours getting food. For example, !Kung adults spend an average of about 17 hours per week collecting food. Even when you add the time spent making tools (about 6 hours a week) and doing housework (about 19 hours a week), the !Kung seem to have more leisure time than many agriculturalists, as we will discuss later.

FOOD PRODUCTION

Beginning about 10,000 years ago, certain peoples in widely separated geographic locations made the revolutionary changeover to **food production.** That is, they began to cultivate and then domesticate plants and animals. (Domesticated plants and animals are different from the ancestral wild forms.)

TABLE 6-1 *Variation in Food-Getting and Associated Features*

| | FOOD COLLECTORS | FOOD PRODUCERS | | |
	Foragers	Horticulturalists	Pastoralists	Intensive Agriculturalists
Population density	Lowest	Low–moderate	Low	Highest
Maximum community size	Small	Small–moderate	Small	Large (towns and cities)
Nomadism/permanence of settlements	Generally nomadic or seminomadic	More sedentary: communities may move after several years	Generally nomadic or seminomadic	Permanent communities
Food shortages	Infrequent	Infrequent	Frequent	Frequent
Trade	Minimal	Minimal	Very important	Very important
Full-time craft specialists	None	None or few	Some	Many (high degree of craft specialization)
Individual differences in wealth	Generally none	Generally minimal	Moderate	Considerable
Political leadership	Informal	Some part-time political officials	Part- and full-time political officials	Many full-time political officials

With domestication of these food sources, people acquired control over certain natural processes, such as animal breeding and seeding. Today, most peoples in the world depend for their food on some combination of domesticated plants and animals.

Anthropologists generally distinguish three major types of food-production systems—horticulture, intensive agriculture, and pastoralism.

Horticulture

The word **horticulture** may conjure up visions of people with "green thumbs" growing orchids and other flowers in greenhouses. But to anthropologists, the word means the growing of crops of *all* kinds with relatively simple tools and methods, in the absence of permanently cultivated fields. The tools are usually hand tools, such as the digging stick or hoe, not plows or other equipment pulled by animals or tractors. And the methods used do not include fertilization, irrigation, or other ways to restore soil fertility after a growing season.

There are two kinds of horticulture. The more common one involves a dependence on **extensive or**

shifting cultivation. The land is worked for short periods and then left idle for some years. During the years when the land is not cultivated, wild plants and brush grow up; when the fields are later cleared by *slash-and-burn* techniques (to be described shortly), nutrients are returned to the soil. The other kind of horticulture involves a dependence on long-growing tree crops. The two kinds of horticulture may be practiced in the same society, but in neither case is there permanent cultivation of field crops.

Most horticultural societies do not rely on crops alone for food. Many also hunt or fish; a few are nomadic for part of the year. For example, the northern Kayapo of the Brazilian Amazon leave their villages for as long as three months at a time to trek through the forest in search of game. The entire village participates in a trek, carrying large quantities of garden produce and moving their camp every day.[13] Other horticulturalists raise domestic animals, but these are usually not large animals such as cattle and camels.[14] More often than not, the animals raised by horticulturalists are smaller ones such as pigs, chickens, goats, and sheep. Let us look now at two horticultural societies, the Yanomamö of the Brazilian-Venezuelan Amazon and the Samoans of the South Pacific.

The Yanomamö. Dense tropical forest covers most of Yanomamö territory. From the air, the typical village is located in a forest clearing and looks like a single large circular lean-to with its inner side open to the central plaza. Each individual family has its own portion of the lean-to under the common roof. Each family's portion of the lean-to has a back wall (part of the closed back wall around the circular village structure), but the portions are open on the sides to each other as well as onto the central plaza of the village. The Yanomamö get most of their calories from garden produce, but according to Raymond Hames the Yanomamö actually spend most of their time foraging.[15]

Before the people can plant, the forest must be cleared of trees and brush. Like most shifting cultivators, the Yanomamö use a combination of techniques: slashing the undergrowth, felling trees, and controlled burning to clear a garden spot (that is why we speak of **slash-and-burn** horticulture). Before the 1950s, the Yanomamö had only stone axes, so felling trees was quite difficult. Now they have steel machetes and axes given or traded to them by missionaries.

Because of the work involved in clearing a garden, the Yanomamö prefer to make use of forest patches that have little thorny brush and not too many large trees.[16] After the ground is cleared, the Yanomamö plant plantains, manioc, sweet potatoes, taro, and a variety of plants for medicine, condiments, and craft materials. Men do the heavy clearing work to prepare a garden, and they as well as women plant the crops. Women usually go to the gardens daily to weed and harvest. After two or three years the yields diminish and the forest starts growing back, making continued cultivation less desirable and more difficult, so they abandon the garden and clear a new one. If they can, they clear adjacent forest, but if gardens are far from the village they will move the village to a new location. Villages are moved about every five years because of gardening needs and warfare. There is a great deal of intervillage raiding, so villages are often forced to flee to another location.

Extensive cultivation requires a lot of territory because new gardens are not cleared until the forest grows back. What is often misunderstood is why it is so important to shift gardens. Not only is a burned field easier to plant, but all the organic matter that is burned provides necessary nutrients for a good yield. If horticulturalists come back too quickly to a spot with little plant cover, a garden made there will not produce a satisfactory yield.

The Yanomamö crops do not provide much protein, so hunting and fishing are quite important to their diet. Men hunt animals such as birds, peccaries, monkeys, and tapir with bows and arrows. Fishing is enjoyed by women, men, and children. They catch fish by hand, with small bows and arrows and by stream poisoning. Everybody gathers honey, hearts of palm, Brazil nuts, and cashews, although the men usually climb trees to shake nuts out. Much of the foraging is done from the village base, but the Yanomamö, like the Kayapo, may go away from the village (on trek) to forage from time to time.

The Samoans. The Samoans numbered about 56,000 persons in 1839, soon after European missionaries arrived.[17] The islands of Samoa, which are about 2,300 miles south of the Hawaiian Islands, are volcanic in origin, with central ridges and peaks as high as 4,000 feet. Though the land is generally steep, the islands have a lush plant cover watered by up to 200 inches of rain a year (about five times the amount of rain that falls on New York City in a year). All that rain does not interfere much with outdoor activity, because the torrential showers do not last long and the water disappears quickly into the porous volcanic soil. The temperature is relatively constant, rarely falling below 70° or rising above 88° F. Strong cooling trade winds blow most of the year, generally from the east or southeast, and on the coasts one constantly hears the low rumble of huge Pacific swells breaking upon the fringing coral reefs offshore.

Samoan horticulture involves mostly three tree crops requiring little work except in harvesting. Once planted, and with hardly more than a few years of waiting, the breadfruit tree continues to produce about two crops a year for up to half a century. Coconut trees may continue to produce for a hundred years. And banana trees make new stalks of fruit, each weighing more than 50 pounds, for many years; merely cutting down one stalk induces the plant to grow another. Young men do most of the harvesting of tree crops. Women do the occasional weeding.

The Samoans also practice some shifting cultivation; men periodically clear small patches of land for taro, a root crop that is a staple food. The taro patches can produce a few crops before they must be allowed to revert to bush so that soil fertility can be restored. But even taro cultivation does not require much work; planting requires nothing more than slightly burying the top sliced off a root

The islands of American Samoa have very little flat land for cultivation. Coconut trees and breadfruit trees grow in the beach area, but taro is grown on the hillside shown behind the houses. To prevent soil erosion, crops are planted interspersed amongst the naturally occurring brush. If land were completely cleared and single-cropped, the frequent torrential rains would quickly wash away the loose volcanic topsoil.

just harvested. (Young men do most of the planting and harvesting.) The taro patches are weeded infrequently, mostly by women. This kind of casual farming behavior prompted Captain Bligh, of *Mutiny on the Bounty* fame, to describe the Tahitians as lazy.[18] Captain Bligh's attitude was ethnocentric. South Pacific islanders such as the Samoans and Tahitians cannot weed as often as European farmers without risking the erosion of their soil, because, in contrast with European farmlands, which are generally flat or only slightly sloping, the land of Samoa and Tahiti is mostly steep. The Samoan and Tahitian practice of not weeding crops and growing them in glorious and messy confusion enables the deep and shallow root structures of the various plants growing together to prevent the loose volcanic soil from being washed away by the torrential showers.

The Samoans keep chickens and pigs, which they eat only occasionally. The major source of animal protein in the Samoan diet is fish caught inside and outside the reef. Younger men may swim in the deep sea outside the reef and use a sling to spear fish; older men are more likely to stand on the reef and throw a four-pointed spear at fish swimming inside the reef. For many years, people in the villages of Samoa have sold copra (the sun-dried meat of the ripe coconut) to the world market for co-

conut oil. Men generally cut the copra from the shells after the ripe coconuts fall by themselves to the ground. With the cash earned from the sale of copra, people buy imported things such as machetes, kerosene, and flour. People in most villages still produce most of the foods they eat, but many have migrated to towns on the bigger islands and to cities in Hawaii and on the U.S. mainland to find wage-paying jobs.

General Features of Horticulturalists. In most horticultural societies, simple farming techniques have tended to yield more food from a given area than is generally available to food collectors. Consequently, horticulture is able to support larger, more densely populated communities. The way of life of horticulturalists is more sedentary than that of food collectors, although communities may move after some years to farm a new series of plots. (Some horticulturalists have permanent villages because they depend mostly on food from trees that keep producing for a long time.) In contrast with most recent food-collecting groups, horticultural societies exhibit the beginnings of social differentiation. For example, some individuals may be part-time craftworkers or part-time political officials, and certain members of a kin group may have more status than other individuals in the society.

Intensive Agriculture

People engaged in **intensive agriculture** use techniques that enable them to cultivate fields permanently. Essential nutrients may be put back through the use of fertilizers, which may be organic material (most commonly dung from humans or other animals) or inorganic (chemical) fertilizers. But there are other ways to restore nutrients. The Luo of western Kenya plant beans around corn plants. Bacteria growing around the roots of the bean plant replace lost nitrogen, and the corn plant conveniently provides a pole for the bean plant to wind around as it grows. Some intensive agriculturalists use irrigation from streams and rivers to ensure an adequate supply of water-borne nutrients. Crop rotation and plant stubble that has been plowed under also restore nutrients to the soil.

In general, the technology of intensive agriculturalists is more complex than that of horticulturalists. Plows rather than digging sticks are generally employed. But there is enormous variation in the degree to which intensive agriculturalists rely on mechanization rather than hand labor. In some societies the most complex machine is an animal-drawn plow; in the corn and wheat belts of the United States, huge tractors till, seed, and fertilize twelve rows at a time.[19]

Let's look now at two groups of intensive agriculturalists; those of rural Greece and those of the Mekong Delta in Vietnam.

Rural Greece. The village of Vasilika is situated at the foot of Mount Parnassus on the Boeotian plain. As described by Ernestine Friedl in the 1950s, its population was about 220 inhabitants.[20]

Grapevines and wheat are cultivated for domestic use. The agricultural year begins in March with pruning of the vines and hoeing of the fields; these tasks are regarded as men's work. Wine making begins in September, after the grain harvest, and involves the whole family. Men, women, and children talk and joke as they pick the grapes and put them into large baskets. After the leaves and stems are removed, the fruit is trampled by the men, and the newly pressed grape juice, or *must,* is transferred to barrels. After adding whatever sugar and alcohol are needed, farmers also add resin to give the wine its characteristic flavor.

The villagers use horses to plow their wheat fields in October, and in November they sow the seed by hand. The wheat crop is harvested the following summer, usually by machine. Wheat consti-

tutes the staple village food and is eaten as bread, as a cereal (called *trakhana*), or as noodles. It is also commonly bartered for other food items, such as fish, olive oil, and coffee.

Cotton and tobacco are the main **cash crops** (crops raised for sale). In this dry plains country, the success of the cotton crop depends on irrigation, and the villagers use efficient diesel pumps to distribute water. The real work in the cotton fields begins after the spring plowing and seeding have been completed. Then the young plants must be hoed and mulched, a task done mostly by women. The season of cotton cultivation is especially hard on women, who must do all the cooking and household chores in addition to working in the cotton fields. Irrigation, which begins in July, is men's work. It is usually done three times a season and involves the clearing of shallow ditches, the mounting of pumps, and the channeling of the water. Cotton picking, which starts in October, is considered women's work. For picking, as well as hoeing and harvesting, a farmer owning more than 5 acres usually hires women from the same village or neighboring villages, and sometimes even from distant towns. The cotton ginning is carried out by centrally located contractors, who are paid on the spot with 6 percent of each farmer's crop. Most of the seed reclaimed in the ginning is used for the next year's planting. The remainder is pressed into cakes to serve as supplementary food for ewes at lambing time. Tobacco yields a larger cash income than cotton, and the tobacco crop fits well into what would otherwise be slack periods in cultivation.

Raising animals plays a relatively minor role in the villagers' economic life. Each farmer has a horse or two for heavy draft work, a mule or donkey, about two dozen sheep, and some fowl.

Farmers at Vasilika are responsive to modern developments; they are prepared to experiment to a certain extent, especially with mechanization. Where the amount of acreage under cultivation warrants the expense, tractors are hired for plowing. Specialists are regularly called in to handle harvesting, cotton ginning, and similar tasks. Indeed, the Greek farmer is content to be a farmer and to rely on the skills of others to repair his roof, maintain his water pump, or provide the mechanical know-how for his production.

Rural Vietnam: The Mekong Delta. The village of Khanh Hau, situated along the flat Mekong Delta, comprised about 600 families when it was described in the late 1950s by Gerald Hickey before the Vietnam War.[21] The delta area has a tropical climate, with a rainy season that lasts from May to November. As a whole, the area has been made habitable only through extensive drainage.

Wet rice cultivation is the principal agricultural activity of Khanh Hau. It is part of a complex, specialized arrangement that involves three interacting components: (1) a complex system of irrigation and water control; (2) a variety of specialized equipment, including plows, water wheels, threshing sledges, and winnowing machines; and (3) a clearly defined set of socioeconomic roles—from those of landlord, tenant, and laborer to those of rice miller and rice merchant.

In the dry season, the farmer decides what sort of rice crop to plant—whether of long (120 days) or short (90 days) maturation. The choice depends on the capital at his disposal, the current cost of fertilizer, and the anticipated demand for rice. The seedbeds are prepared as soon as the rains have softened the ground in May. The soil is turned over (plowed) and broken up (harrowed) as many as six separate times, with two-day intervals for "airing" between operations. During this time, the rice seeds are soaked in water for at least two days to stimulate sprouting. Before the seedlings are planted, the paddy is plowed once more and harrowed twice in two directions at right angles.

Planting is a delicate, specialized operation that must usually be done quickly and is performed most often by hired male laborers. But efficient planting is not enough to guarantee a good crop. Proper fertilization and irrigation are equally important. In the irrigating, steps must be taken to ensure that the water level remains at exactly the proper depth over the entire paddy. Water is distributed by means of scoops, wheels, and mechanical pumps. Successive crops of rice ripen from late September to May; all members of the family may be called upon to help with the harvest. After each crop is harvested, it is threshed, winnowed, and dried. Normally, the rice is sorted into three portions: one is set aside for use by the household in the following year; one is for payment of hired labor and other services (such as loans from agricultural banks); and one is for cash sale on the market. Aside from the harvesting, women do little work in the fields; they spend most of their time on household chores. In families with little land, however, young daughters help in the fields and older daughters may hire themselves out to other farmers.

The villagers also cultivate vegetables, raise pigs, chickens, and the like, and frequently engage in fishing. The village economy usually supports three or four implement makers and a much larger number of carpenters.

General Features of Intensive-Agricultural Societies.
Societies with intensive agriculture are more likely than horticulturalists to have towns and cities, a high degree of craft specialization, complex political organization, and large differences in wealth and power.

Studies suggest that intensive agriculturalists work longer hours than simpler agriculturalists.[22] For example, men engaged in intensive agriculture

Threshing grain on a hillside in Greece on the island of Santorini in the Aegean Sea

average nine hours of work a day, seven days a week; women average almost eleven hours of work per day. Most of the work for women in intensive-agricultural societies involves food processing and work in and around the home, but they also spend a lot of time working in the fields. We discuss some of the implications of the work patterns for women in the chapter on sex, gender, and culture.

Intensive-agricultural societies are more likely than horticultural societies to face food shortages, even though intensive agriculture is generally more productive than horticulture.[23] Why, if more food can be produced per acre, is there more risk of shortage among intensive agriculturalists? Social scientists do not know for sure. One possibility is that intensive agriculturalists rely more often on single crops, and such crops may fail because of fluctuations in weather, plant diseases, or insect pests. Intensive agriculturalists may also be more likely to face food shortages because they are often producing crops for a market. If the market demand drops, they may not have enough cash to buy all the other food they need.

The Commercialization and Mechanization of Agriculture.
Some intensive agriculturalists produce very little for sale; most of what they produce is for their own use. But there is a worldwide trend for intensive agriculturalists to produce more and more for a market. (This trend is called **commercialization,** which may occur in any area of life and which involves increasing dependence on buying and selling, usually with money as the medium of exchange.) The increasing commercialization of agriculture is associated with several other trends. One is that farm work is becoming more and more mechanized as hand labor becomes scarce (because of migration to industrial and service jobs in towns and cities) or too expensive. A second trend is the emergence and spread of *agribusiness,* large corporation-owned farms that may be operated by multinational companies and worked by hired (as opposed to "family") labor. For example, consider how cotton farming has changed in the southeastern United States. In the 1930s, mules and horses used in plowing were replaced by tractors. This change allowed some landowners to evict their sharecroppers and expand their holdings. After World War II, mechanical cotton pickers replaced most of the harvest laborers. But you had to have a good deal of money (or be a corporation) to acquire those machines, each of which cost many tens of thousands of dollars.[24] So the mechanization of cotton farming sent many rural farm laborers off to the cities of the north in search of employment, and the agricultural sector increasingly became big business.

A third trend associated with the commercialization of agriculture (including animal raising) is a reduction in the proportion of the population engaged in food production. In the United States, for example, less than 2 percent of the total population work on farms.[25]

In the next chapter, on economics, and later in the chapter on culture change, we more fully discuss some of the apparent consequences of the worldwide changeover to commercial or market economies.

"Market Foraging" in Industrial Societies.
Food in countries such as the United States and Canada comes largely from intensive agriculture and animal husbandry practiced by a small proportion of the population. Those food specialists make their living by selling animal and plant products to marketers, distributors, and food processors. Indeed, most people know very little about how to grow crops or raise animals. Food appears in markets (or supermarkets) already processed by other specialists. It comes in paper or plastic packages, looking far different from how it originally looked in the field or on the feedlot. Thus, most of us are "market foragers," collecting our food from stores. In some ways, as we shall see in the chapter on psychology and culture, we behave very much like foragers of wild plants and animals. But there are also enormous differences between our kind of foraging and the original kind. If our society did not have very productive intensive agriculture and animal husbandry, we would not have towns and cities, thousands of different full-time occupations (hardly any of which are involved in food-getting), a centralized government, or many of our other characteristics.

Pastoralism

Most agriculturalists raise animals (practice animal husbandry), but a small number of societies depend directly or indirectly on domesticated herds of animals for their living. We call such a system **pastoralism.** We might assume that pastoralists breed animals to eat their meat, but most do not. Pastoralists more often get their animal protein from live animals in the form of milk, and some pastoralists regularly take blood, which is rich in protein, from their animals to mix with other foods. The herds also indirectly provide food because pastoralists trade animal products for plant foods and other necessities. In fact, a large proportion of their food may actually come from trade with agricultural groups.[26] For example, some pastoral groups in the Middle East derive a good deal of their livelihood from the sale of what we call oriental rugs, which are made from the wool of their sheep on hand looms. Two pastoral societies are the Basseri of southern Iran and the Lapps of Scandinavia.

The Basseri. The Basseri, described by Fredrik Barth as of the 1960s, are a tribe of about 16,000 tent-dwelling nomads.[27] Their herds consist principally of sheep and goats, though donkeys and camels are raised for pulling or carrying and the wealthier men have horses for riding. Theirs is a dry, arid habitat, with rainfall averaging no more than 10 inches a year.

The Basseri's pastoral way of life is based on a regular, migratory exploitation of the grazing lands within their territory, which measures about 15,000 square miles in all. In winter, when the mountains to the north are covered with snow, the plains and foothills to the south offer extensive pasturage. During the spring, grazing is excellent on a plateau near the center of the territory. By summer, when most of the lower-lying pastures have dried up, sufficient food for the herds can be found in the mountains at an altitude of nearly 6,000 feet.

Annual migrations are so important to the economies of the Basseri and other pastoralist societies of that region that they have developed the concept of *il-rah,* or "tribal road." A major pastoral tribe such as the Basseri has a traditional route and schedule. The route, consisting of the localities in the order in which each is visited, follows existing passes and lines of communication. The schedule, which regulates the length of time each location will be occupied, depends on the maturation of different pastures and the movements of other tribes. The *il-rah* is regarded, in effect, as the property of the tribe. Local populations and authorities recognize the tribe's right to pass along roads and cultivated lands, to draw water from the public wells, and to pasture flocks on public land.

The Basseri herd sheep and goats together, with one shepherd (a boy or unmarried man) responsible for a flock of 300 to 400 animals. Children of both sexes are usually responsible for herding the baby animals (lambs and kids). Milk and its by-products are the most important commodities, but wool, hides, and meat are also important to the economy of the Basseri. Both wool and hides are traded, but they are even more useful within the tribe. The Basseri, especially the women, are skilled spinners and weavers; much of their time is spent at these activities. Saddlebags and pack bags are woven on horizontal looms from homespun wool and hair, as are carpets, sleeping rugs, and the characteristic black tents made of panels of woven goat hair. This hair provides an exceptionally versatile cloth. For winter use, it retains heat and repels water; in the summer, it insulates against heat and permits free circulation of air.

Lambskin hides also serve many purposes. When plucked and turned inside out, they are made into storage bags to hold water, buttermilk, sour milk, and other liquids.

Most of the Basseri must trade for the necessities and luxury items they do not produce within the community. The staple items they sell are butter, wool, lambskins, rope, and occasionally livestock.

The Lapps. The Lapps practice reindeer herding in northwestern Scandinavia where Finland, Sweden, and Norway share common frontiers. It is a typical Arctic habitat: cold, windswept, with long, dark days for half the year. Considerable change has occurred recently, so we first discuss the food-getting strategy in the 1950s, as described by Ian Whitaker and T. I. Itkonen.[28]

The Lapps herd their reindeer either intensively or, more often, extensively. In the intensive system, the herd is constantly under observation within a fenced area for the whole year. Intensively herded reindeer and other animals are accustomed to human contact. Hence, the summer corralling of the females for milking and the breaking in of the ox-reindeer for use as work animals are not difficult tasks.

The extensive system involves allowing the animals to migrate over a large area. It requires little surveillance and encompasses large herds. Under this system, the reindeer are allowed to move through their seasonal feeding cycles watched by only one or two scouts. The other Lapps stay with the herd only when it has settled in its summer or winter habitat. But milking, breaking in, and corralling are harder in the extensive than in the intensive system because the animals are less accustomed to humans.

Even under the extensive system, which theoretically permits Lapps to engage in subsidiary economic activities such as hunting and fishing, the reindeer herd is the essential, if not the only, source of income. A family might possess as many as 1,000 reindeer, but usually the figure is half that number. Studies show 200 to be the minimum number of reindeer needed to provide for a family of four or five adults. Women may have shared the herding chores in the past under the intensive system, but

A roundup of reindeer in Norwegian Lappland

now under the extensive system men do the herding. Women still do the milking.

The Lapps eat the meat of the bull reindeer; the female reindeer are kept for breeding purposes. Bulls are slaughtered in the fall, after the mating season. Meat and hides are frequently sold or bartered for other food and necessities.

Reindeer are still herded nowadays, but instead of sleds, one sees and hears snowmobiles, all-terrain vehicles, and even helicopters used for herding. Ferries are used to move reindeer to and from different pastures, and the herders communicate by field telephones. With faster transportation, many Lapps now live in permanent homes and can still get to their herds in hours. Lapp children spend much of their time in school and, consequently, do not learn much of the herding ways. The Norwegian government now regulates pastoralism, licensing pastoralists and trying to limit the number of reindeer they can herd.[29]

General Features of Pastoralism. In recent times, pastoralism has been practiced mainly in grassland and other semiarid habitats that are not especially suitable for cultivation without some significant technological input such as irrigation. Most pastoralists are nomadic, moving camp fairly frequently to find water and new pasture for their herds. But other pastoralists have somewhat more sedentary lives—they may move from one settlement to another in different seasons, or they may send some people out to travel with the herds in different seasons. Pastoral communities are usually small, consisting of a group of related families.[30] Individuals or families may own their own animals, but decisions about when and where to move the herds are community decisions.

As we have noted, there is a great deal of interdependence between pastoral and agricultural groups. That is, trade is usually necessary for pastoral groups to survive.

ENVIRONMENTAL RESTRAINTS ON FOOD-GETTING

Of great interest to anthropologists is why different societies have different methods of getting food. Archaeological evidence suggests that major changes in food-getting—such as the domestication of plants and animals—have been independently invented in at least several areas of the world. Yet, despite these comparable inventions and their subsequent spread by diffusion and migration, there is still wide diversity in the means by which people obtain food.

How much does the physical environment affect food-getting? Anthropologists have concluded that the physical environment by itself has a restraining, rather than a determining, effect on the major types of subsistence. Because they have very short growing seasons, cold regions of the earth are not particularly conducive to the growing of plants. No society we know of has practiced agriculture in the Arctic; instead, people who live there rely primarily on animals for food. But both food collection (as among the Inuit) and food production (as among the Lapps) can be practiced in cold areas. Indeed, cross-cultural evidence indicates that neither food collection nor food production is significantly associated with any particular type of habitat.[31]

We know that food collection has been practiced at one time or another in almost all areas of the earth. The physical environment does seem to have some effect on what kind of food collection is practiced, that is, on the extent to which food collectors will depend on plants, animals, or fish. Farther away from the equator, food collectors depend much less on plants for food and much more on animals and fish.[32] Lewis Binford argues that fishing becomes increasingly important in cold climates because food collectors need nonportable housing in severe winters to protect themselves from the cold. Therefore they cannot rely on large animals that usually have to feed themselves by moving over considerable distances in the winter. Fishing is more localized than hunting, and therefore food collectors who rely on fishing can stay in their nonportable houses in winter.[33]

THE EFFECT OF FOOD-GETTING ON THE ENVIRONMENT

Many people are now aware of industrial pollution—the dumping of industrial wastes in the ground or into rivers, the spewing of chemicals into the air through smokestacks. But we don't often realize how much humans have altered the environment by the ways they collect and produce food.

Consider irrigation. There are various ways to capture water for irrigation. Water can be channeled from rivers; rainwater can be caught in terraces carved out of hillsides; ancient water can be pumped up from vast underground "reservoirs" called aquifers. But not all of the water drawn for irrigation seeps into the ground. Much of it evaporates, leaving behind minerals and salts. And the more a piece of land has been irrigated, the saltier the ground becomes. Eventually, the soil becomes too salty to grow crops effectively. Some archaeologists have suggested that the accumulation of toxic salts in the soil at least partially explains the doom or decline of various groups in the past. For example, salinization may have contributed to the decline of the earliest city-states in Mesopotamia (present-day southern Iraq and southwestern Iran). The Hohokam farmers who lived in Arizona had about 150 miles of canals for irrigation; some of their ditches were 15 feet deep and 25 feet wide. In fact, their irrigation networks were comparable to those that served the Aztecs in precolumbian Mexico City. The Hohokam seem to have vanished around A.D. 1400, perhaps because the salty soil "poisoned" their crops. Today much of the soil is still too salty for cultivation.

The lessons of history may not have been learned yet. The San Joaquin Valley of California, perhaps the most productive agricultural area in the world, now has a serious salinization problem. One "solution" in many of the areas of the "Great American Desert" is to pump water up from underground. Indeed, in many places there is a great deal of water underground. For example, the Ogallala aquifer, which underlies parts of Nebraska, Kansas, Texas, Oklahoma, Colorado, and New Mexico, contains water left from the Ice Ages. But the pumping solution, if it is a solution, is only a short-term fix, for the huge Ogallala aquifer is also the fastest-disappearing aquifer. The only question is how long it will take to disappear.

Too many people raising too many animals can also have serious effects on the environment. We can easily imagine how the possibility of profit might inspire people to try to raise more animals than the land will support. For example, 300 years ago the Great American Desert looked like a vast grassland. It supported large herds of buffalo, which in the next 200 years were all but exterminated by overhunting. The white settlers soon discovered they could raise cattle and sheep on this grassland, but in many parts of it the land was overgrazed. It took the swirling dust storms of the 1930s to make people realize that overgrazing as well as poor farming practices could be disastrous. The problems are not just recent ones. The Norse colonized Greenland and Iceland around A.D. 800. But overgrazing of pasture undoubtedly contributed to soil erosion and the disappearance or decline of the colonies by A.D. 1500.

Are environmental problems associated only with food production? Although food producers may be the worst offenders, there is reason to think that foragers may also have sometimes overfished, overgathered, or overhunted. For example, some scholars suspect that the movement of humans into the New World was mainly responsible for the disappearance of the mammoth. Unfortunately, there is little evidence that humans have been good conservers in the past. That does not mean that humans cannot do better in the future. But they have to want to.

Sources: *"Plundering Earth Is Nothing New," Los Angeles Times News Service as reported in the* New Haven Register, *June 12, 1994, pp. A18–19;* Marc Reisner, Cadillac Desert: The American West and Its Disappearing Water, *rev. ed. (New York: Penguin Books, 1993); Robert Dirks, "Hunger and Famine," in Carol R. Ember, Melvin Ember, and Peter N. Peregrine, eds.,* Research Frontiers in Anthropology *(Englewood Cliffs, NJ: Prentice Hall, 1995). Prentice Hall/ Simon & Schuster Custom Publishing.*

There is one habitat that may have precluded food collection until recent times. If it were not for the nearness of food producers (particularly agriculturalists), recent food collectors such as the Mbuti Pygmies (of central Africa) could probably not have supported themselves in the tropical forest habitats where they now live.[34] Tropical forests are lush in plants, but they do not provide much in the way of reachable fruits, seeds, and flowers that can be eaten by humans. Animals are available in tropical forests, but typically they are lean and do not provide humans with sufficient carbohydrates or fat. Like the Pygmy groups who hunt and gather in the forest, many tropical food collectors trade for agricultural products; other collectors cultivate some crops in addition to hunting and gathering. It would seem, then, that food collectors could not survive in tropical forests were it not for the carbohydrates they obtain from agriculturalists (whoever they are).

When we contrast horticulture and intensive agriculture, the physical environment appears to explain some of the variation. Approximately 80 percent of all societies that practice horticulture or simple agriculture are in the tropics, whereas 75 percent of all societies that practice intensive agriculture are *not* in tropical forest environments.[35]

Tropical forests have abundant rainfall. But, despite the attractiveness of lush vegetation and brilliant coloring, tropical forest lands do not usually offer favorable environments for intensive agriculture. Perhaps the heavy rainfall quickly washes away certain minerals from cleared land. Also, the difficulty of controlling insect pests and weeds (which abound in tropical forests)[36] may make intensive agriculture less productive.

But difficulty is not impossibility. Today, there are some areas (for instance, the Mekong Delta of Vietnam) whose tropical forests have been cleared and prevented from growing up again by the intensive cultivation of rice in paddies. And, although cultivation is not normally possible in dry lands (because of insufficient natural rainfall to sustain crops), agriculture can be practiced where there are oases—small, naturally watered areas where crops can be grown with a simple technology—or rivers that can be tapped by irrigation (one of the techniques used with intensive agriculture).

The animals raised by pastoralists depend primarily on grass for food, so it is not surprising that pastoralism is typically practiced in grassland regions of the earth. These regions may be **steppes** (dry, low grass cover), **prairies** (taller, better-watered grass), or **savannas** (tropical grasslands).

The grassland habitat favors large game and hence supports both hunting and pastoral technologies, except where a machine technology makes intensive agriculture possible, as in parts of the United States, Canada, and Ukraine.

Very different strategies of food-getting have been practiced in the same environment over time. For example, a dramatic illustration is the history of the Imperial Valley in California. The complex systems of irrigation now used in that dry-land area have made it a very productive region. Yet about 400 years ago, this same valley supported only hunting and gathering groups who subsisted on wild plants and animals.

It is evident from the Imperial Valley example and many others like it that the physical environment does not by itself account for the system of food-getting in an area. (Even a polar environment could have agriculture with heated greenhouses, but it would be too expensive.) Technological advances as well as enormous capital investment in irrigation, labor, and equipment have made intensive agriculture possible in the Imperial Valley. But the agriculture there is precarious, depending on sources of water and power from elsewhere. In a prolonged drought, it may be difficult or too expensive to obtain the needed water. And should the prices for vegetables fall, the farming businesses in the Imperial Valley could find themselves unable to finance the investment and borrowing they need to continue. So technological and social and political rather than environmental factors mostly determine what kind of food-getting can be practiced in a given environment.

THE ORIGIN OF FOOD PRODUCTION

▼

During the period from about 40,000 years ago to about 15,000 years ago, which we know best archaeologically for Europe, people seem to have gotten most of their food from hunting the available migratory herds of large animals, such as wild cattle, antelope, bison, and mammoths. These hunter-gatherers were probably highly mobile in order to follow the migrations of the animals. Beginning about 14,000 years ago, people in some regions began to depend less on big-game hunting and more on relatively stationary food resources such as fish, shellfish, small game, and wild plants. Salt- and freshwater food supplies may have become more abundant in many areas after the glaciers withdrew.

In the Imperial Valley of Southern California, agriculture is not possible without irrigation. Here we see the irrigated fields next to desert just south of the Salton Sea.

As the ice melted, the level of the oceans rose and formed inlets and bays where crabs, clams, and sea mammals could be found. In some areas, particularly Europe and the Near East, the exploitation of local and relatively permanent resources may have accounted for an increasingly settled way of life.

We see the first evidence of a changeover to food production—the cultivation and domestication of plants and animals—in the Near East about 8000 B.C. This shift occurred, probably independently, in other areas as well. There is evidence of cultivation some time around 6000 B.C. in China, Southeast Asia (what is now Malaysia, Thailand, Cambodia, and Vietnam), and Africa. In the New World, there appear to have been several places of original cultivation and domestication. The highlands of Mexico (about 7000 B.C.) and the central Andes around Peru (by about 6000 B.C.) were probably the most important in terms of food plants used today.

Most peoples currently are food producers rather than food collectors. But why did people start to produce their food? We know that an economic transformation occurred in widely separate areas of the world beginning after about 10,000 years ago, as people began to domesticate plants and animals. But why did domestication occur? And why did it occur independently in different places within a period of a few thousand years? (Considering that people depended only on wild plants and animals for millions of years, the differences in exactly when domestication first occurred in different parts of the world seem small.) There are many theories of why food production developed; most have tried to explain the origin of domestication in the Near East.

Lewis Binford and Kent Flannery suggested that *some change,* not necessarily environmental, in external circumstances must have induced or favored the changeover to food production.[37] As Flannery pointed out, there is no evidence of a great economic incentive for hunter-gatherers to become food producers. In fact, as we have seen, some contemporary hunter-gatherers may actually obtain adequate nutrition with far *less* work than many agriculturalists.

Binford and Flannery thought that the incentive to domesticate animals and plants may have been a desire to reproduce what was wildly abundant in the most bountiful or optimum hunting and gathering areas. Because of population growth in the optimum areas, people might have moved to surrounding areas containing fewer wild resources. It would have been in those marginal areas that people turned to food production in order to reproduce what they used to have.

The Binford-Flannery model seems to fit the archaeological record in the Levant (the southwestern part of the Fertile Crescent), where population increase did precede the first signs of domestication.[38] But as Flannery admitted, in some regions, such as southwestern Iran, the optimum hunting-gathering areas do not show population increase before the emergence of domestication.[39]

The Binford-Flannery model focuses on population pressure in a small area as the incentive to turn to food production. Mark Cohen theorized that it was population pressure on a global scale that explains why so many of the world's peoples adopted agriculture within the span of a few thousand years.[40] He argued that hunter-gatherers all over the world gradually increased in population so that by about 10,000 years ago the world was more or less filled with food collectors. Thus people could no longer relieve population pressure by moving to uninhabited areas. To support their increasing populations, they would have had to exploit a broader range of less desirable wild foods; that is, they would have had to switch to broad-spectrum collecting, or they would have had to increase the yields of the most desirable wild plants by weeding, protecting them from animal pests, and perhaps deliberately planting the most productive among them. Cohen suggested that people might have tried a variety of these strategies to support themselves but would generally have ended up depending on cultivation because that would have been the most efficient way to allow more people to live in one place.

Recently, some archaeologists have returned to the idea that climatic change played a role in the emergence of agriculture. It seems clear from the evidence now available that the climate of the Near East about 13,000–12,000 years ago became more seasonal: the summers got hotter and drier than before and the winters became colder. These climatic changes may have favored the emergence of annual species of grain that archeologically we see proliferating in many areas of the Near East.[41] Some food collectors intensively exploited the seasonal grains, developing an elaborate technology for storing and processing the grains and giving up their previous nomadic existence to do so. The transition to agriculture may have occurred when sedentary food collection no longer provided sufficient resources for the population. This change could have happened because sedentarization led to population increase and therefore resource scarcity,[42] or because local wild resources became depleted after people settled down in permanent villages.[43]

Change to a more seasonal climate might also have led to a shortage of certain nutrients for food collectors. In the dry seasons certain nutrients would have been less available. For example, grazing animals get lean when grasses are not plentiful, and so meat from hunting would have been in short supply in the dry seasons. Although it may seem surprising, some recent hunter-gatherers have starved when they had to rely on lean meat. If they could have somehow increased their carbohydrate or fat intake, they might have been more likely to get through the periods of lean game.[44] So, it is possible that some wild-food collectors in the past thought of planting crops to get them through the dry seasons when hunting, fishing, and gathering did not provide enough carbohydrates and fat for them to avoid starvation.

THE SPREAD AND INTENSIFICATION OF FOOD PRODUCTION

Whatever the reasons for the switch to food production, we still need to explain why food production has supplanted food collection as the primary mode of subsistence. We cannot assume that collectors would automatically adopt production as a superior way of life once they understood the process of domestication. After all, as we have noted, domestication may entail more work and provide less security than the food-collecting way of life.

The spread of agriculture may be linked to the need for territorial expansion. As a sedentary, food-producing population grew, it may have been forced to expand into new territory. Some of this territory may have been vacant, but much of it was probably already occupied by food collectors. Although food production is not necessarily easier than collection, it is generally more productive per unit of land. Greater productivity enables more people to be supported in a given territory. In the competition for land between the faster-expanding food producers and the food collectors, the food producers may have had a significant advantage: they had more people in a given area. Thus, the foraging groups may have been more likely to lose out in the competition for land. Some groups may have adopted cultivation, abandoning the foraging way of life in order to survive. Other groups, continuing as food collectors, may have been forced to retreat into areas not desired by the cultivators. Today, as we have seen, the small number of remaining food collectors inhabit areas not particularly suitable for cultivation—dry lands, dense tropical forests, and polar regions.

Just as prior population growth might account for the origins of domestication, so at later periods further population growth and ensuing pressure on resources might at least partially explain the transformation of horticultural systems into intensive-agricultural systems. Ester Boserup suggested that intensification of agriculture, with a consequent increase in yield per acre, is not likely to develop naturally out of horticulture because intensification requires much more work.[45] She argued that people will be willing to intensify their labor only if they have to. Where emigration is not feasible, the prime mover behind intensification may be prior population growth. The need to pay taxes or tribute to a political authority may also stimulate intensification.

Intensive agriculture has not yet spread to every part of the world. Horticulture continues to be practiced in certain tropical regions, and there still are some pastoralists and food collectors. Some environments may make it difficult to adopt certain subsistence practices. For example, intensive agriculture cannot supplant horticulture in some tropical environments without tremendous investments in chemical fertilizers and pesticides, not to mention the additional labor required.[46] And enormous amounts of water may be required to make agriculturalists out of foragers and pastoralists who now exploit semiarid environments. Hence, the different kinds of food-getting practices we observe today throughout the world are likely to be with us for some time to come.

▼ SUMMARY

1. Food collection or foraging—hunting, gathering, and fishing—depends on wild plants and animals and is the oldest human food-getting technology. Today, however, only a small number of societies practice it, and they tend to inhabit marginal environments.

2. Food collectors can be found in various physical habitats. Most food collectors are nomadic, and population density is low. Usually, the small bands consist of related families, with the division of labor along age and gender lines only. Personal possessions are limited, individual land rights are seldom recognized, and people are not differentiated by class.

3. Beginning about 10,000 years ago, certain peoples in widely separated geographical locations began to make the revolutionary changeover to food production—the cultivation and raising of plants and animals. Over the centuries, food production began to supplant food collection as the predominant mode of subsistence.

4. Horticulturalists farm with relatively simple tools and methods and do not cultivate fields permanently. Their food supply is sufficient to support larger, more densely populated communities than can be fed by food collection. Their way of life is sedentary, although communities may move after some years to farm a new series of plots.

5. Intensive agriculture is characterized by techniques such as fertilization and irrigation that allow fields to be cultivated permanently. In contrast with horticultural societies, intensive agriculturalists are more likely to have towns and cities, a high degree of craft specialization, large differences in wealth and power, and more complex political organization. They are also more likely to face food shortages. In the modern world, intensive agriculture is increasingly mechanized and geared to production for a market.

6. Pastoralism is a subsistence technology involving principally the raising of large herds of animals. It is generally found in low-rainfall areas. Pastoralists tend to be nomadic, to have small communities consisting of related families, and to depend significantly on trade because they do not produce things (including certain types of food) they need.

7. Anthropologists generally agree that the physical environment normally exercises a restraining rather than determining influence on how people in an area get their food; technology and social and political factors may be more important.

8. Because food producers can support more people in a given territory than food collectors can, they may have had a competitive advantage in confrontations with food collectors.

cash crops

commercialization

extensive or shifting
  cultivation

food collection

food production

foragers

horticulture

intensive agriculture

pastoralism

prairie

savanna

slash-and-burn

steppe

subsistence
  technology

▼ CRITICAL QUESTIONS

1. Why might meat be valued more than plant foods in many societies?

2. Why might foragers be less likely than intensive agriculturalists to suffer from food shortages?

3. Why do certain foods in a society come to be preferred?

▼ SUGGESTED READING

BOSERUP, E. *The Conditions of Agricultural Growth: The Economics of Agrarian Change under Population Pressure.* Chicago: Aldine, 1965. The classic discussion of the theory that prior population growth is the major cause of agricultural development, at least in recent times.

EMBER, M., EMBER, C. R., AND LEVINSON, D., EDS. *Portraits of Culture: Ethnographic Originals.* Englewood Cliffs, NJ: Prentice Hall, 1994. Prentice Hall/Simon & Schuster Custom Publishing. This series includes more than forty ethnographic portraits of, among others, foragers, horticulturalists, and intensive agriculturalists.

HARRIS, M., AND ROSS, E. B., EDS. *Food and Evolution: Toward a Theory of Human Food Habits.* Philadelphia: Temple University Press, 1987. A collection of original papers on why humans in different times and places eat what they do. The perspectives of several disciplines are represented, including primatology, nutrition, biological anthropology, archaeology, psychology, and agricultural economics.

JOACHIM, M. "Hunting and Gathering Societies." In D. Levinson and M. Ember, eds., *Encyclopedia of Cultural Anthropology.* New York: Henry Holt, 1995. A discussion of the cultural variability of recent foraging societies in subsistence, settlement pattern, political organization, economics, conflict, and changes.

SALZMAN, P. "Pastoralism." In D. Levinson and M. Ember, eds., *Encyclopedia of Cultural Anthropology.* New York: Henry Holt, 1995. An up-to-date review and discussion of how pastoralists have adjusted to the modern world of industrialized and developing states.

TURNER, B. L., AND BRUSH, S. B. *Comparative Farming Systems.* New York: Guilford, 1987. The contributors to this volume, including anthropologists, economists, geographers, and rural sociologists, discuss the major types of agricultural systems throughout the world and the forces of change acting on them.

▼ NOTES

[1]Carol R. Ember, "Myths about Hunter-Gatherers," *Ethnology,* 17 (1978): 439–48.

[2]Carmel Schrire, ed., *Past and Present in Hunter-Gatherer Studies* (Orlando, FL: Academic Press, 1984); Fred R. Myers, "Critical Trends in the Study of Hunter-Gatherers," *Annual Review of Anthropology,* 17 (1988):261–82.

[3]The discussion of the Australian aborigines is based on Richard A. Gould, *Yiwara: Foragers of the Australian Desert* (New York: Scribner's, 1969).

[4]Victoria K. Burbank, *Fighting Women: Anger and Aggression in Aboriginal Australia* (Berkeley: University of California Press, 1994), p. 23. For a description of daily life see Victoria K. Burbank, "Australian Aborigines: An

Adolescent Mother and Her Family," in Melvin Ember, Carol R. Ember, and David Levinson, eds., *Portraits of Culture: Ethnographic Originals* (Englewood Cliffs, NJ: Prentice Hall, 1995). Prentice Hall/Simon & Schuster Custom Publishing.

[5]Material is drawn from Ernest S. Burch, Jr., "The North Alaskan Eskimos: A Changing Way of Life," in Melvin Ember, Carol R. Ember, and David Levinson, eds., *Portraits of Culture: Ethnographic Originals* (Englewood Cliffs, NJ: Prentice Hall, 1995). Prentice Hall/Simon & Schuster Custom Publishing. Ernest S. Burch, Jr., *The Eskimos* (Norman: University of Oklahoma Press, 1988).

[6]Data from Robert B. Textor, comp., *A Cross-Cultural Summary* (New Haven, CT: HRAF Press, 1967); and Elman R. Service, *The Hunters*, 2nd ed. (Englewood Cliffs, NJ: Prentice Hall, 1979).

[7]Gisli Palsson, "Hunters and Gatherers of the Sea," in Tim Ingold, David Riches, James Woodburn, eds., *Hunters and Gatherers 1: History, Evolution and Social Change* (New York: St. Martin's Press, 1988), pp. 189–204.

[8]George P. Murdock and Caterina Provost, "Factors in the Division of Labor by Sex: A Cross-Cultural Analysis," *Ethnology*, 12 (1973): 207.

[9]Richard B. Lee, "What Hunters Do for a Living, or, How to Make Out on Scarce Resources," in Richard B. Lee and Irven DeVore, eds., *Man the Hunter* (Chicago: Aldine, 1968), pp. 30–48; and Irven DeVore and Melvin J. Konner, "Infancy in Hunter-Gatherer Life: An Ethological Perspective," in N. F. White, ed., *Ethology and Psychiatry* (Toronto: Ontario Mental Health Foundation and University of Toronto Press, 1974), pp. 113–41.

[10]Carol R. Ember, "Myths about Hunter-Gatherers."

[11]Frederick D. McCarthy and Margaret McArthur, "The Food Quest and the Time Factor in Aboriginal Economic Life," in C. P. Mountford, ed., *Records of the Australian-American Scientific Expedition to Arnhem Land. Volume 2: Anthropology and Nutrition* (Melbourne: Melbourne University Press, 1960).

[12]Richard B. Lee, *The !Kung San: Men, Women, and Work in a Foraging Society* (Cambridge: Cambridge University Press, 1979), pp. 256–58, 278–80.

[13]Dennis Werner, "Trekking in the Amazon Forest," *Natural History*, November 1978, 42–54.

[14]Data from Textor, comp., *A Cross-Cultural Summary*.

[15]This section is based largely on Raymond Hames, "Yanomamö: Varying Adaptations of Foraging Horticulturalists," in Melvin Ember, Carol R. Ember, and David Levinson, eds., *Portraits of Culture: Ethnographic Originals* (Englewood Cliffs, NJ: Prentice Hall, 1995). Prentice Hall/Simon & Schuster Custom Publishing.

[16]Napolean Chagnon, *Yanomamö: The Fierce People*, 3rd ed. (New York: Holt, Rinehart & Winston, 1987) p. 60.

[17]This section is based mostly on Melvin Ember's fieldwork on the islands of American Samoa in 1955–1956.

[18]Douglas L. Oliver, *Ancient Tahitian Society. Volume 1: Ethnography* (Honolulu: University of Hawaii Press, 1974), pp. 252–53.

[19]Seth S. King, "Some Farm Machinery Seems Less Than Human," *New York Times*, April 8, 1979, p. E9.

[20]Ernestine Friedl, *Vasilika: A Village in Modern Greece* (New York: Holt, Rinehart & Winston, 1962).

[21]Gerald Cannon Hickey, *Village in Vietnam* (New Haven, CT: Yale University Press, 1964), pp. 135–65.

[22]Carol R. Ember, "The Relative Decline in Women's Contribution to Agriculture with Intensification," *American Anthropologist*, 85 (1983): 289.

[23]Data from Textor, comp., *A Cross-Cultural Summary*.

[24]Peggy F. Barlett, "Industrial Agriculture," in Stuart Plattner, ed., *Economic Anthropology* (Stanford, CA: Stanford University Press, 1989), pp. 253–91.

[25]U.S. Bureau of the Census, *Statistical Abstract of the United States: 1993*, 113th ed. (Washington, D.C.: U.S. Government Printing Office, 1993).

[26]Susan H. Lees and Daniel G. Bates, "The Origins of Specialized Nomadic Pastoralism: A Systemic Model," *American Antiquity,* 39 (1974): 187–93.

[27]Fredrik Barth, *Nomads of South Persia* (Oslo: Universitetsforlaget, 1964; Boston: Little, Brown, 1968).

[28]Ian Whitaker, *Social Relations in a Nomadic Lappish Community* (Oslo: Utgitt av Norsk Folksmuseum, 1955); and T. I. Itkonen, "The Lapps of Finland," *Southwestern Journal of Anthropology,* 7 (1951): 32–68.

[29]Robert Paine, *Herds of the Tundra* (Washington, D.C.: Smithsonian Institution Press, 1994).

[30]Data from Textor, comp., *A Cross-Cultural Summary.*

[31]Ibid.

[32]Lewis R. Binford, "Mobility, Housing, and Environment: A Comparative Study," *Journal of Anthropological Research,* 46 (1990): 119–52; see also Bobbi Low, "Human Responses to Environmental Extremeness and Uncertainty," in Elizabeth Cashdan, ed., *Risk and Uncertainty in Tribal and Peasant Economies* (Boulder, CO: Westview Press, 1990), pp. 242–43.

[33]The few food collectors in cold areas relying primarily on hunting have animals (dogs, horses, reindeer) that can carry transportable housing—see Binford, "Mobility, Housing, and Environment."

[34]Robert C. Bailey, Genevieve Head, Mark Jenike, Bruce Owen, Robert Rectman, and Elzbieta Zechenter, "Hunting and Gathering in Tropical Rain Forest: Is It Possible?" *American Anthropologist,* 91 (1989): 59–82.

[35]Data from Textor, comp., *A Cross-Cultural Summary.*

[36]Daniel H. Janzen, "Tropical Agroecosystems," *Science,* December 21, 1973, 1212–18. For an argument supporting the "weeding" explanation, see Robert L. Carneiro, "Slash-and-Burn Cultivation among the Kuikuru and Its Implications for Settlement Patterns," in Yehudi Cohen, ed., *Man in Adaptation: The Cultural Present* (Chicago: Aldine, 1968).

[37]Lewis R. Binford, "Post-Pleistocene Adaptations," and Kent V. Flannery, "The Origins and Ecological Effects of Early Domestication in Iran and the Near East," in Stuart Struever, ed., *Prehistoric Agriculture* (Garden City, NY: Natural History Press, 1971), pp. 22–49, 50–70.

[38]Gary A. Wright, "Origins of Food Production in Southwestern Asia: A Survey of Ideas," *Current Anthropology,* 12 (1971): 470.

[39]Kent V. Flannery, "The Research Problem," in Kent V. Flannery, ed., *Guila Naquitz: Archaic Foraging and Early Agriculture in Oaxaca, Mexico* (Orlando, FL: Academic Press, 1986), pp. 10–11.

[40]Mark N. Cohen, "Population Pressure and the Origins of Agriculture," in Charles A. Reed, ed., *Origins of Agriculture* (The Hague: Mouton, 1977), pp. 138–41; see also Mark Nathan Cohen, *The Food Crisis in Prehistory: Overpopulation and the Origins of Agriculture* (New Haven, CT: Yale University Press, 1977), p. 279.

[41]Roger Byrne, "Climatic Change and the Origins of Agriculture," in Linda Manzanilla, ed., *Studies in the Neolithic and Urban Revolutions,* British Archaeological Reports International Series 349 (Oxford, 1987), pp. 21–34, referred to in Mark A. Blumler and Roger Byrne, "The Ecological Genetics of Domestication and the Origins of Agriculture," *Current Anthropology,* 32 (1991): 23–35; Donald O. Henry, *From Foraging to Agriculture: The Levant at the End of the Ice Age* (Philadelphia: University of Pennsylvania Press, 1989), pp. 30–38; Joy McCorriston and Frank Hole, "The Ecology of Seasonal Stress and the Origins of Agriculture in the Near East," *American Anthropologist,* 93 (1991): 46–69.

[42]Henry, *From Foraging to Agriculture,* p. 41.

[43]McCorriston and Hole, "The Ecology of Seasonal Stress."

[44]John D. Speth and Katherine A. Spielmann, "Energy Source, Protein Metabolism, and Hunter-Gatherer Subsistence Strategies," *Journal of Anthropological Archaeology,* 2 (1983): 1–31.

[45]Ester Boserup, *The Conditions of Agricultural Growth: The Economics of Agrarian Change under Population Pressure* (Chicago: Aldine, 1965).

[46]Janzen, "Tropical Agroecosystems."

Economic Systems

When we think of economics, we think of things and activities involving money. We think of the costs of goods and services such as food, rent, haircuts, and movie tickets. We may also think of factories, farms, and other enterprises that produce the goods and services we need or think we need. In our society, workers may stand before a moving belt for eight hours, tightening identical bolts that glide by. For this task they are given bits of paper that may be exchanged for food, shelter, and other goods or services. But many societies (indeed, most that are known to anthropology) did not have money or the equivalent of the factory worker. Still, all societies have economic systems, whether or not these involve the use of money. All societies have customs specifying how people gain access to natural resources; customary ways of transforming or converting those resources, through labor, into necessities and other desired goods and services; and customs for distributing (and perhaps exchanging) goods and services.

As we shall see in this chapter, a great deal of the cross-cultural variation in economic systems is predicted by how a society gets its food. Other aspects of the culture also affect the economic system. These other influences, which we cover in subsequent chapters, include the presence or absence of social (class and gender) inequality, family and kinship groups, and the political system.

THE ALLOCATION OF RESOURCES

▼

Natural Resources: Land

Every society has access to natural resources—land, water, plants, animals, minerals. Every society has cultural rules for determining who has access to particular resources and what can be done with them. In societies like our own, where land and many other things may be bought and sold, land is divided into precisely measurable units, the borders of which are sometimes invisible. Relatively small plots of land and the resources on them are usually owned by individuals. Large plots of land are generally owned collectively. The owner may be a government agency, such as the National Parks Service, which owns land on behalf of the entire population of the United States. Or the owner may be what we call a corporation—a private collective of shareholders. In the United States, property ownership entails a more or less exclusive right to use land or other resources

(called "usufruct") in whatever ways the owner wishes, including the right to withhold or prevent use by others. In the United States and many other societies, property ownership also includes the right to "alienate" property—to sell, give away, bequeath, or destroy the resources owned.

Our system of land allocation is unknown to most food collectors and most horticulturalists, for two reasons. First, in their societies, there is no individual ownership of land or ownership by a group of unrelated shareholders. If there is collective ownership, it is always by groups of related people (kinship groups) or by territorial groups (bands or villages). Second, even if there is collective ownership, such ownership is different from ours in that land is not bought and sold.

Thus, it is society, and not the individual, that specifies what is considered property and what are the rights and duties associated with that property.[1] These specifications are social in nature, for they may be changed over time. For example, France declared all its beaches to be public, thereby stating, in effect, that the ocean shore is not a resource that can be owned by an individual. As a result, all the hotels and individuals that had fenced off portions of the best beaches for their exclusive use had to remove the fences.

In our country, people ask whether abuse of the rights of ownership is a factor in the growing pollution of our air and water. Hence, federal, state, and local governments are becoming more active in regulating exactly what people (and even public agencies) can do with the land they own. Such regulation may be new, but our society has always limited the rights of ownership. For example, land may be taken by the government for use in the construction of a highway; we may be paid compensation, but usually we cannot prevent confiscation. Similarly, we are not allowed to burn our houses, nor can we use them as brothels or munitions arsenals. In short, even under our individualistic system of ownership, property is not entirely private.

How societies differ in their rules for access to land and other natural resources seems to be related in part to how they differ in food-getting. Let us now examine how food collectors, horticulturalists, pastoralists, and intensive agriculturalists structure rights to land in different ways. We examine traditional patterns first. As we shall note later, traditional rights to land have been considerably affected by expanding state societies that have spread to and colonized native societies in the New World, Africa, and Asia.

DOES COMMUNAL OWNERSHIP LEAD TO ECONOMIC DISASTER?

A common idea in Western thought is that when land or other resources are held in common, serious damage results because individuals do not see it in their own interest to protect those resources. In a paper called "The Tragedy of the Commons," Garrett Hardin suggested that if animals are grazed on common land it is economically rational for individual animal owners to graze as many animals as possible, since they do not incur the pasture costs. According to Hardin, tragedy results because pasture is degraded by over-grazing and then productivity falls. Similarly, why shouldn't a "fisher" (a person who fishes) take as much fish as possible from the ocean (a kind of commons) and not worry about the consequences? On the other hand, if the resource is privately owned, individuals might try to conserve their resources

because degrading those resources will cost them in the long run by decreasing their yields. The theory then is that, in order to minimize costs and maximize yields, private owners will find it rational to conserve their resources.

Is it really true that communal ownership tends to result in overexploitation of resources and lower yields and private ownership tends to result in conservation of resources and higher yields? We do not have enough studies yet to generalize, but we do know about instances where communal grazing lands have been more productive than private grazing lands in comparable climates. For example, the Borana of Ethiopia, who have communal grazing, produce more animal protein per acre at lower cost than Australian cattle ranches (the climates are similar). And there are instances,

such as the overgrazing in the Great American Desert (described in the box titled "The Effect of Food-Getting on the Environment" in the preceding chapter), where private ownership did lead to degradation of the environment.

We have to remember that communal ownership does not mean that anyone can graze their animals or fish at any time. Communities and kin groups often govern rights to pasturage or fishing, and only members of the group have rights of access and use. As we saw in the last chapter, pastoralists such as the Basseri have well-defined, socially arranged travel routes, moving their herds when conditions demand. For traditional pastoralists, mobility is often the key to prevent overgrazing. Similarly, many groups that fish have strict rules regulating access to fishing grounds, and some have "conser-

Food Collectors. As we have noted, members of food-collecting societies generally do not own land individually. The reason is probably that land itself has no intrinsic value for food collectors; what is of value is the presence of game and wild plant life on the land. If game moves away or food resources become less plentiful, the land is less valuable. Therefore, the greater the possibility that the wild food supply in a particular locale will fluctuate, the less desirable it is to parcel out small areas of land to individuals and the more advantageous it is to make land ownership communal. The Hadza of Tanzania, for example, do not believe that they have exclusive

rights over the land on which they hunt. Any member of the group can hunt, gather, or draw water wherever he or she likes.[2]

Although food collectors rarely practice anything resembling individual ownership of land or other resources, there is considerable variation in the extent of communal "ownership." In some societies, such as the Hadza, groups do not claim or defend particular territories. In fact, the Hadza do not even restrict use of their land to members of their own language group. Even though outsiders have steadily intruded on Hadza territory recently, such encroachment has not been protested. But the vation" rules as well. For example, the Palauans of Micronesia usually allow only members of a cluster of villages to fish in the adjacent lagoon waters inside the fringing reef. Traditionally, people took only what they could eat, and there were "laws" governing the times that people could fish for certain species.

Restricted access to communal property may be the main way that pastoralists and fishers prevent degradation of their environment. Some groups, such as the Palauans, clearly also have conservation rules. But we do not know how many pastoralists and fishers have such rules. For example, the Ponam of New Guinea do not appear to conserve fish resources, even though they restrict access to their communal fishing territories. They do value the prestige associated with generosity, and consequently they try to collect more fish than they need in order to give some away.

Development and commer-cialization may be more important than private versus communal ownership in leading to overgrazing or overfishing, at least initially. In Palau, which had traditional conservation practices, serious overfishing became a problem apparently only when people started to sell fish to Japanese colonists for imported trade goods. Some of those goods (e.g., nets and motors) helped to make fishing easier. Eventually, overfishing resulted in reduced catches and increased costs of fishing, and the Palauans had to buy much of their fish in imported cans. In arid areas of the Sahel in Africa, development may have led to pastoral overgrazing. Boreholes were built by development agencies to increase the water supply, but this practice often made people reluctant to move to new grazing land, so local land was overgrazed. In addition, the development of irrigation agriculture nearby decreased the amount of land available for pasturage.

So which is more likely in general to lead to conservation—communal ownership or private ownership? We cannot say yet. We need more systematic comparisons, of many cases of the two types of system, to tell us.

Sources: *Garrett Hardin, "The Tragedy of the Commons,"* Science, 162(1968): 1243-1248; *Bonnie M. McCay and James M. Acheson, "Introduction,"* and *James G. Carrier, "Marine Tenure and Conservation in Papua New Guinea,"* in Bonnie M. McCay and James M. Acheson, eds., The Question of Commons: The Culture and Ecology of Communal Resources *(Tucson: University of Arizona Press, 1987); Michael M. Horowitz, "Donors and Deserts: The Political Ecology of Destructive Development in the Sahel,"* in Rebecca Huss-Ashmore and Solomon H. Katz, eds., African Food Systems in Crisis. Part Two: Contending with Change *(New York: Gordon and Breach, 1990); R. E. Johannes,* Words of the Lagoon: Fishing and Marine Lore in the Palau District of Micronesia *(Berkeley: University of California Press, 1981); Robert Dirks, "Hunger and Famine,"* in Carol R. Ember, Melvin Ember, and Peter N. Peregrine, eds., Research Frontiers in Anthropology *(Englewood Cliffs, NJ: Prentice Hall, 1995). Prentice Hall/Simon & Schuster Custom Publishing. John J. Poggie, personal communication, 1994.*

Hadza are somewhat unusual—it is more common in food-collecting societies for a group of individuals (usually kin) to "own" land. To be sure, such ownership is not usually exclusive; typically some degree of access is provided to members of neighboring bands.[3]

At the other extreme, local groups in some foraging societies try to maintain exclusive rights to particular territories. The Owens Valley Paiute in the California part of the Great Basin lived all year in permanent villages along streams. A group of villagers claimed and defended a particular territory against intruders, who may or may not have been other Owens Valley Paiute. Why have some food collectors been more territorial than others? One suggestion is that when the plants and animals collected are predictably located and abundant, groups are more likely to be sedentary and to try to maintain exclusive control over territories. In contrast, when plant and animal resources are unpredictable in location or amount, territoriality will tend to be minimal.[4] Territorial food collectors appear to have predictably located resources *and* more permanent villages, so it is hard to know which is more important in determining whether territory will be defended.

Horticulturalists. Like food collectors, most horticulturalists do not have individual or family ownership of land. This may be because rapid depletion of the soil necessitates letting some of the land lie fallow for a period of years or abandoning an area after a few years and moving to a new location. There is no reason for individuals or families to claim permanent access to land that, given their technology, is not usable permanently. But unlike food collectors, horticulturalists do allocate particular plots of land to individuals or families for their use, although these individuals or families do not own the land in our sense of potentially permanent ownership.

Among the Mundurucu of Brazil, the village controls the rights to use land. People in the community can hunt and fish where they like, and they have the right to clear a garden plot wherever land belonging to the community is not being used. Gardens can be cultivated for only two years before the soil is exhausted; the land then reverts to the community. The Mundurucu distinguish between the land and the produce on the land, so that a person who cultivates the land owns the produce. (Similarly, the person who kills an animal or catches a fish owns it, no matter where it was obtained.) But, because all food is shared with others, it does not really matter who owns it. Rights to land became more individualized when Mundurucu men began to tap rubber trees for sale. Rights to a particular path in the forest (where trees were tapped) could not be bought and sold, but the rights could be inherited by a son or son-in-law.[5]

Pastoralists. The territory of pastoral nomads far exceeds that of most horticultural societies. Since their wealth ultimately depends upon two elements—mobile herds and fixed pasturage and water—pastoralists must combine the adaptive potential of both food collectors and horticulturalists. Like food collectors, they must know the potential of their territory—which can extend as much as 1,000 miles—so that they are assured a constant supply of grass and water. And, like horticulturalists, after their herds graze an area clean they must move on and let that land lie fallow until the grass renews itself. Also like horticulturalists, they depend for subsistence on human manipulation of a natural resource—animals, as opposed to the horticulturalists' land.

Although grazing land tends to be communally held, it is customary among pastoralists for animals to be owned by individuals.[6] Fredrik Barth argued that if animals were not so owned, the whole group might be in trouble because the members might be tempted to eat up their productive capital—their animals—in bad times. When animals are owned individually, a family whose herd drops below the minimum number of animals necessary for survival must drop out of nomadic life, at least temporarily, and work for wages in sedentary agricultural communities. But in so doing, such a family does not jeopardize other pastoral families. On the other hand, if the fortunate were to share their herds with the unfortunate, all might approach bankruptcy. Thus, Barth argued, individual ownership is adaptive for a pastoral way of life.[7]

John Dowling questioned that interpretation. As he pointed out, pastoral nomads are not the only ones who have to save some of their "crop" for future production. Horticulturalists must save some of their crop (in the form of seeds or tubers) for future planting. But horticulturalists generally lack private ownership of productive resources, so the necessity to save for future production cannot explain private ownership of animals in pastoral societies. Dowling suggested that private ownership will develop only in pastoral societies that depend on selling their products to nonpastoralists.[8] Thus, it may be the opportunity to sell their products as well as their labor that explains both the possibility of dropping out of nomadic life and the private ownership of animals among most pastoralists.

Intensive Agriculturalists. Individual ownership of land resources—including the right to use the resources and the right to sell or otherwise dispose of them—is common among intensive agriculturalists. The development of such ownership is partly a result of the possibility of using land season after season, which gives the land more or less permanent value. But the concept of individual ownership is also partly a political and social matter. So, for example, the occupation and cultivation of frontier land in the United States was transformed by law into individual ownership. Under the Homestead Act of 1862, if a person cleared a 160-acre piece of land and farmed it for five years, the federal government would consider that person the owner of the land. This practice is similar to the custom in some societies by which a kin group, a chief, or a community is obligated to assign a parcel of land to anyone who wishes to farm it. The difference is that once the American homesteader had become the owner of the land, the laws of this country gave the homesteader the right to dispose of it at will by selling or giving it away. Once individual ownership of land has become established, property owners may use their economic, and hence political, power to pass laws that favor themselves. In the early years of the United States, only property owners could vote.

Private individual ownership is usually associated with intensive agriculture, but not always. As we mentioned in the preceding chapter, intensive agriculture is usually associated with more complex political systems and with differences in wealth and power, so we need to understand the larger political and social context in order to fully understand particular systems of land allocation. For example, under the feudal and manor system in much of medieval Europe, land and protection were granted by a higher aristocrat to a lower aristocrat (vassal) in exchange for military service and other obligations. If the vassal had no heirs, the land reverted to the higher aristocrat. Most of the farming was done by commoners—tenants and serfs. Tenants were granted land by the lord of a manor in return for labor, a portion of the crops, and military service when needed. Tenancy could be passed on to the children, and tenants technically were free to leave, but it was not easy to leave. Serfs, who had similar obligations to the lord of the manor, were bound to the land and could not leave, but neither could they be ejected.

In recent times, some of the communist and socialist nations with intensive agriculture formed agricultural collectives. For example, after World War II, the small-farm holdings in a village in Bulgaria named Zamfirovo were incorporated into a village cooperative. Most of the villagers worked as laborers on the new cooperative, but every household was allocated a small plot by the cooperative on which to grow its own grain, vegetables, and grapes. These plots were fairly productive, and Westerners often attributed their productivity to private enterprise. But the cooperative provided much of the labor needed to plant and plow these plots, so they could hardly be considered private property. In 1989, after the overthrow of the Communist regime, the cooperative was dissolved; the land was divided and sold to private owners.[9]

In the United States and other capitalist societies, it may appear that private property owners have nearly absolute control over the use and disposal of their property. But the nearly absolute control is offset by the real absoluteness with which the owner can lose that property. In our society, the government can take a person's property as the penalty for inability to pay taxes. A lienholder can take it to satisfy a debt. Or the government can decide to take the property for some public purpose (usually with some compensation to the owner) under the right of eminent domain. A family that has farmed its land for a century can lose it in one year. Often, families lose property because of events over which they have no control—a national economic depression, a drought that causes a bad crop year, or a period of economic stagnation such as the one that followed the Civil War. In addition, where individual ownership is the custom, it is nearly always the case that some individuals do not own any land.

Colonialism and Natives' Control Over Land. Almost universally around the world, colonial conquerors and settlers have taken land away from the natives or aborigines. Even if the natives were given other land in exchange, as in Brazil and the United States in the last few hundred years, these reservations were often, if not always, poorer in potential

In societies with intensive agriculture, private ownership of land is common. The boundaries, as on this Minnesota farm, are usually clearly marked.

than the original land. (If the reservation land hadn't been poorer in quality, the settlers would have taken it for themselves.) In addition, the new centralized governments often tried to change how land was owned by the natives, almost always in the direction of individual or private ownership. If kin groups or larger social entities owned the land, it would be more difficult for the settlers to get the natives to give it up, either by sale or threat. Owners who were individuals could be dispossessed more easily.[10]

The newcomers who benefitted from these forced changes were not always people of European background, but they were always people from expanding state societies. Beginning in the late fifteenth century, the expanding groups came mostly from Western Europe. But in recent times (as well as in the millenia before and after the time of Christ), conquerors and settlers have come from India, China, Japan, Arabia, Scandinavia, Russia, and other countries. This is not to say that native peoples in Africa, Asia, and the New World were never guilty of conquering and exploiting others on their continents or elsewhere. They were. The Aztecs in Mexico and Central America, the native kingdoms in West Africa after about 800 years ago, and the Arabs after the rise of Islam were just some of the expanding state societies of the past, before the rise of the West. Wherever there have been "civilized" (urban) societies, there has been imperialism and colonialism.

In North America, the British recognized the principle that lands not ceded to the crown would be Indian hunting grounds, but such recognition of rights by the British and then by the United States remained in force only as long as the various Indian groups remained numerous enough to constitute a threat to the settlers. President Andrew Jackson, for example, called for a removal of all eastern Native American groups to "permanent" settlements west of the Mississippi. Some 90,000 people were removed. But as settlers moved west, native reservations were often reduced in size. Government agents usually assumed that "communal" forms of ownership were detrimental to progress and enacted laws to assign land to individuals.[11] In much of colonial Africa, governments ceded land to European-owned companies for development. Reserves were established for large native populations, who then were invariably forced to work as laborers on European-owned plantations and in European-owned mines. In Kenya, for example, Europeans who constituted less then 1 percent of the population acquired access to or control of 20 percent of the land, mostly in the highlands, where there was the greatest potential for commercial production of tea and coffee.[12]

Technology

In order to convert resources to food and other goods, every society makes use of a technology, which includes tools, constructions (such as fish traps), and required skills (such as how and where to set up a fish trap). Societies vary considerably in their technologies and in the way access to technology is allocated. For example, food collectors and pastoralists typically have fairly small tool kits; they must limit their tools (and their material possessions in general) to what they can comfortably carry with them. As for access to technology, food collectors and horticulturalists generally allow equal opportunity. In the absence of specialization, most individuals have the skills to make what they need. But in an industrial society like our own, the opportunity to acquire or use a particular technology (which may be enormously expensive as well as complex) is hardly available to all. Most of us may be able to buy a drill or a hammer, but few of us can buy the factory that makes it.

The tools most needed by food collectors are weapons for the hunt, digging sticks, and receptacles for gathering and carrying. Most hunters know the bow and arrow; Andaman Islanders used them exclusively for hunting game and large fish. Australian aborigines developed two types of boomerangs: a heavy one for a straight throw in killing game and a light, returning one for playing games or for scaring birds into nets strung between trees. The Semang of Malaya used poisoned darts and blowguns. The Mbuti Pygmies of Zaire still trap elephants and buffalo in deadfalls and nets. Of all food collectors, the Inuit probably had the most sophisticated weapons, including harpoons, compound bows, and ivory fishhooks. Yet the Inuit also had relatively fixed settlements with available storage space and dog teams and sleds for transportation.[13]

Among food collectors, tools are considered to belong to the person who made them. There is no way of gaining superiority over others through possession of tools, because whatever resources for toolmaking are available to one are available to all. In addition, the custom of sharing applies to tools as well as to food. For example, Elizabeth M. Thomas, speaking of the !Kung said, "the few possessions that Bushmen have are constantly circulating among the members of their groups."[14]

Pastoralists, like food collectors, are somewhat limited in their possessions, for they too are nomadic. But pastoralists can use their animals to carry some possessions. Each family owns its own tools, clothes, and perhaps a tent, as well as its own livestock. The livestock are the source of other needed articles, for the pastoralists often trade their herd products for the products of the townspeople.

Horticulturalists, on the other hand, are more self-sufficient than pastoralists. The knife for slashing and the hoe or stick for digging are their principal farming tools. What a person makes is considered his or her own, yet everyone is often obligated to lend tools to others. In Truk society, the owner of a canoe has first use of it. The same is true for farming implements. Yet if a close relative needs the canoe and finds it unused, it may be taken without permission. A distant relative or neighbor must ask permission to borrow any tools, but the owner may not refuse. If owners were to refuse, they would risk being scorned and refused if they were to need tools later.

Societies with intensive agriculture and industrialized societies are likely to have tools made by specialists—which means that tools must be acquired by trade or purchase. Probably because complex tools cost a considerable amount of money, they are less likely than simple tools to be shared except by those who contributed to the purchase price. For example, a diesel-powered combine requires a large amount of capital for its purchase and upkeep. The person who has supplied the capital is likely to regard the machine as individual private property and to regulate its use and disposal. Farmers may not have the capital to purchase the machine they need, so they may have to borrow from a bank. The owner must then use the machine to produce enough surplus to pay for its cost and upkeep as well as for its replacement. The owner may rent the machine to neighboring farmers during slack periods to obtain a maximum return on his or her investment.

Expensive equipment, however, is not always individually owned in societies with intensive agriculture or industrialized economies. Even in capitalist countries, there may be collective ownership of machines by "cooperatives" or co-owning with neighbors.[15]

Some equipment and facilities are too expensive for even a cooperative to afford. Governments may then allocate tax money collected from all the population for constructions or facilities that benefit some productive group as well as the public: airports benefit airlines and travelers; highways benefit truckers, commuters, and travelers; dams benefit power and water companies as well as the consumers of water. Such resources are owned collectively by the whole society. Rights of use depend on the facility.

Anyone can use a highway, but only municipalities can draw upon the water in a dam. Other productive resources in industrial societies, such as factories or service companies, may be owned jointly by shareholders, who purchase a portion of a corporation's assets in return for a proportionate share of its earnings. The proportion of technology and facilities owned by various levels of government also reflects the type of political-economic system: socialist and communist countries have more public ownership than capitalist countries.

THE CONVERSION OF RESOURCES

In all societies, resources have to be transformed or converted through labor into food, tools, and other goods. (These activities constitute what economists call *production*.) In this section, after briefly reviewing different types of production, we examine what may motivate people to work, how societies may divide up the work to be done, and how they may organize work. As we shall see, some aspects of the conversion of natural resources are culturally universal, but there is also an enormous amount of cultural variation.

Types of Economic Production

At least at the times they were first described, most of the societies known to anthropology had a *domestic* (family or kinship) mode of production. People labored to get food and to produce shelter and implements for themselves and their kin. Usually families had the right to exploit productive resources and controlled the products of their labor. Even part-time specialists, such as potters, could still support themselves without that craft if they needed to. At the other extreme are *industrial* societies, where much of the work is based on mechanized production (as in factories, but also in mechanized agriculture). Because machines and materials are so costly, only some individuals (capitalists), corporations, or governments can afford the expenses of production. Therefore, most people in industrial societies labor for others as wage earners. Although wages can buy food, people out of work can easily lose their ability to support themselves (unless they are protected by welfare payments or unemployment insurance). Then there is the *tributary* type of production system, found in nonindustrial societies in which most people can still produce their own food but an elite or aristocracy controls a portion of production (including the products of specialized crafts). The feudal societies of medieval western Europe were examples, as was czarist Russia under serfdom.[16]

Many people have suggested that our own and other developed economies are now moving from *industrialism* to *postindustrialism*. In many areas of commerce, computers have radically transformed the workplace. Computers "drive" machines and robots, and much of the manual work required in industry is disappearing. Businesses are now more knowledge- and service-oriented. Information is more accessible with telecommunication, so much so that *telecommuting* has entered our vocabulary to describe how many people can now work (for wages) at home. This economic transformation has important implications for both home life and the workplace. With inexpensive home computers and speedy data transmission by telephone and otherwise, more and more people can work at home. In addition, when information and knowledge become more important than capital equipment, more and more people can own and have access to the productive resources of society.[17] If who owns what partly determines who has political and other influence, the wider ownership of resources that is possible in postindustrial society may eventually translate into new, more democratic political forms and processes.

Incentives for Labor

Why do people work? Probably all of us have asked ourselves this question at least once in a while. Our concern may not be why other people are working, but why *we* have to work. Clearly, part of the answer is that work is necessary for survival. Although there are always some able-bodied adults who do not work as much as they should and rely on the work of others, no society would survive if most able-bodied adults were like that. In fact, most societies probably succeed in motivating most people to want to do (and even enjoy) what they have to do. But are the incentives for labor the same in all societies? Anthropologists think the answer is yes and no. One reason people may work is because they must. But why do people in some societies apparently work *more* than they must? We can be fairly certain that a particular and often-cited motive— the profit motive, or the desire to exchange something for more than it costs—is not universal or always the dominant motive.

There can be no profit motive among people who produce food and other goods primarily for their own consumption, as do most food collectors, many if not most horticulturalists, and even some intensive agriculturalists. Such societies have what we call a *subsistence economy,* not a money or commercial economy. Anthropologists have noticed that people in subsistence economies (with a domestic mode of production) often work less than people in commercial economies (with tributary or industrial modes of production). Indeed, food collectors appear to have a considerable amount of leisure time, as do many horticulturalists. It has been estimated, for example, that the men of the horticultural Kuikuru tribe in central Brazil spend about three and a half hours a day on subsistence. It appears that the Kuikuru could produce a substantial surplus of manioc, their staple food, by working thirty minutes more a day.[18] Yet they and many other peoples do not produce more than they need. Why should they? They cannot store a surplus for long because it would rot; they cannot sell it because there is no market nearby; and they do not have a political authority that might collect it for some purpose. Although we often think "more is better," a food-getting strategy with such a goal might even be disastrous, especially for food collectors. The killing of more animals than a group could eat might seriously jeopardize the food supply in the future, because overhunting could reduce reproduction among the hunted animals.[19] Horticulturalists might do well to plant a little extra, just in case part of the crop failed, but a great deal extra would be a tremendous waste of time and effort.

It has been suggested that when resources are converted primarily for household consumption, people will work harder if they have more consumers in the household. That is, when there are few able-bodied workers and a proportionately large number of consumers (perhaps because there are many young children and old people), the workers have to work harder. But when there are proportionately more workers, they can work less. This idea is called *Chayanov's rule.*[20] Alexander Chayanov found this relationship in data on rural Russians before the Communist revolution.[21] But it appears to work in other places too. For example, Michael Chibnik found support for Chayanov's rule when he compared data from twelve communities in five areas of the world (the communities ranged in complexity from New Guinea horticulturalists to commercial Swiss farmers). Although Chayanov restricted his theory to farmers who mostly produce for their own consumption and do not hire labor, Chibnik's analysis suggests that Chayanov's rule applies even where labor is often hired.[22]

But there appear to be many societies, even with subsistence economies, in which some people work harder than they need to just for their own families' subsistence. What motivates them to work harder? It turns out that many subsistence economies are not oriented just to household consumption. Rather, sharing and other transfers of food and goods often go well beyond the household, sometimes including the whole community or even groups of communities, as we will see later in the chapter. In such societies, social rewards come to those who are generous, who give things away. Thus, people who work harder than they have to for subsistence may be motivated to do so because they gain respect or esteem thereby.[23] In many societies too, as we shall see in subsequent chapters, extra food and goods may be needed at times for special purposes and occasions; goods and services may be needed to arrange and celebrate marriages, to form alliances, and to perform rituals and ceremonies (including what we would call sporting events). Thus, how the culture defines what one works for and what is needed may go beyond what is necessary.

In commercial economies such as our own—where foods, other goods, and services are sold and bought—people seem to be motivated to keep any extra income for themselves and their families. Extra income is converted into bigger dwellings, more expensive furnishings and food, and other elements of a "higher" standard of living. But the desire to improve one's standard of living is probably not the only motive operating. Some people may work partly to satisfy a need for achievement,[24] or because they find their work enjoyable. In addition, just as in precommercial societies, some people may work partly to gain respect or influence by giving some of their income away. Not only do we respect philanthropists and movie stars for giving to charities; our society encourages such giving by making it an allowable tax deduction! Still, the emphasis on giving in commercial societies is clearly less developed than in subsistence economies. We consider charity by the religious (or rich) appropriate and even admirable, but we would think it foolish or crazy for people to give so much away that they became poverty-stricken.

Forced Labor

Thus far we have mostly discussed *voluntary labor*—voluntary in the sense that no formal organization within the society compels people to work and punishes them for not working. Social training and social pressure are powerful enough to persuade an individual to perform some useful task. In both food-collecting and horticultural societies, individuals who can stand being the butt of jokes about laziness will still be fed. At most, they will be ignored by the other members of the group. There is no reason to punish them and no way to coerce them to do the work expected of them.

More complex societies have ways of forcing people to work for the authorities—whether those authorities be kings or presidents. An indirect form of forced labor is taxation. In 1989, the average tax in the United States (local, state, and federal) was 34 percent of income, which means that the average person worked four months out of the year for the government. (It's about the same now.) If a person decides not to pay the tax, the money will be forcibly taken or the person can be put in prison.

Money is the customary form of tax payment in a commercial society. In a politically complex but nonmonetary society, persons may pay their taxes in other ways—by performing a certain number of hours of labor or by giving up a certain percentage of what they produce. The **corvée**, a system of required labor, existed in the Inca empire in the central Andes before the Spanish conquest. Each male commoner was assigned three plots of land to work: a temple plot, a state plot, and his own plot. The enormous stores of food that went into state warehouses were used to supply the nobles, the army, the artisans, and all other state employees. If labor became overabundant, the people were still kept occupied; it is said that one ruler had a hill moved to keep some laborers busy. In addition to subsistence work for the state, Inca commoners were subject to military service, to duty as personal servants for the nobility, and to other "public" service.[25]

Another example of forced labor is tenant farming. In return for a house or shack and some acreage to farm, the tenant farmer owes a portion of the harvest to the owner. By manipulating the price for the tenant's crop, by making cash loans to the tenant at high interest rates, and by providing a store at which the tenant must buy staple goods at exorbitant prices, the owner manages to keep the tenant working the farm as economically forced labor. If the tenant farmer tries to leave without paying the debts engineered by the owner, the owner can use the power of the state to make him pay. On the other hand, if the tenant farmer becomes obsolete through the introduction of mechanized farming, the owner can use the power of the state to make him leave. Non-farm workers can also find it difficult to leave or quit in "company towns," whether they be in developing countries or in our own country. Access to supplies and housing may be so controlled by the

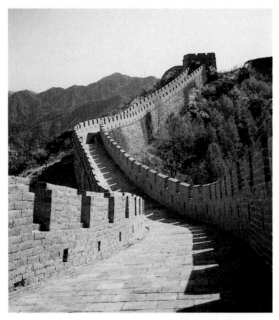

The Great Wall of China, like many monumental works in many ancient societies, was built with forced labor.

In many societies children do a great deal of work. Here a young Mamvu girl in Zaire is minding her two-year-old sibling.

company that people have little choice but to accept inferior conditions of work and living.

The draft or compulsory military service is a form of corvée, in that a certain period of service is required and failure to serve can be punished by a prison term or involuntary exile. Emperors of China had soldiers drafted to defend their territory and had the Great Wall built along the northern borders of the empire. The wall extends over 1,500 miles, and thousands were drafted to work on it.

Slavery is the most extreme form of forced work, in that slaves have little control over their labor. Because slaves constitute a category or class of persons in many societies, we discuss slavery more fully in the chapter on social stratification.

Division of Labor

All societies have some division of labor—some customary assignment of different kinds of work to different kinds of people. Universally, males and females and adults and children do not do the same kinds of work. In a sense, then, division of labor by gender and age is a kind of universal specialization of labor. Many societies known to anthropology divide labor only by gender and age. Other societies, as we will see, have more complex specialization.

By Gender and Age. All societies make use of gender differences to some extent in their customary assignment of labor. In the chapter on sex, gender,

and culture, we discuss the division of labor by gender in detail.

Age is also a universal basis for division of labor. Clearly, children cannot do work that requires a great deal of strength. But in many societies girls and boys contribute much more in labor than do children in our own society. For example, they help in animal tending, weeding, and harvesting, and they do a variety of domestic chores such as child care, fetching water and firewood, and cooking and cleaning. Indeed, in some societies a child six years old is considered old enough to be responsible for a younger sibling for a good part of the day.[26] Animal tending is often important work for children. Children in some societies spend more time at this task than adults.[27]

Why do children do so much work in some societies? If adults (particularly mothers) have heavy workloads, and children are physically and mentally able to do the work, a good part of the work is likely to be assigned to children.[28] As we have seen, food producers probably have more work than food collectors, so we would expect that children would be likely to work more where there is herding and farming. Consistent with this expectation, Patricia Draper and Elizabeth Cashdan found differences in children's work between nomadic and settled !Kung. Even though recently settled !Kung have not switched completely from food collection to food production, children's (as well as adults') activities have changed considerably. The children living in nomadic camps had virtually no work at all—adults did all the gathering and hunting. But the settled children were given lots of chores ranging from helping with animals to helping with the harvest and food processing.[29] When children in a society do a great deal of work, parents may value them more and may consciously want to have more children.[30] This may be one of the reasons birth rates are high in intensive agricultural societies.[31]

In some societies, work groups are formally organized on the basis of age. Among the Nyakyusa of southeastern Africa, for example, cattle are the principal form of wealth, and boys six to eleven years old herd the cattle for their parents' village. The boys join together in herding groups to tend the cattle of their fathers and of any neighboring families that do not have a son of herding age.[32]

Beyond Gender and Age. In societies with relatively simple technologies, there is little specialization of labor beyond that of gender and age. But as a society's technology becomes more complex and it is able to produce large quantities of food, more and more of its people are freed from subsistence work to become specialists in some other tasks—canoe builders, weavers, priests, potters, artists, and the like.

In contrast with food collectors, horticultural societies may have some part-time specialists. Some people may devote special effort to perfecting a particular skill or craft—pottery making, weaving, house building, doctoring—and in return for their products or services be given food or other gifts. Among some horticultural groups, the entire village may partially specialize in making a particular product, which can then be traded to neighboring people.

With the development of intensive agriculture, full-time specialists—potters, weavers, blacksmiths—begin to appear. The trend toward greater specialization reaches its peak in industrialized societies, where workers develop skills in one small area of the economic system. The meaninglessness and dehumanizing effect of much of industrialized work was depicted by Charlie Chaplin in the film *Modern Times:* when he left the factory after repeatedly tightening the same kind of bolt all day long, he could not stop his arms from moving, as if they were still tightening bolts.

In societies with full-time occupational specialization, different jobs are usually associated with differences in prestige, wealth, and power, as we shall see in the next chapter, on social stratification.

The Organization of Labor

The degree to which labor has to be organized reaches its peak in industrial societies, which have great occupational specialization and complex political organization. The coordination required to produce an automobile on an assembly line is obvious; so is the coordination required to collect taxes from every wage earner.

In many food-collecting and horticultural societies there is little formal organization of work. Work groups tend to be organized only when productive work requires it and to dissolve when they are no longer needed. Furthermore, the groups so organized often have changing composition and leadership; participation tends to be individualistic and voluntary.[33] Perhaps this flexibility is possible because when virtually everyone has the same work to do, little instruction is needed and almost anyone can assume leadership. Still, some types of work require more organization than others. Hunting big game usually requires coordinated efforts by a large number of hunters; so might catching fish in large nets. For example, on Moala, a Fijian island in the Pacific, net fishing is a group affair. Saturday is the most popular day for communal netting: a party of twenty to thirty women wade out on the reef and make a semicircle of nets. At a signal from an experienced woman, usually the chief's wife, the women move together at the ends, forming a circle. After the fish are caught in the nets, the women bite them on the backs of their heads to kill them and put them in baskets that they carry ashore. A larger fish drive is undertaken by the village, or several villages, around Christmas. The day before, more than 100 people make a "sweep," some 1,600 yards long, from coconut fronds. The next day, the men, women, and children all participate in the surround, catching thousands of fish.[34]

Kinship ties are an important basis for work organization, particularly in nonindustrial societies. For example, among the horticultural Kapauku of western New Guinea, the male members of a village are a kin group, and all work together to build drainage ditches, large fences, and bridges.[35] Among the pastoral Somali of eastern Africa, a herding

Specialization is more likely in a society that practices intensive agriculture, as among the Huichol of Mexico whose specialists include weavers.

group may consist of brothers, their sons, and all wives, unmarried daughters, and small children. Members of the tribe who decided to settle on farmland apportioned within the British protectorate of Somaliland did so as larger kin groups, not as individuals. As a result, the former cooperating pastoral kin groups became equally cooperative farming villages, depending on kin affiliation for land and other forms of economic help.[36]

With increasing technological complexity, the basis of work organization begins to shift to more formally organized groups. Such a shift usually entails an enforced obligation to participate.[37] Societies with complex political organization, particularly centralized or "state" organization, usually have the power to compel others to work. The power of the state may be employed specifically to draft labor for the construction of public works and buildings, or it may be more generalized, as when the law allows slave owners to compel slaves to work.[38] In our type of industrial society, work is sometimes politically organized, but the predominant basis of organization is the *contract*—the agreement between employers and employees whereby the latter perform a specified amount of work for a specified amount of wages. Although the

arrangement may be entered into voluntarily, laws and the power of the state enforce the obligation of the parties to abide by the contract.

Making Decisions about Work

Food collectors ignore many of the plant and animal species in their environment, choosing to go after only some. Why? The people may say that some animals are taboo whereas others are delicious. But where do such customary beliefs come from? Are they adaptive? And if there are no customary preferences for certain plants and animals, how can we explain why a food collector will go after certain foods and ignore others on a particular day? Food producers also make choices constantly. For example, a farmer has to decide when to plant, what to plant, how much to plant, when to harvest, how much to store, how much to give away or sell. Researchers have recently tried to explain why certain economic decisions become customary and why individuals make certain economic choices in their everyday lives.

A frequent source of ideas about choices is **optimal foraging theory,** which was developed originally by students of animal behavior and which has been applied to decision making by food collectors. Optimal foraging theory assumes that individuals seek to maximize the returns (in calories and nutrients) on their labor in deciding which animals and plants to hunt or collect. Natural selection should favor optimal foraging because "good" decisions would increase the chances of survival and reproduction. Research in different food-collecting societies supports the optimal foraging model.[39] For example, the Aché of eastern Paraguay consistently prefer to hunt peccaries (wild piglike mammals) rather than armadillos. Although peccaries take much longer to find and are harder to kill than armadillos, a day spent hunting peccaries yields more than 4,600 calories per hour of work, whereas hunting armadillos yields only about 1,800 calories an hour.[40] Other factors in addition to calorie yield, such as predictability of resources, may also influence which foods are collected. For example, the !Kung of the Kalahari desert depend largely on mongongo nuts, even though these nuts yield fewer calories per hour of work than does meat. But mongongo nuts in season are more dependable than game is. Once a group of !Kung hike to a grove of ripe mongongo nuts, they know they can obtain food there until the supply is exhausted; they are not as certain of getting game if they leave.[41]

How does a farmer decide whether to plant a particular crop and how much land and labor to devote to it? Christina Gladwin and others suggested that farmers make decisions in steps, with each choice point involving a yes or no answer. For example, in the high-altitude region of Guatemala, farmers could choose to plant about eight possible crops (or combinations of them, such as corn and beans, which grow together well). A farmer will quickly exclude some choices because of the answers to certain questions: Can I afford the seed and fertilizer? Can this crop be watered adequately? Is the altitude appropriate? And so on. If any of the answers is no, the crop is not planted. By a further series of yes or no decisions, farmers presumably decide which of the remaining possibilities will be planted.[42]

Individuals may not always be able to state clearly their rules for making decisions nor do they always have complete knowledge about the various possibilities, particularly when some of the possibilities are new. That does not mean, however, that economic choices cannot be predicted or explained by researchers. For example, Michael Chibnik found that men in two villages in Belize (in Central America) were not able to say why they devoted more or less time to working for wages versus growing crops. But their behavior was still predictable. For example, older men grew crops more, because wage labor was more physically demanding; and in the village with a higher cost of living the men were more likely to work for wages.[43]

THE DISTRIBUTION OF GOODS AND SERVICES

Goods and services are distributed in all societies by systems that, however varied, can be classified under three general types: reciprocity, redistribution, and market or commercial exchange.[44] The three systems often coexist in a society, but one system usually predominates. The predominant system seems to be associated with the society's food-getting technology and, more specifically, its level of economic development.

Reciprocity

Reciprocity consists of giving and taking without the use of money; it ranges from pure gift giving to equal exchanges to cheating. Technically, then, reciprocity may take three forms: **generalized reciprocity, balanced reciprocity,** and **negative reciprocity.**[45]

Generalized Reciprocity. When goods or services are given to another, without any apparent expectation of a return gift, we call it generalized reciprocity. Generalized reciprocity sustains the family in all societies. Parents give food, clothing, and labor to children because they want to (or perhaps feel obliged to), but they do not usually calculate exactly how their children will reciprocate years later. In this sense, all societies have some kind of generalized reciprocity. But some societies depend on it almost entirely to distribute goods and services.

Lorna Marshall recounted how the !Kung divided an eland brought to a site where five bands and several visitors were camping together—more than 100 people in all. The owner of the arrow that had first penetrated the eland was, by custom, the owner of the meat. He first distributed the forequarters to the two hunters who had aided him in the kill. After that, the distribution depended on kinship: each hunter shared with his wives' parents, wives, children, parents, and siblings, and they in turn shared with their kin. Sixty-three gifts of raw meat were recorded, after which further sharing of raw and cooked meat was begun.

The !Kung distribution of large game, clearly generalized reciprocity, is common among foragers. But giving away is not limited to game. For example, when Marshall left the band that had sponsored her in 1951, she gave each woman in the band a present of enough cowrie shells to make a necklace—one large shell and twenty small ones. When she returned in 1952, there were no cowrie-shell necklaces and hardly a single shell among the people in the band. Instead, the shells appeared by ones and twos in the ornaments of the people of neighboring bands.[46]

Although generalized reciprocity may appear to be altruistic or unselfish, researchers have suggested that giving may in fact benefit the givers in various ways. For example, parents who help their children may not only perpetuate their genes (the ultimate biological benefit) but may also be likely when they are old to receive care and affection from their grown-up children. And giving parents may be happier and enjoy life more than nongiving parents. So, in the shorter as well as longer run, givers may derive economic and psychological benefits, in addition to reproductive benefits.

Parent-child giving may seem easy to understand, but giving beyond the family is more of a problem. Why do some societies rely more on generalized reciprocity than others, particularly beyond the family? Sharing may be most likely when people are not sure they can get the food and water they need. In other words, sharing may be most likely if resources are unpredictable. So a !Kung band may share its water with other bands because they may have water now but not in the future. A related group in the Kalahari, the G//ana,[47] has been observed to share less than other groups. It turns out that the resources available to the G//ana are more predictable, because the G//ana supplement their hunting and gathering with plant cultivation and goat herding. Cultivated melons (which store water) appear to buffer the G//ana against water shortages, and goats appear to buffer them against shortages of game. Thus, whereas the !Kung distribute the meat right after a kill, the G//ana dry it and then store it in their houses.[48]

The idea that unpredictability favors sharing may also explain why some foods are more often shared than others. Wild game, for example, is usually unpredictable; when hunters go out to hunt, they cannot be sure that they will come back with meat. Wild plants, on the other hand, are more predictable; gatherers can be sure when they go out that they will come back with at least some plant foods. In any case, it does appear that game tends to be

Hunting success is less predictable than gathering. Like many foragers, the Aché of eastern Paraguay share the meat from hunting.

shared by food collectors much more than wild plant foods.[49] Even among people who depend largely on horticulture, such as the Yanomamö of Venezuela and Brazil, food items that are less predictably obtained (hunted game and fish) are shared more often than the more predictably obtained garden produce.[50]

Does food sharing increase the food supply for an individual? Calculations for the Aché of eastern Paraguay, who get most of their food from hunting when they go on food-collecting trips, suggest that the average individual gets more food when food is shared. Even the males who actually do the hunting get more, although the benefits are greater for the females and children on the trip.[51] Mathematically, the risk that an individual food collector will not find enough food on a particular day will be appreciably reduced if at least six to eight adult collectors share the food they collect. Food-collecting bands may often contain only twenty-five to thirty people, which is about the size that is needed to ensure that there are six to eight adult collectors.[52]

Although giving things to others may be expected in some societies, this does not necessarily mean that everyone does so willingly, or without some social pressure. For example, the !Kung call "far-hearted" anyone who does not give gifts, and they express their disapproval openly. The necessity to reduce tensions, to avoid envy and anger, and to keep all social relations peaceful, not only within their own band but among all !Kung bands, creates continuing cross-currents of obligation and friendship. These are maintained, renewed, or established through the generalized reciprocity of gift giving. In a sense, one can say that in exchange for a gift one gains prestige or perhaps "social credit" for a potential return at some indefinite time in the future. But this gain clearly is not based on explicit return considerations. Among the !Kung as well as other foraging groups, a person who does not hunt will still get a share of meat.

Day-to-day unpredictability is one thing; more prolonged scarcity is another. What happens to a system of generalized reciprocity when resources are scarce because of a drought or other disaster? Does the ethic of giving break down? Evidence from a few societies suggests that the degree of sharing may actually *increase* during the period of food shortage.[53] For example, in describing the Netsilik Inuit, Asen Balikci said, "Whenever game was abundant, sharing among non-relatives was avoided, since every family was supposedly capable of obtaining the necessary catch. In situations of scarcity, however, caribou meat was more evenly distributed throughout camp."[54] Sharing may increase during *mild* scarcity because people can minimize their deprivation. But generalized reciprocity may be strained by extreme scarcity. Ethnographic evidence from a few societies suggests that during famine, when individuals are actually dying from hunger, sharing may be limited to the household.[55]

Balanced Reciprocity. Balanced reciprocity is explicit and short-term in its expectations of return. It involves either an immediate exchange of goods or services or an agreed upon exchange over a limited period of time.

The !Kung, for instance, trade with the Tswana Bantu: a gemsbok hide for a pile of tobacco, five strings of beads made from ostrich eggshells for a spear, three small skins for a good-sized knife.[56] In the 1600s, the Iroquois of the North American Northeast traded deerskin to Europeans for brass kettles, iron hinges, steel axes, woven textiles, and guns.[57] The !Kung and Iroquois acquired trade goods by balanced reciprocity, but such exchanges were not crucial to their economies. In contrast, some societies depend much more heavily on balanced reciprocity. For example, the Efe, who hunt and gather in the Ituri Forest of central Africa, get most of their calories from manioc, peanuts, rice, and plaintains grown by another group—the agricultural Lese. Efe men and women provide labor to the Lese and in exchange receive a portion of the harvest as well as goods such as metal pots and spears.[58] Pastoralists too are rarely self-sufficient, as we mentioned in the preceding chapter; they have to trade their pastoral products to agriculturalists to get the grain and other things they need.

When we say that an exchange is balanced, we do not mean to imply that the things exchanged are exactly equivalent in value or that the exchange is purely economic. In the absence of a money economy, where there is no explicit standard by which value can be judged, there is no way to assess value objectively. The point is that the parties in balanced reciprocity are freely giving each other the respective goods and services they each want; they are not coerced into doing so, so presumably they are not conceiving of the exchange as unbalanced.[59] And when something is valued, it may be valued for other than economic reasons. The exchange itself may also be fun, adventuresome, or aesthetically pleasing, or it may enhance social relationships.

Exchanges can have different motivations and therefore may have different meanings. Consequently, some economic anthropologists now want to distinguish between *gift* and *commodity* exchanges. Gift exchanges are personal and involve the creation or perpetuation of some kind of enduring relationship between people and groups. In our society, the exchange of dinner invitations or Christmas gifts is motivated by social considerations; we are not interested only in the actual food or objects received. As we shall see shortly, some of the exchanges involved in the famous *kula* ring seem mostly to be motivated by the desire to establish or cement trade partnerships. In contrast, commodity exchanges, which can occur even in the absence of money, focus on the objects or services received—the transaction itself is the motive. When the transaction is completed, the relationship between the parties involved usually ends.[60]

THE KULA RING. The horticultural Trobriand Islanders, who live off the eastern coast of New Guinea, have worked out an elaborate scheme for trading food and other items with the people of neighboring islands. Such trade is essential, for some of the islands are small and rocky and cannot produce enough food to sustain their inhabitants, who specialize instead in canoe building, pottery making, and other crafts. Other islands produce far more yams, taro, and pigs than they need. Yet the trade of such necessary items is carefully hidden beneath the panoply of the **kula** **ring,** a ceremonial exchange of valued shell ornaments.[61]

Two kinds of ornaments are involved in the ceremony of exchanges—white shell armbands (*mwali*), which travel around the circle of islands in a counterclockwise direction, and red shell necklaces (*soulava*), which travel in a clockwise direction (see Figure 7–1). The possession of one or more of these ornaments allows a man to organize an expedition to the home of one of his trading partners on another island. The high point of an expedition is the ceremonial giving of the valued *kula* ornaments. Each member of the expedition receives a shell ornament from his trading partner and then remains on the island for two or three days as the guest of that person. During the visit the real trading goes on. Some of the exchange takes the form of gift giving between trading partners. There is also exchange or barter between expedition members and others on the island. By the time the visitors leave, they have accomplished a year's trading without seeming to do so. (A somewhat similar occurrence was the American and Chinese ceremonial exchange of musk oxen and pandas when U.S. President Richard Nixon first visited the People's Republic of China. These animals are valued because they are rare, yet they are practically useless. Immediately after the exchange of the animals, the real trading of goods between the two countries began.)

But the practical advantages of the *kula* ring are not the only gains. There may be purely social ones, for goods are traded with ease and enjoyment. A trading expedition takes on the flavor of adventure rather than business. Many of the traditions of the islands are kept alive: myth, romance, ritual, and history are linked to the circulating ornaments, especially the larger, finer pieces, which are well known and recognized as heirlooms. The *kula* ring also permits wide ownership of valuables. Instead of possessing one valued object permanently, a man is able to possess many valued things within his lifetime, each for a year or so. Each object, when it is received, arouses enthusiasm in a way that one lifelong possession could not do.[62]

Whatever the reasons for the origin of the *kula* ring, which may date back nearly 2,000 years, it continued to be an important institution after Papua New Guinea became an independent country. For example, active participation in the *kula* ring helped candidates in the 1960s and the 1970s to be elected to the national parliament.[63]

FIGURE 7–1
The Kula Ring

In the *kula* ring, red shell necklaces *(soulava)* travel in a clockwise direction; white shell armbands *(mwali)* travel counterclockwise. The solid lines show the overseas trade routes. The dashed circles identify the *(kula)* communities, and the dashed rectangles show the areas indirectly affected by the *kula*.

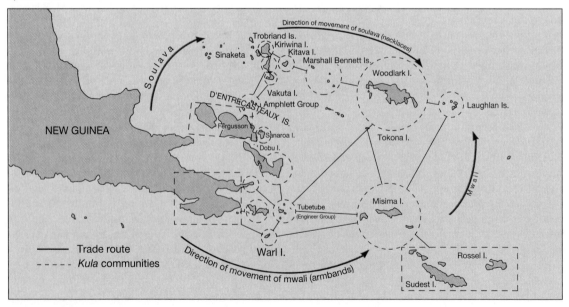

The *kula* is not the only form of exchange in Trobriand life. For example, on the two days following a burial, the kin of the deceased give yams, taro, and valuables to those who helped care for the deceased before death, to those who participated in the burial ceremonies, and to those who came to mourn the deceased. After these initial exchanges, the hamlet settles into mourning. Women from other hamlets bring food to the people in mourning, and the mourning women prepare bundles of banana leaves and weave skirts of banana fiber for later distribution. Husbands help their wives accumulate valuables to "buy" extra bundles of banana leaves. Then the women's mortuary ceremony is held. It is very competitive—each of the mourning women tries to distribute the most bundles and skirts. As many as 5,000 bundles and 30 skirts might be distributed by one mourning woman in a single day! Each of these giveaways completes a balanced reciprocity: the giver is reciprocating for gifts of goods and services received in the past. A woman's brothers gave her yams and taro during the year. She gives her brother's wives bundles or skirts, which are also given to those who helped make the special mourning skirts and to those who brought or cooked food during the mourning period.[64]

OTHER BALANCED SYSTEMS. Balanced reciprocity may involve labor as well as goods. Cooperative work parties exchange or balance gifts of labor. Among the Mundurucu, all men of the village work together to clear gardens; the men and women also work together to plant manioc shoots in each garden.[65] In other societies, a feast may be an additional reciprocation for the gift of labor. A cooperative work party, or *kuu,* among the Kpelle of Liberia may number from six to forty persons, all of whom are generally relatives or friends. In addition to promising return work on a particular date, each farmer rewards the work party's hard day's labor by providing a feast and sometimes rhythmic music to work by.[66]

Sometimes the line between generalized and balanced reciprocity is not so clear. Consider our gift giving at Christmastime. Although such gift giving may appear to be generalized reciprocity, there may be strong expectations of balance. Two friends or relatives may try to exchange presents of fairly equal value, based on calculations of what last year's gift cost. If a person receives a $5 present when he or she gave a $25 present, that person will be hurt and perhaps angry. On the other hand, a person who receives a $500 present when he or she gave a $25 present may well be dismayed.

Negative Reciprocity. Taking without thought of a fair return is to take advantage of another, to get something for nothing or for less than its worth. A mild form is deceitful bargaining; extreme forms are theft and other varieties of seizure. In other words, negative reciprocity ranges from "various degrees of cunning, guile, stealth, and violence to the finesse of a well-conducted horse-raid."[67]

Kinship Distance and Type of Reciprocity. Most food-collecting and horticultural societies depend on some form of reciprocity for the distribution of goods and labor. Sahlins suggested that whether the reciprocity is generalized, balanced, or negative depends largely on the kinship distance between persons. Generalized reciprocity may be the rule for family members and close kinsmen. Balanced reciprocity may be practiced among equals who are not closely related. Persons who would consider it inappropriate to trade with their own families will trade with neighboring groups. Negative reciprocity may be practiced against strangers and enemies.[68] In general, the importance of reciprocity declines with economic development.[69] In societies with intensive agriculture, and even more so in societies that are industrialized, reciprocity distributes only a small proportion of goods and services.

Reciprocity as a Leveling Device. Reciprocal gift giving may do more than equalize the distribution of goods within a community, as in the !Kung's sharing. It may also tend to equalize the distribution of goods between communities.

Many Melanesian societies in and near New Guinea have the custom of holding pig feasts in which 50, 100, or even 2,000 pigs are slaughtered. Andrew Vayda, Anthony Leeds, and David Smith suggested that these enormous feasts, though apparently wasteful, are just one of the outcomes of a complex of cultural practices that are highly advantageous. The people of these societies cannot accurately predict how much food they will produce during the year. Some years there will be bumper crops, other years very poor crops, because of fluctuations in the weather. So it might be wise to overplant just in case the yield is poor. Yet overplanting results in overproduction during average and exceptionally good years. What can be done with this extra food? Root crops such as yams and taro do not keep well over long periods, so any surplus is fed to pigs, which become, in effect, food-storing repositories. Pigs are then available for needed food during lean times. But if there are several years of surpluses, pigs can become too much of a good thing. Pigs wanting food can destroy yam and taro patches. When the pig population grows to menacing proportions, a village may invite other villages to a gigantic feast that results in a sharp reduction of the pig population and keeps the fields from being overrun. Over the years the pig feasts serve to equalize the food consumption, and especially the protein consumption, of all the villages that participate in the feasts.[70] Thus, the custom of pig feasts may be a way for villages to "bank" surplus food by storing up "social credit" with other villages, which will return that credit in subsequent feasts.

In some Melanesian societies, the pig feasts foster an element of competition among the men who give them. "Big men" may try to bolster their status and prestige by the size of their feasts. A reputation is enhanced not by keeping wealth but by giving it away. A similar situation existed among many Native American groups of the Northwest Coast, where a chief might attempt to enhance his status by holding a **potlatch.** At a potlatch, a chief and his group would give away blankets, pieces of copper, canoes, large quantities of food, and other items to their guests. The host chief and his group would later be invited to other potlatches.

The competitive element in the potlatch appears to have intensified after contact with whites. Because of the fur trade, the number of trade goods increased, and so more items could be given away. Possibly more important was the population decline among the Indians, caused by diseases (such as smallpox) introduced by European traders. Distant relatives of chiefs who had no direct heirs might compete for the right to the title, each attempting to give away more than the others.[71] Chiefs may also have attempted to attract men to their half-empty villages by spectacular giveaways.[72] Decimated groups might coalesce in order to maintain the potlatching. For example, when the Tlingit population declined to the low of the 1910s, kin groups coalesced in order to assemble enough resources for a potlatch.[73] Although the potlatch system seems wasteful in that goods were often destroyed in the competition, the system probably also served to equalize the distribution of goods among competing groups.

The Pomo Indians of central California had another way to bank credit for previous generosity. A village with an overabundance of fish or acorns might invite another village to a feast. In return for surplus fish or acorns, the guests would give the host village a certain number of beads. Before beginning the journey to the feast, the chief of the guest village would obtain from each family as many strings of beads as possible. After a few days of feasting at the

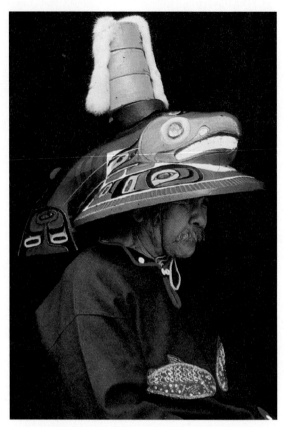

A man on the Northwest Pacific Coast (southeastern Alaska) wears a "potlatch hat" showing how many potlatches he has had.

host village, the chief would trade the beads for the supply of surplus fish or acorns. Each member of the visiting village would be given an equal share of the food, regardless of how many beads had been contributed. But the members of a village would not be invited to a feast unless they brought beads to trade, and they could not obtain beads unless they had given food away themselves sometime in the past. Thus, giving away food and receiving beads in return served as a means of storing social credit for times of scarcity. Later, if food was scarce in the former host village, the villagers could use the beads they had acquired by giving in the past to obtain food from another village with a surplus. The trade feasts, then, had the effect of equalizing the consumption of food not only within a village but over a fairly widespread area.[74]

On one level of analysis, the Melanesian pig feasts, the Northwest Coast potlatches, and the Pomo trade feasts were all reciprocal exchanges between communities or villages. But these exchanges were not just intercommunity versions of reciprocal gift giving between individuals. Because these feasts were organized by people who collected goods, they also involved another mode of distribution, which anthropologists call redistribution.

Redistribution

Redistribution is the accumulation of goods (or labor) by a particular person, or in a particular place, for the purpose of subsequent distribution. Although redistribution is found in all societies, it becomes an important mechanism only in societies that have political hierarchies—that is, chiefs or other specialized officials and agencies. In all societies, there is some redistribution, at least within the family. Members of the family pool their labor or products or income for the common good. But in many societies, there is little or no redistribution beyond the family. It seems that redistribution on a territorial basis emerges when there is a political apparatus to coordinate centralized collection and distribution of goods or to mobilize labor for some public purpose.

In the African state of Bunyoro in western Uganda, for example, the king (called the *mukama*) retained much of the wealth for himself and his close kin. The *mukama* had the authority to grant the use of land and all other natural resources to his subordinate chiefs, and they in turn granted it to the common people. In return, everyone was required to give the *mukama* large quantities of food, crafts, and even labor services. The *mukama* then redistributed these goods and services, in theory at least, to all the people. The *mukama* was praised with names that emphasized his generosity: *Agutamba* ("he who relieves distress") and *Mwebingwa* ("he to whom the people run for help"). But it is clear that much of what the king redistributed did not find its way back to the common people, who produced the bulk of the goods. Instead, the wealth was distributed largely according to rank within the state.[75]

Other redistribution systems are more equal. For example, among the Buin of Melanesia, "the chief is housed, dressed, and fed exactly like his bondsman."[76] Even though the chief owns most of the pigs, everyone shares equally in the consumption of the wealth. In general, where redistribution is important (in societies with higher levels of productivity), the wealthy are more likely than the poor to benefit from the redistributions.[77]

Why do redistribution systems develop? Elman Service suggested that they develop in agricultural societies that contain subregions suited to different kinds of crops or natural resources. Food collectors can take advantage of environmental vari-

ation by moving to different areas. With agriculture, the task is more difficult; it might be easier to move different products across different regions.[78] If the demand for different resources or products becomes too great, reciprocity between individuals might become awkward. So it might be more efficient to have someone—a chief, perhaps—coordinate the exchanges. We saw in the Pomo trade feasts that, although whole communities appeared to be engaged in reciprocal exchanges, the collection of surplus food and beads was handled by village chiefs.

Marvin Harris agreed that redistribution becomes more likely with agriculture, but for a somewhat different reason. He argued that competitive feasting, as in New Guinea, is adaptive because it encourages people to work harder to produce somewhat more than they need. Why would this feature be adaptive? Harris argued that with agriculture, people really have to produce more than they need so that they can protect themselves against crises such as crop failure. The groups that make feasts may be indirectly ensuring themselves against crises by storing up social credit with other villages, who will reciprocate by making feasts for them in the future. On the other hand, inducements to collect more than they need may not be advantageous to food-collecting groups, who might lose in the long run by overcollecting.[79]

Market or Commercial Exchange

When we think of markets we usually think of bustling colorful places in other parts of the world where goods are bought and sold. In our own society we seldom use the word *market*, although we have supermarkets and the stock market and other places for buying and selling that we call shops, stores, and malls. In referring to **market** or **commercial exchange,** economists and economic anthropologists are referring to exchanges or transactions in which the "prices" are subject to supply and demand, whether or not the transactions occur in a marketplace.[80] "Market exchange" involves not only the exchange, or buying and selling, of goods but also transactions of labor, land, rentals, and credit.

On the surface, many market exchanges resemble balanced reciprocity. One person gives something and receives something in return. How then does market exchange differ from balanced reciprocity? It is easy to distinguish market exchange from balanced reciprocity when money is involved, since reciprocity is defined as not involving money. But market exchange need not always involve money.[81] For example, a landowner grants a

IMPACT OF THE WORLD-SYSTEM— DEFORESTATION OF THE AMAZON

When we speak of the economic system of a people, we must keep in mind that probably no group has ever been completely isolated from outside economic, political, social, or environmental events. In the modern world, with the expanding demand and opportunity of a growing world market economy, even the most self-sufficient of groups cannot avoid the effects of their connections to the outside world.

Consider the great rain forest drained by the Amazon River and its tributaries. World demand for wood, hamburger, and gold threatens to diminish the Amazon forest. Covering more than a billion acres, it is not only the home to many, largely self-sufficient indigenous cultures; it also supports about 50 percent of all the earth's plants and animals. Like many tropical forests, the Amazon has large numbers of desirable hardwood trees. Forests in Africa and Asia are already largely depleted, so the demand for wood from the Amazon has grown considerably. In addition, the Amazon Development Agency in Brazil has offered incentives to clear forest for cattle ranching, which can provide hamburger to North American fast-food restaurants. There is lit-

tle concern that a few seasons of overgrazing can make it impossible even for grasses to grow in the soils of the former forest.

The indigenous people often find themselves in a land squeeze, with loggers, cattle ranchers, and miners trying to encroach on their territory. With less land, food-getting and traditional economic practices are in jeopardy. But it is naive to assume that the indigenous people are interested only in maintaining their traditional economies. They often accept the dilemma of economic development: they might lose some land, but selling rights to loggers and miners brings in money, which they can use to buy things they need and want. Researchers and some development experts are searching for ways to achieve development without destroying or degrading the environment. For example, indigenous groups are encouraged to gather Brazil nuts (a wild but renewable resource) for sale. Others are encouraged to harvest latex (natural rubber) and hearts of palm. Medicinal plants have economic value to multinational pharmaceutical and biotechnical companies, which have discovered that the conservation of biodiversity may

be economically advantageous to themselves as well as to the local people and to scientists who want to study the diversity.

Can development be sustainable? That is, are resources (such as hardwoods) renewable so that both economic productivity and the environment can be protected? Even if some kind of sustainable development is possible, arranging it may require concerted effort by all involved, which requires participation by all in decision making.

Whether we like it or not, economic development and the desire for it are not going to go away. But we need to do more than applaud or bemoan economic development. In particular, we need research that reveals what impact particular changes will have on people, other animals and plants, and on the environment. Most of all, for the sake of human rights, we need to listen to the people whose lives will be most affected, to understand their needs as well as the developers'.

Sources: *Marguerite Holloway, "Sustaining the Amazon,"* Scientific American, *July 1993, 91–99; Emilio F. Moran,* Through Amazon Eyes: The Human Ecology of Amazonian Populations *(Iowa City: University of Iowa Press, 1993).*

tenant farmer the right to use the land in exchange for a portion of the crop. So to call a transaction market exchange, we have to ask whether supply and demand determine the price. If a tenant farmer gave only a token gift to the landowner, we would not call it market exchange, just as a Christmas gift to a teacher is not payment for teaching. If tenants, however, were charged a large portion of their crops when the supply of land is short, or if landowners lowered their demands when few people wanted to tenant-farm, then we would call the transactions market or commercial exchange.

Although market exchange need not involve money, most commercial transactions, particularly nowadays, do involve what we call money.

Kinds of Money. Some anthropologists define money according to the functions and characteristics of the **general-purpose money** used in our own and other complex societies, for which nearly all goods, resources, and services can be exchanged. According to this definition, *money* performs the basic functions of serving as an accepted medium of exchange, a standard of value, and a store of wealth. As a medium of exchange, it allows all goods and services to be valued in the same objective way; we say that an object or service is worth so much money. Also, money is nonperishable, and therefore savable or storable, and almost always transportable and divisible, so transactions can involve the buying and selling of goods and services that differ in value. Although money can technically be anything, the first money systems used rare metals such as gold and silver. These metals are relatively soft and therefore can be melted and shaped into standard sizes and weights. The earliest standardized coins we know of were made by the Lydians in Asia Minor and the Chinese, in the seventh century A.D. It is important to realize that money has little or no intrinsic value; it is society that determines its value. In the United States today, paper bills, bank checks, and even debit cards are fully accepted as money. And money is increasingly transferred electronically.

General-purpose money is used both for commercial transactions (buying and selling) and for noncommercial transactions (payment of taxes or fines, personal gifts, contributions to religious and other charities). General-purpose money provides a way of condensing wealth: gold dust or nuggets are easier to carry around than bushels of wheat; paper bills, a checkbook, and plastic cards are handier than a herd of sheep or goats.

In many societies, money is not an all-purpose medium of exchange. Many peoples whose food production per capita is not sufficient to support a large population of nonproducers of food have **special-purpose money.** This consists of objects of value for which only some goods and services can be exchanged on the spot or through balanced reciprocity. In some parts of Melanesia, pigs are assigned value in terms of shell money—lengths of shells strung together in units each roughly as long as the distance covered by a man's outstretched arms. According to its size, a pig will be assigned a value in tens of such units up to 100.[82] But shell money cannot be exchanged for all the goods or services a person might need. Similarly, a Northwest Coast native could exchange food (but not most other goods and services) for a "gift of wealth," such as blankets. The gift was a "receipt" that entitled the person to receive an equal amount of food (but little else) later.

Degrees of Commercialization. Most societies were not commercialized at all, or only barely so, when first described in the ethnographic record (by explorers, missionaries, and anthropologists). That is, most societies as first described did not rely on market or commercial exchange to distribute goods and services. But commercial exchange has become the dominant form of distribution in the modern world. (Most societies of the ethnographic past are now incorporated into larger nation-states; for example, the Trobriand Islanders and other societies in Melanesia are now districts in the nation of Papua New Guinea.) Selling nowadays goes far beyond the nation-state; the world is now a multinational market.[83]

But there is considerable variation in the degree to which societies today depend on market or commercial exchange. Many societies still allocate land without purchase and distribute food and other goods primarily by reciprocity and redistribution, participating only peripherally in market exchange. These are societies in transition: their traditional subsistence economies are gradually becoming commercialized. Among the Luo of western Kenya, for example, most rural families still have land that was allocated to them by their kin groups. The food they eat they mostly produce themselves. But nowadays many men also work for wages—some nearby, others far away in towns and cities (where they spend a year or two). These wages are used to pay government taxes, to pay for children's schooling, and to buy commercially produced items such as clothes, kerosene lamps, radios, fish from Lake Nyanza, tea, sugar, and coffee. Occasionally, families sell agricultural surpluses or craft items such as reed mats.

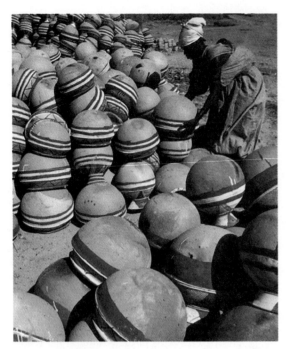
Pots for sale in the market in Timbuktu, Mali

Economies such as that of the Luo are not fully commercialized, but they may become so in the future. In the chapter on culture change, we discuss some of the implications and effects of this transition to a more commercialized economy—a transition that is a worldwide phenomenon.

What anthropologists call *peasant economies* are somewhat more commercialized than transitional subsistence economies such as that of the Luo. Although **peasants** also produce food largely for their own consumption, they *regularly* sell part of their surplus (food, other goods, or labor) to others, and land is one of the commodities they buy, rent, and sell. But, although their production is somewhat commercialized, peasants still are not like the fully commercialized farmers in industrialized societies, who rely on the market to exchange *all* or *almost all* of their crops for *all* or *almost all* of the goods and services they need.

In fully commercialized societies such as our own, market or commercial exchange dominates the economy; prices and wages are regulated, or at least significantly affected, by the forces of supply and demand. A modern industrial or postindustrial economy may involve international as well as national markets, in which everything has a price, stated in the same money terms—natural resources, labor, goods, services, prestige items, religious and ceremonial items. Reciprocity is reserved for family members and friends or remains behind the scene in

business transactions. Redistribution, however, is an important mechanism. It is practiced in the form of taxation and the use of public revenue for transfer payments and other benefits to low-income families—welfare, social security, health care, and so on. But commercial exchange is the major way goods and services are distributed.

Why Do Money and Market Exchange Develop?
Most economists think that money is invented in a society (or borrowed from another society) when trade increases and barter becomes increasingly inefficient. The more important trade is, the more difficult it is to find a person who can give something you want and wants something you have to give. Money is a valuable that can be exchanged for anything and so is an efficient medium of exchange when trade becomes important. In contrast, many anthropologists do not link the origins of money or market exchange to the necessities of trade. Instead they link the origins of money to various noncommercial "payments" such as the *kula* valuables, the Pomo beads, and the taxes that have to be paid to a political authority. All of the available explanations of money suggest that money will be found mostly in societies at higher levels of economic development; and indeed it is. And, if some simpler societies have money, dominant and more complex societies have usually introduced it.[84]

Most theories about the development of money and market exchange assume that producers have regular surpluses they want to exchange. But why do people produce surpluses in the first place? Perhaps they are motivated to produce extra only when they want to obtain goods from a distance and the suppliers of such goods are not well known to them, making reciprocity less likely as a way to obtain those goods. Some theorists suggest that market exchange begins with external (intersocietal) trade; kin would not likely be involved, so transactions would involve bargaining (and therefore market exchange, by definition). Finally, some argue that as societies become more complex and more densely populated, social bonds between individuals become less kinlike and friendly and therefore reciprocity becomes less likely.[85] Perhaps this is why traders in developing areas are often foreigners or recent immigrants.[86]

In any case, Frederic Pryor's cross-cultural research supports the notion that all types of market exchange—of goods, labor, land, and credit—are more likely with higher levels of economic productivity. Pryor also found that market exchange of goods appears at lower levels of economic develop-

Fiesta sponsors spend a great deal of money for food and drink as well as for musicians and dancers. Here we see dancers at a fiesta in Oaxaca, Mexico.

ment than market exchange of labor and credit; market exchange of land, probably because it is associated with private property (individual ownership), appears mostly at the highest levels of productivity. Perhaps surprisingly, smaller societies tend to have more market exchange or trade with other societies. Larger societies can presumably get more of what they need from inside the society; for example, China has had relatively little foreign trade throughout much of its history.[87]

Possible Leveling Devices in Commercial Economies.
As we will see in the next chapter, societies that depend substantially on market or commercial exchange tend to have marked differences in wealth among people. Nonetheless, there may be mechanisms that lessen the inequality, that act at least partially as leveling devices.

Some anthropologists have suggested that the *fiesta complex* in highland Indian communities of Latin America may be a mechanism that tends to equalize income.[88] In these peasant villages, fiestas are held each year to celebrate important village saints. The outstanding feature of this system is the extraordinary amount of money and labor a sponsoring family must contribute. Sponsors must hire ritual specialists, pay for church services, musicians, and costumes for dancers, and cover the complete cost of food and drink for all members of the com-

munity. The costs incurred can very easily amount to a year's wages.[89]

Some anthropologists have suggested that, although the richer Indians who sponsor fiestas are clearly distributing a good deal of wealth to the poorer members of their own and other communities, the fiestas do not really level wealth at all. First, true economic leveling would entail the redistribution of important productive resources such as land or animals; the fiesta only temporarily increases the general level of consumption. Second, the resources expended by the sponsors are usually extra resources that have been accumulated specifically for the fiesta—that is why the sponsors are always appointed in advance. Third, and perhaps most important, the fiestas do not seem to have reduced long-term wealth distinctions within the villages.[90]

In nations such as ours, can the income tax and the social-assistance programs it pays for (such as welfare and disaster relief) be thought of as leveling devices? Theoretically, our tax system is supposed to work that way by taxing higher incomes at higher rates. But we know that in fact it doesn't. Those in higher income brackets can often deduct an appreciable amount from their taxable incomes and therefore pay taxes at a relatively low rate. Our tax system may help some to escape extreme poverty, but, like the fiesta system, it has not eliminated marked distinctions in wealth.

▼ SUMMARY

1. All societies have economic systems, whether or not these involve the use of money. All societies have customs specifying access to natural resources; customary ways of transforming or converting those resources, through labor, into necessities and other desired goods and services; and customs for distributing (and perhaps exchanging) goods and services.

2. Regulation of access to natural resources is a basic factor in all economic systems. The concept of individual ownership of land—including the right to use its resources and the right to sell or otherwise dispose of them—is common among intensive agriculturalists. In contrast, food collectors, horticulturalists, and pastoralists generally lack individual ownership of land. Among pastoral nomads, however, animals are considered family property and are not usually shared.

3. Every society makes use of a technology, which includes tools, constructions, and required skills. Even though food collectors and horticulturalists tend to think of tools as "owned" by the individuals who made them, the sharing of tools is so extensive that individual ownership does not have much meaning. Among intensive agriculturalists, toolmaking tends to be a specialized activity. Tools tend not be shared, except mainly by those who have purchased them together.

4. Incentives for labor vary cross-culturally. Many societies produce just for household consumption: if there are more consumers, producers work harder. In some subsistence economies, people may work harder to obtain the social rewards that come from giving to others. Forced labor generally occurs only in complex societies.

5. Division of labor by gender is universal. In many nonindustrial societies, large tasks are often accomplished through the cooperative efforts of a kinship group. Such cooperation is not as prevalent in industralized societies. In general, the more technically advanced a society is, the more surplus food it produces and the more some of its members engage in specialized work.

6. The organization of labor reaches its peak in complex societies: work groups tend to be formally organized, and sometimes there is an enforced obligation to participate. In food-collecting and horticultural societies, in contrast, there is little formal organization of work.

7. Goods and services are distributed in all societies by systems that can be classified under three types: reciprocity, redistribution, and market or commercial exchange. Reciprocity is giving and taking without the use of money and may assume three forms: generalized reciprocity, balanced reciprocity, and negative reciprocity. Generalized reciprocity is gift giving without any immediate or planned return. In balanced reciprocity, individuals exchange goods and services immediately or in the short term. Negative reciprocity is generally practiced with strangers or enemies: one individual attempts to steal from another or to cheat in trading.

8. Redistribution is the accumulation of goods or labor by a particular person, or in a particular place, for the purpose of subsequent distribution. It becomes an important mechanism of distribution only in societies with political hierarchies.

9. Market or commercial exchange, where "prices" depend on supply and demand, tends to occur with increasing levels of economic productivity. Especially nowadays, market exchange usually involves an all-purpose medium of exchange (money). Most societies today are at least partly commercialized; the world is becoming a single market system.

▼ GLOSSARY TERMS

balanced reciprocity	*kula* ring	optimal foraging theory	reciprocity
corvée	market or commercial exchange	peasants	redistribution
generalized reciprocity	negative reciprocity	potlatch	special-purpose money
general-purpose money			

▼ CRITICAL QUESTIONS

1. What conditions might enable us to achieve a world of sustainable resources?
2. What are the possible effects of a postindustrial economy in which a large proportion of the population has inexpensive access to computers and information?
3. Do you expect any appreciable change in the amount of resources privately owned in the future? State your reasons.

▼ SUGGESTED READING

BLANTON, R. E. "Variation in Economy." In C. R. Ember and M. Ember, eds., *Cross-Cultural Research for Social Science* (Englewood Cliffs, NJ: Prentice Hall, 1995). Prentice Hall/Simon & Schuster Custom Publishing. A brief survey for undergraduates of the concepts and challenges involved in cross-cultural comparisons of variations in economic systems.

CASHDAN, E., ED. *Risk and Uncertainty in Tribal and Peasant Economies.* Boulder, CO: Westview Press, 1990. The contributors to this volume discuss the various ways people in nonindustrial societies respond to unpredictable variation in the environment.

MACLACHLAN, M. D., ED. *Household Economies and Their Transformations.* Monographs in Economic Anthropology, No. 3. Lanham, MD: University Press of America, 1987. The papers in this volume deal with the intensification and transformation of agriculture in many societies of the modern world.

PLATTNER, S., ED. *Economic Anthropology.* Stanford, CA: Stanford University Press, 1989. Covers economic behavior among foragers, horticulturalists, peasants, and industrialized societies, as well as issues such as gender roles, communal ownership, and mass marketing in urban areas.

PRYOR, F. L. *The Origins of the Economy: A Comparative Study of Distribution in Primitive and Peasant Economies.* New York: Academic Press, 1977. A large cross-cultural study of variation in distribution systems and their possible determinants.

▼ NOTES

[1]E. Adamson Hoebel, *The Law of Primitive Man* (New York: Atheneum, 1968 [originally published 1954]), pp. 46–63.

[2]James Woodburn, "An Introduction to Hadza Ecology," in Richard B. Lee and Irven DeVore, eds., *Man the Hunter* (Chicago: Aldine, 1968), pp. 49–55.

[3]Eleanor Leacock and Richard Lee, "Introduction," in Eleanor Leacock and Richard Lee, eds., *Politics and History in Band Societies* (Cambridge: Cambridge University Press, 1982), p. 8.

[4]Rada Dyson-Hudson and Eric Alden Smith, "Human Territoriality: An Ecological Reassessment," *American Anthropologist,* 80 (1978): 21–41.

[5]Robert F. Murphy, *Headhunter's Heritage: Social and Economic Change among the Mundurucu* (Berkeley: University of California Press, 1960), pp. 69, 142–43.

[6]Not all pastoralists have individual ownership. For example, the Tungus of northern Siberia have kin group ownership of reindeer; see John H. Dowling, "Property Relations and Productive Strategies in Pastoral Societies," *American Ethnologist,* 2 (1975): 422.

[7]Fredrik Barth, *Nomads of South Persia* (Oslo: Universitetsforlaget, 1964; Boston: Little, Brown, 1968), p. 124.

[8]Dowling, "Property Relations and Productive Strategies in Pastoral Societies," pp. 419–26.

[9]Gerald W. Creed, "Bulgaria: Anthropological Corrections to Cold War Stereotypes," in Melvin Ember, Carol R. Ember, and David Levinson, eds., *Portraits of Culture: Ethnographic Originals* (Englewood Cliffs, NJ: Prentice Hall, 1995). Prentice Hall/Simon & Schuster Custom Publishing.

[10]John H. Bodley, *Victims of Progress,* 3rd ed. (Mountain View, CA: Mayfield, 1990), pp. 77–93; Edwin N. Wilmsen, ed., *We Are Here: Politics of Aboriginal Land Tenure* (Berkeley, CA: University of California Press, 1989), pp. 1–14.

[11]Bodley, *Victims of Progress,* pp. 79–81.

[12]Ibid., pp. 86–89.

[13]Elman R. Service, *The Hunters,* 2nd ed. (Englewood Cliffs, NJ: Prentice Hall, 1979), p. 10.

[14]Elizabeth Marshall Thomas, *The Harmless People* (New York: Knopf, 1959), p. 22.

[15]B. Lisa Groger, "Of Men and Machines: Cooperation among French Family Farmers," *Ethnology,* 20 (1981): 163–75.

[16]Stuart Plattner, "Marxism," in Stuart Plattner, ed., *Economic Anthropology* (Stanford, CA: Stanford University Press, 1989), pp. 379–96.

[17]Jerald Hage and Charles H. Powers, *Post-Industrial Lives: Roles and Relationships in the 21st Century* (Newbury Park, CA: Sage Publications, 1992).

[18]Robert L. Carneiro, "Slash-and-Burn Cultivation among the Kuikuru and Its Implications for Settlement Patterns," in Yehudi Cohen, ed., *Man in Adaptation: The Cultural Present* (Chicago: Aldine, 1968), cited in Marshall Sahlins, *Stone Age Economics* (Chicago: Aldine, 1972), p. 68.

[19]Marvin Harris, *Cows, Pigs, Wars and Witches: The Riddles of Culture* (New York: Random House, Vintage, 1975), pp. 127–28.

[20]Sahlins, in *Stone Age Economics,* p. 87, introduced North American anthropology to Alexander Chayanov and coined the phrase *Chayanov's rule.*

[21]Alexander V. Chayanov, *The Theory of Peasant Economy,* D. Thorner, B. Kerblay, and R. E. F. Smith, eds. (Homewood, IL: Richard D. Irwin, 1966), p. 78; for a discussion of Chayanov's analysis see E. Paul Durrenberger, "Chayanov's Economic Analysis in Anthropology," *Journal of Anthropological Research,* 36 (1980): 133–48.

[22]Michael Chibnik, "The Economic Effects of Household Demography: A Cross-Cultural Assessment of Chayanov's Theory," in Morgan D. Maclachlan, ed., *Household Economies and Their Transformations,* Monographs in Economic Anthropology, No. 3 (Lanham, MD: University Press of America, 1987), pp. 74–106; E. Paul Durrenberger, "Chayanov's Economic Analysis," also finds some support in an analysis of three northern Thailand groups. For a critique of the equation of Chayanov's rule with Chayanov's analysis, see Nicola Tannenbaum, "The Misuse of Chayanov: 'Chayanov's Rule' and Empiricist Bias in Anthropology," *American Anthropologist,* 86 (1984): 927–42.

[23]Sahlins, *Stone Age Economics,* pp. 101–48.

[24]David C. McClelland, *The Achieving Society* (New York: Van Nostrand, 1961).

[25]Julian H. Steward and Louis C. Faron, *Native Peoples of South America* (New York: McGraw-Hill, 1959), pp. 122–25.

[26]Beatrice B. Whiting and Carolyn P. Edwards, *Children of Different Worlds: The Formation of Social Behavior* (Cambridge, MA: Harvard University Press, 1988), p. 164.

[27]Moni Nag, Benjamin N. F. White, and R. Creighton Peet, "An Anthropological Approach to the Study of the Economic Value of Children in Java and Nepal," *Current Anthropology,* 19 (1978): 295–96.

[28]Whiting and Edwards, *Children of Different Worlds,* pp. 97–107.

[29]Patricia Draper and Elizabeth Cashdan, "Technological Change and Child Behavior among the !Kung," *Ethnology,* 27 (1988): 348.

[30]Nag, White, and Peet, "An Anthropological Approach to the Study of the Economic Value of Children in Java and Nepal," p. 293; see also Candice Bradley, "The Sexual Division of Labor and the Value of Children," *Behavior Science Research,* 19 (1984–1985): 160–64.

[31]Carol R. Ember, "The Relative Decline in Women's Contribution to Agriculture with Intensification," *American Anthropologist,* 85 (1983): 291–97.

[32]Monica Wilson, *Good Company: A Study of Nyakyusa Age Villages* (Boston: Beacon Press, 1963 [originally published 1951]).

[33]Stanley H. Udy, Jr., *Work in Traditional and Modern Society* (Englewood Cliffs, NJ: Prentice Hall, 1970), pp. 35–37.

[34]Marshall D. Sahlins, *Moala: Culture and Nature on a Fijian Island* (Ann Arbor: University of Michigan Press, 1962), pp. 50–52.

[35]Leopold Pospisil, *The Kapauku Papuans of West New Guinea* (New York: Holt, Rinehart & Winston, 1963), p. 43.

[36]I. M. Lewis, *A Pastoral Democracy* (New York: Oxford University Press, 1961), pp. 107–9.

[37]Udy, *Work in Traditional and Modern Society,* pp. 35–39.

[38]Ibid., pp. 39–40.

[39]Eric Alden Smith, "Anthropological Applications of Optimal Foraging Theory: A Critical Review," *Current Anthropology,* 24 (1983): 626.

[40]Kim Hill, Hillard Kaplan, Kristen Hawkes, and A. Magdalena Hurtado, "Foraging Decisions among Aché Hunter-Gatherers: New Data and Implications for Optimal Foraging Models," *Ethology and Sociobiology,* 8 (1987): 17–18.

[41]Andrew Sih and Katharine A. Milton, "Optimal Diet Theory: Should the !Kung Eat Mongongos?" *American Anthropologist,* 87 (1985): 395–401.

[42]Christina H. Gladwin, "A Theory of Real-Life Choice: Applications to Agricultural Decisions," in Peggy F. Barlett, ed., *Agricultural Decision-Making: Anthropological Contributions to Rural Development* (New York: Academic Press, 1980), pp. 45–85.

[43]Michael Chibnik, "The Statistical Behavior Approach: The Choice between Wage Labor and Cash Cropping in Rural Belize," in Barlett, ed., *Agricultural Decision-Making,* pp. 87–114.

[44]Karl Polanyi, "The Economy as Instituted Process," in Karl Polanyi, Conrad Arensberg, and Harry W. Pearson, eds., *Trade and Market in the Early Empires* (New York: Free Press, 1957), pp. 243–70.

[45]Sahlins, *Stone Age Economics,* pp. 188–96.

[46]Lorna Marshall, "Sharing, Talking and Giving: Relief of Social Tensions among !Kung Bushmen," *Africa,* 31 (1961): 239–41.

[47]The // sign in the name for the G//ana people symbolizes a click sound not unlike the sound we make when we want a horse to move faster.

[48]Elizabeth A. Cashdan, "Egalitarianism among Hunters and Gatherers," *American Anthropologist,* 82 (1980): 116–20.

⁴⁹Hillard Kaplan and Kim Hill, "Food Sharing among Aché Foragers: Tests of Explanatory Hypotheses," *Current Anthropology*, 26 (1985): 223–46; Hillard Kaplan, Kim Hill, and A. Magdalena Hurtado, "Risk, Foraging and Food Sharing among the Aché," in Elizabeth Cashdan, ed., *Risk and Uncertainty in Tribal and Peasant Economies* (Boulder, CO: Westview Press, 1990), pp. 107–43.

⁵⁰Raymond Hames, "Sharing among the Yanomamo: Part I, the Effects of Risk," in Cashdan, ed., *Risk and Uncertainty in Tribal and Peasant Economies,* pp. 89–105.

⁵¹Kaplan, Hill, and Hurtado, "Risk, Foraging and Food Sharing among the Aché."

⁵²Bruce Winterhalder, "Open Field, Common Pot: Harvest Variability and Risk Avoidance in Agricultural and Foraging Societies," in Elizabeth Cashdan, ed., *Risk and Uncertainty in Tribal and Peasant Economies,* pp. 67–87.

⁵³Kathleen A. Mooney, "The Effects of Rank and Wealth on Exchange among the Coast Salish," *Ethnology,* 17 (1978): 391–406.

⁵⁴Asen Balikci, *The Netsilik Eskimo* (Garden City, NY: Natural History Press, 1970), quoted in Mooney, "The Effects of Rank and Wealth on Exchange among the Coast Salish," p. 392.

⁵⁵Mooney, "The Effects of Rank and Wealth on Exchange among the Coast Salish," p. 392.

⁵⁶Marshall, "Sharing, Talking and Giving," p. 242.

⁵⁷Thomas S. Abler, "Iroquois: The Tree of Peace and the War Kettle," in Melvin Ember, Carol R. Ember, and David Levinson, eds., *Portraits of Culture: Ethnographic Originals* (Englewood Cliffs, NJ: Prentice Hall, 1994). Prentice Hall/Simon & Schuster Custom Publishing.

⁵⁸Nadine Peacock and Robert Bailey, "Efe: Investigating Food and Fertility in the Ituri Rain Forest," in Melvin Ember, Carol R. Ember, and David Levinson, eds., *Portraits of Culture: Ethnographic Originals* (Englewood Cliffs, NJ: Prentice Hall, 1994). Prentice Hall/Simon & Schuster Custom Publishing.

⁵⁹Caroline Humphrey and Stephen Hugh-Jones, "Introduction: Barter, Exchange and Value," in Caroline Humphrey and Stephen Hugh-Jones, eds., *Barter, Exchange and Value: An Anthropological Approach* (New York: Cambridge University Press, 1992).

⁶⁰Richard E. Blanton, "Variation in Economy," in Carol R. Ember and Melvin Ember, eds., *Cross-Cultural Research for Social Science* (Englewood Cliffs, NJ: Prentice Hall, 1995). Prentice Hall/Simon & Schuster Custom Publishing; C. A. Gregory, *Gifts and Commodities* (New York: Academic Press, 1982).

⁶¹J. P. Singh Uberoi, *The Politics of the Kula Ring: An Analysis of the Findings of Bronislaw Malinowski* (Manchester: University of Manchester Press, 1962).

⁶²Bronislaw Malinowski, " *Kula:* The Circulating Exchange of Valuables in the Archipelagoes of Eastern New Guinea," *Man,* 51, no. 2 (1920): 97–105; and Uberoi, *The Politics of the Kula Ring.*

⁶³Jerry W. Leach, "Introduction," in Jerry W. Leach and Edmund Leach, eds., *The Kula: New Perspectives on Massim Exchange* (Cambridge: Cambridge University Press, 1983), pp. 12, 16.

⁶⁴Annette B. Weiner, *Women of Value, Men of Renown: New Perspectives in Trobriand Exchange* (Austin: University of Texas Press, 1976), pp. 77–117.

⁶⁵Robert F. Murphy, "Matrilocality and Patrilineality in Mundurucu Society," *American Anthropologist,* 58 (1956): 414–34.

⁶⁶James L. Gibbs, Jr., "The Kpelle of Liberia," in Gibbs, ed., *Peoples of Africa,* p. 223. But in other societies the food provided a work party may exceed the value of the labor provided, or there may not be any subsequent reciprocation of labor. Thus, an exchange of food for labor may not always be balanced. See Mahir Saul, "Work Parties, Wages, and Accumulation in a Voltaic Village," *American Ethnologist,* 10 (1983): 77–96.

⁶⁷Sahlins, *Stone Age Economics,* p. 195.

⁶⁸Ibid., pp. 196–204.

⁶⁹Frederic L. Pryor, *The Origins of the Economy: A Comparative Study of Distribution in Primitive and Peasant Economies* (New York: Academic Press, 1977), pp. 204, 276.

⁷⁰Andrew P. Vayda, Anthony Leeds, and David B. Smith, "The Place of Pigs in Melanesian Subsistence," in Viola E. Garfield, ed., *Symposium: Patterns of Land Utilization, and Other Papers,* Proceedings of the Annual Spring Meeting of the American Ethnological Society, 1961 (Seattle: University of Washington Press, 1962), pp. 69–74.

⁷¹Philip Drucker, "The Potlatch," in George Dalton, ed., *Tribal and Peasant Economies: Readings in Economic Anthropology* (Garden City, NY: Natural History Press, 1967), pp. 481–93.

⁷²Harris, *Cows, Pigs, Wars and Witches,* p. 120.

⁷³Kenneth D. Tollefson, "Tlingit: Chiefs Past and Present," in Melvin Ember, Carol R. Ember, and David Levinson, eds., *Portraits of Culture: Ethnographic Originals* (Englewood Cliffs, NJ: Prentice Hall, 1995). Prentice Hall/Simon & Schuster Custom Publishing.

⁷⁴Andrew P. Vayda, "Pomo Trade Feasts," in Dalton, ed., *Tribal and Peasant Economies,* pp. 494–500.

⁷⁵John Beattie, *Bunyoro: An African Kingdom* (New York: Holt, Rinehart & Winston, 1960).

⁷⁶R. C. Thurnwald, "Pigs and Currency in Buin: Observations About Primitive Standards of Value and Economics," *Oceania,* 5 (1934): 125.

⁷⁷Pryor, *The Origins of the Economy,* pp. 284–86.

⁷⁸Elman R. Service, *Primitive Social Organization: An Evolutionary Perspective* (New York: Random House, 1962), pp. 145–46.

⁷⁹Harris, *Cows, Pigs, Wars and Witches,* pp. 118–21.

⁸⁰Stuart Plattner, "Introduction," in Stuart Plattner, ed., *Markets and Marketing,* Monographs in Economic Anthropology, No. 4 (Lanham, MD: University Press of America, 1985), p. viii.

⁸¹Pryor, *The Origins of the Economy,* pp. 31–33.

[82]Thurnwald, "Pigs and Currency in Buin," p. 122.

[83]Plattner, "Introduction," p. xii.

[84]Pryor, *The Origins of the Economy*, pp. 153–83.

[85]Ibid., pp. 109–11.

[86]Brian L. Foster, "Ethnicity and Commerce," *American Ethnologist*, 1 (1974): 437–47.

[87]Pryor, *The Origins of the Economy*, pp. 125–48.

[88]See, for example, Eric Wolf, "Types of Latin American Peasantry: A Preliminary Discussion," *American Anthropologist*, 57 (1955): 452–71; and Pedro Carrasco, "The Civil-Religious Hierarchy in Mesoamerican Communities: Pre-Spanish Background and Colonial Development," *American Anthropologist*, 63 (1961): 483–97.

[89]Waldemar R. Smith, *The Fiesta System and Economic Change* (New York: Columbia University Press, 1977); and Marvin Harris, *Patterns of Race in the Americas* (New York: Walker, 1964).

[90]Smith, *The Fiesta System and Economic Change*; and Harris, *Patterns of Race in the Americas*.

Social Stratification

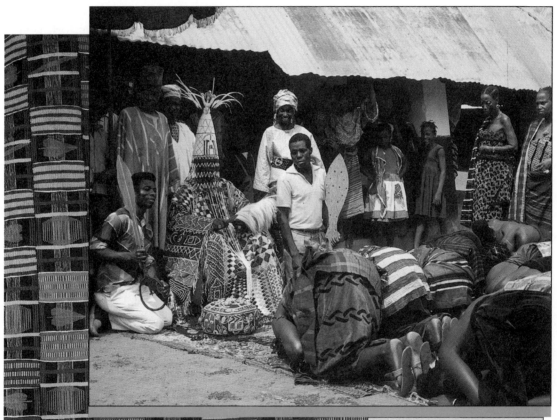

A long-enduring value in the United States is the belief that "all men are created equal." These famous words from our Declaration of Independence do not mean that all people are equal in wealth or status, but rather that all (including women nowadays) are supposed to be equal before the law. In fact, modern industrial societies such as our own are socially stratified—that is, they contain social groups that have unequal access to important advantages, such as economic resources, power, and prestige.

Many sociologists say that all societies are stratified; anthropologists disagree. But the disagreement is really a matter of definition, because sociologists and anthropologists do not usually mean the same thing by the term *stratification*. When sociologists speak of the "universality of stratification," they mean that all societies show some inequality from one *individual* to another. The sociological definition of stratification derives from the observation that in even the simplest societies there are usually some differences in advantages based on age or ability or gender: adults have higher status than children, the skilled more than the unskilled, men more than women. (We discuss sexual or "gender" stratification in the next chapter.) When anthropologists say that stratification is not universal and that egalitarian societies exist, they mean that there are some societies in which all *social groups* (for example, families) have more or less the same access or right to advantages. It is not a question of deciding whether sociologists or anthropologists are correct: both are. For anthropologists, then, human inequality may be universal; social stratification is not.

Systems of social stratification are strongly linked to the customary ways in which economic resources are allocated, distributed, and converted through labor into goods and services. So we would not expect substantial inequality if all people had relatively equal access to economic resources. But stratification cannot be understood solely in terms of economic resources—there are other benefits (such as prestige and power) that may be unequally distributed. After examining how societies vary in their systems of stratification, we will turn to possible explanations of why they vary.

Sharing can occur even in a socially stratified society. Here we see men in a village in Yunnan, China, cutting the meat from a steer into 72 portions for the families of the village.

VARIATION IN DEGREE OF SOCIAL INEQUALITY

Societies vary in the extent to which social groups (as well as individuals) have unequal access to advantages. In this chapter we are concerned with differential or unequal access to three types of advantages: wealth or economic resources, power, and prestige. As we saw in the preceding chapter, resources may range from hunting or fishing grounds to farmland to money; the different social groups in a society may or may not have unequal access to these resources. Power is a second but related advantage. It is the ability to make others do what they do not want to do; power is influence based on the threat of force. When groups in a society have rules or customs that give them unequal access to wealth or resources, they generally also have unequal access to power. So, for example, when we speak of a "company town" in the United States, we are referring to the fact that the company that employs most of the residents of the town usually has considerable control over them. Finally, there is the advantage of prestige. When we speak of prestige we mean that someone or some group is accorded particular respect or honor. Even if it is true that there is always unequal access by individuals to prestige (because of differences in age, gender, or ability), there are some societies in the ethnographic record that have no social groups with unequal access to prestige.

Thus, anthropologists conventionally distinguish three types of society in terms of the degree to which different social groups have unequal access to advantages: *egalitarian, rank,* and *class* societies. Some societies in the ethnographic record do not fit easily into any of these three types; as with any classification scheme, some cases seem to straddle the line between types.[1] But most societies are conventionally classified as belonging to just one of the three types summarized in Table 8–1. **Egalitarian societies** contain no social groups with greater or lesser access to economic resources, power, or prestige. **Rank societies** do not have unequal access to economic resources or to power, but they do contain social groups with unequal access to prestige. Rank societies, then, are partially stratified. **Class societies** have unequal access to all three advantages—economic resources, power, and prestige.

EGALITARIAN SOCIETIES

Egalitarian societies can be found not only among foragers but also among horticulturalists and pastoralists. An important point to keep in mind is that *egalitarian* does not mean that all people within such societies are the *same.* There will always be differences among individuals in age and gender and in such abilities or traits as hunting skill, perception, health, creativity, physical prowess, attractiveness, and intelligence. According to Morton Fried, *egalitarian* means that within a given society "there are as many positions of prestige in any given age/sex grade as there are persons capable of filling them."[2] For instance, if a person can achieve high status by fashioning fine spears, and if every person in the society fashions such spears, then every person acquires high status as a spear maker. If high status is also acquired by carving bones into artifacts, and if only three people are considered expert carvers of bones, then only those three achieve high status as carvers. But the next generation might produce eight spear makers and twenty carvers. In an egalitarian society, the number of prestigious positions is adjusted to fit the number of qualified candidates. We would say, therefore, that such a society is not socially stratified.

There are, of course, differences in position and prestige arising out of differences in ability. Even in an egalitarian society, differential prestige exists.

▼▼▼▼▼▼
TABLE 8–1 *Stratification in Three Types of Societies*

Type of Society	Economic Resources	Power	Prestige	Examples
	SOME SOCIAL GROUPS HAVE GREATER ACCESS TO:			
Egalitarian	No	No	No	!Kung, Mbuti
Rank	No	No	Yes	Trobriand Islands
Class/caste	Yes	Yes	Yes	United States and Canada, India, Rwanda

But, although some persons may be better hunters or more skilled artists than others, there is still equal *access* to status positions for people of the same ability. Any prestige gained by achievement of high status as a great hunter, for instance, is neither transferable nor inheritable. Because a man is a great hunter, it is not assumed that his sons are also great hunters. There may also be individuals with more influence, but it is not bequeathable, and there are no groups with appreciably more influence over time. An egalitarian society keeps inequality at a minimal level.

Any differences in prestige that do exist are not related to economic differences. Egalitarian groups depend heavily on *sharing*, which ensures equal access to economic resources despite differences in acquired prestige. For instance, in some egalitarian communities, some members achieve higher status through hunting. But even before the hunt begins, how the animal will be divided and distributed among the members of the band has already been decided according to custom. The culture works to separate the status achieved by members—recognition as great hunters—from actual possession of the wealth, which in this case would be the slain animal.

Just as egalitarian societies do not have social groups with unequal access to economic resources, they also do not have social groups with unequal access to power. As we will see later in the chapter on political organization, unequal access to power by social groups seems to occur only in state societies, which have full-time political officials and marked differences in wealth.

The Mbuti Pygmies of central Africa provide an example of a society almost totally equal: "Neither in ritual, hunting, kinship nor band relations do they exhibit any discernable inequalities of rank or advantage."[3] Their hunting bands have no leaders; recognition of the achievement of one person is not accompanied by privilege of any sort. Economic resources such as food are communally shared, and even tools and weapons are frequently passed from person to person. Only within the family are rights and privileges differentiated.

RANK SOCIETIES

Most societies with social *ranking* practice agriculture or herding, but not all agricultural or pastoral societies are ranked. Ranking is characterized by social groups with unequal access to prestige or status but *not* significantly unequal access to economic resources or power. Unequal access to prestige is often reflected in the position of chief, a rank to which only some members of a specified group in the society can succeed.

In rank societies, the position of chief is at least partially hereditary. The criterion of superior rank in some Polynesian societies, for example, was genealogical. Usually the eldest son succeeded to the position of chief, and different kinship groups were differentially ranked according to their genealogical distance from the chiefly line.

In rank societies, chiefs are often treated with deference by people of lower rank. For example, among the Trobriand Islanders of Melanesia, people of lower rank must keep their heads lower than a person of higher rank. So, when a chief is standing, commoners must bend low. When commoners have to walk past a chief who happens to be sitting, he may rise and they will bend. If the chief chooses to remain seated, they must crawl.[4]

Chiefs may sometimes look as if they are substantially richer than commoners, for they may receive many gifts and have larger storehouses. In some instances, the chief may be called the "owner" of the land, but other people have the right to use the land. The chief may have bigger storehouses, but his stores may be only temporary accumulations for feasts or other redistributions. The chief in a rank society usually cannot make people give him gifts or work on communal projects. Often the chief can encourage production only by working furiously on his own cultivation.[5]

Unusual among rank societies were the nineteenth-century Native Americans who lived along the Northwest Coast.[6] They were unusual because their economy was based on food collecting. But huge catches of salmon—which were preserved for year-round consumption—enabled them to support fairly large and permanent communities. In many ways, the Northwest Coast societies were similar to food-producing societies, even in their development of social ranking. Still, the principal means of proving one's high status among the Northwest Coast Indians was to give wealth away. The tribal chiefs celebrated solemn rites by grand feasts (potlatches), at which they gave gifts to every guest.[7]

CLASS SOCIETIES

In class societies, as in rank societies, there is unequal access to prestige. But unlike rank societies, class societies are characterized by groups that have substantially greater or lesser access to economic re-

A high chief in Fiji is served the ceremonial drink of kava first.

sources and power. That is, not every social group has the same opportunity to obtain land, animals, money, or other economic benefits or the same opportunity to exercise power that other groups have. Fully stratified or class societies range from somewhat open to virtually closed class, or *caste,* systems.

Open Class Systems

A **class** is a category of persons who all have about the same opportunity to obtain economic resources, power, and prestige. Different classes have differing opportunities. We call class systems *open* if there is some possibility of moving from one class to another. Since the 1920s, there have been innumerable studies of classes in North American towns and cities. Sociologists have produced profiles of these different communities—known variously as Yankee City, Middletown, Jonesville, and Old City—all of which support the premise that the United States has distinguishable, though somewhat open, social classes. Both W. Lloyd Warner and Paul Lunt's Yankee City study[8] and Robert and Helen Lynd's Middletown study[9] concluded that the social status or prestige of a family is generally correlated with the occupation and wealth of the head of the family.

The determinants of class status can change over time. For example, in 1776 the middle class in the United States consisted of the families of self-employed craftspeople, shopkeepers, and farmers. By 1985, only about 8 percent of the population were self-employed, but many more people thought of themselves as belonging to the middle class. Self-employment is now a less important determinant of middle class status than working with one's mind and having authority over others on the job.[10]

How open a class system is, how possible it is to move into a class that is different from the one you were born into, may vary over time. In Britain, it is estimated that only 16.5 percent of the population born before 1890 moved to a higher social class than their parents belonged to; for those born between 1930 and 1947, the percentage moving up was 30.5 percent. Most of this increase in mobility can be explained as the result of a declining number of semiskilled and skilled manual-labor jobs throughout the twentieth century, along with an increase in clerical and service jobs. In short, many working-class individuals were able to move up to more middle-class jobs. But, although there was considerable mobility from working to middle class in Britain, there was much less mobility into the upper class. There was also some downward social mobility, al-

THE WIDENING GAP BETWEEN RICH AND POOR IN THE UNITED STATES

In the 1950s and 1960s, the U.S. economy expanded enormously. Many people grew up during those years assuming that things could only get better. Their parents may have lived through the Great Depression of the 1930s, but that kind of thing could never happen to them. They would have bigger incomes and bigger houses and live the American Dream. But from the mid-1970s through the early 1990s something went wrong. Anthropologist Katherine Newman spent two years interviewing ordinary people in a suburban town she calls "Pleasanton." Lauren's comments are typical: "I'll never have what my parents had. I can't even dream of that. . . . I worked all those years and then I didn't get to candyland." It is not that Lauren didn't follow the

How Wealthy the Wealthy: A History

The purple line shows the percentage of the national wealth held by the richest one percent of Americans, from 1774 to 1989.

The country has gone through several cycles of concentration and redistribution of wealth. Only once before were the rich as rich as they were in 1989 — but that took 150 years to achieve.

The chart data are from estimates by three economists — Claudia Goldin and Bradford DeLong at Harvard University and Edward Wolff at New York University.

1865 Emancipation. Vast "wealth" - in the form of slaves - is lost to Southern landowners and "transferred" to the poor - the newly freed themselves.

AGRARIAN SOCIETY

Colonial era to 1820. Land on frontiers is essentially free for the taking, and the population is small. Labor is expensive, compared to Europe, and industry negligible. Wealth is Southern planters and coastal merchants.

29   27

1862 Homestead Act opens rest of public lands to settlers.

WAVES OF IMMIGRANTS

1870's-1920's. The ranks of labor are swelled by millions, holding down wage growth. Laws restricting immigration are passed in 1921, 1924, and 1929.

14.6%

1787 Under the Northwest Ordinance, new land is distributed as small plots, not huge fiefs.

EARLY INDUSTRIAL REVOLUTION

1820-1850. Rise of railroads and textiles creates fortunes, concentrating wealth.

| 1770's | 1780's | 1790's | 1800's | 1810's | 1820's | 1830's | 1840's | 1850's | 1860's | 1870's | 1880's |

Adapted from Sylvia Nasar, "The Rich Get Richer, But Never the Same Way Twice," New York Times, August 16, 1992, p. E3. Copyright © 1992 by The New York Times Company. Reprinted by permission.

rules. She worked hard to get good grades, she went to college, and she has a respectable job. Yet, even though both she and her husband work, they still cannot afford a house and they are not doing as well as her parents did on just one salary. Not only is housing more expensive. Jobs are less secure and harder to find, and the credentials needed for those jobs are harder to achieve.

The squeeze on the people in the middle is only a small part of the economic picture. Not all segments of society did worse since the mid-1970s. While middle- and working-class people got poorer, the rich got richer. By the end of the 1980s, the richest 1 percent of all Americans owned over 36 percent of all the wealth (assets minus debts) in this country. The only time the very rich owned more was at the end of the 1920s, just before the Great Depression (see the graph). The same trend occurred in the distribution of income—the wealthiest 20 percent of the population earned over 44 percent of all the income in 1991, which was the highest percentage since 1949.

As the graph shows, the degree of economic inequality has fluctuated throughout U.S. history, so the recent increase in inequality may not continue. Change over time in the degree of inequality sometimes has economic causes; the stock market crash in 1929 made the wealthy less wealthy. Some of the change over time is due to shifts in public policy. During the New Deal of the 1930s, tax changes and work programs shifted more income to ordinary people; in the 1980s, tax cuts for the wealthy helped the rich get richer.

Will the gap between rich and poor continue to widen? Only the future will tell. But whatever happens, political events—such as which interest groups can most influence Congress—are likely to be as crucial as the competitive position of the United States in the world economy.

Sources: *Katherine S. Newman,* Declining Fortunes: The Withering of the American Dream *(New York: Basic Books, 1993), quotation from p. 3; Kevin Phillips,* The Politics of Rich and Poor: Wealth and the American Electorate in the Reagan Aftermath *(New York: Random House, 1990); U.S. Bureau of the Census,* Statistical Abstract of the United States: 1993, *113th ed. (Washington, D.C.: U.S. Government Printing Office, 1993).*

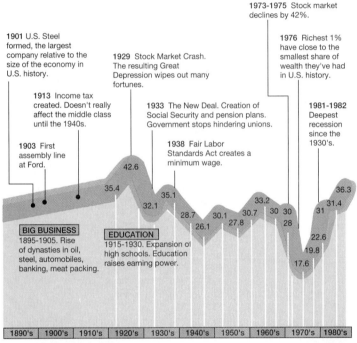

1901 U.S. Steel formed, the largest company relative to the size of the economy in U.S. history.

1913 Income tax created. Doesn't really affect the middle class until the 1940s.

1903 First assembly line at Ford.

1929 Stock Market Crash. The resulting Great Depression wipes out many fortunes.

1933 The New Deal. Creation of Social Security and pension plans. Government stops hindering unions.

1938 Fair Labor Standards Act creates a minimum wage.

1973-1975 Stock market declines by 42%.

1976 Richest 1% have close to the smallest share of wealth they've had in U.S. history.

1981-1982 Deepest recession since the 1930's.

BIG BUSINESS
1895-1905. Rise of dynasties in oil, steel, automobiles, banking, meat packing.

EDUCATION
1915-1930. Expansion of high schools. Education raises earning power.

42.6 35.4 32.1 35.1 28.7 26.1 30.1 27.8 30.7 33.2 30 30 28 31 22.6 19.8 17.6 31.4 36.3

| 1890's | 1900's | 1910's | 1920's | 1930's | 1940's | 1950's | 1960's | 1970's | 1980's |

PROGRESSIVE ERA
1900-1914. Inequality of wealth becomes a national political issue. Child labor laws, wage and hour laws, railroad rate controls created.

1980s
Top tax rate slashed from 70% to less than 30%, shifting tax burden to the middle class. Federal Reserve's anti-inflation stance buoys stocks and bonds. Fluctuating dollar sends manufacturing jobs overseas.

ROARING TWENTIES
1923-1929. Stock market boom expands richest people's fortunes.

WORLD WAR II
1941-1945. The draft dries up the labor supply, putting upward pressure on wages.

RAPID GROWTH
1950-1970. Helped by G.I. bill, many Americans got college educations.

though the rate of it declined over time. Downward mobility in Britain declined from 33 percent for those born before 1890 to 22 percent for those born between 1930 and 1947.[11]

How do the United States and Canada compare with other countries in degree of mobility? Among capitalist countries, Canada and Sweden have more mobility than the United States, France, and Britain. Japan and Italy have less mobility. If we focus on the ease of moving into the highest class, Italy, France, Spain, Germany, and Japan are more difficult than Britain and the United States.[12]

Degree of mobility, however, is not the same as degree of economic inequality. For example, Britain and the United States do not differ that much in rate of mobility, but they do differ considerably in the wealth of the rich compared with the poor. In 1989, the richest 1 percent in Britain held 18 percent of the wealth[13]; in the United States the comparable figure (at the end of the 1980s) was 36.3 percent (see the graph in the box titled "The Widening Gap between Rich and Poor in the United States"). The degree of inequality in Britain has declined enormously since the early 1900s: in 1911–1913, the wealthiest 1 percent held 69 percent of the nation's wealth.[14]

Another way to calculate the disparity between rich and poor is to use the ratio of income held by the top fifth of the population divided by the income held by the bottom fifth. Comparatively speaking, the United States has the biggest discrepancy of any of the developed countries (see Figure 8–1), with a ratio of about 10 to 1; the top 20 percent of the population in this country controls ten times the wealth controlled by the bottom 20 percent. Among the developing countries, Brazil is the most unequal, with a ratio of 30 to 1, but the United States has more inequality than some of the developing countries, such as India, Ghana, Pakistan, and the Philippines.[15]

Obtaining more education, particularly a university education, is one of the most effective ways to move upward in contemporary societies. In fact, in many countries educational attainment predicts one's social class better than parent's occupation does.[16] Lower-class persons may become "resocialized" at the university. Resocialization separates them from their parents and enables them to gradually learn the skills, speech, attitudes, and manners characteristic of the higher class they wish to join. So successful is this process that students from a lower class who move into a higher class may find themselves ashamed to take their new friends to their parents' homes.

But obtaining more education, and particularly higher education, is not so easy. Your chances of doing so are affected by the class you are born into, as are many other aspects of our lives. People of different classes usually live in different neigh-

FIGURE 8–1
Patterns of Income Distribution within Selected Countries

Percentage of total national income received by one-fifth of the population. Dates vary: most are in the late 1980s; the United States data are for 1990.   Source: *From Ruth Leger Sivard,* World Military and Social Expenditures 1993, *15th ed. (Washington, D.C.: World Priorities, 1993).*

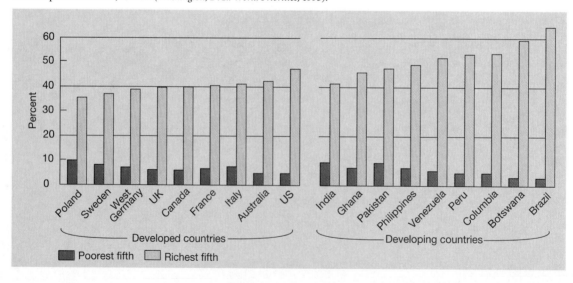

borhoods and go to different grade and secondary schools, and a person's ability to be accepted at a prestigious college might be affected by the grade and secondary schools attended. In addition, having money to spend on private schools and colleges may make it easier to go to the more prestigious schools, which are generally the more expensive schools. The schools we attend are not the only markers of class status. Our identification with a social class begins quite early in life. In addition to their differences in occupation and wealth, social classes vary in many other ways, including religious affiliation, closeness to kin, ideas about child rearing, job satisfaction, leisure-time activities, style of clothes and furniture, and (as we noted in the chapter on communication and language) even in styles of speech.[17]

Although one's adult class status is not fully determined at birth in open class societies, there is a high probability that most people will stay close to the class into which they were born and will marry within that class. That is, even if we do not inherit money from our parents, our chances of being successful are strongly influenced by our class background. The daughter of a wealthy business executive, for example, is likely to attend schools with good reputations. She will learn to speak with an accent that is more "elite." She will be likely to learn to ride horses, play tennis and the piano, and acquire the etiquette appropriate for attending concerts, parties, and teas. If she wants a career, she has a very good chance of getting into a college or graduate school of her choice, and she has social connections that can help her obtain a good starting position. If she gets married, she has a very good chance of marrying a man of similar background, tastes, and likelihood of success.

Class boundaries, though vague, have been established by custom and tradition; sometimes they have been reinforced by the enactment of laws. Many of our laws serve to protect property and thus tend to favor the upper and upper-middle classes. The poor, in contrast, seem to be perennial losers in our legal system. The crimes the poor are most likely to commit are dealt with quite harshly in our judicial system, and poor people rarely have the money to secure effective legal counsel.

Classes tend to perpetuate themselves through the bequeathing of wealth. John Brittain suggested that, in the United States, the transfer of money through bequests accounts for much of the wealth of the next generation. As we might expect, the importance of inheritance seems to increase at higher levels of wealth. That is, the wealth of richer people comes more from inheritance than does the wealth of not-so-rich people.[18]

Caste Systems

Some societies have classes that are virtually closed—these are called *castes*. A **caste** is a ranked group in which membership is determined at birth and marriage is restricted to members of one's own caste. So the only way you can belong is by being born into the group. And since you cannot marry outside the group, your children cannot acquire another caste status either. In India, for example, there are several thousand hereditary castes. Although the precise ranking of these thousands of groups is not completely clear, there appear to be four main levels of hierarchy, with the Brahmans at the top. The castes in India are often thought to be associated with different occupations, but that is not quite true. Most Indians live in rural areas and have agricultural occupations, but their castes vary a lot.[19]

Castes may exist in conjunction with a more open class system. Indeed, in India today, members of a low caste who can get wage-paying jobs (chiefly those in urban areas) may improve their social standing in the same ways available to people in other class societies. In general, however, they still cannot marry someone in a higher caste, so the caste system is perpetuated.

Questions basic to all stratified societies, and particularly to a caste society, were posed by John Ruskin, a nineteenth-century British essayist: "Which of us . . . is to do the hard and dirty work for the rest—and for what pay? Who is to do the pleasant and clean work, and for what pay?"[20] Those questions have been answered in India by the caste system, which mainly dictates how goods and services are exchanged, particularly in rural areas.[21] Who is to do the hard and dirty work for the rest of society is clearly established: a large group of untouchables forms the bottom of the hierarchy. Among the untouchables are subcastes such as the Camars, or leatherworkers, and the Bhangis, who traditionally are sweepers. At the top of the hierarchy, performing the pleasant and clean work of priests, are the Brahmans. Between the two extremes are thousands of castes and subcastes. In a typical village, the potter makes clay drinking cups and larger water vessels for the entire village population. In return, the principal landowner gives him a house site and supplies him twice yearly with grain. Some other castes owe the potter their services: the

A member of the barber caste in India gives the first haircut.

barber cuts his hair; the sweeper carries away his rubbish; the washer washes his clothes; the Brahman performs his children's weddings. The barber serves every caste in the village except the untouchables; he, in turn, is served by half of the others. He has inherited the families he works for, along with his father's occupation. He also receives a house site from the principal landowner and, at each harvest, all the grain he can lift. All castes help at harvest and at weddings for additional payment, which sometimes includes a money payment.

This description is, in fact, an idealized picture of the caste system of India. In reality, the system operates to the advantage of the principal landowning caste—sometimes the Brahmans and sometimes other castes. Also, it is not carried on without some resentment; signs of hostility are shown toward the ruling caste by the untouchables and other lower castes. The resentment does not appear to be against the caste system as such. Instead, the lower castes exhibit bitterness at their own low status and strive for greater equality. For instance, one of the Camars' traditional services is to remove dead cattle; in return, they can have the meat to eat and the hide to tan for their leatherworking. Because handling dead animals and eating beef are both regarded as unclean acts, the Camars of one village refused to continue this service. Thus, they lost a source of free hides and food in a vain attempt to escape unclean status.

Since World War II, the economic basis of the caste system in India has been undermined somewhat by the growing practice of giving cash payment for services. For instance, the son of a barber may be a teacher during the week, earning a cash salary, and confine his haircutting to weekends. But he still remains in the barber caste (Nai) and must marry within that caste.

Perpetuation of the caste system is ensured by the power of those in the upper castes, who derive three main advantages from their position: economic gain, gain in prestige, and sexual gain. The economic gain is the most immediately apparent. An ample supply of cheap labor and free services is maintained by the threat of sanctions. Lower-caste members may have their use of a house site withdrawn; they may be refused access to the village well or to common grazing land for animals; or they may be expelled from the village. Prestige is also maintained by the threat of sanctions; the higher castes expect deference and servility from the lower castes. The sexual gain is less apparent but equally real. The high-caste male has access to two groups of females, those of his own caste and those of lower castes. High-caste females are kept free of the "contaminating" touch of low-caste males because low-caste males are allowed access only to low-caste women. Moreover, the constant reminders of ritual uncleanness serve to keep the lower castes "in their place." Higher castes do not accept water from untouchables, sit next to them, or eat at the same table with them.

Although few areas of the world have developed a caste system like that of India, there are castelike features in some other societies. For example, blacks in the United States used to have a castelike status determined partially by the inherited characteristic of skin color. Until recently, some states had laws prohibiting a black from marrying a white. Even when interracial marriage does occur, children of the union are often regarded as having lower status than white children, even though they may have blonde hair and light skin. In the South, where treatment of blacks as a caste was most apparent, whites traditionally refused to eat with blacks or to sit next to them at lunch counters, on buses, and in schools. Separate drinking fountains and toilets for blacks and whites reinforced the idea of ritual uncleanness. The economic advantages and gains in prestige enjoyed by whites are well documented.[22]

The traditional barriers between blacks and whites in the United States have mostly been lifted in recent years, but the "color line" has not disappeared. Blacks may be found now in all social classes, but they are underrepresented in the wealthiest group and overrepresented at the bottom. Life expectancy for blacks is substantially lower than for whites.[23] Even those blacks who are now part of the elite may experience racism, the belief that blacks are inferior. Thus, blacks may have to be better than whites to get promoted, or it may be assumed that they got ahead just because they were black. Whites often expect them to be "ambassadors," to be called on mainly for knowledge about how to handle situations involving other blacks. They may work with whites, but go home to black neighborhoods. Or they may live in white neighborhoods and experience considerable isolation. Few blacks in the United States can avoid the anguish of racism.[24]

Another example of a caste group in a class society was the *Eta* of Japan. Unlike blacks in America, the Eta (now called the *Dowa Kankeisha*) were physically indistinguishable from other Japanese. Comparable to India's untouchables, they were a hereditary, endogamous (in-marrying) group. Their occupations were traditionally those of farm laborer, leatherworker, and basket weaver; their standard of living was very low. Discrimination against the Dowa Kankeisha was officially abolished by the Japanese government in 1871; more active steps have been taken recently. Since 1965, the government of Japan has been attempting to im-

prove living conditions for the Dowa and discourage discrimination against them.[25]

In Rwanda, a country in east-central Africa, a longtime caste system was overthrown, first by an election and then by a revolution in 1959–1960. Three castes had existed, each distinguished from the others by physical appearance and occupation. The ruling caste, the Tutsi, constituted about 15 percent of the population. They were the landlords and practiced the prestigious occupation of herding. The agricultural caste, the Hutu, made up about 85 percent of the population. As tenants of the Tutsi, they produced most of the country's food. The Twa, accounting for less than 1 percent of the population, were a Pygmy group of foragers who formed the lowest caste. It is believed that the three castes derived from three different language groups who came together through migration and conquest. Later, however, they came to use a common language, although remaining endogamous and segregated by hereditary occupations. When the Hutu united to demand more of the rewards of their labor in 1959, the king and many of the Tutsi ruling caste were driven out of the country. The Hutu then established a republican form of government and declared independence from Belgium. In this new government, however, the forest-dwelling Twa were generally excluded from full citizenship. The interethnic rivalry did not end there. Recently, Rwanda has had mass murders and civil war, largely between the Hutus and the Tutsis, with hundreds of thousands of people killed in 1993–1994.

Slavery

Slaves are persons who do not own their own labor, and as such they represent a class. Slavery has existed in various forms in many times and places, regardless of race and culture. Sometimes it has been a closed class, or caste, system, sometimes a relatively open class system. In different slave-owning societies, slaves have had different, but always some, legal rights.[26]

In ancient Greece, slaves often were conquered enemies. Because city-states were constantly conquering one another or rebelling against former conquerors, slavery was a threat to everyone. After the Trojan War, the transition of Hecuba from queen to slave was marked by her cry "Count no one happy, however fortunate, before he dies."[27] Nevertheless, Greek slaves were considered human beings, and they could even acquire some higher class status along with freedom. Andromache, Hecuba's daughter-in-law, was taken as slave and concubine by one of the Greek heroes. When his legal wife produced no children, Andromache's slave son became heir to his father's throne. Although slaves had no rights under law, once they were freed, either by the will of their master or by purchase, they and their descendants could become assimilated into the dominant group. In other words, slavery in Greece was not seen as the justified position of inferior people. It was regarded, rather, as an act of fate—"the luck of the draw"—that relegated a victim to the lowest class in society.

Among the Nupe, a society in central Nigeria, slavery was of quite another type.[28] The methods of obtaining slaves—as part of the booty of warfare, and later by purchase—were similar to those of Europeans, but the position of the slaves was very different. Mistreatment was rare. Male slaves were given the same opportunities to earn money as other dependent males in the household—younger brothers, sons, or other relatives. A slave might be given a garden plot of his own to cultivate, or he might be given a commission if his master was a craftsman or a tradesman. Slaves could acquire property, wealth, and even slaves of their own. But all of a slave's belongings went to the master at the slave's death.

Manumission, the granting of freedom, was built into the Nupe system. If a male slave could afford the marriage payment for a free woman, the children of the resulting marriage were free; the man himself, however, remained a slave. Marriage and concubinage were the easiest ways out of bondage for a slave woman. Once she had produced a child by her master, both she and the child had free status. The woman, however, was only figuratively free: if a concubine, she had to remain in that role. As might be expected, the family trees of the nobility and the wealthy were liberally grafted with branches descended from slave concubines.

The most fortunate slaves among the Nupe were the house slaves. They could rise to positions of power in the household as overseers and bailiffs, charged with law-enforcement and judicial duties. (Recall the Old Testament story of Joseph, who was sold into slavery by his brothers. Joseph became a household slave of the pharaoh and rose to the position of second in the kingdom because he devised an ingenious system of taxation.) There was even a titled group of Nupe slaves—the Order of Court Slaves—who were trusted officers of the king and members of an elite. Slave status in general, though, placed one at the bottom of the social ladder. In

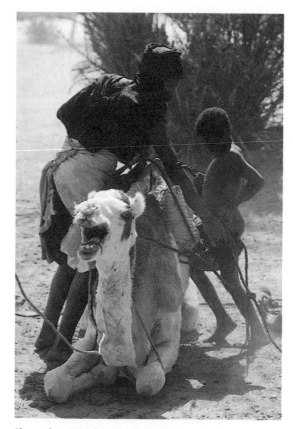

Slavery has existed in many societies. This Niger Republic boy, formerly a Tuareg slave but now a servant, helps load skins filled with water onto a camel's back.

the Nupe system, few slaves, mainly princes from their own societies, ever achieved membership in the titled group.

In the United States, slavery originated as a means of obtaining cheap labor, but the slaves soon came to be regarded as deserving of their low status because of their alleged inherent inferiority. Because the slaves were black, some whites justified slavery and belief in black people's inferiority by quoting Scripture out of context ("they shall be hewers of wood and drawers of water"). Slaves could not marry or make any other contracts, nor could they own property. In addition, their children were also slaves, and the master had sexual rights over the female slaves. Because the status of slavery was determined by birth in the United States, slaves constituted a caste. During the days of slavery, therefore, the United States had both a caste and a class system. And even after the abolition of slavery, as we have noted, some castelike elements remained.

As for why slavery may have developed in the first place, the cross-cultural evidence is as yet inconclusive. We do know, however, that slavery is not an inevitable stage in economic development, contrary to what some persons have assumed. In other words, slavery is *not* found mainly in certain economies, such as those dependent on intensive agriculture. (Unlike the United States until the Civil War, many societies with intensive agriculture did not develop any variety of slavery.) Also, the hypothesis that slavery develops where available resources are plentiful but labor is scarce is not supported by the cross-cultural evidence. All we can say definitely is that slavery does not occur in developed or industrial economies; either it disappears or it was never present in them.[29]

THE EMERGENCE OF STRATIFICATION

Anthropologists are not certain why social stratification developed. Nevertheless, they are reasonably sure that higher levels of stratification emerged relatively recently in human history. Archaeological sites dating before about 7,500 years ago do not show extensive evidence of inequality. Houses do not appear to vary much in size or content, and burials seem to be more or less the same, suggesting that their occupants were treated the same in life and death. Another indication that stratification is a relatively recent development in human history is the fact that certain cultural features associated with stratification also developed relatively recently. For example, most societies that depend primarily on agriculture or herding have social classes.[30] Agriculture and herding developed within the past 10,000 years, so we may assume that most food collectors in the distant past lacked social classes. Other recently developed cultural features associated with class stratification include fixed settlements, political integration beyond the community level, the use of money as a medium of exchange, and the presence of at least some full-time specialization.[31]

In 1966, the comparative sociologist Gerhard Lenski suggested that the 10,000-year-old trend toward increasing inequality was reversing. He argued that inequalities of power and privilege in industrial societies—measured in terms of the concentration of political power and the distribution of income—are less pronounced than inequalities in complex preindustrial societies. Technology in industrialized societies is so complex, he suggested, that those in power are compelled to delegate some authority to subordinates if the system is to work. In addition, a decline in the birth rate in industrialized societies, coupled with the need for skilled labor, has pushed the average wage of workers far above the subsistence level, resulting in greater equality in the distribution of income. Finally, Lenski also suggested that the spread of the democratic ideology, and particularly its acceptance by elites, has significantly broadened the political power of the lower classes.[32] A few studies have tested and supported Lenski's hypothesis that inequality has decreased with industrialization. In general, nations that are highly industrialized exhibit a lower level of inequality than nations that are only somewhat industrialized.[33] But, as we have seen, even the most industrialized societies may still have an enormous degree of inequality.

Why did social stratification develop in the first place? On the basis of his study of Polynesian societies, Marshall Sahlins suggested that an increase in agricultural productivity results in social stratification.[34] According to Sahlins, the degree of stratification is directly related to the production of a surplus, which is made possible by greater technological efficiency. The higher the level of productivity and the larger the agricultural surplus, the greater the scope and complexity of the distribution system. The status of the chief, who serves as redistributing agent, is in turn enhanced. Sahlins argued that the differentiation between distributor and producer inevitably gives rise to differentiation in other aspects of life:

> First, there would be a tendency for the regulator of distribution to exert some authority over production itself—especially over productive activities which necessitate subsidization, such as communal labor or specialist labor. A degree of control of production implies a degree of control over the utilization of resources, or, in other words, some preeminent property rights. In turn, regulation of these economic processes necessitates the exercise of authority in interpersonal affairs; differences in social power emerge.[35]

Sahlins later rejected the idea that a surplus leads to chiefships, postulating instead that the relationship may be the other way around—that is, leaders encourage the development of a surplus so as to enhance their prestige through feasts, potlatches, and other redistributive events.[36] Of course, both trajectories are possible: surpluses may generate stratification, and stratification may generate surpluses. Those two possibilities are not mutually exclusive.

Lenski's theory of the causes of stratification is similar to Sahlins's original idea. Lenski, too, argued that production of a surplus is the stimulus in the de-

IS INEQUALITY BETWEEN COUNTRIES INCREASING?

When people support themselves by what they collect and produce themselves, as most people the world over did until a few thousand years ago, it is difficult to compare the standards of living of different societies because we cannot translate what people have into market or monetary value. It is only where people are at least partially involved in the world market economy that we can measure the standard of living in monetary terms. Nowadays, this comparison is possible for most of the world; many people in most societies depend on buying and selling for a living. And the more people there are who depend on international exchange, the more possible it is to compare them in terms of standard economic indicators. We do not have such indicators for all the different societies, but we do have them for many countries. Those indicators suggest that the degree of economic inequality in the world is not only

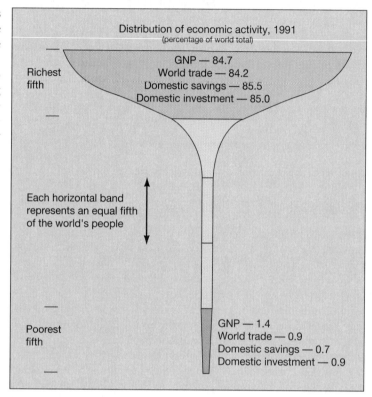

Distribution of economic activity, 1991
(percentage of world total)

Richest fifth

GNP — 84.7
World trade — 84.2
Domestic savings — 85.5
Domestic investment — 85.0

Each horizontal band represents an equal fifth of the world's people

Poorest fifth

GNP — 1.4
World trade — 0.9
Domestic savings — 0.7
Domestic investment — 0.9

Source: *From* Human Development Report 1994, *Published for the United Nations Development Programme (New York: Oxford University Press, 1994).*

velopment of stratification, but he focused primarily on the conflict that arises over control of that surplus. Lenski concluded that the distribution of the surplus will be determined on the basis of power. Thus, inequalities in power promote unequal access to economic resources and simultaneously give rise to inequalities in privilege and prestige.[37]

The "surplus" theories of Sahlins and Lenski do not really address the question of why the redistributors or leaders will want, or be able, to acquire greater control over resources. After all, the redis-

tributors or leaders in many rank societies do not have greater wealth than others, and custom seems to keep things that way. One suggestion is that as long as followers have mobility, they can vote with their feet by moving away from leaders they do not like. But when people start to make more permanent "investments" in land or technology (for example, irrigation systems or weirs for fishing), they are more likely to put up with a leader's aggrandizement in exchange for protection.[38] Another suggestion is that access to economic resources be-very substantial but is increasing.

The "champagne glass" figure conveys how unequal are the rich and poor of the world. If you consider gross national product (GNP), which is a measure for each country of how much is produced (in U.S. dollars), and compare it across countries, the richest fifth (20 percent) of the world's population controls 84.7 percent of the world's total gross national product. The poorest fifth (20 percent) controls only 1.4 percent of the world's output. As the figure shows, similar disparities exist if you compare trade, domestic savings, or domestic investment. To evaluate changes over time, we can compare the ratio between the richest and poorest fifths over time. In 1991 the ratio was 60.5 to 1, which is calculated by dividing the 84.7 percent for the top fifth by 1.4 for the bottom fifth. That ratio has increased since the 1960s. In 1960 the ratio was 30 to 1, in 1970 it was 32 to 1, in 1980 it was 45 to 1.

If the world as a whole is see-ing improvements in technology and economic development, why is inequality in the world increasing? As we shall see later, in the chapter on culture change, it is often the rich within a society who benefit most from new technology, at least initially. They are not only the most likely to be able to afford it; they also are the only ones who can afford to take the risks that it involves. The same may be true for nations. Those that already have capital are more likely than the poorer nations to take advantage of improvements in technology. In addition, the poorer countries generally have the highest rates of population growth, so income per capita can fall if population increases faster than the rate of economic development. Economists tell us that a developing country may, at least initially, experience an increase in inequality, but the inequality often decreases over time. Will the inequalities among countries also decrease as the world economy develops further?

The picture is not entirely bleak. It is true that the disparity between rich and poor countries has increased in recent years, but it is also true that the world economy has improved in some respects. The United Nations Organization has computed a "human development index" for 114 countries, combining measures of life expectancy, literacy, and a measure of per capita purchasing power. According to this index, all countries have improved over a period of 30 years, many of them substantially. If this trend continues, there might be less inequality among countries in the future.

Sources: Human Development Report 1994, *published for the United Nations Development Programme (New York: Oxford University Press, 1994), pp. 90–106;* State of the World 1994: A Worldwatch Institute Report on Progress toward a Sustainable Society *(New York: W. W. Norton, 1994), pp. 1–8;* Peter Donaldson, Worlds Apart: The Economic Gulf between Nations *(London: British Broadcasting Corporation, 1971);* Philips Foster, The World Food Problem: Tackling the Causes of Undernutrition in the Third World *(Boulder, CO: Lynne Rienner, 1992), pp. 149–51.*

comes unequal only when there is population pressure on resources in rank or chiefdom societies.[39] Such pressure may be what induces redistributors to try to keep more land and other resources for themselves and their families.

C. K. Meek offered an example of how population pressure in northern Nigeria may have led to economic stratification. At one time, a tribal member could obtain the right to use land by asking permission of the chief and presenting him with a token gift in recognition of his higher status. But by 1921, the reduction in the amount of available land had led to a system under which applicants offered the chief large payments for scarce land. As a result of these payments, farms came to be regarded as private property, and differential access to such property became institutionalized.[40]

Future research by archaeologists, sociologists, historians, and anthropologists should provide more understanding of the emergence of social stratification in human societies and how and why it may vary in degree.

▼ SUMMARY

1. Whereas sociologists contend that social stratification is universal because individual inequalities exist in all societies, anthropologists argue that egalitarian societies exist in the sense that there are societies in which access to advantages is equally available to all social groups.

2. The presence or absence of customs or rules that give certain groups unequal access to economic resources, power, and prestige can be used to distinguish three types of societies. In egalitarian societies, social groups do not have unequal access to economic resources, power, or prestige—they are unstratified. In rank societies, social groups do not have unequal access to economic resources or power, but they do have unequal access to prestige. Rank societies, then, are partially stratified. In class societies, social groups have unequal access to economic resources, power, and prestige. They are more completely stratified than are rank societies.

3. Stratified societies range from somewhat open class systems to caste systems, which are extremely rigid, since caste membership is fixed permanently at birth.

4. Slaves are persons who do not own their own labor; as such, they represent a class and sometimes even a caste. Slavery has existed in various forms in many times and places, regardless of race and culture. Sometimes slavery is a rigid and closed, or caste, system; sometimes it is a relatively open class system.

5. Social stratification appears to have emerged relatively recently in human history, about 7,500 years ago. This conclusion is based on archaeological evidence and on the fact that certain cultural features associated with stratification developed relatively recently.

6. One type of theory suggests that social stratification developed as productivity increased and surpluses were produced. Another suggestion is that stratification can develop only when people have "investments" in land or technology and therefore cannot move away from leaders they do not like. A third type of theory suggests that stratification emerges only when there is population pressure on resources in rank societies.

▼ GLOSSARY TERMS

caste	class societies	manumission	slaves
class	egalitarian societies	rank societies	

▼ CRITICAL QUESTIONS

1. What might be the social consequences of large differences in wealth?
2. Is an industrial or developed economy incompatible with a more egalitarian distribution of resources?
3. Why do you suppose the degree of inequality has decreased in some countries in recent years?

▼ SUGGESTED READING

BENJAMIN, L. *The Black Elite: Facing the Color Line in the Twilight of the Twentieth Century* (Chicago: Nelson-Hall, 1991). On the basis of interviews with 100 successful African Americans, the author documents how the "color line" continues to affect their lives.

BERREMAN, G. D., ED. *Social Inequality: Comparative and Developmental Approaches.* New York: Academic Press, 1981. Chapters in this book discuss inequality in different societies, unstratified and stratified. Inequality is examined in relation to degree of economic development, colonialism, and education, among other factors.

FRIED, M. H. *The Evolution of Political Society: An Essay in Political Anthropology.* New York: Random House, 1967. Beginning with definitions of commonly used terms and drawing from several disciplines, this classic work suggests a theoretical approach to questions about the origins of ranking, social stratification, and the state.

KLASS, M. "Is There 'Caste' Outside of India?" In Carol R. Ember and Melvin Ember, eds., *Cross-Cultural Research for Social Science,* Englewood Cliffs, NJ: Prentice Hall, 1995. Prentice Hall/Simon & Schuster Custom Publishing. A discussion of what "caste" is like in contemporary Hindu India and whether anything like it is found in other societies.

NEWMAN, K. S. *Declining Fortunes: The Withering of the American Dream.* New York: Basic Books, 1993. An in-depth study of ordinary Americans in a suburban town who are trying to understand why they are not better off than their parents.

PEREGRINE, P. N. "Variation in Stratification." In Carol R. Ember and Melvin Ember, eds., *Cross-Cultural Research for Social Science,* Englewood Cliffs, NJ: Prentice Hall, 1995. Prentice Hall/Simon & Schuster Custom Publishing. A discussion, with examples, of egalitarian, rank, and class-stratified societies, and what may account for the variation.

PRYOR, F. L. *The Origins of the Economy: A Comparative Study of Distribution in Primitive and Peasant Economies.* New York: Academic Press, 1977. A large cross-cultural study of variation in distribution systems and their possible determinants. Chapter 8, on the varieties of slavery, is particularly relevant to this chapter.

▼ NOTES

[1]In an analysis of many native societies in the New World, Gary Feinman and Jill Neitzel argue that egalitarian and rank societies ("tribes" and "chiefdoms," respectively) are not systematically distinguishable. See their "Too Many Types: An Overview of Sedentary Prestate Societies in the Americas," in Michael B. Schiffer, ed., *Advances in Archaeological Method and Theory* (Orlando, FL: Academic Press, 1984), vol. 7, p. 57.

[2]Morton H. Fried, *The Evolution of Political Society: An Essay in Political Anthropology* (New York: Random House, 1967), p. 33.

[3]Michael G. Smith, "Pre-Industrial Stratification Systems," in Neil J. Smelser and Seymour Martin Lipset, eds., *Social Structure and Mobility in Economic Development* (Chicago: Aldine, 1966), p. 152.

[4]Elman R. Service, *Profiles in Ethnology,* 3rd ed. (New York: Harper & Row, Pubishers, 1978), p. 249.

[5]Marshall Sahlins, *Social Stratification in Polynesia* (Seattle: University of Washington Press, 1958), pp. 80–81.

[6]See, for example, the description of a Kwakiutl group called the Nimpkish in Donald Mitchell, "Nimpkish: Complex Foragers on the Northwest Coast of North America," in Melvin Ember, Carol R. Ember, and David Levinson, eds., *Portraits of Culture: Ethnographic Originals* (Englewood Cliffs, NJ: Prentice Hall, 1994). Prentice Hall/Simon & Schuster Custom Publishing.

[7]Philip Drucker, *Cultures of the North Pacific Coast* (San Francisco: Chandler, 1965), pp. 56–64.

[8]W. Lloyd Warner and Paul S. Lunt, *The Social Life of a Modern Community* (New Haven, CT: Yale University Press, 1941).

[9]Robert S. Lynd and Helen Merrell Lynd, *Middletown* (New York: Harcourt, Brace, 1929); and Robert S. Lynd and Helen Merrell Lynd, *Middletown in Transition* (New York: Harcourt, Brace, 1937).

[10]Reeve Vanneman and Lynn Weber Cannon, *The American Perception of Class* (Philadelphia: Temple University Press, 1987), pp. 53-91.

[11]Michael Argyle, *The Psychology of Social Class* (New York: Routledge, 1994), pp. 3–6; Vanneman and Cannon, *The American Perception of Class,* pp. 283–84.

[12]Argyle, *The Psychology of Social Class,* pp. 36–37, 178.

[13]Ibid., p. 19.

[14]Ibid.

[15]Ruth Leger Sivard, *World Military and Social Expenditures 1993,* 15th ed. (Washington, D.C.: World Priorities, 1993).

[16]Donald J. Treiman and Harry B. G. Ganzeboom, "Cross-National Comparative Status-Attainment Research," *Research in Social Stratification and Mobility,* 9 (1990): 117; David L. Featherman and Robert M. Hauser,

Opportunity and Change (New York: Academic Press, 1978), pp. 4, 481.

[17]Argyle, *The Psychology of Social Class.*

[18]John A. Brittain, *Inheritance and the Inequality of Material Wealth* (Washington, D.C.: Brookings Institution, 1978).

[19]Morton Klass, "Is There 'Caste' Outside of India?", in Carol R. Ember and Melvin Ember, eds., *Cross-Cultural Research for Social Science* (Englewood Cliffs, NJ: Prentice Hall, 1995). Prentice Hall/Simon & Schuster Custom Publishing.

[20]John Ruskin, "Of Kings' Treasures," in John D. Rosenberg, ed., *The Genius of John Ruskin: Selections from His Writings* (New York: Braziller, 1963), pp. 296–314.

[21]See Oscar Lewis, with the assistance of Victor Barnouw, *Village Life in Northern India* (Urbana: University of Illinois Press, 1958).

[22]Gerald D. Berreman, "Caste in India and the United States," *American Journal of Sociology,* 66 (1960): 120–27.

[23]U.S. Bureau of the Census. *Statistical Abstract of the United States: 1993,* 113th ed. (Washington, D.C.: U.S. Government Printing Office, 1993), p. 463.

[24]Lois Benjamin, *The Black Elite: Facing the Color Line in the Twilight of the Twentieth Century* (Chicago: Nelson-Hall, 1991); see also Melvin D. Williams, "Racism," in Carol R. Ember, Melvin Ember, and Peter N. Peregrine, eds., *Research Frontiers in Anthropology.* (Englewood Cliffs, NJ: Prentice Hall, 1995). Prentice Hall/Simon & Schuster Custom Publishing.

[25]For more information about caste in Japan and in Rwanda, see Gerald D. Berreman, *Caste in the Modern World* (Morristown, NJ: General Learning Press, 1973) and "Race, Caste and Other Invidious Distinctions in Social Stratification," *Race,* 13 (1972): 403–14. Information about what the Japanese government has done in regard to the Dowa was provided to us by the Japanese consulate in New York City.

[26]Frederic L. Pryor, *The Origins of the Economy: A Comparative Study of Distribution in Primitive and Peasant Economies* (New York: Academic Press, 1977), p. 219.

[27]Euripides, "The Trojan Women," in Edith Hamilton, trans., *Three Greek Plays,* New York: Norton, 1937, p. 52.

[28]S. F. Nadel, *A Black Byzantium: The Kingdom of Nupe in Nigeria* (London: Oxford University Press, 1942). The Nupe abolished slavery at the beginning of this century.

[29]Pryor, *The Origins of the Economy,* pp. 217–47.

[30]Data from Robert B. Textor, comp., *A Cross-Cultural Summary* (New Haven, CT: HRAF Press, 1967).

[31]Ibid.

[32]Gerhard Lenski, *Power and Privilege: A Theory of Social Stratification* (Chapel Hill: University of North Carolina Press, 1984 [first published 1966]), pp. 308–18.

[33]Treiman and Ganzeboom, "Cross-National Comparative Status-Attainment Research," p. 117; Phillips Cutright, "Inequality: A Cross-National Analysis," *American Sociological Review,* 32 (1967): 564.

[34]Sahlins, *Social Stratification in Polynesia.*

[35]Ibid., p. 4.

[36]Marshall D. Sahlins, *Stone Age Economics* (Chicago: Aldine, 1972).

[37]Lenski, *Power and Privilege.*

[38]Antonio Gilman, "The Development of Social Stratification in Bronze Age Europe," *Current Anthropology* 22: 1–23.

[39]See Fried, *The Evolution of Political Society,* pp. 201–2; and Michael J. Harner, "Scarcity, the Factors of Production, and Social Evolution," in Steven Polgar, ed., *Population, Ecology, and Social Evolution* (The Hague: Mouton, 1975), pp. 123–38.

[40]C. K. Meek, *Land Law and Custom in the Colonies* (London: Oxford University Press, 1940), pp. 149–50.

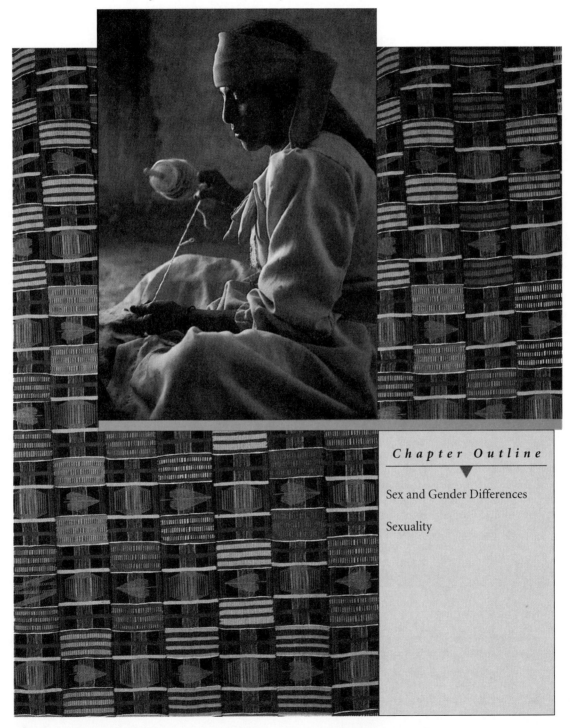

9

Sex, Gender, and Culture

We all know that humans come in two major varieties—female and male. The contrast is one of the facts of life we share with most animal species. But the fact that males and females always have different organs of reproduction does not explain why males and females may also differ in some other physical ways. After all, there are many animal species—such as pigeons, gulls, and laboratory rats—in which the two sexes differ little in appearance.[1] Thus, the fact that we are a species with two sexes does not really explain why human females and males typically look different. Also, the fact that humans reproduce sexually does not explain why human males and females should differ in behavior or be treated differently by society. Yet no society we know of treats females and males in exactly the same way; indeed, females usually have fewer advantages than males. That is why in the last chapter we were careful to say that egalitarian societies have no *social groups* with unequal access to resources, power, and prestige. But within social groups (for example, families), even egalitarian societies usually allow males greater access to resources, power, and prestige.

Because many of the differences between females and males may reflect cultural expectations and experiences, many researchers now prefer to speak of **gender differences** (reserving the term *sex differences* for purely biological differences).[2] Unfortunately, biological and cultural influences are not always clearly separable, so it is sometimes hard to know which term to use. As long as societies treat males and females differently, we may not be able to separate the effects of biology from the effects of culture, and both may be present. Although we focus in this chapter on differences and similarities between females and males, it is important to keep in mind that not all cultures conceive of gender as including just two categories. Sometimes "maleness" and "femaleness" are thought of as opposite ends of a continuum, or there might be three or more categories of gender (such as "female," "male," and "other").[3]

In this chapter we discuss what we know cross-culturally about how and why females and males may differ physically, in gender roles, and in personality. We also discuss how and why sexual behavior, and attitudes about sex, vary from culture to culture.

SEX AND GENDER DIFFERENCES

▼

Physique and Physiology

As we noted at the outset, males and females of many animal species cannot readily be distinguished. Although they differ in chromosome makeup and in their external and internal organs of reproduction, they do not differ otherwise. In contrast, humans are **sexually dimorphic**—that is, the females and males of our species exhibit fairly marked differences in size and appearance. Females have proportionately wider pelvises. Males typically are taller and have heavier skeletons than females. Females have a larger proportion of their body weight in fat; males have a larger proportion of body weight in muscle. Males typically have greater grip strength, proportionately larger hearts and lungs, and greater aerobic work capacity (greater maximum uptake of oxygen during exercise).

There is a tendency in our society to view "taller" and "more muscled" as better, which may reflect the bias toward males in our culture. Natural selection may have favored these traits in males but different ones in females. For example, because females bear children, selection may have favored earlier cessation of growth (and therefore less ultimate height) in females so that the nutritional needs of a fetus would not compete with a growing mother's needs.[4] (Females achieve their ultimate height shortly after puberty, but boys continue to grow for longer after puberty.) Similarly, there is some evidence that females are less affected than males by nutritional shortages, presumably because they tend to be shorter and have proportionately more fat.[5] Natural selection may have favored those traits in females if they resulted in greater reproductive success.

Female and male athletes can build up their muscle strength and increase their aerobic work capacity through training. Given that fact, then, cultural factors (such as how much a society expects and allows males and females to engage in muscular activity) could influence the degree to which females and males differ muscularly and in aerobic work capacity. Similar training may account for the recent trend toward decreasing differences between females and males in certain athletic events, such as marathons and swim meets.

Even when it comes to female and male physique and physiology, then, what we see may be the result of both culture and genes.[6]

Gender Roles

Productive and Domestic Activities. In the chapter on economic systems, we noted that all societies assign or divide labor at least somewhat differently between females and males. Because role assignments have a clear cultural component, we can speak of them as gender roles. What is of particular interest here about the gender division of labor is not so much that every society has different work

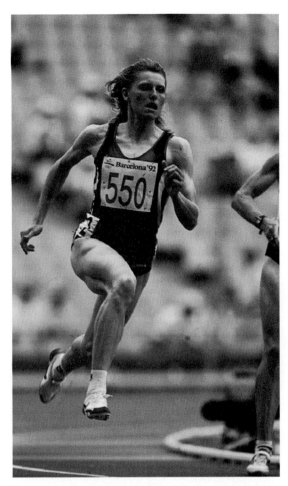

Training can increase muscle strength and aerobic work capacity. As women get more involved in competitive sports, we can expect their records to improve and the differences between male and female performance to decrease.

for males and females, but rather that so many societies divide up work in similar ways. The question, then, is why there are universal or near-universal patterns in such assignments.

Table 9–1 summarizes the worldwide patterns. We note which activities are performed by which gender in all or almost all societies, which activities are usually performed by one gender, and which activities are commonly assigned to either gender or both. Does the distribution of activities in the table suggest why females and males generally do different things?

One possible explanation may be labeled the *strength theory.* The greater strength of males, and their superior capacity to mobilize strength in quick bursts of energy (because of their greater aerobic work capacity), has commonly been cited as the reason for the universal or near-universal patterns in the division of labor by gender. Certainly, activities that require lifting heavy objects (hunting large animals, butchering, clearing land, working with stone, metal, or lumber), throwing weapons, and running with great speed (as in hunting) may generally be performed best by males. And none of the activities females usually perform, with the possible exception of collecting firewood, seems to require the same degree of physical strength or quick bursts of energy. But the strength theory is not completely convincing, if only because it cannot readily explain all the observed patterns. For example, it is not clear that the male activities of trapping small animals, collecting wild honey, or making musical instruments require much physical strength.

Another possible explanation of the worldwide patterns in division of labor can be called the *compatibility-with-child-care theory.* The argument here is that women's tasks tend to be those that are compatible with child care. Although males can take care of infants, most traditional societies rely on breast-feeding of infants, which men cannot do. (In most societies, women breast-feed their children for two years on the average.) Women's tasks may be those that do not take them far from home for long periods, that do not place children in potential danger if they are taken along, and that can be stopped and resumed if an infant needs care.[7]

The compatibility theory may explain why *no* activities other than infant care are listed in the right-hand column of Table 9–1. That is, it may be that there are practically no universal or near-universal women-only activities because until recently most women have had to devote much of their time to nursing and caring for infants, as well as usually caring for other children. The compatibility theory may also explain why men usually do tasks such as hunting, trapping, fishing, collecting honey, lumbering, and mining. Those tasks are dangerous for infants to be around and in any case would be difficult to coordinate with infant care.[8]

Finally, the compatibility theory may also explain why men seem to take over certain crafts in societies with full-time specialization. Although the distinction is not shown in Table 9–1, crafts such as making baskets, mats, and pottery are women's activities in noncommercial societies but tend to be men's activities in societies with full-time craft specialists.[9] Cooking is a good example in our own society. Women may be fine cooks, but chefs and bakers tend to be men, even though women traditionally do most of the cooking at home. Women might be more likely to work as cooks and chefs if

TABLE 9–1 *Worldwide Patterns in the Division of Labor by Gender*

TYPE OF ACTIVITY	MALES ALMOST ALWAYS	MALES USUALLY	EITHER GENDER OR BOTH	FEMALES USUALLY	FEMALES ALMOST ALWAYS
Primary subsistence activities	Hunt and trap animals, large and small	Fish Herd large animals Collect wild honey Clear land and prepare soil for planting	Collect shellfish Care for small animals Plant crops Tend crops Harvest crops Milk animals	Gather wild plants	
Secondary subsistence and household activities		Butcher animals	Preserve meat and fish	Care for children Cook Prepare • vegetable food • drinks • dairy products Launder Fetch water Collect fuel	Care for infants
Other	Lumber Mine and quarry Make • boats • musical instruments • bone, horn, and shell objects Engage in combat	Build houses Make • nets • rope Exercise political leadership	Prepare skins Make • leather products • baskets • mats • clothing • pottery	Spin yarn	

Sources: *Mostly adapted from George P. Murdock and Caterina Provost, "Factors in the Division of Labor by Sex: A Cross-Cultural Analysis,"* Ethnology, *12 (1973): 203–25. The information on political leadership and warfare comes from Martin K. Whyte, "Cross-Cultural Codes Dealing with the Relative Status of Women,"* Ethnology, *17 (1978): 217. The information on child care comes from Thomas S. Weisner and Ronald Gallimore, "My Brother's Keeper: Child and Sibling Caretaking,"* Current Anthropology, *18 (1977): 169–80.*

they could leave their babies and young children in safe places to be cared for by other people.

But the compatibility theory does not explain why men usually prepare soil for planting, make things (such as musical instruments) out of wood, or work bone, horn, and shell. All of those tasks could probably be stopped to tend to a child, and none of them is any more dangerous to children nearby than is cooking. Why, then, do males tend to do them? Additional considerations, such as *economy of effort,* may help explain patterns that cannot readily be explained by the strength and compatibility theories. For example, it may be advantageous for men to make musical instruments because men generally collect the hard materials involved (for example, by lumbering).[10] And because they collect those materials, men may be more knowledgeable about their physical properties and so more likely to know how to work with them. The economy-of-effort interpretation also suggests that it would be advantageous for one gender to perform tasks that are located near each other. Thus, if women have to be near home to take care of young children, it would be economical for them to do other chores that are located in or near the home.

A fourth explanation of division of labor can be called the *expendability theory.* This theory suggests that men, rather than women, will tend to do the dangerous work in a society because men are more expendable, because the loss of men is less disadvantageous reproductively than the loss of women. If some men lose their lives in hunting,

Certain tasks are incompatible with child care. Although tilling a field and carrying a child are not the easiest tasks, this peasant woman in Chikoku, Japan, is clearly managing to do both at the same time.

haps strength is more a function of training than we have traditionally believed.

The compatibility theory also has some problems. It suggests that labor is divided to conform to the requirements of child care. But sometimes it seems the other way around. For example, women who spend a good deal of time in agricultural work outside the home often ask others to watch and feed their infants while they are unavailable to nurse.[13] Consider too the mountain areas of Nepal, where agricultural work is quite incompatible with child care; heavy loads must be carried up and down steep slopes, fields are far apart, and labor takes up most of the day. Yet women do this work anyway and leave their infants with others for long stretches of time.[14] And in some societies women hunt: one of the activities most incompatible with child care and generally not done by women. For example, many Agta women of the Philippines regularly hunt wild pig and deer; women alone or in groups kill almost 30 percent of the large game.[15] The women's hunting does not seem to be incompatible with child care. Women take nursing babies on hunting trips, and the women who hunt do not have lower reproductive rates than the women who choose not to hunt. Of course, Agta women may find it possible to hunt because the hunting grounds are only about a half-hour from camp, the dogs that accompany the women assist in the hunting and protect the women and babies, and the women generally hunt in groups, so others can help carry babies as well as carcasses.

As the cases just described suggest, we need to know a lot more about labor requirements. More precisely, we need to know exactly how much strength is required in particular tasks, exactly how dangerous those tasks are, and whether a person could stop working at a task to care for a child. So far, we have mostly guesses. When there is more systematically collected evidence on such aspects of particular tasks, we will be in a better position to evaluate the theories we have discussed. In any case, it should be noted that none of the available theories implies that the worldwide patterns of division of labor shown in Table 9–1 will persist. As we know from our own and other industrial societies, when machines replace human strength, when women have fewer children, and when women can assign child care to others, a strict gender division of labor begins to disappear.

Relative Contributions to Subsistence. In our society, the stereotype of the husband is that he is the breadwinner in the family; the wife is the manager

deep-water fishing, mining, quarrying, lumbering, and the like, reproduction need not suffer so long as most fertile women have sexual access to men, as for example if the society permits two or more women to be married to the same man.[11] When would anybody, male or female, be willing to do dangerous work? Perhaps only when society glorifies the roles and endows them with high prestige and other rewards.

Although the various theories, singly or in combination, seem to explain much of the division of labor by gender, there are some unresolved problems. Critics of the strength theory have pointed out that in some societies women engage in very heavy labor.[12] If women in some societies can develop the strength to do such work, per-

WOMEN'S ELECTORAL SUCCESS ON THE NORTHWEST COAST

Political life has changed dramatically since first contact with Europeans for most Native American groups, including the Coast Salish of western Washington State and British Columbia. With impetus from the U.S. and Canadian governments, each of the recognized Coast Salish communities now has an elected council. But who is getting elected? Even though women did not have much of a role in traditional politics, now the Coast Salish groups are electing a lot of women. From the 1960s to the 1980s, women held over 40 percent of the council seats in the twelve Washington State groups, and in the 1990s women held 28 percent of the seats in the fifty British Columbian groups. What accounts for the women's electoral success? And why does that success vary from one group to another, even though the groups are closely related culturally? (The proportion of women on the councils varies from 6 percent among the Tulalip to 62 percent among the Stillaguamish.)

According to Bruce Miller, who did a comparative study of women's electoral success

in Coast Salish communities, women generally have more of a political role now perhaps because new economic opportunities in the service and technical sectors allow women to contribute more to the household economy. But why do women win proportionately more council seats in some communities than in others? Miller found that women win proportionately more seats in communities with less income, the least income derived from fishing, and the smallest populations. Why should lower household income predict more electoral success for women? Miller suggests that it is not so much the amount of income but rather the degree to which women (compared with men) contribute to household income. In groups with economic difficulties, the jobs women are able to get play a vital role in the household. Women were helped by federally funded programs (such as the War on Poverty) to acquire technical skills and jobs. Simultaneously, many men in some communities lost their jobs in logging and agriculture.

But a high dependence on

fishing income seems to favor men politically. Families that operate purse-seine vessels to catch fish at sea can make hundreds of thousands of dollars a year. Such fishing is predominantly done by men, and where there is such lucrative fishing, the successful men dominate the councils. Even though women may have jobs too, their income is not as great as the successful fisherman's.

Why should women be more successful politically in smaller communities? Miller suggests that women have a better chance to be known personally when the community is small, even though working outside the home in technical or service jobs cuts down on the time women can devote to tribal ceremonials and other public events.

Does female income relative to male and community size help explain the relative political success of women elsewhere? We do not yet know, but subsequent research may help us find out.

Source: Bruce G. Miller, "Women and Politics: Comparative Evidence from the Northwest Coast," Ethnology, 31 (1992): 367–82.

of the house and children. As we know, the stereotype is becoming more myth than reality; in addition to the many women who are single parents, many married women (in the United States, more than 50 percent) now work outside the home.

Among married women with children 6–17 years old, more than 70 percent are employed.[16]

The concept of breadwinner in our society emphasizes the person—traditionally the male—who "brings in the bread" (the food, or money to buy it) from the outside. In focusing on the breadwinner, however, we may minimize the contributions of the person who works primarily inside the home.

How should we judge who contributes more to subsistence? Most anthropologists distinguish between **primary subsistence activities** and **secondary subsistence activities** (see Table 9–1). The primary activities are the food-getting activities discussed earlier: gathering, hunting, fishing, herding, and agriculture. Many of the secondary activities involve preparing and processing food for eating or storing. We know a considerable amount about how and possibly why women's and men's relative contributions to primary subsistence activities vary cross-culturally. We know much less about contributions to secondary subsistence activities. Researchers have focused mostly on primary subsistence activities, and they usually measure how much each gender's work in these activities contributes to the diet (in terms of caloric intake). Alternatively, contribution to primary subsistence activities (which are generally "outside" activities, away from the home) can be measured in terms of time spent doing them. Measures of caloric versus time contribution, however, can yield very different results. As we saw in the chapter on getting food, more time is spent by the Yanomamö in hunting than in horticulture, but horticulture yields more calories.

In some societies women have traditionally contributed more to the economy than men by any measure. For example, among the Tchambuli of New Guinea in the 1930s the women did all the fishing—going out early in the morning by canoe to their fish traps and returning when the sun was hot. Some of the catch was traded for sago (a starch) and sugarcane, and it was the women who went on the long canoe trips to do the trading.[17]

The stereotype of husband as breadwinner no longer fits our society. But it does fit the Toda of India, as they were described early in the twentieth century. They depended for subsistence almost entirely on the dairy products of their water buffalo, either by using the products directly or by selling them for grain. Women were not allowed to have anything to do with dairy work; only men tended the buffalo and prepared the dairy products. Women's work was largely household work. Women prepared the purchased grain for cooking, cleaned house, and decorated clothing.[18]

A survey of a wide variety of societies has revealed that both women and men typically contribute to primary food-getting activities—but men usually contribute more in terms of calories.[19] Women are almost always occupied with infant- and child-care responsibilities in most societies, so it is not surprising that men usually do most of the pri-

Even when women and men both contribute labor to an activity, women and men may or may not work together. This Nduma man and woman in Papua New Guinea are digging out an earth oven for a village feast.

mary food-getting work, which generally has to be done away from the home.

In some societies women contribute more (in the caloric sense) to primary subsistence activities than do men. In societies that depend on hunting, fishing, and herding—generally male activities—for most of their calories, men usually contribute more than women.[20] For example, among the Inuit, who traditionally depended mostly on hunting and fishing, and among the Toda, who depended mostly on herding, men did most of the primary subsistence work. But the predominant type of food-getting is not always predictive: among the Tchambuli, who depended mostly on fishing, women did most of the work. In societies that depend on gathering—primarily women's work—women tend to do most of the food-getting (in terms of calories). The !Kung are an example. But most societies known to anthropology depend primarily on agriculture, not on hunting or gathering, for their calories. And, with the exception of clearing land and preparing the soil, which are usually men's tasks, the work of planting, crop tending (weeding, irrigating), and harvesting crops is done by men *or* women or both (see Table 9–1). So we need some explanation of why women do most of the agriculture in some societies and men in others. Different patterns predominate in different areas of the world. In Africa south of the Sahara, women generally do most of the agriculture. But in much of Asia

and in Europe and the areas around the Mediterranean, men do more.[21]

One apparently explanatory factor is the kind of agriculture done. Many writers have pointed out that with intensive agriculture, particularly plow agriculture, men's caloric contribution to primary subsistence tends to be much higher than women's. In horticultural societies, in contrast, women's contribution is relatively high compared with men's. Figure 9–1 shows the relationship between women's relative contribution to primary subsistence and the type of cultivation practiced. As the graph indicates, women contribute the most when horticulture is practiced—either root and tree crop horticulture (labeled Horticulture) or shifting/slash-and-burn cultivation (labeled Extensive or Shifting Agriculture). According to Ester Boserup, when population increases and there is pressure to make more intensive use of the land, cultivators begin to use the plow and irrigation, and males start to do more.[22] But it is not quite clear why.

Why should women not continue to contribute a lot to agriculture just because plows are used? In trying to answer this question, most researchers shift to considering how much time males and females spend in various agricultural tasks, rather than estimating the total caloric contribution of females versus males. The reason for this shift is that gender contribution to agriculture varies sub-

FIGURE 9–1
Relationship between Type and Intensity of Agriculture and Average Percentage of Women's Contribution to Subsistence

Source: *Peggy R. Sanday, "Toward a Theory of the Status of Women," American Anthropologist, 75 (1973); 1691. Reproduced by permission of the American Anthropological Association.* Not for sale or further reproduction.

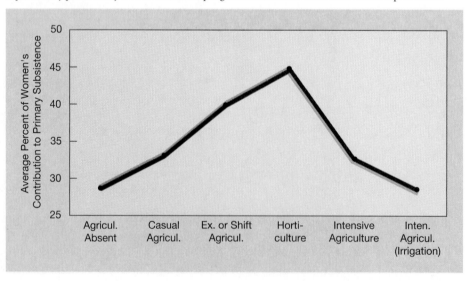

stantially over the various phases of the production sequence, as well as from one crop to another. Thus, the total amount of time females versus males work at agricultural tasks is easier to estimate than how much each gender contributes to the diet in terms of calories. How would caloric contribution be judged, for example, if men do the clearing and plowing, women do the planting and weeding, and both do the harvesting?

One suggestion about why males contribute more to agriculture when the plow is used is that plow agriculture involves a great deal of labor input in the clearing and preparation phases of cultivation, and at the same time minimizes subsequent weeding time. Men usually clear land anyway, but clearing is a more time-consuming process if intensive agriculture is practiced. It has been estimated that in one district in Nigeria, 100 days of work are required to clear one acre of virgin land for plowing by tractor; only 20 days are required to prepare the land for shifting cultivation. Weeding is a task that probably can be combined with child care, and perhaps for that reason it may have been performed mostly by women previously.[23] But the fact that men do the plowing, which may take a lot of time, does not explain why women do relatively less of all agricultural tasks, including weeding, in societies that have the plow.[24]

Another explanation for why women contribute less time than men to intensive agriculture is that household chores increase with intensive agriculture and thus limit the time women can spend in the fields. Intensive agriculturalists typically rely heavily on grain crops, which take much more work to make edible. Cereal grains (corn, wheat, oats) are usually dried before storing. They therefore take a long time to cook if they are left whole. More cooking requires more time to collect water and firewood (usually women's work) and more time to clean pots and utensils. A variety of techniques can reduce cooking time (such as soaking, grinding, or pounding), but the process that speeds up cooking the most—grinding—is itself time-consuming (unless done by machine). Finally, household work may increase substantially with intensive agriculture because women in such societies have more children than women in horticultural societies. If household work increases in these ways, it is easy to understand why women cannot contribute more time than men, or as much time as men, to intensive agriculture. But women's contribution—although less than men's—is nonetheless quite substantial: they seem to work outside the home four and a half hours a day, seven days a week, on the average.[25]

We still have not explained why women contribute so much to horticulture in the first place. They may not have as much household work as intensive-agricultural women, but neither do the men. Why, then, don't men do relatively more in horticulture also? One possibility is that in horticultural societies men are often drawn away from cultivation into other types of activities. There is evidence that if males are engaged in warfare when primary subsistence work has to be done, then the women must take care of that work.[26] Men may also be withdrawn from primary subsistence work if they have to work in distant towns and cities for wages or if they periodically go on long-distance trading trips.[27]

When women contribute a lot to primary food-getting activities we might expect their behavior and attitudes concerning children to be affected. Several cross-cultural studies suggest that this expectation is correct. In societies with a high female contribution to primary subsistence (in terms of contributing calories), infants are fed solid foods earlier (so that other persons besides mothers can feed them) than in societies with a low female contribution.[28] Girls are likely to be trained to be industrious (probably to help their mothers out), and girl babies are more valued.[29]

It is important to realize that what we conclude about gender contribution to subsistence depends largely on how we measure it. Most of our discussion until now has focused on contribution to primary subsistence activities. If we change our perspective for a moment and count all kinds of work, we see a different picture of men's versus women's contribution to making a living. Adding up all work time, including activities outside the home (mostly food-getting activities) and activities inside the home (mostly preparing and cooking food), women typically work more total hours per day than men in both intensive agricultural and horticultural societies.[30]

Political Leadership and Warfare.   In almost every society we know about, men rather than women are the leaders in the political arena. One cross-cultural survey found that, in about 85 percent of the surveyed societies, only men were leaders. In the societies in which some women occupied leadership positions, the women were either outnumbered by or less powerful than the men leaders.[31] Whether or not we consider warfare to be part of the political sphere of life (see the chapter on political life), we find an almost universal dominance of males in that arena. In 87–88 percent of the world's societies, women never participate actively in war.[32] (See the box titled "Why Do Some Societies Allow Women to Participate in Combat?" for a discussion of women in combat in the remaining 12–13 percent of societies.)

Even in *matrilineal* societies, which seem to be oriented around women (see the chapter on marital residence and kinship), men usually occupy political positions. For example, among the Iroquois of what is now New York State, women had control over resources and a great deal of influence. But men, not women, held political office. The highest political body among the League of the Iroquois (which comprised five tribal groups) was a council of fifty male chiefs. Although women could not serve on the council, they could nominate, elect, and impeach their male representatives. Women also could decide between life and death for prisoners of war, they could forbid the men of their households to go to war, and they could intervene to bring about peace.[33]

Why have men (at least so far) almost always dominated the political sphere of life? Some scholars have suggested that men's role in warfare gives them the edge in all kinds of political leadership, particularly because they control weapons—an important resource.[34] But evidence suggests that force is rarely used to obtain leadership positions[35]; superior strength is not the deciding factor. Still, warfare may be related to political leadership for another reason. Warfare clearly affects survival, and it occurs regularly in most of the societies we know about. Therefore, decision making about war may be among the most important kinds of politics in most societies. If it is, then the persons who know the most about warfare should be making the decisions about it.

To explain why males and not females usually engage in fighting, let us refer to three of the possible explanations of the worldwide patterns in the gender division of labor. Warfare, like hunting, probably requires strength (for throwing weapons)

New Perspectives on Gender

WHY DO SOME SOCIETIES ALLOW WOMEN TO PARTICIPATE IN COMBAT?

U.S. women can serve in the military but usually are excluded from combat. Some women feel that such exclusion is unfair and decreases their chances of promotion in the military. Other people (including some women) insist that female participation in combat would be detrimental to military performance or is inappropriate for women.

Why then do some societies allow women to be warriors? Psychologist David Adams compared about 70 societies studied by anthropologists to try to answer that question. Although most societies exclude women from war, Adams found that

women are active warriors, at least occasionally, in 13 percent of the sample societies. In native North America, such societies included the Comanche, Crow, Delaware, Fox, Gros Ventre, and Navaho. In the Pacific, there were active warrior women among the Maori of New Zealand, on Majuro in the Marshall Islands, and among the Orokaiva of New Guinea. In none of these societies were the warriors usually women, but women were allowed to engage in combat if they wanted to.

How are the societies with women warriors different from those that exclude women from

combat? They differ in one of two ways. Either they conduct war only against people in other societies (this is called "purely external" war) or they marry within their own community. Adams argues that these two conditions, which are not particularly common, preclude the possibility of conflicts of interest between wives and husbands, and therefore women can be permitted to engage in combat because their interests are the same as their husbands'. Because marriages in most cases involve individuals from the same society, husbands and wives will have the same loyalties if the society has and quick bursts of energy (for running). And certainly combat is one of the most dangerous and uninterruptible activities imaginable, hardly compatible with child care. Also, even if they do not at the moment have children, women may generally be kept out of combat because their potential fertility is more important to a population's reproduction and survival than their potential usefulness as warriors.[36] So, the strength theory, the compatibility theory, and the expendability theory might all explain the predominance of men in warfare.

Two other factors may be involved in male predominance in politics. One is the generally greater height of men. Why height should be a factor in leadership is unclear, but studies suggest that taller persons are more likely to be leaders.[37] Finally, there is the possibility that men dominate politics because they get around more in the outside world than do women. Men's activities typically take them farther from home; women tend to work more around the home. If societies choose leaders at least in part because of what they know about the larger world, then men will generally have some advantage. In support of this reasoning, Patricia Draper found that in !Kung bands that had settled down women no longer engaged in long-distance gathering, and they lost much of their former influence in making decisions.[38] Involvement in child care may also detract from such influence. In a study of village leadership among the Kayapo of Brazil, Dennis Werner found that women with heavy child-care burdens were less influential than women not as involved in child care; perhaps they had fewer friends and missed many details of what was going on in the village.[39]

These various explanations suggest why men generally dominate politics, but we still need to explain why women participate in politics more in some societies than in others. Marc Ross investigated this question in a cross-cultural survey of ninety societies.[40] In that sample, the degree of fe-

purely external war. And even if war occurs between communities and larger groups in the same society (what we call "internal" war), there will be no conflict of interest between husband and wife if they both grew up in the same community. In contrast, there is internal war at least occasionally in most societies, and wives usually marry in from other communities. In this situation, there may often be a conflict of interest between husband and wife; if women were to engage in combat, they might have to fight against their fathers, paternal uncles, and brothers. And wouldn't we expect the wives to try to warn kin in their home communities if the husbands planned to attack them? Indeed, the men's likely fear of their wives' disloyalty would explain why women in these societies are forbidden to make or handle weapons or go near meetings in which war plans are discussed.

Many countries today engage in purely external war, so other things being equal, we would not expect conflicts of interest to impede women's participation in combat. Therefore, extrapolating from Adams's findings, we might expect that the barriers against female participation in combat will disappear completely. But other conditions may have to be present before women and men participate equally in combat. In Adams's study, not all societies with purely external war or intracommunity marriage had women warriors. So we may also have to consider the degree to which the society seeks to maximize reproduction (and therefore protect women from danger) and the degree to which the society depends on women for subsistence during wartime.

There are other related questions to explore. Does military participation by women increase women's participation in politics? Does the presence of war in a society decrease or increase women's political participation? Does women's participation in politics or in the military change the nature of war?

Source: *David B. Adams, "Why There Are So Few Women Warriors,"* Behavior Science Research, *18 (1983): 196–212.* Reprinted by permission of Sage Publications, Inc.

male participation in politics varied considerably. For example, among the Mende of Sierra Leone women regularly held high office, but among the Azande of Zaire women took no part in public life. One factor that appeared to predict the exclusion of women from politics was the organization of communities around male kin. As we will see later, women when they marry usually have to leave their communities and move to their husband's place. If women are "strangers" in a community with many related males, then the males will have political advantages because of their knowledge of community members and past events.

The Relative Status of Women. There are probably as many definitions of status as there are researchers interested in the topic. To some, the relative status of the sexes means how much importance society confers on females versus males. To others, it means how much power and authority men and women have relative to each other. And to still others, it means what kinds of rights women and men possess to do what they want to do. In any case, many social scientists are asking why the status of women appears to vary from one society to another. Why do women have few rights and little influence in some societies and more of each in other societies? Or, in other words, why is there variation in degree of *gender stratification?*

In the small Iraqi town of Daghara, women and men live very separate lives.[41] In many respects, women appear to have very little status. Like women in much of the Islamic world, women in Daghara live their lives mostly in seclusion: they stay in their houses and interior courtyards. If women must go out, which they can do only with male approval, they must shroud their faces and bodies in long, black cloaks. These cloaks must be worn in mixed company, even at home. Women are essentially excluded from political activities. Legally, they are considered to be under the authority of their fathers and husbands. Even the sexuality of women is controlled. There is strict emphasis on virginity before marriage. Because women are not permitted even casual conversations with strange men, the possibilities for extramarital or even premarital relationships are very slight. In contrast, hardly any sexual restrictions are imposed on men.

But some societies, such as the Mbuti Pygmies, seem to approach equal status for males and females. Like most food collectors, the Mbuti have no formal political organization to make decisions or to settle disputes. Public disputes occur, and both women and men take part in the uproar that is part of such disputes. Not only do women make their positions known, but their opinions are often heeded. Even in domestic quarrels involving physical violence between husband and wife, others usually intervene to stop them, regardless of who hit whom first.[42] Women control the use of dwellings; they usually have equal say over the disposal of resources they or the men collect, over the upbringing of their children, and about whom their children should marry. One of the few signs of inequality is that women are somewhat more restricted than men with respect to extramarital sex.[43]

There are many theories about why women have relatively high or low status. One of the most common is that women's status will be high when they contribute substantially to primary subsistence activities. According to this theory, then, women should have very little status when food-getting depends largely on hunting, herding, or intensive agriculture. A second theory suggests that where warfare is especially important, men will be more valued and esteemed than women. A third theory suggests that where there are centralized political hierarchies, men will have higher status. The reasoning in the last theory is essentially the same as

In some societies women are secluded in their houses and courtyards. This woman in South Yemen is obliged to wear a veil whenever she goes out.

Women as well as men serve on political councils in many Coast Salish communities. Here we see a swearing-in ceremony for the Special Chief's Council of the Stó:lo Nation in Sardis, British Columbia.

that in the warfare theory—men usually play the dominant role in political behavior, so men's status should be higher wherever political behavior is more important or frequent. Finally, there is the theory that women will have higher status where kin groups and couples' place of residence after marriage are organized around women.

One of the problems in evaluating these theories is that decisions have to be made about the meaning of status. Does it mean value? Rights? Influence? And do all these aspects of status vary together? Cross-cultural research by Martin Whyte suggests that they do not. For each sample society in his study, Whyte rated fifty-two items that might be used to define the relative status of the sexes. These items included things such as which sex can inherit property, who has final authority over disciplining unmarried children, and whether the gods in the society are male, female, or both. The results of the study indicate that very few of these items are related. Therefore, Whyte concluded, we cannot talk about status as a single concept. Rather, it seems more appropriate to talk about the relative status of women in different spheres of life.[44]

Even though Whyte found no necessary connection between one aspect of status and another, he decided to ask whether some of the theories just mentioned correctly predict why some societies have many (as opposed to few) areas in which the status of women is high. Let us turn first to the ideas that are *not* supported by the available cross-cultural evidence. The idea that generally high status derives from a greater caloric contribution to primary subsistence activities is not supported at all.[45] Women in intensive-agricultural societies (who contribute less than men to primary subsistence) do tend to have lower status in many areas of life, just as in the Iraqi case described above. But in societies that depend mostly on hunting (where women also do little of the primary subsistence work), women seem to have higher status—which contradicts the theoretical expectation. Similarly, there is no consistent evidence that a high frequency of warfare generally lowers women's status in different spheres of life.[46]

What does predict higher status for women in many areas of life? Although the results are not that strong, there is some support in Whyte's study for the theory that where kin groups and marital residence are organized around women, women have somewhat higher status (we discuss these features of society more fully in the chapter on marital residence and kinship). The Iroquois are a good example. Even though Iroquois women could not hold political office, they had considerable authority within and beyond the household. Related women lived together in longhouses with husbands who belonged to other kin groups. In the longhouse, the women's authority was clear and they could ask objectionable men to leave. The women controlled the allocation of the food they produced. Allocation could influence the timing of war parties, since men could not undertake a raid without provisions. Women were involved in the selection of religious leaders, half of whom were women. Even in politics, although women could not speak or serve on the council, they largely controlled the selection of councilmen and could institute impeachment proceedings against those to whom they objected.[47]

A generally lower status for women does appear to be found in societies with political hierarchies.[48] Lower status for women appears to be associated with other indicators of cultural complexity as well as with political hierarchies. Societies with social stratification, plow and irrigation agriculture, large settlements, private property, and craft specialization tend to have lower status for women. (One type of influence for women increases with cultural complexity—informal influence. But as Whyte pointed out, informal influence may simply reflect a lack of *real* influence.[49]) Why cultural complexity is associated with women having less authority in the home, less control over property, and more restricted sexual lives is not yet understood.

Western colonialism also appears to have been generally detrimental to women's status, perhaps because Westerners have been accustomed to dealing with men. There are plenty of examples of Europeans restructuring land ownership around men and teaching men modern farming techniques, even in places where women were usually the farmers. In addition, men more often than women could earn cash through wage labor or through sales of goods (such as furs) to Europeans.[50] Although the relative status of men and women may not have been equal before the Europeans arrived, colonial influences seem generally to have undermined the position of women.

We are beginning to understand some of the conditions that may enhance or decrease certain aspects of women's status. If we can understand which of these conditions are most important, society may (if it wants to) be able to reduce gender inequality.[51]

Personality

Reporting on three tribes in New Guinea, Margaret Mead said that "many, if not all, of the personality traits we have called masculine or feminine are as lightly linked to sex as are the clothing, the manners, and the form of head-dress that a society at a given period assigns to either sex."[52] In other words, she suggested that there were *no* universal or near-universal personality differences between the sexes. Rather, societies were free to create any such differences. She described Arapesh females and males as essentially alike: both sexes were gentle, cooperative, and nurturing. She also described the Mundugumor males and females as similar, but in this case both sexes exhibited violence and aggression. Finally, she described the Tchambuli as having substantial female-male differences in temperament, but oppo-

When a society has very different role expectations for boys and girls, it is difficult to know how much of the sex difference in aggression is due to biology and how much is due to learning. This Yanomamö boy, as in many societies, starts to learn about weapons for hunting and war at a very early age.

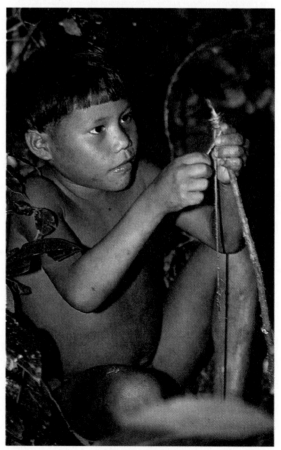

site to what we might expect. The women were domineering, practical, and impersonal and were the chief economic providers; the men were sensitive and delicate and devoted their time to their appearance and to artistic pursuits.

But research conducted in recent years does not support Mead's view that there are no consistent sex differences in temperament. On the contrary, some sex differences in behavior occur consistently and in quite diverse societies. (This does not mean that Mead was wrong about the three New Guinea societies she studied—it is possible that they were unusual cases. Nancy McDowell reanalyzed Mead's Mundugumor notes and studied a group of related neighboring people; she found no reason to doubt Mead's conclusion that female and male temperaments were similar.[53]) It is also possible that Mead might have found some gender differences if she had employed the kinds of observation techniques (particularly systematic and randomized behavior observations) that have been employed in recent field studies. Such studies systematically record the minute details of behavior of a substantial number of males and females. Any conclusions about female-male differences in aggressiveness, for example, are based on actual counts of the number of times a particular individual tried to hurt or injure another person in a fixed amount of observation time.

Which differences in personality are suggested by these more systematic studies? Most of them have observed children in different cultural settings. The most consistent difference is in the area of aggression: boys try to hurt others more frequently than girls do. In an extensive comparative study of children's behavior—the Six Cultures project—this difference showed up as early as three to six years of age.[54] Research done in the United States is consistent with the cross-cultural findings.[55] In a large number of observational and experimental studies, boys exhibited more aggression than girls.

Other female-male differences have turned up with considerable consistency, but we have to be more cautious in accepting them, either because they have not been documented as well or because there are more exceptions. There seems to be a tendency for girls to exhibit more responsible behavior, including nurturance (trying to help others). Girls seem more likely to conform to adult wishes and commands. Boys try more often to exert dominance over others in order to get their own way. In play, boys and girls show a preference for their own gender. Boys seem to play in large groups, girls in small ones. And boys seem to maintain more distance between each other than girls do.[56]

If we assume that these differences are consistent across cultures, how can we explain them? Many writers and researchers believe that because certain female-male differences are so consistent, they are probably rooted in the biological differences between the two sexes. Aggression is one of the traits talked about most often in this connection, particularly because this male-female difference appears so early in life.[57] But an alternative argument is that societies bring up boys and girls differently because they almost universally require adult males and females to perform different types of roles. If most societies expect adult males to be warriors or to be prepared to be warriors, shouldn't we expect most societies to encourage or idealize aggression in males? And if females are almost always the caretakers of infants, shouldn't we also expect societies generally to encourage nurturant behaviors in females?

Researchers tend to adopt either the biological or the socialization view, but it is quite possible that both kinds of causes are important in the development of gender differences. For example, parents might turn a slight genetic difference into a large gender difference by maximizing that difference in the way they socialize boys versus girls.

It is difficult for researchers to distinguish the influence of genes (or other biological conditions) from the influence of socialization. We do have research indicating that as early as birth parents treat boy and girl infants differently.[58] In spite of the fact that objective observers can see no major "personality" differences between girl and boy infants, parents often claim to.[59] But parents may unconsciously want to see differences and may therefore produce them in socialization. So even early differences could be learned rather than genetic. Remember too that researchers cannot do experiments with people—for example, parents' behavior cannot be manipulated to find out what would happen if boys and girls were treated in exactly the same way.

However, there is considerable experimental research on aggression in nonhuman animals. These experiments suggest that the male hormone androgen is partly responsible for higher levels of aggression. For example, in some experiments, females injected with androgen at around the time the sexual organs develop (before or shortly after birth) behave more aggressively when they are older than do females without the hormone. These results may or may not apply to humans of course, but some researchers have investigated human females who were "androgenized" in the womb because of drugs given to their mothers to prevent miscarriages. By and large the results of these studies are similar to the experimental studies—androgenized human females show similar patterns of higher aggression.[60] Some scholars take these results to indicate that biological differences between males and females are responsible for the male-female difference in aggression[61]; others suggest that even these results are not conclusive, because females who get more androgen show generally disturbed metabolic systems, and general metabolic disturbance may itself increase aggressiveness. Furthermore, androgen-injected females look more like males because they develop male genitals; therefore, they may be treated like males.[62]

Is there any evidence that socialization differences may account for differences in aggression? Although a cross-cultural survey of ethnographers' reports on 101 societies does show that more societies encourage aggression in boys than in girls, *most* societies show no difference in aggression training.[63] The few societies that show differences in aggression training can hardly account for the widespread sex differences in actual aggressiveness. But the survey does not necessarily mean that there are no consistent differences in aggression training for boys and girls. All it shows is that there are no *obvious* differences. For all we know, the learning of aggression and other "masculine" traits by boys could be produced by subtle types of socialization.

One possible type of subtle socialization that could create gender differences in behavior is the type of chores children are assigned. It is possible that little boys and girls learn to behave differently because their parents ask them to do different kinds of work. Beatrice and John Whiting reported from the Six Cultures project that in societies where children were asked to do a great deal of work, they generally showed more responsible and nurturant behavior. Because girls are almost always asked to do more work than boys, they may be more responsible and nurturant for that reason alone.[64] If this reasoning is correct, we should find that if boys are asked to do girls' work, they will learn to behave more like girls.

A study of Luo children in Kenya supports that view.[65] Girls were usually asked to babysit, cook, clean house, and fetch water and firewood. Boys were usually asked to do very little because boys' traditional work was herding cattle—and most families in the community studied had few cattle. But for some reason more boys than girls had been born, and many mothers without girls at home asked their sons to do girls' chores. Systematic behavior observations showed that much of the behavior of the boys who did girls' work was

intermediary between the behavior of other boys and the behavior of girls. The boys who did girls' work were more like girls in that they were less aggressive, less domineering, and more responsible than other boys, even when they weren't working. So it is possible that task assignment has an important influence on how boys and girls learn to behave. These and other subtle forms of socialization need to be investigated more thoroughly; research may help us to understand better the origins of female-male differences in behavior.

Misconceptions about Differences in Behavior. Before we leave the subject of behavior differences, we should note some widespread beliefs about them that are unsupported. Some of these mistaken beliefs are that girls are more dependent than boys, that girls are more sociable, and that girls are more passive. The results obtained by the Six Cultures project cast doubt on all those notions.[66] First, if we think of dependency as seeking help and emotional support from others, girls are generally no more likely to behave this way than boys. To be sure, the results do indicate that boys and girls have somewhat different styles of dependency. Girls more often seek help and contact; boys more often seek attention and approval. As for sociability, which means seeking and offering friendship, the Six Cultures results showed no reliable differences between the sexes. Of course, boys and girls may be sociable in different ways because boys generally play in larger groups than girls. As for the supposed passivity of girls, the evidence is also not particularly convincing. Girls in the Six Cultures project did not consistently withdraw from aggressive attacks or comply with unreasonable demands. The only thing that emerged as a female-male difference was that older girls were less likely than boys to respond to aggression with aggression. But this finding may not reflect passivity as much as the fact that girls are less aggressive than boys—which we already knew.

So some of our common ideas about female-male differences are unfounded. Others, such as those dealing with aggression and responsibility, cannot be readily dismissed and should be investigated further.

SEXUALITY

In view of the way the human species reproduces, it is not surprising that sexuality is part of our nature. But no society we know of leaves sexuality to na-

Societies vary markedly in their rules about modesty. But these cultural rules change over time. In the past, both women and men in the United States were expected to cover much of their bodies on the beach.

ture; all have at least some rules governing "proper" conduct. There is much variation from one society to another in the degree of sexual activity permitted or encouraged before marriage, outside marriage, and even within marriage. And societies vary markedly in their tolerance of nonheterosexual sexuality.

Cultural Regulation of Sexuality: Permissiveness versus Restrictiveness

All societies seek to regulate sexual activity to some degree, and there is a lot of variation cross-culturally. Some societies allow premarital sex, others forbid it. The same is true for extramarital sex. In addition, a society's degree of restrictiveness is not always consistent through the life span or for all aspects of sex. For example, quite a number of societies ease sexual restrictions somewhat for adolescents, and many become more restrictive for adults.[67] Then, too, societies change over time. Our own society has traditionally been rather restrictive, but until recently (before the emergence

of the AIDS epidemic) more permissive attitudes were gaining acceptance.

Premarital Sex. The degree to which sex before marriage is approved or disapproved of varies greatly from society to society. The Trobriand Islanders, for example, approved of and encouraged premarital sex, seeing it as an important preparation for later marriage roles. Both girls and boys were given complete instruction in all forms of sexual expression at the onset of puberty and were allowed plenty of opportunity for intimacy. Some societies not only allow premarital sex on a casual basis, but specifically encourage trial marriages between adolescents. Among the Ila-speaking peoples of central Africa, at harvest time girls were given houses of their own where they could play at being wife with the boys of their choice. It is said that among these people virginity did not exist beyond the age of ten.[68]

On the other hand, in many societies premarital sex was discouraged. For example, among the Tepoztlan Indians of Mexico, a girl's life became "crabbed, cribbed, confined" from the time of her first menstruation. A girl was not to speak to or encourage boys in the least way. To do so would be to court disgrace, to show herself to be crazy. The responsibility of guarding the chastity and reputation of one or more daughters of marriageable age was often felt to be a burden by the mother. One mother said she wished her fifteen-year-old daughter would marry soon because it was inconvenient to "spy" on her all the time.[69]

In many Muslim societies, a girl's premarital chastity was tested after her marriage. After the wedding night, blood-stained sheets were displayed as proof of the bride's virginity.

Extramarital Sex. Extramarital sex is not uncommon in many societies. In about 69 percent of the world's societies men have extramarital sex more than occasionally, and in about 57 percent so do women. The frequency of such sexual activity is higher than we might expect, given that only a slight majority of societies (54 percent) say they allow extramarital sex for men, and only a small number (11 percent) say they allow it for women.[70]

In several societies, then, there is quite a difference between the restrictive code and actual practice. The Navaho of the 1940s were said to forbid adultery, but young married men under thirty had 27 percent of their heterosexual contacts with women other than their wives.[71] And, although people in the United States in the 1970s almost overwhelmingly rejected extramarital sex, 41 percent of married men and about 18 percent of married women had had extramarital sex. (Proportionately more men and women in the 1990s reported that they had been faithful to their spouses.)[72] Cross-culturally, most societies have a double standard with regard to men and women: restrictions are considerably greater for women.[73] A substantial number of societies openly accept extramarital relationships. The Chukchee of Siberia, who often traveled long distances, allowed a married man to engage in sex with his host's wife, with the understanding that he would offer the same hospitality when the host visited him.[74]

Sex within Marriage. There is as much variety in the way coitus is performed as there is in sexual attitudes in general. Privacy is a nearly universal requirement. But, whereas a North American will usually find this in the bedroom, many other peoples are obliged to go out into the bush. The Siriono of Bolivia, for example, had as many as fifty hammocks 10 feet apart in their small huts.[75] In some cultures coitus often occurs in the presence of others, who may be sleeping or simply looking the other way.

Time and frequency of coitus are also variable. Night is generally preferred, but some peoples, such as the Rucuyen of Brazil and the Yapese of the Pacific Caroline Islands, specifically opted for day. The Chenchu of India believed that a child conceived at night might be born blind. People in most societies abstain from intercourse during menstruation, during at least part of pregnancy, and for a period after childbirth. The Lesu, a people of New Ireland, an island off New Guinea, prohibited all members of the community from engaging in sex between the death of any member and burial.[76] Some societies prohibit sexual relations before various activities, such as hunting, fighting, planting, brewing, and iron smelting. Our own society is among the most lenient regarding restrictions on coitus within marriage, imposing only rather loose restraints during mourning, menstruation, and pregnancy.

Homosexuality. The range in permissiveness or restrictiveness toward homosexual relations is as great as that for any other kind of sexual activity. Among the Lepcha of the Himalayas, a man was believed to become homosexual if he ate the flesh of an uncastrated pig. But the Lepcha said that homosexual behavior was practically unheard of, and they viewed it with disgust.[77] Perhaps because many societies deny that homosexuality exists, little is known about homosexual practices in the restrictive societies. Among the permissive ones, there is variation in the pervasiveness of homosexuality. In some societies homosexuality is accepted but limited to certain times and certain individuals. For example, among the Papago of the southwestern United States there were "nights of saturnalia," in which homosexual tendencies could be expressed. The Papago also had many male transvestites, who wore women's clothing, did women's chores, and, if not married, could be visited by men.[78] A woman did not have quite the same freedom of expression. She could participate in the saturnalia feasts only with her husband's permission, and female transvestites were nonexistent.

Homosexuality occurs even more widely in other societies. The Siwans of North Africa expected all males to engage in homosexual relations. In fact, fathers made arrangements for their unmarried sons to be given to an older man in a homosexual arrangement. Siwan custom limited a man to one boy. Fear of the government made this a secret matter, but before 1909 such arrangements were made openly. Almost all men were reported to have engaged in a homosexual relationship as boys; later, when they were between sixteen and twenty, they married girls.[79] Among the most extremely prohomosexual societies, the Etoro of New Guinea preferred homosexuality to heterosexuality. Heterosexuality was prohibited as many as 260 days a year and was forbidden in or near the house and gardens. Male homosexuality, on the other hand, was not prohibited at any time and was believed to make crops flourish and boys become strong.[80]

Reasons for Restrictiveness

Before we deal with the question of why some societies are more restrictive than others, we must first ask whether all forms of restrictiveness go together. The research to date suggests that societies that are restrictive with regard to one aspect of heterosexual sex tend to be restrictive with regard to other aspects. Thus, societies that frown on sexual expression by young children also punish premarital and extramarital sex.[81] Furthermore, such societies tend to insist on modesty in clothing and are constrained in their talk about sex.[82] But societies that are generally restrictive about heterosexuality are not necessarily restrictive about homosexuality. Societies restrictive about premarital sex are neither more nor less likely to restrict homosexuality. In the case of extramarital sex, the situation is somewhat different. Societies that have a considerable amount of male homosexuality tend to disapprove of males having extramarital heterosexual relationships.[83] If we are going to explain restrictiveness, then, it appears we have to consider heterosexual and homosexual restrictiveness separately.

Let us consider homosexual restrictiveness first. The ethnographic material indicates an extremely broad range of societal reactions to homosexual relationships. Why? Why do homosexual relationships occur more frequently in some societies, and why are some societies intolerant of such relationships? There are many psychological interpretations of why some people become interested in homosexual relationships, and many of these interpretations relate the phenomenon to early parent-child relationships. So far the research has not yielded any clear-cut predictions, although several cross-cultural predictors about male homosexuality are intriguing.

One such finding is that societies that forbid abortion and infanticide for married women (most societies permit these practices for illegitimate births) are likely to be intolerant of male homosexuality. This and other findings are consistent with the point of view that homosexuality is less tolerated in societies that would like to increase population.

Such societies may be intolerant of all kinds of behaviors that minimize population growth. Homosexuality would have this effect, if we assume that a higher frequency of homosexual relations is associated with a lower frequency of heterosexual relations. The less frequently heterosexual relations occur, the lower the number of conceptions there might be. Another indication that intolerance may be related to a desire for population growth is that societies with famines and severe food shortages are more likely to allow homosexuality. Famines and food shortages suggest population pressure on resources; under these conditions homosexuality and other practices that minimize population growth may be tolerated or even encouraged.[84]

The history of the Soviet Union may provide some other relevant evidence. In 1917, in the turmoil of revolution, laws prohibiting abortion and homosexuality were revoked and reproduction was discouraged. But in the period 1934–1936 the policy was reversed. Abortion and homosexuality were again declared illegal, and homosexuals were arrested. At the same time, awards were given to mothers who had more children.[85] Population pressure may also explain why our own society has become somewhat more tolerant of homosexuality recently. Of course, population pressure does not explain why certain individuals become homosexual or why most individuals in some societies engage in such behavior, but it might explain why some societies view such behavior more or less permissively.

Let us turn now to heterosexual behavior. What kinds of societies are more permissive than others? Although we do not as yet understand the reasons, we do know that greater restrictiveness toward premarital sex tends to occur in more complex societies—societies that have hierarchies of political officials, part-time or full-time craft specialists, cities and towns, and class stratification.[86] It may be that as social inequality increases and various groups come to have differential wealth, parents become more concerned with preventing their children from marrying "beneath them." Permissiveness toward premarital sexual relationships might lead a person to become attached to someone who would not be considered a desirable marriage partner. Even worse (from the family's point of view), such "unsuitable" sexual liaisons might result in a pregnancy that could make it impossible for a girl to marry "well." Controlling mating, then, may be a way of trying to control property. Consistent with this view is the finding that virginity is emphasized in rank and stratified societies, in which families are likely to exchange goods and money in the course of arranging marriages.[87]

As is apparent from our review in this chapter, the biological fact that humans depend on sexual reproduction does not by itself help us explain why females and males differ in so many ways across cultures, or why societies vary in the way they handle male and female roles. We are only beginning to investigate these questions. When we eventually understand more about how and why females and males are different or the same in roles, personality, and sexuality, we may be better able to decide how much we want the biology of sex to shape our lives.

▼ SUMMARY

1. That humans reproduce sexually does not explain why males and females tend to differ in appearance and behavior, and to be treated differently, in all societies.

2. All or nearly all societies assign certain activities to females and other activities to males. These worldwide gender patterns of division of labor may be explained by male-female differences in strength, by differences in compatibility of tasks with child care, or by economy-of-effort considerations, and/or the expendability of men.

3. Perhaps because women almost always have infant- and child-care responsibilities, men in most societies contribute more to primary subsistence activities (in terms of calories). But women contribute substantially to primary subsistence activities in societies that depend heavily on gathering and horticulture and in which warfare occurs while primary subsistence work has to be done. When primary *and* secondary subsistence work are counted, women typically work more hours than men. In most societies men are the leaders in the political arena, and warfare is almost exclusively a male activity.

4. The relative status of women (compared with that of men) seems to vary from one area of life to another: whether women have relatively high status in one area does not necessarily indicate that they will have high status in another. Less complex societies, however, seem to approach more equal status for males and females in a variety of areas of life.

5. Recent field studies have suggested some consistent female-male differences in personality: boys tend to be more aggressive than girls, and girls seem to be more responsible and helpful than boys.

6. Although all societies regulate sexual activity to some extent, societies vary considerably in the degree to which various kinds of sexuality are permitted. Some societies allow both masturbation and sex play among children, whereas others forbid such acts. Some societies allow premarital sex; others do not. Some allow extramarital sex in certain situations; others forbid it generally.

7. Societies that are restrictive toward one aspect of heterosexual sex tend to be restrictive with regard to other aspects. And more complex societies tend to be more restrictive toward premarital heterosexual sex than less complex societies.

8. Societal attitudes toward homosexuality are not completely consistent with attitudes toward sexual relationships between the sexes. Societal tolerance of homosexuality is associated with tolerance of abortion and infanticide and with famines and food shortages.

▼ GLOSSARY TERMS

gender differences
primary subsistence activities

secondary subsistence activities
sexually dimorphic

▼ CRITICAL QUESTIONS

1. Would you expect female-male differences in personality to disappear in a society with complete gender equality in the workplace?
2. Under what circumstances would you expect male-female differences in athletic performance to disappear?
3. What conditions make the election of a female head of state most likely?

▼ SUGGESTED READING

BROUDE, G. J. "Variations in Sexual Attitudes, Norms and Practices." In C. R. Ember and M. Ember, eds., *Cross-Cultural Research for Social Science.* Englewood Cliffs, NJ: Prentice Hall, 1995. Prentice Hall/Simon & Schuster Custom Publishing. An exploration of the ways in which cultures vary in their sexual attitudes and practices and the possible reasons for the variation.

EMBER, C. R. "Universal and Variable Patterns of Gender Difference." In C. R. Ember and M. Ember, eds., *Cross-Cultural Research for Social Science.* Englewood Cliffs, NJ: Prentice Hall, 1995. Prentice Hall/Simon & Schuster Custom Publishing. A review of what we know and do not know about sex and gender differences cross-culturally and a critical evaluation of the theories that might explain the universal and variable patterns.

MORGEN, S. *Gender and Anthropology: Critical Reviews for Research and Teaching.* Washington, D.C.: American Anthropological Association, 1989. Designed to bring the insights of feminist anthropology to all four subfields of anthropology. Most relevant here are the chapters on different culture areas.

SANDAY, P. R., AND GOODENOUGH, R. G., EDS. *Beyond the Second Sex: New Directions in the Anthropology of Gender.* Philadelphia: University of Pennsylvania Press, 1990. The authors of the chapters in this volume reexamine theoretical notions about gender symbolism, gender roles, and male-female relationships in particular reference to the societies they have studied.

SCHLEGEL, A. "The Status of Women." In C. R. Ember and M. Ember, eds., *Cross-Cultural Research for Social Science.* Englewood Cliffs, NJ: Prentice Hall, 1995. Prentice Hall/Simon & Schuster Custom Publishing. A critical discussion of the comparative research on variation in women's status with an analysis of different kinds of equality and inequality in four ethnographic cases.

WOMACK, M. AND MARTI, J. *The Other Fifty Percent: Multicultural Perspectives on Gender Relations* (Prospect Heights, IL: Waveland Press, 1993). A collection of twenty-four readings about women in different societies—their roles in marriage, economic decision making, politics, and religion.

▼ NOTES

[1]Lila Leibowitz, *Females, Males, Families: A Biosocial Approach* (North Scituate, MA: Duxbury, 1978), pp. 43–44.

[2]Alice Schlegel, "Gender Issues and Cross-Cultural Research," *Behavior Science Research,* 23 (1989): 266; Cynthia Fuchs Epstein, *Deceptive Distinctions: Sex, Gender, and the Social Order* (New York: Russell Sage Foundation, 1988), pp. 5–6; Janet Saltzman Chafetz, *Gender Equity: An Integrated Theory of Stability and Change,* Sage Library of Social Research No. 176 (Newbury Park, CA: Sage Publications, 1990), p. 28.

[3]Sue-Ellen Jacobs and Christine Roberts, "Sex, Sexuality, Gender and Gender Variance," in Sandra Morgen, ed., *Gender and Anthropology: Critical Reviews for Research and Teaching* (Washington, D.C.: American Anthropological Association, 1989), pp. 438–62.

[4]William A. Stini, "Evolutionary Implications of Changing Nutritional Patterns in Human Populations," *American Anthropologist,* 73 (1971): 1019–30.

[5]David W. Frayer and Milford H. Wolpoff, "Sexual Dimorphism," *Annual Review of Anthropology,* 14 (1985): 431–32.

[6]For reviews of theories and research on sexual dimorphism and possible genetic and cultural determinants of variation in degree of dimorphism over time and place, see Frayer and Wolpoff, "Sexual Dimorphism"; and J. Patrick Gray, *Primate Sociobiology* (New Haven, CT: HRAF Press, 1985), pp. 201–9, 217–25.

[7]Judith K. Brown, "A Note on the Division of Labor by Sex," *American Anthropologist,* 72 (1970): 1074.

[8]Among the Aché hunter-gatherers of Paraguay, women collect the type of honey produced by stingless bees (men collect other honey); this division of labor is consistent with the compatibility theory. See Ana Magdalena Hurtado, Kristen Hawkes, Kim Hill, and Hillard Kaplan, "Female Subsistence Strategies among the Aché Hunter-Gatherers of Eastern Paraguay," *Human Ecology,* 13 (1985): 23.

[9]George P. Murdock and Caterina Provost, "Factors in the Division of Labor by Sex: A Cross-Cultural Analysis," *Ethnology,* 12 (1973): 213; Bryan Byrne, "Access to Subsistence Resources and the Sexual Division of Labor among Potters," *Cross-Cultural Research,* 28 (1994): 225–50.

[10]Douglas R. White, Michael L. Burton, and Lilyan A. Brudner, "Entailment Theory and Method: A Cross-Cultural Analysis of the Sexual Division of Labor," *Behavior Science Research,* 12 (1977): 1–24.

[11]Carol C. Mukhopadhyay and Patricia J. Higgins, "Anthropological Studies of Women's Status Revisited: 1977–1987," *Annual Review of Anthropology,* 17 (1988): 473.

[12]Brown, "A Note on the Division of Labor by Sex," pp. 1073–78; and White, Burton, and Brudner, "Entailment Theory and Method," pp. 1–24.

[13]Sara B. Nerlove, "Women's Workload and Infant Feeding Practices: A Relationship with Demographic Implications," *Ethnology,* 13 (1974): 201–14.

[14]Nancy E. Levine, "Women's Work and Infant Feeding: A Case from Rural Nepal," *Ethnology,* 27 (1988): 231–51.

[15]Madeleine J. Goodman, P. Bion Griffin, Agnes A. Estioko-Griffin, and John S. Grove, "The Compatibility of Hunting and Mothering among the Agta Hunter-Gatherers of the Philippines," *Sex Roles,* 12 (1985): 1199–209.

[16]John J. Macionis, *Sociology,* 4th ed. (Englewood Cliffs, NJ: Prentice Hall, 1993), p. 362.

[17]Margaret Mead, *Sex and Temperament in Three Primitive Societies* (New York: Mentor, 1950 [originally published 1935]), pp. 180–84.

[18]W. H. R. Rivers, *The Todas* (Oosterhout, N.B., The Netherlands: Anthropological Publications, 1967 [originally published 1906]), p. 567.

[19]Melvin Ember and Carol R. Ember, "The Conditions Favoring Matrilocal versus Patrilocal Residence," *American Anthropologist,* 73 (1971): 573, table 1.

[20]Alice Schlegel and Herbert Barry III, "The Cultural Consequences of Female Contribution to Subsistence," *American Anthropologist,* 88 (1986): 142–50.

[21]Ester Boserup, *Woman's Role in Economic Development* (New York: St. Martin's Press, 1970), pp. 22–25; see also Schlegel and Barry, "The Cultural Consequences of Female Contribution to Subsistence," pp. 144–45.

[22]Boserup, *Woman's Role in Economic Development,* pp. 22–25.

[23]Ibid., pp. 31–34.

[24]Carol R. Ember, "The Relative Decline in Women's Contribution to Agriculture with Intensification," *American Anthropologist,* 85 (1983): 286–87; data from Murdock and Provost, "Factors in the Division of Labor by Sex," p. 212; Candice Bradley, "Keeping the Soil in Good Heart: Weeding, Women and Ecofeminism," in Karen Warren, ed., *Ecofeminism: Multidisciplinary Perspectives* (Bloomington: Indiana University Press, 1995).

[25]Ember, "The Relative Decline in Women's Contribution to Agriculture with Intensification," pp. 287–93.

[26]Ember and Ember, "The Conditions Favoring Matrilocal versus Patrilocal Residence," pp. 579–80.

[27]Ibid., p. 581; see also Peggy R. Sanday, "Toward a Theory of the Status of Women," *American Anthropologist,* 75 (1973): 1684.

[28]Nerlove, "Women's Workload and Infant Feeding Practices," pp. 207–14.

[29]Schlegel and Barry, "The Cultural Consequences of Female Contribution to Subsistence," 142–50.

[30]Carol R. Ember, "The Relative Decline in Women's Contribution to Agriculture with Intensification," pp. 288–89.

[31]Martin K. Whyte, "Cross-Cultural Codes Dealing with the Relative Status of Women," *Ethnology,* 17 (1978): 217.

[32]Ibid.; and David B. Adams, "Why There Are So Few Women Warriors," *Behavior Science Research,* 18 (1983): 196–212.

[33]Judith K. Brown, "Economic Organization and the Position of Women among the Iroquois," *Ethnohistory,* 17 (1970): 151–67.

[34]Peggy R. Sanday, "Female Status in the Public Domain," in Michelle Z. Rosaldo and Louise Lamphere, eds., *Woman, Culture, and Society* (Stanford, CA: Stanford University Press, 1974), pp. 189–206; and William T. Divale and Marvin Harris, "Population, Warfare, and the Male Supremacist Complex," *American Anthropologist,* 78 (1976): 521–38.

[35]Naomi Quinn, "Anthropological Studies on Women's Status," *Annual Review of Anthropology,* 6 (1977): 189–90.

[36]Susan Brandt Graham, "Biology and Human Social Behavior: A Response to van den Berghe and Barash," *American Anthropologist,* 81 (1979): 357–60.

[37]Dennis Werner, "Chiefs and Presidents: A Comparison of Leadership Traits in the United States and among the Mekranoti-Kayapo of Central Brazil," *Ethos,* 10 (1982): 136–48; and Ralph M. Stogdill, *Handbook of Leadership: A Survey of Theory and Research* (New York: Macmillan, 1974), cited in ibid.; see also W. Penn Handwerker and Paul V. Crosbie, "Sex and Dominance," *American Anthropologist,* 84 (1982): 97–104.

[38]Patricia Draper, "!Kung Women: Contrasts in Sexual Egalitarianism in Foraging and Sedentary Contexts," in Rayna R. Reiter, ed., *Toward an Anthropology of Women* (New York: Monthly Review Press, 1975), p. 103.

[39]Dennis Werner, "Child Care and Influence among the Mekranoti of Central Brazil," *Sex Roles,* 10 (1984): 395–404.

[40]Marc H. Ross, "Female Political Participation: A Cross-Cultural Explanation," *American Anthropologist,* 88 (1986): 843–58.

[41]This description is based on the fieldwork of Elizabeth and Robert Fearnea (1956–1958), as reported in M. Kay Martin and Barbara Voorhies, *Female of the Species* (New York: Columbia University Press, 1975), pp. 304–31.

[42]Elsie B. Begler, "Sex, Status, and Authority in Egalitarian Society," *American Anthropologist,* 80 (1978): 571–88.

[43]Ibid. See also Whyte, "Cross-Cultural Codes Dealing with the Relative Status of Women," pp. 229–32.

[44]Martin K. Whyte, *The Status of Women in Preindustrial Societies* (Princeton, NJ: Princeton University Press, 1978), pp. 95–120. For a similar view, see Quinn, "Anthropological Studies on Women's Status."

[45]Whyte, *The Status of Women in Preindustrial Societies,* pp. 124–29, 145; see also Sanday, "Toward a Theory of the Status of Women."

[46]Whyte, *The Status of Women in Preindustrial Societies,* pp. 129–30.

[47]Brown, "Economic Organization and the Position of Women among the Iroquois."

[48]Whyte, *The Status of Women in Preindustrial Societies,* pp. 135–36.

[49]Ibid., p. 135.

[50]Quinn, "Anthropological Studies on Women's Status," p. 85; see also Mona Etienne and Eleanor Leacock, eds., *Women and Colonization: Anthropological Perspectives* (New York: Praeger, 1980), pp. 19–20.

[51]Chafetz, *Gender Equity,* pp. 11–19.

[52]Mead, *Sex and Temperament in Three Primitive Societies,* p. 206.

[53]Nancy McDowell, "Mundugumor: Sex and Temperament Revisited," in Melvin Ember, Carol R. Ember, and David Levinson, eds., *Portraits of Culture: Ethnographic Originals* (Englewood Cliffs, NJ: Prentice Hall, 1994). Prentice Hall/Simon & Schuster Custom Publishing.

[54]Beatrice B. Whiting and Carolyn P. Edwards, "A Cross-Cultural Analysis of Sex Differences in the Behavior of Children Aged Three through Eleven," *Journal of Social Psychology,* 91 (1973): 171–88.

[55]Eleanor E. Maccoby and Carol N. Jacklin, *The Psychology of Sex Differences* (Stanford CA: Stanford University Press, 1974).

[56]For a more extensive discussion of behavior differences and possible explanations of them, see Carol R. Ember, "A Cross-Cultural Perspective on Sex Differences," in Ruth H. Munroe, Robert L. Munroe, and Beatrice B. Whiting, eds., *Handbook of Cross-Cultural Human Development* (New York: Garland Press, 1981), pp. 531–80.

[57]Whiting and Edwards, "A Cross-Cultural Analysis of Sex Differences in the Behavior of Children Aged Three through Eleven."

[58]For references to this research, see Ember, "A Cross-Cultural Perspective on Sex Differences," p. 559.

[59]J. Z. Rubin, F. J. Provenzano, and R. F. Haskett, "The Eye of the Beholder: Parents' Views on the Sex of New Borns," *American Journal of Orthopsychiatry,* 44 (1974): 512–19.

[60]For a discussion of this evidence see Lee Ellis, "Evidence of Neuroandrogenic Etiology of Sex Roles from a Combined Analysis of Human, Nonhuman Primate and Nonprimate Mammalian Studies," *Personality and Individual Differences,* 7 (1986): 525–27; Ember, "A Cross-Cultural Perspective on Sex Differences," pp. 531–80.

[61]For example Ellis, in "Evidence of Neuroandrogenic Etiology of Sex Roles," considers the evidence for the biological view of aggression "beyond reasonable dispute."

[62]For a discussion of other possibilities see Ember, "A Cross-Cultural Perspective on Sex Differences."

[63]Ronald P. Rohner, "Sex Differences in Aggression: Phylogenetic and Enculturation Perspectives," *Ethos,* 4 (1976): 57–72.

[64]Beatrice B. Whiting and John W. M. Whiting (in collaboration with Richard Longabaugh), *Children of Six Cultures: A Psycho-Cultural Analysis* (Cambridge, MA: Harvard University Press, 1975); see also Beatrice B. Whiting and Carolyn P. Edwards, *Children of Different Worlds: The Formation of Social Behavior* (Cambridge, MA: Harvard University Press, 1988), p. 273.

[65]Carol R. Ember, "Feminine Task Assignment and the Social Behavior of Boys," *Ethos,* 1 (1973): 424–39.

[66]Whiting and Edwards, "A Cross-Cultural Analysis of Sex Differences in the Behavior of Children Aged Three through Eleven," pp. 175–79; see also Maccoby and Jacklin, *The Psychology of Sex Differences.*

[67]David R. Heise, "Cultural Patterning of Sexual Socialization," *American Sociological Review,* 32 (1967): 726–39.

[68]Ford and Beach, *Patterns of Sexual Behavior,* p. 191.

[69]Oscar Lewis, *Life in a Mexican Village: Tepoztlan Revisited* (Urbana: University of Illinois Press, 1951), p. 397.

[70]Gwen J. Broude and Sarah J. Greene, "Cross-Cultural Codes on Twenty Sexual Attitudes and Practices," *Ethnology,* 15 (1976): 409–29.

[71]Clyde Kluckhohn, "As an Anthropologist Views It," in A. Deutsch, ed., *Sex Habits of American Men* (Englewood Cliffs, NJ: Prentice Hall, 1948), p. 101.

[72]Morton Hunt, *Sexual Behavior in the 1970s* (Chicago: Playboy Press, 1974), pp. 254-57; Tamar Lewin,

"Sex in America: Faithfulness in Marriage Is Overwhelming," *New York Times (National)*, October 7, 1994, pp. A1, A18.

[73]Gwen J. Broude, "Extramarital Sex Norms in Cross-Cultural Perspective," *Behavior Science Research,* 15 (1980): 184.

[74]Ford and Beach, *Patterns of Sexual Behavior,* p. 114.

[75]Ibid., p. 69.

[76]Ibid., p. 76.

[77]John Morris, *Living with Lepchas: A Book about the Sikkim Himalayas* (London: Heinemann, 1938), p. 191.

[78]Ruth M. Underhill, *Social Organization of the Papago Indians* (New York: Columbia University Press, 1938), pp. 117, 186.

[79]Mahmud M. 'Abd Allah, "Siwan Customs," *Harvard African Studies,* 1 (1917): 7, 20.

[80]Raymond C. Kelly, "Witchcraft and Sexual Relations: An Exploration in the Social and Semantic Implications of the Structure of Belief," paper presented at the annual meeting of the American Anthropological Association, Mexico City, 1974.

[81]Data from Robert B. Textor, comp., *A Cross-Cultural Summary* (New Haven, CT: HRAF Press, 1967).

[82]William N. Stephens, "A Cross-Cultural Study of Modesty," *Behavior Science Research,* 7 (1972): 1–28.

[83]Gwen J. Broude, "Cross-Cultural Patterning of Some Sexual Attitudes and Practices," *Behavior Science Research,* 11 (1976): 243.

[84]Dennis Werner, "A Cross-Cultural Perspective on Theory and Research on Male Homosexuality," *Journal of Homosexuality,* 4 (1979): 345–62; see also Dennis Werner, "On the Societal Acceptance or Rejection of Male Homosexuality," M.A. thesis, Hunter College of the City University of New York, 1975, p. 36.

[85]Werner, "A Cross-Cultural Perspective on Theory and Research on Male Homosexuality," p. 358.

[86]Data from Textor, comp., *A Cross-Cultural Summary.*

[87]Alice Schlegel, "Status, Property, and the Value of Virginity," *American Ethnologist,* 18 (1991): 719–34.

Marriage and the Family

Whatever a society's attitudes toward male-female relationships, one such relationship is found in all societies—marriage. Why marriage is customary in every society we know of is a classic and perplexing question—and one we attempt to deal with in this chapter.

The universality of marriage does not mean that everyone in every society gets married. It means only that most (usually nearly all) people in every society get married at least once in their lifetime. In addition, when we say that marriage is universal, we do not mean that marriage and family customs are the same in all societies. On the contrary, there is much variation from society to society in how one marries, whom one marries, and even how many persons one marries. The only cultural universal about marriage is that no society permits people to marry parents, brothers, or sisters.

Families also are universal. All societies have parent-child social groups, although the form and size of family may vary from one society to another. Some societies have large extended families with two or more related parent-child groups; others have smaller independent families. Nowadays, marriage is not always the basis for family life. One-parent families are becoming increasingly common in our own and other societies. Marriage has not disappeared in these places—it is still customary to marry—but more individuals are choosing now to have children without being married.

MARRIAGE

▼

When anthropologists speak of marriage, they do not mean to imply that couples everywhere must get marriage certificates or have wedding ceremonies, as in our own society. **Marriage** merely means a socially approved sexual and economic union between a woman and a man. It is presumed, both by the couple and by others, to be more or less permanent, and it subsumes reciprocal rights and obligations between the two spouses and between spouses and their future children.[1]

It is a socially approved sexual union in that a married couple does not have to hide the sexual nature of their relationship. A woman might say "I want you to meet my husband," but she could not say "I want you to meet my lover" without causing some embarrassment in most societies. Although the union may ultimately be dissolved by divorce, couples in all societies begin marriage with some idea of permanence in mind. Implicit too in mar-

Some societies have ceremonies marking the onset of marriage, and some do not. Here we see the bride and groom at a Shinto wedding in Japan.

riage are reciprocal rights and obligations. These may be more or less specific and formalized regarding matters of property, finances, and child rearing.

Marriage entails both a sexual and an economic relationship:

> Sexual unions without economic co-operation are common, and there are relationships between men and women involving a division of labor without sexual gratification, e.g., between brother and sister, master and maidservant, or employer and secretary, but marriage exists only when the economic and the sexual are united in one relationship, and this combination occurs only in marriage.[2]

As we will see, the event that marks the commencement of marriage varies in different societies. A Winnebago bride, for example, knew no formal ritual such as a wedding ceremony. She went with her groom to his parents' house, took off her "wedding" clothes and finery, gave them to her mother-in-law, received plain clothes in exchange, and that was that.[3]

The Nayar "Exception"

There is one group of people in the ethnographic literature that did not have marriage, as we have defined it. In the nineteenth century, a caste group in southern India called the Nayar seem to have treated sex and economic relations between men and women as things separate from marriage. About the time of puberty, Nayar girls took ritual husbands. The union was publicly established in a ceremony during which the husband tied a gold ornament around the neck of his bride. But from that time on, he had no more responsibility for her. Usually, he never saw her again.

The bride lived in a large household with her family, where she was visited over the subsequent years by other "husbands." One might be a passing guest, another a more regular visitor; it did not matter, providing the "husband" met the caste restrictions and was approved by her kin group. He came at night and left the following day. If a regular visitor, he was expected to make small gifts of cloth, betel nuts, and hair and bath oil. If the father of her child, or one of a group who might be, he was expected to pay the cost of the midwife. But at no time was he responsible for the support of the woman or her child, nor did he have any say in the upbringing of his biological children. Rather, her blood relatives retained such responsibilities.[4]

Whether or not the Nayar had marriage depends, of course, on how we choose to define marriage. Certainly, Nayar marital unions involved no regular sexual component or economic cooperation, nor did they involve important reciprocal rights and obligations. According to our definition, then, the Nayar did not have marriage. But the Nayar were not a separate society—only a caste group whose men specialized in soldiering. The Nayar situation seems to have been a special response to the problem of extended male absence during military service. In more recent times, military service has ceased to be a common occupation of the Nayars and stable married relationships have become the norm.[5] Because the Nayar were not a separate society, the Nayar are not really an exception to our statement that marriage, as we have defined it, has been customary in all societies known to anthropology.

Rare Types of Marriage

In addition to the usual male-female marriages, some societies recognize marriages between persons of the same biological sex. But such marriages are not typical in any known society and do not completely fit our definition of marriage. First, the unions are not between a male and a female. Second, they are not necessarily sexual unions, as we will see. But these "marriages" are socially approved unions, usually modeled after regular marriages, and they often entail a considerable number of reciprocal rights and obligations. Sometimes the marriages involve an individual who is considered a "woman" or "man" even though "she" or "he" is not that sex biologically. For example, the Cheyenne

Indians allowed married men to take on **berdaches,** or male transvestites, as second wives.[6] (The term *two-spirits* is often used now instead of *berdache.*)

Although it is not clear that the Cheyenne male-male marriages involved homosexual relationships, it is clear that temporary homosexual marriages did occur among the Azande of Africa. Before the British took control over what is known as the Sudan, Azande warriors who could not afford wives often married "boy-wives" to satisfy their sexual needs. As in normal marriages, gifts (although not as substantial) were given by the "husband" to the parents of his boy-wife. The husband performed services for the boy's parents and could sue any other lover in court for adultery. The boy-wives not only had sexual relations with their husbands but also performed many of the chores female wives traditionally performed for their husbands.[7]

Female-female marriages are reported to have occurred in many African societies, but there is no evidence of any sexual relationship between the partners. It seems rather that female-female marriages were a socially approved way for a woman to take on the legal and social roles of a father and husband.[8] For example, among the Nandi, a pastoral and agricultural society of Kenya, about 3 percent of the marriages are female-female marriages. Such marriages appear to be a Nandi solution to the problem of a regular marriage's failing to produce a male heir to property. The Nandi solution is to have the woman, even if her husband is still alive, become a "husband" to a younger female and "father" the younger woman's children. The female husband provides the marriage payments required for obtaining a wife, renounces female work, and takes on the obligations of the husband to that woman. Although no sexual relations are permitted between the female husband and the new wife (or between the female husband and her own husband), the female husband arranges a male consort so that the new wife can have children. Those children, however, consider the female husband to be their father because she (or more aptly the gender role "he") is the socially designated father. If asked who their father is, a child of such a marriage will name the female who is the husband.[9]

WHY IS MARRIAGE UNIVERSAL?

Because all societies practice female-male marriage as we have defined it, we can assume that the custom is adaptive. But saying that does not specify exactly how it may be adaptive. Several interpretations have traditionally been offered to explain why all human societies have the custom of marriage. Each suggests that marriage solves problems found in all societies—how to share the products of a gender division of labor; how to care for infants, who are dependent for a long time; and how to minimize sexual competition. To evaluate the plausibility of these interpretations, we must ask whether marriage provides the best or the only reasonable solution to each problem. After all, we are trying to explain a custom that is presumably a universal solution. The comparative study of other animals, some of which have something like marriage, may help us to evaluate these explanations, as we will see.

Gender Division of Labor

We noted in the preceding chapter that every society known to anthropology has had a gender division of labor. Males and females in every society perform different economic activities. This gender division of labor has often been cited as a reason for marriage.[10] As long as there is a division of labor by gender, society has to have some mechanism by which women and men share the products of their labor. Marriage would be one way to solve that problem. But it seems unlikely that marriage is the only possible solution. The hunter-gatherer rule of sharing could be extended to include all the products brought in by both women and men. Or a small group of men and women (such as brothers and sisters) might be pledged to cooperate economically. Thus, although marriage may solve the problem of sharing the fruits of a division of labor, it clearly is not the only possible solution.

Prolonged Infant Dependency

Humans exhibit the longest period of infant dependency of any primate. The child's prolonged dependence places the greatest burden on the mother, who is the main child tender in most societies. The burden of prolonged child care by human females may limit the kinds of work they can do. They may need the help of a man to do certain types of work, such as hunting, that are incompatible with child care. Because of this prolonged dependency, it has been suggested, marriage is necessary.[11] But here the argument becomes essentially the same as the division-of-labor argument, and it has the same logical weakness. It is not clear why a group of women and men, such as a hunter-gatherer band, could not cooperate in providing for dependent children without marriage.

Sexual Competition

Unlike most other female primates, the human female may engage in intercourse at any time throughout the year. Some scholars have suggested that more or less continuous female sexuality may have created a serious problem—considerable sexual competition between males for females. It is argued that society had to prevent such competition in order to survive—that it had to develop some way of minimizing the rivalry between males for females in order to reduce the chance of lethal and destructive conflict.[12]

There are several problems with this argument. First, why should continuous female sexuality make for more sexual competition in the first place? One might argue the other way around: there might be more competition over the scarcer resources that would be available if females were less frequently interested in sex. Second, males of many animal species, even some that have relatively frequent female sexuality (as do many of our close primate relatives), do not show much aggression over females. Third, why couldn't sexual competition, even if it existed, be regulated by cultural rules other than marriage? For instance, society might have adopted a rule whereby men and women circulated among all the opposite-sex members of the group, each person staying a specified length of time with each partner. Such a system presumably would solve the problem of sexual competition. On the other hand, such a system might not work particularly well if individuals came to prefer certain other individuals. Jealousies attending those attachments might give rise to even more competition.

Other Mammals and Birds: Postpartum Requirements

None of the theories we have discussed explains convincingly why marriage is the only or the best solution to a particular problem. Also, we now have some comparative evidence on mammals and birds that casts doubt on those theories.[13] How can evidence from other animals help us evaluate theories about human marriage? If we look at the animals that (like humans) have some sort of stable female-male mating, as compared with those that are completely promiscuous, we can perhaps see what sorts of factors may predict male-female bonding in the warm-blooded animal species. (Most species of birds, and wolves and beavers have "marriage.") Among forty mammal and bird species, none of the three factors discussed above—division of labor, prolonged infant dependency, and greater female sexuality—predicts or is correlated strongly with male-female bonding. With respect to division of labor by sex, most other animals have nothing comparable to a humanlike division of labor, but many have stable female-male matings anyway. The two other supposed factors—prolonged infant dependency and female sexuality—predict just the opposite of what we might expect. Mammal and bird species that have longer dependency periods or more female sexuality are *less* likely to have stable matings.

Does anything predict male-female bonding? One factor does among mammals and birds, and it may also help explain human marriage. Animal species in which females can simultaneously feed themselves and their babies after birth *(postpartum)* tend not to have stable matings; species in which postpartum mothers cannot feed themselves and their babies at the same time tend to have stable matings. Among the typical bird species, a mother would have difficulty feeding herself and her babies simultaneously. Because the young cannot fly for a while and must be protected in a nest, the mother risks losing them to other animals if she goes off to obtain food. But if she has a male bonded to her (as most bird species do), he can bring back food or take a turn watching the nest. Among animal species that have no postpartum feeding problem, babies almost immediately after birth are able to travel with the mother as she moves about to eat (as do grazers such as horses), or the mother can transport the babies as she moves about to eat (as do baboons and kangaroos). We think the human female has a postpartum feeding problem. When humans lost most of their body hair, babies could not readily travel with the mother by clinging to her fur. And when humans began to depend on certain kinds of food-getting that could be dangerous (such as hunting), mothers could not engage in such work with their infants along.

Even if we assume that human mothers have a postpartum feeding problem, we still have to ask if marriage is the most likely solution to the problem. We think so, because other conceivable solutions probably would not work as well. For example, if a mother took turns babysitting with another mother, neither might be able to collect enough food for both mothers and the two sets of children dependent on them. But a mother and father share the *same* set of children, and therefore it would be easier for them to feed themselves and their children adequately. Another possible solution is no pair bonding at all, just a promiscuous group of males and females. But in that kind of arrangement, we think, a particular mother probably would not always be able to count on some male to watch her baby when she had to go out for food or to bring her food when she had to watch her baby. Thus, it seems to us that the problem of postpartum feeding by itself helps to explain why some animals (including humans) have relatively stable male-female bonds. Of course, there is still the question of whether research on other animals can be applied to human beings. We think it can, but not everybody will agree.

HOW DOES ONE MARRY?

When we say that marriage is a socially approved sexual and economic union, we mean that all societies have some way of marking the onset of a marriage, but the ways of doing so vary considerably. For reasons that we don't fully understand, some cultures mark marriages by elaborate rites and celebrations; others mark marriages in much more informal ways. And most societies have economic transactions before, during, or even after the onset of the marriages.

Marking the Onset of Marriage

Many societies have ceremonies marking the beginning of marriage. But others, such as the Taramiut Inuit, the Trobriand Islanders of the South Pacific, and the Kwoma of New Guinea, use different social signals to indicate that a marriage has taken place.

"I do love you. But, to be perfectly honest, I would have loved any other lovebird who happened to turn up." (© 1978 Punch/Rothco)

Among the Taramiut Inuit, the betrothal is considered extremely important and is arranged between the parents at or before the time their children reach puberty. Later, when the youth is ready, he moves in with his betrothed's family for a trial period. If all goes well—that is, if the girl gives birth to a baby within a year or so—the couple are considered married. At this time, the wife goes with her husband to his camp.[14]

In keeping with the general openness of their society's attitudes toward sexual matters, a Trobriand couple advertise their desire to marry "by sleeping together regularly, by showing themselves together in public, and by remaining with each other for long periods at a time."[15] When a girl accepts a small gift from a boy, she demonstrates that her parents favor the match. Before long, she moves to the boy's house, takes her meals there, and accompanies her husband all day. Then the word goes around that the two are married.[16]

The Kwoma of New Guinea practice a trial marriage followed by a ceremony that makes the couple husband and wife. The girl lives for a while in the boy's home. When the boy's mother is satisfied with the match and knows that her son is too, she waits for a day when he is away from the house. Until that time, the girl has been cooking only for herself, and the boy's food has been prepared by his womenfolk. Now the mother has the girl prepare his meal. The young man returns and begins to eat his soup. When the first bowl is nearly finished, his mother tells him that his betrothed cooked the meal, and his eating it means that he is now married. At this news, the boy customarily rushes out of the house, spits out the soup, and shouts, "Faugh! It tastes bad! It is cooked terribly!" A ceremony then makes the marriage official.[17]

Among those societies that have ceremonies marking the onset of marriage, feasting is a common element. It expresses publicly the unification of the two families by marriage. The Reindeer Tungus of Siberia set a wedding date after protracted negotiations between the two families and their larger kin groups. Go-betweens assume most of the responsibility for the negotiating. The wedding day opens with the two kin groups, probably numbering as many as 150 people, pitching their lodges in separate areas and offering a great feast. After the groom's gifts have been presented, the bride's dowry is loaded onto reindeer and carried to the groom's lodge. There the climax of the ceremony takes place. The bride takes the wife's place—that is, at the right side of the entrance of the lodge—and members of both families sit in a circle. The groom enters and

follows the bride around the circle, greeting each guest, while the guests, in their turn, kiss the bride on the mouth and hands. Finally, the go-betweens spit three times on the bride's hands, and the couple are formally husband and wife. More feasting and revelry bring the day to a close.[18]

In many cultures, marriage includes ceremonial expressions of hostility. One form of this custom is the trading of insults between kin groups, such as occurs on the Polynesian atoll of Pukapuka. Mock fights are staged in many societies. On occasion, hostility can have genuinely aggressive overtones, as among the Gusii of Kenya:

> Five young clansmen of the groom come to take the bride and two immediately find the girl and post themselves at her side to prevent her escape, while the others receive the final permission of her parents. When it has been granted the bride holds onto the house posts and must be dragged outside by the young men. Finally she goes along with them, crying and with her hands on her head.[19]

But the battle is not yet over. Mutual antagonism continues right onto the marriage bed, even up to and beyond coitus. The groom is determined to display his virility; the bride is equally determined to test it. "Brides," Robert and Barbara LeVine remarked, "are said to take pride in the length of time they can hold off their mates." Men can also win acclaim. If the bride is unable to walk the following day, the groom is considered a "real man."[20]

Such expressions of hostility usually occur in societies in which the two sets of kin are actual or potential rivals or enemies. In many societies, it is common to marry women from "enemy" villages.

As this example suggests, marriage ceremonies often symbolize important elements of the culture. Whereas the Gusii ceremony may symbolize hostility between the two families, in other societies the ceremony may promote harmony between the families. For example, on the Polynesian island of Rotuma, a female clown is an important part of the ceremony. She is responsible for creating an enjoyable, joking atmosphere that facilitates interaction between the two sides.[21]

Economic Aspects of Marriage

"It's not man that marries maid, but field marries field, vineyard marries vineyard, cattle marry cattle." In its down-to-earth way, this German peasant saying indicates that in many societies marriage involves economic considerations. In our culture, economic considerations may or may not be explicit. However, in about 75 percent of the societies known to anthropology,[22] one or more explicit economic transactions take place before or after the marriage. The economic transaction may take several forms: bride price, bride service, exchange of females, gift exchange, dowry, and indirect dowry. The distribution of those forms among societies that have economic marriage transactions is shown in Figure 10–1.

Bride Price. **Bride price** (or **bride wealth**) is a gift of money or goods from the groom or his kin to the bride's kin. The gift usually grants the groom the right to marry the bride and the right to her children. Of all the forms of economic transaction involved in marriage, bride price is the most common. In one cross-cultural sample, 44 percent of the societies with economic transactions at marriage practiced bride price; in almost all of those societies the bride price was substantial.[23] Bride price occurs all over the world but is especially common in Africa and Oceania. Payment can be made in different currencies; livestock and food are two of the more common. With the increased importance of commercial exchange, money has increasingly become part of the bride price payments. Among the Nandi, the bride price consists of about five to seven cattle, one or two sheep and goats, cowrie shells and money equivalent to the value of one cow. Even in unusual female-female marriages, the female "husband"

must pay a bride price to arrange the marriage and be considered the "father."[24]

The Subanun of the Philippines have an expensive bride price—several times the annual income of the groom *plus* three to five years of bride service (described in the next section).[25] Among the Manus of the Admiralty Islands off New Guinea, a groom requires an economic backer—usually an older brother or an uncle—if he is to marry, but it will be years before he can pay off his debts. Depending on the final bride price, payments may be concluded at the time of the marriage, or they may continue for years afterward.[26]

Despite the connotations that bride price may have for us, the practice does not reduce a woman to the position of slave (although it is associated, as we shall see, with relatively low status for women). The bride price may be important to the woman and her family. Indeed, the fee they receive can serve as a security. If the marriage fails through no fault of hers and the wife returns to her kin, the family might not return the bride price to the groom. On the other hand, the wife's kin may pressure her to remain with her husband, even though she does not wish to, because they do not want to return the bride price or are unable to do so.

What kinds of societies are likely to have the custom of bride price? Cross-culturally, societies with bride price are likely to practice horticulture

FIGURE 10–1
Distribution of Economic Marriage Transactions among Societies That Have Them

Twenty-five percent of the societies in the ethnographic record lack any substantial economic transactions at marriage. Source: *Alice Schlegel and Rohn Eloul, "Marriage Transactions: Labor, Property, and Status,"* American Anthropologist *90 (1988): 291–309.*

The bride at an Islamic wedding in central Turkey wears some of the bride price on her veil.

North Alaskan Eskimo, for example, the boy works for his in-laws after the marriage is arranged. To fulfill his obligation, he may simply catch a seal for them. The marriage may be consummated at any time while he is in service.[30] In some societies, bride service sometimes substitutes for bride price. An individual might give bride service in order to reduce the amount of bride price required. Native American societies (in North and South America) were likely to practice bride service, particularly if they were egalitarian food collectors.[31]

Exchange of Females. Of the societies that have economic transactions at marriage, 6 percent have the custom whereby a sister or female relative of the groom is exchanged for the bride. Among these societies are the Tiv of West Africa and the Yanomamö of Venezuela-Brazil. These societies tend to be horticultural, egalitarian, and to have a relatively high contribution of women to primary subsistence.[32]

Gift Exchange. Gift exchange, which involves the exchange of gifts of about equal value by the two kin groups about to be linked by marriage, occurs somewhat more often than the exchange of females (about 11 percent of those with economic transactions).[33] For example, among the Andaman Islanders, as soon as a boy and girl indicate their intention to marry, their respective sets of parents cease all communication and begin sending gifts of food and other objects to each other through a third party. This arrangement continues until the marriage is completed and the two kin groups are united.[34]

Dowry. A **dowry** is usually a substantial transfer of goods or money from the bride's family to the bride.[35] Unlike the types of transactions we have discussed so far, the dowry (which occurs in about 8 percent of the societies with economic transactions) is usually not a transaction between the kin of the bride and the kin of the groom. A family has to have wealth to give a dowry, but because the goods go to the bride, no wealth comes back to the family that gave the dowry. Payment of dowries was common in medieval and Renaissance Europe, where the size of the dowry often determined the desirability of the daughter. The custom is still practiced in parts of eastern Europe and in sections of southern Italy and France, where land is often the major item provided by the bride's family. Parts of India also practice the dowry.

In contrast to societies with bride price, societies with dowry tend to be those in which women

and lack social stratification. Bride price is also likely where women contribute a great deal to primary subsistence activities[27] and where they contribute more than men to all kinds of economic activities.[28] Although these findings might suggest that women are highly valued in such societies, recall that the status of women relative to men is *not* higher in societies in which women contribute a lot to primary subsistence activities. Indeed, bride price is likely to occur in societies in which men make most of the decisions in the household,[29] and decision making by men is one indicator of lower status for women.

Bride Service. **Bride service,** which is the next most common type of economic transaction at marriage (occurring in about 19 percent of the societies with economic transactions), requires the groom to work for the bride's family, sometimes before the marriage begins, sometimes after. Bride service varies in duration. In some societies it lasts for only a few months; in others it lasts as long as several years. Among the contribute relatively little to primary subsistence activities, there is a high degree of social stratification, and a man is not allowed to be married to more than one woman simultaneously.[36] Why does dowry tend to occur in these types of societies? One theory suggests that the dowry is intended to guarantee future support for a woman (and her children), even though she will not do much primary subsistence work. Another theory is that the dowry is intended to attract the best bridegroom for a daughter in monogamous societies with a high degree of social inequality. (The dowry strategy is presumed to increase the likelihood that the daughter and her children will do well reproductively.) Both theories are supported by recent cross-cultural research, with the second predicting dowry better.[37] But many stratified societies (including our own) in which women and men have only one spouse (at a time) do not practice dowry. Why this is so still needs to be explained.

Indirect Dowry. The dowry is provided by the bride's family to the bride. But sometimes the payments to the bride originate from the groom's family; because the goods are sometimes first given to the bride's father who passes most if not all of them to her, this kind of transaction is called **indirect dowry**.[38] Indirect dowry occurs in about 12 percent of the societies in which marriage involves an economic transaction. For example, among the Basseri of southern Iran, the groom's father assumes the expense of setting up the couple's new household. He gives cash to the bride's father, who uses at least some of the money to buy his daughter household utensils, blankets, and rugs.[39]

RESTRICTIONS ON MARRIAGE: THE UNIVERSAL INCEST TABOO

▼

Hollywood and its press agents notwithstanding, marriage is not always based solely on mutual love, independently discovered and expressed by the two life-partners-to-be. Nor is it based on sex or wealth alone. Even when love, sex, and economics are contributing factors, regulations specify whom one may or may not marry. Perhaps the most rigid regulation, found in *all* cultures, is the **incest taboo,** which prohibits sexual intercourse or marriage between some categories of kin.

The most universal aspect of the incest taboo is the prohibition of sexual intercourse or marriage between mother and son, father and daughter, and brother and sister. No society in recent times has permitted either sexual intercourse or marriage between those pairs. A few societies in the past, however, did permit incest, mostly within the royal and aristocratic families, though generally it was forbidden to the rest of the population. For example, the Incan and Hawaiian royal families allowed marriages within the family. Probably the best-known example of allowed incest involved Cleopatra of Egypt.

It seems clear that the Egyptian aristocracy and royalty indulged in father-daughter and brother-sister marriages. (Cleopatra was married to two of her younger brothers at different times.)[40] The reasons seem to have been partly religious—a member of the family of Pharaoh, who was a god, could not marry any "ordinary" human—and partly economic, for marriage within the family kept the royal property undivided. In the Egyptian case, between 30 B.C. and A.D. 324, incest was allowed not just in the royal family; an estimated 8 percent of commoner marriages were brother-sister marriages.[41]

But, despite these exceptions, the fact remains that no cultures we know of today permit or accept incest within the nuclear family. Why is the familial incest taboo universal? Several explanations have been suggested.

Childhood-Familiarity Theory

The childhood-familiarity theory, suggested by Edward Westermarck, was given a wide hearing in the early 1920s. Westermarck argued that persons who have been closely associated with each other since earliest childhood, such as siblings, are not sexually attracted to each other and therefore would avoid marriage with each other.[42] This theory was subsequently rejected because of evidence that some children *were* sexually interested in their parents and siblings. Studies have suggested, however, that there might be something to Westermarck's theory.

Yonina Talmon investigated marriage patterns among the second generation of three well-established collective communities (*kibbutzim*) in Israel. In these collectives, children live with many members of their peer group in quarters separate from their families. They are in constant interaction with their peers, from birth to maturity. The study revealed that among 125 couples, there was "not one instance in which both mates were reared from birth in the same peer group,"[43] despite parental encouragement of marriage within the peer group. Children reared in common not only avoided marriage, they also avoided any sexual relations among themselves.

Talmon stated that the people reared together firmly believed that overfamiliarity breeds sexual

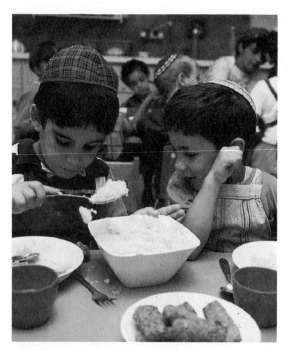

Research has indicated that people who grow up together are not interested in each other sexually when they are adults. On an Israeli kibbutz, children spend much of their time together in a communal children's house. Although parents would like the children from the same kibbutz to marry, they are not likely to be interested.

disinterest. As one of them told her, "We are like an open book to each other. We have read the story in the book over and over again and know all about it."[44] Talmon's evidence reveals not only the onset of disinterest and even sexual antipathy among children reared together, but a correspondingly heightened fascination with newcomers or outsiders, particularly for their "mystery."

Arthur Wolf's study of the Chinese in northern Taiwan also supports the idea that something about being reared together produces sexual disinterest. Wolf focused on a community still practicing the Chinese custom of *t'ung-yang-hsi*, or "daughter-in-law raised from childhood."

> When a girl is born in a poor family . . . she is often given away or sold when but a few weeks old, or one or two years old, to be the future wife of a son in the family of a friend or relative which has a little son not betrothed in marriage. . . . The girl is called a "little bride" and taken home and brought up in the family together with her future husband.[45]

Wolf's evidence indicates that this arrangement is associated with sexual difficulties when the child-

hood "couple" later marry. Informants implied that familiarity results in disinterest and lack of stimulation. As an indication of their disinterest, these couples produce fewer offspring than spouses not raised together, they are more likely to seek extra-marital sexual relationships, and they are more likely to get divorced.[46]

The Talmon and Wolf studies suggest, then, that children raised together are not likely to be sexually interested in each other when they grow up. Such disinterest is consistent with Westermarck's notion that the incest taboo may be more an avoidance of certain matings than a prohibition of them. There is one other piece of evidence consistent with his explanation of the incest taboo. Hilda and Seymour Parker compared two samples of fathers: those who had sexually abused their daughters and those who supposedly had not.[47] (To maximize their similarities otherwise, the Parkers selected the two samples of fathers from the same prisons and psychiatric facilities.) The Parkers found that the fathers who had committed incest with their daughters were much more likely than the other sample of fathers to have had little to do with bringing up their daughters, because they were not at home or hardly at home during the daughters' first three years of life. In other words, the fathers who avoided incest had been more closely associated with their daughters in childhood. That finding again is consistent with Westermarck's suggestion that the incest taboo is a result of familiarity in childhood.

Although Westermarck was talking about the development of sexual aversion during early childhood, some researchers have asked how the childhood-familiarity theory could explain the extension of incest taboos to first cousins. The familiarity argument implies that first-cousin marriage should be prohibited in societies in which first cousins grow up together in the same community. But that is not the case. Such societies are not more likely to prohibit first-cousin marriage.[48]

Even if there is something about familiarity in childhood that normally leads to sexual disinterest,[49] we still are left with the question of why societies have to prohibit marriages that would voluntarily be avoided because of disinterest.

Freud's Psychoanalytic Theory

Sigmund Freud proposed that the incest taboo is a reaction against unconscious, unacceptable desires.[50] He suggested that the son is attracted to his mother (as the daughter is to her father) and as a result feels jealousy and hostility toward his father. But the son knows that these feelings cannot continue, for they might lead the father to retaliate against him; therefore, they must be renounced or repressed. Usually the feelings are repressed and retreat into the unconscious. But the desire to possess the mother continues to exist in the unconscious, and, according to Freud, the horror of incest is a reaction to, or a defense against, the forbidden unconscious impulse. Although Freud's theory may account for the aversion felt toward incest, or at least the aversion toward parent-child incest, it does not explain why society needs an explicit taboo, particularly on brother-sister incest. Nor does it account for the findings of sexual disinterest we discussed above in connection with the Westermarck hypothesis.

Family-Disruption Theory

The family disruption theory, often associated with Bronislaw Malinowski,[51] can best be summed up as follows: sexual competition among family members would create so much rivalry and tension that the family could not function as an effective unit. Because the family must function effectively for society to survive, society has to curtail competition within the family. The familial incest taboo is thus imposed to keep the family intact.

But there are inconsistencies in this approach. Society could have shaped other rules about the sexual access of one member of the family to another that would also eliminate potentially disruptive competition. Also, why would brother-sister incest be so disruptive? As we noted, such marriages did exist in ancient Egypt. Brother-sister incest would not disrupt the authority of the parents if the children were allowed to marry when mature. The family-disruption theory, then, does not explain the origin of the incest taboo.

Cooperation Theory

The cooperation theory was proposed by the early anthropologist Edward B. Tylor and was elaborated by Leslie A. White and Claude Lévi-Strauss. It emphasizes the value of the incest taboo in promoting cooperation among family groups and thus helping communities to survive. As Tylor saw it, certain operations necessary for the welfare of the community can be accomplished only by large numbers of people working together. In order to break down suspicion and hostility between family groups and make such cooperation possible, early humans developed the incest taboo to ensure that individuals would marry members of other families. The ties created

by intermarriage would serve to hold the community together. Thus, Tylor explained the incest taboo as an answer to the choice "between marrying out and being killed out."[52]

The idea that marriage with other groups promotes cooperation sounds plausible, but is there evidence to support it? After all, there are societies such as the Gusii in which marriage is often between hostile groups. But is that society an exception? Does marriage promote cooperation? Because people in all recent societies marry outside the family, we cannot test the idea that such marriages promote cooperation more than marriages within the family. We can, however, ask whether other kinds of out-marriage, such as marriage with other communities, promote cooperation with those communities. The evidence on that question does not support the co-operation theory. There is no greater peacefulness between communities when marriages are forbidden within the community, and always arranged with other communities, than when they are not.[53] But even if marriage outside the family promoted cooperation with other groups, why would it be necessary to prohibit all marriages within the family? Couldn't families have required some of their members to marry outside the family if they thought it necessary for survival but permitted incestuous marriages when such alliances were not needed? Although the incest taboo might enhance cooperation between families, the need for cooperation does not adequately explain the existence of the incest taboo in all societies; other customs might also promote alliances. Furthermore, the cooperation theory does not explain the sexual aspect of the incest taboo. Societies could conceivably allow incestuous sex and still insist that children marry outside the family.

Inbreeding Theory

One of the oldest explanations for the incest taboo, the inbreeding theory focuses on the potentially damaging consequences of inbreeding, or marrying within the family. People within the same family are likely to carry the same harmful recessive genes. Inbreeding, then, will tend to produce offspring who are more likely to die early of genetic disorders than are the offspring of unrelated spouses. For many years this theory was rejected because, on the basis of dog-breeding practices, it was thought that inbreeding need not be harmful. The inbreeding practiced to produce prize-winning dogs, however, is not a good guide to whether inbreeding is harmful; dog breeders don't count the runts they cull when they try to breed for success in dog shows. We now have a good deal of evidence, from humans as well as other animals, that the closer the degree of inbreeding, the more harmful the genetic effects.[54]

Genetic mutations occur frequently. Although many pose no harm to the individuals who carry a single recessive gene, matings between two persons who carry the same gene often produce offspring with a harmful or lethal condition. Close blood relatives are much more likely than unrelated individuals to carry the same harmful recessive gene. So if close relatives mate, their offspring have a higher probability than the offspring of nonrelatives of inheriting the harmful trait.

One study compared children produced by familial incest and children (of the same mothers) produced by nonincestuous unions. About 40 percent of the incestuously produced children had serious abnormalities compared with about 5 percent of the other children.[55] Matings between other kinds of relatives, not as closely related, also show harmful (but not as harmful) effects of inbreeding. These results are consistent with inbreeding theory: the likelihood that a child will inherit a double dose of a harmful recessive gene is lower the more distantly the child's parents are related. Also consistent with inbreeding theory is the fact that rates of abnormality are consistently higher in the offspring of uncle-niece marriages (which are allowed in some societies) than in the offspring of cousin marriages; for the offspring of uncle-niece marriages, the likelihood of inheriting a double dose of a harmful recessive is twice that for the offspring of first cousins.[56]

Although most scholars acknowledge the harmful effects of inbreeding, some question whether people in former days would have deliberately invented or borrowed the incest taboo because they knew that inbreeding was biologically harmful. William Durham's recent cross-cultural survey suggests that they did. Ethnographers do not always report the perceived consequences of incest, but in 50 percent of the reports Durham found, biological harm to the offspring was mentioned.[57] For example, Raymond Firth reported on the Tikopia, who live on an island in the South Pacific:

> The idea is firmly held that unions of close kin bear with them their own doom, their *mara*. . . . The idea [*mara*] essentially concerns barrenness. . . . The peculiar barrenness of an incestuous union consists not in the absence of children, but in their illness or death, or some other mishap. . . . The idea that the offspring of a marriage between near kin are weakly and likely to die

young is stoutly held by these natives and examples are adduced to prove it.[58]

So, if the harm of inbreeding was widely recognized, people may have deliberately invented or borrowed the incest taboo.[59] But whether or not people actually recognized the harmfulness of inbreeding, the demographic consequences of the incest taboo would account for its universality, since reproductive and hence competitive advantages probably accrued to groups practicing the taboo. Thus, although cultural solutions other than the incest taboo might provide the desired effects assumed by the family-disruption theory and the cooperation theory, the incest taboo is the only possible solution to the problem of inbreeding.

As we shall see toward the end of the next section, a society may or may not extend the incest taboo to first cousins. That variation is also predictable from inbreeding theory, which provides additional support for the theory that the incest taboo was invented or borrowed to avoid the harmful consequences of inbreeding.

WHOM SHOULD ONE MARRY?

Probably every child in our society knows the story of Cinderella—the poor, downtrodden, but lovely girl who accidentally meets, falls in love with, and eventually marries a prince. It is a charming tale, but as a guide to mate choice in our society it is quite misleading. The majority of marriages simply do not occur in so free and coincidental a way in any society. In addition to the incest taboo, societies often have rules restricting marriage with other persons, as well as preferences about which other persons are the most desirable mates.

Even in a modern, urbanized society such as ours, where mate choice is theoretically free, people tend to marry within their own class and geographical area. For example, studies in the United States consistently indicate that a person is likely to marry someone who lives close by.[60] Neighborhoods are frequently made up of people from similar class backgrounds, so it is unlikely that many of these alliances are Cinderella stories.

Arranged Marriages

In an appreciable number of societies, marriages are arranged: negotiations are handled by the immediate families or by go-betweens. Sometimes betrothals

THE HUSBAND-WIFE RELATIONSHIP:
VARIATION IN LOVE, INTIMACY, AND SEXUAL JEALOUSY

Americans believe that love should be a basis of marriage. Does this ideal characterize most societies? We know the answer to that question—the answer is no. In fact, in many places romantic love is believed to be a poor basis for marriage and is strongly discouraged. However, even though romantic love may not be the basis for marriage everywhere, it does occur almost everywhere. A recent cross-cultural survey suggests that about 88 percent of the world's societies show signs of romantic love—accounts of personal longing, love songs or love depicted in folklore, elopement because of affection, and passionate love described by informants quoted in ethnographies. So if love is nearly universal, why is it often discouraged as a basis for marriage?

Two conditions appear to predict such discouragement. One is that the husband and wife live in an extended family. In this situation, people seem more concerned with how the person marrying into the family gets along with others, and less concerned with whether the husband and wife love each other. A second condition predicting the discouragement of romantic love (as a basis for mar-

riage) is that one of the spouses does most of the primary subsistence work or earns most of the couple's income. In this situation too, marrying for love appears to be discouraged. In general, then, romantic love is discouraged as a basis for marriage if one of the spouses is highly dependent on the other or the other's kin.

Intimacy is different from romantic love. It refers to how close the married couple are to each other—eating together, sleeping in the same bed, spending their leisure time together, as well as having frequent sex. In some societies couples are together a lot; in others they spend very little time together. Foraging societies seem on average to have more intimacy between couples than more complex herding and agricultural societies, but the reason is not entirely clear. A high involvement in war also seems to detract from intimacy between couples.

When it comes to sexual jealousy, men are far more likely to be violent than women. Anthropologists with a biological orientation point out that fathers always have some uncertainty about who their children are, so males are much

more likely for that reason alone to try to guard against "rival" males. But how can we account for the considerable variation in jealousy from one society to another? It does seem that the more a society emphasizes the importance of getting married, the more it limits sex to the marriage relationship, the more it emphasizes property, and the more its males appear to exhibit sexual jealousy.

How are these various aspects of marriage related to each other? Does romantic love as a basis for marriage increase or decrease sexual jealousy? Does romantic love predict intimacy, or is romantic love more likely with less frequent contact between the spouses? We are still far from understanding how these different aspects are related. All we know is that an emphasis on love and intimacy does not preclude marital violence or marital dissolution.

Sources: Lewellyn Hendrix, "Varieties of Marital Relationships," in Carol R. Ember and Melvin Ember, eds., Cross-Cultural Research for Social Science (Englewood Cliffs, NJ: Prentice Hall, 1995). Prentice Hall/Simon & Schuster Custom Publishing. William R. Jankowiak and Edward F. Fischer, "A Cross-Cultural Perspective on Romantic Love," Ethnology, 31 (1992): 149–55.

are completed while the future partners are still children. This was formerly the custom in much of Hindu India, China, Japan, and eastern and southern Europe. Implicit in the arranged marriage is the conviction that the joining together of two kin groups to form new social and economic ties is too important to be left to free choice and romantic love.

An example of a marriage arranged for reasons of prestige comes from Clellan Ford's study of the Kwakiutl of British Columbia. Ford's informant described his marriage as follows:

> When I was old enough to get a wife—I was about 25—my brothers looked for a girl in the same position that I and my brothers had. Without my consent, they picked a wife for me—Lagius' daughter. The one I wanted was prettier than the one they chose for me, but she was in a lower position than me, so they wouldn't let me marry her.[61]

In many places arranged marriages are beginning to disappear, and couples are beginning to have more say about their marriage partners. As recently as 1960 marriages were still arranged on the Pacific island of Rotuma, and sometimes the bride and groom did not meet until the wedding day. Nowadays, weddings are much the same, but cou-ples are allowed to "go out" and have a say about whom they wish to marry.[62] In a small Moroccan town, arranged marriages are still the norm, although a young man may ask his mother to make a marriage offer to a particular girl's parents, who may ask her whether she wants to accept the marriage offer. But dating is still not acceptable, so getting acquainted is hard to arrange.[63]

Exogamy and Endogamy

Marriage partners often must be chosen from *outside* one's own kin group or community; this is known as a rule of **exogamy.** Exogamy can take many forms. It may mean marrying outside a particular group of kin or outside a particular village or group of villages. Often, then, spouses come from quite a distance. For example, in Rani Khera, a village in India, 266 married women had come from about 200 different villages averaging between 12 and 24 miles away; 220 local women had gone to 200 other villages to marry. As a result of these exogamous marriages, Rani Khera, a village of 150 households, was linked to 400 other nearby villages.[64] When there are rules of exogamy, violations are often believed to cause harm. On the is-

The female clown at a wedding ceremony on Rotuma tries to create an enjoyable atmosphere, which increases the likelihood that the two sides will get along.

lands of Yap in Micronesia, people who are related through women are referred to as "people of one belly." The elders say that if two people from the same kinship group married they would not have any female children and the group would die out.[65]

A rule of **endogamy** obliges a person to marry *within* some group. The caste groups of India have traditionally been endogamous. The higher castes believed that marriage with lower castes would "pollute" them, and such unions were forbidden. Caste endogamy is also found in some parts of Africa. In East Africa, a Masai warrior would never stoop to marry the daughter of an ironworker, nor would a former ruling-caste Tutsi in Rwanda (in central Africa) think of marrying a person from the hunting caste Twa.

Cousin Marriages

Kinship terminology for most people in the United States does not differentiate between types of cousins. In other societies such distinctions may be important, particularly with regard to first cousins; the terms for the different kinds of first cousin may indicate which cousins are suitable marriage partners (sometimes even preferred mates) and which are not. Although most societies prohibit marriage with all types of first cousins,[66] some societies allow and even prefer particular kinds of cousin marriage.

Cross-cousins are children of siblings of the opposite sex; that is, a person's cross-cousins are father's sisters' children and mother's brothers' children. **Parallel cousins** are children of siblings of the same sex; a person's parallel cousins, then, are father's brothers' children and mother's sisters' children. The Chippewa Indians used to practice cross-cousin marriage, as well as cross-cousin joking. With his female cross-cousins, a Chippewa man was expected to exchange broad, risqué jokes, but he would not do so with his parallel cousins, with whom severe propriety was the rule. In general, in any society in which cross-cousin marriage is allowed but parallel-cousin is not, there is a joking relationship between a man and his female cross-cousins. This attitude contrasts with the formal and very respectful relationship the man maintains with female parallel cousins. Apparently, the joking relationship signifies the possibility of marriage, whereas the respectful relationship signifies the extension of the incest taboo to parallel cousins.

When first-cousin marriage is allowed or preferred it is usually with some kind of cross-cousin. Parallel-cousin marriage is fairly rare, but Muslim societies usually prefer such marriages, allowing other cousin marriages as well. The Kurds, who are mostly Sunni Muslims, prefer a young man to marry his father's brother's daughter (for the young woman this would be her father's brother's son). The father and his brother usually live near each other, so the woman will stay close to home in such a marriage. The bride and groom are also in the same kin group, so marriage in this case also entails kin group endogamy.[67]

What kinds of societies allow or prefer first-cousin marriage? One cross-cultural study presented evidence that cousin marriages are most apt to be permitted in relatively large and densely populated societies. Perhaps this is because the likelihood of such marriages, and therefore the risks of inbreeding, are minimal in those societies. Many small, sparsely populated societies, however, permit or even sometimes prefer cousin marriage. How can these cases be explained? They seem to cast doubt on the interpretation that cousin marriage should be prohibited in sparsely populated societies, in which marriages between close relatives are more likely just by chance and the risks of inbreeding should be greatest. It turns out that most of the small societies that permit cousin marriage have lost a lot of people to epidemics. Many peoples around the world, particularly in the Pacific and in North and South America, suffered severe depopulation in the first generation or two after contact with Europeans, who introduced diseases (such as measles, pneumonia, and smallpox) to which the native populations had little or no resistance. Such societies may have had to permit cousin marriage in order to provide enough mating possibilities among the reduced population of eligible mates.[68]

Levirate and Sororate

In many societies, cultural rules oblige individuals to marry the spouse of deceased relatives. **Levirate** is a custom whereby a man is obliged to marry his brother's widow. **Sororate** obliges a woman to marry her deceased sister's husband. Both customs are exceedingly common, being the obligatory form of second marriage in a majority of societies known to anthropology.[69]

Among the Chukchee of Siberia, levirate obliges the next oldest brother to become the successor husband. He cares for the widow and children, assumes the sexual privileges of the husband, and unites the deceased's reindeer herd with his own, keeping it in the name of his brother's children. If there are no brothers, the widow is married to a cousin of her first husband. The Chukchee regard the custom more as a duty than as a right. The nearest relative is obliged to care for a woman left with children and a herd.[70]

HOW MANY DOES ONE MARRY?

We are accustomed to thinking of marriage as involving just one man and one woman at a time (**monogamy**), but most societies known to anthropology have allowed a man to be married to more than one woman at the same time (**polygyny**). At any given moment, however, the majority of men in societies permitting polygyny are married monogamously; few or no societies have enough women to permit most men to have at least two wives. Polygyny's mirror image—one woman being married to more than one man at the same time (**polyandry**)—is practiced in very few societies. Polygyny and polyandry are the two types of **polygamy**, or plural marriage. **Group marriage**, in which more than one man is married to more than one woman at the same time, sometimes occurs but is not customary in any known society. The four possible forms of marriage are illustrated in Table 10–1.

Polygyny

The Old Testament has many references to men with more than one wife simultaneously: King David and King Solomon are just two examples of men polygynously married. Just as in the society described in the Old Testament, polygyny in many societies is a mark of a man's great wealth or high status. In such societies only the very wealthy can, and are expected to, support more than one wife. Some Muslim societies, especially Arabic-speaking ones, still view polygyny in this light. But a man does not always have to be wealthy to be polygynous; indeed, in some societies in which women are important contributors to the economy, it seems that men try to have more than one wife in order to become wealthier.

Among the Siwai, a society in the South Pacific, status is achieved through feast giving. Pork is the main dish at these feasts, so the Siwai associate pig raising with prestige. This great interest in pigs sparks an interest in wives, because in Siwai society women raise the food needed to raise pigs. Thus, although having many wives does not in itself confer status among the Siwai, the increase in pig herds that may result from polygyny is a source of prestige for the owner.[71]

Polygynously married Siwai men do seem to have greater prestige, but they complain that a household with multiple wives is difficult. Sinu, a Siwai, described his plight:

> There is never peace for a long time in a polygynous family. If the husband sleeps in the house of one wife, the other one sulks all the next day. If the man is so stupid as to sleep two consecutive nights in the house of one wife, the other one will refuse to cook for him, saying, "So-and-so is your wife; go to her for food. Since I am not good enough for you to sleep with, then my food is not good enough for you to eat." Frequently the co-wives will quarrel and fight. My uncle formerly had five wives at one time and the youngest one was always raging and fighting the others. Once she knocked an older wife senseless and then ran away and had to be forcibly returned.[72]

Jealousy between co-wives is reported in many polygynous societies, but it seems not to be present in some. For example, Margaret Mead reported that married life among the Arapesh of New Guinea, even in the polygynous marriages, was "so even and contented that there is nothing to relate of it at all."[73]

Why might there be little or no jealousy between co-wives in a society? One possible reason is that a man is married to two or more sisters (**sororal polygyny**); it seems that sisters, having grown up together, are more likely to get along and cooperate as

▼▼▼▼▼▼▼
TABLE 10–1
Four Possible Forms of Marriage

FORM OF MARRIAGE	MALES	FEMALES
Monogamy	△	= ○
Polygamy		
Polygyny	△	= ○ + ○ + . . .
Polyandry	△ + △ + . . .	= ○
Group marriage	△ + △ + . . .	= ○ + ○ + . . .

△ represents male; ○, female; and =, marriage.

co-wives than are co-wives who are not also sisters (**nonsororal polygyny**). Other customs may also lessen jealousy between co-wives:

1. Co-wives who are not sisters tend to have separate living quarters; sororal co-wives almost always live together. Among the Plateau Tonga in Africa, who practice nonsororal polygyny, the husband shares his personal goods and his favors among his wives, who live in separate dwellings, according to principles of strict equality. The Crow Indians practiced sororal polygyny, and co-wives usually shared a tepee.

2. Co-wives have clearly defined equal rights in matters of sex, economics, and personal possessions. For example, the Tanala of Madagascar require the husband to spend a day with each co-wife in succession. Failure to do so constitutes adultery and entitles the slighted wife to sue for divorce and alimony of up to one-third of the husband's property. Furthermore, the land is shared equally among all the women, who expect the husband to help with its cultivation when he visits them.

3. Senior wives often have special prestige. The Tonga of Polynesia, for example, grant to the first wife the status of "chief wife." Her house is to the right of her husband's and is called "the house of the father." The other wives are called "small wives," and their houses are to the left of the husband's. The chief wife has the right to be consulted before the small wives, and her husband is expected to sleep under her roof before and after a journey. Although this rule might seem to enhance the jealousy of the secondary wives, later wives are usually favored somewhat because they tend to be younger and more attractive. By this custom, then, the first wife may be compensated for her loss of physical attractiveness by increased prestige.[74]

We must remember that, although jealousy is commonly mentioned in polygynous marriages, people who practice polygyny think it has considerable advantages. In a study conducted by Philip and Janet Kilbride in Kenya, female as well as male married people agreed that polygyny had economic and political advantages. Because they tend to be large, polygynous families provide plenty of farm labor and extra food that can be marketed. They also tend to be influential in their communities and are likely to produce individuals who become government officials.[75]

How can we account for the fact that polygyny is allowed and often preferred in most of the societies known to anthropology? Linton suggested that polygyny derives from the general primate urge to collect females.[76] But if that were so, then why wouldn't all societies allow polygyny? Other explanations of polygyny have been suggested. We restrict our discussion here to those that statistically and strongly predict polygyny in worldwide samples of societies.

One theory is that polygyny will be permitted in societies that have a long **postpartum sex taboo**.[77] In these societies, a couple must abstain from intercourse until their child is at least a year old. John Whiting suggested that couples abstain from sexual intercourse for a long time after their child is born for health reasons. A Hausa woman reported that

> a mother should not go to her husband while she has a child she is suckling. If she does, the child gets thin; he dries up, he won't be strong, he won't be healthy. If she goes after two years it is nothing, he is already strong before that, it does not matter if she conceives again after two years.[78]

The Mormons who settled in Utah practiced polygyny. Here we see two men and their wives walking to church.

The symptoms the woman described seem to be those of *kwashiorkor.* Common in tropical areas, kwashiorkor is a protein-deficiency disease that occurs particularly in children suffering from intestinal parasites or diarrhea. By observing a long postpartum sex taboo, and thereby ensuring that her children are widely spaced, a woman can nurse each child longer. If a child gets protein from mother's milk during its first few years, the likelihood of contracting kwashiorkor may be greatly reduced. Consistent with Whiting's interpretation is the fact that societies with low-protein staples (those whose principal foods are root and tree crops such as taro, sweet potatoes, bananas, and breadfruit) tend to have a long postpartum sex taboo. Societies with long postpartum sex taboos also tend to be polygynous. Perhaps, then, a man's having more than one wife is a cultural adjustment to the taboo. As a Yoruba woman said,

> When we abstain from having sexual intercourse with our husband for the two years we nurse our babies, we know he will seek some other woman. We would rather have her under our control as a co-wife so he is not spending money outside the family.[79]

Even if we agree that men will seek other sexual relationships during the period of a long postpartum sex taboo, it is not clear why polygyny is the only possible solution to the problem. After all, it is conceivable that all of a man's wives might be subject to the postpartum sex taboo at the same time. Furthermore, there may be sexual outlets outside marriage.

Another explanation of polygyny is that it is a response to an excess of women over men. Such an imbalanced sex ratio may occur because of the prevalence of warfare in a society. Because men and not women are generally the warriors, warfare almost always takes a greater toll of men's lives. Given that almost all adults in noncommercial societies are married, polygyny may be a way of providing spouses for surplus women. Indeed, there is evidence that societies with imbalanced sex ratios in favor of women tend to have both polygyny and high male mortality in warfare. Conversely, societies with balanced sex ratios tend to have both monogamy and low male mortality in warfare.[80]

A third explanation is that a society will allow polygyny when men marry at an older age than women. The argument is similar to the sex ratio interpretation. Delaying the age of marriage for men would produce an artificial, though not an actual, excess of marriageable women. Why marriage for men is delayed is not clear, but the delay does predict polygyny.[81]

Is one of these explanations better than the others, or are all three factors (long postpartum sex taboo, an imbalanced sex ratio in favor of women, and delayed age of marriage for men) important in explaining polygyny? One way of trying to decide among alternative explanations is to do what is called a statistical-control analysis, which allows us to see if a particular factor still predicts when the effects of other possible factors are removed. In this case, when the possible effect of sex ratio is removed, a long postpartum sex taboo no longer predicts polygyny and hence is probably not a cause of polygyny.[82] But both an actual excess of women and a late age of marriage for men seem to be strong predictors of polygyny. Added together, these two factors predict even more strongly.[83]

Polyandry

George Peter Murdock's *World Ethnographic Sample* included only four societies (less than 1 percent of the total) in which polyandry, or the marriage of several men to one woman, was practiced.[84] Polyandry can be **fraternal** (when the husbands are brothers) or **nonfraternal.**

Some Tibetans, the Toda of India, and the Sinhalese of Sri Lanka have practiced fraternal polyandry. Among the Tibetans who practice fraternal polyandry, biological paternity seems to be of no particular concern; there is no attempt to link children biologically to a particular brother, and all children are treated the same.[85]

One possible explanation for some of the societies with polyandry is a shortage of women. The Toda practiced female infanticide;[86] the Sinhalese had a shortage of women but denied the practice of female infanticide.[87] A correlation between shortage of women and polyandry would account for why polyandry is so rare in the ethnographic record; an excess of men is rare cross-culturally.

Another possible explanation is that polyandry is an adaptive response to severely limited resources. Melvyn Goldstein studied Tibetans who live in the northwestern corner of Nepal, above 12,000 feet in elevation. Cultivable land is extremely scarce there; most families have less than an acre. The people say they practice fraternal polyandry in order to prevent the division of a family's farm (and animals). Instead of dividing up their land among them and each taking a wife, brothers preserve the family farm by sharing a wife. Although not recognized by the Tibetans, their practice of polyandry minimizes population growth. There are as many women as men of marriageable age. But about 30 percent of the women do not marry, and, although these women do have some children, they have far fewer than married women. Thus, the practice of polyandry minimizes the number of mouths to feed and therefore maximizes the standard of living of the polyandrous family. In contrast, if the Tibetans practiced monogamy and almost all women married, the birthrate would be much higher and there would be more mouths to feed with the severely limited resources.[88]

THE FAMILY

Although family form varies from one society to another and even within societies, all societies have families. A **family** is a social and economic unit consisting minimally of one or more parents and their children. Members of a family always have certain reciprocal rights and obligations, particularly economic ones. Family members usually live in one household, but common residence is not a defining feature of families. In our society, children may live away while they go to college. Some members of a family may deliberately set up separate households in order to manage multiple business enterprises while maintaining economic unity.[89] In simpler societies, the family and the household tend to be indistinguishable; it is only in more complex societies, and in societies becoming dependent on commercial exchange, that some members of a family may live elsewhere.[90]

The family provides a learning environment for children. Although some animals, such as fish, do take care of themselves after birth or hatching, no mammal is able to care for itself at birth, and a human is exceptional in that he or she is unable to do so for many years afterward. Since, biologically, humans mature late, they have few if any inborn or instinctive responses that will simplify adjustment to their surroundings. Consequently, they have to learn a repertoire of beliefs and habits (most of which are cultural) in order to become functioning adults in society. A family cares for and protects children while they acquire the cultural behavior, beliefs, and values necessary for their own, and their society's, survival.

Variation in Family Form

Most societies have families that are larger than the single-parent family (the parent in such families is usually the mother, in which case the unit is called the **matrifocal family),** the monogamous (single-couple) family (called the **nuclear family**), or the polygamous (usually polygynous) family. The **extended family** is the prevailing form of family in more than half the societies known to anthropology.[91] It may consist of two or more single-parent, monogamous, polygynous, or polyandrous families linked by a blood tie. Most commonly, the extended family consists of a married couple and one or more of the married children, all living in the same house or household. The constituent nuclear families are normally linked through the parent-child tie. An extended family, however, is sometimes composed of families linked through a sibling tie. Such a family might consist of two married brothers, their wives, and their children. Extended families may be quite large, containing many relatives and including three or four generations.

Extended-Family Households

In a society composed of extended-family households, marriage does not bring as pronounced a change in life-style as it does in our culture, where the couple typically move to a new residence and form a new, and basically independent, family unit. In extended families, the newlyweds are assimilated into an existing family unit. Margaret Mead described such a situation in Samoa:

> In most marriages there is no sense of setting up a new and separate establishment. The change is felt in the change of residence for either husband or wife and in the reciprocal relations which spring up between the two families. But the young couple live in the main household, simply receiving a bamboo pillow, a mosquito net and a pile of mats for their bed. . . . The wife works with all the women of the household and waits on all the men. The husband shares the enterprises of the other men and boys. Neither in personal service given or received are the two marked off as a unit.[92]

A young couple in Samoa, as in other societies with extended families, generally has little decision-making power over the governing of the household.

ONE-PARENT FAMILIES: WHY THE RECENT INCREASE?

Not only is the custom of marriage almost universal, but in most societies known to anthropology most people marry. And they usually remarry if they divorce. This means that, except for the death of a spouse, or temporarily during times of divorce or separation, one-parent families are relatively uncommon in most societies.

In many Western countries, however, there has been a dramatic increase recently in the percentage of families that are one-parent families, most of which (about 90 percent) are female-headed families. So for example, in the 1960s about 9 percent of families in the United States were one-parent families, but in the mid-1980s the figure jumped to about 24 percent. Whereas Sweden once led the Western countries in percentage of one-parent families (about 13 percent in the 1970s), the United States now has the highest percentage. Before we try to examine the reasons for the increase, we need to consider that there are a

variety of ways to become a one-parent family. First, many one-parent families result from the divorce or separation of two-parent families. Second, many one-parent families result from births out of wedlock. In addition, some result from the death of a spouse and others from the decision by a single person to adopt a child.

Many researchers suggest that the ease of divorce is largely responsible for the increase in one-parent families. On the face of it, this explanation seems plausible. But it is flawed. In many countries during the late 1960s and early 1970s, changes in the law made getting a divorce much easier, and the percentage of one-parent families did rise after that. But why did so many countries ease divorce restrictions at the same time? Did attitudes about marriage change first? A high divorce rate by itself will make for a higher percentage of one-parent households only *if* individuals do not remarry quickly. In the United States, for example, remarriage rates did

decline sharply in the mid-1960s, particularly among younger, better educated women, and so the percentage of one-parent households may have risen for that reason. In many other countries, divorce rates stabilized in the 1980s, but the percentage of one-parent families still increased. Thus, easier divorce does not fully explain the increase in number of one-parent families.

Although some parents are clearly choosing to stay single, many might prefer to marry if they could find an appropriate spouse. In some countries, and among some ethnic groups within some countries, there are many fewer males than females, and sometimes a high proportion of the males have poor economic prospects. In the former Soviet Union, there are many more women than men; males were more likely to have died from war, alcoholism, and accidents. The United States does not have such a skewed sex ratio, but in some neighborhoods, particularly poor neighborhoods,

---

Often the responsibility of running the household rests with the senior male. Nor can the new family accumulate its own property and become independent; it is a part of the larger corporate structure:

> So the young people bide their time. Eventually, when the old man dies or retires, *they* will own the homestead, they will run things. When their son grows up and marries, he will create a new subsidiary family, to live with them, work for the

greater glory of *their* extended family homestead, and wait for them to die.[93]

The extended family is thus more likely than the independent nuclear family to perpetuate itself as a social unit. In contrast with the independent nuclear family, which by definition disintegrates with the death of the senior members (the parents), the extended family is always adding junior families (monogamous or polygamous or both), whose there are very high mortality rates for young males. And many males in such neighborhoods do not have work. One study by Daniel Lichter and his colleagues estimated that for every 100 African American women between the ages of 21 and 28, there were fewer than 80 available African American men. If we count only men who are employed (full- or part-time), the number of available men per 100 women drops below 50. So there may be considerable merit to the argument that one-parent families (usually headed by women) will be likely when a spouse (particularly an employed one) is hard to find.

Another popular explanation for the rise in number of one-parent families is that, in contrast to the past, women can manage without husbands because of support from the state. This scenario seems to fit Sweden, where unmarried and divorced mothers receive many social supports and allowances for maternity and educational leave. But Iceland has few social supports from the government and yet has the highest

rate of out-of-wedlock births of all the Scandinavian countries. In the United States, the welfare argument fails to predict changes over time. The program called Aid to Families with Dependent Children provides aid largely to single mothers. If the theory about government help were correct, increases in such aid would generally predict increases in the percentage of mother-headed households. But, in fact, during the 1970s the percentage of families receiving aid (and the value of aid) decreased, while the percentage of mother-headed households increased. And in the 1980s it was more difficult to go "on welfare," but the percentage of mother-headed households increased anyway. Women might be more able to manage alone if they have high-paying employment, and therefore we might expect more one-parent families by choice, as more women enter the job market. But, although this may explain the choices of some women, recent research finds that employed women generally are *more* rather than less likely to marry!

In any case, there seems to be a general association between commercial economies and the possibility of one-parent families. Is there something about subsistence economies that promotes marriage and something about commercial economies that detracts from it? Although marriage is not universally based on love or companionship, it entails a great deal of economic and other kinds of interdependence, particularly in not-so-commercial economies. Market economies allow other possibilities; goods and services can be bought and sold and governments may take over functions normally handled by kin and family. So the one-parent family is likely to remain an option—either a choice or a necessity—for some people.

Sources: *Alisa Burns and Cath Scott*, Mother-Headed Families and Why They Have Increased *(Hillsdale, NJ: Lawrence Erlbaum Associates, 1994); David Popenoe*, Disturbing the Nest: Family Change and Decline in Modern Societies *(New York: Aldine de Gruyter, 1988); Daniel T. Lichter, Diane K. McLaughlin, George Kephart, and David J. Landry, "Race and the Retreat from Marriage: A Shortage of Marriageable Men?"* American Sociological Review, *57 (1992): 781–99.*

members eventually become the senior members when their elders die.

Possible Reasons for Extended-Family Households

Why do most societies known to anthropology commonly have extended-family households? Extended-family households are found most frequently in societies with sedentary agricultural economies, so economic factors may play a role in determining household type. M. F. Nimkoff and Russell Middleton suggested how agricultural life, as opposed to hunting-gathering life, may favor extended families among agriculturalists. The extended family may be a social mechanism that prevents the economically ruinous division of family property in societies in which property such as cultivated land is important. Conversely, the need for mobility in hunter-gatherer societies may make

A Slovakian extended family

it difficult to maintain extended-family households. During certain seasons, the hunter-gatherers may be obliged to divide into nuclear families that scatter into other areas.[94]

But agriculture is only a weak predictor of extended-family households. Many agriculturalists lack them, and many nonagricultural societies have them. A different theory is that extended-family households come to prevail in societies that have incompatible activity requirements—that is, requirements that cannot be met by a mother or a father in a one-family household. In other words, the suggestion is that extended-family households are generally favored when the work a mother has to do outside the home (cultivating fields or gathering foods far away) makes it difficult for her to also care for her children and do other household tasks; similarly, extended families may be favored when the re-

quired outside activities of a father (warfare, trading trips, or wage labor far away) make it difficult for him to do the subsistence work required of males. There is cross-cultural evidence that societies with such incompatible activity requirements are more likely to have extended-family households than societies with compatible activity requirements, *regardless* of whether or not the society is agricultural. Even though they have incompatible activity requirements, however, societies with commercial or monetary exchange may not have extended-family households. In commercial societies, a family may be able to obtain the necessary help by "buying" the required services.[95]

Of course, even in societies with money economies, not everyone can buy required services. Those who are poor may need to live in extended families, and extended-family living may become more common even in the middle class when the economy is depressed. As a 1983 article in a popular magazine noted,

> Whatever happened to the all-American nuclear family—Mom, Pop, two kids and a cuddly dog, nestled under one cozy, mortgaged roof? What happened was an economic squeeze: layoffs, fewer jobs for young people, more working mothers, a shortage of affordable housing and a high cost of living. Those factors, along with a rising divorce rate, a trend toward later marriages and an increase in the over sixty-five population, all hitting at once, are forcing thousands of Americans into living in multigenerational families.[96]

In many societies there are kin groups even larger than extended families. The next chapter discusses the varieties of such groupings.

▼ SUMMARY

1. All societies known today have the custom of marriage. Marriage is a socially approved sexual and economic union between a man and a woman that is presumed to be more or less permanent and that subsumes reciprocal rights and obligations between the two spouses and between the spouses and their children.

2. The way marriage is socially recognized varies greatly: it may involve an elaborate ceremony or none at all. Variations include childhood be-

trothals, trial-marriage periods, feasting, and the birth of a baby.

3. Marriage arrangements often include an economic element. The most common form is the bride price, in which the groom or his family gives an agreed-upon amount of money or goods to the bride's family. Bride service exists when the groom works for the bride's family for a specified period. In some societies, a female from the groom's family is exchanged for the bride; in others, gifts are ex-

changed between the two families. A dowry is a payment of goods or money by the bride's family usually to the bride. Indirect dowry is provided by the groom's family to the bride (sometimes through the bride's father).

4. No society in recent times has allowed sex or marriage between brothers and sisters, mothers and sons, or fathers and daughters.

5. Every society tells people whom they cannot marry, whom they can marry, and sometimes even whom they should marry. In quite a few societies, marriages are arranged by the couple's kin groups. Implicit in arranged marriages is the conviction that the joining of two kin groups to form new social and economic ties is too important to be left to free choice and romantic love. Some societies have rules of exogamy, which require marriage outside one's own kin group or community; others have rules of endogamy, requiring marriage within one's group. Although most societies prohibit all first-cousin marriages, some permit or prefer marriage with cross-cousins (children of siblings of the opposite sex) and parallel cousins (children of siblings of the same sex). Many societies have customs providing for the remarriage of widowed persons. Levirate is a custom whereby a man marries his brother's widow. Sororate is the practice whereby a woman marries her deceased sister's husband.

6. We think of marriage as involving just one man and one woman at a time (monogamy), but most societies allow a man to be married to more than one woman at a time (polygyny). Polyandry—the marriage of one woman to several husbands—is rare.

7. The prevailing form of family in most societies is the extended family. It consists of two or more single-parent, monogamous (nuclear), polygynous, or polyandrous families linked by blood ties.

▼ GLOSSARY TERMS

berdaches	extended family	marriage	polyandry
bride price (or bride wealth)	family	matrifocal family	polygamy
bride service	fraternal polyandry	monogamy	polygyny
cross-cousins	group marriage	nonfraternal polyandry	postpartum sex taboo
dowry	incest taboo	nonsororal polygyny	sororal polygyny
endogamy	indirect dowry	nuclear family	sororate
exogamy	levirate	parallel cousins	

▼ CRITICAL QUESTIONS

1. Will it remain customary in this society to marry, and why do you think it will or will not?
2. Do you think extended-family households will become more frequent in this society, and why do you think so?
3. Why is polyandry so much less frequent than polygyny?

▼ SUGGESTED READING

EMBER, M., AND EMBER, C. R. *Marriage, Family, and Kinship: Comparative Studies of Social Organization.* New Haven, CT: HRAF Press, 1983. A collection of reprinted cross-cultural and cross-species studies testing possible explanations of some aspects of human social organization. Relevant to this chapter are the studies of male-female bonding, the incest taboo, polygyny, and the extended family.

FOX, R. *Kinship and Marriage: An Anthropological Perspective.* Cambridge: Cambridge University Press,

1983. An introduction to problems and theory in the study of kinship and marriage. Chapters 1 and 2 are of particular relevance to our discussion.

HENDRIX, L. "Varieties of Marital Relationships." In C. R. Ember and M. Ember, eds., *Cross-Cultural Research for Social Science* (Englewood Cliffs, NJ: Prentice Hall, 1995). Prentice Hall/Simon & Schuster Custom Publishing. A recent review of what is known cross-culturally about love, intimacy, jealousy, violence, and fear of sex within the marital relationship, as well as the circumstances under which divorce rates are high.

LEVINSON, D., AND MALONE, M. J., eds. *Toward Explaining Human Culture: A Critical Review of the Findings of Worldwide Cross-Cultural Research.* New Haven, CT: HRAF Press, 1980. Chapters 6, 7, and 8 review the cross-cultural research literature on marriage, the family, and the incest taboo.

MURDOCK, G. P. *Social Structure.* New York: Macmillan, 1949. A classic cross-cultural analysis of variation in social organization. Chapters 1, 2, 9, and 10—on the nuclear family, composite forms of the family, the regulation of sex, and incest taboos and their extensions—are particularly relevant.

PASTERNAK, B. *Introduction to Kinship and Social Organization.* Englewood Cliffs, NJ: Prentice Hall, 1976. Chapters 3, 5, 6, and 7 present a survey and critique of theories and evidence about variation in marriage and the family. Also see the section on family in Pasternak's "Family and Household: Who Lives Where, Why Does It Vary, and Why Is It Important?" In C. R. Ember and M. Ember, eds., *Cross-Cultural Research for Social Science* (Englewood Cliffs, NJ: Prentice Hall, 1995). Prentice Hall/Simon & Schuster Custom Publishing.

▼ NOTES

[1] William N. Stephens, *The Family in Cross-Cultural Perspective* (New York: Holt, Rinehart & Winston, 1963), p. 5.

[2] George Peter Murdock, *Social Structure* (New York: Macmillan, 1949), p. 8.

[3] Stephens, *The Family in Cross-Cultural Perspective*, pp. 170–71.

[4] E. Kathleen Gough, "The Nayars and the Definition of Marriage," *Journal of the Royal Anthropological Institute*, 89 (1959): 23–34; N. Prabha Unnithan, "Nayars: Tradition and Change in Marriage and Family," in Melvin Ember, Carol R. Ember, and David Levinson, eds., *Portraits of Culture: Ethnographic Originals* (Englewood Cliffs, NJ: Prentice Hall, 1994). Prentice Hall/Simon & Schuster Custom Publishing.

[5] Unnithan, *Nayars*.

[6] E. Adamson Hoebel, *The Cheyennes: Indians of the Great Plains* (New York: Holt, Rinehart & Winston, 1960), p. 77.

[7] E. E. Evans-Pritchard, "Sexual Inversion among the Azande," *American Anthropologist*, 72 (1970): 1428–34.

[8] Denise O'Brien, "Female Husbands in Southern Bantu Societies," in Alice Schlegel, ed., *Sexual Stratification: A Cross-Cultural View* (New York: Columbia University Press, 1977), pp. 109–26; see also Regina Smith Oboler, "Is the Female Husband a Man? Woman/Woman Marriage among the Nandi of Kenya," *Ethnology*, 19 (1980): 69–88.

[9] Regina Smith Oboler, "Nandi: From Cattle-Keepers to Cash-Crop Farmers," in Melvin Ember, Carol R. Ember, and David Levinson, eds., *Portraits of Culture: Ethnographic Originals* (Englewood Cliffs,

NJ: Prentice Hall, 1994). Prentice Hall/Simon & Schuster Custom Publishing.

[10] Murdock, *Social Structure*, pp. 7–8.

[11] Ibid., pp. 9–10.

[12] See, for example, Ralph Linton, *The Study of Man* (New York: Appleton-Century-Crofts, 1936), pp. 135–36.

[13] Melvin Ember and Carol R. Ember, "Male-Female Bonding: A Cross-Species Study of Mammals and Birds," *Behavior Science Research*, 14 (1979): 37–56.

[14] Nelson H. Graburn, *Eskimos without Igloos* (Boston: Little, Brown, 1969), pp. 188–200.

[15] Bronislaw Malinowski, *The Sexual Life of Savages in Northwestern Melanesia* (New York: Halcyon House, 1932), p. 77.

[16] Ibid., p. 88.

[17] John W. M. Whiting, *Becoming a Kwoma* (New Haven, CT: Yale University Press, 1941), p. 125.

[18] Elman R. Service, *Profiles in Ethnology*, 3rd ed. (New York: Harper & Row, 1978).

[19] Robert A. LeVine and Barbara B. LeVine, "Nyansongo: A Gusii Community in Kenya," in Beatrice B. Whiting, ed., *Six Cultures* (New York: John Wiley, 1963), p. 65.

[20] Ibid.

[21] For an extensive discussion of the symbolism of Rotuman weddings see Alan Howard and Jan Rensel, "Rotuma: Interpreting a Wedding," in Melvin Ember, Carol R. Ember, and David Levinson, eds., *Portraits of Culture: Ethnographic Originals* (Englewood Cliffs, NJ: Prentice Hall, 1995). Prentice Hall/Simon & Schuster Custom Publishing.

[22]Alice Schlegel and Rohn Eloul, "A New Coding of Marriage Transactions," *Behavior Science Research,* 21 (1987): 119.

[23]Alice Schlegel and Rohn Eloul, "Marriage Transactions: Labor, Property, and Status," *American Anthropologist,* 90 (1988): 295, table 1. We used the data to calculate the frequency of various types of economic transaction in a worldwide sample of 186 societies.

[24]Oboler, "Nandi."

[25]Charles O. Frake, "The Eastern Subanun of Mindanao," in George P. Murdock, ed., *Social Structure in Southeast Asia,* Viking Fund Publications in Anthropology, No. 29 (Chicago: Quadrangle, 1960), pp. 51–64.

[26]Margaret Mead, *Growing Up in New Guinea* (London: Routledge & Kegan Paul, 1931), pp. 206–8.

[27]Alice Schlegel and Rohn Eloul, "Marriage Transactions," pp. 298–99.

[28]Frederic L. Pryor, *The Origins of the Economy: A Comparative Study of Distribution in Primitive and Peasant Economies* (New York: Academic Press, 1977), pp. 363–64.

[29]Ibid.

[30]Robert F. Spencer, "Spouse-Exchange among the North Alaskan Eskimo," in Paul Bohannan and John Middleton, eds., *Marriage, Family and Residence* (Garden City, NY: Natural History Press, 1968), p. 136.

[31]Schlegel and Eloul, "Marriage Transactions," pp. 296–97.

[32]Ibid.

[33]Ibid.

[34]A. R. Radcliffe-Brown, *The Andaman Islanders: A Study in Social Anthropology* (London: Cambridge University Press, 1922), p. 73.

[35]Jack Goody, "Bridewealth and Dowry in Africa and Eurasia," in Jack Goody and S. H. Tambiah, eds., *Bridewealth and Dowry* (Cambridge: Cambridge University Press, 1973), pp. 17–21.

[36]Pryor, *The Origins of the Economy,* pp. 363–65; Schlegel and Eloul, "Marriage Transactions," pp. 296–99.

[37]Research is reported in Steven J. C. Gaulin and James S. Boster, "Dowry as Female Competition," *American Anthropologist,* 92 (1990): 994–1005. The first theory discussed herein is associated with Ester Boserup, *Woman's Role in Economic Development* (New York: St. Martin's Press, 1970). The second is put forward by Gaulin and Boster.

[38]Schlegel and Eloul, in "Marriage Transactions," following Jack Goody, "Bridewealth and Dowry in Africa and Eurasia," p. 20.

[39]Fredrik Barth, *Nomads of South Persia* (Boston: Little, Brown, 1961), pp. 18–19; as reported in (and coded as indirect dowry by) Schlegel and Eloul, "A New Coding of Marriage Transactions." p. 131.

[40]Russell Middleton, "Brother-Sister and Father-Daughter Marriage in Ancient Egypt," *American Sociological Review,* 27 (1962): 606.

[41]William H. Durham, *Coevolution: Genes, Culture, and Human Diversity* (Stanford, CA: Stanford University Press, 1991), pp. 293–94, citing research by K. Hopkins, "Brother-Sister Marriage in Roman Egypt," *Comparative Studies of Society and History* 22 (1980): 303–54.

[42]Edward Westermarck, *The History of Human Marriage* (London: Macmillan, 1894).

[43]Yonina Talmon, "Mate Selection in Collective Settlements," *American Sociological Review,* 29 (1964): 492.

[44]Ibid., p. 504.

[45]Arthur Wolf, "Adopt a Daughter-in-Law, Marry a Sister: A Chinese Solution to the Problem of the Incest Taboo," *American Anthropologist,* 70 (1968): 864.

[46]Arthur P. Wolf and Chieh-shan Huang, *Marriage and Adoption in China, 1845–1945* (Stanford, CA: Stanford University Press), 1980, pp. 159, 170, 185.

[47]Hilda Parker and Seymour Parker, "Father-Daughter Sexual Abuse: An Emerging Perspective," *American Journal of Orthopsychiatry,* 56 (1986): 531–49.

[48]Melvin Ember, "On the Origin and Extension of the Incest Taboo," *Behavior Science Research,* 10 (1975): 249–81; Durham, *Coevolution,* pp. 341–57.

[49]For a discussion of mechanisms that might lead to sexual aversion, see Seymour Parker, "The Precultural Basis of the Incest Taboo: Toward a Biosocial Theory," *American Anthropologist,* 78 (1976): 285–305; also see Seymour Parker, "Cultural Rules, Rituals, and Behavior Regulation," *American Anthropologist,* 86 (1984): 584–600.

[50]Sigmund Freud, *A General Introduction to Psychoanalysis* (Garden City, NY: Garden City Publishing, 1943 [originally published in German in 1917]).

[51]Bronislaw Malinowski, *Sex and Repression in Savage Society* (London: Kegan Paul, Trench, Trubner, 1927).

[52]Quoted in Leslie A. White, *The Science of Culture: A Study of Man and Civilization* (New York: Farrar, Straus, & Cudahy, 1949), p. 313.

[53]Gay Elizabeth Kang, "Exogamy and Peace Relations of Social Units: A Cross-Cultural Test," *Ethnology* 18 (1979): 85–99.

[54]Curt Stern, *Principles of Human Genetics,* 3rd ed. (San Francisco: W. H. Freeman, 1973), pp. 494–95, as cited in Ember, "On the Origin and Extension of the Incest Taboo," p. 256. For a recent review of the theory and evidence, see Durham, *Coevolution.*

[55]Eva Seemanova, "A Study of Children of Incestuous Matings," *Human Heredity,* 21 (1971): 108–28, as cited in Durham, *Coevolution,* pp. 305–9.

[56]Durham, *Coevolution,* pp. 305–9.

[57]Ibid., pp. 346–52.

[58]Raymond Firth, *We, the Tikopia* (Boston: Beacon Press, 1957), pp. 287–88, cited (somewhat differently) in Durham, *Coevolution,* pp. 349–50.

[59]A mathematical model of early mating systems suggests that people may have noticed the harmful effects of inbreeding once populations began to expand as a re-

sult of agriculture; people may therefore have deliberately adopted the incest taboo to solve the problem of inbreeding. See Ember, "On the Origin and Extension of the Incest Taboo." For a similar suggestion, see Durham, *Coevolution*, pp. 331–39.

[60]William J. Goode, *The Family*, 2nd ed. (Englewood Cliffs, NJ: Prentice Hall, 1982), pp. 61–62.

[61]Clellan S. Ford, *Smoke from Their Fires* (New Haven, CT: Yale University Press, 1941), p. 149.

[62]Howard and Rensel, "Rotuma."

[63]Susan Schaefer Davis, "Morocco: Adolescents in a Small Town." In Ember, Ember, and Levinson, eds., *Portraits of Culture*, 1994.

[64]W. J. Goode, *World Revolution and Family Patterns* (New York: Free Press, 1970), p. 210.

[65]Sherwood G. Lingenfelter, "Yap: Changing Roles of Men and Women." In Ember, Ember, and Levinson, eds., *Portraits of Culture*.

[66]Ember, "On the Origin and Extension of the Incest Taboo," p. 262, table 3.

[67]Annette Busby, "Kurds: A Culture Straddling National Borders," In Ember, Ember, and Levinson, eds., *Portraits of Culture*, 1994.

[68]Ember, "On the Origin and Extension of the Incest Taboo," pp. 260–69; see also Durham, *Coevolution*, pp. 341–57.

[69]Murdock, *Social Structure*, p. 29.

[70]Waldemar Bogoras, "The Chukchee," pt. 3, *Memoirs of the American Museum of Natural History*, 2 (1909); cited in Stephens, *The Family in Cross-Cultural Perspective*, p. 195.

[71]Douglas Oliver, *A Solomon Island Society* (Cambridge, MA: Harvard University Press, 1955), pp. 352–53.

[72]Ibid., pp. 223–24; quoted in Stephens, *The Family in Cross-Cultural Perspective*, p. 58.

[73]Margaret Mead, *Sex and Temperament in Three Primitive Societies* (New York: New American Library, 1950 [originally published 1935]), p. 101.

[74]The discussion of these customs is based on Stephens, *The Family in Cross-Cultural Perspective*, pp. 63–67.

[75]Philip L. Kilbride and Janet C. Kilbride, "Polygyny: A Modern Contradiction?" in Philip L. Kilbride and Janet C. Kilbride, *Changing Family Life in East Africa: Women and Children at Risk* (University Park, PA: Pennsylvania State University Press, 1990), pp. 202–06.

[76]Linton, *The Study of Man*, p. 183.

[77]John W. M. Whiting, "Effects of Climate on Certain Cultural Practices," in Ward H. Goodenough, ed., *Explorations in Cultural Anthropology: Essays in Honor of George Peter Murdock* (New York: McGraw-Hill, 1964), pp. 511–44.

[78]Ibid., p. 518.

[79]Ibid., pp. 516–17.

[80]Melvin Ember, "Warfare, Sex Ratio, and Polygyny," *Ethnology*, 13 (1974): 197–206. Bobbi Low, in "Marriage Systems and Pathogen Stress in Human Societies," *American Zoologist* 30 (1990): 325–39, has suggested that a high incidence of disease also may reduce the prevalence of "healthy" men. In such cases it may be to a woman's advantage to marry a "healthy" man even if he is already married, and it may be to a man's advantage to marry sev-

eral unrelated women to maximize genetic variation (and disease resistance) among his children.

[81]Melvin Ember, "Alternative Predictors of Polygyny," *Behavior Science Research*, 19 (1984–1985): 1–23. The statistical relationship between late age of marriage for men and polygyny was first reported by Stanley R. Witkowski, "Polygyny, Age of Marriage, and Female Status," paper presented at the annual meeting of the American Anthropological Association, San Francisco, 1975.

[82]Ember, "Warfare, Sex Ratio, and Polygyny," pp. 202–5.

[83]Ember, "Alternative Predictors of Polygyny." For other predictors of polygyny, see Douglas R. White and Michael L. Burton, "Causes of Polygyny: Ecology, Economy, Kinship, and Warfare," *American Anthropologist*, 90 (1988): 871–87; and Low, "Marriage Systems and Pathogen Stress in Human Societies."

[84]Allan D. Coult and Robert W. Habenstein, *Cross Tabulations of Murdock's World Ethnographic Sample* (Columbia, MO: University of Missouri Press, 1965); George Peter Murdock, "World Ethnographic Sample," *American Anthropologist* 59 (1957): 664–87.

[85]Melvyn C. Goldstein, "When Brothers Share a Wife," *Natural History*, March 1987, p. 39.

[86]Stephens, *The Family in Cross-Cultural Perspective*, p. 45.

[87]L. R. Hiatt, "Polyandry in Sri Lanka: A Test Case for Parental Investment Theory," *Man*, 15 (1980): 583–98.

[88]Goldstein, "When Brothers Share a Wife," pp. 39–48. Formerly, in feudal Tibet, a class of serfs who owned small parcels of land also practiced polyandry. Goldstein suggested that a shortage of land would explain their polyandry too. See Melvyn C. Goldstein, "Stratification, Polyandry, and Family Structure in Central Tibet," *Southwestern Journal of Anthropology*, 27 (1971): 65–74.

[89]For example, see Myron L. Cohen, *House United, House Divided: The Chinese Family in Taiwan* (New York: Columbia University Press, 1976).

[90]Burton Pasternak, *Introduction to Kinship and Social Organization* (Englewood Cliffs, NJ: Prentice Hall, 1976), p. 96.

[91]Allan D. Coult and Robert W. Habenstein, *Cross Tabulations of Murdock's World Ethnographic Sample* .

[92]Margaret Mead, *Coming of Age in Samoa* (New York: Morrow, 1928), quoted in Stephens, *The Family in Cross-Cultural Perspective*, pp. 134–35.

[93]Mead, *Coming of Age in Samoa*, quoted in Stephens, *The Family in Cross-Cultural Perspective*, p. 135.

[94]M. F. Nimkoff and Russell Middleton, "Types of Family and Types of Economy," *American Journal of Sociology*, 66 (1960): 215–25.

[95]Burton Pasternak, Carol R. Ember, and Melvin Ember, "On the Conditions Favoring Extended Family Households," *Journal of Anthropological Research*, 32 (1976): 109–23.

[96]Jean Libman Block, "Help! They've *All* Moved Back Home!" *Woman's Day*, April 26, 1983, pp. 72–76.

Marital Residence
and Kinship

In the United States and Canada, and in many other industrial societies, a young man and woman usually establish a place of residence apart from their parents or other relatives when they marry, if they have not already moved away before that. Our society is so oriented toward this pattern of marital residence—*neolocal (new-place) residence*—that it seems to be the obvious and natural one to follow. Some upper-income families begin earlier than others to train their children to live away from home by sending them to boarding schools at age thirteen or fourteen, or to sleep-away summer camps. Young adults of all income levels learn to live away from home most of the year, if they join the army or attend an out-of-town college. In any case, when a young person marries, he or she generally lives apart from family.

So familiar is neolocal residence to us that we tend to assume that all societies practice the same pattern. On the contrary, of the 565 societies in George Peter Murdock's *World Ethnographic Sample,* only about 5 percent followed this practice.[1] About 95 percent of the world's societies have some pattern of residence whereby a new couple settles within, or very close to, the household of the parents or some other close relative of either the groom or the bride. When married couples live near kin, it stands to reason that kinship relationships will figure prominently in the social life of the society. Marital residence largely predicts the types of kin groups found in a society, as well as how people refer to and classify their various relatives.

As we will see, kin groups that include several or many families and hundreds or even thousands of people are found in many societies and structure many areas of social life. Kin groups may have important economic, social, political, and religious functions.

PATTERNS OF MARITAL RESIDENCE

In societies in which newly married couples customarily live with or close to their kin, several residence patterns may be established. Children in all societies are required to marry outside the nuclear family (because of the incest taboo), and couples in almost all societies live together after they are married (with a few exceptions); therefore some children have to leave home when they marry. But which married children remain at home and which reside elsewhere? Societies vary in the way they deal with this question, but there are not many different patterns. Actually, only four occur with any sizable frequency (the percentages shown below do not sum to 100 because of rounding):

1. **Patrilocal residence:** The son stays and the daughter leaves so that the married couple lives with or near the husband's parents (67 percent of all societies).
2. **Matrilocal residence:** The daughter stays and the son leaves so that the married couple lives with or near the wife's parents (15 percent of all societies).
3. **Bilocal residence:** Either the son or the daughter leaves so that the married couple lives with or near either the wife's or the husband's parents (7 percent of all societies).
4. **Avunculocal residence:** Both son and daughter normally leave, but the son and his wife settle with or near his mother's brother (4 percent of all societies).[2]

In these definitions, we use the phrase "the married couple lives *with or near*" a particular set of in-laws. When couples live with or near the kin of a spouse, the couple may live in the same household with those kin, creating an *extended-family* household, or they may live separately in an *independent-family* household, but nearby.

A fifth pattern of residence, of course, is neolocal, in which the newly married couple does not live with or near kin.

5. **Neolocal residence:** Both son and daughter leave; married couples live apart from the relatives of both spouses (5 percent of all societies).

Figure 11–1 graphically shows the percentage of societies in the ethnographic record that practice each of the five marital residence patterns.

How does place of residence affect the social life of the couple? Because the pattern of residence governs with whom or near whom individuals live, it largely determines which people those individuals interact with and have to depend on. If a married couple is surrounded by the kin of the husband, for example, the chances are that those relatives will figure importantly in the couple's future. Whether the couple lives with or near the husband's or the wife's kin can also be expected to have important consequences for the status of the husband or wife. If married couples live patrilocally, as occurs in most societies, the wife may be far from her own kin. In any case, she will be an outsider among

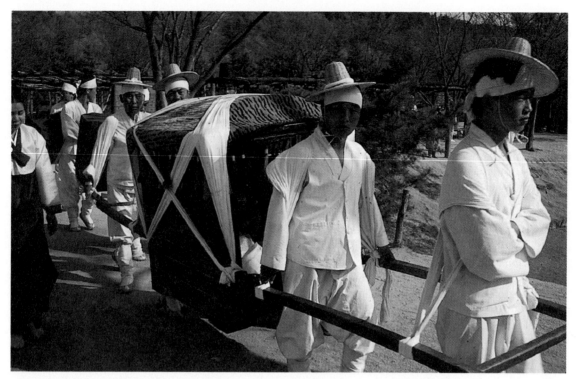

In most societies known to anthropology, the bride leaves her home to live with or near her husband's parents when she marries. A Korean bride was traditionally carried in a litter to the home of the groom.

FIGURE 11–1
Percentage of Societies in the Ethnographic Record with Various Marital Residence Patterns

Source: *Calculated from Allan D. Coult and Robert W. Habenstein, Cross Tabulations of Murdock's World Ethnographic Sample (Columbia: University of Missouri Press, 1965).*

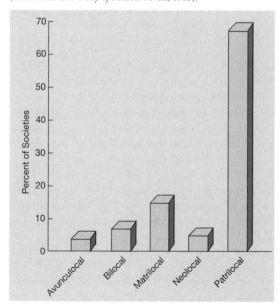

a group of male relatives who have grown up together. The feeling of being an outsider is particularly strong when the wife has moved into a patrilocal extended-family household.

Among the Tiv of central Nigeria,[3] the patrilocal extended family consists of the "great father," who is the head of the household, and his younger brothers, his sons, and his younger brothers' sons. Also included are the in-marrying wives and all unmarried children. (The sisters and daughters of the household head who have married would have gone to live where their husbands lived.) Authority is strongly vested in the male line, particularly the eldest of the household, who has authority over bride price, disputes, punishment, and plans for new buildings.

A somewhat different situation exists if the husband comes to live with or near his wife's parents. In this case, the wife and her kin take on somewhat greater importance, and the husband is the outsider. As we shall see, however, the matrilocal situation is not quite the mirror image of the patrilocal, because in matrilocal societies the husband's kin often are not far away. Moreover, even though residence is matrilocal, women often do not have as much to say in decision making as their brothers do.

If the married couple does not live with or near the parents or close kin of either spouse, the situation is again quite different. It should not be surprising that relatives and kinship connections do not figure very largely in everyday life in neolocal residence situations.

EXPLANATIONS OF VARIATION IN RESIDENCE

Questions can be raised as to why different societies have different patterns of residence. If in most societies married couples live with or near kin (as in patrilocal, matrilocal, bilocal, and avunculocal residence), then why in some societies, such as our own, do couples typically live apart from kin? And, among the societies in which couples live with or near kin, why do most choose the husband's side (patrilocal residence) but some the wife's side (matrilocal residence)? Why do some nonneolocal societies allow a married couple to go to either the wife's or the husband's kin (bilocal residence), whereas most others do not allow a choice? (Because matrilocal, patrilocal, and avunculocal residence specify just one pattern, they are often called nonoptional or **unilocal residence** patterns.)

Neolocal Residence

Many anthropologists have suggested that neolocal residence is somehow related to the presence of a money or commercial economy. They argue that when people can sell their labor or their products for money, they can buy what they need to live, without having to depend on kin. Because money is not perishable (unlike crops and other foods in a world largely lacking refrigeration), it can be stored for exchange at a later time. Thus, a money-earning family can resort to its own savings during periods of unemployment or disability (or it might be able to rely on monetary aid from the government, as in our own society). This strategy is impossible in non-money economies, where people must depend on relatives for food and other necessities if for some reason they cannot provide their own.

There is some cross-cultural evidence to support this interpretation. Neolocal residence tends to occur in societies with monetary or commercial exchange, whereas societies without money tend to have patterns of residence that locate a couple near or with kin.[4] The presence of money, then, appears to be related to neolocal residence: money seems to

allow couples to live on their own. Still, this fact does not quite explain why they choose to do so.

One reason may be that in commercial societies couples do better on their own because the jobs available require physical or social mobility. Or perhaps couples prefer to live apart from kin because they want to avoid some of the interpersonal tensions and demands that may be generated by living with or near kin. But why couples, when given money, should *prefer* to live on their own is not yet completely understood.

Matrilocal versus Patrilocal Residence

Traditionally, it has been assumed that in societies in which married children live near or with kin, residence will tend to be patrilocal if males contribute more to the economy and matrilocal if women contribute more. However plausible that assumption may seem, the cross-cultural evidence does not support it. Where men do most of the primary subsistence work, residence is patrilocal no more often than would be expected by chance. Conversely, where women do an equal amount or more of the subsistence work, residence is no more likely to be matrilocal than patrilocal.[5] And if we counted all work in and outside the home, most societies should be matrilocal because women usually do more. But that is not true either—most societies are not matrilocal.

We can predict whether residence will be matrilocal or patrilocal, however, from the type of warfare practiced in a society. In most societies known to anthropology, neighboring communities or districts are enemies. The type of warfare that breaks out periodically between such groups is called internal, because the fighting occurs between groups that speak the same language. In other societies, the warfare is never within the same society but only with other language groups. This pattern of warfare is referred to as purely external. Cross-cultural evidence suggests that in societies where warfare is at least sometimes internal, residence is almost always patrilocal rather than matrilocal. In con-trast, residence is usually matrilocal when warfare is purely external.[6]

How can we explain this relationship between type of warfare and matrilocal versus patrilocal residence? One theory is that patrilocal residence tends to occur with internal warfare because there may be concern over keeping sons close to home to help with defense. Because women do not usually constitute the fighting force in any society, having sons reside at home after marriage might be favored as a means of maintaining a loyal and quickly mobilized

NEOLOCALITY AND ADOLESCENT REBELLION: ARE THEY RELATED?

In our society it is taken for granted that adolescence means turmoil and parent-child conflict. Teenagers, parents, and educators worry about how to reduce the conflict. But few in our society ask why the conflict occurs in the first place. Is it "natural" for adolescents to be rebellious? Are they rebellious in all cultures? If not, why do we have conflict in this society?

This issue was first raised by Margaret Mead. In her best-selling *Coming of Age in Samoa* (originally published in 1928), she said that conflict during adolescence was minimal in Samoa. Some researchers have recently criticized her analysis (see our discussion in the chapter on psychology and culture), but many field and comparative studies by anthropologists have since found that adolescence is *not* experienced in the same way in all societies. For example, in their systematic cross-cultural study of adolescence, Alice Schlegel and Herbert Barry concluded that relations between adolescents and their families were generally harmonious around

the world. They suggested that when family members need each other throughout their lives, independence (as expressed in adolescent rebelliousness) would be quite foolhardy. Indeed, Schlegel and Barry found that adolescents are likely to be rebellious only in societies (like our own) that have *neolocal* residence and considerable job and geographical mobility.

Why should this be? We might speculate that adolescent rebellion is an elaborate psychodrama played out by both parents and children to prepare themselves for moving apart. Children spend a considerable part of their lives being *dependent* on their parents. But they know they must move away, and that prospect may arouse anxiety. Children want to be independent, but independence is scary. Dependence is nice in some ways—at least it can make life easier (someone else cooks for you and so on)—but it is also less grown-up than independence. So what pushes a child to leave? Perhaps the conflict itself propels the departure. Teenagers

ask for things they want, but they may know (at least unconsciously) that their parents will say no. And parents often do say no, so the teenager gets angry and can't wait to be on her own. Parents are also ambivalent. They want their children to grow up, but they miss them when they leave. After a period of conflict, it may be a relief for all concerned when parents and children go their separate ways.

What if our social structure were different? What if parents and children knew that some of the children were going to spend the rest of their lives *with or near* the parents? And even those children who moved away (as some would have to in societies practicing matrilocal, patrilocal, avunculocal, or bilocal residence) would know they were going to spend the rest of their lives *with or near* their in-laws. Could teenagers in non-neolocal societies afford to have serious conflict with their parents? Could the parents afford to have serious conflict with the teenagers who will be staying put after their marriages? We think

fighting force in case of surprise attack from nearby. If warfare is purely external, however, people may not be so concerned about keeping their sons at home because families need not fear attack from neighboring communities or districts.

With purely external warfare, then, residence

may be determined by other considerations, especially economic ones. If in societies with purely external warfare the women do most of the primary subsistence work, families might want their daughters to remain at home after marriage, so the pattern of residence might become matrilocal.

not. We suggest that adolescent conflict would be very disadvantageous in a nonneolocal society, and therefore we would expect its minimization or suppression when the residence pattern is other than neolocal.

There is another reason why rebelliousness might be associated with neolocality; it has to do with the fact that neolocality is predicted by commercial exchange. In the modern world, commercial societies are likely to have a great deal of occupational specialization and people with many different values. Thus children are presented with a great many choices in a rapidly changing culture. Let us consider the effect of a rapidly changing technology. If children have to know and do things that the parents do not know about, how can we expect the children to want to follow in their parents' footsteps?

But a rapidly changing culture is not necessarily accompanied by parent-child conflict. Other conditions are probably also necessary to generate the conflict, if the situation in a Moroccan town is any guide. As part of a comparative research project on adolescence, Susan and Douglas Davis interviewed young people in a small town in Morocco. The culture had changed a lot recently. Parents mostly worked at jobs in and related to agriculture; children aspired to white-collar jobs. Grandparents rarely saw a car; teenagers took trains to the capital. Only a few parents went to school; most teenagers did. Yet the Davises reported little serious parent-child conflict, despite the cultural changes. For example, 40 percent of the teenagers said that they had never disagreed with their mothers. Perhaps then we need to consider other facets of the culture. For one thing, Morocco has an authoritarian political structure with a monarchy and a clear pyramid of offices; perhaps parent-child conflict is unlikely in such a political system because it emphasizes and requires obedience. A second possible consideration is that group life is more important than the individual—the family is the most important social group and as such cannot tolerate adolescent rebelliousness. A third possible consideration is that adults are supposed to avoid open conflict. The study by the Davises implies then that adolescent rebelliousness is likely only in societies like the United States that emphasize individuality, personal autonomy, and individual achievement.

What we need is research that tries to untangle the various causal possibilities. To discover the possible effect of neolocality, or rapid change, or a cultural emphasis on individual autonomy, or an authoritarian political system, we need to study samples of cultures that have different combinations of those traits. It is possible that they all are influential, or that some are more important than others, or that some *cause* the others. Whatever we discover about the causality in the future, we know now that adolescent rebelliousness is not inevitable or natural—that it is probably linked to some other aspects of cultural variation—as Margaret Mead suggested many years ago.

Sources: *Margaret Mead,* Coming of Age in Samoa *(New York: Morrow, 1928); Alice Schlegel and Herbert Barry III,* Adolescence: An Anthropological Inquiry *(New York: Free Press, 1991); Susan Schaefer Davis, "Rebellious Teens? A Moroccan Instance," paper presented at annual meeting of the Middle East Studies Association, November 1993; Susan Schaefer Davis, "Morocco: Adolescents in a Small Town," in Melvin Ember, Carol R. Ember, and David Levinson, eds.,* Portraits of Culture: Ethnographic Originals *(Englewood Cliffs, NJ: Prentice Hall, 1994). Prentice Hall/Simon & Schuster Custom Publishing.*

(If warfare is purely external but men still do more of the primary subsistence work, residence should still be patrilocal.) Thus, the need to keep sons at home after marriage when there is internal warfare may take precedence over any considerations based on division of labor. It is perhaps only when internal warfare is nonexistent that a female-dominant division of labor may give rise to matrilocal residence.[7]

The frequent absence of men because of long-distance trade or wage labor in distant places may also provide an impetus for matrilocal residence even after warfare ceases. For example, among the Miskito of eastern Central America, matrilocality allowed domestic and village life to continue without interruption when men were away from home for long periods of time, working as lumberers, miners, and river transporters. These jobs were not always available, but when they were the men went away to work at them in order to earn money. Even though some men would always be away from home, the Miskito continued to get food in their traditional ways, from farming (done mostly by the women) and from hunting and fishing (which was mostly men's work).[8]

Bilocal Residence

In societies that practice bilocal residence, a married couple goes to live with or near either the husband's or the wife's parents. Although this pattern seems to involve a choice for the married couple, theory and research suggest that bilocal residence may occur out of necessity instead. Elman Service suggested that bilocal residence is likely to occur in societies that have recently suffered a severe and drastic loss of population because of the introduction of new infectious diseases.[9] Over the last 400 years, contact with Europeans in many parts of the world has resulted in severe population losses among non-European societies that lacked resistance to the Europeans' diseases. If couples need to live with some set of kin in order to make a living in noncommercial societies, it seems likely that couples in depopulated, noncommercial societies might have to live with whichever spouse's parents (and other relatives) are still alive. This interpretation seems to be supported by the cross-cultural evidence. Recently depopulated societies tend to have bilocal residence or frequent departures from unilocality, whereas societies that are not recently depopulated tend to have one pattern or another of unilocal residence.[10]

In hunter-gatherer societies, a few other circumstances may also favor bilocal residence. Bilocality tends to be found among those hunter-gatherers who have very small bands or unpredictable and low rainfall. Residential "choice" in these cases may be a question of adjusting marital residence to where the couple will have the best chance to survive or to find close relatives with whom to live and work.[11]

Figure 11–2 illustrates the main predictors of the various marital residence patterns.

FIGURE 11–2
The Main Predictors of Marital Residence Patterns

An arrow indicates the suggested causal direction.   Source: *Adapted from Melvin Ember and Carol R. Ember,* Marriage, Family, and Kinship: Comparative Studies of Social Organization *(New Haven, CT: HRAF Press, 1983).*

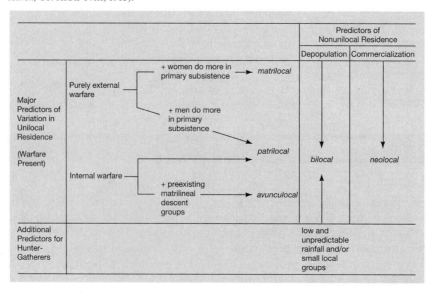

THE STRUCTURE OF KINSHIP

In noncommercial societies, kinship connections structure many areas of social life—from the kind of access an individual has to productive resources to the kind of political alliances formed between communities and larger territorial groups. In some societies, in fact, kinship connections have an important bearing on matters of life and death.

Recall the social system described in Shakespeare's *Romeo and Juliet*. The Capulets and the Montagues were groups of kin engaged in lethal competition with each other, and the fatal outcome of Romeo and Juliet's romance was related to that competition. Although Romeo and Juliet's society had a commercial economy (but not, of course, an industrialized one), the political system of the city they lived in was a reflection of the way kinship was structured. Sets of kin of common descent lived together, and the various kin groups competed (and sometimes fought) for a prominent, or at least secure, place in the political hierarchy of the city-state.

If a preindustrial commercial society could be so structured by kinship, we can imagine how much more important kinship connections and kin groups are in many noncommercial societies that lack political mechanisms such as princes and councils of lords who try to keep the peace and initiate other activities on behalf of the community. It is no wonder that anthropologists often speak of the web of kinship as providing the main structure of social action in noncommercial societies.

If kinship is important, there is still the question of which set of kin a person affiliates with and depends on. After all, if every single relative were counted as equally important, there would be an unmanageably large number of people in each person's kinship network. Consequently, in most societies in which kinship connections are important, rules allocate each person to a particular and definable set of kin.

Rules of Descent

Rules that connect individuals with particular sets of kin because of known or presumed common ancestry are called **rules of descent.** By the particular rule of descent operating in their society, individuals can know more or less immediately which set of kin to turn to for support and help.

Kin group rivalry between the Capulets and the Montagues made it unacceptable for Romeo and Juliet to court or wed.

There are only three known rules of descent that affiliate individuals with different sets of kin:

1. **Patrilineal descent** (the most frequent rule) affiliates an individual with kin of both sexes related to him or her *through men only*. As Figure 11–3 indicates, in patrilineal systems the children in each generation belong to the kin group of their father; their father, in turn, belongs to the group of his father; and so on. Although a man's sons and daughters are all members of the same descent group, affiliation with that group is transmitted only by the sons to their children.

2. **Matrilineal descent** affiliates an individual with kin of both sexes related to him or her *through women only*. In each generation, then, children belong to the kin group of their mother (see Figure 11–4). Although a woman's sons and daughters are all members of the same descent group, only her daughters can pass on their descent affiliation to their children.

3. **Ambilineal descent** affiliates an individual with kin related to him or her through men *or* women. In other words, some people in the society affiliate with a group of kin through their fathers; others, through their mothers. Consequently, the descent groups show both female and male genealogical links, as illustrated in Figure 11–5.

These three rules are usually, but not always, mutually exclusive. Most societies can be character-

FIGURE 11–3
Patrilineal Descent

Individuals 4 and 5, who are the children of 1 and 2, affiliate with their father's patrilineal kin group, represented by the color. In the next generation, the children of 3 and 4 also belong to the color kin group, since they take their descent from their father, who is a member of that group. However, the children of 5 and 6 do not belong to this patrilineal group, since they take their descent from their father, who is a member of a different group. That is, although the mother of 12 and 14 belongs to the color patrilineal group, she cannot pass on her descent affiliation to her children, and, since her husband (6) does not belong to her patrilineage, her children (12 and 14) belong to their father's group. In the fourth generation, only 15 and 16 belong to the color patrilineal group, since their father is the only male member of the preceding generation who belongs to the color patrilineal group. In this diagram, then, 1, 4, 5, 8, 10, 15, and 16 are affiliated by patrilineal descent; all the other individuals belong to other patrilineal groups.

FIGURE 11–4
Matrilineal Descent

Individuals 4 and 5, who are the children of 1 and 2, affiliate with their mother's kin group, represented by the color. In the next generation, the children of 5 and 6 also belong to the color kin group since they take their descent from their mother, who is a member of that group. However, the children of 3 and 4 do not belong to this matrilineal group since they take their descent from their mother, who is a member of a different group; their father, although a member of the color matrilineal group, cannot pass his affiliation on to them under the rule of matrilineal descent. In the fourth generation, only 21 and 22 belong to the color matrilineal group, since their mother is the only female member of the preceding generation who belongs. Thus, individuals 2, 4, 5, 12, 14, 21, and 22 belong to the same matrilineal group.

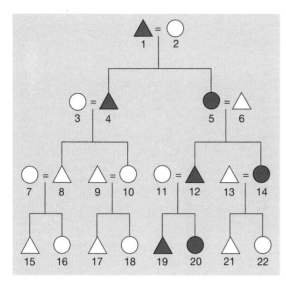

FIGURE 11–5
Ambilineal Descent

A hypothetical ambilineal group of kin is indicated by the color. Members 4 and 5 belong to this group because of a male link, their father (1); members 12 and 14 belong because of a female link, their mother (5); and members 19 and 20 belong because of a male link, their father (12). This is a hypothetical example because any combination of lineal links is possible in an ambilineal descent group.

ized as having only one rule of descent, but sometimes two principles are used to affiliate individuals with different sets of kin for different purposes. Some societies have then what is called **double descent,** or **double unilineal descent,** whereby an individual affiliates for some purposes with a group of matrilineal kin and for other purposes with a group of patrilineal kin. Thus, two rules of descent, each traced through links of one sex only, are operative at the same time. For example, if there is a patrilineal system and a matrilineal one, individuals would belong to *two* groups at birth: the matrilineal group of the mother *and* the patrilineal group of the father. Imagine combining Figures 11–3 and 11–4. Individuals 4 and 5 would belong to both the patrilineal group (purple on Figure 11–3) to which their father belongs and the matrilineal group (green on Figure 11–4) to which their mother belongs.

The way a society assigns names does not necessarily convey any information about a rule of descent. It is customary in North American society for children to have a last (or "family") name; it is usually their father's last name. All the people with the same last name do not conceive of themselves as descended from the same common ancestor; all Smiths do not consider themselves related. Nor do such

people act together for any particular purpose. And many societies, even with rules of descent, do not give individuals the name of their kin group, or of their father or mother. For example, among the patrilineal Luo of Kenya, babies were traditionally given names that described the circumstances of their birth ("born-in-the-morning"); their names did not include their father's or kin group's name. (Only after the British established a colony in Kenya, and continuing after independence, did children get their father's personal name as a family name.)

BILATERAL KINSHIP

Many societies, including our own, do not have lineal (matrilineal, patrilineal, or ambilineal) descent groups—sets of kin who believe they descend from a common ancestor. These are societies with **bilateral kinship.** *Bilateral* means "two-sided," and in this case it refers to the fact that one's relatives on both mother's and father's sides are equal in importance or (more usually) in unimportance. Kinship reckoning in bilateral societies does not refer to common descent, but rather is horizontal (see Figure 11–6), moving outward from close to more distant relatives, rather than upward to common ancestors.

The term **kindred** describes a person's bilateral set of relatives who may be called upon for some purpose. In our society, we think of the kindred as including the people we might invite to weddings, funerals, or some other ceremonial occasion; the kindred, however, is not usually a definite group. As anyone who has been involved in the planning of a wedding-invitation list knows, a great deal of time may be spent deciding which relatives ought to be invited and which ones can legitimately be excluded. Societies with bilateral kinship differ in precisely how distant relatives have to be before they are lost track of or before they are not included in ceremonial activities. In societies such as our own, in which kinship is relatively unimportant, fewer relatives are included in the kindred. In other bilateral societies, however, where kinship connections are somewhat more important, more would be included.

The distinctive feature of bilateral kinship is that, aside from brothers and sisters, no two persons belong to exactly the same kin group. Your kindred contains close relatives spreading out on both your mother's and father's sides, but the members of your kindred are affiliated only by way of their connection to you (**ego,** or the focus). Thus, the kindred is an *ego-centered* group of kin. Because different people (except for brothers and sisters) have differ-

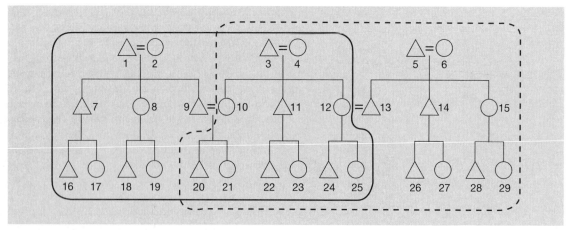

FIGURE 11–6
Bilateral Kinship

In a bilateral system the kindred is ego-centered; hence, it varies with different points of reference (except for brothers and sisters). In any bilateral society, the kindred minimally includes parents, grandparents, aunts, uncles, and first cousins. So, if we look at the close kindred of the brother and sister 20 and 21 (enclosed by the solid line), it would include their parents (9 and 10), their aunts and uncles (7, 8, 11, 12), their grandparents (1, 2, 3, 4) and their first cousins (16–19, 22–25). But the kindred of the brother and sister 24 and 25 (shown by the dashed line) includes only some of the same people (3, 4, 10–12, 20–23); in addition, the kindred of 24 and 25 includes people not in the kindred of 20 and 21 (5, 6, 13–15, 26–29).

ent mothers and fathers, your first cousins will have different kindreds, and even your own children will have a different kindred from yours. It is the ego-centered nature of the kindred that makes it difficult for it to serve as a permanent or persistent group. The only thing the people in a kindred have in common is the ego who brings them together. The kindred usually has no name, no common purpose, and only temporary meetings centered around the ego.[12] Furthermore, because everyone belongs to many different and overlapping kindreds, the society is not divided into clear-cut groups.

UNILINEAL DESCENT

Both matrilineal and patrilineal rules of descent are **unilineal descent** rules, in that a person is affiliated with a group of kin through descent links of one sex only—either males only or females only. Unilineal rules of descent affiliate an individual with a line of kin extending back in time and into the future. By virtue of this line of descent (whether it extends through males or females), some very close relatives are excluded. For example, in a patrilineal system, your mother and your mother's parents do not belong to your patrilineal group, but your father and

his father (and their sisters) do. In your own generation in a matrilineal or patrilineal system, some cousins are excluded, and in your children's generation, some of your nieces and nephews are excluded.

However, although unilineal rules of descent exclude certain relatives from membership in one's kin group (just as practical considerations restrict the effective size of kinship networks in our own society), the excluded relatives are not necessarily ignored or forgotten. Indeed, in many unilineal societies they may be entrusted with important responsibilities. For example, when a person dies in a patrilineal society, some members of his or her mother's patrilineal descent group may customarily be accorded the right to perform certain rituals at the funeral.

Unlike bilateral kinship, unilineal rules of descent can form clear-cut, and hence unambiguous, groups of kin, which can act as separate units even after the death of individual members. Referring again to Figures 11–3 and 11–4, we can see that the individuals in the highlight color belong to the same patrilineal or matrilineal descent group without ambiguity—an individual in the fourth generation belongs to the group just as much as one in the first generation. If we imagine that the patrilineal group, for instance, has a name, say the Hawks, then an individual knows immediately whether or not she or he is a Hawk. If the individual is not a Hawk, then he or she belongs to some other group—for each person belongs to only one line.

This fact is important if kin groups are to act as separate or nonoverlapping units. It is difficult for people to act together unless they know exactly who should get together. And it is easier for individuals to act together as a group if each one belongs to only one such group or line. Recall that in a bilateral system, not only is it sometimes unclear where the boundary of the kindred is, but one person belongs to many different kindreds—one's own and others' (children's, cousins', and so forth). Consequently, it is not surprising that a kindred gets together only temporarily for ceremonial occasions.

Types of Unilineal Descent Groups

In a society with unilineal descent, people usually refer to themselves as belonging to a particular unilineal group or set of groups because they believe they share common descent in either the male line (patrilineal) or the female line (matrilineal). These people form what is called a *unilineal descent group.* Several types of unilineal descent groups are distinguished by anthropologists: lineages, clans, phratries, and moieties.

Lineages. A **lineage** is a set of kin whose members trace descent from a common ancestor through known links. There may be **patrilineages** or **matrilineages,** depending, of course, on whether the links are traced through males only or through females only. Lineages are often designated by the name of the common ancestor or ancestress. In some societies, people belong to a hierarchy of lineages. That is, they first trace their descent back to the ancestor of a minor lineage, then to the ancestor of a larger and more inclusive major lineage, and so on.

Clans. A **clan** (also called a **sib**) is a set of kin whose members believe themselves to be descended from a common ancestor or ancestress, but the links back to that ancestor are not specified. In fact, the common ancestor may not even be known. Clans with patrilineal descent are called **patriclans;** clans with matrilineal descent are called **matriclans.** Clans often are designated by an animal or plant name (called a **totem**), which may have some special significance for the group and at the very least provides a means of group identification. Thus, if someone says she or he belongs to the Bear, Wolf, or Turtle clan, for example, others will know whether or not that person is a clan member.

The word *totem* comes from the Ojibwa Indian word *ototeman,* "a relative of mine." In some societies, people have to observe taboos relating to their clan totem animal. For example, clan members may be forbidden to kill or eat their totem.

Although it may seem strange to us that an animal or plant should be a symbol of a kin group, animals as symbols of groups are familiar in our own culture. Football and baseball teams, for example, are often named for animals (Detroit Tigers, Los Angeles Rams, Philadelphia Eagles, Chicago Bears). Voluntary associations, such as men's clubs,

Many Northwest Pacific Coast Indians constructed totem poles representing the animal totems and human ancestors of their clans. Shown here are totem poles and a reconstructed house in Victoria, British Columbia.

are sometimes called by the name of an animal (Elks, Moose, Lions). Entire nations may be represented by an animal; we speak, for instance, of the American Eagle and the British Lion.[13] Why humans so often choose animal names to represent groups is an intriguing question to which we have no tested answer as yet.

Phratries. A **phratry** is a unilineal descent group composed of supposedly related clans or sibs. As with clans, the descent links in phratries are unspecified.

Moieties. When a whole society is divided into two unilineal descent groups, we call each group a **moiety.** (The word *moiety* comes from a French word meaning "half.") The people in each moiety believe themselves to be descended from a common ancestor, although they cannot specify how. Societies with moiety systems usually have relatively small populations (fewer than 9,000 people). Societies with phratries and clans tend to be larger.[14]

Combinations. Although we have distinguished several different types of unilineal descent groups, we do not wish to imply that all unilineal societies have only one type of descent group. Many societies have two or more types in various combinations. For example, some societies have lineages and clans; others may have clans and phratries but no lineages; and still others may have clans and moieties but neither phratries nor lineages. Aside from the fact that a society that has phratries must also have clans (since phratries are combinations of clans), all combinations of descent groups are possible. Even if societies have more than one type of unilineal kin group—for example, lineages and clans—there is no ambiguity about membership: small groups are simply subsets of larger units. The larger units include people who say they are unilineally related further back in time.

Patrilineal Organization

Patrilineal organization is the most frequent type of descent system. The Kapauku Papuans, a people living in the central highlands of western New Guinea, are an example of a patrilineal society with many types of descent groups.[15] The hierarchy of groups to which Kapauku are affiliated by virtue of the patrilineal descent system plays an extremely important part in their lives. Every Kapauku belongs to a patrilineage, to a patriclan that includes his or her lineage, and to a patriphratry that includes his or her clan.

The male members of a patrilineage—all the living males who can trace their actual relationship through males to a common ancestor—constitute the male population of a single village or, more likely, a series of adjoining villages. In other words, the lineage is a *territorial* unit. The male members of the lineage live together by virtue of a patrilocal rule of residence and a fairly stable settlement pattern. A son stays near his parents and brings his wife to live in or near his father's house; the daughters leave home and go to live with their husbands. If the group lives in one place over a long period, the male descendants of one man will live in the same territory. If the lineage is large, it may be divided into sublineages composed of people who trace their descent from one of the sons of the lineage ancestor. The male members of a sublineage live in a contiguous block within the larger lineage territory.

The members of the same patrilineage address each other affectionately, and within this group law and order are maintained by a headman. Killing within the lineage is considered a serious offense, and any fighting that takes place is done with sticks rather than lethal weapons such as spears. The sublineage headman tries to settle any kind of grievance within the sublineage as quickly and as peacefully as possible. If a sublineage mate commits a crime against outsiders, all members of the sublineage may be considered responsible and their property seized, or a member of the sublineage may be killed in revenge by the victim's kin.

The Kapauku also belong to larger and more inclusive patrilineal descent groups—clans and phratries. All the people of the same clan believe they are related to each other in the father's line, but they are unable to say how they are related. If a member of the patriclan eats the clan's plant or animal totem, it is believed that the person will become deaf. A Kapauku is also forbidden to marry anyone from his or her clan. In other words, the clan is exogamous.

Unlike the members of the patrilineage, the male members of the patriclan do not all live together. Thus, the lineage is the largest group of patrilineal kinsmen that is localized. The lineage is also the largest group of kinsmen that acts together politically. Among clan members there is no mechanism for resolving disputes, and members of the same patriclan (who belong to different lineages) may even go to war with one another.

The most inclusive patrilineal descent group among the Kapauku is the phratry, each of which is composed of two or more clans. The Kapauku believe that the phratry was originally one clan, but that in a conflict between brothers of the founding family the younger brother was expelled and formed a new clan. The two resulting clans are, of course, viewed as patrilineally related, since their founders are said to have been brothers. The members of a phratry observe all the totemic taboos of the clans that belong to that phratry. Intermarriage of members of the same clan is forbidden, but members of the same phratry (if they belong to different clans) may marry.

The Kapauku, then, are an example of a unilineal society with many types of descent groups. They have lineages with demonstrated kinship links and two kinds of descent groups with unknown descent links (clans and phratries).

Matrilineal Organization

Although societies with matrilineal descent seem in many respects like mirror images of their patrilineal counterparts, they differ in one important way. That difference has to do with who exercises authority. In patrilineal systems, descent affiliation is transmitted through males, and it is also the males who exercise authority. Consequently, in the patrilineal system, lines of descent and of authority converge. In a matrilineal system, however, although the line of descent passes through females, females rarely exercise authority in their kin groups—usually males do.

Thus, the lines of authority and descent do not converge.[16] Anthropologists do not quite understand why this is so, but it is an ethnographic fact. In any case, since males exercise authority in the kin group, an individual's mother's brother becomes an important authority figure, because he is the individual's closest male matrilineal relative in the parental generation. The individual's father does not belong to the individual's own matrilineal kin group and thus has no say in kin group matters.

The divergence of authority and descent in a matrilineal system has some effect on community organization and marriage. Most matrilineal societies practice matrilocal residence. Daughters stay at home after marriage and bring their husbands to live with them; sons leave home to join their wives. But the sons who are required to leave will be the ones who eventually exercise authority in their kin groups. This situation presents a problem. The solution that seems to have been arrived at in most matrilineal societies is that, although the males move away to live with their wives, they usually do not move too far away—indeed, they often marry women who live in the same village. Thus, matrilineal societies tend not to be locally exogamous—that is, members often marry people from inside the village—whereas patrilineal societies are often locally exogamous.[17]

The matrilineal organization on Truk, a group of small islands in the Pacific, illustrates the

Reconstruction of an Iroquois longhouse, which housed a matrilineal descent group

general pattern of authority in matrilineal systems.[18] The Trukese have both matrilineages and matriclans. The matrilineage is a property-owning group whose members trace descent from a known common ancestress in the female line. The female lineage members and their husbands occupy a cluster of houses on the matrilineage's land. The property of the lineage group is administered by the oldest brother of the group. He allocates the productive property of his matrilineage and directs the work of the members. The oldest brother of the lineage also represents the group in dealings with the district chief and all outsiders, and he must be consulted on any matter that affects the group. There is also a senior woman of the lineage who exercises some authority, but only insofar as the activities of the women are concerned. She may supervise the women's cooperative work (they usually work separately from the men) and manage the household.

Within the nuclear family, the father and mother have the primary responsibility for raising and disciplining their children. When a child reaches puberty, however, the father's right to discipline or exercise authority over the child ceases. The mother continues to exercise her right of discipline, and her brother may interfere. A woman's brother rarely interferes with his sister's child before puberty, but after puberty he may exercise some authority, especially since he is an elder in the child's own matrilineage. On Truk, men rarely move far from their birthplace. As Ward Goodenough pointed out, "Since matrilocal residence takes the men away from their home lineages, most of them marry women whose lineage houses are within a few minutes' walk of their own."[19]

Although there are some differences between patrilineal and matrilineal systems, there are many similarities. In both types of systems there may be lineages, clans, phratries, and moieties, alone or in any combination. These kin groups, in either matrilineal or patrilineal societies, may perform any number of functions. They may regulate marriage; they may come to each other's aid either economically or politically; and they may perform rituals together.

Now that we have learned something about matrilineal systems, the avunculocal pattern of residence, whereby married couples live with or near the husband's mother's brother, may become clearer. Although avunculocal residence is relatively rare, just about all avunculocal societies are matrilineal. As we have seen, the mother's brother plays an important role in decision making in most matrilineal societies. Aside from his brothers, who is a boy's closest male matrilineal relative? His mother's

brother. Going to live with mother's brother, then, provides a way of localizing male matrilineal relatives. But why should some matrilineal societies practice that form of residence? The answer may involve the prevailing type of warfare.

Avunculocal societies, in contrast with matrilocal societies, fight internally. Just as patrilocality may be a response to keep (patrilineally) related men home after marriage, so avunculocality may be a way of keeping related (in this case, matrilineally related) men together after marriage to provide for quick mobilization in case of surprise attack from nearby. Societies that already have strong, functioning matrilineal descent groups may, when faced with fighting close to home and high male mortality, choose to practice avunculocality rather than switch to patrilocality.[20]

Functions of Unilineal Descent Groups

Unilineal descent groups exist in societies at all levels of cultural complexity.[21] Apparently however, they are most common in noncommercial food-producing (as opposed to food-collecting) societies.[22] Unilineal descent groups often have important functions in the social, economic, political, and religious realms of life.

Regulating Marriage.   In unilineal societies, individuals are not usually permitted to marry within their own unilineal descent groups. In some, however, marriage may be permitted within more inclusive kin groups but prohibited within smaller kin groups. In a few societies, marriage within the kin group is actually preferred.

But in general, the incest taboo in unilineal societies is extended to all presumed unilineal relatives. For example, on Truk, which has matriclans and matrilineages, a person is forbidden by the rule of descent group exogamy to marry anyone from her or his matriclan. The matrilineage is included within the matriclan, so the rule of descent group exogamy also applies to the matrilineage. Among the Kapauku, who have patriphratries, patriclans, and patrilineages, the largest descent group that is exogamous is the patriclan. The phratry may once have been exogamous, but the exogamy rule no longer applies to it. Some anthropologists have suggested that rules of exogamy for descent groups may have developed because the alliances between descent groups generated by such rules may be selectively favored under the conditions of life faced by most unilineal societies.

Economic Functions. Members of a person's lineage or clan are often required to side with that person in any quarrel or lawsuit, to help him or her get established economically, to contribute to a bride price or fine, and to support the person in life crises. Mutual aid often extends to economic cooperation on a regular basis. The unilineal descent group may act as a corporate unit in land ownership. For example, house sites and farmland are owned by a lineage among the Trukese and the Kapauku. Descent group members may also support one another in such enterprises as clearing virgin bush or forest for farmland and providing food and other things for feasts, potlatches, curing rites, and ceremonial occasions, such as births, initiations, marriages, and funerals.

Money earned—either by harvesting a cash crop or by leaving the community for a time to work for cash wages—is sometimes viewed by the descent group as belonging to all. In recent times, however, young people in some places have shown an unwillingness to part with their money, viewing it as different from other kinds of economic assistance.

Political Functions. The word *political,* as used by members of an industrialized society, generally does not apply to the rather vague powers that may be entrusted to a headman or the elders of a lineage or clan. But these persons may have the right to assign land for use by a lineage member or a clan member. Headmen or elders may also have the right to settle disputes between two members within a lineage, although they generally lack power to force a settlement. And they may act as intermediaries in disputes between a member of their own clan and a member of an opposing kin group.

Certainly one of the most important political functions of unilineal descent groups is their role in warfare—the attempt to resolve disputes within and without the society by violent action. In societies without towns or cities, the organization of such fighting is often in the hands of descent groups. The Tiv of central Nigeria, for instance, know quite well at any given moment which lineages they will fight against, which lineages they will join as allies in case of a fight, which they will fight against using only sticks, and which must be attacked using bows and arrows.

Religious Functions. A clan or lineage may have its own religious beliefs and practices, worshiping its own gods or goddesses and ancestral spirits. The Tallensi of West Africa revere and try to pacify their ancestors. They view life as we know it as only a part of human existence: for them, life existed before birth and will continue after death. The Tallensi believe that the ancestors of their descent groups have changed their form but have retained their interest in what goes on within their society. They can show their displeasure by bringing sudden disaster or minor mishap and their pleasure by bringing unexpected good fortune. But people can never tell what will please them; ancestral spirits are, above all, unpredictable. Thus, the Tallensi try to account for unexplainable happenings by attributing them to the ever-watchful ancestors. Belief in the presence of ancestors also provides security; if their ancestors have survived death, so will they. The Tallensi religion is thus a descent-group religion. The Tallensi are not concerned with other people's ancestors; they believe it is only one's own ancestors who plague or protect one.[23]

Development of Unilineal Systems

Unilineal kin groups play very important roles in the organization of many societies. But not all societies have such groups. In societies that have complex systems of political organization, officials and agencies take over many of the functions that might be performed by kin groups, such as the organization of work and warfare and the allocation of land. But not all societies that lack complex political organization have unilineal descent systems. Why, then, do some societies have unilineal descent systems but others do not?

It is generally assumed that unilocal residence (patrilocal or matrilocal) is necessary for the development of unilineal descent. Patrilocal residence, if practiced for some time in a society, will generate a set of patrilineally related males who live in the same territory. Matrilocal residence over time will similarly generate a localized set of matrilineally related females. It is no wonder, then, that matrilocal and patrilocal residence are cross-culturally associated with matrilineal and patrilineal descent, respectively.[24]

But, although unilocal residence might be necessary for the formation of unilineal descent groups, it is apparently not the only condition required. For one thing, many societies with unilocal residence lack unilineal descent groups. For another, merely because related males or related females live together by virtue of a patrilocal or matrilocal rule of residence, it does not necessarily follow that the related people will actually view themselves as a descent group and function as such. Thus, it appears that other conditions are needed to supply the impetus for the formation of unilineal descent groups.

There is some evidence that unilocal societies that engage in warfare are more apt to have unilineal descent groups than unilocal societies without warfare.[25] It may be, then, that the presence of fighting in societies lacking complex systems of political organization provides an impetus to the formation of unilineal descent groups. Unilineal descent groups provide individuals with unambiguous groups of persons who can fight or form alliances as discrete units.[26] There is no ambiguity about an individual's membership. It is perfectly clear whether someone belongs to a particular clan, phratry, or moiety. It is this feature of unilineal descent groups that enables them to act as separate and distinct units—mostly, perhaps, in warfare.

Bilateral systems, in contrast, are ego-centered, and every person, other than siblings, has a slightly different set of kin to rely on. Consequently, in bilateral societies it is often not clear to whom one can turn and which person has responsibility for aiding another. Such ambiguity, however, might not be a liability in societies without warfare or in societies with political systems that organize fighting on behalf of large populations.

New Perspectives on Gender

VARIATION IN RESIDENCE AND KINSHIP: WHAT DIFFERENCE DOES IT MAKE TO WOMEN?

When we say that residence and kinship have profound effects on people's lives, what exactly do we mean? We may imagine that it is hard for a woman in a patrilocal society to move at marriage into another village where her husband has plenty of relatives and she has few. But do we have evidence of that? Most ethnographies usually do not give details about people's feelings. But some do. For example, Leigh Minturn gives us the text of a letter that one new Rajput bride (who grew up in the village of Khalapur, India) sent to her mother shortly after she married into her husband's village. The letter was written when the bride had been gone six weeks, but she repeatedly asked if her mother, her father, her aunts had forgotten her. She begged to be called home and said her bags were packed. She described herself as

"a parrot in a cage" and complained about her in-laws. The bride's mother was not alarmed; she knew that such complaints were normal, reflections of her daughter's separation anxiety. Seven years later when Minturn returned to India, the daughter was reported by the mother to be happy. Still, a few other brides did have more serious symptoms: ghost possession, twenty-four to thirty-six hour comas, serious depression, or suicide. What research has not told us yet is whether these serious symptoms among women are present more often in patrilocal, patrilineal societies than in other societies (particularly matrilocal, matrilineal societies). Conversely, do men have some symptoms in matrilocal, matrilineal societies that they do not have in patrilocal societies? We do not know yet.

What about the status of women? Some research suggests that matrilocality and matrilineality enhance some aspects of women's status, but perhaps not as much as we might think. (Even in matrilineal societies, men are usually the political leaders.) The main effect of matrilocality and matrilineality appears to be that women control property, but they also tend to have more domestic authority in the home, more equal sexual restrictions, and more value placed on their lives. Alice Schlegel pointed out that women's status is not always relatively high in matrilineal societies, because they can be dominated by the husband or by brothers (because brothers play important roles in their kin groups). It is only when neither the husband nor the brother dominates that women may have considerable control

AMBILINEAL SYSTEMS

Societies with ambilineal descent groups are far less numerous than unilineal or even bilateral societies. Ambilineal societies, however, resemble unilineal ones in many ways. For instance, the members of an ambilineal descent group believe that they are descended from a common ancestor, though frequently they cannot specify all the genealogical links. The descent group is commonly named and may have an identifying emblem or even a totem; land and other productive resources may be owned by the descent group; and myths and religious practices are often associated with the group. Marriage is often regulated by group membership, just as in unilineal systems, though kin group exogamy is not nearly as common as in unilineal systems. Moreover, ambilineal societies resemble unilineal ones in having various levels or types of descent groups. They may have lineages and higher orders of descent groups, distinguished (as in unilineal systems) by whether or not all the genealogical links to the supposed common ancestors are specified.[27]

over their own lives. Certainly the combination of matrilocality *and* matrilineality is better for women's status than patrilocality and patrilineality. Matrilocality and matrilineality might not enhance women's status because of the dominance of male matrilineal kin, but patrilocality and patrilineality are very likely to detract from women's status. Norma Diamond stated that even after the Chinese Communist revolution, which abolished the landholding estates of patrilineages and gave women access to education as well as jobs outside the home, male dominance continued. The mode of production and labor changed, but patrilocality did not. Women were still usually the in-marrying strangers, and members of the patrilineage became a work team on the collective farm. Diamond pointed out that those few women who became local leaders were likely to have atypical marriages that allowed them to live in the villages of their birth.

Residence and descent also predict societal attempts to control reproduction. According to Suzanne Frayser, patrilineal societies have several sexual and reproductive dilemmas.One dilemma is the contradiction between the importance of males in kinship and the women's role in reproduction. If patrilineal societies denigrate women too much, women may try to decrease their reproduction. If patrilineal societies exalt women too much, that exaltation may detract from the value of men. A second dilemma has to do with paternity, which is essential for patrilineal descent but harder than maternity to be certain of. Frayser argued that because kin group links are traced through males in patrilineal societies, they will do more to assure that the man a woman marries *is* the father. Frayser suggested that patrilineal societies therefore will be more restrictive about a woman's sexuality. Indeed, the results of her crosscultural study indicate that patrilineal societies are more likely than other societies to prohibit premarital and extramarital sex for women, and they are more likely to make it very difficult for a woman to divorce her husband.

Sources: *Leigh Minturn*, Sita's Daughters: Coming Out of Purdah: The Rajput Women of Khalapur Revisited *(New York: Oxford University Press, 1993), pp. 54–71; Martin King Whyte,* The Status of Women in Preindustrial Societies *(Princeton, NJ: Princeton University Press, 1978), pp. 132–34; Alice Schlegel, "The Status of Women," in Carol R. Ember and Melvin Ember, eds.,* Cross-Cultural Research for Social Science *(Englewood Cliffs, NJ: Prentice Hall, 1995). Prentice Hall/Simon & Schuster Custom Publishing. Norma Diamond, "Collectivization, Kinship, and the Status of Women in Rural China," in Rayna R. Reiter,* Toward an Anthropology of Women *(New York: Monthly Review Press, 1975); Suzanne G. Frayser,* Varieties of Sexual Experience *(New Haven, CT: HRAF Press, 1985), pp. 338–47.*

The Samoans of the South Pacific are an example of an ambilineal society.[28] There are two types of ambilineal descent groups in Samoa, corresponding to what would be called clans and subclans in a unilineal society. Both groups are exogamous. Associated with each ambilineal clan are one or more chiefs. A group takes its name from the senior chief; subclans, of which there are always at least two, may take their names from junior chiefs.

The distinctiveness of the Samoan ambilineal system, compared with unilineal systems, is that because an individual may be affiliated with an ambilineal group through her or his father or mother (and her or his parents, in turn, could be affiliated with any of their parents' groups), there are a number of ambilineal groups to which that individual could belong. Affiliation with a Samoan descent group is optional, and a person may theoretically affiliate with any or all of the ambilineal groups to which she or he is related. In practice, however, a person is primarily associated with one group—the ambilineal group whose land he or she actually lives on and cultivates—although he or she may participate in the activities (house building, for example) of several groups. Because a person may belong to more than one ambilineal group, the society is not divided into separate kin groups, in contrast with unilineal societies. Consequently, the core members of each ambilineal group cannot all live together (as they could in unilineal societies), because each person belongs to more than one group and cannot live in several places at once.

Not all ambilineal societies have the multiple descent group membership that occurs in Samoa. In some ambilineal societies, a person may belong (at any one time) to only one group. In such cases, the society can be divided into separate, nonoverlapping groups of kin.

Why do some societies have ambilineal descent groups? Although the evidence is not clear-cut on this point, it may be that societies with unilineal descent groups are transformed into ambilineal ones under special conditions—particularly in the presence of depopulation. We have already noted that depopulation may transform a previously unilocal society into a bilocal society. If that previously unilocal society also had unilineal descent groups, the descent groups may become transformed into ambilineal groups. If a society used to be patrilocal and patrilineal, for example, but some couples began to live matrilocally, then their children would be associated with a previously patrilineal descent group (on whose land they may be living) through their mother. Once this situation

happens regularly, the unilineal principle may become transformed into an ambilineal principle.[29] Thus, ambilineal descent systems may have developed recently as a result of depopulation caused by the introduction of European diseases.

KINSHIP TERMINOLOGY

Our society, like all others, refers to a number of different kin by the same **classificatory term.** Most of us probably never stop to think about why we name relatives the way we do. For example, we call our mother's brother and father's brother (and often mother's sister's husband and father's sister's husband) by the same term— *uncle.* It is not that we are unable to distinguish between our mother's or father's brother or that we do not know the difference between **consanguineal kin** (blood kin) and **affinal kin** (kin by marriage, or what we call *in-laws*). Instead, it seems that in our society we do not usually find it necessary to distinguish between various types of uncles.

However natural our system of classification may seem to us, countless field studies by anthropologists have revealed that societies differ markedly in how they group or distinguish relatives. The kinship terminology used in a society may reflect its prevailing kind of family, its rule of residence and its rule of descent, and other aspects of its social organization. Kin terms may also give clues to prior features of the society's social system, if, as many anthropologists believe,[30] the kin terms of a society are very resistant to change. The major systems of kinship terminology are the Omaha system, the Crow system, the Iroquois system, the Sudanese system, the Hawaiian system, and the Inuit (Eskimo) system.

Because it is the most familiar to us, let us first consider the kinship terminology system employed in our own and many other commercial societies. But it is by no means confined to commercial societies—in fact, this system is found in many Inuit (Eskimo) societies.

Inuit, or Eskimo, System

The distinguishing features of the Inuit, or Eskimo, system (see Figure 11–7) are that all cousins are lumped together under the same term but are distinguished from brothers and sisters, and all aunts and uncles are lumped under the same terms but are distinguished from mother and father. In Figure 11–7 and in subsequent figures, the kin types that

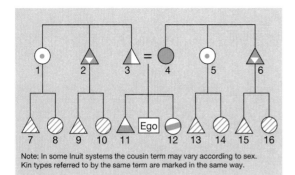

Note: In some Inuit systems the cousin term may vary according to sex. Kin types referred to by the same term are marked in the same way.

FIGURE 11–7
Inuit (Eskimo) Kinship Terminology System

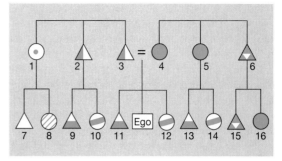

FIGURE 11–8
Omaha Kinship Terminology System

are referred to by the same term are colored and marked in the same way; for example, in the Inuit system, kin types 2 (father's brother) and 6 (mother's brother) are referred to by the same term (*uncle* in English). Note that in this system, in contrast to the others we examine below, no other relatives are generally referred to by the same terms used for members of the nuclear family—mother, father, brother, and sister.

The Inuit type of kinship terminology is not generally found where there are unilineal or ambilineal descent groups; the only kin group that appears to be present is the bilateral kindred.[31] Remember that the kindred in a bilateral kinship system is an ego-centered group. Although relatives on both my mother's and my father's sides are equally important, my most important relatives are generally those closest to me. This is particularly true in our society, where the nuclear family generally lives alone, separated from and not particularly involved with other relatives except on ceremonial occasions. Because the nuclear family is most important, we would expect to find that the kin types in the nuclear family are distinguished terminologically from all other relatives. And the mother's and father's sides are equally important (or unimportant), so it makes sense that we use the same terms (*aunt, uncle,* and *cousin*) for both sides of the family.

Omaha System

The Omaha system of kin terminology is named after the Omaha of North America, but the system is found in many societies around the world, usually those with patrilineal descent.[32] Referring to Figure 11–8, we can see immediately which types of kin are lumped together in an Omaha system. First, father and father's brother (numbers 2 and 3) are both referred to by the same term. This way of classifying relatives contrasts markedly with ours, in which no term that applies to a member of the nuclear family (father, mother, brother, sister) is applied to any other relative. What could account for the Omaha system of lumping? One interpretation is that father and father's brother are lumped in this system because most societies in which this system is found have patrilineal kin groups. Both father and father's brother are in the parental generation of my patrilineal kin group and may behave toward me similarly. My father's brother also probably lives near me, since patrilineal societies usually have patrilocal residence. The term for father and father's brother, then, might be translated "male member of my patrilineal kin group in my father's generation."

A second lumping (which at first glance appears similar to the lumping of father and father's brother) is that of mother and mother's sister (4 and 5), both of whom are called by the same term. But more surprisingly, mother's brother's daughter (16) is also referred to by this term. Why? If we think of the term as meaning "female member of my mother's patrilineage of *any* generation," then the term makes sense. Consistent with this view, all the male members of my mother's patrilineage of any generation (mother's brother, 6; mother's brother's son, 15) are also referred to by one term.

It is apparent, then, that relatives on the father's and the mother's sides are grouped differently in this system. For members of my mother's patrilineal kin group, I lump all male members together and all female members together regardless of their generation. Yet, for members of my father's patrilineal kin group, I have different terms for the male and female members of different generations. George Peter Murdock suggested that a society lumps kin types when there are more similarities than differences among them.[33]

Using this principle, and recognizing that societies with an Omaha system usually are patrilineal,

I realize that my father's patrilineal kin group is the one to which I belong and in which I have a great many rights and obligations. Consequently, persons of my father's generation are likely to behave quite differently toward me than are persons of my own generation. Members of my patrilineal group in my father's generation are likely to exercise authority over me, and I am required to show them respect. Members of my patrilineal group in my own generation are those I am likely to play with as a child and to be friends with. Thus, in a patrilineal system, persons on my father's side belonging to different generations are likely to be distinguished. On the other hand, my mother's patrilineage is relatively unimportant to me (since I take my descent from my father). And because my residence is probably patrilocal, my mother's relatives will probably not even live near me. Thus, inasmuch as my mother's patrilineal relatives are comparatively unimportant in such a system, they become similar enough to be lumped together.

Finally, in the Omaha system, I refer to my male parallel cousins (my father's brother's son, 9, and my mother's sister's son, 13) in the same way I refer to my brother (number 11). I refer to my female parallel cousins (my father's brother's daughter, 10, and my mother's sister's daughter, 14) in the same way I refer to my sister (12). Considering that my father's brother and mother's sister are referred to by the same terms I use for my father and mother, this lumping of parallel cousins with **siblings** (brothers and sisters) is not surprising. If I call my own mother's and father's children (other than myself) "Brother" and "Sister," then the children of anyone whom I also call "Mother" and "Father" ought to be called "Brother" and "Sister" as well.

Crow System

The Crow system, named after another North American culture, has been called the mirror image of the Omaha system. The same principles of lumping kin types are employed, except that the Crow system is associated with matrilineal descent,[34] so the individuals in my mother's matrilineal group (which is my own) are not lumped across generations, whereas the individuals in my father's matrilineal group are. By comparing Figure 11–9 with Figure 11–8, we find that the lumping and separating of kin types are much the same in both, except that the lumping across generations in the Crow system appears on the father's side rather than on the mother's side. In other words, I call both my mother and my mother's sister by the

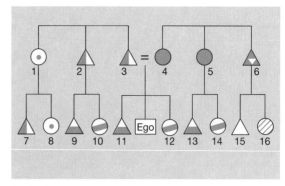

FIGURE 11–9
Crow Kinship Terminology System

same term (since both are female members of my matrilineal descent group in my mother's generation). I call my father, my father's brother, and my father's sister's son by the same term (all male members of my father's matrilineal group in any generation). I call my father's sister and my father's sister's daughter by the same term (both female members of my father's matrilineal group). And I refer to my parallel cousins in the same way I refer to my brother and sister.

Iroquois System

The Iroquois system, named after the Iroquois of North America, is similar to both the Omaha and Crow systems in the way in which I refer to relatives in my parents' generation (see Figure 11–10). That is, my father and my father's brother (2 and 3) are referred to by the same term, and my mother and my mother's sister (4 and 5) are referred to by the same term. However, the Iroquois system differs from the Omaha and Crow systems regarding my own generation. In the Omaha and Crow systems, one set of cross-cousins was lumped in the kinship

FIGURE 11–10
Iroquois Kinship Terminology System

Note: Although not shown in this diagram, in the Iroquois system, parallel cousins are sometimes referred to by different terms than one's own brother or sister.

terminology with the generation above. In the Iroquois system both sets of cross-cousins (mother's brother's children, 15 and 16, and father's sister's children, 7 and 8) are referred to by the same terms, distinguished by sex. That is, mother's brother's daughter and father's sister's daughter are both referred to by the same term. Also, mother's brother's son and father's sister's son are referred to by the same term. Parallel cousins always have terms different from those for cross-cousins and are sometimes, but not always, referred to by the same terms as one's brother and sister.

Like the Omaha and Crow systems, the Iroquois system has different terms for relatives on the father's and mother's sides. Such differentiation tends to be associated with unilineal descent, which is not surprising since unilineal descent involves affiliation with either mother's or father's kin. Why Iroquois, rather than Omaha or Crow, terminology occurs in a unilineal society requires explanation. One possible explanation is that Omaha or Crow is likely to occur in a developed, as opposed to a developing or decaying, unilineal system.[35] Another possible explanation is that Iroquois terminology emerges in societies that prefer marriage with both cross-cousins,[36] who are differentiated from other relatives in an Iroquois system.

Sudanese System

One other system of kinship terminology is associated with unilineal descent—the Sudanese system. But, unlike the Omaha, Crow, and Iroquois systems we have examined so far, the Sudanese system usually does not lump any relatives in the parents' and ego's generations. That is, the Sudanese system is usually a *descriptive* system, in which a different **descriptive term** is used for *each* of the relatives shown in Figure 11–11. What kinds of societies are likely to have such a system? Although societies with Sudanese terminology are likely to be patrilineal, they probably are different from most patrilineal societies that have Omaha or Iroquois terms. Sudanese terminology is associated with relatively great political complexity, class stratification, and occupational specialization. It has been suggested that under such conditions, a kinship system may reflect the need to make fine distinctions among members of descent groups who have different opportunities and privileges in the occupational or class system.[37]

The Omaha, Crow, Iroquois, and Sudanese systems, although different from one another and associated with somewhat different predictors, share one important feature: the terms used for the mother's and father's side of the family are not the same. If you imagine folding the kinship terminology diagrams in half, the two sides would not be the same. As we have seen, in the Inuit system, however, the terms on the mother's and father's side of the family are *exactly* the same. This feature suggests that the two sides of the family are equally important, or equally unimportant. The next system—Hawaiian—also has the same terms on both sides, but kinship outside the nuclear family is more important.

Hawaiian System

The Hawaiian system of kinship terminology is the least complex in that it uses the smallest number of terms. In this system, all relatives of the same sex in the same generation are referred to by the same term (see Figure 11–12). Thus, all my female cousins are referred to by the same term as my sister; all male cousins are referred to by the same term as my brother. Everyone known to be related to me in my parents' generation is referred to by one term if female (including my mother) and by another term if male (including my father).

The fact that societies with Hawaiian kin terminology tend not to have unilineal descent groups[38] helps explain why kinship terms are the same on both sides of the family. Why are the

FIGURE 11–11
Sudanese Kinship Terminology System

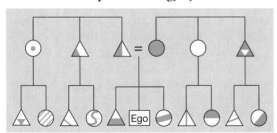

FIGURE 11–12
Hawaiian Kinship Terminology System

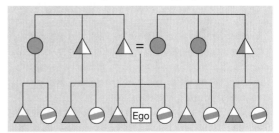

terms for mother, father, sister, and brother used for other relatives? Perhaps because societies with Hawaiian terminology are likely to have large extended families[39] to which every type of relative in Figure 11–12 may belong because of alternative (bilocal) residence patterns.[40] So, in contrast to our own society, many kin are quite important, a fact that seems to be reflected in the practice of referring to other relatives with the same terms that are used for nuclear family members.

▼ SUMMARY

1. In our society, and in many other industrial societies, a newly married couple usually establishes a place of residence apart from parents or relatives (neolocal residence). But about 95 percent of the world's societies have some pattern of residence whereby the new couple settles within, or very close to, the household of the parents or some other close relative of the groom or bride.

2. The four major patterns in which married couples live with or near kinsmen are these:
   a. Patrilocal residence. The couple lives with or near the husband's parents (67 percent of all societies).
   b. Matrilocal residence. The couple lives with or near the wife's parents (15 percent of all societies).
   c. Bilocal residence. The couple lives with or near either the husband's parents or the wife's parents (7 percent of all societies).
   d. Avunculocal residence. The son and his wife settle with or near his mother's brother (4 percent of all societies).

3. In most societies in which kinship connections are important, a rule allocates each person to a particular and definable set of kin. The rules affiliating individuals with sets of kin are called rules of descent.

4. Rules of descent affiliate individuals with different sets of kin. There are only three known rules of descent:
   a. Patrilineal descent affiliates an individual with kin of both sexes related to him or her through men only. In each generation, then, children belong to the kin group of their father.
   b. Matrilineal descent affiliates an individual with kin related to her or him through women only. In each generation, then, children belong to the kin group of their mother.
   c. Ambilineal descent affiliates an individual with kin related to him or her through either men or women. Consequently, the descent groups show both female and male genealogical links.

5. Societies without lineal descent rules are bilateral societies. Relatives on both the mother's and father's sides of the family are of equal importance or (more usually) unimportance. Kindreds are ego-centered sets of kin who may be called together temporarily for some purpose.

6. With unilineal descent (patrilineal or matrilineal), people usually refer to themselves as belonging to a particular unilineal group or set of groups because they believe they share common descent in either the male or the female line. These people form what is called a unilineal descent group. There are several types:
   a. Lineages are sets of kin whose members trace descent from a common ancestor through known links.
   b. Clans are sets of kin who believe they are descended from a common ancestor but cannot specify the genealogical links.
   c. Phratries are groups of supposedly related clans.
   d. Moieties are said to exist when the whole society is divided into two unilineal descent groups without specified links to the supposed common ancestor of each.

7. Unilineal descent groups are most common in societies in the middle range of cultural complexity—that is, in noncommercial food-producing (as opposed to food-collecting) societies. In such societies, unilineal descent groups often have important functions in the social, economic, political, and religious realms of life.

8. Societies differ markedly in how they group or distinguish relatives under the same or different kinship terms. The major systems of terminology are the Inuit (Eskimo), Omaha, Crow, Iroquois, Sudanese, and Hawaiian systems.

▼ GLOSSARY TERMS

affinal kin
ambilineal descent
avunculocal residence
bilateral kinship
bilocal residence
clan or sib
classificatory term
consanguineal kin

descriptive term
double descent or double
  unilineal descent
ego
kindred
lineage
matriclans
matrilineage

matrilineal descent
matrilocal residence
moiety
neolocal residence
patriclans
patrilineage
patrilineal descent
patrilocal residence

phratry
rules of descent
siblings
totem
unilocal residence
unilineal descent

▼ CRITICAL QUESTIONS

1. What other things about our society would change if we practiced other than neolocal residence?

2. Why does kinship provide the main structure of social action in non-commercial societies?

3. Why might it be important for unilineal descent groups to be nonoverlapping in membership?

▼ SUGGESTED READING

EMBER, M., AND EMBER, C. R. *Marriage, Family, and Kinship: Comparative Studies of Social Organization.* New Haven, CT: HRAF Press, 1983. A collection of reprinted cross-cultural and cross-species studies testing possible explanations of some aspects of human social organization. Relevant to this chapter are the studies of variation in marital residence and the development of unilineal descent.

FOX, R. *Kinship and Marriage: An Anthropological Perspective.* Cambridge: Cambridge University Press, 1983. An introduction to social organization, focusing on issues and principles in the study of various kinship groups.

LEVINSON, D., AND MALONE, M. J., eds. *Toward Explaining Human Culture: A Critical Review of the Findings of Worldwide Cross-Cultural Research.* New Haven, CT: HRAF Press, 1980. Chapter 9 reviews the cross-cultural research literature on marital residence, descent groups, and kinship terminology.

MURDOCK, G. P. *Social Structure.* New York: Macmillan, 1949. A pioneering cross-cultural analysis of variation in aspects of social organization, including the family and marriage, kin groups, kinship terminology, the incest taboo and its extensions, and the regulation of sex.

PASTERNAK, B. "Family and Household: Who Lives Where, Why Does It Vary, and Why Is It Important?" In C. R. Ember and M. Ember, *Cross-Cultural Research for Social Science* (Englewood Cliffs, NJ: Prentice Hall, 1995). Prentice Hall/Simon & Schuster Custom Publishing. The first part of this chapter, written especially for undergraduates, discusses the variation in marital residence practices. Also discussed is why residence matters so much. See also Pasternak's *Introduction to Kinship and Social Organization.* Englewood Cliffs, NJ: Prentice Hall, 1976. Chapters 4, 8, and 9 present a survey and critique of theories and evidence about variation in residence and kinship.

▼ NOTES

[1]Allan D. Coult and Robert W. Habenstein, *Cross Tabulations of Murdock's World Ethnographic Sample* (Columbia: University of Missouri Press, 1965); George Peter Murdock, "World Ethnographic Sample," *American Anthropologist* 59 (1957): 664–87.

[2]Percentages calculated from Coult and Habenstein, *Cross Tabulations of Murdock's World Ethnographic Sample.*

[3]Laura Bohannan and Paul Bohannan, *The Tiv of Central Nigeria* (London: International African Institute, 1953).

[4]Melvin Ember, "The Emergence of Neolocal Residence," *Transactions of the New York Academy of Sciences,* 30 (1967): 291–302.

[5]Melvin Ember and Carol R. Ember, "The Conditions Favoring Matrilocal versus Patrilocal Residence," *American Anthropologist,* 73 (1971): 571–94. See also William T. Divale, "Migration, External Warfare, and Matrilocal Residence," *Behavior Science Research,* 9 (1974): 75–133.

[6]Ember and Ember, "The Conditions Favoring Matrilocal versus Patrilocal Residence," pp. 583–85; and Divale, "Migration, External Warfare, and Matrilocal Residence," p. 100.

[7]Ember and Ember, "The Conditions Favoring Matrilocal versus Patrilocal Residence." For a different theory—that matrilocal residence precedes, rather than follows, the development of purely external warfare—see Divale, "Migration, External Warfare, and Matrilocal Residence."

[8]See Mary W. Helms, "Miskito: Adaptations to Colonial Empires, Past and Present," in Melvin Ember, Carol R. Ember, and David Levinson, eds., *Portraits of Culture: Ethnographic Originals* (Englewood Cliffs, NJ: Prentice Hall, 1994). Prentice Hall/Simon & Schuster Custom Publishing. See also Ember and Ember, "The Conditions Favoring Matrilocal versus Patrilocal Residence."

[9]Elman R. Service, *Primitive Social Organization: An Evolutionary Perspective* (New York: Random House, 1962), p. 137.

[10]Carol R. Ember and Melvin Ember, "The Conditions Favoring Multilocal Residence," *Southwestern Journal of Anthropology,* 28 (1972): 382–400.

[11]Carol R. Ember, "Residential Variation among Hunter-Gatherers," *Behavior Science Research,* 9 (1975): 135–49.

[12]J. D. Freeman, "On the Concept of the Kindred," *Journal of the Royal Anthropological Institute,* 91 (1961): 192–220.

[13]George Peter Murdock, *Social Structure* (New York: Macmillan, 1949), pp. 49–50.

[14]Carol R. Ember, Melvin Ember, and Burton Pasternak, "On the Development of Unilineal Descent," *Journal of Anthropological Research,* 30 (1974): 84–89.

[15]Leopold Pospisil, *The Kapauku Papuans of West New Guinea* (New York: Holt, Rinehart & Winston, 1963).

[16]David M. Schneider, "The Distinctive Features of Matrilineal Descent Groups," in David M. Schneider and Kathleen Gough, eds., *Matrilineal Kinship* (Berkeley: University of California Press, 1961), pp. 1–35.

[17]Ember and Ember, "The Conditions Favoring Matrilocal vesus Patrilocal Residence," p. 581.

[18]David M. Schneider, "Truk," in Schneider and Gough, eds., *Matrilineal Kinship*, pp. 202–33.

[19]Ward H. Goodenough, *Property, Kin, and Community on Truk* (New Haven, CT: Yale University Press, 1951), p. 145.

[20]Melvin Ember, "The Conditions That May Favor Avunculocal Residence," *Behavior Science Research*, 9 (1974): 203–9.

[21]Coult and Habenstein, *Cross Tabulations of Murdock's World Ethnographic Sample*.

[22]Data from Robert B. Textor, comp., *A Cross-Cultural Summary* (New Haven, CT: HRAF Press, 1967).

[23]Meyer Fortes, *The Web of Kinship among the Tallensi* (New York: Oxford University Press, 1949).

[24]Data from Textor, comp., *A Cross-Cultural Summary*.

[25]Ember, Ember, and Pasternak, "On the Development of Unilineal Descent."

[26]The importance of warfare and competition as factors in the formation of unilineal descent groups is also suggested by Service, *Primitive Social Organization;* and Marshall D. Sahlins, "The Segmentary Lineage: An Organization of Predatory Expansion," *American Anthropologist*, 63 (1961): 332–45.

[27]William Davenport, "Nonunilinear Descent and Descent Groups," *American Anthropologist*, 61 (1959): 557–72.

[28]The description of the Samoan descent system is based on Melvin Ember's 1955–1956 fieldwork. See also his "The Nonunilinear Descent Groups of Samoa," *American Anthropologist*, 61 (1959): 573–77; and Davenport, "Nonunilinear Descent and Descent Groups."

[29]Ember and Ember, "The Conditions Favoring Multilocal Residence."

[30]See, for example, Murdock, *Social Structure*, pp. 199–222.

[31]Reported in Textor, comp., *A Cross-Cultural Summary*.

[32]The association between the Omaha system and patrilineality is reported in Textor, comp., *A Cross-Cultural Summary*.

[33]Murdock, *Social Structure*, p. 125.

[34]The association between the Crow system and matrilineality is reported in Textor, comp., *A Cross-Cultural Summary*.

[35]See Leslie A. White, "A Problem in Kinship Terminology," *American Anthropologist*, 41 (1939): 569–70.

[36]Jack Goody, "Cousin Terms," *Southwestern Journal of Anthropology*, 26 (1970): 125–42.

[37]Burton Pasternak, *Introduction to Kinship and Social Organization* (Englewood Cliffs, NJ: Prentice Hall, 1976), p. 142.

[38]Reported in Textor, comp., *A Cross-Cultural Summary*.

[39]Ibid.

[40]This conjecture is based on our unpublished cross-cultural research.

12

Associations and Interest Groups

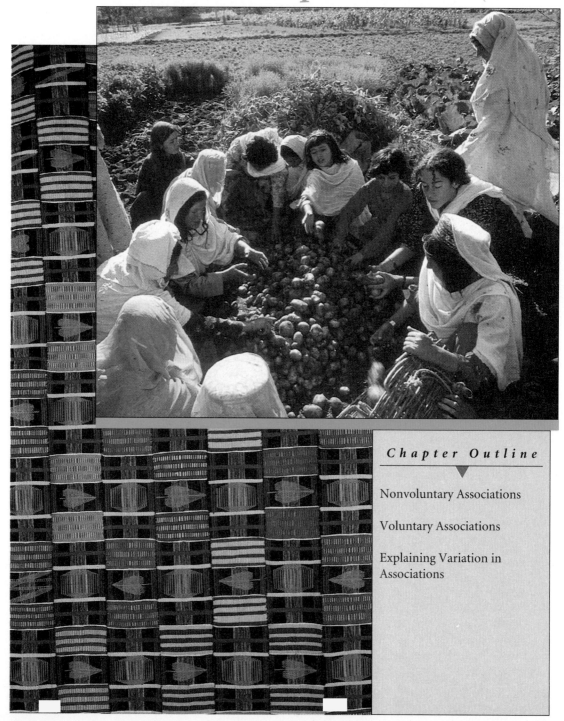

Samuel Johnson, the eighteenth-century English author, was once asked to describe James Boswell, his companion and biographer. "Boswell," he boomed, "is a very clubable man." Johnson did not mean that Boswell deserved to be attacked with bludgeons. He was referring to Boswell's fondness for all sorts of clubs and associations, a fondness he shared with many of his contemporaries. The tendency to form associations was not unique to eighteenth-century England. At all times and in all areas of the world, we find evidence of human beings' "clubability."

The notion of clubs may make us think of something extracurricular and not terribly important, but associations play very important roles in the economy and political life of many societies. In this chapter, we examine the various kinds of associations formed in different societies, how these groups function, and what general purposes they serve. When we speak of **associations,** we mean different kinds of groups that are not based on kinship, as in the preceding chapter, or on territory, as in the next chapter. Associations, then, are nonkin and nonterritorial groups. And, although they vary a lot, they also have several common characteristics: (1) some kind of formal, institutionalized structure; (2) the exclusion of some people; (3) members with common interests or purposes; and (4) members with a discernible sense of pride and feeling of belonging. Contemporary American society has an abundance of *interest groups*—to use the terminology of the political scientist—that display these general characteristics of associations. Such groups vary considerably in size and social significance, ranging from national organizations such as the Democratic and Republican parties to more local organizations such as college sororities and fraternities.

But societies differ considerably in the degree to which they have such associations and, if they do have them, in what kind they have. To make our discussion somewhat easier, we focus on two dimensions of how associations vary from one society to another. One is whether recruitment into the association is voluntary or not. In our society, with the exception of the government's right to draft men into the military, just about all our associations are voluntary—that is, people can choose to join or not join. But in many societies, particularly the more egalitarian ones, membership is nonvoluntary: all people of a particular category must belong.

A second dimension of variation in associations is what qualifies a person for membership. There are two possible kinds of qualifications: those that are achieved and those that are ascribed.

Achieved qualities are those an individual acquires during his or her lifetime, such as superior skills in a sport or the skills required to be an electrician. **Ascribed qualities** are those determined for a person at birth, either because of genetic makeup (for instance, sex) or because of family background (for instance, ethnicity, place of birth, religion, social class). We speak of two kinds of ascribed qualities or characteristics: **universally ascribed qualities,** those that are found in all societies (such as age and sex), and **variably ascribed qualities,** those that are found only in some societies (such as ethnic, religious, or social-class differences). Table 12–1 gives these two dimensions of variation in associations (voluntary versus nonvoluntary recruitment and criteria for membership) and some kinds of associations that fit neatly into our classification. Of course, some associations do not fit so neatly—for example, the criteria that qualify someone for Girl Scout membership include an interest in joining (an achieved quality) as well as biological sex (an ascribed characteristic).

NONVOLUNTARY ASSOCIATIONS

Although complex societies may have nonvoluntary associations, such associations are more characteristic of relatively unstratified or egalitarian societies. In relatively unstratified societies, associations tend to be based on the universally ascribed characteris-

▼▼▼▼▼▼▼
TABLE 12–1 *Some Examples of Associations*

MEMBERSHIP CRITERIA	RECRUITMENT	
	Voluntary	*Nonvoluntary*
Universally ascribed		Age-sets Most unisex associations
Variably ascribed	Ethnic associations Regional associations	Conscripted army
Achieved	Occupational associations Political parties Special interest groups	

tics of age and sex. Such associations take two forms: age-sets and male or female (unisex) associations.

Age-Sets

All societies use a vocabulary of age terms, just as they use a vocabulary of kinship terms. For instance, as we distinguish among *brother, uncle,* and *cousin,* so we differentiate *infant, adolescent,* and *adult.* Age terms refer to categories based on age, or *age-grades.* An **age-grade** is simply a category of persons who happen to fall within a particular, culturally distinguished age range. **Age-set,** on the other hand, is the term for a group of persons of similar age and the same sex who move through some or all of life's stages together. For example, all the boys of a certain age range in a particular district might simultaneously become ceremonially initiated into "manhood." Later in life, the group as a whole might become "elders," and still later "retired elders." Entry into an age-set system is generally nonvoluntary and is based on the universally ascribed characteristics of sex and age.

Kinship forms the basis of the organization and administration of most noncommercial societies. In some societies, however, age-sets crosscut kinship ties and form strong supplementary bonds. Two such societies are the Karimojong of East Africa and the Shavante of Brazil.

Karimojong Age-Sets. The Karimojong number some 60,000 people. Predominantly cattle herders, they occupy about 4,000 acres of semiarid country in northeastern Uganda. Their society is especially interesting because of its organization into combinations of age-sets and generation-sets. These groupings provide "both the source of political authority and the main field within which it is exercised."[1]

A Karimojong age-set comprises all the men who have been initiated into manhood within a span of about five to six years. A generation-set consists of a combination of five such age-sets, covering twenty-five to thirty years. Each generation-set is seen as "begetting" the one that immediately follows it, and at any one time two generation-sets are in

Some circumstances have changed, but the age-sets of the Nandi of Kenya still have importance. This warrior-aged Nandi man (in a suit) is told by a traditional spiritual leader (in a skin cloak): "In the past, when our young warriors went out for the first time, we gave them spears and shields and told them to bring back wealth to the community. Today we give you a pen and paper and ask the same."

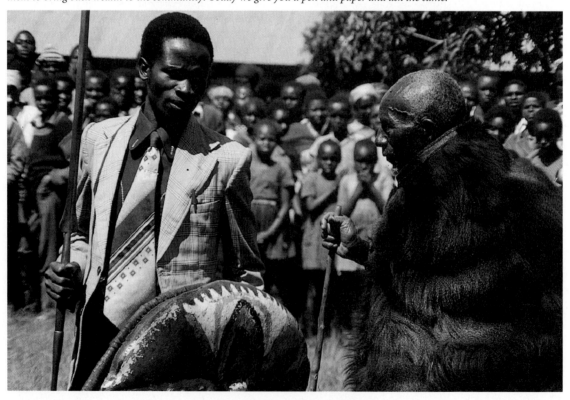

corporate existence. The senior unit—whose members perform the administrative, judicial, and priestly functions—is closed; the junior unit, whose members serve as warriors and police, is still recruiting. When all five age-sets in the junior generation-set are established, that generation-set will be ready (actually impatient) to assume the status of its senior predecessor. Eventually, grumbling but realistic, the elders will agree to a succession ceremony, moving those who were once in a position of obedience to a position of authority.

The Karimojong age system, then, comprises a cyclical succession of four generation-sets in a predetermined continuing relationship. The *retired generation-set* consists of elders who have passed on the mantle of authority, since most of the five age-sets within the retired generation-set are depleted, if not defunct. The *senior generation-set* contains the five age-sets that actively exercise authority. The *junior generation-set* is still recruiting members and, although obedient to elders, has some administrative powers. The *noninitiates* are starting a generation-set. Figure 12–1 illustrates the Karimojong age system.

Once initiated, a boy has become a man, one with a clearly defined status and the ultimate certainty of exercising full authority together with his set partners. Indeed, a Karimojong is not expected

FIGURE 12–1

The Karimojong age system is composed of four distinct generation-sets (labeled A, B, C, and D in this diagram), which succeed each other cyclically. Each generation-set, in turn, is divided into five age-sets or potential age-sets. The senior generation-set (A) exercises authority. The junior age set (B)—the warriors and policemen—is still recruiting. Generation-set D consists of retired age-sets. Noninitiated and not-yet-born boys constitute the potential age-sets C1–C5.

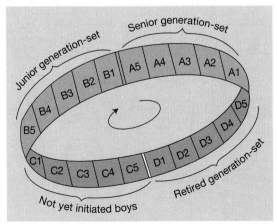

to marry—and is certainly barred from starting a family—until he has been initiated. The initiation ceremony itself illustrates the essential political and social characteristics of the age-set system. Without the authority of the elders, the ceremony cannot be held; throughout the proceedings their authority is explicit. The father-son relationship of adjacent generation-sets is emphasized, for fathers are initiating their sons.

Shavante Age-Sets. The Shavante inhabit the Mato Grosso region of Brazil. Until recently, they were extremely hostile to Brazilians of European ancestry who tried to move into their territory. It was not until the 1950s that peaceful contact with the 2,000 or so Shavante was achieved. Although the Shavante have some agriculture, they rely primarily on food collection. Wild roots, nuts, and fruits are their staple foods, and hunting is their passion.[2] The Shavante have villages, but they rarely stay in them for more than a few weeks at a time. Instead they make frequent community treks lasting six to twenty-four weeks to hunt or collect. They spend no more than four weeks a year at their gardens, which are located at least a day's journey from the villages.

Age-sets are an extremely important part of Shavante society, particularly for males. Boys emerge from the status of childhood when they are formally inducted into a named age-set and take up residence in the "bachelor hut." An induction ceremony takes place every five years, and boys from seven to twelve years of age are inducted at the same time. The five-year period of residence in the bachelor hut is relatively free of responsibility: the boys' families provide food for them, and they go out hunting and collecting when they feel like it. But during the five-year period they are instructed in hunting, weapon making, and ceremonial skills. At the end of this period, a much more elaborate series of initiation ceremonies marks the entry by these boys into a different status—that of "young men." The day they emerge from the bachelor hut for the last time, during the final rites of initiation, the whole age-set is married, each to a small girl, usually not yet mature, chosen by the boys' parents. Marriages cannot be consummated at this time, because the young men must wait until their wives are more mature. When the ceremonies are over, the young men make war clubs, for they are thought of now as the warriors of the community, and they earn the privilege of sitting in the evening village council. But they have no authority at this stage and few responsibilities.

The next stage is that of the "mature men," and when an age-set is inducted into this stage the members begin to experience some authority. It is in the mature men's council that important community decisions are made. This last status position actually consists of five consecutive age-sets (because new age-sets are formed every five years and each one continues in existence until the death of its members). Among the mature men the oldest sets are considered senior to the younger ones. Members of the most junior mature men's age-set rarely talk in the council; they assert themselves more as they progress in the system.

In contrast to the Karimojong, who have age-sets just for males, the Shavante also have them for females. Shavante girls are inducted into an age-set when boys about their age enter the bachelor hut, but they belong to the age-set in name only. They do not participate in the bachelor hut (nor do they have their own equivalent), they are not initiated, and they cannot participate in the village council, which makes community decisions. About the only thing the age-set gives them is occasional participation with males in a few ceremonies. For Shavante women, then, the age-set system does not function as an association.

Unisex Associations

Unisex, as used here, has quite a different meaning from its current connotation in our own society, where it signifies something that is suitable for both sexes. We use the word **unisex** to describe a type of association that restricts its membership to one sex, usually male. Sex as a qualification is directly related to the purpose of the unisex association. In many male unisex associations, this purpose is to strengthen the concept of male superiority and to offer men a refuge from females. In noncommercial societies, men's associations are similar to age-sets, except that there are only two sets, or stages—mature males, who are association members, and immature males, who are nonmembers. Like societies with age-sets, societies with male unisex associations are very likely to have traumatic and dramatic male ceremonies initiating males into the group of "mature" men. We will discuss these ceremonies further in the chapter on psychology and culture.

In most noncommercial societies, women have few associations perhaps because in such societies the men are dominant in the kinship, property, and political spheres of life. (There is also the possibility that anthropologists, most of whom were

A men's house in a Chimbu village in the highlands of New Guinea

men, have given women's associations less attention than men's associations.) In some partly commercialized economies, such as in West Africa, women's associations are more common.[3] Unisex associations or clubs are also a feature of very industrialized societies. The Boy Scouts and the Kiwanis, the Girl Scouts and the League of Women Voters, are cases in point. Admission to these clubs, however, is voluntary; in noncommercial and less complex societies, recruitment is more often nonvoluntary.

Mae Enga Bachelor Associations. The Mae Enga are a subgroup of about 30,000 sedentary horticulturalists living in the New Guinea highlands. Their society has received a great deal of attention from anthropologists for its practice of sexual segregation—indeed, for the strain of active hostility to women that runs through its culture.[4] It is the custom for Mae men to live in a separate, communal house. Up to the age of five, a young boy is permitted to live in his mother's house, although he is unconsciously aware of the "distance" between his father and mother. As he grows older, this awareness is made explicit by his father and elder clansmen. It is undesirable, he is told, to be so much in the company of women; it is better that he join the menfolk in their house and in their activities. As the boy grows up, the need to avoid contact with women is made abundantly clear to him. He is told that contact with menstrual blood or menstruating women, if not countered by magic rites, can "pollute" a man. It can "corrupt his vital juices so that his skin darkens and wrinkles and his flesh wastes, permanently dull his wits, and eventually lead to a slow decline and death."[5]

Because Mae culture regards a woman as potentially unclean, to say the least, it enforces strict codes of male-female behavior. These codes are designed to safeguard male integrity, strength, and possession of crops and other property. So strict are these regulations that many young men are reluctant to marry. But the elders do try to impress upon the young men their duty to marry and reproduce. The men's association attempts to regulate the males' sexual relationships. The association is said to have several purposes: to cleanse and strengthen its members; to promote their growth; to make them attractive to women; and, most important, to supervise contact between the sexes so that ultimately the "right" wives are procured for the men and the "right" children are born into the clan.

By the time he is fifteen or sixteen, a Mae youth has joined the village bachelors' association. He agrees to take scrupulous care neither to copulate with a woman nor to accept food from her hands. As a club member, he will participate in the *sanggai* rituals. Bachelors, under the supervision of senior club members, go into seclusion, in a clubhouse deep in the forest, to undergo "purification." During four days of "exercises" (which are rather similar in purpose to those of a religious retreat), each youth observes additional prohibitions to protect himself from all forms of sexuality and impurity. For instance, pork is denied him (women have cared for the pigs), and he may not look at the ground during excursions into the forest, lest he see feminine footprints or pig feces. His body will be scrubbed, his dreams discussed and interpreted. Finally, together with his club, now restored to purity and reprotected at least for a while against contamination, he will participate in organized dances and feasting with his chosen lady.

The *sanggai* festivals afford the entire clan an opportunity to display its size, solidarity, and magnificence to its enemies, whom on other occasions it fights. Hostility toward women may not be surprising in view of the fact that a man's wife and mother come from neighboring clans (the Mae clan villages are exogamous) perpetually in conflict with his own. Male-female hostility, then, seems to reflect the broader, interclan hostility. The Mae have a succinct way of describing the situation: "We marry the people we fight."[6]

Men's houses, and occasionally women's, are found among many peoples, especially in Melanesia, Polynesia, Africa, and South America. Men's associations generally involve bachelors, although older married men will often come by to instruct the youngsters and pass on the benefits of their experience. In more militant days, men's houses acted as fortresses and arsenals—even as sanctuaries for fugitives. By and large, they serve to strengthen—certainly to symbolize—male power and solidarity. As do age-sets, men's clubs often provide ties that cut across and supplement kinship bonds. Hence, they permit a given group of men in a given society to act together toward the realization of mutually agreed-upon objectives, irrespective of kin relationships.

Poro and Sande. There is usually some secrecy in all associations, as in social life in general. In the examples we discussed above, many of the details of male initiation ceremonies usually are kept secret. But more secrecy seems to be required in the *Poro* and *Sande* associations of West Africa.

The Poro and Sande associations exist in several cultural groups that speak Mande languages and are located in what is now Liberia, Sierra Leone, the Ivory Coast, and Guinea. In Guinea, the Poro and the Sande were recently declared illegal, but in the other countries they are not only legal—they are an integral part of local political structure. Membership in them is public and nonvoluntary; all men in the community must belong to the Poro, and all women must belong to the Sande.[7]

Where the Poro and the Sande associations are legal, the community has two political structures—the "secular" and the "sacred." The secular structure consists of the town chief, neighborhood and kin group headmen, and elders. The sacred structure, or *Zo*, consists of the hierarchies of "priests" in the Poro and Sande associations. Among the Kpelle of Liberia, for example, the Poro and Sande Zo take turns in assuming responsibility for dealing with in-town fighting, murder, rape, incest, and disputes over land.

So in what sense are the Poro and Sande secret? If all adults belong to them, their membership and what they do can hardly be described as secret. Furthermore, anthropologists have not only written about these associations; some have even joined them. Beryl Bellman, who joined the Poro of the Kpelle,[8] suggested that what is "secret" about these associations is the necessity for members to learn to keep secrets, particularly about how people are initiated into membership. Only when people learn to keep secrets are they considered trustworthy for participation in political life.

The Poro leadership establishes the place where the initiates will undergo scarification and live in seclusion for about a year (formerly it was three or four years). The boys are taken out of town, where they engage in a mock battle with a *ngamu* (a member of the Poro masquerading as a forest "devil") who incises marks on their necks, chests, and backs. These marks symbolize being killed and eaten by the devil; but then the initiates are "reborn." In the initiation "village" outside of town, the boys learn crafts, hunting, and the use of basic medicines. The children of the Zo are given special instruction so that they can take over the rituals from their fathers. Some are trained to perform as "devils." At the end of the year, the initiates are given Poro names, by which they will be known from then on. Secrecy is attached to events surrounding the initiates; everyone knows that the boys are not killed and eaten by the devil, but only some can speak of it. For example, women must say that the boys are in the devil's stomach; if they say otherwise, they might be killed in punishment.[9]

The initiation of females into the Sande also involves taking the initiates into the forest for a year (formerly three years). The girls not only undergo scarification; they also undergo a clitoridectomy (removal of the clitoris). Like the boys, the girls receive training in adult activities. In the years just before and during the Sande initiation (which occurs every seven years or so), the women are responsible for the moral behavior of the community. Persons who commit crimes are first brought before the women; if a man is the accused, he is tried by the Poro Zo, but a portion of any fine is given to the women.[10]

The Poro and Sande Zo are held in great respect, and the devils are viewed with fear and awe for the powers they possess. Some authors suggest that fear of the Poro and the Sande strengthens the hands of secular political authority, because chiefs and landowners occupy the most powerful positions in the associations.[11]

Secret associations are common in many areas of the world—the Pacific, North and South America, as well as various parts of Africa—although they may be voluntary organizations in some places. In Africa, according to a recent cross-cultural study, secret associations are usually involved in political activities, as are the Poro and Sande. These activities punish persons who, according to the secret society, have committed some wrongs. The fact that the punished persons almost never seem to be members of the native elite or foreign rulers supports the observation about the Poro and Sande that they typically strengthen the hand of existing political authority.[12]

Ijaw Women's Associations. Among the Ijaw of southern Nigeria, only women in the northern part of this society are organized into associations. In one northern Ijaw village there are seven women's associations.[13] Once a married woman shows herself capable of supporting a household independent of her mother-in-law, which she does by engaging in marketing and trading, she has to belong to the women's association linked to her husband's patrilineage. Membership in such an association is nonvoluntary; all eligible women must join, and members are fined if they do not come to meetings or come late.

The women's associations act as mediators in disputes and impose punishments even in cases that have gone to court. For example, an association may impose fines for "crimes" such as defaming a woman's character or adultery. An association may also adopt rules for proper behavior. Judgments and rules are arrived at by consensus of all the women members. If a punished member does not accept a judgment, the other members might get together and taunt the woman or take some important item

The Samba clubs or "schools" of Rio de Janeiro, Brazil, are voluntary associations that compete during carnival time in the Sambadrome before hundreds of thousands of spectators. Before the competition a Samba "school" participates in a parade. To become champion is like winning the Superbowl in the United States.

from her house and refuse to have anything to do with her.

Some of the larger associations also act as lending institutions, using their cash reserves from fines to lend to members or nonmembers at an interest rate of 50 percent or more. Even a male in debt to the association might be held captive in his own house until he pays his debt. (It is no wonder, then, that few resist an association's judgment for long.) Although it is not clear why women's associations such as the Ijaw's are common in West Africa, one of the factors that may have been important is the women's participation in marketing and trade, which allows them to be financially independent of men.

We shall see in the next section that women are increasingly forming voluntary self-help groups to improve themselves economically.

VOLUNTARY ASSOCIATIONS

Voluntary associations such as the military associations of the Cheyenne of North America (see below)

may be found in some relatively simple societies. But voluntary associations tend to be more common in stratified and complex societies, presumably because stratified societies are composed of people with many different, and often competing, interests. We deal here with some examples of voluntary associations that are not familiar in American experience.

Military Associations

Military associations in noncommercial societies may be compared to our own American Legion or Veterans of Foreign War posts. They all seem to exist to unite members through their common experiences as warriors, to glorify the activities of war, and to perform certain services for the community. Membership in such associations is usually voluntary and based on the achieved criterion of participation in war. Among the North American Plains Indians, military societies were common. The Cheyenne, for example, had military associations that were not ranked by age, but were open to any boy or man ready to go to war.[14]

In the beginning of the nineteenth century the Cheyenne had five military associations: the Fox, the Dog, the Shield, the Elk (or Hoof Rattle), and the Bowstring (or Contrary). The last-named association was annihilated by the Pawnee in the middle of the nineteenth century. Later, two new associations were established, the Wolf and the Northern Crazy Dogs. Although the various associations may have had different costumes, songs, and dances, they were alike in their internal organization, each being headed by four leaders who were among the most important war chiefs.

Several of the Cheyenne military associations selected four virgin daughters of tribal leaders to serve as "maids of honor." These girls participated in the associations' ceremonies and sat with the war chiefs during council meetings. Although women had no political authority, they were highly respected among the Cheyenne. The maids of honor of the military associations were looked upon as reflecting the ideals of female chastity and deportment. So important was the virtue of female chastity among the Cheyenne that a defiled maid of honor was believed to bring bad luck to the warriors of the association. As a result, the Dog and Contrary associations were unwilling to take the risk of having maids of honor affiliated with them.

When various Plains groups were confined to reservations, the military associations lost many of their old functions. But they did not entirely disappear. For example, among the Lakota, warrior soci-

DO SEPARATE WOMEN'S ASSOCIATIONS INCREASE WOMEN'S STATUS AND POWER?

Some women's associations, like those of the Ijaw of southern Nigeria, are reported to have considerable power. Do women generally have more power where women create and join their own associations? We might assume that the existence of such organizations would increase the status of women overall, or at least lead to more equality with men. But it could also be argued the other way around, that "separate" does not generally lead to more equality; it may just increase separateness. As far as we know, researchers have not yet tried to assess the cross-cultural effect of women's associations on female status in various domains of life, but there has been one cross-cultural attempt to see if the presence of women's associations predicts various aspects of women's participation in the political process.

Marc Howard Ross looked at four aspects of women's political participation: (1) the degree of inequality between women's and men's participation in public or community decision making; (2) the degree to which women participate in politics privately, (3) the degree to which women have access to positions of authority, and (4) the degree to which women have separate associations that are under their exclusive control. It is this last domain that concerns us here. Does the presence of separate women's associations increase women's participation in public decision making and their access to positions of authority? Ross's cross-cultural data indicate that the answer is no. The presence of separate women's organizations *does not* generally increase the participation of women in public decision making, their access to positions of authority, or even their private participation in politics. This is not to say that women in organizations do not have influence. They do, but probably only or mainly within their organizations. The influ-ence of women in their organizations, however, does not carry over into other political arenas.

Of course, we might need to consider other possible factors in future research. Perhaps women's participation in political arenas is more likely if female organizations control important economic resources. Such resources may give women more leverage politically. Also, some types of female organizations may have more power than others; for example, stand-alone organizations may have more power than those that are connected to male organizations. But it is also possible that adding these additional conditions would not change the basic finding—separate female organizations (perhaps because they are separate) do not have any impact on women's participation in other political arenas.

Recently, people in the United States have started to discuss a related issue—the possible effects of female "separateness" on

eties continue to be an important part of social life because many men and women have engaged in military activity on behalf of the United States in World Wars I and II, in Korea and Vietnam, and in Desert Storm. Returning soldiers are welcomed with traditional songs of honor and victory dances.[15]

Regional Associations

Regional associations are clubs that bring together migrants from a common geographical background. Thus, they are often found in urban centers, which traditionally have attracted settlers from rural areas. In the United States, for example, migrants from rural Appalachia have formed associations in Chicago and Detroit. Many of these organizations have become vocal political forces in municipal government. Regional associations often form even when migrants have come from a considerable distance. For example, in the Chinatowns of the United States and Canada, there were many associations women's success. For example, do separate math and science classes for women lead to more equality between women and men in academic performance, in obtaining advanced degrees in math and science, and in access to high-paying positions in those areas? It is well known that women are very underrepresented in the math and physical science professions in the United States. For example, only 11 percent of persons who hold doctorates in physics and 16 percent in computer science are women; but in the social sciences and humanities the numbers of men and women are approximately equal.

These differences could be mostly a result of social conditions that discourage females in various subjects and professions. Researchers have found that teachers of math and science pay more attention to boys. When boys give wrong answers, teachers are apt to challenge them; when girls give wrong answers, teachers tend to express sympathy. Boys are more likely to operate scientific equipment; girls are more likely to take notes. In the seventh grade, girls perform similarly to boys in math and science, but girls display less confidence in their abilities. By the time they graduate from high school, women have taken fewer math and science courses, so they are at a disadvantage for continuing in those fields.

If the dampening effects on women are social, or mostly social, what can be done? Because current research suggests that girls do best in learning science and math without boys, some researchers have advocated separate math and science activities (classes and clubs). So, for example, voluntary girls' clubs (Operation SMART) have been set up in 240 locations to interest elementary and junior high school girls in science. A majority of the girls from those schools voluntarily attend. Moreover, many of them now say they want to go into science. Whether they stay in science, or how well they do if they stay, is not clear yet. But if these programs work, we would have to conclude that "separate" is more equal than "together."

The two situations we have described here do not seem to be parallel in their effects on women's status. Separate women's associations do not make (by themselves) for equality between the genders in political participation. But separate training for girls in math and science may make for more equality. What is different about the two situations? At least one thing is different. Separate women's associations are usually nonvoluntary; women more or less have to join because that's how the society structures what women can do. Separate training for females in math and science is usually voluntary; girls may opt for the separateness in order to acquire the skills and the confidence they need to move into arenas *open* to both genders. In other words, when achievement and not gender defines how far you can go, temporary separateness for women might increase the likelihood of gender equality in professions that do not have it now.

Sources: *Marc Howard Ross, "Female Political Participation: A Cross-Cultural Explanation,"* American Anthropologist, *88 (1986): 843–58;* "Women in Science '93: Gender and the Culture of Science," Science, April 16, 1993, 383–430.

based on district of origin in China as well as on surname. The regional and family organizations were in turn incorporated into more inclusive ethnic associations, as we shall see later in this chapter.[16]

William Mangin described the role of regional associations in helping rural migrants adapt to urban life in Lima, Peru.[17] During the 1950s, Mangin studied a group of migrants from the rural mountains, the *serranos* from Ancash. Typically these *serranos,* about 120,000 in number, lived in a slum-like urban settlement called a *barriada*. The *barriada* was not officially recognized by either the national government or the city authorities. Accordingly, it lacked all normal city services, such as water supply, garbage removal, and police protection. Its inhabitants had left their rural birthplaces for reasons typical of such population movements, wherever they occur. These reasons were social and economic; most were related to population and land pressure, but the higher expectations associated with the

WHY DO STREET GANGS DEVELOP, AND WHY ARE THEY VIOLENT?

The street gangs of young people that we read and hear about so often are voluntary associations. They are a little like age-sets in that the members are all about the same age, but they are unlike age-sets in being voluntary and they do not "graduate" through life stages together. Nobody has to join, although there may be strong social pressure to join the neighborhood gang. Gangs have a clear set of values, goals, roles, group functions, symbols, and initiations. Street gangs are also often like military associations in their commitment to violence in the defense of gang interests.

Violent street gangs are found in many U.S. cities, particularly in poor neighborhoods. But poverty alone does not appear sufficient to explain the existence of gangs. For example, there was plenty of poverty in Mexico, but gangs did not develop there. In Mexico there was a *palomilla* (age-cohort) tradition; age-mates hung out together and continued their friendship well into adulthood, but there were no gangs as we know them. Mexican American gangs did develop in the *barrios* of cities such as Los Angeles. When we realize that *most* youths in poor neighborhoods do not join gangs, it is clear that poor neighborhoods cannot explain gangs. (It is estimated that only 3 to 10 percent of Mexican American young people join gangs.)

But why do some young people join and not others? If we look at who joins a gang, it seems to be those children who are sub-ject to the most domestic stress. The gang "joiners" are likely to come from poor families, have several siblings, and have no father in the household. They seem to have had difficulty in school and have gotten into trouble early. What about gangs appeals to them? Most adolescents in this country have a difficult time deciding who they are and what kind of person they want to be, but young people who join gangs seem to have more identity problems. One eighteen-year-old said he "joined the gang for my ego to go higher," reflecting a low self-esteem. Those who are raised in female-centered households seem to be looking for a way to show how "masculine" they are. They look up to the tough male street gang members

big city—better education, social mobility, wage labor—were also compelling considerations.

Typically also, the *serranos* from Ancash formed a regional association. Club membership was open to both sexes. Men generally controlled the executive positions, and club leaders were often men who achieved political power in their hometowns. Women, who had relatively less economic and social freedom, nevertheless played an important part in club activities.

The *serrano* regional association performed three main services for its members. First, it lobbied the central government on matters of community importance—for example, the supplying of sewers, clinics, and similar public services. A club member had to follow a piece of legislation through the channels of government to make certain it was not forgotten or abandoned. Second, the *serrano* association assisted in acculturating newly arrived *serranos* to the urban life in Lima. The most noticeable rural traits—coca chewing, and hairstyle and clothing peculiarities—were the first to disappear, with the men generally able to adapt faster than the women. The association also provided opportunities for fuller contact with the national culture. And finally, the group organized social activities such as fiestas, acted as the clearinghouse for information transmitted to and from the home area, and supplied a range of other services to help migrants adapt to their new environment while retaining ties to their birthplace.

The functions of regional associations may change over time as social conditions change. For example, during the plantation period in Hawaii, many and want to act like them. But getting into a gang requires initiation. Most gangs have their own stylized rituals; for example, Mexican American gangs physically beat the initiate, who must show bravery and courage. As happens in most initiation ceremonies, the gang initiate identifies even more strongly with the group afterward. So, belonging to a gang may make some youths feel as if they belong to something important. This is a kind of psychological adjustment, but is it adaptive? Does being in a gang help such youths survive in a neighborhood where young men are often killed? Or are gang members *less* likely to survive? We really don't know the answers to those questions.

Why did gangs develop in the United States and not in Mexico? Were there some things different about life for Mexican Ameri-cans in the cities of the United States? Life in the United States was more difficult in several respects. First, many Mexican immigrants had to settle for very low pay and housing in marginal areas of the city. Second, they were subject to a lot of social and job discrimination. Third, they were immersed in a new culture that differed in many ways from their own. The young people who were least able to cope with these stresses were probably most likely to join gangs. But what explains the culture of violence of these gangs? Some scholars have suggested that the need to show exaggerated "masculine" behavior is a response to the absence of male models in the household. The association of many young men who have this same need may explain the violence of gangs. If aggressiveness is part of the male role (for example, until recently only males were allowed to engage in military combat), then a young man who wants to exhibit his masculinity may be extremely aggressive.

We need much more research to uncover why gangs develop more often in some societies than in others, and why they often are violent. Are there places where aggressiveness is not so much part of the male role, and are they therefore less likely to have violent gangs?

Sources: *James Diego Vigil, "Group Processes and Street Identity: Adolescent Chicano Gang Members," Ethos, 16 (1988): 421–45; James Diego Vigil, "Mexican Americans: Growing Up on the Streets of Los Angeles," in Melvin Ember, Carol R. Ember, and David Levinson, eds., Portraits of Culture: Ethnographic Originals (Englewood Cliffs, NJ: Prentice Hall, 1994). Prentice Hall/Simon & Schuster Custom Publishing. Carol R. Ember and Melvin Ember, "Issues in Cross-Cultural Studies of Interpersonal Violence,"* Violence and Victims, 8 (1994): 217–33.

Filipino migrants joined hometown associations that served as mutual aid societies. As more and more Filipinos went to Hawaii, however, more people had kin to whom they could turn. The hometown associations continue to have some economic functions, such as assistance in times of emergency, serious illness, or death, and some scholarship aid, but meetings are infrequent and most members do not attend. Those members who are active seem to want the recognition and prestige that can be attained through leadership positions in the hometown association, which is much more than they can achieve in the wider Hawaiian arena.[18]

Although regional clubs may help to integrate their members into a more complex urban or changing environment, the presence of many such groups may increase divisiveness and rivalry among groups. In some areas the smaller groups have banded together and become quite powerful. For example, within each Chinatown of a major U.S. or Canadian city, the various regional and family associations formed a Chinese Benevolent Association. This larger association, usually controlled by the wealthiest Chinese merchants, acted to oversee business, settle disputes, and to organize against discrimination from the outside.[19] Thus, by banding together, the regional and family associations formed ethnic associations.

Ethnic Associations

There are many types of ethnic associations or interest groups, and they are found in cities all over the world. Membership in these associations is based

In most major cities with Chinatown, as in San Francisco, many regional and family associations merged together to form larger associations, like Hop Sing Tong, a fraternal organization established in 1870 that acted to oversee business, settle disputes, and fight against discrimination.

on ethnicity. Ethnic associations are particularly widespread in urban centers of West Africa. There, accelerated cultural change—reflected in altered economic arrangements, in technological advances, and in new urban living conditions—has weakened kinship relations and other traditional sources of support and solidarity.[20] Sometimes it is difficult to say whether a particular association is ethnic or regional in origin; it may be both.

Tribal unions are frequently found in Nigeria and Ghana. These are typical of most such associations in that they are extraterritorial (that is, they recruit members who have left their tribal locations), they have a formal constitution, and they have been formed to meet certain needs arising out of conditions of urban life. One such need is to keep members in touch with their traditional culture. The Ibo State Union, for example, in addition to providing mutual aid and financial support in case of unemployment, sickness, or death, performs the service "of fostering and keeping alive an interest in tribal song, history, language and moral beliefs and thus maintaining a person's attachment to his native town or village."[21] Some tribal unions collect money to improve conditions in their ancestral homes. Education, for example, is an area of particular concern. Others publish newsletters that report members' activities. Most unions have a young membership that exercises a powerful democratizing influence in tribal councils, and the organizations provide a springboard for those with national political aspirations.

Friendly societies differ from tribal unions in that their objectives are confined for the most part to mutual aid. Such a club was formed by the wives of Kru migrants in Freetown, Sierra Leone. Kru men normally go to sea—still a hazardous occupation. The club is classified into three grades. An admission fee permits entry into the lowest grade. Elevation to higher grades depends on further donations. At the death of a member or her husband, the family receives a lump sum commensurate with her status in the club. The Yoruba Friendly Society in Nigeria uses another approach to mutual aid. At regular intervals all members contribute a fixed sum, and the total is given to one member at a time. In this way, significant amounts of capital are available, in rotation, for each member to buy trading stock, to purchase expensive new clothes (to keep up appearances in a government post, for example), or even to pay a bride price. Rotating credit associations, such as the Yoruba Friendly Society, are found throughout Nigeria and in other countries of sub-Saharan Africa, and in Southeast Asia as well.

West African occupational clubs also fall into the ethnic category. They are African versions of trade unions, organized along tribal as well as craft lines. Their principal concern is the status and remuneration of their members as workers. The Motor Drivers' Union of Keta, in Ghana, was formed to fund insurance and legal costs, to contribute to medical care in case of accident or illness, and to help pay for funeral expenses.

Finally, clubs that concentrate on entertainment and recreation are very common in West Africa. The dancing *compin* of Sierra Leone is typical. Kenneth Little described it as

> a group of young men and women concerned with the performance of "plays" of traditional music and dancing and with the raising of money for mutual benefit. . . . A "play" is generally given in connection with some important event . . . or as part of the ceremonies celebrating a wedding or a funeral. The general public as well as the persons honored by the performance are expected to donate money to the compin on these occasions. Money is also collected in the form of weekly subscriptions from the members.[22]

Some observers have suggested that the widespread incidence of ethnic associations in West Africa has virtually amounted to a resurgence of tribalism. The presence of such interest groups in urban areas has indeed seemed to slow the development of national identity and loyalty. On the other hand, the evidence indicates that these clubs serve important adaptive and integrative functions for both men and women, just as regional associations do in other areas of the world. As Little stated, "Their combination of modern and traditional

The Kafaina women's savings and loan associations in New Guinea often encourage relatives to start "daughter" organizations. At a ceremony for the new organization a "daughter" doll is displayed.

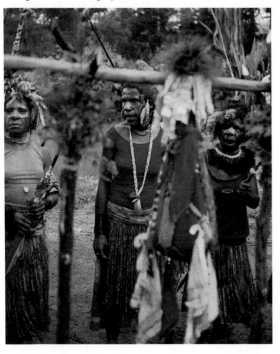

traits constitutes a cultural bridge which conveys, metaphorically speaking, the tribal individual from one kind of sociological universe to another."[23]

Multi-Ethnic Associations

Although many voluntary associations draw on people from the same regional or ethnic background, increasingly in the modern world voluntary groups draw members from many different backgrounds. For example, the Kafaina, or *Wok Meri* ("women's work"), associations in Papua New Guinea are savings and loan associations that link thousands of women from different tribal areas.[24] Originally, there were smaller groups that started as savings associations in particular localities, but links between groups developed as women who married out of a village encouraged a relative back home or in another village to start a "daughter" group. "Mother-daughter" visits between groups can last for three days as one group hosts another and the groups exchange money. All money received from another group is placed in a netbag that is hidden and cannot be touched, so the savings grow over time. When a group accumulates a certain amount, a building the size of a men's house is built for the association and a very large ceremony is held. Does the development of these women's associations translate into new power for women in their traditionally male-dominated societies? That has yet to happen (see the box titled "Do Separate Women's Associations Increase Women's Status and Power?"). Apparently frustrated by their exclusion from local politics, the women are increasingly participating in the Kafaina movement. They may have intergroup exchanges and they may now engage in public speaking, but so far their arena is still separate from the men's arena.

Just as the Kafaina women's associations seem to be a response to perceived deprivation, the formation of associations with multi-ethnic or regional membership is not unusual where colonialism or other political domination is recognized as a common problem. For example, in Alaska in the 1960s Native Americans felt threatened by proposals for economic development that they thought would threaten their subsistence resources. Many regional and ethnic associations formed during this crisis, but perhaps more significant (from the point of view of achieving substantial compensation and titles to land) was the formation of a pan-Alaska association called the Alaska Federation of Natives. What made the amalgamation possible? Like the leaders of multi-ethnic movements in many places, the leaders at the highest levels seem to have had a lot of things in common. They were educated, urban dwellers who worked at professional occupations. Perhaps most important, many of them had attended the same schools.[25]

Multi-ethnic and multiregional associations have often been involved in independence movements all over the world. Often, revolutionary political parties develop out of such associations and lead the efforts to gain independence. Why independence movements develop in some places but not in others is not yet understood.

Other Interest Groups

Societies such as the United States consist of people from many different ethnic backgrounds. Often there are voluntary ethnic and regional associations. But the majority of the voluntary associations in our own and other complex societies have members who belong because of common, achieved interests. These common interests include occupation (so we have trade unions and professional associations), political affiliation (as in national political parties and political action groups), recreation (such as sports and game clubs, fan clubs, music and theater groups), charities, and social clubs. The larger and more diversified the society, the more different kinds of associations there are. They bring together sets of people with common interests, aspirations, or qualifications, and they provide opportunities to work for social causes, for self-improvement, or to satisfy a need for new and stimulating experiences. We join clubs and other interest groups because we want to achieve particular goals. Not the least of such goals is identification with a "corporate" group and through it the acquisition of status and influence.

Joining clubs is much more important in some societies than in others. Norway is an example of a society with a rich organizational life. Even in areas with small communities there are many different clubs. For example, Douglas Caulkins found that in the municipality of Volda, a town of about 7,000, there were 197 organizations. People were expected to be active in at least a couple of organizations, and these groups met regularly. In fact, there were so many meetings that organizations were expected to coordinate their calendars so that the meetings would not interfere with one another.[26] Why some societies, like Norway, have so much involvement with voluntary associations is not well understood. Nor do we understand what the consequences of such involvement may be. Norway happens to have a particularly low rate of crime and it scores high on other indicators of social and economic health.[27] Does the complexity of its organizational life, and its many overlapping involvements, play a role in its social health? We don't yet know, because cross-cultural studies to test that possibility have not yet been done.

EXPLAINING VARIATION IN ASSOCIATIONS

Anthropologists are not content to provide descriptions of the structure and operation of human associations. They also seek to understand why different types of associations develop. For example, what may account for the development of age-set systems?

S. N. Eisenstadt's comparative study of African age-sets led him to the hypothesis that when kinship groups fail to carry out functions important to the integration of society—such as political, educational, and economic functions—age-set systems arise to fill the void. Age-set systems may provide a workable solution to a society's need for functional divisions among its members, because age is a criterion that can be applied to all members of society in the allocation of roles.[28] But it is not at all clear why age-set systems arise to fill the void left by lack of kinship organization. Many societies have kin structures that are limited in scope, yet the majority of them have not adopted an age-set system.

B. Bernardi, in his critical evaluation of Nilo-Hamitic age-set systems,[29] also suggested that age-set systems arise to make up for a deficiency in social organization. But, in contrast with Eisenstadt, Bernardi specifically suggested why more social organization is necessary and what particular deficiencies in the previous form of organization should favor development of age-sets. He hypothesized that age-set systems arise in societies that have a history of territorial rivalry, lack central authority, and have only dispersed kin groups. When all three factors are present, he argued, the need for a mechanism of territorial integration is supplied by an age-set system.

One cross-cultural study suggests that territorial rivalry, as indicated by warfare, may favor the development of age-set systems, but this study found no evidence to support Bernardi's hypothesis that age-sets develop in societies that lack central authority and have only dispersed kin groups.[30] So it does not seem that age-set societies are deficient in political or kinship organization. An alternative explanation, which is consistent with the cross-cultural evidence, is that age-set systems arise in societies that have both frequent warfare and local groups that change in size and composition throughout the year. In such situations, men may not always be able to rely on their kinsmen for co-operation in warfare because the kinsmen are not always nearby. Age-sets, however, can provide allies *wherever* one happens to be.[31] This interpretation suggests that age-set systems arise *in addition to,* rather than as alternatives to, kin-based and politically based forms of integration.[32]

As for voluntary associations whose membership is variably ascribed (that is, determined at birth but not found in all persons of a given age-sex category), it is difficult to say exactly what causes them to arise. As already noted, there are suggestions that voluntary associations of all types become more numerous (and more important) as the society harboring them advances in technology, complexity, and scale. No definitive evidence is yet available to support this explanation, but the following trends seem to be sufficiently established to merit consideration.

First, there is urbanization. Developing societies are becoming urban, and as their cities grow, so does the number of people separated from their traditional kinship ties and local customs. It is not surprising, then, that the early voluntary associations should be mutual-aid societies, established first to take over kin obligations in case of death, and later broadening their benefits in other directions. In this respect, the recent associations of the developing African societies closely resemble the early English laboring-class associations. Those clubs also served to maintain the city migrant's contacts with former traditions and culture. The regional associations in Latin America resemble the regional associations of European immigrants in the United States. Such associations also seem to arise in response to the migrant's or immigrant's needs in the new home.

Second, there is an economic factor. Migrants and immigrants try to adapt to new economic conditions, and group interests in the new situations have to be organized, promoted, and protected.

Why, then, do variably ascribed associations tend to be replaced by clubs of the achieved category in highly industrialized societies? Perhaps the strong focus on specialization in industrialized societies is reflected in the formation of specialized groups. Possibly the emphasis on achievement in industrialized societies is another contributing factor. Perhaps, too, the trend toward uniformity, encouraged by mass marketing and the mass media, is progressively weakening the importance of regional and ethnic distinctions. The result seems to be that the more broadly based organizations are being replaced by more narrowly based associations that are more responsive to particular needs not being met by the institutions of mass society.

▼ SUMMARY

1. Associations or interest groups have the following characteristics in common: (a) some kind of formal, institutional structure exists; (b) some people are excluded from membership; (c) membership is based on commonly shared interests or purposes; and (d) there is a clearly discernible sense of mutual pride and belonging. Membership varies according to whether it is voluntary or not and according to whether the qualities of members are universally ascribed, variably ascribed, or achieved.

2. Age-sets are nonvoluntary associations whose members belong because of universally ascribed characteristics. They are composed of groups of persons of similar age and sex who move through life's stages together. Entry into the system is usually by an initiation ceremony. Transitions to new stages are usually marked by succession rituals. Unisex associations restrict membership to one sex. In noncommercial societies membership in such associations (usually male) is generally nonvoluntary.

3. Regional and ethnic organizations are voluntary associations whose members belong because of variably ascribed characteristics. Both usually occur in societies where technological advance is accelerating, bringing with it economic and social complexity. Despite a variety of types, regional and ethnic associations have in common an emphasis on (a) helping members adapt to new conditions; (b) keeping members in touch with home-area traditions; and (c) promoting improved living conditions for members who have recently migrated to urban areas.

4. Associations whose members belong because of variably ascribed characteristics tend to be replaced in highly industrialized societies by associations whose membership is based on achieved qualities.

▼ GLOSSARY TERMS

achieved qualities   ascribed qualities   universally ascribed qualities

age-grade   associations   variably ascribed qualities

age-set   unisex association

▼ CRITICAL QUESTIONS

1. How could young people who might join gangs be encouraged not to?
2. What associations do you belong to and why?
3. Many formerly unisex associations have opened their membership to the opposite sex. What might be the results of this change?

▼ SUGGESTED READING

BERNARDI, B. "The Age-System of the Nilo-Hamitic Peoples." *Africa,* 22 (1952): 316–32. A theoretical discussion of why age-set systems occur in some societies and not in others.

CAULKINS, D. D., "Norwegians: Cooperative Individualists." In M. Ember, C. R. Ember, and D. Levinson, eds., *Portraits of Culture: Ethnographic Originals* (Englewood Cliffs, NJ: Prentice Hall, 1994). Prentice Hall/Simon & Schuster Custom Publishing. This narrative of fieldwork in two coastal towns describes how the numerous voluntary organizations structure much of social life. Personal profiles illustrate the diversity of life-styles. Particular attention is paid to the role of women's organizations.

EISENSTADT, S. N. *From Generation to Generation: Age Groups and Social Structure.* New York: Free Press, 1956. A comparative and theoretical analysis of age groups in different societies. Chapters 2–5 give a detailed presentation of age groupings in a wide variety of societies.

LOWIE, R. H. *Primitive Society.* New York: Liveright, 1970 (originally published 1920). A classic comparative study of various elements of social organization. Chapters 10 and 11 contain comparative discussions of clubs and age groups in simpler societies.

RITTER, M. "The Conditions Favoring Age-Set Organization." *Journal of Anthropological Research,* 36 (1980): 87–104. Evaluates the various theories about the development of age-sets and presents a new theory, which is supported by cross-cultural evidence.

THOMPSON, R. H. "Chinatowns: Immigrant Communities in Transition." In M. Ember, C. R. Ember, and D. Levinson, eds., *Portraits of Culture: Ethnographic Originals* (Englewood Cliffs, NJ: Prentice Hall, 1994). Prentice Hall/Simon & Schuster Custom Publishing. The author discusses how regional, familial, and ethnic associations have played important roles in the changes that have occurred in Chinatowns in the United States and Canada.

▼ NOTES

[1]Neville Dyson-Hudson, *Karimojong Politics* (Oxford: Clarendon Press, 1966), p. 155. This section draws from this source.

[2]This section is based on David Maybury-Lewis, *Akwe-Shavante Society* (Oxford: Clarendon Press, 1967).

[3]Nancy B. Leis, "Women in Groups: Ijaw Women's Associations," in Michelle Z. Rosaldo and Louise Lamphere, eds., *Woman, Culture, and Society* (Stanford, CA: Stanford University Press, 1974), pp. 223–42.

[4]M. J. Meggitt, "Male-Female Relationships in the Highlands of Australian New Guinea," *American Anthropologist*, 66 (special issue, 1964): 204–24.

[5]Ibid., p. 207. For why men in some societies may fear sex with women, see Carol R. Ember, "Men's Fear of Sex with Women: A Cross-Cultural Study," *Sex Roles*, 4 (1978): 657–78.

[6]Meggitt, "Male-Female Relationships in the Highlands of Australian New Guinea," p. 218.

[7]Beryl L. Bellman, *The Language of Secrecy: Symbols and Metaphors in Poro Ritual* (New Brunswick, NJ: Rutgers University Press, 1984), pp. 8, 25–28, 33.

[8]Ibid., p. 8.

[9]Ibid., pp. 8, 80–88.

[10]Ibid., pp. 33, 80; also Caroline H. Bledsoe, *Women and Marriage in Kpelle Society* (Stanford, CA: Stanford University Press, 1980), p. 67.

[11]Kenneth Little, "The Political Function of the Poro," *Africa*, 35 (1965): 349–65; and 36 (1966): 62–71; Bledsoe, *Women and Marriage in Kpelle Society*, pp. 68–70.

[12]Karen Paige Ericksen, "Male and Female Age Organizations and Secret Societies in Africa," *Behavior Science Research*, 23 (1989): 234–64.

[13]Leis, "Women in Groups."

[14]E. Adamson Hoebel, *The Cheyennes: Indians of the Great Plains* (New York: Holt, Rinehart & Winston, 1960).

[15]William K. Powers and Marla N. Powers, "Lakota: A Study in Cultural Continuity," in Melvin Ember, Carol R. Ember, and David Levinson, eds., *Portraits of Culture: Ethnographic Originals* (Englewood Cliffs, NJ: Prentice Hall, 1994). Prentice Hall/Simon & Schuster Custom Publishing.

[16]Richard H. Thompson, "Chinatowns: Immigrant Communities in Transition," in Melvin Ember, Carol R. Ember, and David Levinson, eds., *Portraits of Culture: Ethnographic Originals* (Englewood Cliffs, NJ: Prentice Hall, 1994). Prentice Hall/Simon & Schuster Custom Publishing.

[17]William P. Mangin, "The Role of Regional Associations in the Adaptation of Rural Migrants to Cities in Peru," in Dwight B. Heath and Richard N. Adams, eds., *Contemporary Cultures and Societies of Latin America* (New York: Random House, 1965), pp. 311–23.

[18]Jonathan Y. Okamura, "Filipino Hometown Associations in Hawaii," *Ethnology*, 22 (1983): 341–53.

[19]Thompson, "Chinatowns."

[20]See Kenneth Little, *West African Urbanization* (New York: Cambridge University Press, 1965); and Claude Meillassoux, *Urbanization of an African Community* (Seattle: University of Washington Press, 1968).

[21]Kenneth Little, "The Role of Voluntary Associations in West African Urbanization," *American Anthropologist*, 59 (1957): 582. The rest of this section draws on this source.

[22]Ibid., pp. 586–87.

[23]Ibid., p. 593.

[24]Wayne Warry, "Kafaina: Female Wealth and Power in Chuave, Papua New Guinea," *Oceania*, 57 (1986): 4–21.

[25]Alexander M. Ervin, "Styles and Strategies of Leadership During the Alaskan Native Land Claims Movement: 1959–71," *Anthropologica*, 29 (1987): 21–38.

[26]D. Douglas Caulkins, "Norwegians: Cooperative Individualists," in Melvin Ember, Carol R. Ember, and David Levinson, eds., *Portraits of Culture: Ethnographic Originals* (Englewood Cliffs, NJ: Prentice Hall, 1994). Prentice Hall/Simon & Schuster Custom Publishing.

[27]Raoul Naroll, *The Moral Order: An Introduction to the Human Situation* (Beverly Hills, CA: Sage Publications, 1983), pp. 74–75.

[28]S. N. Eisenstadt, "African Age Groups," *Africa*, 24 (1954): 102.

[29]B. Bernardi, "The Age-System of the Nilo-Hamitic Peoples," *Africa*, 22 (1952): 316–32.

[30]Madeline Lattman Ritter, "The Conditions Favoring Age-Set Organization," *Journal of Anthropological Research*, 36 (1980): 87–104.

[31]Ibid.

[32]For an explanation of age-sets among North American Plains Indians, see Jeffery R. Hanson, "Age-Set Theory and Plains Indian Age-Grading: A Critical Review and Revision," *American Ethnologist*, 15 (1988): 349–64.

Political Life: Social Order and Disorder

For people in the United States, the phrase *political life* has many connotations. It may call to mind the various branches of government: the executive branch, from the president on the national level to governors on the state level to mayors on the local level; legislative institutions, from Congress to state legislatures to city councils; and administrative bureaus, from federal-government departments to local agencies.

Political life may also evoke thoughts of political parties, interest groups, lobbying, campaigning, and voting. In other words, when people living in the United States think of political life, they may think first of "politics," the activities (not always apparent) that influence who is elected or appointed to political office, what public policies are established, how they get established, and who benefits from those policies.

But *political life* involves even more than government and politics in the United States and many other countries. Political life also involves ways of preventing or resolving troubles and disputes both within and outside the society. Internally, a complex society such as ours may employ mediation or arbitration to resolve industrial disputes, a police force to prevent crimes or track down criminals, and courts and a penal system to deal with lawbreakers as well as with social conflict in general. Externally, such a society may establish embassies in other nations and develop and utilize its armed forces both to maintain security and to support domestic and foreign interests.

By means of all these informal and formal political mechanisms, complex societies establish social order and minimize, or at least deal with, social disorder.

Formal governments have become more and more widespread around the world over the last 100 years, as powerful colonizing countries have imposed political systems upon others or as people less formally organized realized that they needed governmental mechanisms to deal with the larger world. But many societies known to anthropology did not have political officials or political parties or courts or armies. Indeed, the band or village was the largest autonomous political unit in 50 percent of the societies in the ethnographic record, as of the times they were first described. And those units were only informally organized; that is, they did not have individuals or agencies formally authorized to make and implement policy or resolve disputes. Does this mean they did not have political life? If we mean political life as we know it in our own society, then the answer has to be that they did not. But if we look beyond our formal institutions and mechanisms—if we ask what functions these institutions and mechanisms perform—we find that all societies have had political activities and beliefs that are ways of creating and maintaining social order and coping with social disorder.

Many of the kinds of groups we discussed in the three previous chapters (families, descent groups, and associations) have political functions. But when anthropologists talk about *political organization* or *political life,* they are particularly focusing on activities and beliefs pertaining to *territorial groups.* Territorial groups, in whose behalf political activities may be organized, range from small communities (bands, villages) to large communities (towns, cities) to multilocal groups such as districts or regions, entire nations, or even groups of nations.

As we shall see, the different types of political organization, as well as how people participate in politics and how they cope with conflict, are often strongly linked to variation in food-getting, economy, and social stratification.

VARIATION IN TYPES OF POLITICAL ORGANIZATION

▼

Societies in the ethnographic record vary in *level of political integration* (the largest territorial group on whose behalf political activities are organized) and in the degree to which political authority is centralized or concentrated in the integrated group. When we describe the political integration of particular societies in this section, we focus on their traditional political systems. In many societies known to anthropology, the small community (band or village) was traditionally the largest territorial group on whose behalf political activities were organized. The authority structure in such societies did not involve any centralization: there was no political authority whose jurisdiction included more than one community. In other societies known to anthropology, political activities were traditionally organized sometimes on behalf of a multilocal group, but there was no permanent authority at the top. And in still other societies known to anthropology, political activities were often traditionally organized on behalf of multilocal territorial groups, and there was a centralized or supreme political authority at the top. In the modern world, every society has been incorporated into some larger, centralized political system. With a handful of exceptions, there are no politically autonomous bands or tribes or chiefdoms in the world any more.

Many anthropologists classify societies, present and past, in terms of the highest level of political integration that occurs and in terms of the nature of the political authority structure. For example, Elman Service suggested that most societies can be classified into four principal types of political organization: bands, tribes, chiefdoms, and states.[1] We shall examine how political life is organized in each of these types of society in order to see how societies vary in the ways they try to create and maintain social order. We may use the present tense in our discussion, because that is the convention in ethnographic writing, but the reader should remember that most societies that used to be organized at the band, tribe, and chiefdom levels are now incorporated into larger political entities.

Band Organization

Some societies were composed of fairly small and usually nomadic groups of people. Each of these groups is conventionally called a **band** and is politically autonomous. That is, in **band organization** the local group or community is the largest group that acts as a political unit. Because most recent food collectors had band organization, some anthropologists contend that this type of political organization characterized nearly all societies before the development of agriculture, or until about 10,000 years ago. But we have to remember that almost all of the described food-collecting societies are or were located in marginal environments; and almost all were affected by more dominant societies nearby.[2] So it is possible that what we call "band organization" may not have been typical of food collectors in the distant or prehistoric past.

Bands are typically small, and societies with bands have a low population density. Julian Steward estimated that density in band societies ranged from a maximum of about one person per 5 square miles to a minimum of one person per 50 or so square miles.[3] Of course, by the time they were described by anthropologists, many band societies had been severely depopulated by introduced European diseases. So band size in the ethnographic record varies considerably. The Guayaki of the Amazon Basin had about 20 individuals in their local bands; the Semang of the Malay Peninsula had 50; the Patagonian Tehuelche of South America numbered 400 to 500, perhaps the largest of all.[4] Band size often varies by season, with the band breaking up or recombining according to the quantity of food resources available at a given time and place. Inuit bands, for example, are smaller in the winter, when food is hard to find, and larger in the summer, when there is sufficient food to feed a larger group.

Political decision making within the band is generally informal. The "modest informal authority"[5] that does exist can be seen in the way decisions affecting the group are made. Because the formal, permanent office of leader typically does not exist, decisions such as when camp has to be moved or how a hunt is to be arranged are either agreed upon by the community as a whole or made by the best-qualified member. Leadership, when it is exercised by an individual, is not the consequence of bossing or throwing one's weight about. Each band may have its informal **headman,** or its most proficient hunter, or a person most accomplished in rituals. There may be one person with all these qualities, or several persons, but such a person or persons will have gained status through the community's recognition of skill, good sense, and humility. Leadership, in other words, stems not from power but from influence, not from office but from admired personal qualities.

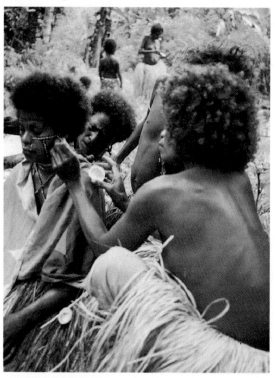

In many egalitarian societies leadership shifts informally from one person to another. In much of New Guinea there is more competition for achieving "big" status. On Vanatinai the people competing are women as well as men, and so there are "big women" as well as "big men." Here a "big woman" paints the face of her cousin's widow for a feast honoring the dead man.

In Inuit bands, each settlement may have its headman, who acquires his influence because the other members of the community recognize his good judgment and superior skills. The headman's advice concerning the movement of the band and other community matters is generally heeded, but he possesses no permanent authority and has no power to impose sanctions of any kind. Inuit leaders are male. But men often consult their wives in private, and women who hunt seem to have more influence than those who do not.[6] In any case, leadership exists only in a very restricted sense, as among the Iglulik Inuit, for example.

> Within each settlement . . . there is as a rule an older man who enjoys the respect of the others and who decides when a move is to be made to another hunting center, when a hunt is to be started, how the spoils are to be divided, when the dogs are to be fed. . . . He is called *isumaitoq*, "he who thinks." It is not always the oldest man, but as a rule an elderly man who is a clever hunter or, as head of a large family, exercises great authority. He cannot be called a chief; there is no obligation to follow his counsel; but they do so in most cases, partly because they rely on his experience, partly because it pays to be on good terms with this man.[7]

A summary of the general features associated with band organization can be found in Table 13–1. But there are exceptions to these generalizations. For example, not all known food collectors are organized at the band level or have all the features of a band type of society. The classic exceptions are the Native American societies of the Northwest Coast, who had enormous resources of salmon and other fish, relatively large and permanent villages, and political organization beyond the level of the typical band societies in the ethnographic record.

Tribal Organization

When local communities mostly act autonomously but there are kinship groups (such as clans) or associations (such as age-sets) that can potentially integrate several local groups into a larger unit (**tribe**), we say that the society has **tribal organization.** Unfortunately, the term "tribe" is sometimes used to refer to an entire society. That is, the entire language group may be called a tribe. But a tribal type of political system does not usually permit the entire society to act as a unit; all the communities in a tribal society may be linked only occasionally for some political (usually military) purpose. Thus, what distinguishes tribal from band political organization is the presence in the former of some multilocal (but

not usually societywide) integration. The multilocal integration, however, is *not permanent,* and it is *informal* in the sense that it is not headed by political officials. Frequently, the integration is called into play only when an external threat arises; when the threat disappears, the local groups revert to self-sufficiency.[8] Tribal organization may seem fragile—and of course it usually is—but the fact that there are social ways to integrate local groups into larger political entities means that societies with tribal organization are militarily a good deal more formidable than societies with band organization.

Societies with tribal political organization are similar to band societies in their tendency to be egalitarian (see Table 13–1). At the local level, informal leadership is also characteristic. In those tribal societies where kinship provides the basic framework of social organization, the elders of the local kin groups tend to have considerable influence; where age-sets are important, a particular age-set is looked to for leadership. But, in contrast to band societies, societies with tribal organization generally are food producers. And because cultivation and animal husbandry are generally more productive than hunting and gathering, the population density of tribal societies is generally higher, local groups are larger, and the way of life is more sedentary than in hunter-gatherer bands.

Kinship Bonds. Frequently communities are linked to each other by virtue of belonging to the same kin group, usually a unilineal group such as a lineage or clan. Kin group elders may act to settle disputes between kin group members or even attempt to punish wrongs committed against members by people belonging to different groups. In addition, kinship bonds often tend to unite members of the same descent group during periods of warfare; in many societies, as we noted previously, the organization of warfare is often the responsibility of the kin group.[9]

The **segmentary lineage system** is one type of tribal integration based on kinship. A society with such a system is composed of segments or parts, each similar to the others in structure and function. Every local segment belongs to a hierarchy of lineages stretching farther and farther back genealogically. The hierarchy of lineages, then, unites the segments into larger and larger genealogical groups. The closer two groups are genealogically, the greater their general closeness. In the event of a dispute between members of different segments, people related more closely to one contestant than to another take the side of their nearest kinsman.

▼▼▼▼▼▼ TABLE 13–1   *Suggested Trends in Political Organization and Other Social*
Characteristics

TYPE OF ORGANIZATION	HIGHEST LEVEL OF POLITICAL INTEGRATION	SPECIALIZATION OF POLITICAL OFFICIALS	PREDOMINANT MODE OF SUBSISTENCE	COMMUNITY SIZE AND POPULATION DENSITY	SOCIAL DIFFERENTIATION	MAJOR FORM OF DISTRIBUTION
Band	Local group or band	Little or none; informal leadership	Food collecting	Very small communities, very low density	Egalitarian	Mostly reciprocity
Tribe	Sometimes multilocal group	Little or none; informal leadership	Extensive (shifting) agriculture and/or herding	Small communities, low density	Egalitarian	Mostly reciprocity
Chiefdom	Multilocal group	Some	Extensive or intensive agriculture and/or herding	Large communities, medium density	Rank	Reciprocity and redistribution
State	Multilocal group, often entire language group	Much	Intensive agriculture and herding	Cities and towns, high density	Class and caste	Mostly market exchange

The Tiv of northern Nigeria offer a classic example of a segmentary lineage system, one that happens to link all the Tiv into a single genealogical structure or tribe. The Tiv are a large society, numbering more than 800,000. Figure 13–1 is a representation of the Tiv lineage structure as described by Paul Bohannan:

> The lineage whose apical ancestor is some three to six generations removed from living elders and who are associated with the smallest discrete territory *(tar)* I call the minimal segment; . . . it can vary in population from 200 people to well over a thousand. . . . The territory of a minimal segment adjoins the territory of its sibling minimal segment. Thus, the lineage comprising two minimal segments also has a discrete territory, and is in turn a segment of a more inclusive lineage, and of its more inclusive territory. In [Figure 13–1], the whole system can be seen: the father or founder of segment *a* was a brother of the founder of segment *b.* Each is a minimal segment today, and each has its own territory. The two segments taken together are all descended from 1, and are known by his name—the children of 1. In the same way, the territory of lineage 1, made up as it is of the combined minimal territories *a* and *b,* combines with the territory of lineage 2, made up of the combined minimal territories of *c* and *d,* to form territory A, occupied by lineage segment A, all descended from a single ancestor "A." This process is extended indefinitely, right up to the apex of the genealogy, back in time to the founder who [is said to have] begot the entire people; and outwards in space to the edges of Tivland. The entire 800,000 Tiv form a single "lineage" *(nongo)* and a single land called *Tar Tiv.*[10]

Tiv lineage organization is the foundation of Tiv political organization. A look at Figure 13–1 helps to explain how. A dispute between lineages (and territories) *a* and *b* remains minor, since no more than "brother" segments are involved. But a dispute between *a* and *c* now involves lineages 1 and 2 as well, with the requirement that *b* assist *a* and *d* support *c.* This process of mutual support, often called **complementary opposition,** means that segments will unite only in a confrontation with some other group. Groups that will fight with each other in a minor dispute might coalesce at some later time against a larger group.

Externally, the segmentary lineage system was presumably very effective in allowing the Tiv to intrude into new territory and take land from other tribal societies with smaller descent groups. Individual Tiv lineage segments could call on support from related lineages when faced with border troubles.

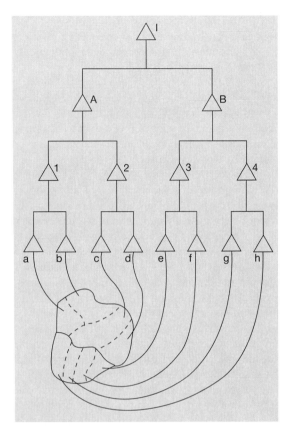

FIGURE 13–1
Tiv Lineage Segments and Their Territories

Source: *Adapted from Paul Bohannan, "The Migration and Expansion of the Tiv,"* Africa, 24 (1954): 3

Conflicts within the society (between segments), especially in border areas, were often turned outward, "releasing internal pressure in an explosive blast against other peoples."[11]

Segmentary lineage systems may have military advantages even when they do not unite the entire society. A classic example is the Nuer of the Upper Nile region, who had tribal (but not societywide) organization because of their segmentary lineages. In the early 1800s the Nuer had a territory of about 8,700 square miles and the neighboring Dinka had ten times that much. But by 1890, the Nuer had cut a hundred-mile swath through Dinka territory, increasing Nuer territory to 35,000 square miles. Even though the Nuer and Dinka were culturally very similar, the segmentary lineage organization of the Nuer seems to have given them a significant military advantage in their incursions into Dinka territory.[12]

A segmentary lineage system may generate a formidable military force, but the combinations of manpower it produces are temporary, forming and dissolving as the occasion demands.[13] Tribal political organization does not make for a political system that more or less permanently integrates a number of communities.

Age-Set Systems. In the previous chapter we described age-set systems in general. Here we discuss how age-sets can function as the basis of a tribal type of political organization, as among the Karimojong of northeastern Uganda.[14]

The Karimojong depend on cattle herding and agriculture for their livelihood. Their political community includes elders who direct day-to-day affairs, large-herd owners whose wealth enables them to have a say in certain activities, and initiated adult males whose responsibility it is to implement policy once it has been decided. Initiation into an age-set, and public acceptance of tribal customs, means that a Karimojong will ultimately become an elder and perhaps a leader of his local community.

The Karimojong age-set system has an important bearing on day-to-day tribal life. As herders, Karimojong adults are often separated from their usual settlements. Herders will meet, mingle for a while, then go their separate ways, but each may call upon other members of his age-set wherever he goes. The age-set system is important among the Karimojong because it immediately allocates to each individual a place in the system and thereby establishes for him an appropriate pattern of response. A quarrel in camp will be settled by the representatives of the senior age-set who are present, regardless of which section of the tribe they may belong to.

Among the Karimojong, political leaders are not elected from among the elders of a particular age-set, nor are they appointed; they acquire their positions informally. Usually a man's background, and the ability he has demonstrated in public debates over a period of time, will result in his being considered by the men of his neighborhood to be their spokesman. His function is to announce what course of action seems required in a particular situation, to initiate that action, and then to coordinate it after it has begun.

Most political leaders exercise their authority within the local sphere because the pastoral nature of the Karimojong economy, with its dispersed groups and movement from one feeding ground to another, offers no alternative. From time to time an elder may acquire the status of a prophet and be awarded respect and obedience on a tribal scale. He will be called upon to lead sacrifices (to avert misfortune), to undertake rainmaking (to bring prosperity), and so on. Yet even a prophet's prestige and authority do not warrant him a position of overlord or chief.[15]

Chiefdom Organization

Whereas a tribe has some informal mechanism that can integrate more than one community, a **chiefdom** has some *formal* structure that integrates more than one community into a political unit. The formal structure could consist of a council with or without a chief, but most commonly there is a person—the **chief**—who has higher rank or authority than others. Most societies at the chiefdom level of organization contain more than one multicommunity political unit or chiefdom, each headed by a district chief or a council. There may also be more than one level of chief beyond the community, such as district chiefs and higher level chiefs. Compared with tribal societies, societies with chiefdoms are more densely populated and their communities more permanent, partly as a consequence of their generally higher economic productivity (see Table 13–1).

The position of chief, which is sometimes hereditary and generally permanent, bestows high status on its holder. Most chiefdoms have social ranking and accord the chief and his family greater access to prestige. The chief may redistribute goods, plan and direct the use of public labor, supervise religious ceremonies, and direct military activities on behalf of the chiefdom.

In South Pacific chiefdoms, the chiefs carried out most of the duties we have just described. In Fijian chiefdoms, for example, the chief was responsible for the redistribution of goods and the coordination of labor:

> [The chief] could summon the community's labor on his own behalf, or on behalf of someone else who requested it, or for general purposes. . . . Besides his right to summon labor he accumulated the greater proportion of the first fruits of the yam crop . . . and he benefited from other forms of food presentation, or by the acquisition of special shares in ordinary village distribution. . . . Thus, the paramount [chief] would collect a significant part of the surplus production of the community and redistribute it in the general welfare.[16]

In contrast to leaders in tribal societies, who generally have to earn their privileges by their personal qualities, hereditary chiefs are said to have those qualities in their "blood." A high-ranking chief in Polynesia, that huge triangular area of islands in the South Pacific, inherited special religious power called *mana.* Mana sanctified his rule and protected him.[17] Chiefs in Polynesia had so

Chiefs in Tahiti directed military activities. Captain Cook encountered their war canoes when he visited in 1774.

much religious power that the missionaries could convert people to Christianity only after their chiefs had been converted.[18]

In most chiefdoms, the chiefs did not have the power to compel people to obey them; people would act in accordance with the chief's wishes because the chief was respected and often had religious authority. But in the most complex paramount chiefdoms, such as those of Hawaii and Tahiti, the chiefs seemed to have more compelling sanctions than the "power" of respect or mana. Substantial amounts of goods and services collected by the chiefs were used to support subordinates, including specialists such as high priests, political envoys, and warriors who could be sent to quell rebellious factions.[19] When redistributions do not go to everybody and a chief begins to use armed force, the political system is on the way to becoming what we call a state. Why chiefs sometimes are allowed to keep items for their own purposes is still a puzzle.

State Organization

A **state,** according to one more or less standard definition, is "an autonomous political unit, encompassing many communities within its territory and having a centralized government with the power to collect taxes, draft men for work or war, and decree and enforce laws."[20] States, then, have a complex, centralized political structure, which includes a wide range of permanent institutions with legislative, executive, and judicial functions, and a large bureaucracy. Central to this definition is the concept of legitimate force used to implement policies both internally and externally. In states, the government tries to maintain a monopoly on the use of physical force.[21] This monopoly can be seen in the development of formal and specialized instruments of social control: a police force, a militia, a standing army.

Just as a particular society may contain more than one band, tribe, or chiefdom, so may it contain more than one state. The contiguously distributed population speaking a single language may or may not be politically unified in a single state. Ancient Greece was composed of many city-states. So too was Italy until the 1870s. German speakers are also not politically unified; Austria and Germany are separate states, and Germany itself was not politically unified until the 1870s. We say that a society has **state organization** when it is composed of one or more political units that are states.

A state may include more than one society. Multisociety states often are the result of conquest or colonial control when the dominant political authority, itself a state, imposes a centralized government over a territory with many different societies and cultures (as the British did in Nigeria and Kenya). Nearly all of the new multisociety states that emerged after World War II were the results of successful independence movements against colonial powers.[22] Most have retained their political unity despite the fact that they contain many different societies. For example, even Nigeria remains unified despite a civil war; the eastern section called Biafra (mostly populated by people of Ibo culture) tried unsuccessfully 30 years ago to secede, and subsequently there has been serious conflict between some of the constituent societies. Multisociety or multi-ethnic states may also form voluntarily, in reaction to external threat. Switzerland comprises cantons, each of which speaks mainly French, German, Italian, or Romansch; the various cantons confederated originally to shake off control by the Holy Roman Empire.

In addition to their strictly political features, states have class stratification and hence unequal access to economic resources. State-organized societies are generally supported by intensive agriculture. The high productivity of the agriculture presumably allows for the emergence of cities, a high degree of economic and other kinds of specialization, market or commercial exchange, and class stratification (see Table 13–1).

When states come into existence, people's access to scarce resources is radically altered. So too is their ability to *not* listen to leaders: you cannot refuse to pay taxes and go unpunished! Of course, the rulers of a state do not maintain the social order by force alone. The people must believe, at least to some extent, that those in power have a legitimate right to govern. If the people think otherwise, history suggests that those in power may eventually lose their ability to control. Witness the recent downfall of Communist parties throughout most of Eastern Europe and the former Soviet Union.

So force and the threat of force are not enough to explain the legitimacy of power, and the inequities that occur commonly, in state societies. But then what does? There are various theories. The rulers of early states often claimed divine descent to buttress their legitimacy, but this claim is rare nowadays. Parents may teach their children to accept all authority; such lessons may generalize to the acceptance of political authority. Some analysts think that people accept state authority for no good reason; the rulers are just able to fool them. Finally, some theorists think that states must provide people with real or rational advantages; otherwise people would not think that the rulers deserve to exercise authority. Legitimacy is not an all-or-none phenomenon; it varies in degree. Why it has varied, in different times and places, remains a classic question in the social sciences, including anthropology, as well as in philosophy and other humanistic disciplines.[23]

A state society can retain its legitimacy, or at least its power, for a long time. For example, the Roman Empire was a complex state society that dominated the Mediterranean and Near East for hundreds of years. It began as a city-state that waged war to acquire additional territory. At its height, the Roman Empire embraced more than 55 million

All governments, even state societies, ultimately depend on the people's sense of legitimacy. This toppled statue of Lenin symbolizes the recent breakup of the Soviet Union and the overthrow of rule by the Communist party.

people;[24] the capital city of Rome had a population of well over a million.[25] The empire included parts of what are now Great Britain, France, Spain, Portugal, Germany, Rumania, Turkey, Greece, Armenia, Egypt, Israel, and Syria.

Another example of a state society was the kingdom of Nupe in West Africa, now part of the nation-state of Nigeria. As is characteristic of state societies, Nupe society was quite rigidly stratified. At the top of the social system was the king, or *etsu*. Beneath the king, members of the royal family formed the highest aristocratic class. Next in order were two other classes of nobility—the local chiefs and the military leaders. At the bottom were the commoners, who had neither prestige nor power, and no share in political authority.

The Nupe king possessed ultimate authority in many judicial matters. Minor disputes and civil cases were handled by local village councils, but serious criminal cases were the prerogative of the king. Such cases, referred to as "crimes for the king," were brought before the royal court by the king's local representatives. The king and his counselors judged the cases and determined suitable punishments.

The most powerful influence of the state over the Nupe people was in the area of taxation. The king was given the power to impose taxes and collect them from every household. Payment was made either in money (cowrie shells originally, and later British currency) or certain gifts, such as cloth, mats, and slaves. Much of the revenue collected was kept by the king, and the remainder was shared with his local representatives and lords. In return for the taxes they paid, the people received security—protection against invasion and domestic disorder.[26]

Factors Associated with Variation in Political Organization

The kinds of political organization we call band, tribal, chiefdom, and state are points on a continuum of levels of political integration or unification, from small-scale local autonomy to large-scale regional unification. There also is variation in political authority, from a few temporary and informal political leaders to large numbers of permanent, specialized political officials, from the absence of coercive political power to the monopoly of public force by a central authority. These aspects of variation in political organization are generally associated with shifts from food collection to more intensive food production, from small to large communities, from low to high population densities, from an emphasis on reciprocity to redistribution to market exchange, and from egalitarian to rank to fully stratified class societies.

The associations just outlined, which seem to be confirmed by the available cross-cultural evidence, are summarized in Table 13–1. With regard to the relation between level of subsistence technology and political complexity, one cross-cultural study employing a small random sample of societies found that the greater the importance of agriculture in a society, the larger the population that is politically unified and the greater the number and types of political officials.[27] A massive cross-cultural survey reported a similar trend: the more intensive the agriculture, the greater the likelihood of state organization; conversely, societies with no more than local political institutions are likely to depend on hunting, gathering, and fishing.[28] With regard to community size, the first of these studies also suggested that the larger the leading community, the wider the range of political officials in the society.[29]

Robert Textor presented a similar finding: societies with state organization tend to have cities and towns, whereas those with only local political organization are more likely to have communities with an average population of fewer than 200 persons.[30] Cross-cultural research also tends to confirm that societies with higher levels of political integration are more likely to exhibit social differentiation, especially in the form of class distinctions.[31]

Does this evidence provide us with an explanation for why political organization varies? Clearly, the data indicate that several factors are associated with political development, but exactly why changes in organization occur is not yet understood. Although economic development may be a necessary condition for political development,[32] that relation does not fully explain why political organization should become more complex just because the economy can support it. Some theorists have suggested that competition between groups may be a more important reason for political consolidation. For example, Elman Service suggested competition as a reason why a society might change from a band level of political organization to a tribal level. Band societies are generally hunter-gatherers. With a changeover to agriculture, population density and competition between groups may increase. Service believes that such competition will foster the development of some informal organization beyond the community—namely, tribal organization—for offense and defense.[33] Indeed, as we saw in the chapters on residence and kinship and associations, unilineal kinship groups and age-set systems both seem to be associated with warfare.

Among agriculturalists, defensive needs might also be the main reason for switching from informal multivillage political organization to more formal chiefdom organization. Formally organized districts are probably more likely to defeat autonomous villages or even segmentary lineage systems.[34] In addition, there may be economic reasons for political development. With regard to chiefdoms, Service suggested that chiefdoms will emerge when redistribution between communities becomes important or when large-scale coordinated work groups are required. The more important these activities are, the more important (and hence more "chiefly") the organizer and his family presumably become.[35] But redistribution is far from a universal activity of chiefs,[36] so Service's explanation of chiefdoms is probably not sufficient either by itself.

Theory and research on the anthropology of political development have focused mostly on the high end of the scale of political complexity, and particularly on the origins of the first state societies. Those earliest states apparently arose independently of one another, after about 3500 B.C., in what is now southern Iraq, Egypt, northwestern India, northern China, and central Mexico. Several theories have been proposed to explain the earliest states, but no one theory seems to fit all of the known archaeological sequences culminating in early state formation. The reason may be that different conditions in different places favored the emergence of centralized government. The state, by definition, implies the power to organize large populations for collective purposes. In some areas, the purpose may have been the need to organize necessary local or long-distance trade or both. In other cases, the state may have emerged as a way to control defeated populations that could not flee. In still other instances, other factors or a combination of factors may have fostered the development of the state type of political system. It is still not clear what the specific conditions were that led to the emergence of the state in each of the early centers.[37]

The Spread of State Societies

For whatever reasons the earliest states developed, the state level of political development has come to dominate the world. Societies with states have larger communities and higher population densities than do band, tribal, and chiefdom societies. They also have armies that are ready to fight at almost any time. State systems that have waged war against chiefdoms and tribes have almost always won, and the result has usually been the political incorporation of the losers. For example, the British and later the United States colonization of much of North America led to the defeat and incorporation of many Native American societies.

The defeat and incorporation of the Native Americans was at least partially due to the catastrophic depopulations they suffered because of epidemic diseases (such as smallpox and measles) that colonists introduced. Catastrophic depopulation was commonly the outcome of the first contacts between Euro-Americans and the natives of North and South America, as well as the natives of the far islands in the Pacific. People in the New World and the Pacific had not previously been exposed (and therefore were not resistant) to the diseases the Euro-Americans carried with them when they began to colonize the world. Before the expansion of Europeans, the people of the New World and the Pacific had been separated for a long time from the people and diseases on that geographically continuous land mass we separate into Europe, Africa, and Asia. Smallpox, measles, and the other former scourges of Europe had largely become childhood diseases that most individuals of European ancestry survived.[38]

Whether by depopulation, conquest, or intimidation, the number of independent political units in the world has decreased strikingly in the last 3,000 years, and especially in the last 200 years.

Robert Carneiro estimated that in 1000 B.C., there may have been between 100,000 and 1 million separate political units in the world; today there are

State societies frequently try to expand by conquering other peoples, as the Spanish did in Mexico. This Aztec drawing depicts a 1530 Spanish battle in which a non-Aztec group fought together with the Spanish against another non-Aztec group.

fewer than 200.[39] In the ethnographic record, about 50 percent of the 2,000 or so societies described within the last 150 years had only local political integration. That is, the highest level of political integration in 1 out of 2 fairly recent societies was the local community.[40] Thus, most of the decrease in the number of independent political units has occurred fairly recently.

But the recent secessions from the former Soviet Union and Yugoslavia, and other separatist movements around the world, suggest that ethnic rivalries may make for departures from the trend toward larger and larger political units. Ethnic groups that have been dominated by others in multinational states may opt for political autonomy, at least for a while. On the other hand, the separate nations of Western Europe are becoming more unified every day, both politically and economically. So the trend toward larger and larger political units may be continuing, even if there are departures from it now and then.

Extrapolating from past history, a number of investigators have suggested that the entire world will eventually come to be politically integrated, perhaps as soon as the twenty-third century and no later than A.D. 4850.[41] Only the future will tell if this prediction will come true. And only the future will tell if further political integration in the world will occur peacefully—with all parties agreeing—or by force or the threat of force, as has happened so often in the past.

VARIATION IN POLITICAL PROCESS

Anthropologists nowadays are increasingly interested in the politics, or political processes, of the societies they study: who acquires influence or power, how they acquire it, and how political decisions are made. But even though we have descriptive accounts of politics in many societies, there is as yet little comparative or cross-cultural research on what may explain variation in politics.[42]

Getting to Be a Leader

In those societies that have hereditary leadership, which is common in rank societies and in state societies with monarchies, rules of succession usually establish how leadership is inherited. Such leaders are often identifiable in some obviously visible way; they may be permanently marked or tattooed, as in

chiefdoms in Polynesia, or they may wear elaborate dress and insignia, as in class-stratified societies (see the discussion of body adornment in the chapter on the arts). But for societies whose leaders are *chosen* (either as informal leaders or as political officials), we need a lot more research to understand why some kinds of people are chosen over others.

We do have a few studies that investigated the personal qualities of leaders in tribal societies. One study, conducted among the Mekranoti-Kayapo of central Brazil, found that leaders (in contrast to followers) tend to be rated by their peers as higher on intelligence, generosity, knowledgeability, ambitiousness, and aggressiveness. Leaders also tend to be older and taller. And despite the egalitarian nature of Mekranoti society (at least with respect to sharing resources), sons of leaders are more likely than others to become leaders.[43]

Research in another Brazilian society, the Kagwahiv of the Amazon region, suggests another personal quality of leaders—they seem to have positive feelings about their fathers and mothers.[44] In many respects, studies of leaders in the United States show them to be not that different from their counterparts in Brazil. But there is one major difference. Mekranoti and Kagwahiv leaders are not wealthier than others; in fact, they give their wealth away. U.S. leaders are wealthier than others.[45]

"Big Men". In some egalitarian tribal societies, the quest for leadership seems quite competitive. In parts of New Guinea and South America, "big men" compete with other ambitious men to attract followers. Men who want to compete must show that they have magical powers, success in gardening, and bravery in war. But, most important, they have to collect enough goods to throw big parties at which the goods are given away. Big men have to work very hard to attract and keep their followings; dissatisfied followers can always join other aspiring men.[46] The wives of big men are often leaders too. Among the Kagwahiv, for example, a headman's wife is usually the leader of the women in the community; she is responsible for much of the planning for feasts and often distributes the meat at them.[47]

Although the phenomenon of big men leaders is common throughout New Guinea, researchers are beginning to see variation in the type and extent of "bigmanship" in different areas of New Guinea. For example, in the southern Highlands, groups of men (not just big men) may engage in large-scale giveaways, so big men are not so different from ordinary men. In the northwestern Highlands, on the other hand, big men stand out from other men in striking ways. They make policy for groups of people and organize collective events, they have substantial access to pigs or to valuables acquired in exchanges, and they have control over a substantial amount of labor (more than one wife and fellow kin).[48]

So we know that some big men are bigger than others, but how does a man get to be a big man? Among the Kumdi-Engamoi, a central Highlands group, a man who wants to be considered a *wua nium* (literally a "great-important-wealthy man") needs to have many wives and daughters, because the amount of land controlled by a man and how much can be produced on that land depend on the number of women in his family. (The more wives he has, the more land he is given to cultivate.) He must also be a good speaker. Everyone has the right to speak and give speeches, but to get to be known as a big man requires speaking well and forcefully and knowing when to sum up a consensus. It usually takes a man until his thirties or forties to acquire more than one wife and to make his name through exchanges. When a man wants to inaugurate an exchange, he needs to get shells and pigs from his family and relatives. Once he has achieved a reputation as a *wua nium,* he can keep it only if he continues to perform well, that is, if he continues to distribute fairly, make wise decisions, speak well, and conduct exchanges.[49]

"Big Women". In contrast to most of mainland New Guinea, the islands off the southeastern coast are characterized by matrilineal descent. But like the rest of New Guinea, the islands also usually have a shifting system of leadership in which people compete for "big" status. Here, though, the people competing are women as well as men, and so there are "big women" as well as "big men." On the island of Vanatinai, for example, women and men compete with each other to exchange valuables. Women lead canoe expeditions to distant islands to visit male as well as female exchange partners, women mobilize relatives and exchange partners to mount large feasts, and the women get to keep the ceremonial valuables exchanged, at least for a while.[50]

The prominence of women on Vanatinai island may be linked to the disappearance of warfare (the colonial powers imposed peace—we call this "pacification"). Interisland exchanges grew in frequency when war became rarer in the early twentieth century, giving women and men more freedom to travel. For men, but not women, war provided a path to leadership—champion warriors would acquire great renown and influence. It is not that women did not participate in war; they did (which is unusual cross-culturally). But a woman could not become a war leader. Now, in the absence of war, women have an opportunity (through exchanges) to become leaders, or "big women."

In one respect, however, women have less of an opportunity to acquire influence now. There are local government councils now, but all the councillors are male. Why? Some women were nominated for the posts, but they withdrew in embarrassment because they could not speak English. Big men or big women do not automatically have a path to these new positions—it is mostly young males who know English and become the councillors. But this situation may change. With the opening of a government primary school in 1984, girls and boys are both learning English, so women in the future may be more likely to achieve leadership by becoming councillors.

Political Participation

The political scientist Marc Ross conducted cross-cultural research on variation in degree of political participation. As Ross phrased the research question: "Why is it that in some polities there are relatively large numbers of persons involved in political life, while in others political action is the province of very few?"[51]

Political participation in preindustrial societies ranges from widespread to low or nonexistent. Widespread participation (in 16 percent of the societies examined) means that decision-making forums are *open* to all adults (not necessarily that all adults participate); the forums may be formal (councils and other governing bodies) or informal. Next in degree of political participation are societies (37 percent) that have widespread participation by some but not all adults (men but not women, certain classes but not others). Next are societies (29 percent) that have some but not much input by the community. Finally, 18 percent of the societies have low or nonexistent participation, which means that leaders make most decisions and involvement of the average person is very limited.

Degree of political participation seems to be high in small-scale societies, as well as in modern democratic nation-states, but not in between (feudal states and preindustrial empires). Why? In small-scale societies leaders do not have the power to force people to act; thus a high degree of political participation may be the only way to get people to go along with decisions. In modern democracies, which have many powerful groups outside the government (corporations, unions, other associations), the central authorities may only theoretically have the power to force people to go along; in reality, they have to rely mostly on voluntary compliance. For example, the U.S. government failed when it tried with force (during Prohibition, 1920–1933) to stop the manufacture, transportation, and sale of alcoholic beverages.

A high degree of political participation seems to have an important consequence. In the modern world, democratically governed states rarely go to war with each other. This does not mean that modern democracies are more peaceful in general; on the contrary, they are as likely to go to war as other kinds of political systems, but not so much with each other.[52] So, for example, troops from the United States invaded three countries between 1980 and 1993 (Grenada, Panama, Iraq), but no democracies. Similarly, it appears that more participatory (more "democratic") political units in the ethnographic record fight with each other significantly less often than do less participatory political units, just as seems to be the case among modern nation-states.[53] Exactly why more participation or more democracy may lead to peace still remains to be established; we explore the implications of the relationship in our final chapter on applied anthropology and social problems.

RESOLUTION OF CONFLICT

As we noted in the beginning of the chapter, political life involves more than the making of policy, its administration, and its enforcement. It also involves the resolution of conflict, which may be accomplished peacefully by avoidance, community action, mediation or the negotiation of compromises, apology, appeal to supernatural forces, or adjudication by a third party (for example, a court). As we shall see, the procedures used usually vary with degree of social complexity; decisions by third parties are more likely in more hierarchical societies.[54] But peaceful solutions are not always possible, and disputes may erupt into violent conflict. When violence occurs within a political unit in which disputes are usually settled peacefully, we call such violence **crime,** particularly when committed by an individual. When the violence occurs between groups of people from separate political units—groups between which there is no procedure for settling disputes—we usually call such violence **warfare.** (When violence occurs between subunits of a population that had been politically unified, we call it "civil war.")

Peaceful Resolution of Conflict

Most modern industrialized states have formal institutions and offices such as police, district attorneys, courts, and penal systems to deal with minor disputes and more serious conflicts that may arise in society. All these institutions generally operate according to **codified laws**—that is, a set of explicit (usually, written) rules stipulating what is permissible and what is not. Transgression of the law by individuals gives the state the right to take action against them. The state has a monopoly on the legitimate use of force in the society, for it alone has the right to coerce subjects into agreement with regulations, customs, political edicts, and procedures.

Many societies lack such specialized offices and institutions for dealing with conflict. Yet, because all societies have peaceful, regularized ways of handling at least certain disputes, some anthropologists speak of the universality of law. E. Adamson Hoebel, for example, stated the principle as follows:

> Each people has its system of social control. And all but a few of the poorest of them have as a part of the control system a complex of behavior patterns and institutional mechanisms that we may properly treat as law. For, "anthropologically considered, law is merely one aspect of our culture—the aspect which employs the force of organized society to regulate individual and group conduct and to prevent redress or punish deviations from prescribed social norms."[55]

Law, then, whether informal as in simpler societies, or formal as in more complex societies, provides a means of dealing peacefully with whatever conflicts develop. That does not mean that conflicts are always resolved peacefully.

Avoidance. Violence can often be avoided if the parties to a dispute voluntarily avoid each other or are separated until emotions cool down. Anthropologists have frequently remarked that foragers are particularly likely to make use of this technique. People may move to other bands or move their dwellings to opposite ends of camp. Shifting horticulturalists may also split up when conflicts get too intense. Avoidance is obviously easier in societies, such as band societies, that are nomadic or seminomadic and in which people have temporary dwellings. And avoidance is more feasible when people live independently and self-sufficiently (for example, in cities and suburbs).[56] But even if conditions in such societies may make avoidance

DEMOCRACY AND ECONOMIC DEVELOPMENT: HOW AND WHY ARE THEY RELATED?

The subsistence economies traditionally studied by anthropologists are becoming more and more commercialized as people increasingly produce goods and services for a market. And the pace of economic development is quickening, particularly in places that until recently lacked industrial wage labor, as their economies are increasingly integrated into the same world system. What effect, if any, does economic development have on political participation? Can we speculate about the future on the basis of comparative research?

Most of the comparative research on the relationship between economic development and political participation has been cross-national, comparing data on different countries. Some countries are more democratic

than others, on the basis of traits such as contested elections, an elected head of state, an elected powerful legislature, and the protection of civil liberties. In capitalist countries, more democracy is generally associated with higher levels of economic development (as measured by indicators such as per capita output). In countries that are not very industrialized, there is little democracy at the national level. Why should more democracy be associated with more economic development? The prevailing opinion is that economic development increases the degree of social equality in the country, and the more equality among interest groups, the more they demand participation in the political process, and hence the more democracy. Or, to put this theory another way, as

the economy develops, the more what we might call the middle and working classes can demand rewards and power, and therefore the less power the elite can retain.

What about the societies usually studied by anthropologists (what we call the cross-cultural or ethnographic record)? We know that some of the highest levels of political participation occur in the least complex societies, such as foraging societies. Many adults in such societies have a say in decisions and leadership is informal; leaders can retain their roles only if people voluntarily go along with them. Concentrated power and less political participation are more likely in chiefdoms and states than in band and tribal societies. The more hierarchical chiefdoms and states usually depend on

---

easier, we still need to know *why* some societies use avoidance more than confrontation as a way of resolving conflict.

Community Action. Societies have found various ways of resolving disputes peacefully. One such way involves action by a group or the community as a whole; collective action is common in simpler societies that lack powerful authoritarian leaders.[57] Many Inuit societies, for example, frequently resolve disputes through community action. Within local groups, kinship ties are not particularly emphasized, and the family is regarded as autonomous in most matters. They believe that spirits—particularly if displeased—can determine much of a person's fate. Consequently, people carry out their

daily tasks within a complex system of taboos. This system of taboos is so extensive that the Inuit, at least in the past, may have had no need for a formal set of laws.

Nevertheless, conflicts do arise and have to be resolved. Accordingly, "principles" act as guides to the community in settling trouble cases. An individual's failure to heed a taboo or to follow the suggestions of a shaman leads to expulsion from the group, because the community cannot accept a risk to its livelihood. A person who fails to share goods voluntarily will find them confiscated and distributed to the community, and he or she may be executed in the process. A single case of murder, as an act of vengeance (usually because of the abduction of a wife or as part of a blood feud), does not conagriculture, particularly intensive agriculture, which can produce more goods and services per capita than foraging economies can. So the relationship between economic development and political participation in the ethnographic record is *opposite* to what we find cross-nationally. That is, the more economic development, the *less* political participation, in the societies studied by anthropologists. Why should this be so? It seems that social equality *decreases* with economic development in the ethnographic record (which does not include many industrialized societies). In that record, an economically developed society is likely to have features such as plowing, fertilizers, and irrigation, which make permanent cultivation of the fields and permanent communities possible. Such intensive agricultural activity is more conducive to concentrated

wealth than is hunter-gatherer subsistence or shifting cultivation (horticulture). Thus, in the ethnographic record, the more economically developed societies have *more* social inequality and therefore *less* democracy.

The two sets of findings (the cross-national and the cross-cultural) are not that hard to reconcile. Social (and economic) inequality appears to work against democracy and extensive political participation. Social inequality increases with the switch from foraging to agriculture. But social inequality decreases with the switch from preindustrial agriculture to high (industrial) levels of economic development. Political participation decreases with the first switch and increases with the second, because social inequality first increases and then decreases.

So what does comparative research suggest about the future?

If the middle and working classes feel they are not getting a fair return on their labor, their demands should increase. The elite may be willing to satisfy those increased demands; if they do, their power will be reduced. Or the elite may be forced by the electoral process to accommodate those increased demands. In either case, unless the elite try to retain their power at any cost, there should be more political participation and more democracy, at least in the long run.

Sources: *Kenneth A. Bollen, "Liberal Democracy: Validity and Method Factors in Cross-National Measures,"* American Journal of Political Science, 37 (1993) 1207–30; *Edward N. Muller, "Economic Determinants of Democracy,"* and *Melvin Ember, Carol R. Ember, and Bruce Russett, "Inequality and Democracy in the Anthropological Record," papers presented at a conference on inequality and democracy, organized by Manus Midlarsky at Rutgers University, February 1994; Marc Howard Ross, "Political Participation," in Carol R. Ember and Melvin Ember, eds.,* Cross-Cultural Research for Social Science (Englewood Cliffs, NJ: Prentice Hall, 1995). Prentice Hall/Simon & Schuster Custom Publishing.

cern the community, but repeated murders do. Franz Boas gave a typical example:

> There was a native of Padli by the name Padlu. He had induced the wife of a native of Cumberland Sound to desert her husband and follow him. The deserted husband, meditating revenge . . . visited his friends in Padli, but before he could accomplish his intention of killing Padlu, the latter shot him. . . . A brother of the murdered man went to Padli to avenge the death . . . but he also was killed by Padlu. A third native of Cumberland Sound, who wished to avenge the death of his relatives, was also murdered by him.
>
> On account of these outrages the natives wanted to get rid of Padlu, but yet they did not dare to attack him. When the *pimain* (headman) of the Akudmurmuit learned of these events he started south-

> ward and *asked every man in Padli whether Padlu should be killed. All agreed;* so he went with the latter deer hunting . . . and . . . shot Padlu in the back.[58]

The killing of an individual is the most extreme action a community can take—we call it capital punishment. The community as a whole or a political official or a court may decide to administer such punishment, but capital punishment seems to exist in nearly all societies, from the simplest to the most complex.[59] It is often assumed that capital punishment deters crime. If it did, we would expect the abolition of capital punishment to be followed by an increase in homicide rates. But that does not seem to happen. A cross-national study indicated that the abolition of capital punishment tends to be followed by a *decrease* in homicide rates.[60]

Negotiation and Mediation. In many conflicts, the parties to a dispute may come to a settlement themselves by *negotiation*. There aren't necessarily any rules for how they will do so, but any solution is "good" if it restores peace.[61]

Sometimes an outside or third party is used to help bring about a settlement between the disputants. We call it *mediation* when the outside person tries to help bring about a settlement, but that person does not have the formal authority to force a settlement. Both negotiation and mediation are likely when the society is relatively egalitarian and it is important for people to get along.[62] Among the Nuer of East Africa, a pastoral and horticultural people, disputes within the community can be settled with the help of an informal mediator called the "leopard-skin chief." This man is not a political chief but a mediator. His position is hereditary, has religious overtones, and makes its holder responsible for the social well-being of the district.

Matters such as cattle stealing rarely come to the attention of the leopard-skin chief; the parties involved usually prefer to settle in their own private way. But if, for example, a murder has been committed, the culprit will go at once to the house of the leopard-skin chief. Immediately the chief cuts the culprit's arm so that blood flows; until the cut has been made the murderer may not eat or drink. If the murderer is afraid of vengeance by the slain man's family, he will remain at the house of the leopard-skin chief, which is considered sanctuary. Then, within the next few months, the chief attempts to mediate between the parties to the crime.

The chief elicits from the slayer's kin that they are prepared to pay compensation to avoid a feud, and he persuades the dead man's kin that they ought to accept compensation, usually in the form of cattle. During this period neither party may eat or drink from the same vessels as the other, and they may not, therefore, eat in the house of the same third person. The chief then collects the cattle—some forty to fifty beasts—and takes them to the dead man's home, where he performs various sacrifices of cleansing and atonement.[63]

The chief acts throughout as a go-between. He has no authority to force either of the parties to negotiate, and he has no power to enforce a solution once it has been arrived at. However, he is able to take advantage of the fact that because both parties to the dispute belong to the same community and are anxious to avoid a blood feud, they usually are willing to come to terms.

Ritual Reconciliation—Apology. The desire to restore a harmonious relationship may also explain ceremonial apologies. An apology is based on deference—the guilty party shows obeisance and asks for forgiveness. Such ceremonies tend to occur in recent chiefdoms.[64] Among the Fijians of the South Pacific, there is a strong ethic of harmony and mutual assistance, particularly within a village. When a person offends someone of higher status, the offended person and other villagers begin to avoid, and gossip about, the offender. If the offender is sensitive to village opinion, he or she will perform a ceremony of apology called *i soro*. One of the meanings of *soro* is "surrender." In the ceremony the offender keeps her or his head bowed and remains silent while an intermediary speaks, presents a token gift, and asks the offended person for forgiveness. The apology is rarely rejected.[65]

Oaths and Ordeals. Still another way of peacefully resolving disputes is through oaths and ordeals, both of which involve appeals to supernatural power. An **oath** is the act of calling upon a deity to bear witness to the truth of what one says. An **ordeal** is a means used to determine guilt or innocence by submitting the accused to dangerous or painful tests believed to be under supernatural control.[66]

Oaths, as one would expect, vary widely in content according to the culture in which they are found. The Rwala Bedouin, for example, do the following:

> In serious disputes the judge requires the *msabba* oath, so called from the seven lines drawn with a saber on the ground. The judge first draws a circle with a saber, then its diameter; then he intersects with five vertical lines, inviting the witness to step inside and, facing south, to swear: "A false oath is the ruin of the descendants, for he who [swears falsely] is insatiable in his desire [of gain] and does not fear for his Lord."[67]

Scarcely is the oath finished when the witness jumps out of the circle and, full of rage, runs at his opponent, who has made him swear. The people present at the trial have to surround and hold him until he calms down.

A common kind of ordeal, found in almost every part of the world, is scalding. Among the Tanala of Madagascar, the accused person, having first had his hand carefully examined for protective covering, has to reach his hand into a cauldron of boiling water and grasp, from underneath, a rock suspended there. He then plunges his hand into cold water, has it bandaged, and is led off to spend the night under guard. In the morning his hand is unbandaged and examined. If there are blisters, he is guilty.

Oaths and ordeals have also been practiced in Western societies. Both were common in medieval Europe. Even today, in our own society, vestiges of oaths can be found: children can be heard to say "Cross my heart and hope to die," and witnesses in courts of law are obliged to swear to tell the truth.

Why do some societies use oaths and ordeals? John Roberts suggested that they tend to be found in fairly complex societies in which political officials lack sufficient power to make and enforce judicial decisions or would make themselves unnecessarily vulnerable were they to attempt to do so. So the officials may use oaths and ordeals to let the gods decide guilt or innocence. When political officials gain more power, oaths and ordeals seem to decline or disappear.[68] In contrast, smaller and less complex societies probably have no need for elaborate mechanisms such as courts and oaths and ordeals to ascertain guilt. In such societies, everyone is aware of what crimes have been committed and who the guilty parties probably are.

Adjudication, Courts, and Codified Law.   We call it *adjudication* when a third party acting as judge makes a decision that the disputing parties have to accept. Judgment may be rendered by one person (a judge), a panel of judges, a jury, or a political agent or agency (a chief, a royal personage, a council). Courts are often open to an audience, but they need not be. Judges and courts may rely on codified law and stipulated punishments, but codified law is not necessary for decisions to be made. Our own society relies heavily on codified law and courts to resolve disputes peacefully, but courts often if not usually rely on precedent (the outcomes of previous, similar cases). Codified laws and courts are not limited to Western societies. From the late seventeenth to the early twentieth century, for example, the Ashanti of West Africa had a complex political system with elaborate legal arrangements. The Ashanti state was a military-based empire possessing legal codes that resembled those of many ancient civilizations.[69]

The most effective sanction underpinning Ashanti law and its enforcement was the intense respect—almost religious deference—accorded the wishes of the ancestors and also the elders as custodians of the ancestral tradition. Ashanti law was based on a concept of natural law—a belief that there is an order of the universe whose principles lawmakers should follow in the decisions they make and in the regulations they design. Criminal and religious law were merged by the Ashanti: crimes—especially homicide, cursing of a chief, cowardice, and sorcery—were regarded as sins against the ancestral spirits. In Ashanti court procedure, elders examined and cross-examined witnesses as well as parties to the dispute. There were also quasiprofessional advocates, and appeals against a verdict could be made directly to a chief. Particularly noteworthy was the emphasis on intent when assessing guilt. Drunkenness constituted a valid defense for all crimes except murder and cursing a chief, and a plea of insanity, if proved, was upheld for all offenses.

Ashanti punishments could be severe. Physical mutilation, such as slicing off the nose or an ear—even castration in sexual offenses—was often employed. Fines were more frequent, however, and death sentences could often be commuted to banishment and confiscation of goods.

Why do some societies have codified systems while others do not? One explanation, advanced by E. Adamson Hoebel, A. R. Radcliffe-Brown, and others, is that in small, closely knit communities there is little need for formal legal guidelines because competing interests are minimal. Hence, simple societies need little codified law: there are relatively few matters to quarrel about, and the general will of the group is sufficiently well known and demonstrated frequently enough to deter transgressors.

This point of view is echoed in Richard Schwartz's study of two Israeli settlements. In one communal kibbutz, a young man aroused a good deal of community resentment because he had accepted an electric teakettle as a gift. It was the general opinion that he had overstepped the code about not having personal possessions, and he was so informed. Accordingly, he gave the kettle to the communal infirmary. Schwartz observed that "no organized enforcement of the decision was threatened, but had he disregarded the expressed will of the community, his life . . . would have been made intolerable by the antagonism of public opinion."[70]

In this community, where people worked and ate together, not only did everyone know about transgressions, but a wrongdoer could not escape public censure. Thus, public opinion was an effective sanction. In another Israeli community, however, where individuals lived in widely separated houses and worked and ate separately, public opinion did not work as well. Not only were community members less aware of problems, but they had no quick way of making their feelings known.

As a result, they established a judicial body to handle trouble cases.

Larger, more heterogeneous and stratified societies are likely to have more frequent disputes, which at the same time are less visible to the public. Individuals in stratified societies are generally not so dependent on community members for their well-being and hence are less likely to know of, or care about, others' opinions. It is in such societies that codified laws and formal authorities for resolving disputes develop—in order, perhaps, that disputes may be settled impersonally enough so that the parties can accept the decision and social order can be restored.

A good example of how more formal systems of law develop is the experience of towns in the American West during the gold-rush period. These communities were literally swamped by total strangers. The townsfolk, having no control (authority) over these intruders because the strangers had no local ties, looked for ways to deal with the troublesome cases that were continually flaring up. A first attempt at a solution was to hire gun-slingers—who were also strangers—to act as peace officers or sheriffs, but this strategy usually failed.

Eventually, towns succeeded in having federal authorities send in marshals backed by federal power.

Is there some evidence to support the theory that codified law is necessary only in larger, more complex societies? Data from a large, worldwide sample of societies suggest that codified law is associated with political integration beyond the local level. Murder cases, for example, are dealt with informally in societies that have only local political organization. In societies with multilocal political units, murder cases tend to be judged or adjudicated by specialized political authorities.[71] There is also some cross-cultural evidence that violence within a society tends to be less frequent when there are formal authorities (chiefs, courts) who have the power to punish murderers.[72] In general, adjudication or enforced decisions by outside authorities tend to occur in hierarchical societies with social classes and centralized power.[73]

Violent Resolution of Conflict

People are likely to resort to violence when regular, effective alternative means of resolving a conflict are not available. Some societies consider violence be-

Many societies have adopted peaceful ways of resolving disputes, even between different societies. This meeting between the Hopi and the Navaho of the U.S. Southwest is an attempt to work out a dispute between them.

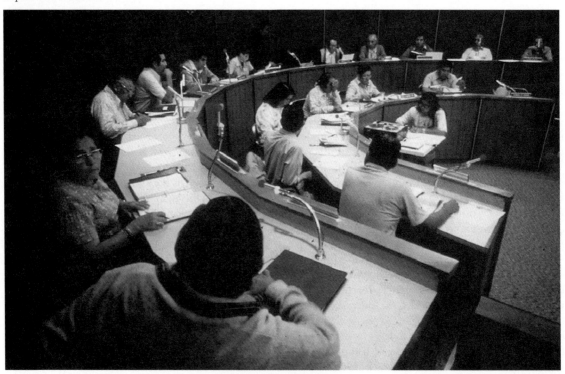

NEW COURTS ALLOW WOMEN TO ADDRESS GRIEVANCES IN PAPUA NEW GUINEA

In most societies in New Guinea, women did not traditionally participate in the resolution of disputes. And they could not themselves bring actions against men. But when village courts were introduced, women began to go to court to redress offenses against them.

In colonial times, the introduced Western-style courts followed Western law (primarily Australian and British common law), not native customary law. After Papua New Guinea became an independent country, those courts remained in place. The lowest of the courts, called Local Courts, were located in town centers, often far from villages, so villagers rarely brought cases to them. But in 1973 a new kind of court was created. Called Village Courts, they were designed to settle local disputes in the villages, using a blend of customary law (relying on compromise) and Western law. In contrast to the Local Courts, magistrates in the Village Courts were not outsiders but were selected from the pool of traditional and local leaders who knew the local people.

When Richard Scaglion studied changes in village courts among the Abelam from 1977 to 1987, he noticed a shift toward the increased use of these courts by women. In 1977, most of the complainants were male, but by 1987 most of them were female. In a wider study of court cases over many regions of Papua New Guinea, Scaglion and Rose Whittingham found that most of the cases in which women were the plaintiffs were attempts to redress sex-related offenses (sexual jealousy, rape, incest, domestic disputes) committed by males. Most disputes in New Guinea villages are settled informally by self-help or by appeal to a "big man"; the courts are appealed to only as a last resort. But serious sex-related cases are unlikely to be settled informally and are more likely to be settled in the Village Court. Apparently women do not believe that they can get satisfaction informally. So they go to the Village Court, where they win some sort of punishment for the defendant in about 60 percent of the cases, just about the same rate that men achieve when they bring a case seeking punishment.

Culture change introduced from the outside often works against native peoples. But Papuan New Guinea women have benefited from the new Village Court system, particularly in redressing grievances against males. The traditional system for resolving disputes was largely male-dominated (women could not be plaintiffs) and so the possibility of taking disputes to the new courts has given women some measure of legal equality with men.

Sources: *Richard Scaglion, "Legal Adaptation in a Papua New Guinea Village Court,"* Ethnology *29 (1990): 17–33; Richard Scaglion and Rose Whittingham, "Female Plaintiffs and Sex-Related Disputes in Rural Papua New Guinea,"* in S. Toft, ed., Domestic Violence in Papua New Guinea, *Monograph No. 3 (Port Moresby, Papua New Guinea: Law Reform Commission, 1985), pp. 120–33.*

tween individuals to be appropriate under certain circumstances; we generally do not and call it crime. When violence occurs between political entities such as communities, districts, or nations, we call it warfare. The type of warfare, of course, varies in scope and complexity from society to society. Sometimes a distinction is made among feuding, raiding, and large-scale confrontations.

Some scholars talk about a cultural pattern of violence. But are some cultures more violent than others? The answer seems to be yes. More often than not, societies with one type of violence have others. Societies with more war tend to have warlike sports, malevolent magic, severe punishment for crimes, high murder rates, feuding, and family violence. What might explain this tendency? One suggestion is that if war is frequent, the society may have to encourage boys to be aggressive, so that they can grow up to be effective warriors. But this socializing for aggression can spill over into other areas of life;

high rates of crime and other violence may be inadvertent or unintended consequences of the encouragement of aggressiveness.[74]

Individual Violence. Although it may at first seem paradoxical, violent behavior itself is often used to try to control behavior. In some societies it is considered necessary for parents to beat children who misbehave. They don't consider this criminal behavior or child abuse; they consider it punishment (see our discussion of family violence in the chapter on applied anthropology and social problems). Similar views may attach to interpersonal behavior between adults. If a person trespasses on your property or hurts someone in your family, some societies consider it appropriate or justified to kill or maim the trespasser. Is this social control, or is it just lack of control? Most societies have norms about when such "punishment" is or is not appropriate, so the behavior of anyone who contemplates doing something wrong, as well as the behavior of the person wronged, is likely to be influenced by the "laws" of their society. For example, systems of individual self-help are characteristic of egalitarian societies.[75] How is this different from "community action," which we classified above under peaceful resolution of conflict? Because community action is explicitly based on obtaining a consensus, it is likely to lead to the ending of a particular dispute. Individual action, or self-help, particularly if it involves violence, is not.

Feuding. *Feuding* is an example of how individual self-help may not lead to a peaceful resolution of conflict. **Feuding** is a state of recurring hostilities between families or groups of kin, usually motivated by a desire to avenge an offense—whether insult, injury, deprivation, or death—against a member of the group. The most characteristic feature of the feud is that responsibility to avenge is carried by all members of the kin group. The killing of any member of the offender's group is considered appropriate revenge, because the kin group as a whole is regarded as responsible. Nicholas Gubser told of a feud within a Nunamiut Inuit community, caused by a husband's killing of his wife's lover, that lasted for decades. The Nunamiut take feuds seriously, as do many societies, especially when murder has been committed. Gubser described what happens when a man is killed:

> The closely related members of his kindred do not rest until complete revenge has been achieved. The immediate relatives of the deceased . . . recruit as much support from other relatives as they can.

Their first action, if possible, is to kill the murderer, or maybe one of his closest kin. Then, of course, the members of the murderer's kindred are brought into the feud. These two kindreds may snipe at each other for years.[76]

Feuds are by no means limited to small-scale societies; they occur as frequently in societies with high levels of political organization.[77]

Raiding. **Raiding** is a short-term use of force, planned and organized, to realize a limited objective. This objective is usually the acquisition of goods, animals, or other forms of wealth belonging to another (often a neighboring) community.

Raiding is especially prevalent in pastoral societies, in which cattle, horses, camels, or other animals are prized and an individual's own herd can be augmented by theft. Raids are often organized by temporary leaders or coordinators whose authority may not endure beyond the planning and execution of the venture. Raiding may also be organized for the purpose of capturing people. Sometimes people are taken to marry (the capture of women to be wives or concubines is fairly common)[78] or to be slaves. Slavery has been practiced in about 33 percent of the world's known societies; war has been one way of obtaining slaves either to keep or to trade for other goods.[79]

Large-Scale Confrontations. Both feuding and raiding usually involve relatively small numbers of persons and almost always an element of surprise. Because they are generally attacked without warning, the victims are often unable to muster an immediate defense. Large-scale confrontations, in contrast, involve a large number of persons and planning by both sides of strategies of attack and defense.

Large-scale warfare is usually practiced among societies with intensive agriculture or industrialization. Only these societies possess a technology sufficiently advanced to support specialized armies, military leaders, strategists, and so on. But large-scale confrontations are not limited to state societies: they occur, for example, among the horticultural Dugum Dani of central New Guinea.

The military history of the Dani, with its shifting alliances and confederations, is reminiscent of that of Europe, although Dani battles involve far fewer fighters and less sophisticated weaponry. Among the Dani, long periods of ritual warfare are characterized by formal battles announced through a challenge sent by one side to the opposing side. If the challenge is accepted, the protagonists meet at

Warfare among the Asmat of Indonesian New Guinea is sometimes internal, as when one village attacks another.

the agreed-upon battle site to set up their lines. Fighting with spears, sticks, and bows and arrows begins at midmorning and continues either until nightfall or until rain intervenes. There may also be a rest period during the midday heat during which the two sides shout insults at each other or talk and rest among themselves.

The front line of battle is composed of about a dozen active warriors and a few leaders. Behind them is a second line, still within arrow range, composed of those who have just left the forward line or are preparing to join it. The third line, outside arrow range, is composed of noncombatants—males too old or too young to participate and those recovering from wounds. This third line merely watches the battle taking place on the grassy plain. On the hillsides far back from the front line, some of the old men help to direct ancestral ghosts to the battle by gouging a line in the ground that points in the direction of the battlefield.[80]

Yet, as total as large-scale confrontations may be, even warfare has cultural rules. Among the Dani, for instance, no fighting occurs at night, and weapons are limited to simple spears and bows and arrows. Similarly, in state societies, governments will sign "self-denying" pacts restricting the use of poison gas, germ warfare, and so forth. Unofficially, private arrangements are common. One has only to glance through the memoirs of national leaders of the two world wars to become aware of locally arranged truces, visits to one another's front positions, exchanges of prisoners of war, and so on.

Explaining Warfare

Most societies anthropology knows about have had warfare between communities or larger territorial groups. (The vast majority of the societies in a recent cross-cultural study had at least occasional wars when they were first described, unless they had been pacified or incorporated by more dominant societies.[81]) Yet relatively little research has been done on the possible causes of war and why it varies in type and frequency. Why have some people fought a great deal, and others only infrequently? Why in some societies does warfare occur internally (within the society or language group)?

We have tentative and perhaps only partial answers to some of those questions. There is evidence that people in preindustrial societies go to war mostly out of fear—particularly a fear of expectable but unpredictable natural disasters (e.g., droughts, floods, locust infestations) that will destroy food resources. People may think they can protect themselves against such disasters ahead of time by taking things from defeated enemies. In any case, preindustrial societies with higher frequencies of war are very likely to have had a history of expectable but unpredictable disasters. The fact that chronic (annually recurring and therefore predictable) food shortages do not predict higher frequencies of war suggests that people go to war in an attempt to cushion the impact of the disasters they expect to occur in the future but cannot predict. Consistent with this tentative conclusion is the fact that the victors in war almost always take land or other resources from the defeated. And this is true for simpler as well as more complex preindustrial societies.[82] Might similar motives affect decisions about war and peace in the modern world?

We know that complex or politically centralized societies are likely to have professional armies, hierarchies of military authority, and sophisticated weapons.[83] But surprisingly, the frequency of warfare seems to be not much greater in complex societies than in simple band or tribal societies.[84]

We have some evidence that warfare is unlikely to occur internally (within a society) if it is small in population (21,000 or fewer people) or territory; in a larger society there is a high likelihood of warfare within the society, between communities or larger territorial divisions.[85] In fact, complex societies, even if they are politically unified, are not less likely than simpler societies to have internal warfare.[86]

What, if anything, do we know about recent warfare between nation-states? Here we also have some surprising findings. Although many people think that military alliances lessen the chance of war, it turns out that nations formally allied with other nations have gone to war more often than nations lacking formal alliances. Also, trade relationships do not appear to lessen the chance of war. Rather, disputes between trading partners escalate to war more frequently than disputes between nations that do not trade much with each other. Finally, military equality between nations, particularly when preceded by a rapid military buildup, seems to increase rather than lessen the chance of war between those nations.[87]

Clearly, these findings contradict some traditional beliefs about how to prevent war. If alliances, trade, and military buildups do *not* make war less likely, what may? We have already noted that participatory ("democratic") political systems are less likely to go to war with each other than are authoritarian political systems. Later, in the chapter on applied anthropology and social problems, we discuss how the results of these studies may translate into policies that could minimize the risk of war in the world.

▼ SUMMARY

1. All societies have customs or procedures that, organized on behalf of territorial groups, result in decision making and the resolution of disputes. These ways of creating and maintaining social order and coping with social disorder vary from society to society.

2. Societies with a band type of political organization are composed of fairly small, usually nomadic groups. Each of these bands is politically autonomous, the band being the largest group that acts as a political unit. Authority within the band is usually informal. Societies with band organization generally are egalitarian hunter-gatherers. But band organization may not have been typical of food collectors in the distant past.

3. Societies with tribal organization are similar to those with band organization in being egalitarian. But in contrast with band societies, they generally are food producers, have a higher population density, and are more sedentary. Tribal organi-

zation is defined by the presence of groupings (such as clans and age-sets) that can integrate more than one local group into a larger whole.

4. The personal qualities of leaders in tribal societies seem to be similar to the qualities of leaders in the United States, with one major difference: United States leaders are wealthier than others in their society.

5. Chiefdom organization differs from tribal organization in having formal authority structures that integrate multicommunity political units. Compared with societies with tribal organization, societies with chiefdoms are more densely populated and their communities are more permanent. In contrast to "big men" in tribal societies, who generally have to earn their privileges by their personal qualities, chiefs generally hold their positions permanently. Most chiefdom societies have social ranking.

6. A state has been defined as a political unit composed of many communities and having a cen-

tralized government with the authority to make and enforce laws, collect taxes, and draft men for military service. In state societies, the government tries to maintain a monopoly on the use of physical force. In addition, states are generally characterized by class stratification, intensive agriculture (the high productivity of which presumably allows the emergence of cities), commercial exchange, a high degree of economic and other specialization, and extensive foreign trade. The rulers of a state cannot depend forever on the use or threat of force to maintain their power; the people must believe that the rulers are legitimate or have the right to govern.

7. Degree of political participation varies in the societies studied by anthropologists, just as among modern nation-states. Degree of political participation seems to be high in small-scale societies, as well as in modern democratic nation-states, but not in between (feudal states and preindustrial empires).

8. Many societies lack specialized offices and institutions for dealing with conflict. Yet all societies have peaceful, regularized ways of handling at least certain disputes. Avoidance, community action, and negotiation and mediation are more common in simpler societies. Ritual apology occurs frequently in chiefdoms. Oaths and ordeals tend to occur in complex societies in which political officials lack power to enforce judicial decisions. Adjudication is more likely in stratified, more complex societies. Capital punishment seems to exist in nearly all societies, from the simplest to the most complex.

9. People are likely to resort to violence when regular, effective alternative means of resolving a conflict are not available. Violence can occur between individuals, within communities, and between communities. Violence that occurs between political entities such as communities, districts, or nations is generally referred to as warfare. The type of warfare varies in scope and complexity from society to society. Preindustrial societies with higher warfare frequencies are likely to have had a history of unpredictable disasters that destroyed food supplies. More often than not, societies with one type of violence have others.

▼ GLOSSARY TERMS

band	complementary opposition	ordeal	state organization
band organization	crime	raiding	tribal organization
chief	feuding	segmentary lineage system	tribe
chiefdom	headman	state	warfare
codified laws	oath		

▼ CRITICAL QUESTIONS

1. When, if ever, do you think the world will be politically unified, and why do you think so?
2. Why don't informal methods of social control work well in societies like our own? Why don't formal methods work better than they do?
3. What does research on war and violence suggest about how to minimize them?

▼ SUGGESTED READING

FERGUSON, R. B., AND WHITEHEAD, N. L., EDS. *War in the Tribal Zone: Expanding States and Indigenous Warfare.* Santa Fe, NM: School of American Research Press, 1992. An examination of the role of European colonialism in generating or changing the nature of warfare among a selection of non-Western peoples.

HAAS, J., ed. *The Anthropology of War.* Cambridge: Cambridge University Press, 1990. The contributors to this volume discuss war in general and in particular places, focusing on explanatory models of warfare, origins versus persistence of warfare, and causes versus effects of warfare in nonstate societies.

MCGLYNN, F., AND TUDEN, A., eds. *Anthropological Approaches to Political Behavior.* Pittsburgh: University of Pittsburgh Press, 1991. A compilation of articles that discuss political processes in a variety of societies. The editors provide an overview of the central concerns of political anthropology and its different approaches.

ROSS, M. H. "Political Participation." In C. R. Ember and M. Ember, eds., *Cross-Cultural Research for Social Science* (Englewood Cliffs, NJ: Prentice Hall, 1995). Prentice Hall/Simon & Schuster Custom Publishing. This chapter, written especially for undergraduates, discusses variation in political participation (decision making and demand making) in societies and nations. The author also discusses why political participation varies.

SCAGLION, R. "Law and Society." In C. R. Ember and M. Ember, eds., *Cross-Cultural Research for Social Science.* (Englewood Cliffs, NJ: Prentice Hall, 1995). Prentice Hall/Simon & Schuster Custom Publishing. Written especially for undergraduates, this chapter reviews some of the comparative research on law and summarizes two approaches to the study of law in anthropology—the rule-centered approach and the processual approach.

UPHAM, S., ed. *The Evolution of Political Systems: Sociopolitics in Small-Scale Sedentary Societies.* Cambridge: Cambridge University Press, 1990. The contributors to this volume offer different and sometimes contradictory ideas about political organization and change in sedentary societies. They explore fundamental questions such as how people come to give up local autonomy and equality for bigger, hierarchical political units.

▼ NOTES

[1]Elman R. Service, *Primitive Social Organization: An Evolutionary Perspective* (New York: Random House, 1962).

[2]Carmel Schrire, "Wild Surmises on Savage Thoughts," in Carmel Schrire, ed., *Past and Present in Hunter Gatherer Studies* (Orlando, FL: Academic Press, 1984), pp. 1–25; see also Eleanor Leacock and Richard Lee, "Introduction," in Eleanor Leacock and Richard Lee, eds., *Politics and History in Band Societies* (Cambridge: Cambridge University Press, 1982), p. 8.

[3]Julian Steward, *Theory of Culture Change* (Urbana: University of Illinois Press, 1955), p. 125.

[4]Morton H. Fried, *The Evolution of Political Society: An Essay in Political Anthropology* (New York: Random House, 1967), p. 68.

[5]Service, *Primitive Social Organization,* p. 109.

[6]Jean L. Briggs, "Eskimo Women: Makers of Men," in Carolyn J. Matthiasson, *Many Sisters: Women in Cross-Cultural Perspective* (New York: Free Press, 1974), pp. 261–304.

[7]Therkel Mathiassen, *Material Culture of the Iglulik Eskimos* (Copenhagen: Glydendalske, 1928), as quoted in E. M. Weyer, *The Eskimos: Their Environment and Folkways* (New Haven, CT: Yale University Press, 1932), p. 213.

[8]Service, *Primitive Social Organization,* pp. 114–15.

[9]Ibid., p. 126.

[10]Paul Bohannan, "The Migration and Expansion of the Tiv," *Africa,* 24 (1954): 3.

[11]Marshall D. Sahlins, "The Segmentary Lineage: An Organization of Predatory Expansion," *American Anthropologist,* 63 (1961): 342.

[12]Raymond C. Kelly, *The Nuer Conquest: The Structure and Development of an Expansionist System* (Ann Arbor: University of Michigan Press, 1985), p. 1.

[13]Sahlins, "The Segmentary Lineage," p. 345.

[14]Neville Dyson-Hudson, *Karimojong Politics* (Oxford: Clarendon Press, 1966), chapters 5 and 6.

[15]Ibid.

[16]Marshall Sahlins, Moala: *Culture and Nature on a Fijian Island* (Ann Arbor: University of Michigan Press, 1962), pp. 293–94.

[17]Marshall D. Sahlins, "Poor Man, Rich Man, Big-Man, Chief: Political Types in Melanesia and Polynesia," *Comparative Studies in Society and History,* 5 (1963): 295.

[18]Marshall Sahlins, "Other Times, Other Customs: The Anthropology of History," *American Anthropologist,* 85 (1983): 519.

[19]Sahlins, "Poor Man, Rich Man, Big-Man, Chief," p. 297.

[20]Robert L. Carneiro, "A Theory of the Origin of the State," *Science,* August 21, 1970, p. 733.

[21]See Max Weber, *The Theory of Social and Economic Organization,* trans. A. M. Henderson and Talcott Parsons (New York: Oxford University Press, 1947), p. 154.

[22]Hakan Wiberg, "Self-Determination as an International Issue," in I. M. Lewis, ed., *Nationalism and Self-Determination in the Horn of Africa* (London: Ithaca Press, 1983), pp. 43–65.

[23]For an extensive review of the various theories about legitimacy, see Ronald Cohen, "Introduction," in Ronald Cohen and Judith D. Toland, eds., *State Forma-*

tion and Political Legitimacy, vol. 1: Political Anthropology (New Brunswick, NJ: Transaction Books, 1988), pp. 1–3.

[24] M. I. Finley, Politics in the Ancient World (Cambridge: Cambridge University Press, 1983).

[25] Jerome Carcopino, Daily Life in Ancient Rome: The People and the City at the Height of the Empire, edited with bibliography and notes by Henry T. Rowell, translated from the French by E. O. Lorimer (New Haven, CT: Yale University Press, 1940), pp. 18–20.

[26] Our discussion of Nupe is based on S. F. Nadel, "Nupe State and Community," Africa, 8 (1935): 257–303.

[27] Melvin Ember, "The Relationship between Economic and Political Development in Nonindustrialized Societies," Ethnology, 2 (1963): 228–48.

[28] Data from Robert B. Textor, comp., A Cross-Cultural Summary (New Haven, CT: HRAF Press, 1967).

[29] Ember, "The Relationship between Economic and Political Development in Nonindustrialized Societies."

[30] Data from Textor, comp., A Cross-Cultural Summary.

[31] Raoul Naroll, "Two Solutions to Galton's Problem," Philosophy of Science, 28 (January 1961): 15–39. See also Marc H. Ross, "Socioeconomic Complexity, Socialization, and Political Differentiation: A Cross-Cultural Study," Ethos, 9 (1981): 217–47.

[32] Ember, "The Relationship between Economic and Political Development in Nonindustrialized Societies," pp. 244–46.

[33] Service, Primitive Social Organization; see also David P. Braun and Stephen Plog, "Evolution of 'Tribal' Social Networks: Theory and Prehistoric North American Evidence," American Antiquity, 47 (1982): 504–25; Jonathan Haas, "Warfare and the Evolution of Tribal Polities in the Prehistoric Southwest," in Jonathan Haas, ed., The Anthropology of War (New York: Cambridge University Press, 1990), pp. 171–89.

[34] Allen Johnson and Timothy Earle, The Evolution of Human Societies: From Foraging Group to Agrarian State (Stanford, CA: Stanford University Press, 1987), p. 158; Robert L. Carneiro, "Chiefdom-Level Warfare as Exemplified in Fiji and the Cauca Valley," in Haas, ed., The Anthropology of War, pp. 190–211.

[35] Service, Primitive Social Organization, pp. 112, 145.

[36] Gary Feinman and Jill Nietzel, "Too Many Types: An Overview of Sedentary Prestate Societies in the Americas," in Michael B. Schiffer, ed., Advances in Archaeological Method and Theory, vol. 7, (Orlando, FL: Academic Press, 1984), pp. 39–102.

[37] For a more detailed description and evaluation of the available theories, see Chapter 9 in Carol R. Ember and Melvin Ember, Anthropology, 8th ed. (Upper Saddle River, NJ: Prentice Hall, 1996). See also Ronald Cohen and Elman R. Service, eds., Origins of the State: The Anthropology of Political Evolution (Philadelphia: Institute for the Study of Human Issues, 1978).

[38] William H. McNeill, Plagues and Peoples (Garden City, NY: Doubleday Anchor, 1976).

[39] Robert L. Carneiro, "Political Expansion as an Expression of the Principle of Competitive Exclusion," in Cohen and Service, eds., Origins of the State, p. 215.

[40] Data from Textor, comp., A Cross-Cultural Summary.

[41] Carneiro, "Political Expansion as an Expression of the Principle of Competitive Exclusion." See also Hornell Hart, "The Logistic Growth of Political Areas," Social Forces, 26 (1948): 396–408; Raoul Naroll, "Imperial Cycles and World Order," Peace Research Society: Papers, 7, Chicago Conference (1967): 83–101; and Louis A. Marano, "A Macrohistoric Trend toward World Government," Behavior Science Notes, 8 (1973): 35–40.

[42] For a review of the descriptive literature until the late 1970s, see Joan Vincent, "Political Anthropology: Manipulative Strategies," Annual Review of Anthropology, 7 (1978): 175–94.

[43] Dennis Werner, "Chiefs and Presidents: A Comparison of Leadership Traits in the United States and among the Mekranoti-Kayapo of Central Brazil," Ethos, 10 (1982): 136–48.

[44] Waud H. Kracke, Force and Persuasion: Leadership in an Amazonian Society (Chicago: University of Chicago Press, 1979), p. 232.

[45] Werner, "Chiefs and Presidents."

[46] Sahlins, "Poor Man, Rich Man, Big-Man, Chief," pp. 285–303.

[47] Kracke, Force and Persuasion, p. 41.

[48] Rena Lederman, "Big Men, Large and Small? Towards a Comparative Perspective," Ethnology, 29 (1990): 3–15.

[49] Ernest Brandewie, "The Place of the Big Man in Traditional Hagen Society in the Central Highlands of New Guinea," in Frank McGlynn and Arthur Tuden, eds., Anthropological Approaches to Political Behavior (Pittsburgh: University of Pittsburgh Press, 1991), pp. 62–82.

[50] Maria Lepowsky, "Big Men, Big Women and Cultural Autonomy," Ethnology, 29 (1990): 35–50.

[51] Marc Howard Ross, "Political Organization and Political Participation: Exit, Voice, and Loyalty in Preindustrial Societies," Comparative Politics, 21 (1988): 73. The discussion in this section draws mostly from ibid., pp. 73–89 and from Marc Howard Ross, "Political Participation," in Carol R. Ember and Melvin Ember, eds., Cross-Cultural Research for Social Science (Englewood Cliffs, NJ: Prentice Hall, 1995). Prentice Hall/Simon & Schuster Custom Publishing.

[52] For studies of international relations that support these conclusions, see footnotes 2 and 3 in Carol R. Ember, Melvin Ember, and Bruce Russett, "Peace between Participatory Polities: A Cross-Cultural Test of the 'Democracies Rarely Fight Each Other' Hypothesis," World Politics, 44 (1992): 573–99.

[53] Ibid.

[54] Richard Scaglion, "Law and Society," in Carol R. Ember and Melvin Ember, eds., Cross-Cultural Research for Social Science (Englewood Cliffs, NJ: Pren-

tice Hall, 1995). Prentice Hall/Simon & Schuster Custom Publishing.

[55]E. Adamson Hoebel, *The Law of Primitive Man* (New York: Atheneum, 1968 [originally published 1954]), p. 4; quoting S. P. Simpson and Ruth Field, "Law and the Social Sciences," *Virginia Law Review,* 32 (1946): 858.

[56]Donald Black, *The Social Structure of Right and Wrong* (San Diego: Academic Press, 1993), pp. 79–83.

[57]Ross, "Political Organization and Political Participation."

[58]Franz Boas, *Central Eskimos,* Bureau of American Ethnology, Annual Report no. 6 (Washington, D.C., 1888), p. 668.

[59]Keith F. Otterbein, *The Ultimate Coercive Sanction: A Cross-Cultural Study of Capital Punishment* (New Haven, CT: HRAF Press, 1986), p. 107.

[60]Dane Archer and Rosemary Gartner, *Violence and Crime in Cross-National Perspective* (New Haven, CT: Yale University Press, 1984), pp. 118–39.

[61]Scaglion, "Law and Society"; Black, *The Social Structure of Right and Wrong,* pp. 83–86.

[62]Ibid.

[63]E. E. Evans-Pritchard, "The Nuer of the Southern Sudan," in M. Fortes and E. E. Evans-Pritchard, eds., *African Political Systems* (New York: Oxford University Press, 1940), p. 291. The discussion of Nuer follows this source.

[64]Letitia Hickson, "The Social Contexts of Apology in Dispute Settlement: A Cross-Cultural Study," *Ethnology,* 25 (1986): 283–94.

[65]Ibid.; and Klaus-Friedrich Koch, Soraya Altorki, Andrew Arno, and Letitia Hickson, "Ritual Reconciliation and the Obviation of Grievances: A Comparative Study in the Ethnography of Law," *Ethnology,* 16 (1977): 279.

[66]John M. Roberts, "Oaths, Autonomic Ordeals, and Power," in Clellan S. Ford, ed., *Cross-Cultural Approaches: Readings in Comparative Research* (New Haven, CT: HRAF Press, 1967), p. 169. The discussion follows ibid.

[67]Alois Musil, *The Manners and Customs of the Rwala Bedouins,* American Geographical Society, Oriental Exploration Studies, no. 6 (New York, 1928), p. 430, as cited in Roberts, "Oaths, Autonomic Ordeals, and Power," pp. 169–70.

[68]Roberts, "Oaths, Autonomic Ordeals, and Power," p. 192.

[69]Hoebel, *The Law of Primitive Man,* chapter 9.

[70]Richard D. Schwartz, "Social Factors in the Development of Legal Control: A Case Study of Two Israeli Settlements," *Yale Law Journal,* 63 (February 1954): 475.

[71]Textor, comp., *A Cross-Cultural Summary.*

[72]Wilfred T. Masumura, "Law and Violence: A Cross-Cultural Study," *Journal of Anthropological Research,* 33 (1977): 388–99.

[73]Scaglion, "Law and Society"; Black, *The Social Structure of Right and Wrong,* pp. 83–86; Katherine S.

Newman, *Law and Economic Organization: A Comparative Study of Preindustrial Societies* (Cambridge, MA: Cambridge University Press, 1983), p. 131.

[74]Carol R. Ember and Melvin Ember, "War, Socialization, and Interpersonal Violence," *Journal of Conflict Resolution,* 38 (1994): 620–46.

[75]Newman, *Law and Economic Organization,* p. 131.

[76]Nicholas J. Gubser, *The Nunamiut Eskimos: Hunters of Caribou* (New Haven, CT: Yale University Press, 1965), p. 151.

[77]Keith F. Otterbein and Charlotte Swanson Otterbein, "An Eye for an Eye, A Tooth for a Tooth: A Cross-Cultural Study of Feuding," *American Anthropologist,* 67 (1965): 1476.

[78]Douglas R. White, "Rethinking Polygyny: Co-Wives, Codes, and Cultural Systems," *Current Anthropology,* (1988): 529–58.

[79]Orlando Patterson, *Slavery and Social Death: A Comparative Study* (Cambridge, MA: Harvard University Press, 1982), pp. 345–52.

[80]Karl Heider, *The Dugum Dani* (Chicago: Aldine, 1970), pp. 105–11. See also Karl Heider, *Grand Valley Dani: Peaceful Warriors* (New York: Holt, Rinehart & Winston, 1979), pp. 88–99.

[81]Melvin Ember and Carol R. Ember, "Cross-Cultural Studies of War and Peace: Recent Achievements and Future Possibilities," in S. P. Reyna and R. E. Downs, eds., *Studying War: Anthropological Perspectives* (New York: Gordon & Breach, 1992), pp. 188–189.

[82]Carol R. Ember and Melvin Ember, "Resource Unpredictability, Mistrust, and War: A Cross-Cultural Study," *Journal of Conflict Resolution,* 36 (1992): 242–62. See also Melvin Ember, "Statistical Evidence for an Ecological Explanation of Warfare," *American Anthropologist,* 84 (1982): 645–49. For a discussion of how Dani warfare seems to be motivated mainly by economic considerations, see Paul Shankman, "Culture Contact, Cultural Ecology, and Dani Warfare," *Man,* 26 (1991): 299–321.

[83]Keith Otterbein, *The Evolution of War* (New Haven, CT: HRAF Press, 1970).

[84]Ember and Ember, "Resource Unpredictability, Mistrust, and War." See also Otterbein, *The Evolution of War;* and Colin K. Loftin, "Warfare and Societal Complexity: A Cross-Cultural Study of Organized Fighting in Preindustrial Societies," Ph.D. dissertation, University of North Carolina at Chapel Hill, 1971.

[85]Carol R. Ember, "An Evaluation of Alternative Theories of Matrilocal versus Patrilocal Residence," *Behavior Science Research,* 9 (1974): 135–49.

[86]Keith F. Otterbein, "Internal War: A Cross-Cultural Study," *American Anthropologist,* 70 (1968): 283. See also Marc H. Ross, "Internal and External Conflict and Violence," *Journal of Conflict Resolution,* 29 (1985): 547–79.

[87]J. David Singer, "Accounting for International War: The State of the Discipline," *Annual Review of Sociology,* 6 (1980): 349–67.

Psychology and Culture

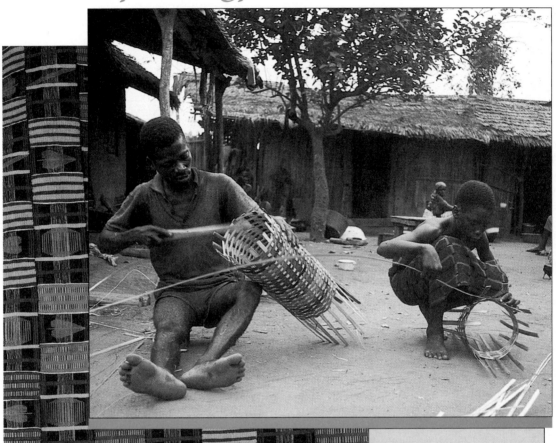

Visitors to another society often come to feel that the people there think differently, or have different reactions to situations, that they seem to have different **personalities** (distinctive ways of thinking, feeling, and behaving) compared with people back home. Stereotypes are born from these casual observations: certain peoples are thought to be reserved, others authoritarian, still others hot-tempered. Although anthropologists generally reject such stereotypes because they are often based on hasty, even ethnocentric judgments, they do not reject the idea that there may be differences from society to society in the frequencies of some aspects of thinking, feeling, and behaving. Individuals may be frequently reserved in some societies, for example.

Consider the contrast in feelings and behavior between the Semai of central Malaya and the Yanomamö of the Brazil-Venezuela border—a contrast that clearly expresses differences in personality. The Semai are famous in Malaya for their timidity and have never been described as hostile or surly. When asked about anger, the Semai say, "We do not get angry."[1] The Yanomamö, on the other hand, are famous for their fierceness. They not only have chronic warfare between villages, but frequently show aggression within a village. Shouting and threatening to obtain demands are frequent, as are wife beating and bloody fights with clubs. Men are proud of their scars and sometimes shave their heads to display them.[2]

Even though there may be psychological differences between societies, there also are psychological similarities. After all, we are all human. People the world over cry or weep when a loved one dies, laugh or smile when something good happens, learn from mistakes, and have many of the same needs. Anthropologists who are interested in psychological differences between and within societies and in psychological similarities across the broad range of human societies call themselves *psychological anthropologists.* (Psychologists who study people in two or more societies call themselves *cross-cultural psychologists.*) Four main questions seem to characterize psychological anthropology: To what extent do all human beings develop psychologically in the same ways? If there are differences, what are they and what may account for them? How do people in different societies conceive of personality and psychological development? What kinds of cultural variation might be explained by psychological factors? This chapter discusses some of the attempts made by researchers to answer these questions.

THE UNIVERSALITY OF PSYCHOLOGICAL DEVELOPMENT

Anthropologists became interested in psychology in the early years of this century, partly because they did not believe that human nature was completely revealed in Western societies, as psychologists then generally assumed. Only recently have many psychologists joined anthropologists in questioning the assumption that humans are exactly the same psychologically in all societies. Psychologist Otto Klineberg, for example, scolded his colleagues in 1974: "My contact with anthropology affected me somewhat like a religious conversion. How could psychologists speak of *human* attributes and *human* behavior when they knew only one kind of human being?"[3]

How can we know what is universal about human behavior and what is variable until we study all kinds of humans? Because humans the world over are the same species and share a very large proportion of genes, we might assume that there is a good deal of similarity across societies in the way people develop psychologically from birth to maturity or in the way people think, feel, and behave. We have already discussed many universals (culture, language, marriage, the incest taboo), but here we discuss some that are related more to psychology. Donald Brown complied a list of probable human universals in the psychological realm.[4] They include the ability to create taxonomies, make binary contrasts, order phenomena, use logical operators (e.g., *and, not, equals),* plan for the future, and have an understanding of the world and what it is about. With regard to ideas about people, it seems universal to have a concept of the self or person, to recognize individual faces, to try to discern other persons' intentions from observable clues (in their faces, utterances, and actions), and to imagine what others are thinking. With regard to emotions, people seem universally to be able to empathize with the feelings of others, facially communicate and recognize (as well as hide or mimic) the emotions of happiness, sadness, anger, fear, surprise, disgust, and contempt (see the box titled "Do Masks Show Emotion in Universal Ways?" in the chapter on the arts), smile when friendly, cry when in pain or unhappy, play for fun, show and feel affection for others, feel sexual attraction, envy, and jealousy, and have similar childhood fears (e.g., fear of strangers).

What about psychological development? We saw in the chapter on communication and language that certain aspects of language acquisition appear to be universal across cultures. In what respects is psychological development the same the world over? In what respects is it different?

Early Research on Emotional Development

When Margaret Mead went to American Samoa in the mid-1920s, psychologists believed that adolescence was universally a period of "storm and stress" because of the physiological changes that occur at puberty. Mead's observations of, and interviews with, Samoan adolescent girls led her to doubt the idea that adolescence was necessarily a time of turmoil. The Samoan girls apparently showed little evidence of emotional upheaval and rebelliousness, and therefore it was questionable whether psychological development in adolescence was the same in all societies.[5]

Bronislaw Malinowski was another early anthropologist who questioned the universality of an assumption about emotional development, in this case Freud's assumption that young boys universally see themselves (unconsciously) as sexual rivals of their fathers for possession of their mothers. Freud had called these feelings the Oedipus complex, after the character in Greek mythology who killed his father and married his mother without knowing that they were his parents. Freud thought that all boys before the age of seven or so would show hostility toward their fathers, but Malinowski disagreed on the basis of his fieldwork in the matrilineal Trobriand Islands.[6]

Malinowski suggested that young boys in nonmatrilineal societies may feel hostility toward the father not as a sexual rival but as the disciplinarian. Malinowski proposed this theory because he thought that the Oedipus complex works differently in matrilineal societies. Boys in matrilineal societies may feel more hostile toward their mother's brother—who is the main authority figure in the matrilineal kin group—than toward their father.

Derek Freeman criticized Mead's conclusions about Samoa,[7] and Melford Spiro challenged Malinowski's conclusions about the Trobriand Islanders.[8] Mead and Malinowski may or may not have been correct about the societies they studied (we really cannot know for sure because we cannot travel back in time), but the issues they raised remain crucial to the question of whether psychological development is similar in all societies. To find out, we need research in *many* societies, not just a few. Only on the basis of extensive cross-cultural research will we be able to decide whether

Adolescence in many societies is a time for developing work skills. An Asmat boy in Indonesian New Guinea is learning to carve and an adult is supervising.

stages of emotional development can be affected by cultural differences.

For example, it is only recently that adolescence has been systematically studied cross-culturally. Alice Schlegel and Herbert Barry reported that adolescence is generally not a period of overt rebelliousness. The reason, they suggested, is related to the fact that most people in most societies live with or near (and depend on) close kin before and after they grow up. Only in societies like our own, where children leave home when they grow up, might adolescents be rebellious, possibly to prepare emotionally for going out on their own.[9] (Recall the box titled "Neolocality and Adolescent Rebellion: Are They Related?" in the chapter on marital residence and kinship.)

Research on Cognitive Development

One day the two of us went out for pizza. The pizza maker was laughing hilariously, and we asked what was so funny. He told us: "I just asked the guy ahead of you, 'How many slices do you want me to cut the pizza into, six or eight?' 'Six,' he said, 'I'm not very hungry.'"

According to a theory of cognitive (intellectual) development suggested by Jean Piaget, the renowned Swiss psychologist, the "not very hungry" guy may not have acquired the concept of *conservation,* which characterizes a stage of thinking normally acquired by children between the ages of seven and eleven in Western societies.[10] The pizza customer ahead of us, like many very young children, seemed not to understand that certain properties of an object (such as quantity, weight, and volume) remain constant even if the object is divided into small pieces or removed to a container of a different shape. They have not acquired the mental image of *reversibility,* the ability to imagine that if you put the pizza back together again it would be the same size whether you had previously cut it into eight or six slices. To the child or adult who has not acquired the ability to reverse actions mentally, eight slices may seem like more pizza than six slices, because eight is more than six.

Piaget's theory says that the development of thinking in humans involves a series of stages, each of which is characterized by different mental skills. To get to a higher stage of thinking, one has to pass through a lower stage. So, Piaget's theory would predict that the pizza customer would not be able to think systematically about the possible outcomes of hypothetical situations (a defining feature of Piaget's *formal-operational* stage) because he had not acquired the notion of conservation and the other mental skills that characterize the previous *(concrete-operational)* stage of cognitive development.

What does the available evidence suggest about the universality of Piaget's supposed stages? And do people the world over get to each stage at the same age? The first stage of development *(sensorimotor)* has not been investigated in many societies, but the results of studies conducted so far are remarkably consistent. They support Piaget's notion that there is a predictable order in the sequence of stages.[11] And, on the basis of their reactions to the same conditions, babies in different places seem to think similarly. For example, a comparison of French babies and Baoulé babies in the Ivory Coast (West Africa) showed that the Baoulé babies, who had never seen objects such as red plastic tubes and paper clips, nevertheless tried to pass the clips through the tubes in the same way the French babies did. The two sets of babies even made the same kinds of errors.[12] And even though they have few

toys, the Baoulé babies showed advances over French babies on tasks such as using instruments to increase the reach of the arm. But Baoulé babies are allowed to touch all kinds of objects, even things that Europeans consider dangerous.[13]

Most of the cross-cultural studies of Piaget's stages have focused on the transition between the second *(preoperational)* and third *(concrete-operational)* stages, particularly the attainment of the concept of conservation. The results of many of these studies are somewhat puzzling. Although older children are generally more likely to show conservation than younger children, it is not clear what to make of the apparent finding that the attainment of conservation is much delayed in many non-Western populations. Indeed, in some places most of the adults tested do not appear to understand one or more of the conservation properties.

Can this be true? Do people in different cultures differ that much in intellectual functioning, or is there some problem with the way conservation is measured? Is it possible that an adult who just brought water from the river in a large jug and poured it into five smaller containers does not know that the quantity of water is still the same? We may also be skeptical about the findings on the formal-operational stage. Most of the studies of formal-operational thinking have found little evidence of such thinking in non-Western populations. But people in nonliterate societies surely have formal-operational thinking if they can navigate using the stars, remember how to return to camp after a 15-mile trek, or identify how people are related to each other three and more generations back.

A girl four-and-a-half-years-old is being tested for conservation (of area).

One reason to be skeptical about the apparent findings regarding delay of conservation and formal-operational thinking is that most of the cross-cultural psychologists have taken tests developed here (in our own and other Western countries) to measure cognitive development elsewhere.[14] This procedure puts non-Westerners at a considerable disadvantage, because they are not as familiar as Westerners with the test materials and the whole testing situation. In tests of conservation, for example, researchers have often used strange-looking glass cylinders and beakers. Some researchers who have used natively familiar materials, however, have gotten different results. Douglass Price-Williams found no difference between Tiv (West Africa) and European children in understanding the conservation of earth, nuts, and number.[15] Also, some researchers have retested children after brief training sessions and found that they improved substantially. It would seem then that children anywhere can acquire the concept of conservation if they have had preparatory life experiences or appropriate training.[16]

The results of tests elsewhere on formal-operational thinking may also be questionable. Such tests ask questions dealing with content that is taught here in science and mathematics classes. It should not be surprising then that schooled individuals usually do better than the nonschooled on tests of formal-operational thinking. And where compulsory schooling is lacking, we should not expect people to do well on tests of such thinking.[17]

In trying to find out what may be universal in emotional and cognitive development, researchers have discovered some apparent differences between societies. These differences, which we now turn to, need to be explored and explained.

CROSS-CULTURAL VARIATION IN PSYCHOLOGICAL CHARACTERISTICS

Thinking about personality differences seems to come easily to many North Americans. We like to talk about the psychology of those we know. We speculate why one friend is emotional, why another has a hot temper, why another is shy. We may also wonder why one friend is likely to remember faces and why another is a whiz at computers. We are interested in personality as an individual characteristic, and we emphasize the uniqueness of each individual. Indeed, because every person has a unique combination of genetic traits and life experiences, we can say that in some ways no person is like any other person. But anthropologists are interested in approaching personality from a different perspective. Instead of focusing on the uniqueness of an individual, psychological anthropologists are interested in those aspects of personality that may be common in a population.

Why should we expect different societies to differ in some personality characteristics? It is generally agreed that our personalities are the result of an interaction between genetic inheritance and life experiences. But a considerable portion of one's life experiences (as well as one's genes) is shared with others. Parents undoubtedly exert a major influence on the way we grow up. Because family members share similar life experiences (as well as genes), they may be somewhat similar in personality. But we have to consider why a particular family raises children the way it does. To some extent, all families are unique. Yet much of the way parents rear children is influenced by their culture—by typical patterns of family life and by shared conceptions of the way to bring up children.

It is not easy to determine the extent to which members of a society share conceptions about child rearing. As we look around at families in our own society we see differences in upbringing that reflect different ideas about the "right" way to raise children. Indeed, some parents seem determined to bring up their children in unconventional (in terms of our society) ways. Still, in a study of unconventional California families (headed by single mothers, unmarried couples, or living in communes), researchers found that compared with parents in other societies, these so-called unconventional parents did not differ that much from conventional parents (married, living in nuclear families).[18] For example, even though unconventional California mothers breast-fed their children for a significantly longer period than conventional mothers did, both types of mothers usually stopped breast-feeding after about a year, which is far below the worldwide average. In 70 percent of the world's societies, mothers typically breast-feed children for at least two years; last-born children may be weaned even later. In a few societies, such as the Chenchu of India, children typically were not weaned until they were five or six years old.[19] Both the unconventional and conventional California parents differed in other ways too, compared with parents in most other societies. In the California study, no parent (conventional or unconventional) was observed to carry a baby more than 25 percent of the time, but it is common in many preindustrial societies for babies to be held more than half the day.[20]

It is only when we examine other societies and their patterns of child rearing that our own cultural conceptions begin to become apparent. Consider how societies vary in how quickly parents respond to an infant's needs, in other words, the degree of "indulgence." In many aspects of indulgence—amount of time holding, feeding on demand, responding to crying—industrialized societies such as the United States tend to indulge babies less than do preindustrialized societies. In contrast to those preindustrial societies in which babies are held more than half the day, consider the United States, England, and the Netherlands, where babies may spend most of the day in cagelike devices such as playpens or cribs. It is estimated that babies are held or touched only 12–20 percent of their daytime hours in these countries (and in Japan). The same pattern continues at nighttime. In preindustrial societies, babies are much more apt to be close to another person, usually sleeping with the mother in the same bed or, if not in the same bed, in the same room. During the day, babies are breast-fed in all preindustrial societies, usually on demand. In industrialized societies, bottle-feeding is common, and feeding is usually spaced out every few hours; in some preindustrial societies babies are fed twenty to forty times a day. And in many preindustrial societies people respond very quickly to an infant's crying. For example, among the Efe of the Ituri Forest in central Africa, a three-

One major difference in childrearing between the West and other places is the degree to which an infant is held by a caretaker during the day. In the United States and other Western countries, an infant spends much of the day in a crib, playpen, or stroller. This Bai baby from Yunnan Province in China spends a good deal of the day in physical contact with the mother.

month-old infant who cries gets a response within 10 seconds 75 percent of the time. In the United States, a caregiver deliberately *does not* respond at all 44–46 percent of the time.[21]

The cross-cultural variation just described seems to reflect cultural attitudes toward child rearing. Parents in the United States say that they do not want their babies to be dependent and clingy—they want to produce independent and self-reliant children. Whether children become self-reliant because of our kind of child rearing is debatable,[22] but our attitudes about child rearing are certainly consistent with our practices.

Let us again consider the Yanomamö and the Semai. With respect to aggression, the two societies have very different ways of dealing with children. (The difference is not surprising, in view of the way adult behaviors and attitudes differ in the two societies.) Yanomamö boys are encouraged to be fierce and are rarely punished for hitting either their parents or the girls in the village. One father, for example, lets his son Ariwari

> beat him on the face and head to express his anger and temper, laughing and commenting on his ferocity. Although Ariwari is only about four years old, he has already learned that the appropriate response to a flash of anger is to strike someone with his hand or with an object, and it is not uncommon for him to give his father a healthy smack in the face whenever something displeases him. He is frequently goaded into hitting his father by teasing, being rewarded by gleeful cheers of assent from his mother and from the other adults in the household.[23]

Whereas the Yanomamö clearly and actively encourage aggression, the Semai communicate nonviolence in more subtle ways. They say, in fact, that they do not teach children. The Semai expect children to be nonviolent and are shocked when they are not. When a child loses her temper, an adult will simply cart her off and bring her home. The Semai do not physically punish a child's aggression—and this approach may be one of the most important teaching devices of all. With such teaching—by example—a child hardly ever sees an aggressive model and has no aggression to imitate.[24] In comparison with the ways Semai and Yanomamö parents treat their children, most North American parents are probably somewhere in the middle. Hardly any North American parents would encourage children to hit them in the face or encourage them to hit other children. Yet many North American

parents probably use physical punishment sometimes, and many feel that boys especially should "stand up for themselves" if another child provokes a fight.

As these examples suggest, societies vary in how they raise children. We assume that the way children are reared determines in part the type of personality they will have in adulthood. In other words, different societies, with different customs of child rearing, will probably tend to produce different kinds of people. Other cultural differences also may produce differences in typical personality characteristics. As we will see, growing up in an extended family and going to school seem to affect personality development. We do not mean to suggest, however, that all personalities in a society are alike. An individual's uniqueness is derived from her or his distinctive genetic endowment and life experiences—and thus one personality will be somewhat different from another within the same culture or subculture.

Cultural anthropologists are interested in common or shared patterns of behavior, belief, feeling, and thinking. Psychological anthropologists are therefore often interested in those aspects of personality that are common or typically shared with others—other members of the society or other members of some subcultural group. Personality attributes are not all-or-nothing characteristics but usually need to be described or measured in terms of degree. So, for example, aggressiveness is not present or absent in a person, but is found to a greater or lesser degree in some people than in others. Similarly, when we say that a great deal of physical or verbal aggression is a characteristic personality trait in a particular society, we are making a relative judgment. For example, when we compare ethnographic descriptions of the Yanomamö and Semai, we can be fairly certain that the Yanomamö typically display much more aggression than the Semai. If fieldworkers based their judgments on systematic comparisons of behavior, we could say how often aggressive behavior is exhibited in a culture, and we could calculate the *modal* frequency of aggression among individuals within a given period of time. That modal frequency could then be compared with the modal frequencies of such behavior in other societies.

Just as culture is never fixed or static, so typical personality characteristics are never static. Individuals often alter their behavior in adapting to changing circumstances. When enough individuals in a society have altered their own behavior or the way they bring up their children, typical personality characteristics will also presumably have changed.

Yanomamö men dueling while a child watches

Child-Rearing Explanations

Many researchers have tried to discover if variation in child-rearing customs can account for observed psychological differences. **Socialization** is a term used by both anthropologists and psychologists to describe the development, through the influence of parents and other people, of patterns of behavior in children (and attitudes and values) that conform to cultural expectations. Parents and others often try to socialize children directly by rewarding certain behaviors and ignoring or punishing other behaviors. Socialization can be indirect or subtle as well as direct. In assigning tasks to children, parents are not only encouraging specific skills needed for adult life, but they may also be subtly communicating what kind of person they want their children to become. Whether children go to school may affect their psychological (particularly cognitive) development. Finally, parents may affect the psychological development of their children by the way they generally feel about them.

Parental Acceptance and Rejection. In a classic study of personality, Cora Du Bois spent almost eighteen months on the island of Alor in eastern Indonesia studying the native Alorese. To understand the Alorese personality, she broke new ground by asking specialists in various fields to assess and interpret her field data independently. These authorities were given no background briefing on Alorese culture or attitudes, nor were they permitted to see Du Bois's general ethnographic notes or interpretations. To a remarkable degree, their findings concurred with hers.[25]

A rather unfavorable picture of the typical Alorese personality emerged from this many-sided investigation. Alorese of both sexes were described by Du Bois and her colleagues as suspicious and antagonistic, prone to violent, emotional, and often jealous outbursts. They tended to be uninterested in the world around them, slovenly in workmanship, and indifferent to goals.

Turning to the possible causal influences, Du Bois and her co-researchers focused on the experiences of the Alorese infant, particularly time gaps between breast-feedings. At the root of much of Alorese personality development, they suggested, is the mother's long absence from the baby during the day; she returns to agricultural work about ten days to two weeks after the birth. Women are the major food suppliers, working daily in the family gardens; men occupy themselves with commercial affairs, usually the trading of pigs, gongs, and kettledrums. The infant is left in the care of the father, an older sibling, or a grandparent, but it is deprived of the breast as well as the mother for most of the day. Substitute foods are given, but infants often spit them out, suggesting that they are not satisfactory. In Freudian terms, the infant experiences oral frustration and resultant anxiety. At the same time, the baby suffers bewildering switches in attention, from loving and petting to neglect and bad-tempered rejection. Thus, maternal neglect in infancy is viewed as being largely responsible for Alorese personality.

But how do we know that maternal neglect is really responsible for the seeming suspiciousness and outbursts of jealousy among the Alorese? Perhaps maternal neglect is responsible, but the cause or causes could also be any number of other conditions of Alorese life. For example, some critics have suggested that the high prevalence of debilitating diseases in Alor may be responsible for much of the behavior of the Alorese.[26] For us to be more certain that a particular aspect of child rearing produces certain effects on Alorese personality, we must compare the people of Alor with people in other societies. Do other societies with this kind of maternal neglect show the same pattern of personality traits? If they do, then the presumed association becomes more plausible. If they do not, then the interpretation becomes questionable.

Although subsequent researchers have not specifically followed up on the possible effects of time gaps between breast-feedings, Ruth and Robert Munroe studied the effects of more versus less holding by the mother in infancy on Logoli children.[27] The Munroes had observational information on how often infants were held, and they were able to interview many of these individuals as children five years later. They were interested in seeing whether children who had been held more often by their mothers were more secure, trusting, and optimistic. So they designed a series of personality measures appropriate for young children. As a measure of optimism, they showed children smiling faces and nonsmiling faces and asked which they preferred. As measures of trust, they looked to see how long a child was willing to stay in a room with a stranger or play with new toys. The results of the study suggest that children who were often held or carried by their mothers as infants are significantly more trusting and optimistic at age five than are other children. Somewhat to their surprise, the Munroes found that, although time held by other caregivers did not predict more trust and optimism, the sheer number of different people who had held the infant did predict more trust and optimism. Holding by the mother was important, but trust was even greater if the baby had been held by a large number of other persons. One possible explanation is that a highly trusting mother is likely to allow many others to hold the baby; by doing so she conveys trust to the baby.

What about the quality of parenting? Are there positive effects on personality when parents show love, warmth, and affection to their children and negative effects when parents are indifferent or hostile to their children? These questions are difficult to investigate cross-culturally because cultures may vary in the ways feeling is expressed. If love and affection are not expressed in the same ways, outsiders may misinterpret parental behavior. Nevertheless, Ronald Rohner and his colleagues did extensive work on the effects of parental acceptance

and rejection on children after infancy. In a cross-cultural comparison of 101 societies, using measures based on ethnographic materials, Rohner found that children tend to be hostile and aggressive when they are neglected and not treated affectionately by their parents. In societies in which children tend to be rejected, adults seem to view life and the world as unfriendly, uncertain, and hostile.[28] Other studies have compared individuals in different cultures to see if the cross-cultural findings were supported. In general, they were. In addition to finding the world more unfriendly and hostile, individuals who think they were rejected are likely to have negative evaluations of themselves.[29]

Under what conditions is parental rejection likely in childhood? The Rohner study suggests that rejection is likely where mothers get no relief from child care; when fathers and grandparents play a role in child care, rejection is less likely. Food-collecting societies (those dependent on wild food resources) tend to show warmth and affection to their children. More complex societies are less likely to be affectionate to their children.[30] It is not clear why this should be, but perhaps parental rejection is more likely where parents have less leisure time. Less leisure time may make parents more tired and irritable, and they may therefore have less patience with their children. As we noted in the chapter on economic systems, leisure time probably decreases as cultural complexity increases. More complex societies, which rely on intensive agriculture, also tend to have more economic uncertainty, as we noted in the chapter on getting food. Not only do they tend to have more risk of famines and food shortages, but they also tend to have social inequality. In societies

A father in Laos bathes his child. In societies where fathers and grandparents help to care for children, the children are less likely to be rejected.

with social classes, many families may not have enough food and money to satisfy their needs, and this factor can also produce frustration in the parents. Whatever the reasons for parental rejection, it seems to perpetuate itself—children who were rejected tend to reject their own children.

Task Assignment. In our society, young children are not expected to help much with chores. If there are any chores for them (such as tidying up their rooms), they are not likely to affect the welfare of the family or its ability to survive. In contrast, there are societies known to anthropology in which young children, even three- and four-year-olds, are expected to help prepare food, care for animals, and carry water and firewood, as well as clean. A child between five and eight years of age may even be given the responsibility of caring for an infant or toddler for much of the day while the mother works in the fields.[31] What are the effects of such task assignment on personality development?

We now have evidence from more than ten cultures that children who regularly babysit are more nurturant (offer more help and support to others) than are other children, even when they are not babysitting. Some of this evidence comes from a project known as the Six Cultures study, in which different research teams observed children's behavior in Kenya (Nyansongo), Mexico, India, the Philippines, Okinawa, and the United States (New England).[32] Ruth and Robert Munroe collected data on children's behavior in four other cultures that show the same relationship between babysitting and nurturant behavior; the Munroes' data come from Kenya (Logoli), Nepal, Belize, and American Samoa.[33] Clearly, children who babysit infrequently are less attuned to others' needs than are children who babysit often.

Why might task assignment affect the behaviors of children? One possibility is that children learn certain behaviors during performance of the task, and these behaviors become habitual. For example, a responsible babysitter is supposed to offer help. Mothers might directly instruct the babysitter to make sure that happens. But there is probably also an intrinsic satisfaction in doing a job well. For example, it is pleasurable to see an infant smile and laugh, but it is unpleasant to hear a baby cry. We might therefore expect that a child who is assigned babysitting would learn for himself or herself that comforting a baby brings its own rewards.[34]

Children who are assigned many tasks may spend their day in different kinds of settings, and these settings may indirectly influence behavior. For example, children who are asked to do many household chores are apt to be around both adults and younger children. Children who are assigned few or no tasks are freer to play with their agemates. Some of the results of the Six Cultures project suggest that children tend to be more aggressive the more they associate with other children of the same age. In contrast, children tend to inhibit aggression when they are around adults more.[35] We have already noted that being around younger children may make older children more nurturant. So the kinds of tasks assigned to children may influence behavior not only because certain tasks require certain behaviors (for example, babysitting requires nurturance) but also because the kinds of tasks assigned will place children in different social contexts that may also affect how they behave.

Schooling. Most researchers focus on the parents when they investigate how children are brought up. But in our own and other societies, children may spend a substantial part of their time in school from the age of three or so. What influence does school have on children's social behavior and on how they think as measured by tests? To investigate the effect of schooling, researchers have compared children (or adults) who have not gone to school with those who have. All of this research has been done in societies that do not have compulsory schooling; otherwise we could not compare the schooled with the unschooled. We know relatively little about the influence of school on social behavior. In contrast, we know more about how schooling influences performance on cognitive tests.

Schooling clearly predicts "superior" performance on many cognitive tests, and within the same society schooled individuals will generally do better than the unschooled on those tests. So, for example, nonschooled individuals in non-Western societies are not as likely as schooled individuals to perceive depth in two-dimensional pictures, do not perform as well on tests of memory, are not as likely to classify items in certain ways, and (as we discussed earlier in the chapter) do not display evidence of formal-operational thinking.[36] But schooling does not always produce superior performance on tests of inferential reasoning.[37]

Why does schooling have these effects? Although it is possible that something about schooling creates higher levels of cognitive thinking in some respects, there are other possible explanations. The observed differences may be due to the advantages that schoolchildren have because of their experiences in school, advantages that have nothing to do

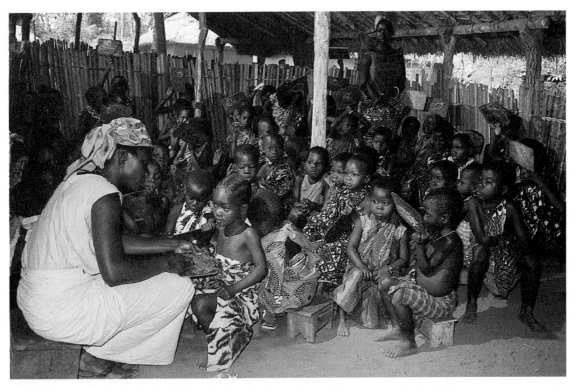

Attending school has become customary in many parts of the world, as among the Baoulé tribe of the Ivory Coast. Schooling seems to affect cognitive development, but we do not know exactly how or why.

with general cognitive ability. For example, consider research that asks people to classify or group drawings of geometric shapes that belong together. Suppose a person is shown three cards—a red circle, a red triangle, and a white circle—and is asked which two are most alike. A person could choose to classify in terms of color or in terms of shape. In the United States, young children usually classify by color, and as they get older they classify more often by shape. Many psychologists assume that classification by color is more "concrete" and classification by shape or function is more "abstract." Unschooled adults in many parts of Africa sort by color, not by shape. Does this mean that they are classifying less abstractly? Not necessarily. It may just be that nonschooled Africans classify differently because they are likely to be unfamiliar with the test materials (drawings on paper, geometric shapes).

How can people classify "abstractly" (for example, by shape) if they have never had the experience of handling or seeing shapes that are drawn in two dimensions? Is it likely that they would classify things as triangles if they had never seen a three-pointed figure with straight sides? In contrast, consider how much time teachers in this country spend exposing and drilling children on various geometric

shapes. People who are familiar with certain materials may for that reason alone do better on cognitive tests that use those materials.[38]

A comparative study of Liberian rice farmers in West Africa and U.S. undergraduates also illustrates the point that choice of materials may influence research results. The comparison involved a set of materials familiar to the rice farmers (bowls of rice) and a set of materials (geometric cards) familiar to the undergraduates. Rice farmers appeared to classify more "abstractly" than undergraduates when they were asked to classify rice, and undergraduates seemed to classify more "abstractly" than rice farmers when they classified geometric cards.[39]

Schooled individuals may also enjoy an advantage on many cognitive tests just because they are familiar with tests and the way tests ask them to think of new situations. For example, consider the reaction of a nonschooled person in central Asia who was asked the following question by a Russian psychologist interested in measuring logical thinking: "In the Far North where there is snow, all bears are white. Novaya Zemlya is in the Far North and there is always snow there. What color are the bears there?" The reply was, "We don't talk about what we haven't seen." Such a reply was typical of non-

DO SCHOOLS TEACH VALUES?

In the United States there is controversy nowadays about the teaching of values. Many people think that the schools should teach values; others think that the teaching of values should be left to parents and family. But whether or not schools should explicitly teach values, research on schools in different countries suggests that they do at least implicitly teach values. They do not just teach content.

Joseph Tobin, David Wu, and Dana Davidson videotaped preschool classroom scenes in Japan, China, and the United States. In each country they asked children, teachers, parents, and school administrators to comment on the scenes in all three countries. We can get a feel for how different values are implicitly taught in each country by reviewing the comments.

When individuals in the United States viewed the Japanese tape, they were generally bothered by two things. One was the fact that children in Japan often did the same things simultaneously as a group. For example, the teacher showed what to fold first (and subsequently) to make an origami bird figure, and the children followed along.

U.S. parents and teachers said that children should have more choice in what to do and how to do it. The second thing that bothered people in the United States (as well as in China) was that the teacher in Japan appeared to ignore what we might consider "unruly" behavior by the children. For example, when children got restless during a group workbook activity, they would leave their seats, joke with friends, or go to the bathroom. In the tape, a particularly troublesome boy talked loudly, sometimes purposely hurt other children, and threw ,things around, but the teacher seemed to ignore these behaviors. People in this country and China thought that the teacher should try to do something in such situations. In Japan, however, most of the teachers preferred not to call attention to, or single out, a troublesome child. Japanese teachers expect such a child eventually to behave more appropriately, and they encourage the other children to exert social pressure in that direction. In Lois Peak's words: "Learning to go to school in Japan is primarily defined as training in group life."

Most of the activities in the Chinese preschool were highly structured. For example, the first task of the day was building with blocks, but in contrast to the style at the Japanese preschool the children in China were expected to complete the task on their own and to do so in silence. If they spoke, the teacher reprimanded them. They used a picture as a guide to what to do. When they were done, the teachers checked their work. If they got it right, they took it apart and rebuilt it; if they got it wrong they were asked to correct it. An arithmetic lesson followed. Children then ate the lunch that was brought for them into the classroom. Teachers monitored the lunch to make sure that the children ate all their food and ate in silence. After an afternoon nap, the children listened to a patriotic story and then had relay races, which were followed by fifteen minutes of free play. Supper was served at 5:00 P.M. and parents came at 6:00. In seeing the videotapes, Americans and Japanese were bothered by the rigidity and "overcontrol" of the children and by the lack of privacy in their communal bathroom.

schooled individuals; they did not even try to answer the question because it was not part of their experience.[40] Clearly, we cannot judge whether people think logically if they do not want to play a cognitive game.

Much research needs to be done on exactly how and why schooling affects cognition. Is it important which specific things are taught? Is it important to be asked to attend to questions that are out of context? Is being literate a factor? This last ques-

In the United States preschool (in Honolulu), as in Japan, parents brought their children at different times, but some parents stayed with the child for as long as a half hour. Compared with the other preschools, the U.S. preschool emphasized individual participation and individualized activity. For example, "show and tell" was voluntary; sometimes only three kids decided to get up and talk. In an activity involving a feltboard, each child was asked to add something to the board. Much of the rest of the day was spent in "learning centers"; the teachers helped the children decide which center they would like to go to. Children started at one activity but could change if they wished. Even lunch was more individual. Each child took out her or his lunch box and took it to a big table where they all ate and talked animatedly. Many kids went home after lunch; those who stayed had naptime followed by relatively free play. The U.S. teacher, in contrast to the Japanese teacher, intervened when a child misbehaved, such as when one boy grabbed a block from another. Without raising her voice, the teacher asked the two children to talk to each other about the disagreement. She resorted to a "time-out" (a period of isola-tion) when the dispute was not settled by talking.

Even though they do not teach values explicitly, these preschools clearly convey values by how they deal with the children. First is the importance of the group versus the individual. In the U.S. preschool, most of the daily activities allowed individual choice of some kind; in both Japan and China group activities predominated, although the Japanese preschool allowed flexible arrival times, more free play, and more freedom to talk or move about than the Chinese preschool. Second is the source of control. The Japanese teachers relied informally on the group to control the children's behavior. For example, after nine months the unruly boy sat by himself at lunch; the other children did not want to sit with him. In contrast, the Chinese teachers saw to it that the children behaved like others in the group by exerting strong control over the children's behavior. The U.S. teachers also intervened in response to unruly behavior.

Cultural values are not unchanging. Although many Japanese educational administrators thought that the Japanese preschool was quite "Japanese" in style, and therefore quite satis-factory, a considerable number of Japanese parents and teachers were critical of the school and said there were "better" schools in Japan that were more like the U.S. preschool. And some Japanese thought that more attention should be paid to the individual needs of troubled children. Some Chinese complained, when they saw the tapes of the Chinese school, that it was too "old-fashioned." Yet even they agreed that the amount of freedom displayed at the Japanese and U.S. schools was too much. And the Chinese stressed the importance of schools' not "spoiling" children, especially now that parents are not supposed to have more than one child.

Whether or not they consciously intend to, preschools in different countries do seem to socialize their children according to what is valued in the culture.

Sources: *Joseph J. Tobin, David Y. H. Wu, and Dana H. Davidson,* Preschool in Three Cultures: Japan, China, and the United States *(New Haven, CT: Yale University Press, 1989); Lois Peak,* Learning to Go to School in Japan: The Transition from Home to Preschool *(Berkeley: University of California Press, 1991); Margaret Lock, "Japan: Glimpses of Everyday Life," in Melvin Ember, Carol R. Ember, and David Levinson, eds.,* Portraits of Culture: Ethnographic Originals *(Englewood Cliffs, NJ: Prentice Hall, 1994). Prentice Hall/Simon & Schuster Custom Publishing.*

tion was the subject of research among the Vai of Liberia, who had a somewhat unusual situation in that schooling and literacy were not completely confounded. The Vai had an indigenous script learned outside of school. Thus, researchers Sylvia Scribner and Michael Cole were able to see how Vai individuals who were literate but not formally schooled compared with others who were formally schooled (and literate) and those who were unschooled (and illiterate). They found some, but relatively minor, effects of literacy itself; cognitive test performance was much more affected by the number of years of schooling. Similar results come from a study of the Cree of northern Ontario who have their own syllabic script learned outside of school.[41] These comparisons suggest that some other aspects of schooling are more important than literacy as determinants of cognitive performance.

By studying other societies where schooling is not universal, we may be better able to understand just what role schooling plays in cognitive and other development. That schooling makes for so much difference in cognitive performance raises the serious issue of how much of what we observe about child development in our society and in other Western societies is simply a function of what children are taught in school. After all, children who grow up in this society not only get older each year, they also go one year further in school.

Schools are not just places to learn a particular curriculum. Children learn to interact with one another and with adults who are not parents and family. Therefore we might expect that schools not only shape cognition but also convey important cultural attitudes, values, and appropriate ways of behaving toward others (see the box titled "Do Schools Teach Values?").

General Cultural Themes as Explanations

Many of the aspects of socialization we have discussed are fairly specific—customs such as how often a baby is held, whether children are encouraged to be aggressive, what kinds of tasks are assigned to children, and whether they attend formal schools. As we have suggested, many of these specific aspects of socialization may have important effects on how a person grows up psychologically. But children may also be influenced by more general themes or ideas prevalent in the culture. Earlier, for example, when we discussed various aspects of infant care—how often babies are held, how quickly they are responded to—we mentioned that many customs seem to be aspects of a larger pattern, such as high or low indulgence. But what ideas underlie and possibly explain these larger patterns? One likely general theme in the United States is many parents' belief that the child should not grow up spoiled or dependent. Perhaps then there are general ideas or themes *behind* a culture's specific socialization patterns. These general themes may be expressed in a variety of ways.

Concepts of the Self. Anthropologists have begun to study different cultural ideas of personhood or concept of the "self." Many have concluded that the concept of self in many non-Western societies is quite different from the Western conception. Clifford Geertz described the Western conception of the person as "bounded, unique, . . . a dynamic center of awareness, emotion, judgment, and action organized into a distinctive whole."[42] He claimed, on the basis of his fieldwork in Java, Bali, and Morocco, that those societies have very different conceptions of a person, not only different from each other, but quite different from the Western conception. For example, he said that the Balinese describe a person as having many different roles, like an actor who plays different characters. The unique characteristics of a person are not emphasized; what is emphasized are the "masks" people wear and the "parts" they play.

Geertz focused on the variation and uniquenesses in different cultures' conceptions of the self. But other scholars think that there are recognizable and predictable patterns in this variation. One of the most talked about patterns is the Western emphasis on the self as an autonomous individual and the non-Western emphasis on the relations a person has with others.[43] Labels used to describe such Western/non-Western cultural differences are "individualism" versus "holism" or "collectivism," "egocentric" versus "sociocentric," and the like. For example, the Japanese concept of self is often described as "relational" or "situational": people exist in networks of relationships and the ideal person has the ability to shift easily from one social situation to another.[44]

There are two major objections to the idea that the Western sense of self should be contrasted with the non-Western. The first is that studies of other cultures have suggested other dimensions of variation besides "individualism" versus "collectivism." For example, the traditional Inuit concept *inummarik,* "a genuine person," seems to include a lifelong process of ecological involvement—interacting with animals and the environment as well as people.[45] A culture's concept of self then may include other dimensions besides individual versus collective. A second objection to the Western/non-Western contrast is that it may not be based on adequate evidence. As Melford Spiro pointed out, it is necessary to find out how a sample of individuals in a society actually view themselves. The ideal in the culture might be different from the actual.[46] For example, individuals even in the United States do not just describe themselves as autonomous. When Jane Wellenkamp and Douglas Hollan interviewed individuals in this country about their feelings about the death of someone close, they got statements about autonomy (such as "I can stand on my own" and "At least you have yourself"), but they also got statements reflecting interdependence ("You realize that they're gone and that a part of you has gone with them").[47] This is not to say that the autonomy of the individual isn't important in the United States. It is. But individuals also realize that they are interdependent. How we actually think of ourselves may not be so different from how people in other societies think of themselves.

If a cultural theme such as individualism is important, societies may express or convey this theme in many ways. It may start right after birth, as when a baby is put in a crib or bassinet to sleep alone rather than with someone in the family. Young children may be given their "own" toys. They may go to preschool or daycare, where they are encouraged to make their own choices (see the box titled "Do Schools Teach Values?"). And schools for older children may require individual, not group, achievement. Does the theme of individualism have to be taught explicitly? Probably not, because it can be conveyed in so many different ways.

Adaptational Explanations

The cultural anthropologist seeks not only to establish connections between child-rearing customs and personality traits but also to learn why those customs differ in the first place. Some anthropologists believe that child-rearing practices are largely adaptive—that a society produces the kinds of personalities best suited to performance of the activities necessary for the survival of the society. As John Whiting and Irvin Child expressed it, "The economic, political and social organs of a society—the basic customs surrounding the nourishment, sheltering and protection of its members . . . seem a likely source of influence on child training practices."[48] The belief that child-rearing practices are adaptive does not mean that societies always produce the kinds of persons they need. Just as in the biological realm, where we see poor adaptations and extinctions of species and subspecies, so we may expect that societies sometimes produce personality traits that are maladapted to the requirements of living in that society. So we cannot assume that just because a trait is present it must be adaptive. We cannot come to that conclusion unless we carefully investigate whether the trait is beneficial or harmful.[49] But we do expect that most societies that have survived to be

recorded have produced personality traits that are mostly adaptive.

Robert LeVine suggested an adaptational explanation for the frequent holding and feeding of infants, and quick response of caretakers to them, in preindustrial societies.[50] Only 1 percent of infants die in industrial societies in the first year of life, but typically more than 20 percent die in preindustrial societies. What can parents do? Parents often do not have access to modern medical care, but they can respond to a baby's fussing immediately if the baby is with them. Also, babies may be safer off the ground if there are cooking fires, dangerous insects, and snakes in the vicinity. When survival is not so much at issue, LeVine suggested, parents can safely leave babies more on their own.

Herbert Barry, Irvin Child, and Margaret Bacon cross-culturally investigated the possibility that child-training practices are adapted to the economic requirements of a society. Such requirements, they theorized, might explain why some societies strive to develop "compliant" (responsible, obedient, nurturant) children while others aim more for "assertiveness" (independence, self-reliance, and achievement).[51] The cross-cultural results indicated that agricultural and herding societies are likely to stress responsibility and obedience, whereas hunting-and-gathering societies tend to stress self-reliance and individual assertiveness. The investigators suggested that agricultural and herding societies cannot afford departures from established routine, because departures might jeopardize the food supply for long periods. Such societies are therefore likely to emphasize compliance with tradition. Departures from routine in a hunter-gatherer society cannot cause much damage to a food supply that has to be collected anew almost every day. So, hunter-gatherers can afford to emphasize individual initiative.

Although our own society relies on food production and has large stores of accumulated food, we seem more like hunter-gatherers in emphasizing individual initiative. Are we then exceptions to the Barry, Child, and Bacon findings? Not really. Hardly any of us are farmers (in the United States, only 2 percent of the total population is still on the farm), and most of us expect that we can "forage" in the supermarket or "store" just about anytime. Perhaps more important is the fact that our highly commercial economy, with most people dwelling in or near cities, requires us to compete to get jobs to make a living. In our kind of economy, then, individual initiative is important too. Consider the results of a cross-national comparison of eight countries in which the researchers asked parents what quality

People relying greatly on food production tend to stress responsibility and obedience. A Taos Pueblo girl helps others husk corn.

they most wanted their school-age children to have. Independence and self-reliance were seldom mentioned by parents in the more rural countries (Indonesia, Philippines, and Thailand), but they were often mentioned in the more urban countries (Korea, Singapore, and the United States).[52]

Child-rearing practices may also be affected by household characteristics. Leigh Minturn and William Lambert reported, on the basis of data from the Six Cultures study, that children of families who live in cramped quarters tend to be punished more strongly for fighting with others than are children of families who have ample space. The more people living in a house, the less apt a parent is to permit disobedience.[53] This observation is consistent with the finding of a cross-cultural study, conducted by John Whiting, that societies with extended-family households are more likely than societies with nuclear families to severely punish aggression in children.[54]

Whether adults express aggression freely may be related to a society's economy and social environment. In a comparative study of personality differences between pastoralists and farmers in four societies in East Africa, Robert Edgerton found that pastoralists were more willing than farmers to express aggression openly. As a matter of fact, pastoralists seemed freer to express all kinds of emotion—including sadness and depression. Although farmers displayed reluctance to express overt aggression themselves, they were quite willing to talk about witchcraft and sorcery practiced by others. How can we explain these personality differences? Edgerton proposed that the life-style of farmers, who must spend their lives cooperating with a fixed set of neighbors, requires them to contain their feelings, particularly hostile feelings. (But these

feelings may not go away, and so the farmers might "see them" in others.) Pastoralists, on the other hand, can more readily move away in conflict situations because they are not as dependent on a fixed set of individuals. Not only might they be able to express aggression more openly, but such aggression may even be adaptive. The pastoralists studied by Edgerton engaged frequently in raids and counter-raids involving cattle stealing, and the most aggressive individuals may have had the best chance of surviving the skirmishes.[55]

Might the environment influence the way people in different societies think and perceive (interpret sensory information)? John Berry suggested that different perceptual and cognitive processes may be selected and trained for in societies that differ in their adaptational requirements.[56] Berry's particular focus was on what psychologists call *field independence* and *field dependence*.[57] Field independence means being able to isolate a part of a situation from the whole. The opposite perceptual style, field dependence, means that parts are not perceived separately; rather, the whole situation is focused on.

The contrast between field independence and field dependence may become clear if we look at some of the ways they are measured. In the rod-and-frame test, a person seated in a darkened room is asked to adjust a tilted luminous rod so that it is upright within a luminous frame. Individuals are considered field dependent if they adjust the rod to line up with the frame when the frame is tilted. Individuals are considered field independent if they adjust the rod to a truly upright position even though the frame is tilted. Field independence is also measured by the ability to see a simply drawn figure when it is included but somewhat hidden in a more complex picture.

Why should some societies produce people who are more field independent or dependent? Berry suggested that people who rely a lot on hunting must be field independent to be successful, because hunting requires the visual isolation of animals from their backgrounds. Hunters must also learn to visualize themselves in precise relationship to their surroundings so that they can find animals and get back home. In a comparative study of communities in four societies, Berry found that degree of reliance on hunting predicted field independence. The more a community relied on hunting, the more the individuals showed field independence on tests. Those communities more reliant on agriculture tested out to be more field dependent. How might hunters develop field independence as a cognitive style? Different child training might be involved. In the United States and a few other societies, it has been found that children whose parents are very strict are less likely to develop field independence than are children whose parents are lenient.[58] It seems that emotional independence from parents is necessary for the perceptual style of field independence to develop. No matter what the precise mechanism is, we know from the Barry, Child, and Bacon study that hunter-gatherers are more likely to train children to be individualistic and assertive, and that agriculturalists and herders are more likely to train their children to be compliant. So hunter-gatherers may get their children to develop field independence by stressing emotional independence in childhood.

Investigations have shown that there are gender differences in the United States and other (but not all) cultures in degree of field dependence versus independence.[59] Perhaps these differences reflect the fact that girls are more encouraged to be obedient and responsible and boys more to be independent and self-reliant. And perhaps too gender differences in field dependence versus independence may be related to the fact that girls work more in and around the home, close to others. If so, we might expect that girls who are more field dependent are also more likely to have a morality that stresses interpersonal concerns (see the box titled "Do Women Have a Different Morality?").

Possible Genetic and Physiological Influences

Some researchers have suggested that genetic or physiological differences between populations predispose them to have different personality characteristics. Daniel Freedman found differences in "temperament" in newborn babies of different ethnic groups; because he observed newborns, the differences between them were presumed to be genetic. Comparing Chinese and Caucasian newborns (with the families matched on income, number of previous children, and so on), Freedman found that Caucasian babies cried more easily, were harder to console, and fought experimental procedures more. Chinese babies, on the other hand, seemed calmer and more adaptable. Navaho babies were similar to the Chinese, showing even more calmness.[60] Freedman also suggested that an infant's behavior can influence how the parents respond. A calm baby may encourage a calm parental response; a more active baby may encourage a more active response.[61] So, in Freedman's view, babies' genetically determined behavior can lead to ethnic differences in adult personality and caretaking styles.

But we cannot rule out nongenetic explanations of babies' behavior. For example, the mother's diet or her blood pressure could affect the baby's behavior. And it may be that the baby can learn even in the womb. After all, babies in the womb apparently can hear sounds and respond to other stimuli. Therefore, it is possible that in societies in which pregnant women are calm, their babies may have learned calmness even before they were born. Last, we still do not know if the initial differences observed in newborn babies persist to become personality differences in adulthood.

Just as the diet of the mother (including the intake of alcohol and drugs) may affect the developing fetus, the diet of infants and children may also affect their intellectual development and their behavior. Studies have shown that malnutrition is associated with lower levels of activity, less attentiveness, lack of initiative, and low tolerance of frustration. Behavior of children can change with short-term nutrition supplements. For example, Guatemalan children who were given nutritional supplements were observed to have less anxiety, more exploratoriness, and greater involvement in games than children who were not given supplements.[62] The problem of malnutrition is not just a matter of nutrition. Other kinds of care may also be reduced. For example, caretakers of malnourished children may interact with them less than do caretakers of healthy children. As a malnourished child shows reduced activity, caretakers tend to respond to the child with lower frequency and less enthusiasm. Then the child withdraws from interaction, creating a potentially serious vicious cycle.[63]

DO WOMEN HAVE A DIFFERENT MORALITY?

There is widespread agreement that as children mature they develop a sense of self that distinguishes themselves from others. But *what kind* of sense of self do they develop? Some researchers suggest that different cultures have different conceptions of the self. In particular, the West seems to emphasize the separateness of each person; other cultures emphasize the connection of the self to others.

Several psychologists, including Carol Gilligan, proposed that women, in contrast to men, are more likely to develop a sense of themselves that involves social interaction and connectedness. Gilligan proposed that women also tend to have a different sense

of morality, one that is more apt to consider the feelings of others and the preservation of relationships. Men, she suggested, are more likely to emphasize rules or principles that are applied equally and impartially to individuals. Is there any substantial evidence for her claims about gender differences in morality?

Some studies have interviewed females and males and explicitly compared their statements about themselves and about solutions to moral dilemmas. The responses are coded for the degree to which the self is described as "autonomous" or as "connected" and the degree to which responses to moral dilemmas are couched in "justice" or "care"

terms. "Well, you have to think about whether it is right . . . or whether it is wrong," is an example of a statement couched in justice terms. "I wanted them to get along . . . I didn't want anybody getting in fights or anything" is an example of a statement couched in "care" terms.

So far the research, conducted mostly in the United States among well-educated populations, suggests that, although women more often than men do tend to describe themselves as "connected" and more often display a "caring" morality, there is no absolute separation between the genders. Most people, regardless of gender, give "connected" and "autonomous" statements

Physiological (not necessarily genetic) differences between populations may also be responsible for some personality differences in adulthood. Research by Ralph Bolton suggests that a physiological condition known as hypoglycemia may be responsible for the high levels of aggression recorded among the Qolla of Peru.[64] (People with hypoglycemia experience a big drop in their blood sugar level after they ingest food.) Bolton found that about 55 percent of the males he tested in a Qolla village had hypoglycemia. Moreover, those men with the most aggressive life histories tended to be hypoglycemic. Whether hypoglycemia is induced by genetic or environmental factors (or both), the condition can be alleviated by a change in diet.

Mental Illness

So far in this chapter, we have discussed cross-cultural universals and societal differences in "normal" behavior, but anthropologists have also been

intrigued by questions about similarities and differences in *abnormal* behavior. Central to the study of abnormal behavior is how to define it. Is abnormality relative? That is, can what is normal in one society be abnormal in another? Or, alternatively, are there universals in abnormality cross-culturally?

In a very widely read book, Ruth Benedict suggested that abnormality was relative. In her view, behavior thought to be appropriate and normal in one society can be considered abnormal in another.[65] Many German officials, for instance, were regarded in every way as normal by their neighbors and co-workers during the period of Nazi control. Yet these officials committed acts of inhumanity so vicious that to many observers in other Western societies they appeared criminally insane. The Saora of Orissa (India) provide another example of behavior normal to one society that would be abnormal to another society. The Saora took for granted that certain of their womenfolk regularly were courted by lovers from the supernatural world, married them, about themselves, and most people express "justice" and "care" concerns with regard to moral dilemmas. If there is a difference between the genders in a culture, it is only in tendency not in a completely different approach to morality.

Although moral development in childhood has been studied in several cultures, there is relatively little research that directly addresses the issues raised by Gilligan. To be sure, research by David Stimpson and his colleagues compared educated university students in Korea, China, Thailand, and the United States and found support for the idea that women were more concerned with affection, compassion, and sensitivity to the needs of others, as compared with men. But that study did not specifically ask for responses to moral dilemmas. Some other researchers suggest that the picture may be more complicated, because concepts of morality may vary quite a bit from the two types described by Gilligan. For example, Joan Miller found that middle-class Hindu Indians generally had a very strong sense of interpersonal morality compared with people in the United States. But the Hindu Indian morality was not based on individual concern for others; rather their responses to moral dilemmas were strongly influenced by considerations of *social duty*. And Miller found no gender differences in responses.

All we can conclude now is that the genders may have somewhat different moralities in *some* cultures. We need more research on how morality may vary by gender as well as by culture.

Sources: *Carol Gilligan*, In a Different Voice: Psychological Theory and Women's Development *(Cambridge, MA: Harvard University Press, 1982); Nona Plessner Lyons, "Two Perspectives: On Self, Relationships, and Morality," and Carol Gilligan and Jane Attanucci, "Two Moral Orientations," in Carol Gilligan, Janie Victoria Ward, and Jill McLean Taylor, eds.,* Mapping the Moral Domain: A Contribution of Women's Thinking to Psychological Theory and Education *(Cambridge, MA: Harvard University Press, 1988), pp. 22–45 and 73–86, respectively; David Stimpson, Larry Jensen and Wayne Neff, "Cross-Cultural Gender Differences in Preference for a Caring Morality," Journal of Social Psychology, 132 (1992): 317–22; Joan G. Miller, "Cultural Diversity in the Morality of Caring: Individually Oriented versus Duty-Based Interpersonal Moral Codes," Cross-Cultural Research, 28 (1994): 3–39.*

and had children (who were never seen, yet allegedly were suckled at night).[66] Behavior that is so alien to our own makes it no easy task for researchers to identify mental illness in other societies, let alone compare more complex and less complex societies on rates of mental disorder.

When anthropologists first started describing mental illness elsewhere, there seemed to be unique illnesses in different cultures. These are referred to as *culture-bound syndromes*. For example, a mental disorder called *pibloktoq* occurred among some Eskimo adults of Greenland, usually women, who became oblivious to their surroundings and acted in agitated, eccentric ways. They might strip themselves naked and wander across the ice and over hills until they collapsed of exhaustion. Another disorder, *amok*, occurred in Malaya, Indonesia, and New Guinea, usually among males. It was characterized by John Honigmann as a "destructive maddened excitement . . . beginning with depression and followed by a period of brooding and withdrawal [culminating in] the final mobilization of tremendous energy during which the 'wild man' runs destructively berserk."[67] *Anorexia nervosa*, the disorder involving aversion to food, may be unique to the relatively few societies that idealize slimness.[68]

Some scholars think that each society's views of personality and concepts of mental illness have to be understood in their own terms. Western understandings and concepts cannot be applied to other cultures. For example, Catherine Lutz suggested that the Western concept of depression cannot be applied to the Pacific island of Ifaluk. The people there have many words for thinking or feeling about "loss and helplessness," but all their words are related to a *specific* need for someone (such as when someone dies or leaves the island). Such thoughts and feelings of loss are considered perfectly normal, and there is no word in their language for general hopelessness or "depression."[69] Therefore Lutz questioned the applicability of the Western concept of depression as well as other Western psychiatric categories.

Other researchers are not so quick to dismiss the possible universality of psychiatric categories. Some think they have found a considerable degree of cross-cultural uniformity in conceptions of mental illness. Jane Murphy studied descriptions by Eskimos and Yoruba (in Nigeria) of severely disturbed persons. She found that their descriptions not only were similar to each other but also corresponded to North American descriptions of schizophrenia. The Eskimo word for "crazy" is *nuthkavihak.* They use this word when something inside a person seems to be out of order. *Nuthkavihak* people are described as talking to themselves, believing themselves to be animals, making strange faces, becoming violent, and so on. The Yoruba have a word *were* for people who are "insane." People described as *were* sometimes hear voices, laugh when there is nothing to laugh at, and take up weapons and suddenly hit people.[70] Robert Edgerton found similarities in conceptions of mental illness in four East African societies. He noted not only that the four groups essentially agreed on the symptoms of psychosis but also that the symptoms they described were the same ones that are considered psychotic here.[71] Edgerton believed that the lack of exact translation in different cultures, such as the one pointed out by Lutz regarding Ifaluk, does not make comparison impossible. If researchers can come to understand another culture's views of personality *and* the researchers can manage to communicate these views to people of other cultures, we can compare the described cases and try to discover what may be universal and what may be found only in some cultures.[72]

Some mental illnesses, such as schizophrenia and depression, seem so widespread that many researchers think they are probably universal. Still, cultural factors may influence the risk of developing such diseases, the specific symptoms that are expressed, and the effectiveness of different kinds of treatment.[73] There may be some truly culture-bound (nearly unique) syndromes, but others thought at one time to be unique may be culturally varying expressions of conditions that occur widely. *Pibloktoq,* for example, may be a kind of hysteria.[74]

Biological factors may be quite important in the etiology of some of the widespread disorders such as schizophrenia.[75] With regard to hysteria, Anthony Wallace theorized that nutritional factors such as calcium deficiency may cause hysteria and that dietary improvement may account for the decline of this illness in the Western world since the nineteenth century.[76] By the early twentieth century, the discovery of the value of good nutrition, coupled with changes in social conditions, had led many people to drink milk, eat vitamin-enriched foods, and spend time in the sun. These changes in diet and activity increased their intake of vitamin D and helped them to maintain a proper calcium level. Concurrently, the number of cases of hysteria declined. Regarding *pibloktoq,* Wallace suggested that a complex set of related variables may cause the disease. The Eskimos live in an environment that supplies only a minimum amount of calcium. A diet low in calcium could result in two different conditions. One condition, rickets, would produce physical deformities potentially fatal in the Eskimos' hunting economy. Persons whose genetic makeup made them prone to rickets would be eliminated from the population through natural selection. A low level of calcium in the blood could also cause muscular spasms known as tetany. Tetany, in turn, may cause emotional and mental disorientation similar to the symptoms of *pibloktoq.* Such attacks last for only a relatively short time and are not fatal, so people who developed *pibloktoq* would have a far greater chance of surviving in the Arctic environment with a calcium-deficient diet than would those who had rickets.

Although researchers disagree about the comparability of mental illnesses among cultures, most realize that effective treatment requires understanding a culture's ideas about a mental illness—why it occurs, what treatments are believed to be effective, and how families and others respond to those afflicted.[77]

PSYCHOLOGICAL EXPLANATIONS OF CULTURAL VARIATION

We have been talking only about societal variation in psychological characteristics and the possible *causes* of that variation. But psychological anthropologists, as well as other social scientists, have also investigated the possible *consequences* of psychological variation, particularly how psychological characteristics may help us understand certain aspects of cultural variation. For example, David McClelland's research suggests that societies that develop high levels of achievement motivation in individuals (a personality trait) will be likely to experience high rates of economic growth. Economic decline, McClelland suggested, will follow a decline in achievement motivation.[78] Differences in achievement motivation may even have political consequences. For example, Robert LeVine, who studied achievement motivation in three Nigerian ethnic groups, noted that the entry of one of them (the Ibo) into higher education and into many emerging professions may have been resented by the traditionally more influential groups.[79] Soon after LeVine's book was published, the friction between the rival groups escalated into rebellion by the Ibo and the defeat of a separatist Ibo state named Biafra.

Psychological factors may also help us explain why some aspects of culture are statistically associated with others. Abram Kardiner originally suggested that cultural patterns influence personality development through child training and that the resulting personality characteristics in turn influence the culture. He believed that *primary institutions,* such as family organization and subsistence techniques, give rise to certain personality characteristics. Once the personality is formed, though, it can have its own impact on culture. In Kardiner's view, the *secondary institutions* of society, such as religion and art, are shaped by common (he called them *basic*) personality characteristics. Presumably, these secondary institutions have little relation to the adaptive requirements of the society. But they may reflect and express the motives, conflicts, and anxieties of typical members of the society.[80] Thus, if we can understand why certain typical personality characteristics develop, we might, for example, be able to understand why certain kinds of art are associated with certain kinds of social systems. Whiting and Child used the phrase **personality integration of culture** to refer to the possibility that an understanding of personality might help us explain connections between primary and secondary institutions.[81] As examples of how personality may integrate culture, we turn to some suggested explanations for cultural preferences in games and for the custom of male initiation ceremonies.

In a cross-cultural study conducted by John Roberts and Brian Sutton-Smith, cultural preferences for particular types of games were found to be related to certain aspects of child rearing. The researchers suggested that these associations are a consequence of conflict generated in many people in a society by particular types of child-rearing pressures. Games of strategy, for example, are associated with child training that emphasizes obedience. Roberts and Sutton-Smith proposed that severe obedience training can create a conflict between the need to obey and the desire not to obey, a conflict that arouses anxiety. Such anxiety may or may not manifest itself against the person who instigates the anxiety. In any event, the conflict and the aggression itself can be played out on the miniature battlefields

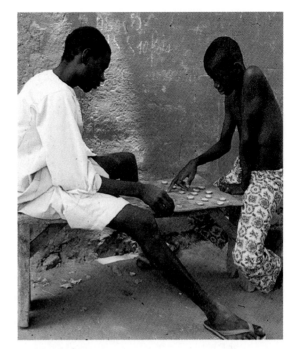

Games of strategy, such as this game played in Mali, tend to occur where societies are hierarchical and where obedience is stressed.

of games of strategy such as chess or the Japanese game of *go.* Similarly, games of chance may represent defiance of societal expectations of docility and responsibility. The general interpretation suggested by Roberts and Sutton-Smith is that players (and societies) initially become curious about games, learn them, and ultimately develop high involvement in them because of the particular kinds of psychological conflicts that are handled or expressed, but not necessarily resolved, by the games.[82]

The possible role of psychological processes in connecting different aspects of culture is also illustrated in cross-cultural work on initiation ceremonies for boys at adolescence. In the ceremonies, boys are subjected to painful tests of manhood, usually including genital operations, which indicate the boys' transition to adulthood. Roger Burton and John Whiting found that initiation ceremonies tend to occur in patrilocal societies in which infant boys initially sleep exclusively with their mothers. They suggest that initiation rites in such societies are intended to break a conflict in sex identity. The conflict is believed to exist because boys in these societies would initially identify with their mothers, who exercise almost complete control over them in infancy. Later, when the boys discover that men dominate the society, they will identify secondarily with their fathers. This sex-role conflict is assumed to be resolved by the initiation ceremony, which demonstrates a boy's manhood, thus strengthening the secondary identification.[83]

In the next two chapters we discuss cultural variation in religion and the arts. In doing so we refer to some psychological explanations. Some researchers feel that such explanations may help us understand why gods in some societies are viewed as mean, why artists in some societies prefer repetitive designs, and why strangers in some societies tend to be the "bad ones" in folktales. It is often assumed by psychological anthropologists that conceptions of gods and artistic creations are not constrained by any objective realities, so people are free to create them as they wish. In other words, people may tend to *project* their personalities—their feelings, their conflicts, their concerns—into these areas. This idea of projection underlies what psychologists call **projective tests.** In such tests, which presumably reveal personality characteristics, subjects are given stimuli that are purposely ambiguous. So, for example, in the *Thematic Apperception Test* (TAT), subjects are shown vague drawings and asked what they think is going on in them, what happened before, and how they think things will turn out. Because the test materials give few instructions about what to say, it is assumed that subjects will interpret the materials by projecting their own personalities. As we will see, some aspects of religion and the arts may be similar to TAT stories and may express or reflect the common personality characteristics of a society.

▼ SUMMARY

1. Psychological anthropologists are interested in the psychological differences and similarities between societies. Their research has focused mainly on four questions: Do all human beings develop psychologically in much the same ways? What may explain the apparent differences in personality characteristics from one society to another? How do people in different societies conceive of personality and psychological development? What kinds of cultural variation might be explained by psychological factors?

2. Early research in psychological anthropology was concerned mainly with how supposedly universal stages of emotional development seem to be affected by cultural differences. Some doubt has been cast on the idea that adolescence is necessarily a time of "storm and stress" and that the Oedipus complex (at least in the form stated by Freud) is universal.

3. Recent research on universals in psychological development has been concerned more with cognitive (intellectual) development. In looking for universals, many researchers have discovered some apparent differences. But most of the tests used in research may favor people in Western cultures and those who attend formal schools.

4. To understand cross-cultural variation in psychological characteristics, many researchers have tried to discover if variation in child-rearing customs can account for the observed psychological differences.

5. *Socialization* is a term used by anthropologists and psychologists to describe the development, through the influence of parents and others, of patterns of behavior in children that conform to cultural expectations.

6. Socialization can be direct or indirect. Indirectly, the degree to which parents like children, the kinds of work children are asked to do, and whether children go to school may at least partly influence how children develop psychologically.

7. Anthropologists seek not only to establish connections between child-rearing customs and personality traits but also to learn why those customs originated. Some anthropologists believe societies produce the kinds of personality best suited to performance of the activities necessary for the survival of the society.

8. Anthropologists are also interested in mental illness. Some mental illnesses are believed to be more or less universal, but the ways they are expressed, their frequencies, and the outcomes of treatment may vary from culture to culture. Some syndromes may be unique to some cultures.

9. Psychological anthropologists are interested not only in the possible causes of psychological differences between societies but also in the possible consequences of psychological variation, particularly how psychological characteristics may help us understand statistical associations between various aspects of culture.

▼ GLOSSARY TERMS

personality   projective tests
personality integration of culture   socialization

▼ CRITICAL QUESTIONS

1. Do you think indulging children makes them more or less self-reliant as adults? Why do you think so?
2. What may explain adolescent rebelliousness?
3. Agriculturalists and foragers seem to have somewhat different personalities, so method of food-getting may be related to personality. Do you think there is a similar relationship between occupation and personality? If so, why?

▼ SUGGESTED READING

BARRY, H. B., III. "Childhood Socialization." In C. R. Ember and M. Ember, eds., *Cross-Cultural Research for Social Science.* Englewood Cliffs, NJ: Prentice Hall, 1995. Prentice Hall/Simon & Schuster Custom Publishing. A review of how childhood socialization varies cross-culturally and why it may vary.

BURBANK, V. K. "Adolescent Socialization and Initiation Ceremonies." In C. R. Ember and M. Ember, eds., *Cross-Cultural Research for Social Science.* Englewood Cliffs, NJ: Prentice Hall, 1995. Prentice Hall/Simon & Schuster Custom Publishing. A review of how and why socialization in adolescence varies, with a special focus on initiation ceremonies and gender differences.

HEWLETT, B. S. "Diverse Contexts of Human Infancy." In C. R. Ember and M. Ember, eds., *Cross-Cultural Research for Social Science.* Englewood Cliffs, NJ: Prentice Hall, 1995. Prentice Hall/Simon & Schuster Custom Publishing. Examines North American and Western European biases in what is considered "normal" in infancy by cross-culturally examining the diverse practices regarding childbirth, infant care, and characteristics of infant caretakers.

MUNROE, R. H., MUNROE, R. L., AND WHITING, B. B., eds. *Handbook of Cross-Cultural Human Development.* New York: Garland Press, 1981. A massive collection of papers, prepared especially for this volume, on many aspects of human development that have been investigated cross-culturally.

ROGOFF, B. *Apprenticeship in Thinking: Cognitive Development in Social Context.* New York: Oxford University Press, 1990. This book suggests that children's cognitive development is an apprenticeship, that the particular cognitive skills developed are rooted in the particular historical and cultural activities of the society.

SEGALL, M. H., DASEN, P. R., BERRY, J. W., AND POORTINGA, Y. H. *Human Behavior in Global Perspective: An Introduction to Cross-Cultural Psychology.* New York: Pergamon Press, 1990. An introduction to research in many societies around the world on the ways in which perception, cognition, motivation, and other aspects of human behavior are influenced by variable social and cultural factors.

WHITING, B. B., AND EDWARDS, C. P. (in collaboration with C. R. Ember, G. M. Erchak, S. Harkness, R. L. Munroe, R. H. Munroe, S. B. Nerlove, S. Seymour, C. M. Super, T. S. Weisner, and M. Wenger). *Children of Different Worlds: The Formation of Social Behavior.* Cambridge, MA: Harvard University Press, 1988. On the basis of data collected in the Six Cultures project, the authors explore the ways in which age, gender, and culture affect the social behavior of children. Knowledge of the company children keep, and of the proportion of time they spend with various categories of people, makes it possible to predict important aspects of children's interpersonal behavior.

▼ NOTES

[1]Robert K. Dentan, *The Semai: A Nonviolent People of Malaya* (New York: Holt, Rinehart & Winston, 1968), pp. 55–56.

[2]Napoleon A. Chagnon, *Yanomamö: The Fierce People*, 3rd ed. (New York: CBS College Publishing, 1983).

[3]Quoted in Otto Klineberg, "Foreword," in Marshall H. Segall, *Cross-Cultural Psychology: Human Behavior in Global Perspective* (Monterey, CA: Brooks/Cole, 1979), p. v.

[4]Donald E. Brown, *Human Universals* (Philadelphia: Temple University Press, 1991).

[5]Margaret Mead, *Coming of Age in Samoa*, 3rd ed. (New York: Morrow, 1961 [originally published 1928]).

[6]Bronislaw Malinowski, *Sex and Repression in Savage Society* (Cleveland: World, 1968; London: Kegan Paul, Trench, Trubner, 1927).

[7]Derek Freeman, *Margaret Mead and Samoa: The Making and Unmaking of an Anthropological Myth* (Cambridge, MA: Harvard University Press, 1983). For reasons to be skeptical about Freeman's criticism, see Melvin Ember, "Evidence and Science in Ethnography: Reflections on the Freeman-Mead Controversy," *American Anthropologist,* 87 (1985): 906–9.

[8]Melford E. Spiro, *Oedipus in the Trobriands* (Chicago: University of Chicago Press, 1982).

[9]Alice Schlegel and Herbert Barry III, *Adolescence: An Anthropological Inquiry* (New York: Free Press, 1991), p. 44.

[10]Jean Piaget, "Piaget's Theory," in Paul Mussen, ed., *Carmichael's Manual of Child Psychology,* vol. 1, 3rd ed. (New York: John Wiley, 1970), 703–32.

[11]John W. Berry, Ype H. Poortinga, Marshall H. Segall, and Pierre R. Dasen, *Cross-Cultural Psychology: Research and Applications* (New York: Cambridge University Press, 1992), p. 40.

[12]Ibid., pp. 40–41.

[13]Pierre R. Dasen and Alastair Heron, "Cross-Cultural Tests of Piaget's Theory," in Harry C. Triandis and Alastair Heron, eds., *Handbook of Cross-Cultural Psychology,* vol. 4, *Developmental Psychology* (Boston: Allyn & Bacon, 1981), pp. 305–6.

[14]Carol R. Ember, "Cross-Cultural Cognitive Studies," *Annual Review of Anthropology,* 6 (1977): 33–56; and Barbara Rogoff, "Schooling and the Development of Cognitive Skills," in Triandis and Heron, eds., *Handbook of Cross-Cultural Psychology,* vol. 4, *Developmental Psychology,* pp. 233–94.

[15]Douglass Price-Williams, "A Study Concerning Concepts of Conservation of Quantities among Primitive Children," *Acta Psychologica,* 18 (1961): 297–305.

[16]Marshall H. Segall, Pierre R. Dasen, John W. Berry, and Ype H. Poortinga, *Human Behavior in Global Perspective: An Introduction to Cross-Cultural Psychology* (New York: Pergamon Press, 1990), p. 149.

[17]Rogoff, "Schooling and the Development of Cognitive Skills," pp. 264–67.

[18]Thomas S. Weisner, Mary Bausano, and Madeleine Kornfein, "Putting Family Ideals into Practice: Pronaturalism in Conventional and Nonconventional California Families," *Ethos,* 11 (1983): 278–304.

[19]John W. M. Whiting and Irvin L. Child, *Child Training and Personality: A Cross-Cultural Study* (New Haven: Yale University Press, 1953), pp. 69–71.

[20]Weisner, Bausano, and Kornfein, "Putting Family Ideals into Practice," p. 291; Barry S. Hewlett, "Diverse Contexts of Human Infancy," in Carol R. Ember and Melvin Ember, eds., *Cross-Cultural Research for Social Science* (Englewood Cliffs, NJ: Prentice Hall, 1995). Prentice Hall/Simon & Schuster Custom Publishing.

[21]See the research cited in Hewlett, "Diverse Contexts of Human Infancy."

[22]Ibid.

[23]Chagnon, *Yanomamö,* p. 115.

[24]Dentan, *The Semai,* p. 61.

[25]Cora Du Bois, *The People of Alor: A Social-Psychological Study of an East Indian Island* (Minneapolis: University of Minnesota Press, 1944).

[26]Victor Barnouw, *Culture and Personality,* 4th ed. (Homewood, IL: Dorsey Press, 1985), p. 118.

[27]Ruth H. Munroe and Robert L. Munroe, "Infant Experience and Childhood Affect among the Logoli: A Longitudinal Study," *Ethos,* 8 (1980): 295–315.

[28]Ronald P. Rohner, *They Love Me, They Love Me Not: A Worldwide Study of the Effects of Parental Acceptance and Rejection* (New Haven, CT: HRAF Press, 1975), pp. 97–105.

[29]See studies reported in Ronald P. Rohner and Evelyn Rohner, eds., "Special Issue on Worldwide Tests of Parental Acceptance-Rejection Theory: An Overview," *Behavior Science Research* 15 (1980), pp. v–88; also, Zdenek Matejcek, "Perceived Parental Acceptance-Rejection and Personality Organization among Czech Elementary School Children," *Behavior Science Research,* 18 (1983): 259–68.

[30]Rohner, *They Love Me, They Love Me Not,* pp. 112–16.

[31]Beatrice B. Whiting and John W. M. Whiting (in collaboration with Richard Longabaugh), *Children of Six Cultures: A Psycho-Cultural Analysis* (Cambridge, MA: Harvard University Press, 1975), p. 94. See also Ruth H. Munroe, Robert L. Munroe, and Harold S. Shimmin, "Children's Work in Four Cultures: Determinants and Consequences," *American Anthropologist,* 86 (1984): 369–79.

[32]Beatrice B. Whiting and Carolyn Pope Edwards (in collaboration with Carol R. Ember, Gerald M. Erchak, Sara Harkness, Robert L. Munroe, Ruth H. Munroe, Sara B. Nerlove, Susan Seymour, Charles M. Super, Thomas S. Weisner, and Martha Wenger), *Children of Different Worlds: The Formation of Social Behavior* (Cambridge, MA: Harvard University Press, 1988), p. 265.

[33]Munroe, Munroe, and Shimmin, "Children's Work in Four Cultures," pp. 374–76; see also Carol R. Ember, "Feminine Task Assignment and the Social Behavior of Boys," *Ethos,* 1 (1973): 424–39.

[34]Whiting and Whiting, *Children of Six Cultures,* p. 179.

[35]Ibid., pp. 152–63; and Carol R. Ember, "A Cross-Cultural Perspective on Sex Differences," in Ruth H. Munroe, Robert L. Munroe, and Beatrice B. Whiting, eds., *Handbook of Cross-Cultural Human Development* (New York: Garland Press, 1981), p. 560.

[36]Ember, "Cross-Cultural Cognitive Studies"; and Rogoff, "Schooling and the Development of Cognitive Skills."

[37]Rogoff, "Schooling and the Development of Cognitive Skills," p. 285.

[38]For how school experiences may improve particular cognitive skills, rather than higher levels of cognitive development in general, see Barbara Rogoff, *Apprenticeship in Thinking: Cognitive Development in Social Context* (New York: Oxford University Press, 1990), pp. 46–49.

[39]Marc H. Irwin, Gary N. Schafer, and Cynthia P. Feiden, "Emic and Unfamiliar Category Sorting of Mano Farmers and U.S. Undergraduates," *Journal of Cross-Cultural Psychology,* 5 (1974): 407–23.

[40]A. R. Luria, *Cognitive Development: Its Cultural and Social Foundations* (Cambridge, MA: Harvard University Press, 1976), p. 108; quoted in Rogoff, "Schooling and the Development of Cognitive Skills," p. 254.

[41]Sylvia Scribner and Michael Cole, *The Psychology of Literacy* (Cambridge, MA: Harvard University Press, 1981); J. W. Berry and J. Bennett, "Syllabic Literacy and Cognitive Performance among the Cree," *International Journal of Psychology* 24 (1989): 429–50 as reported in Berry, Poortinga, Segall, and Dasen, *Cross-Cultural Psychology: Research and Applications,* pp. 123–24.

[42]Clifford Geertz, "'From the Native's Point of View': On the Nature of Anthropological Understanding," in Richard A. Shweder and Robert A. LeVine, eds., *Culture Theory: Essays on Mind, Self, and Emotion* (New York: Cambridge University Press, 1984), pp. 123–36.

[43]Although Melford Spiro does not believe that this Western/non-Western pattern exists, the reader is referred to his article for the many references to the works of those who do. "Is the Western Conception of the Self 'Peculiar' within the Context of the World Cultures?" *Ethos,* 21 (1993): 107–53.

[44]Jane M. Bachnik, "The Two 'Faces' of Self and Society in Japan," *Ethos,* (1992): 3–32.

[45]Arlene Stairs, "Self-Image, World-Image: Speculations on Identity from Experiences with Inuit," *Ethos,* 20 (1992): 116–26.

[46]Spiro, "Is the Western Conception of the Self 'Peculiar?'"

[47]Research reported in Douglas Hollan, "Cross-Cultural Differences in the Self," *Journal of Anthropological Research,* 48 (1992): 289–90.

[48]Whiting and Child, *Child Training and Personality,* p. 310.

[49]Robert B. Edgerton, *Sick Societies: Challenging the Myth of Primitive Harmony* (New York: The Free Press, 1992), p. 206.

[50]Robert A. LeVine, "Human Parental Care: Universal Goals, Cultural Strategies, Individual Behavior," in Robert A. LeVine, Patrice M. Miller, and Mary Maxwell West, eds., *Parental Behavior in Diverse Societies* (San Francisco: Jossey-Bass, 1988), pp. 4–6; see also discussion in Hewlett, "Diverse Contexts of Human Infancy."

[51]Herbert Barry III, Irvin L. Child, and Margaret K. Bacon, "Relation of Child Training to Subsistence Economy," *American Anthropologist,* 61 (1959): 51–63. For a somewhat different analysis of the data used in the Barry, Child, and Bacon study, see Llewellyn Hendrix, "Economy and Child Training Reexamined," *Ethos,* 13 (1985): 246–61.

[52]Lois Wladis Hoffman, "Cross-Cultural Differences in Childrearing Goals," in LeVine, Miller, and West, eds., *Parental Behavior in Diverse Societies,* pp. 101–3.

[53]Leigh Minturn and William W. Lambert, *Mothers of Six Cultures: Antecedents of Child Rearing* (New York: John Wiley, 1964), p. 289.

[54]John W. M. Whiting, "Cultural and Sociological Influences on Development," in *Growth and Development of the Child in His Setting* (Maryland Child Growth and Development Institute, 1959), pp. 5–9.

[55]Robert B. Edgerton, *The Individual in Cultural Adaptation: A Study of Four East African Peoples* (Berkeley: University of California Press, 1971).

[56]John W. Berry, *Human Ecology and Cognitive Style* (New York: John Wiley, 1976).

[57]Herman A. Witkin, "A Cognitive Style Approach to Cross-Cultural Research," *International Journal of Psychology,* 2 (1967): 233–50.

[58]J. L. M. Dawson, "Cultural and Physiological Influences upon Spatial-Perceptual Processes in West Africa," *International Journal of Psychology,* 2 (1967): 115–28, 171–85; and John W. Berry, "Ecological and Cultural Factors in Spatial Perceptual Development," *Canadian Journal of Behavioural Science,* 3 (1971): 324–36.

[59]Carol R. Ember, "Universal and Variable Patterns of Gender Difference," in Carol R. Ember and Melvin Ember, eds., *Cross-Cultural Research for Social Science* (Englewood Cliffs, NJ: Prentice Hall, 1995). Prentice Hall/Simon & Schuster Custom Publishing.

[60]Daniel G. Freedman, "Ethnic Differences in Babies," *Human Nature,* January 1979, 36–43.

[61]Ibid., pp. 40–41. For a discussion of possible genetic influences on the social environment, see Sandra Scarr and Kathleen McCartney, "How People Make Their Own Environments: A Theory of Genotype→Environment Effects," *Child Development,* 54 (1983): 424–35.

[62]See P. R. Dasen, J. W. Berry, and N. Sartorius, eds., *Health and Cross-Cultural Psychology: Toward Applications* (Newbury Park, CA: Sage Publications, 1988), pp. 116–18 for references to research, particularly by D. E.

Barrett, "Malnutrition and Child Behavior: Conceptualization, Assessment and an Empirical Study of Social-Emotional Functioning," in J. Brozek and B. Schürch, eds., *Malnutrition and Behavior: Critical Assessment of Key Issues* (Lausanne, Switzerland: Nestlé Foundation, 1984), pp. 280–306.

[63]Dasen, Berry, and Sartorius, eds., *Health and Cross-Cultural Psychology,* pp. 117–18, 126–28.

[64]Ralph Bolton, "Aggression and Hypoglycemia among the Qolla: A Study in Psychobiological Anthropology," *Ethnology,* 12 (1973): 227–57.

[65]Ruth Benedict, *Patterns of Culture* (New York: Mentor, 1959 [originally published 1934]).

[66]Verrier Elwin, *The Religion of an Indian Tribe* (London: Oxford University Press, 1955); cited in Barnouw, *Culture and Personality,* p. 356.

[67]John J. Honigmann, *Personality in Culture* (New York: Harper & Row, 1967), p. 406.

[68]Arthur Kleinman, *Rethinking Psychiatry: From Cultural Category to Personal Experience* (New York: Macmillan, 1988), p. 3.

[69]Catherine Lutz, "Depression and the Translations of Emotional Worlds," in Arthur Kleinman and Byron Good, eds., *Culture and Depression: Studies in the Anthropology and Cross-Cultural Psychiatry of Affect and Disorder* (Berkeley: University of California Press, 1985), pp. 63–100.

[70]Jane Murphy, "Abnormal Behavior in Traditional Societies: Labels, Explanations, and Social Reactions," in Munroe, Munroe, and Whiting, eds., *Handbook of Cross-Cultural Human Development,* p. 813.

[71]Robert B. Edgerton, "Conceptions of Psychosis in Four East African Societies," *American Anthropologist,* 68 (1966): 408–25.

[72]Edgerton, *Sick Societies,* pp. 16–45.

[73]Kleinman, *Rethinking Psychiatry,* pp. 34–52; Berry, Poortinga, Segall, and Dasen, *Cross-Cultural Psychology,* pp. 357–64.

[74]Honigmann, *Personality in Culture,* p. 401.

[75]Kleinman, *Rethinking Psychiatry,* p. 19.

[76]Anthony F. C. Wallace, "Mental Illness, Biology and Culture," in F. L. K. Hsu, ed., *Psychological Anthropology,* 2nd ed. (Cambridge, MA: Schenkman, 1972), pp. 363–402.

[77]Kleinman, *Rethinking Psychiatry,* pp. 167–85.

[78]David C. McClelland, *The Achieving Society* (New York: Van Nostrand, 1961).

[79]Robert A. LeVine, *Dreams and Deeds: Achievement Motivation in Nigeria* (Chicago: University of Chicago Press, 1966), p. 2.

[80]Abram Kardiner, with Ralph Linton, *The Individual and His Society* (New York: Golden Press, 1946 [originally published 1939]), p. 471.

[81]Whiting and Child, *Child Training and Personality,* pp. 32–38.

[82]John M. Roberts and Brian Sutton-Smith, "Child Training and Game Involvement," *Ethnology,* 1 (1962): 178.

[83]Roger V. Burton and John W. M. Whiting, "The Absent Father and Cross-Sex Identity," *Merrill-Palmer Quarterly of Behavior and Development,* 7, no. 2 (1961): 85–95. See also Robert L. Munroe, Ruth H. Munroe, and John W. M. Whiting, "Male Sex-Role Resolutions," in Munroe, Munroe, and Whiting, eds., *Handbook of Cross-Cultural Human Development,* pp. 611–32; for a recent review of cross-cultural research on initiation see Victoria K. Burbank, "Adolescent Socialization and Initiation Ceremonies," in Ember and Ember, eds., *Cross-Cultural Research for Social Science.*

15

Religion and Magic

As far as we know, all societies have possessed beliefs that can be grouped under the term *religion*. These beliefs vary from culture to culture and from year to year. Yet, whatever the variety of beliefs in things supernatural, we shall define **religion** as any set of attitudes, beliefs, and practices pertaining to *supernatural power,* whether that power be forces, gods, spirits, ghosts, or demons.

In our society, we divide phenomena into the natural and the supernatural, but not all languages or cultures make such a neat distinction. Moreover, what is considered **supernatural**—powers believed to be not human or not subject to the laws of nature—varies from society to society. Some of the variations are determined by what a society regards as natural. For example, some illnesses commonly found in our society are believed to result from the natural action of bacteria and viruses. In other societies (and even among some people in our own society), illness is thought to result from supernatural forces, and thus it forms a part of religious belief.

Beliefs about what is, or is not, a supernatural occurrence also vary within a society at a given time or over time. In Judeo-Christian traditions, for example, floods, earthquakes, volcanic eruptions, comets, and epidemics were once considered evidence of supernatural powers intervening in human affairs. It is now generally agreed that they are simply natural occurrences (but many still believe that supernatural forces may be involved). Thus, the line between the natural and the supernatural appears to vary in a society according to what people believe about the causes of things and events in the observable world.

In many cultures, what we would consider religious is embedded in other aspects of everyday life. That is, it is often difficult to separate the religious (or economic or political) from other aspects of the culture. Such cultures have little or no specialization of any kind; there are no full-time priests, no purely religious activities. So the various aspects of culture we distinguish (for example, in the chapter titles of this book) are not separate and easily recognized in many societies, as they are in complex societies such as our own. However, it is sometimes difficult even for us to agree whether a particular custom of ours is religious or not. After all, the categorizing of beliefs as religious or political or social is a relatively new custom. The ancient Greeks, for instance, did not have a word for religion, but they did have many concepts concerning the behavior of their gods and their own expected duties to the gods.

When people's duties to their gods are linked with duty to their princes, it is difficult to separate

religious from political ideas. As an example of our own difficulty in labeling a particular class of actions or beliefs as religious or social, consider our attitudes about wearing clothes. Is our belief that it is necessary to wear clothing, at least in the company of nonlovers, a religious principle, or is it something else? Recall that in Genesis, the wearing of clothes, or fig leaves, is distinctly associated with the loss of innocence: Adam and Eve, after eating the apple, covered their nakedness. Accordingly, when Christian missionaries first visited islands in the Pacific in the nineteenth century, they forced the native women to wear more clothes, particularly to cover their sexual parts. Were the missionaries' ideas about sex religious or social, or perhaps both?

THE UNIVERSALITY OF RELIGION

Religious beliefs and practices are found in all known contemporary societies, and archaeologists think they have found signs of religious belief associated with *Homo sapiens* who lived at least 60,000 years ago. People then deliberately buried their dead, and many graves contain the remains of food, tools, and other objects that were probably thought to be needed in an afterlife. Some of the artistic productions of modern humans after about 30,000 years ago may have been used for religious purposes. For example, sculptures of females with ample secondary sex characteristics may have been fertility charms. Cave paintings in which the predominant images are animals of the hunt may reflect a belief that the image had some power over events. Perhaps early humans thought that their hunting could be made more successful if they drew images depicting good fortune in hunting. The details of religions practiced in the distant past cannot be recovered. Yet evidence of ritual treatment of the dead suggests that early people believed in the existence of supernatural spirits and tried to communicate with, and perhaps influence, them.

We may reasonably assume the existence of prehistoric religion and we have evidence of the universality of religion in historic times, so we can understand why the subject of religion has been the focus of much speculation, research, and theorizing. As long ago as the fifth century B.C., Herodotus made fairly objective comparisons among the religions of the fifty or so societies he traveled to from his home in Greece. He noted many similarities among their gods and pointed out evidence of diffusion of religious worship. During the 2,500 years since Herodotus's time, scholars, theologians, historians, and philosophers have speculated about religion. Some have claimed superiority for their own forms of religion; others have derided the naive simplicity of others' beliefs; and some have expressed skepticism concerning all beliefs.

Speculation about which religion is superior is not an anthropological concern. What is of interest to anthropologists is why religion is found in all societies and how and why it varies from society to society. Many social scientists—particularly anthropologists, sociologists, and psychologists—have offered theories to account for the universality of religion. Most think that religions are created by humans in response to certain universal needs or conditions. Four such needs or conditions have been discussed: a need for intellectual understanding; reversion to childhood feelings; anxiety and uncertainty; and a need for community.

The Need to Understand

One of the earliest social scientists to propose a major theory of the origin of religion was Edward Tylor. In his view, religion originated in people's speculation about dreams, trances, and death. The dead, the distant, those in the next house, animals—all seem real in dreams and trances. Tylor thought that the lifelike appearances of these imagined persons and animals suggests a dual existence for all things—a physical, visible body and a psychic, invisible soul. In sleep, the soul can leave the body and appear to other people; at death, the soul permanently leaves the body. Because the dead appear in dreams, people come to believe that the souls of the dead are still around.

Tylor thought that the belief in souls was the earliest form of religion; **animism** is the term he used to refer to belief in souls.[1] But many scholars criticized Tylor's theory for being too intellectual and not dealing with the emotional component of religion. One of Tylor's students, R. R. Marett, felt that Tylor's animism was too sophisticated an idea to be the origin of religion. Marett suggested that **animatism**—a belief in impersonal supernatural forces (for example, the power of a rabbit's foot)—preceded the creation of spirits.[2]

Reversion to Childhood Feelings

Sigmund Freud believed that early humans lived in groups each of which was dominated by a tyrannical man who kept all the women for himself.[3] Freud postulated that the sons on maturing were driven out of the group. Later they got together to kill and eat the hated father. But then the sons felt enormous guilt and remorse, which they expressed (projected) by prohibiting the killing of a totem animal (the father-substitute). Subsequently, on ritual occasions, the cannibalistic scene was repeated in the form of a totem meal. Freud believed that these early beliefs gradually became transformed into the worship of deities or gods modeled after the father.

Freud's interpretation of the origin of religion is not accepted by most social scientists today. But there is widespread agreement with his idea that events in infancy can have long-lasting and powerful effects on beliefs and practices in adult life. Helpless and dependent on parents for many years, infants and children inevitably and unconsciously view their parents as all-knowing and all-powerful. When adults feel out of control or in need, they may unconsciously revert to their infantile and childhood feelings. They may then look to gods or magic to do what they cannot do for themselves, just as they looked to their parents to take care of their needs. As we shall see, there is evidence that feelings about the supernatural world parallel feelings in everyday life.

Anxiety and Uncertainty

Freud thought that humans would turn to religion during times of uncertainty, but he did not view religion positively, believing that humans would eventually outgrow the need for religion. Others viewed religion more positively. Bronislaw Malinowski noted that people in all societies are faced with anxiety and uncertainty. They may have skills and knowledge to take care of many of their needs, but knowledge is not sufficient to prevent illness, accidents, and natural disasters. The most frightening prospect is death itself. Consequently, there is an intense desire for immortality. As Malinowski saw it, religion is born from the universal need to find comfort in inevitable times of stress. Through religious belief, people affirm their convictions that death is neither real nor final, that people are endowed with a personality that persists even after death. In religious ceremony, humans can commemorate and communicate with those who have died, and in these ways achieve some measure of comfort.[4]

Theorists such as William James, Carl Jung, Erich Fromm, and Abraham Maslow have viewed religion even more positively: it is not just a way of relieving anxiety; it is thought to be therapeutic. William James suggested that religion provides a feeling of union with something larger than

THE USEFULNESS OF RELIGION: TABOOS AMONG NEW ENGLAND FISHERMEN

People engaged in risky activities may try to ensure their safety by carrying or wearing lucky charms. They believe the charms protect them by invoking the help of supernatural beings or forces. We might also believe we can protect ourselves by *not* doing some things. For example, baseball players on a hitting streak may choose *not* to change their socks or sweatshirt for the next game (to continue their luck). Or we obey a prohibition because we think that by doing so we can avoid supernatural punishment. For example, we may fast or give up certain foods for a period of time. Why? God knows!

Whether or not religious beliefs and practices can affect our success or reduce our risk, we may consider them useful or adaptive if they reduce our anxieties. And reducing anxiety might indirectly maximize our success. Doesn't an actor try to reduce his or her "stage fright" before a performance? Prohibitions (taboos) are perhaps particularly likely to be adaptive in this way. Consider some research on New England fishermen that suggests that their taboos, or "rituals of avoidance," may reduce anxiety.

John Poggie and Richard Pollnac interviewed a random sample of 108 commercial fisher-

men from three New England ports. They were trying to explain the number of taboos among the fishermen, as measured by asking them to describe all the superstitions related to fishing they could remember. The fishermen were often embarrassed when they talked about their ritual beliefs and practices. They would say they did not really believe in their taboos, but they admitted that they would not break them while fishing. The taboos prohibited saying or doing a certain thing, or something bad would happen. Most frequently mentioned were "Don't turn a hatch cover upside down," "Don't whistle on a boat," and "Don't mention the word *pig* on board." When the fishermen were asked what these taboos meant, they talked about personal safety and preventing bad luck.

The results of the study suggest that anxiety about personal danger while fishing is the main stimulus for the taboo behavior observed among the fishermen. For example, there are more taboos reported when the duration of exposure to danger is longer. Fishermen who go out just for the day report significantly fewer taboos than fishermen who go out for longer periods of time. And longer trips

are clearly more dangerous because they are farther from shore. If there is a storm, the farther out you are, the more risk of disaster because you are exposed longer to rough seas. And it is more difficult to deal with illness, injury, breakdowns, and damage to the boat far from shore. Also consistent with the conclusion that the fishermen's taboos reduce anxiety is the fact that inshore fishermen (those who are after shellfish close to shore) report a significantly smaller number of taboos than offshore fishermen (who go out farther in trawlers).

On shore, the fishermen express some disbelief in the effectiveness of their taboos. (They *are* called "superstitions," you know!) But at sea it seems that the omnipresence of danger raises anxiety levels and discourages the fishermen from testing their disbelief. It won't hurt to practice the taboo at sea, they say, but it might hurt not to!

Sources: *John J. Poggie, Jr., and Richard B. Pollnac, "Danger and Rituals of Avoidance among New England Fishermen,"* MAST: Maritime Anthropological Studies, *1 (1988): 66–78; John J. Poggie, Jr., Richard B. Pollnac, and Carl Gersuny, "Risk as a Basis for Taboos among Fishermen in Southern New England,"* Journal for the Scientific Study of Religion, *15 (1976): 257–62.

oneself.[5] Carl Jung suggested that it helps people resolve their inner conflicts and attain maturity.[6] Erich Fromm proposed that religion helps provide people with a framework of values,[7] and Abraham Maslow argued that it provides people with a transcendental understanding of the world.[8]

The Need for Community

All those theories of religion agree on one thing: whatever the beliefs or rituals, religion may satisfy psychological needs common to all people. But some social scientists believe that religion springs from society and serves social, rather than psychological, needs.

Émile Durkheim, a French sociologist, pointed out that living in society makes humans feel pushed and pulled by powerful forces. These forces direct their behavior, pushing them to resist what is considered wrong, pulling them to do what is considered right. These are the forces of public opinion, custom, and law. Because they are largely invisible and unexplained, people would feel them as mysterious forces and therefore come to believe in gods and spirits. Durkheim suggested that religion arises out of the experience of living in social groups; religious belief and practice affirm a person's place in society, enhance feelings of community, and give people confidence. Durkheim proposed that society is really the object of worship in religion.

Consider how Durkheim explained totemism, so often discussed by early religious theorists. He thought that nothing inherent in a lizard, rat, or frog (animal totems for some Australian aborigine groups) would be sufficient to make them *sacred*. The totem animal must therefore be a symbol. But a symbol of what? Durkheim noted that the people are organized into clans, and each clan has its own totem animal; the totem distinguishes one clan from another. So the totem is the focus of the clan's religious rituals and symbolizes both the clan and the clan's spirits. It is the clan with which people mostly identify, and it is the clan that is affirmed in ritual.[9]

Guy Swanson accepted Durkheim's belief that certain aspects or conditions of society generate the responses we call religious. But Swanson thought that Durkheim was too vague about exactly what in society would generate the belief in spirits or gods. So what might? Swanson suggested that the belief in spirits derives from the existence of *sovereign groups* in a society. These are the groups that have independent jurisdiction (decision-making powers) over some sphere of life—the family, the clan, the village, the state. Such groups are not mortal: they persist beyond the lifetimes of their individual members. According to Swanson, then, the spirits or gods that people invent personify or represent the powerful decision-making groups in their society. Just like sovereign groups in a society, the spirits or gods are immortal and have purposes and goals that supersede those of an individual.[10]

VARIATION IN RELIGIOUS BELIEFS

There seems to be no general agreement among scholars as to why people need religion, or how spirits, gods, and other supernatural beings and forces come into existence. (Any or all of the needs we have discussed, psychological or social, may give rise to religious belief and practice.) Yet there is general recognition of the enormous variation in the details of religious beliefs and practices. Societies differ in the kinds of supernatural beings or forces they believe in and the character of those beings. They also differ in the structure or hierarchy of those beings, in what the beings actually do, and in what happens to people after death. Variation exists also in the ways in which the supernatural is believed to interact with humans.

Types of Supernatural Forces and Beings

Supernatural Forces. Some supernatural forces have no personlike character. As we discussed earlier, Marett referred to such religious beliefs as ani-

"There's room in the world for all religions—those who believe in rocks, those who believe in trees, those who believe in clouds. . . " (© 1984 by Sidney Harris)

matism. For example, a supernatural, impersonal force called **mana,** after its Malayo-Polynesian name, is thought to inhabit some objects but not others, some people but not others. A farmer in Polynesia places stones around a field; the crops are bountiful; the stones have mana. During a subsequent year the stones may lose their mana and the crops will be poor. People may also possess mana, as, for example, the chiefs in Polynesia were said to do. However, such power is not necessarily possessed permanently: chiefs who were unsuccessful in war or other activities were said to have lost their mana.

The word *mana* may be Malayo-Polynesian, but a similar concept is also found in our own society. We can compare mana to the power golfers may attribute to some but, unhappily not all, of their clubs. A ballplayer might think a certain sweatshirt or pair of socks has supernatural power or force and that more runs or points will be scored when they are worn. A four-leaf clover has mana; a three-leaf clover does not.

Objects, persons, or places can be considered **taboo.** Anthony Wallace distinguished mana from taboo by pointing out that things containing mana are to be touched, whereas taboo things are not to be touched, for their power can cause harm.[11] Thus, those who touch them may themselves become taboo. Taboos surround food not to be eaten, places not to be entered, animals not to be killed, people not to be touched sexually, people not to be touched at all, and so on. An Australian aborigine could not normally kill and eat the animal that was his totem; Hebrew tribesmen were forbidden to touch a woman during menstruation or for seven days afterward.

Supernatural Beings. Supernatural beings fall within two broad categories: those of nonhuman origin, such as gods and spirits, and those of human origin, such as ghosts and ancestral spirits. Chief among the beings of nonhuman origin, **gods** are named personalities. They are often anthropomorphic—that is, conceived in the image of a person—although they are sometimes given the shapes of other animals or of celestial bodies such as the sun or moon. Essentially, the gods are believed to have created themselves, but some of them then created, or gave birth to, other gods. Although some are seen as creator gods, not all peoples include the creation of the world as one of the acts of gods.

After their efforts at creation, many creator gods retire. Having set the world in motion, they are not interested in its day-to-day operation. Other creator gods remain interested in the ordinary af-fairs of human beings, especially the affairs of one small, chosen segment of humanity. Whether a society has a creator god or not, the job of running the creation is often left to lesser gods. The Maori of New Zealand, for example, recognize three important gods: a god of the sea, a god of the forest, and a god of agriculture. They call upon each in turn for help and try to get all three to share their knowledge of how the universe runs. The gods of the ancient Romans, on the other hand, specialized to a high degree. There were three gods of the plow, one god to help with the sowing, one for weeding, one for reaping, one for storing grain, one for manuring, and so on.[12]

Beneath the gods in prestige, and often closer to people, are multitudes of unnamed **spirits.** Some may be guardian spirits for people. Some, who become known for particularly efficacious work, may be promoted to the rank of named gods. Some spirits who are known to the people but never invoked by them are of the hobgoblin type: they delight in mischief and can be blamed for any number of small mishaps. Other spirits take pleasure in deliberately working evil on behalf of people.

Many Native American groups believed in guardian spirits that had to be sought out, usually in childhood. For example, among the Sanpoil of northeastern Washington, boys and sometimes girls would be sent out on overnight vigils to acquire their guardians. Most commonly the spirits were animals, but they could also be uniquely shaped rocks, lakes, mountains, whirlwinds, or clouds. The vigil was not always successful. When it was, the guardian spirit appeared in a vision or dream, and always at first in human form. Conversation with the spirit would reveal its true identity.[13]

Ghosts and **ancestor spirits** are among the supernatural beings who were once human. The belief that ghosts or their actions can be perceived by the living is apparently almost universal.[14] The near-universality of the belief in ghosts may not be difficult to explain. There are many cues in everyday experience that are associated with a loved one, and even after her or his death those cues might arouse the feeling that the dead person is still somehow present. The opening of a door or the smell of tobacco or cologne in a room may evoke the idea that the person is still present, if only for a moment. Then, too, loved ones live on in dreams. Small wonder, then, that most societies believe in ghosts. If the idea of ghosts is generated by these familiar associations, we might expect that ghosts in most societies would be close relatives and friends, not strangers—and they are.[15]

Although the belief in ghosts is nearly universal, the spirits of the dead do not play an active role in the life of the living in all societies. In his cross-cultural study of fifty societies, Swanson found that people are likely to believe in active ancestral spirits where descent groups are important decision-making units. The descent group is an entity that exists over time, back into the past as well as forward into the future, despite the deaths of individual members.[16] The dead feel concern for the fortunes, the prestige, and the continuity of their descent group as strongly as the living. As a Lugbara elder (in northern Uganda in Africa) put it, "Are our ancestors not people of our lineage? They are our fathers and we are their children whom they have begotten. Those that have died stay near us in our homes and we feed and respect them. Does not a man help his father when he is old?"[17]

The Character of Supernatural Beings

Whatever types they may be, the gods or spirits venerated in a given culture tend to have certain personality or character traits. They may be unpredictable or predictable, aloof from or interested in human affairs, helpful or punishing. Why do the gods and spirits in a particular culture exhibit certain character traits rather than others?

We have some evidence from cross-cultural studies that the character of supernatural beings may be related to the nature of child training. Melford Spiro and Roy D'Andrade suggested that the god-human relationship is a projection of the parent-child relationship, in which case child-training practices might well be relived in dealings with the supernatural.[18] For example, if a child was nurtured immediately by her parents when she cried or waved her arms about or kicked, she might grow up expecting to be nurtured by the gods when she attracted their attention by performing a ritual. On the other hand, if her parents often punished her, she would grow up expecting the gods to punish her if she disobeyed them. William Lambert, Leigh Minturn Triandis, and Margery Wolf, in another cross-cultural study, found that societies with hurtful or punitive child-training practices are likely to believe that their gods are aggressive and malevolent; societies with less punitive child training are more likely to believe that the gods are benevolent.[19] These results are consistent with the Freudian notion that the supernatural world should parallel the natural. It is worth noting in this context that some peoples refer to the god as their father and to themselves as his children.

Structure or Hierarchy of Supernatural Beings

The range of social structures in human societies from egalitarian to highly stratified has its counterpart in the supernatural world. Some societies have gods or spirits that are not ranked; one god has about as much power as another. Other societies have gods or spirits that are ranked in prestige and power. For example, on the Pacific islands of Palau, which was a rank society, gods were ranked as people were. Each clan worshiped a god and a goddess that had names or titles similar to clan titles. Although a clan god was generally important only to the members of that clan, the gods of the various clans in a village were believed to be ranked in the same order that the clans were. Thus, the god of the highest-ranking clan was respected by all the clans of the village. Its shrine was given the place of honor in the center of the village and was larger and more elaborately decorated than other shrines.[20]

Although the Palauans did not believe in a high god or supreme being who outranked all the other gods, some societies do. Consider Judaism, Christianity, and Islam, which we call **monotheistic** religions. Although *monotheism* means "one god," most monotheistic religions actually include more than one supernatural being (e.g., demons, angels, the Devil). But the supreme being or high god, as the creator of the universe or the director of events (or both), is believed to be ultimately responsible for all events.[21] A **polytheistic** religion recognizes many important gods, no one of which is supreme.

Why do some societies have a belief in a high god while others do not? Recall Swanson's suggestion that people invent gods who personify the important decision-making groups in their society. He therefore hypothesized that societies with hierarchical political systems should be more likely to believe in a high god. In his cross-cultural study of fifty societies (none of which practiced any of the major world religions), he found that belief in a high god is strongly associated with three or more levels of "sovereign" (decision-making) groups. Of the twenty sample societies that had a hierarchy of three or more sovereign groups—for instance, family, clan, and chiefdom—seventeen possessed the idea of a high god. Of the nineteen societies that had fewer than three levels of decision-making groups, only two had a high god.[22] Consistent with Swanson's findings, societies dependent on food production are more likely to have a belief in a high god than are food-collecting societies.[23] These results strongly suggest, then, that the realm of

Most religions that we call monotheistic have other, minor supernatural beings. This painting (ca. 1805) by Blake portrays good and bad angels struggling over a child.

the gods parallels and may reflect the everyday social and political world.

Intervention of the Gods in Human Affairs

According to Clifford Geertz, it is when faced with ignorance, pain, and the unjustness of life that a person explains events by the intervention of the gods.[24] Thus, in Greek religion the direct intervention of Poseidon as ruler of the seas prevented Odysseus from getting home for ten years. In the Old Testament, the direct intervention of Yahweh caused the great flood that killed most of the people in the time of Noah. In other societies, people may search their memories for a violated taboo that has brought punishment through supernatural intervention.

In addition to unasked-for divine interference, there are numerous examples of requests for divine intervention, either for good for oneself and friends or for evil for others. Gods are asked to intervene in the weather and make the crops grow, to send fish to the fisherman and game to the hunter,

to find lost things, and to accompany travelers and prevent accidents. They are asked to stop the flow of lava down the side of a volcano, to stop a war, or to cure an illness.

The gods do not intervene in all societies. In some they intervene in human affairs; in others, they are not the slightest bit interested; and in still others they interfere only occasionally. We have little research on why gods are believed to interfere in some societies and not in others. We do, however, have some evidence suggesting when the gods will take an interest in the morality or immorality of human behavior.

Swanson's study suggests that the gods are likely to punish people for immoral behavior when there are considerable differences in wealth in the society. Swanson's interpretation was that the gods in such societies are interested in supporting the inequalities.[25] It may be that supernatural support of moral behavior is particularly useful where inequalities tax the ability of the political system to maintain social order and minimize social disorder. Envy of others' privileges may motivate some people to behave immorally; the belief that the gods will punish such behavior might deter it.

Life after Death

In many societies, ideas about an afterlife are vague and seemingly unimportant, but many other peoples have very definite and elaborate ideas of what happens after death. The Lugbara see the dead as joining the ancestors of the living and staying near the family homesite. They retain an interest in the behavior of the living, both rewarding and punishing them. The Zuni of the southwestern United States think the dead join the past dead, known as the *katcinas,* in a katcina village at the bottom of a nearby lake. There they lead a life of singing and dancing and bring rain to the living Zuni. They are also swift to punish the priest who fails in his duty or the people who impersonate them in masks during the dance ceremonies.[26]

The Chamulas have merged the ancient Mayan worship of the sun and moon with the Spanish conquerors' Jesus and Mary. Their vision of life after death contains a blending of the two cultures. All souls go to the underworld, where they live a humanlike life except that they are incapable of sexual intercourse. After the sun travels over the world, it travels under the underworld, so that the dead have sunlight. Only murderers and suicides are punished, being burned by the Christ-sun on their journey.[27]

Many Christians believe that the dead are divided into two groups: the unsaved are sent to everlasting punishment and the saved to everlasting reward. Accounts differ, but hell is often associated with torture by fire, heaven with mansions. Several societies see the dead as returning to earth to be reborn. The Hindus use this pattern of reincarnation to justify one's caste in this life and to promise eventual release from the pain of life through the attainment of *nirvana,* or inclusion into the One.

The afterworld in many religions may resemble the everyday world, but we still lack comparative studies that show exactly how.

VARIATION IN RELIGIOUS PRACTICES

▼

Beliefs are not the only elements of religion that vary from society to society. There is also variation in how people interact with the supernatural. The manner of approach to the supernatural varies from supplication (requests, prayers, and so on) to manipulation. And societies vary in the kinds of religious practitioners they have.

Ways to Interact with the Supernatural

How to get in touch with the supernatural has proved to be a universal problem. Wallace identified a number of ways used by people the world over, though not necessarily all together, including (but not limited to): prayer (asking for supernatural help), physiological experience (doing things to the body and mind), simulation (manipulating imitations of things), feasts, and sacrifices.[28]

Prayer can be spontaneous or memorized, private or public, silent or spoken. The Lugbara do not say the words of a prayer aloud, for doing so would be too powerful; they simply think about the things that are bothering them. The gods know all languages.

Doing things to the body or mind may involve drugs (hallucinogenics such as peyote or opiates) or alcohol; social isolation or sensory deprivation; dancing or running till exhausted; being deprived of food, water, and sleep; and listening to repetitive sounds such as drumming. Such behaviors may induce trances or altered states of consciousness.[29] Erika Bourguignon found that achieving these altered states (which she generally referred to as trances) is part of religious practice in 90 percent of the world's societies.[30] In some societies, trances are thought to involve the presence of a spirit or power inside a person that changes or displaces that person's personality or soul. These types are referred to as possession trances. Other types of trances may involve the journey of a person's soul, experiencing visions, or transmitting messages from spirits. Possession trances are especially likely in societies that depend on agriculture and have social stratification, slavery, and more complex political hierarchies. Nonpossession trances are most likely to occur in food-collecting societies. Societies with moderate levels of social complexity have both possession and nonpossession trances.[31]

Voodoo employs simulation, or the imitation of things. Dolls are made in the likeness of an enemy and then are maltreated in hopes that the original enemy will experience pain and even death. Simulation is often employed during **divination,** or getting the supernatural to provide guidance. Many people in our society have their fortunes read in crystal balls, tea leaves, Ouija boards, or cards. Or they may choose a course of action by a toss of a coin or a

Although all societies have religious beliefs and practices, the pictures here hint at the range of variation. People make offerings and worship at a shrine in Bangkok, Thailand; prayer time before a soccer game in Riyadh, Saudi Arabia; memorial ceremony in honor of Confucius's birthday in Taipei, Taiwan; and a rabbi blowing a ram's horn on a high holiday.

throw of dice. All are variations of methods used in other cultures.

Omar Moore suggested that among the Naskapi hunters of Labrador, divination is an adaptive strategy for successful hunting. The Naskapi consult the diviner every three or four days when they have no luck in hunting. The diviner holds a caribou bone over the fire, and the burns and cracks that appear in it indicate where the group should hunt. Moore, unlike the Naskapi, did not believe that the diviner really can find out where the animals will be; the cracks in the bones merely provide a way of randomly choosing where to hunt. Because humans are likely to develop customary patterns of action, they might be likely to look for game according to some plan. But game might learn to avoid hunters who operate according to a plan. Thus, any method of ensuring against patterning or predictable plans—any random strategy—may be advantageous. Divination by "reading" the bones

would seem to be a random strategy. It also relieves any individual of the responsibility of deciding where to hunt, a decision that might arouse anger if the hunt failed.[32]

The eating of a sacred meal is found in many religions. For instance, Holy Communion is a simulation of the Last Supper. Australian aborigines, normally forbidden to eat their totem animal, have one totem feast a year at which they eat the totem. Feasts are often part of marriage and funeral ceremonies, as well as a fringe benefit of the sacrifice of food to the gods.

Some societies make sacrifices to a god in order to influence the god's action, either to divert anger or to attract goodwill. Characteristic of all sacrifices is that something of value is given up to the gods, whether it be food, drink, sex, household goods, or the life of an animal or person. Some societies feel that the god is obligated to act on their behalf if they make the appropriate sacrifice. Others use the sacrifice in an attempt to persuade the god, realizing there is no guarantee that the attempt will be successful.

Of all types of sacrifice, we probably think that the taking of human life is the ultimate. Nevertheless, human sacrifice is not rare in the ethnographic and historical records. Why have some societies practiced it? One cross-cultural study found that among preindustrial societies, those with full-time craft specialists, slavery, and the corvée are most likely to practice human sacrifice. The suggested explanation is that the sacrifice mirrors what is socially important: societies that depend mainly on human labor for energy (rather than animals or machines) may think of a human life as an appropriate offering to the gods when people want something very important.[33]

Magic

All these modes of interacting with the supernatural can be categorized in various ways. One dimension of variation is how much people in society rely on pleading or asking or trying to persuade the supernatural to act on their behalf, as opposed to whether they believe they can compel the supernatural to help by performing certain acts. For example, prayer is asking; performing voodoo is presumably compelling. When people believe their action can compel the supernatural to act in some particular and intended way, anthropologists often refer to the belief and related practice as **magic.**

Magic may involve manipulation of the supernatural for good or for evil purposes. Many societies have magical rituals designed to ensure good crops, the replenishment of game, the fertility of domestic animals, and the avoidance and cure of illness in humans. We tend to associate the belief in magic with societies simpler than our own. But as many as 80,000 people in the United States take magic seriously.[34] Many claim to be witches. Why magic appeals to some individuals but not others in our own society may someday help us explain why magic is an important part of religious behavior in many societies.

As we will see, the witch doctor and the shaman often employ magic to effect a cure. But the use of magic to bring about harm has evoked perhaps the most interest.

Sorcery and Witchcraft. Sorcery and witchcraft are attempts to invoke the spirits to work harm against people. Although the words *sorcery* and *witchcraft* are often used interchangeably, they are also often distinguished. **Sorcery** may include the use of materials, objects, and medicines to invoke supernatural malevolence. **Witchcraft** may be said to accomplish the same ills by means of thought and emotion alone. Evidence of witchcraft can never be found. This lack of visible evidence makes an accusation of witchcraft both harder to prove and harder to disprove.

To the Azande of Zaire (central Africa), witchcraft was part of everyday living. It was not used to explain events for which the cause was known, such as carelessness or violation of a taboo, but to explain the otherwise unexplainable. A man is gored by an elephant. He must have been bewitched, because he had not been gored on other elephant hunts. A man goes to his beer hut at night, lights some straw, and holds it aloft to look at his beer. The thatch catches fire and the hut burns down. The man has been bewitched, for huts did not catch fire on hundreds of other nights when he and others did the same thing. Some of the pots of a skilled potter break; some of the bowls of a skilled carver crack. Witchcraft: other pots, other bowls treated exactly the same have not broken.[35]

The witch craze in Europe during the sixteenth and seventeenth centuries and the witch trials in 1692 in Salem, Massachusetts, remind us that the fear of others, which the belief in witchcraft presumably represents, can increase and decrease in a society within a relatively short period of time. Many scholars have tried to explain these witch hunts. One factor often suggested is political turmoil, which may give rise to widespread distrust and a search for scapegoats. In the case of western Europe during the sixteenth and seventeenth centuries, small regional political units were being incorporated into national states, and political allegiances were in flux. In addition, as Swanson noted, the commercial revolution and related changes were producing a new social class, the middle class, and "were promoting the growth of Protestantism and other heresies from Roman Catholicism."[36] In the case of Salem, the government of the colony of Massachusetts was unstable and there was much internal dissension. In 1692, the year of the witchcraft hysteria, Massachusetts was left without an English governor, and judicial practices broke down. These extraordinary conditions saw the accusation of a single person for witchcraft become the accusation of hundreds and the execution of twenty. Swanson suggested that the undermining of legitimate political procedures may have generated the widespread fear of witches.[37]

In Salem, Massachusetts, in 1692 there was an epidemic of witchcraft accusations. Some scholars have suggested that ergot poisoning made people act and feel as if they were bewitched.

It is also possible that epidemics of witchcraft accusation, as in Salem as well as other New England and European communities, may be the result of real epidemics—epidemics of disease. The disease implicated in Salem and elsewhere is the fungus disease called ergot, which can grow on rye plants. (The rye flour that went into the bread that the Salem people ate may have been contaminated by ergot.) It is now known that people who eat grain products contaminated by ergot suffer from convulsions, hallucinations, and other symptoms such as crawling sensations in the skin. We also now know that ergot contains LSD, the drug that produces hallucinations and other delusions that resemble those occurring in severe mental disorders.

The presumed victims of bewitchment in Salem and other places had symptoms similar to victims of ergot poisoning today. They suffered from convulsions and the sensations of being pricked, pinched, or bitten. They had visions and felt as if they were flying through the air. We cannot know for sure that ergot poisoning occurred during those times when witchcraft accusations flourished. There is no direct evidence, of course, since the "bewitched" were not medically tested. But we do have some evidence that seems to be consistent with the

ergot theory. Ergot is known to flourish on rye plants under certain climatic conditions—particularly a very cold winter followed by a cool, moist spring and summer. Tree-ring growth indicates that the early 1690s were particularly cold in eastern New England; and the outbreaks of witchcraft accusation in Europe seem to have peaked with colder winter temperatures.[38] Interestingly too, when witchcraft hysteria was greatest in Europe, Europeans were using an ointment containing a skin-penetrating substance that we now know produces hallucinations and a vivid sensation of flying.[39] It may not be cause for wonder then that our popular image of witches is one of people flying through the air on broomsticks.

But whether or not epidemics of witchcraft hysteria are due to epidemics of ergot poisoning or episodes of political turmoil or both, we still have to understand why so many societies in the ethnographic record believe in witchcraft and sorcery in the first place. Why do so many societies believe that there are ways to invoke the spirits to work harm against people? One possible explanation, suggested by Beatrice Whiting, is that sorcery or witchcraft will be found in societies that lack procedures or judicial authorities to deal with crime and other offenses.

Her theory is that all societies need some form of social control—some way of deterring most would-be offenders and of dealing with actual offenders. In the absence of judicial officials who (if present) might deter and deal with antisocial behavior, sorcery may be a very effective social-control mechanism. If you misbehave, the person you mistreated might cause you to become ill or even die. The cross-cultural evidence seems to support this theory: sorcery is more important in societies that lack judicial authorities than in those that have them.[40]

Types of Practitioner

Individuals may believe that they can directly contact the supernatural, but almost all societies also have part-time or full-time religious or magical practitioners. Recent research suggests there are four major types of practitioner: shamans, sorcerers or witches, mediums, and priests. As we shall see, the number of types of practitioner in a society seems to vary with degree of cultural complexity.[41]

The Shaman.   The **shaman** is usually a part-time male specialist who has fairly high status in his community and is often involved in healing.[42] Westerners often call shamans witch doctors because they don't believe that shamans can effectively cure people. Do shamans effectively cure? Actually, Westerners are not the only skeptics. A Native American named Quesalid from the Kwakiutl of the Northwest Coast didn't believe that shamanism was effective either. So he began to associate with the shamans in order to spy on them and was taken into their group. In his first lessons, he learned

a curious mixture of pantomime, prestidigitation, and empirical knowledge, including the art of simulating fainting and nervous fits, . . . sacred song, the technique for inducing vomiting, rather precise notions of auscultation or listening to sounds within the body to detect disorders and obstetrics, and the use of "dreamers," that is, spies who listen to private conversations and secretly convey to the shaman bits of information concerning the origins and symptoms of the ills suffered by different people. Above all, he learned the *ars magna.* . . . The shaman hides a little tuft of down in the corner of his mouth, and he throws it up, covered with blood at the proper moment—after having bitten his tongue or made his gums bleed—and solemnly presents it to his patient and the onlookers as the pathological foreign body extracted as a result of his sucking and manipulations.[43]

His suspicions were confirmed, but his first curing was a success. The patient had heard that Quesalid had joined the shamans and believed that only he could heal him. Quesalid remained with the shamans for the four-year apprenticeship, during which he could take no fee, and he became increasingly aware that his methods worked. He visited other villages, competed with other shamans in curing hopeless cases and won, and finally seemed convinced that his curing system was more valid than those of other shamans. Instead of denouncing the trickery of shamans, he continued to practice as a renowned shaman.[44]

After working with shamans in Africa, E. Fuller Torrey, a psychiatrist and anthropologist, concluded that they use the same mechanisms and techniques to cure patients as psychiatrists and

Healers commonly go into trance to bring about a cure. This !Kung San healer is being held by others so he doesn't injure himself while he is in a trance.

achieve about the same results. He isolated four categories used by healers the world over:

1. *The naming process.* If a disease has a name—"neurasthenia" or "phobia" or "possession by an ancestral spirit" will do—then it is curable; the patient realizes that the doctor understands his case.

2. *The personality of the doctor.* Those who demonstrate some empathy, nonpossessive warmth, and genuine interest in the patient get results.

3. *The patient's expectations.* One way of raising the patient's expectations of being cured is the trip to the doctor; the longer the trip—to the Mayo Clinic, Menninger Clinic, Delphi, or Lourdes—the easier the cure. An impressive setting (the medical center) and impressive paraphernalia (the stethoscope, the couch, attendants in uniform, the rattle, the whistle, the drum, the mask) also raise the patient's expectations. The healer's training is important: the Ute has dreams analyzed; the Blackfoot has a seven-year training course; the American psychiatrist spends four years in medical school and three in hospital training and has diplomas on the wall. High fees also help to raise a patient's expectations. (The Paiute doctors always collect their fees before starting a cure; if they don't, it is believed that they will fall ill.)

4. *Curing techniques.* Drugs, shock treatment, conditioning techniques, and so on have long been used in many different parts of the world.[45]

Medical research suggests that psychological factors are sometimes very important in illness. Patients who believe that medicine will help them often recover quickly even if the medicine is only a sugar pill. Patients who "lose the will to live" may succumb to illness easily. Still, as pharmaceutical companies have discovered, many "folk medicines" collected in anthropological fieldwork do work.

Shamans may coexist with medical doctors. Don Antonio, a respected Otomi Indian shaman in central Mexico, has many patients, perhaps not as many as before modern medicine, but still plenty. In his view, when he was born God gave him his powers to cure, but his powers are reserved for removing "evil" illnesses (those caused by sorcerers). "Good" illnesses can be cured by herbs and medicine, and he refers patients with those illnesses to doctors; he believes that doctors are more effective

than he could be in those cases. The doctors, however, do not seem to refer any patients to Don Antonio or other shamans![46]

Sorcerers and Witches. In contrast with shamans, who have fairly high status, sorcerers and witches of both sexes tend to have very low social and economic status in their societies.[47] Suspected sorcerers and witches are usually feared because they are thought to know how to invoke the supernatural to cause illness, injury, and death. Because sorcerers use materials for their magic, evidence of sorcery can be found, and suspected sorcerers are often killed for their malevolent activities. Because witchcraft supposedly is accomplished by thought and emotion alone, it may be harder to prove that someone is a witch, but the difficulty of proving witchcraft has not prevented people from accusing and killing others for being witches.

Mediums. **Mediums** tend to be females. These part-time practitioners are asked to heal and divine while in possession trances—that is, when they are thought to be possessed by spirits. Mediums are described as having tremors, convulsions, seizures, and temporary amnesia.

Priests. **Priests** are generally full-time male specialists who officiate at public events. They have very high status and are thought to be able to relate to superior or high gods who are beyond the ordinary person's control. In most societies with priests, the people who get to be priests obtain their offices through inheritance or political appointment.[48] Priests are sometimes distinguished from other people by special clothing or a different hairstyle. The training of a priest can be vigorous and long, including fasting, praying, and physical labor as well as learning the dogma and the ritual of his religion. Priests in the United States complete four years of theological school and sometimes serve first as apprentices under established priests. The priest does not receive a fee for each of his services but is supported by donations from parishioners or followers. Priests often have some political power as a result of their office—the chief priest is sometimes also the head of state or is a close adviser to the chief of state—and their material well-being is a direct reflection of their position in the priestly hierarchy.

It is the dependence on memorized ritual that both marks and protects the priest. If a shaman repeatedly fails to effect a cure, he will probably lose his following, for he has obviously lost the support of the spirits. But if a priest performs his ritual perfectly and the gods choose not to respond, the priest will usually retain his position and the ritual will preserve its assumed effectiveness. The nonresponse of the gods will be explained in terms of the people's unworthiness of supernatural favor.

Practitioners and Social Complexity. More complex societies tend to have more types of religious or magical practitioners. If a society has only one type of practitioner, it is almost always a shaman; such societies tend to be nomadic or seminomadic food collectors. Societies with two types of practitioner (usually shaman-healers and priests) have agriculture. Those with three types of practitioner are agriculturalists or pastoralists with political integration beyond the community (the additional practitioner type tends to be either a sorcerer-witch or a medium). Finally, societies with all four types of practitioners have agriculture, political integration beyond the community, and social classes.[49]

RELIGION AND ADAPTATION

▼

Following Malinowski, many anthropologists take the view that religions are adaptive because they reduce the anxieties and uncertainties that afflict all people. We do not really know that religion is the only means of reducing anxiety and uncertainty, or even that individuals or societies *have* to reduce their anxiety and uncertainty. Still, it seems likely that certain religious beliefs and practices have directly adaptive consequences.

For example, the Hindu belief in the sacred cow has seemed to many to be the very opposite of a useful or adaptive custom. Their religion does not permit Hindus to slaughter cows. Why do the Hindus retain such a belief? Why do they allow all those cows to wander around freely, defecating all over the place, and not slaughter any of them? The contrast with our own use of cows could hardly be greater.

Marvin Harris suggested that the Hindu use of cows may have beneficial consequences that some other use of cows would not have. Harris pointed out that there may be a sound economic reason for not slaughtering cattle in India. The cows (and the males they produce) provide resources that could not easily be provided otherwise. At the same time, their wandering around to forage is no strain on the food-producing economy.

The resources provided by the cows are varied. First, a team of oxen and a plow are essential for the many small farms in India. The Indians could

produce oxen with fewer cows, but to do so they would have to devote some of their food production to the feeding of those cows. In the present system, they do not feed the cows, and even though poor nutrition makes the cows relatively infertile, males (which are castrated to make oxen) are still produced at no cost to the economy. Second, cow dung is essential as a cooking fuel and fertilizer. The National Council of Applied Economic Research estimated that an amount of dung equivalent to 45 million tons of coal is burned annually. Moreover, it is delivered practically to the door each day at no cost. Alternative sources of fuel, such as wood, are scarce or costly. In addition, about 340 million tons of dung are used as manure—essential in a country obliged to derive three harvests a year from its intensively cultivated land. Third, although Hindus do not eat beef, cattle that die naturally or are butchered by non-Hindus are eaten by the lower castes, who, without the upper-caste taboo against eating beef, might not get this needed protein. Fourth, the hides and horns of the cattle that die are used in India's enormous leather industry. Therefore, because the cows do not themselves consume resources needed by people and it would be impossible to provide traction, fuel, and fertilizer as cheaply by other means, the taboo against slaughtering cattle may be quite adaptive.[50]

Religious Change as Revitalization

The long history of religion includes periods of strong resistance to change as well as periods of radical change. Anthropologists have been especially interested in the founding of new religions or sects. The appearance of new religions is one of the things that may happen when cultures are disrupted by contact with dominant societies. Various terms have been suggested for these religious movements—cargo cults, nativistic movements, messianic movements, millenarian cults. Wallace suggested that they are all examples of **revitalization movements,** efforts to save a culture by infusing it with a new purpose and new life.[51] We turn to examples of such movements from North America and Melanesia.

The Seneca and the Religion of Handsome Lake. The Seneca reservation of the Iroquois on the Allegheny River in New York State was a place of "poverty and humiliation" by 1799.[52] Demoralized by whiskey and dispossessed from their traditional lands, unable to compete with the new technology because of illiteracy and lack of training, the Seneca were at an impasse. In this setting, Handsome Lake,

ONE APPEAL OF RELIGION MAY BE THE WISH FOR A BETTER WORLD

There are many religions in the United States today, and new sects (often derisively called cults) emerge regularly. Few of us realize that nearly all of the major churches or religions in the world began as minority sects or cults. Indeed, some of the most established and prestigious Protestant churches were radical social movements at first. For example, what we now know as the United Church of Christ, which includes the Congregational Church, was founded by radicals in England who wanted church governance to be in the hands of the local congregation. Many of these radicals became the people we call Pilgrims, who had to flee to the New World. But they were very fundamentalist in their beliefs too; for example, as late as the 1820s, Congregationalist-dominated towns in Connecticut prohibited celebrations of Christmas outside of church because they were not mentioned in the Bible. Nowadays, Congregationalists are among the most liberal Protestants.

We should not be surprised to learn that most of the various Protestant churches today, including some considered very conservative, began as militant sects that set out to achieve a better world. After all, that's why we call them "Protestant." At first, the rebellion was against Rome and the Catholic Church. Later, sects developed in opposition to church and government hierarchies. And remember that Christianity itself began as a radical group in the hinterland of the Roman Empire. So new sects or cults were probably always political and social, as well as religious, movements. Recall that the word *millennium,* as used in discussions of religious movements, refers to a wished-for or expected future time when human life and society will be perfect and free of troubles; the world will then be prosperous and happy and peaceful. Nowadays, the wish for a better world may or may not be religiously inspired. Some people who seek a more perfect world believe that humans alone must achieve it.

How should we categorize this wish for a better world? Should we call it "conservative" because the imagined world may have existed in the past? If the imagined world does not yet exist, is it "radical" to believe it can be achieved? Maybe the wish for a more perfect world is neither conservative nor radical. Maybe it is just that people who are not satisfied with the world as it is think that something can be done to improve things, with or without divine assistance. However it will come, the "millennium" will be different from now, and better.

Ideas about the millennium, and the origins of new cults and religions, might best be viewed then as human hopes: Which ones do people have? Do they vary from culture to culture (and why)? Are some hopes universal? And how might they be achieved?

Sources: *Rodney Stark,* The Future of Religion: Secularization, Revival and Cult Formation *(Berkeley: University of California Press, 1985);* G. W. Trompf, ed., *Cargo Cults and Millenarian Movements: Transoceanic Comparisons of New Religious Movements *(Berlin: Mouton de Gruyter, 1990).*

the fifty-year-old brother of a chief, had the first of a number of visions. In them, he met with emissaries of the Creator who showed him heaven and hell and commissioned him to revitalize Seneca religion and society. This he set out to do for the next decade and a half. He used as his principal text the *Gaiwiio,* or "Good Word," a gospel that contains statements about the nature of religion and eternity and a code of conduct for the righteous. The *Gaiwiio* is interesting both for the influence of Quaker Christianity it clearly reveals[53] and for the way the new material was merged with traditional Iroquois religious concepts.

The first part of the "Good Word" has three main themes, one of which is the concept of an apocalypse. Handsome Lake offered many signs by

A revitalization movement that became known as the Ghost Dance spread eastward from the Northwest in the 1870s to the 1890s. Although many elements differed from place to place, it was generally believed that if people did the dance correctly, ghosts would come to life with sufficient resources to allow the people to return to their old ways. And, in the course of some cataclysm, the whites would disappear. This painting depicts the Ghost Dance as practiced by the Sioux or Lakota.

which the faithful could recognize impending, cosmic doom. Great drops of fire would rain from the skies and a veil would be cast over the earth. False prophets would appear, witch women would openly cast spells, and poisonous creatures from the underworld would seize and kill those who had rejected the *Gaiwiio*. Second, the *Gaiwiio* emphasized sin. The great sins were disbelief in the "good way," drunkenness, witchcraft, and abortion. Sins had to be confessed and repented. Finally, the *Gaiwiio* offered salvation. Salvation could be won by following a code of conduct, attending certain important traditional rites, and performing public confession.

The second part of the *Gaiwiio* sets out the code of conduct. This code seems to orient the Seneca toward advantageous Euro-American practices without separating them from their culture. The code has five main sections:

1. *Temperance.* All Seneca leaders were fully aware of the social disorders arising out of abuse of liquor. Handsome Lake went to great lengths to illustrate and explain the harmfulness of alcohol.

2. *Peace and social unity.* Seneca leaders were to cease their futile bickering, and all were to be united in their approach to the larger society.

3. *Preservation of tribal lands.* Handsome Lake, fearing the piecemeal alienation of Seneca lands, was far ahead of his contemporaries in demanding a halt in land sales to non-Seneca.

4. *Proacculturation.* Though individual property and trading for profit were prohibited, the acquisition of literacy in English was encouraged so that people would be able to read and understand treaties and to avoid being cheated.

5. *Domestic morality.* Sons were to obey their fathers, mothers should avoid interfering with daughters' marriages, and husbands and wives should respect the sanctity of their marriage vows.

Handsome Lake's teaching seems to have led to a renaissance among the Seneca. Temperance was widely accepted, as were schooling and new farming methods. By 1801, corn yields had been increased tenfold, new crops had been introduced (oats, potatoes, flax), and public health and hygiene had improved considerably. Handsome Lake himself acquired great power among his people. He spent the remainder of his life fulfilling administrative duties, acting as a representative of the Iroquois in Washington, and preaching his gospel to neighboring tribes. By the time of Handsome Lake's death in 1815, the Seneca clearly had undergone a dramatic rebirth, attributable at least in part to the new religion. Later in the century, some of Handsome Lake's disciples founded a church in his name that, despite occasional setbacks and political disputes, survives to this day.

Although many scholars believe cultural stress gives rise to these new religious movements, it is still important to understand exactly what the stresses are and how strong they have to become before a new movement emerges. Do different kinds of stresses produce different kinds of movements? And does the nature of the movement depend on the cultural elements already present? Let us consider some theory and research on the causes of the millenarian cargo cults that began to appear in Melanesia from about 1885 on.

Cargo Cults.   The cargo cults can be thought of as religious movements "in which there is an expectation of, and preparation for, the coming of a period of supernatural bliss."[54] Thus, an explicit belief of the cargo cults was the notion that some liberating power would bring all the Western goods (*cargo* in pidgin English) the people might want. For example, around 1932, on Buka in the Solomon Islands, the leaders of a cult prophesied that a tidal wave would sweep away the villages and a ship would arrive with iron, axes, food, tobacco, cars, and arms. Work in the gardens ceased, and wharves and docks were built for the expected cargo.[55]

What may explain such cults? Peter Worsley suggested that an important factor in the rise of cargo cults and millenarian movements in general is the existence of oppression—in the case of Melanesia, colonial oppression. He suggested that the reactions in Melanesia took religious rather than political forms because they were a way of pulling together people who previously had no political unity and who lived in small, isolated social groups.[56] Other scholars, such as David Aberle, suggested that *relative deprivation* is more important than oppression in explaining the origins of cults; when people feel that they could have more, and they have less than what they used to have or less than others, they may be attracted to new cults.[57] Consistent with Aberle's general interpretation, Bruce Knauft's comparative study of cargo cults found that such cults were more important in Melanesian societies that had had *decreasing* cultural contact with the West, and presumably decreasing contact with valued goods, within the year prior to the cult's emergence.[58]

If the recent as well as distant past is any guide, we can expect religious belief and practice to be revitalized periodically, particularly during periods of stress. Thus, we can expect the world to continue to have religious variation.

▼ SUMMARY

1. Religion is any set of attitudes, beliefs, and practices pertaining to supernatural power. Such beliefs may vary within a culture as well as among societies, and they may change over time.

2. Religious beliefs are evident in all known cultures and are inferred from artifacts associated with *Homo sapiens* since at least 60,000 years ago.

3. Theories to account for the universality of religion suggest that humans create it in response to certain universal needs or conditions, including a need for understanding, reversion to childhood feelings, anxiety or uncertainty, and a need for community.

4. There are wide variations in religious beliefs. Societies vary in the number and kinds of supernatural entities in which they believe. There may be impersonal supernatural forces (e.g., mana and taboo), supernatural beings of nonhuman origin (gods and spirits), and supernatural beings of human origin (ghosts and ancestor spirits). The religious belief system of a society may include any or all such entities.

5. Gods and spirits may be unpredictable or predictable, aloof from or interested in human affairs, helpful or punishing. In some societies, all gods are equal in rank; in others, there is a hierarchy of prestige and power among gods and spirits, just as among the humans in those societies.

6. A monotheistic religion is one in which there is one high god, as the creator of the universe or the director of events (or both); all other supernatural beings are either subordinate to, or function as alternative manifestations of, this god. A high god is generally found in societies with a high level of political development.

7. Faced with ignorance, pain, and injustice, people frequently explain events by claiming intervention by the gods. Such intervention has also been sought by people who hope it will help them achieve their own ends. The gods are likely to punish the immoral behavior of people in societies that have considerable differences in wealth.

8. Various methods have been used to attempt communication with the supernatural. Among them are prayer, doing things to the body and mind, simulation, feasts, and sacrifices.

9. When people believe that their actions can compel the supernatural to act in a particular and intended way, anthropologists refer to the belief and related practice as magic. Sorcery and witchcraft are attempts to make the spirits work harm against people.

10. Almost all societies have part-time or full-time religious or magical practitioners. Recent cross-cultural research suggests that there are four major types of practitioner: shamans, sorcerers or witches, mediums, and priests. The number of types of practitioner seems to vary with degree of cultural complexity: the more complex the society, the more types of practitioners.

11. The history of religion includes periods of strong resistance to change and periods of radical change. One explanation for this cycle is that religious practices always originate during periods of stress. Religious movements have been called revitalization movements—efforts to save a culture by infusing it with a new purpose and new life.

▼ GLOSSARY TERMS

ancestor spirits	gods	polytheistic	sorcery
animatism	magic	priests	spirits
animism	mana	religion	supernatural
divination	mediums	revitalization movements	taboo
ghosts	monotheistic	shaman	witchcraft

▼ CRITICAL QUESTIONS

1. How does your conception of God compare with supernatural beings in other religious systems?
2. What do you think is the future of religion?
3. Could any of the religious practices you know about be classified as magic? Are they associated with anxiety-arousing situations?

▼ SUGGESTED READING

CHILD, A. B., AND CHILD, I. L. *Religion and Magic in the Life of Traditional Peoples.* Englewood Cliffs, NJ: Prentice Hall, 1993. Based on a review of ethnographic data from all over the world, this book discusses the features common to traditional religions everywhere, as well as the factors that may account for variation in religion.

EMBER, M., EMBER, C. R., AND LEVINSON, D. eds. *Portraits of Culture: Ethnographic Originals.* Englewood Cliffs, NJ: Prentice Hall, 1994 and 1995. Prentice Hall/Simon & Schuster Custom Publishing. Several chapters deal extensively with religious belief and practice as seen in a particular culture: G. Brandon, "African-Americans: Getting into the Spirit"; J. W. Dow, "Sierra Otomí: People of the Mexican Mountains"; W. K. Powers and M. N. Powers, "Lakota: A Study in Cultural Continuity"; S. B. Schaefer, "Huichol: Becoming a Godmother"; J. R. Sosa, "Maya: The Sacred in Everyday Life."

LEHMANN, A. C., AND MYERS, J. E. *Magic, Witchcraft, and Religion: An Anthropological Study of the Supernatural.* Palo Alto, CA: Mayfield, 1985. A collection of readings from anthropology and other disciplines on topics in the study of the supernatural.

MALINOWSKI, B. *Magic, Science and Religion and Other Essays.* Garden City, NY: Doubleday, 1954. A classic collection of papers representing some of Malinowski's work on ritual and religious behavior and the nature of primitive cults, magic, and faith.

MATLOCK, J. G. "Universals and Variation in Religious Belief and Practice." In C. R. Ember and M. Ember, eds., *Cross-Cultural Research for Social Science.* Englewood Cliffs, NJ: Prentice Hall, 1995. Prentice Hall/Simon & Schuster Custom Publishing. An up-to-date review of cross-cultural studies of religious diversity, suggesting how religious beliefs and practices change in response to changes in social and political organization and subsistence strategy.

MORRIS, B. *Anthropological Studies of Religion: An Introductory Text.* Cambridge: Cambridge University Press, 1987. A review of theories about the origin and persistence of religion.

SWANSON, G. E. *The Birth of the Gods: The Origin of Primitive Beliefs.* Ann Arbor: University of Michigan Press, 1969. A pioneering cross-cultural study that explores the origins of religious beliefs and examines how various aspects of religion may be related to social and political organization.

▼ NOTES

[1]Edward B. Tylor, "Animism" (originally published 1871), in William A. Lessa and Evon Z. Vogt, eds., *Reader in Comparative Religion: An Anthropological Approach,* 4th ed. (New York: Harper & Row, 1979), pp. 9–18.

[2]R. R. Marett, *The Threshold of Religion* (London: Methuen, 1909).

[3]Sigmund Freud, *Moses and Monotheism,* trans. Katherine Jones (New York: Vintage Books, 1967 [originally published 1939]); Christopher Badcock, *Essential Freud* (Oxford: Basil Blackwell, 1988), pp. 126 27, 133–36.

[4]Bronislaw Malinowski, "The Group and the Individual in Functional Analysis," *American Journal of Sociology,* 44 (1939): 959; Bronislaw Malinowski, "Magic, Science, and Religion," in *Magic, Science, and Religion and Other Essays* (Garden City, NY: Doubleday, 1948), pp. 50–51.

[5]William James, *The Varieties of Religious Experience: A Study in Human Nature* (New York: Modern Library, 1902).

[6]Carl G. Jung, *Psychology and Religion* (New Haven: Yale University Press, 1938).

[7]Erich Fromm, *Psychoanalysis and Religion* (New Haven, CT: Yale University Press, 1950).

[8]Abraham H. Maslow, *Religions, Values, and Peak-Experiences* (Columbus: Ohio State University Press, 1964).

[9]Émile Durkheim, *The Elementary Forms of the Religious Life,* trans. Joseph W. Swain (New York: Collier Books, 1961 [originally published 1912]).

[10]Guy E. Swanson, *The Birth of the Gods: The Origin of Primitive Beliefs* (Ann Arbor: University of Michigan Press, 1969), pp. 1 31.

[11]Anthony Wallace, *Religion: An Anthropological View* (New York: Random House, 1966), pp. 60–61.

[12]Annemarie De Waal Malefijt, *Religion and Culture: An Introduction to Anthropology of Religion* (New York: Macmillan, 1968), p. 153.

[13]Verne F. Ray, *The Sanpoil and Nespelem: Salishan Peoples of Northeastern Washington* (New Haven, CT: Human Relations Area Files, 1954), pp. 172–89.

[14]Paul C. Rosenblatt, R. Patricia Walsh, and Douglas A. Jackson. *Grief and Mourning in Cross-Cultural Perspective* (New Haven, CT: HRAF Press, 1976), p. 51.

[15]Ibid., p. 55.

[16]Swanson, *The Birth of the Gods,* pp. 97–108; see also Dean Sheils, "Toward a Unified Theory of Ancestor Worship: A Cross-Cultural Study," *Social Forces,* 54 (1975): 427–40.

[17]John Middleton, "The Cult of the Dead: Ancestors and Ghosts," in William A. Lessa and Evon Z. Vogt, eds., *Reader in Comparative Religion: An Anthropological Approach,* 3rd ed. (New York: Harper & Row, 1971), p. 488.

[18]Melford E. Spiro and Roy G. D'Andrade, "A Cross-Cultural Study of Some Supernatural Beliefs," *American Anthropologist,* 60 (1958): 456–66.

[19]William W. Lambert, Leigh Minturn Triandis, and Margery Wolf, "Some Correlates of Beliefs in the Malevolence and Benevolence of Supernatural Beings: A Cross-Societal Study," *Journal of Abnormal and Social Psychology,* 58 (1959): 162–69. See also Ronald P. Rohner, *They Love Me, They Love Me Not: A Worldwide Study of the Effects of Parental Acceptance and Rejection* (New Haven, CT: HRAF Press, 1975), p. 108.

[20]H. G. Barnett, *Being a Palauan* (New York: Holt, Rinehart & Winston, 1960), pp. 79–85.

[21]Swanson, *The Birth of the Gods,* p. 56.

[22]Ibid., pp. 55–81; see also William D. Davis, "Societal Complexity and the Nature of Primitive Man's Conception of the Supernatural," Ph.D. dissertation, University of North Carolina, Chapel Hill, 1971.

[23]Robert B. Textor, comp., *A Cross-Cultural Summary* (New Haven, CT: HRAF Press, 1967); see also Ralph Underhill, "Economic and Political Antecedents of Monotheism: A Cross-Cultural Study," *American Journal of Sociology,* 80 (1975): 841–61.

[24]Clifford Geertz, "Religion as a Cultural System," in Michael Banton, ed., *Anthropological Approaches to the Study of Religion,* Association of Social Anthropologists of the Commonwealth, Monograph No. 3 (New York: Praeger, 1966), pp. 1–46.

[25]Swanson, *The Birth of the Gods,* pp. 153–74.

[26]Ruth Bunzel, "The Nature of Katcinas," in Lessa and Vogt, eds., *Reader in Comparative Religion,* 3rd ed., pp. 493–95.

[27]Gary H. Gossen, "Temporal and Spiritual Equivalents in Chamula Ritual Symbolism," in Lessa and Vogt, eds., *Reader in Comparative Religion,* 4th ed., pp. 116–28.

[28]Wallace, *Religion: An Anthropological View,* pp. 52–67.

[29]Michael Winkelman, "Trance States: A Theoretical Model and Cross-Cultural Analysis," *Ethos,* 14 (1986): 178–83.

[30]Erika Bourguignon, "Introduction: A Framework for the Comparative Study of Altered States of Consciousness," in Erika Bourguignon, *Religion, Altered States of Consciousness, and Social Change* (Columbus: Ohio State University Press, 1973), pp. 3–35.

[31]Erika Bourguignon and Thomas L. Evascu, "Altered States of Consciousness within a General Evolutionary Perspective: A Holocultural Analysis," *Behavior Science Research,* 12 (1977): 197–216. See also Winkelman, "Trance States," pp. 196–98.

[32]Omar Khayyam Moore, "Divination: A New Perspective," *American Anthropologist,* 59 (1957): 69–74.

[33]Dean Sheils, "A Comparative Study of Human Sacrifice," *Behavior Science Research,* 15 (1980): 245–62.

[34]M. Adler, *Drawing Down the Moon* (Boston: Beacon, 1986), p. 418, as referred to in T. M. Luhrmann, *Persuasions of the Witch's Craft: Ritual Magic and Witchcraft in Present-Day England* (Oxford: Basil Blackwell, 1989), pp. 4–5.

[35]E. E. Evans-Pritchard, "Witchcraft Explains Unfortunate Events," in Lessa and Vogt, eds., *Reader in Comparative Religion,* 4th ed., pp. 362–66.

[36]Swanson, *The Birth of the Gods,* p. 150. See also H. R. Trevor-Roper, "The European Witch-Craze of the Sixteenth and Seventeenth Centuries," in Lessa and Vogt, eds., *Reader in Comparative Religion,* 3rd ed., pp. 444–49.

[37]Swanson, *The Birth of the Gods,* pp. 150–51.

[38]Linnda R. Caporael, "Ergotism: The Satan Loosed in Salem?" *Science,* April 2, 1976, pp. 21–26; Mary K. Matossian, "Ergot and the Salem Witchcraft Affair," *American Scientist,* 70 (1982): 355–57; and Mary K. Matossian, *Poisons of the Past: Molds, Epidemics, and History* (New Haven, CT: Yale University Press, 1989), pp. 70–80. For possible reasons to dismiss the ergot theory, see Nicholas P. Spanos, "Ergotism and the Salem Witch Panic: A Critical Analysis and an Alternative Conceptualization," *Journal of the History of the Behavioral Sciences,* 19 (1983): 358–69.

[39]Michael Harner, "The Role of Hallucinogenic Plants in European Witchcraft," in Michael Harner, ed., *Hallucinogens and Shamanism* (New York: Oxford University Press, 1972), pp. 127–50.

[40]Beatrice B. Whiting, *Paiute Sorcery,* Viking Fund Publications in Anthropology, No. 15 (New York: Wenner-Gren Foundation, 1950), pp. 36–37. See also Swanson, *The Birth of the Gods,* pp. 137–52, 240–41.

[41]Michael Winkelman, "Magico-Religious Practitioner Types and Socioeconomic Conditions," *Behavior Science Research,* 20 (1986): 17–46.

[42]Ibid., pp. 28–29.

[43]Claude Lévi-Strauss, "The Sorcerer and His Magic," in Claude Lévi-Strauss, *Structural Anthropology,* trans. Claire Jacobsen and Brooke Grundfest Schoepf (New York: Basic Books, 1963), p. 169.

[44]Franz Boas, *The Religion of the Kwakiutl,* Columbia University Contributions to Anthropology, vol. 10, pt. 2 (New York: Columbia University, 1930), pp. 1–41. Reported in Lévi-Strauss, *Structural Anthropology,* pp. 169–73.

[45]E. Fuller Torrey, *The Mind Game: Witchdoctors and Psychiatrists* (New York: Emerson Hall, n.d.).

[46]James Dow, *The Shaman's Touch: Otomi Indian Symbolic Healing* (Salt Lake City: University of Utah Press, 1986), pp. 6–9, 125.

[47]Winkelman, "Magico-Religious Practitioner Types and Socioeconomic Conditions," pp. 27–28.

[48]Ibid., p. 27.

[49]Ibid., pp. 35–37.

[50]Marvin Harris, "The Cultural Ecology of India's Sacred Cattle," *Current Anthropology,* 7 (1966): 51–63.

[51]Wallace, *Religion,* p. 30.

[52]Anthony Wallace, *The Death and Rebirth of the Seneca* (New York: Knopf, 1970), p. 239.

[53]The Quakers, long-time neighbors and trusted advisers of the Seneca, took pains not to interfere with Seneca religion, principles, and attitudes.

[54]Peter Worsley, *The Trumpet Shall Sound: A Study of "Cargo" Cults in Melanesia* (London: MacGibbon & Kee, 1957), p. 12.

[55]Ibid., pp. 11, 115.

[56]Ibid., p. 122.

[57]David Aberle, "A Note on Relative Deprivation Theory as Applied to Millenarian and Other Cult Movements," in Lessa and Vogt, eds., *Reader in Comparative Religion,* 3rd ed., pp. 528–31.

[58]Bruce M. Knauft, "Cargo Cults and Relational Separation," *Behavior Science Research,* 13 (1978): 185–240.

The Arts

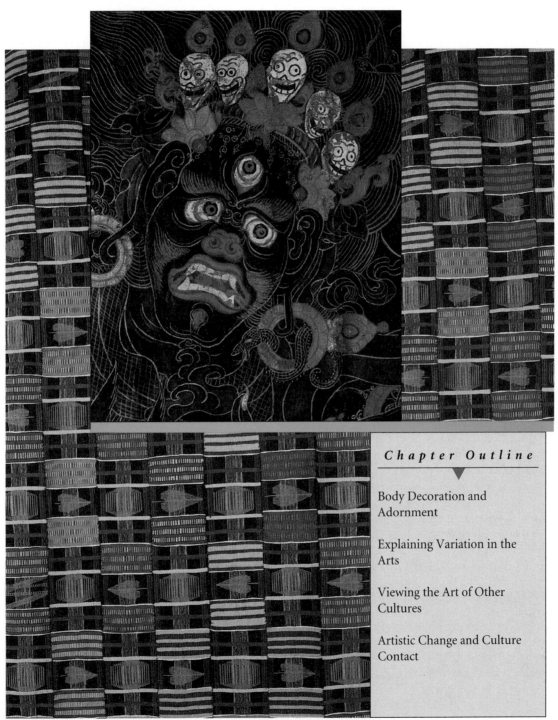

Most societies do not have a word for art.[1] Perhaps because art, particularly in societies with relatively little specialization, is often an integral part of religious, social, and political life. Indeed, most of the aspects of culture we have already discussed—economics, kinship, politics, religion—are also not easily separated from the rest of social life.[2]

Art seems to appear in human history at least as far back as 30,000 years ago. We say that those earliest known carvings, beads, and cave paintings are art, but what do we mean by "art"? A stone spear point, a bone fish hook, obviously required skill and creativity to make. But we do not call them art. Why do we feel that some things are art and others are not?

Some definitions of art emphasize its evocative quality. From the viewpoint of the person who creates it, art expresses feelings and ideas; from the viewpoint of the observer or participant, it evokes feelings and ideas. The feelings and ideas on each side may or may not be exactly the same. And they may be expressed in a variety of ways—drawing, painting, carving, weaving, body decoration, music, dance, story. An artistic work or performance is intended to excite the senses, to stir the emotions of the beholder or participant. It may produce feelings of pleasure, awe, repulsion, fear, but usually not indifference.[3]

But emphasizing the evocative quality of art may make it difficult to compare the art of different cultures because what is evocative in one culture may not be evocative in another. For example, what is a humorous story in one culture may not be funny in another. Thus, most anthropologists agree that art is more than an attempt by an individual to express or communicate feelings and ideas. There is also some cultural patterning or meaning; societies vary in their characteristic kinds and styles of art.[4]

Artistic activities are always in part cultural, involving shared and learned patterns of behavior, belief, and feeling. What are some of the ideas about art in our own culture? We tend to think that anything useful is not art. If the basket has a design that was not necessary to its function, we may possibly consider it art, especially if we keep it on a shelf; but the basket with bread on the table would probably not be considered art. The fact that such a distinction is not made in other societies strongly suggests that our ideas about art are cultural. Among Native Americans on the Northwest Coast, elaborately carved totem poles not only displayed the crests of the lineages of their occupants; they also supported the house.[5] The fact that artistic activities are partly cultural is evident when we compare how people in different societies treat the outsides of their houses. Most North Americans share the value of decorating the interiors of their homes with pictures—paintings, prints, or photographs hung on the walls. But they do not share the value of painting pictures on the outside walls of their houses, as Native Americans did on the Northwest Coast.

In our society, we also insist that to be considered art, a work must be unique. This aspect is clearly consistent with our emphasis on the individual. However, even though we require that artists be unique and innovative, the art they produce must still fall within some range of acceptable variation. Artists must communicate to us in a way we can relate to, or at least learn to relate to. Often, they must follow certain current styles of expression that have been set by other artists or by critics, if they hope to have their art accepted by the public. The idea that an artist should be original is a cultural idea—in some societies the ability to replicate a traditional pattern is more valued than originality.

So art seems to have several qualities. It expresses as well as communicates. It stimulates the senses, affects emotions, and evokes ideas. It is produced in culturally patterned ways and styles; it has cultural meaning. In addition, some people are thought to be better at it than others.[6] Art does not require some people to be full-time artistic specialists; many societies in the ethnographic record had no full-time specialists of any kind. But, although everyone in some societies may participate in some arts (dancing, singing, body decoration), it is usually thought that certain individuals have superior artistic skill.

To illustrate the cross-cultural variation that exists in artistic expression, we will consider first the art of body decoration and adornment.

BODY DECORATION AND ADORNMENT

In all societies, people decorate or adorn their bodies. The decorations may be permanent—scars, tattoos, changes in the shape of a body part. Or they may be temporary—in the form of paint or objects such as feathers, jewelry, skins, and clothing that are not strictly utilitarian. Much of this decoration seems to be motivated by esthetic considerations, which, of course, may vary from culture to culture. The actual form of the decoration depends on cultural traditions. Body ornamentation includes the pierced noses of some women in India, the elongated necks of the Mangebetu of central Africa, the tattooing of North American males, the body painting of the Caduveo of South America, and the varying ornaments found in almost every culture.

However, in addition to satisfying esthetic needs, body decoration or adornment may be used to delineate social position, rank, sex, occupation, local and ethnic identity, or religion within a society. Along with social stratification come visual means of declaring status. The symbolic halo (the crown) on the king's head, the scarlet hunting jacket of the English gentleman, the eagle feathers of the Native American chief's bonnet, the gold-embroidered jacket of the Indian rajah—each of these marks of high status is recognized in its own society. Jewelry in the shape of a cross or the Star of David indicates Christian or Jewish inclinations. Clothes may set apart the priest or the nun or the member of a sect such as the Amish.

The erotic significance of some body decoration is also apparent. Women draw attention to

Body tattooing sometimes is used to permanently mark status, as with chiefs in Polynesia. But in many places, like among the Dayak of Borneo, tattooing is more personal; people choose to decorate their bodies however they wish.

erogenous zones of the body by painting, as on the lips, and by attaching some object—an earring, a flower behind the ear, a necklace, bracelet, brooch, anklet, or belt. Men draw attention too, by beards, tattoos, and penis sheaths (in some otherwise naked societies) that point upward. We have only to follow the fashion trends for women of Europe and North America during the past 300 years, with their history of pinched waists, ballooned hips, bustled rumps, exaggerated breasts, painted faces, and exposed bosoms, to realize the significance of body adornment for sexual provocation. Why some societies emphasize the erotic adornment of women and others emphasize it in men is not yet understood.

In many societies the body is permanently marked or altered, often to indicate a change in status. For example, in the Poro initiation ceremony practiced by the Kpelle of Liberia, newly circumcised boys spent a period of seclusion in the forest with the older men. They returned with scars down their backs, symbolic tooth marks indicative of their close escape from *ngamu,* the Great Masked Figure, which ate the child but disgorged the young adult.[7]

The tendency to decorate the human body is probably universal. We have noted some of the various methods people have used to adorn themselves in different societies. We are also aware of body-decoration practices that raise questions to which we have no ready answers. What explains adornment of the body by permanent marking such as scarification, or by bound feet, elongated ears and necks, shaped heads, pierced ears and septums, and filed teeth? (See the box titled "Politics and Art" for suggestions about the relationship between permanent body marking and politics.) Why do different societies adorn, paint, or otherwise decorate different parts of the body for sexual (or other) reasons? And what leads some members of our society to transfer body decoration to their animals? Why the shaped hair of the poodle, the braided manes of some horses, and diamond collars, painted toenails, coats, hats, and even boots for some pets?

EXPLAINING VARIATION IN THE ARTS

In our society we stress the freedom of the artist, so it may seem to us that art is completely free to vary. But our emphasis on uniqueness obscures the fact that different cultures not only use or emphasize different materials and have different ideas of beauty, but they also may have characteristic styles

POLITICS AND ART

Art is exceedingly variable cross-culturally. But that does not mean that the variability is unexplainable, not linkable to other aspects of human existence. The various findings described in this chapter indicate that much of art *is* linkable to other aspects of culture. Here we consider the possibility that even politics, that messy and sometimes volatile arena of human social life, may have reflections in art.

For example, Christopher Steiner's article, "Body Personal and Body Politic," focuses on four forms of self-decoration—body painting, tattooing, masking, and "crowning." (A mask conceals the face and head of the wearer; a crown or other headdress draws attention to, or identifies, the wearer.) Steiner first discusses how body decoration reflects politics in the islands of Melanesia and Polynesia (in the Pacific).

In Melanesia, political leadership is typically of the "big man" type. There is no fixed authority; big men gain influence by attracting followers, who may not follow for long. There are no political offices or permanent positions of authority. And of course there are no centralized chiefdoms and no hierarchy of influential or powerful people. The whole system is fragile and subject to change. In Polynesia, in contrast, there are permanent systems of authority, usually integrating large populations, with a chief or king at the top whose position is usually inherited. Leaders do not achieve their positions by personal action; they succeed to their positions by genealogical right. The system is permanent or nonshifting as well as hierarchical.

Now consider how body adornment may reflect politics in the two areas. Melanesians paint their bodies, and the painting is ephemeral. It disappears within a short time, or after the first wash, just as a big man's status may go up or down quite quickly, depending on what he has done lately for his former followers. Polynesians decorate their bodies with tattoos, which are permanent, as are their systems of leadership. Just as the chief retains his status over time, so a tattoo does not wash away. In Samoa, for example, tattoos distinguished the chiefly class from commoners. Bands and stripes were restricted to persons of high status; low-status persons could have tattoos only of solid black and only from waist to knees. Within the ruling class, the number of tattooed triangles down a

and themes. It is easy to see styles when we look at art that is different from our own; it is harder to see similarity when we look at the art of our own culture. If we look at dance styles, for example, we may think that the dance style of the 1940s is completely different from the dance style of the 1990s. But it might take an outsider to notice that in our culture we still generally see couples dancing as a pair rather than in a group line or circle (as in dances we call "folk dances"). And, in our culture females and males dance together rather than separately. Furthermore, our popular music still has a beat (or combination of beats) and is made by many of the same kinds of instruments as in the past.

But where do these similarities in form and style come from? Much of the recent research on variation in the arts supports the idea that form and style in visual art, music, dance, and folklore are very much influenced by other aspects of culture. Some psychological anthropologists, as we saw in the chapter on psychology and culture, would go even further, suggesting that art, like religion, expresses the typical feelings, anxieties, and experiences of people in a culture. And the typical feelings and anxieties in turn are influenced by basic institutions such as child rearing, economy, social organization, and politics.

Consider how the physical form of art preferred by a society may reflect its way of life. For example, Richard Anderson pointed out that the art of traditionally nomadic people such as the !Kung, Inuit, and Australian aborigines is mostly carryable.[8] Song, dance, and oral literature are very important in those societies and are as portable as you can get. Those societies decorate useful objects man's leg indicated his relative rank. Because tattooing is permanent, it is a form of body decoration well suited to a society with inherited social stratification.

The traditional political systems of Africa ranged from centralized kingdoms (on the complex end of the continuum) to village-based or segmentary lineage systems in which leadership was ephemeral or secret (tied to secret societies). Masks that conceal identity are often used in the uncentralized systems; crowns or other headdresses indicating high status are frequent in the kingdoms. Among the uncentralized Ibo of eastern Nigeria, masks are often worn by the young men of a village when they criticize the behavior of the village elders. In the kingdom of Ngoyo, in western Zaire, the king's status is indicated by his special cap as well as by his special three-legged stool.

If art may reflect politics on the cultural level, it may also do so on the psychological or individual level. Lewis Austin found that a person's preferences in visual (graphic) symbols can often be predicted from the person's political ideology. Experimental subjects from Japan and the United States were asked to locate themselves on a continuum from radical to conservative and to indicate their preferences in pairs of visual symbols—unbalanced versus balanced, uneven versus even, incomplete versus complete, varying versus uniform. So, for example, a set of bars (as in a bar graph) of the same height is even; bars of different heights are uneven. Conservatives preferred symbols that were orderly (bars side by side ordered from small to large, versus unequal-sized bars lying at angles to each other), passive (a flat line, versus a squiggle or sine wave), and uniform (four

squares, versus three squares and a circle). In these terms, the Japanese subjects were more conservative than the American. But in both countries artistic preferences varied in similar ways with political ideology.

If preferences in visual images have a metaphorical significance that is associated with political preferences, perhaps other style preferences (in clothing, furniture, architecture, and so on) also reflect political ideology. Only future research will tell.

Sources: *Christopher B. Steiner, "Body Personal and Body Politic: Adornment and Leadership in Cross-Cultural Perspective,"* Anthropos, 85 *(1990): 431–45; Lewis Austin, "Visual Symbols, Political Ideology, and Culture,"* Ethos, 5 *(1977): 306–25.*

that they carry with them—harpoons for the Inuit, boomerangs for the Australian aborigines, ostrich egg "canteens" for the !Kung San. But they don't have bulky things such as sculpture or elaborate costumes. And what about the presence of artists or art critics? Although some people in smaller-scale societies are more artistic than others, specialized artists (as well as critics or theoreticians of art) tend to be found only in societies with a complex and specialized division of labor.

Visual Art

Perhaps the most obvious way artistic creations reflect how we live is by mirroring the environment—the materials and technologies available to a culture. Stone, wood, bones, tree bark, clay, sand, charcoal, berries for staining, and a few mineral-derived ochers are generally available materials. In addition, depending on the locality, other resources are accessible: shells, horns, tusks, gold, copper, and silver. The different uses to which societies put these materials are of interest to anthropologists, who may ask, for example, why a people chooses to use clay and not copper when both items are available. Although we have no conclusive answers as yet, such questions have important ramifications. The way in which a society views its environment is sometimes apparent in its choice and use of artistic materials. The use of certain metals, for example, may be reserved for ceremonial objects of special importance. Or the belief in the supernatural powers of a stone or tree may cause a sculptor to be sensitive to that particular material.[9]

The same materials may be used artistically in different societies. In Japan sand is raked into traditional patterns. A Navaho in the southwestern United States creates a sand painting.

What is particularly meaningful to anthropologists is the realization that, although the materials available to a society may to some extent limit or influence what it can do artistically, the materials by no means determine what is done. Why does the artist in Japanese society rake sand into patterns, the artist in Navaho society paint sand, and the artist in Roman society melt sand to form glass? Moreover, even when the same material is used in the same way by members of different societies, the form or style of the work varies enormously from culture to culture.

A society may choose to represent objects or phenomena that are especially important to its population or elite. An examination of the art of the Middle Ages tells us something about the medieval preoccupation with theological doctrine. In addition to revealing the primary concerns of a society, the content of that society's art may also reflect the culture's social stratification. Authority figures may be represented in rather obvious ways. In the art of ancient Sumerian society, the sovereign was portrayed as being much larger than his followers, and the most prestigious gods were given oversized eyes. Also, as we have seen, differences in clothing and jewelry styles within a society usually reflect social stratification.

Certain possible relationships between the art of a society and other aspects of its culture have always been recognized by art historians. Much of this attention has been concentrated on the content of art, since European art has been representational for such a long time. But the style of the art may reflect other aspects of culture. John Fischer, for example, examined the stylistic features of art with the aim of discovering "some sort of regular connection between some artistic feature and some social situation."[10] He argued that the artist expresses a form of social fantasy. In other words, in a stable society artists will respond to those conditions in the society that bring them, and the society, security or pleasure.

Assuming that "pictorial elements in design are, on one psychological level, abstract, mainly unconscious representations of persons in the society,"[11] Fischer reasoned that egalitarian societies would tend to have different stylistic elements in their art than stratified societies. Egalitarian societies are generally composed of small, self-sufficient communities that are structurally similar and have little differentiation between persons. Stratified societies, on the other hand, generally have larger and more interdependent (and dissimilar) communities

TABLE 16–1 Artistic Differences in Egalitarian and Stratified Societies

EGALITARIAN SOCIETY	STRATIFIED SOCIETY
Repetition of simple elements	Integration of unlike elements
Much empty or "irrelevant" space	Little empty space
Symmetrical design	Asymmetrical design
Unenclosed figures	Enclosed figures

Source: *Based on John Fischer, "Art Styles as Cultural Cognitive Maps,"* American Anthropologist, 63 (1961).

and great differences among persons in prestige, power, and access to economic resources. Fischer hypothesized, and found in a cross-cultural study, that certain elements of design were strongly related to the presence of social hierarchy. His findings are summarized in Table 16–1.

Repetition of a simple element, for example, tends to be found in the art of egalitarian societies, which have little political organization and few authority positions. If each element unconsciously represents individuals within the society, the relative sameness of people seems to be reflected in the repetitiveness of design elements. Conversely, the combining of different design elements in complex patterns that tends to be found in the art of stratified societies seems to reflect the high degree of social differentiation that exists in such societies.

According to Fischer, the egalitarian society's empty space in a design represents the society's relative isolation. Because egalitarian societies are usually small and self-sufficient, they tend to shy away from foreigners, preferring to find security within their own group. On the other hand, the art of stratified societies is generally crowded. The hierarchical society does not seek to isolate individuals or communities within the group because they must be interdependent, each social level ideally furnishing services for those above it and help for those beneath it. As Fischer suggested, we can, in general, discern a lack of empty space in the designs of societies in which security is not sought by avoiding strangers, but rather "security is produced by incorporating strangers into the hierarchy, through dominance or submission as the relative power indicates."[12]

Symmetry, the third stylistic feature related to type of society, is similar to the first. Symmetry may suggest likeness or an egalitarian society; asymmetry

suggests difference and perhaps stratification. The fourth feature of interest here, the presence or absence of enclosures or boundaries ("frames" in our art), may indicate the presence or absence of hierarchically imposed rules circumscribing individual behavior. An unenclosed design may reflect free access to most property; in egalitarian societies the fencing off of a piece of property for the use of only one person is unknown. In the art of stratified societies, boundaries or enclosures may reflect the idea of private property. Or they may symbolically represent the real differences in dress, occupation, type of food allowed, and manners that separate the different classes of people.

Studies such as Fischer's offer anthropologists new tools with which to evaluate ancient societies that are known only by a few pieces of pottery or a few tools or paintings. If art reflects certain aspects of a culture, then the study of whatever art of a people has been preserved may provide a means of testing the accuracy of the guesses we make about their culture on the basis of more ordinary archaeological materials. For example, even if we did not know from classical Greek writings that Athens became more and more socially stratified between 1000 B.C. and 450 B.C., we might guess that such a transformation had occurred because of the changes we can see over time in the way the Athenians decorated vases. Consistent with Fischer's cross-cultural findings, as Athens became more stratified, its vase painting became more complex, more crowded, and more enclosed.[13]

Music

When we hear the music of another culture, we often don't know what to make of it. We may say it does not "mean" anything to us, hardly realizing that the meaning of music has been programmed into us by our culture. In music as well as in art, our culture largely determines what we consider acceptable variation, what we say has "meaning" to us. Even a trained musicologist, listening for the first time to music of a different culture, will not be able to hear the subtleties of tone and rhythm that members of the culture hear with ease. His or her predicament is similar to that of the linguist who, exposed to a foreign language, cannot at first distinguish phonemes, morphemes, and other regular patterns of speech.

Not only do instruments vary, but music itself varies widely in style from society to society. For example, in some societies people prefer music with a regularly recurring beat; in others they prefer changes in rhythm. There are also variations in

DO MASKS SHOW EMOTION IN UNIVERSAL WAYS?

Anthropologists have documented how forms and styles in art vary from culture to culture. But with all this variation, it seems that certain forms of art may show emotion in universally similar ways. For example, recent research on masks from different cultures supports the conclusion that masks (like faces) tend to represent certain emotions in the same ways.

Face masks are commonly used in rituals and performances. They not only hide the real face of the mask wearer but they often evoke powerful emotions in the audience—anger, fear, sadness, joy. You might think, because so many things vary cross-culturally, that the ways in which emotion is displayed and recognized in the face vary too. But apparently they do not. We now have some evidence

that the symbolism used in masks is often universal.

The research on masks builds on work done by Ekman and Izard, who used photographs of individuals experiencing (or actors simulating) various emotions. Ekman and Izard showed photographs to members of different cultural groups and asked them to identify the emotions displayed in the photographs. A particular emotion was identified correctly by most viewers, whatever the viewer's native culture. The results for the viewers from less Westernized cultures paralleled the results for viewers from more Westernized cultures. Coding schemes were developed to enable researchers to compare the detailed facial positions of individual portions of the face (eyebrows, mouth, etc.) for dif-

ferent emotions. What exactly do we do when we scowl? We contract the eyebrows and lower the corners of the mouth; in geometric terms, we make angles and diagonals on our faces. When we smile, we raise the corners of the mouth; we make it curved.

Psychologist Joel Aronoff and his colleagues compared two types of wooden face masks from many different societies—masks described as threatening (for example, designed to frighten off evil spirits) versus masks associated with nonthreatening functions (for example, a courtship dance). As suspected, the two sets of masks had significantly different proportions of certain facial elements. The threatening masks had eyebrows and eyes facing inward and downward and a downward-facing mouth.

singing styles. In some places it is customary to have different vocal lines for different people; in other places people all sing together in the same way.

Is variation in music, as in the other arts, related to other aspects of culture? On the basis of a cross-cultural study of more than 3,500 folk songs from a sample of the world's societies, Alan Lomax and his co-researchers found that song style seems to vary with cultural complexity. As we will see, these findings about variation in song style are similar to Fischer's findings about variation in art.

Lomax and his co-researchers found some features of song style to be correlated with cultural complexity. (The societies classified as more complex tend to have higher levels of food-production technology, social stratification, and higher levels of political integration.) For example, wordiness and

clearness of enunciation were found to be associated with cultural complexity. The association is a reasonable one: the more a society depends on verbal information, as in giving complex instructions for a job or explaining different points of law, the more strongly will clear enunciation in the transmitting of information be a mark of its culture. Thus, hunter-gatherer bands, in which people know their productive role and perform it without ever being given complex directions, are more likely than we are to base much of their singing on lines of nonwords, such as our refrain line "tra-la-la-la-la." Their songs are characterized by lack of explicit information, by sounds that give pleasure in themselves, by much repetition, and by relaxed, slurred enunciation.[14]

Examples of the progression from repetition or nonwords to wordy information are found

The threatening masks also were more likely to have pointed heads, chins, beards, and ears, as well as projections from the face such as horns. In more abstract or geometrical terms, threatening features generally tend to be angular or diagonal, and non-threatening features tend to be curved or rounded. A face with a pointed beard is threatening; a baby's face is not. The theory (originally suggested by Charles Darwin, the evolutionist) is that humans express and recognize basic emotions in uniform ways because all human faces are quite similar, skeletally and muscularly.

But is it the facial features themselves that convey threat or is it the design elements of angularity and diagonality that convey threat? To help answer this question, students in this country were asked to associate adjectives with drawings of abstract pairs of design features (for example, a *V* shape and a *U* shape). Even with abstract shapes, the angular patterns were thought of as less "good," more "powerful" and as "stronger" than the curved shapes.

We should not be surprised to discover that humans all over the world use their faces (and masks) to show emotions in the same ways. Aren't we all members of the same species? Our skin color may vary from dark brown to white (or "swine pink," according to some). Our hair may be straight or wavy or kinky—or skimpy. We vary in the percentages of a lot of characteristics. But those are the characteristics we see. We are not so likely to notice the things about us (by far *most* of the things about us) that don't vary—such as how we show emotion in our faces. That's why a movie made in Hollywood or Beijing may evoke the same feelings wherever people see it. The universality of human emotion as expressed in the face becomes obvious only when we see faces (and masks) from elsewhere, showing emotions in ways that are unmistakable to us.

Thus, we become aware of universality (in masks as well as other cultural things) in the same way we become aware of variation—by exposure though reading and direct experience to the ways cultures do and do not vary.

Sources: *Joel Aronoff, Andrew M. Barclay, and Linda A. Stevenson, "The Recognition of Threatening Facial Stimuli,"* Journal of Personality and Social Psychology, 54 (1988): 647–55; *Joel Aronoff, Barbara A. Woike, and Lester M. Hyman, "Which Are the Stimuli in Facial Displays of Anger and Happiness? Configurational Bases of Emotion Recognition,"* Journal of Personality and Social Psychology, 62 (1992): 1050–66.

within our society. The most obvious (and universal) example of a song made entirely of repetition is the relaxed lullaby of a mother repeating a comforting syllable to her baby while improvising her own tune. But this type of song is not characteristic of our society. Although our songs sometimes have single lines of nonwords, it is rare for an entire song to be made of them. Usually, the nonwords act as respites from information:

> *Zippity do dah*
> *Zippety ay*
> *My o my*
> *What a wonderful day*[15]

In associating variation in music with cultural complexity, Lomax found that elaboration of song parts also corresponds to the complexity of a society. Societies in which leadership is informal and temporary seem to symbolize their social equality by an *interlocked* style of singing: each person sings independently but within the group, and no one singer is differentiated from the others. Rank societies, in which there is a leader with prestige but no real power, are characterized by a song style in which one "leader" may begin the song, but the others soon drown out his voice. In stratified societies, where leaders have the power of force, choral singing is generally marked by a clear-cut role for the leader and a secondary "answering" role for the others. Societies marked by elaborate stratification show singing parts that are differentiated and in which the soloist is deferred to by the other singers.

Symmetry and the repetition of design elements tend to be found in the art of unstratified societies, as in this Navaho blanket, ca. 1887. Stratified societies are more likely to have asymmetry and different design elements, as in this nineteenth-century Japanese painting.

Lomax also found a relationship between **polyphony** (two or more melodies sung simultaneously) and a high degree of female participation in food-getting. In societies in which women's work is responsible for at least half of the food, songs are likely to contain more than one simultaneous melody, with the higher tunes usually sung by women. Moreover:

Counterpoint was once believed to be the invention of European high culture. In our sample it turns out to be most frequent among simple producers, especially gatherers, where women supply the bulk of the food. Counterpoint and perhaps even polyphony may then be very old feminine inventions. . . . Subsistence complementarity is at its maximum among gatherers, early gardeners, and horticulturalists. It is in

In this "Devil Dance" in Yare, Venezuela, males wearing masks try to get rid of the "devil" inside themselves. Like many masks around the world that are supposed to be frightening, these masks have sharp angular lines manifested in a variety of ways, such as the large ears.

such societies that we find the highest occurrence of polyphonic singing.[16]

In societies in which women do not contribute much to production, the songs are more likely to have a single melody and to be sung by males.[17]

In some societies, survival and social welfare are based on a unified group effort; in those cultures, singing tends to be marked by cohesiveness. That is, cohesive work parties, teams of gatherers or harvesters and kin groups who work voluntarily for the good of the family or community, seem to express their interconnectedness in song by blending both tone and rhythm.

Some variations in music may be explained as a consequence of variation in child-rearing practices. For example, researchers are beginning to explore child-rearing practices as a way to explain why some societies respond to, and produce, regular rhythm in their music, whereas others enjoy free rhythm that has no regular beat but instead approximates the rhythm of speech.

One hypothesis is that a regular beat in music is a simulation of the regular beat of the heart. For nine months in the womb, the fetus feels the mother's regular eighty or so heartbeats a minute. Moreover, mothers generally employ rhythmic tactics in quieting crying infants—patting their backs or rocking them. But the fact that children respond positively to an even tempo does not mean that the regular heartbeat is completely responsible for their sensitivity to rhythm. In fact, if the months in the womb were sufficient to establish a preference for rhythm, then every child would be affected in exactly the same manner by a regular

beat, and all societies would have the same rhythm in their music.

Barbara Ayres suggested that the importance of regular rhythm in the music of a culture is related to the rhythm's *acquired reward value*—that is, its associations with feelings of security or relaxation. In a cross-cultural study of this possibility, Ayres found a strong correlation between a society's method of carrying infants and the type of musical rhythm the society produced. In some societies, the mother or an older sister carries the child, sometimes for two or three years, in a sling, pouch, or shawl, so that the child is in bodily contact with her for much of the day and experiences the motion of her rhythmic walking. Ayres discovered that such societies tend to have a regularly recurring beat in their songs. Societies in which the child is put into a cradle or is strapped to a cradleboard tend to have music based either on irregular rhythm or on free rhythm.[18]

The question of why some societies have great tonal ranges in music whereas others do not was also studied by Ayres, who suggested that this difference too might be explained by certain child-rearing practices. Ayres theorized that painful stimulation of infants before weaning might result in bolder, more exploratory behavior in adulthood, which would be apparent in the musical patterns of the culture. This hypothesis was suggested to her by laboratory experiments with animals. Contrary to expectations, those animals given electric shocks or handled before weaning showed greater than usual physical growth and more exploratory behavior when placed in new situations as adults. Ayres equated the range of musical notes (from low to high) with the exploratory range of animals and forcefulness of accent in music with boldness in animals.

The kinds of stress Ayres looked for in ethnographic reports were those that would be applied to all children or to all of one sex—for example, scarification; piercing of the nose, lips, or ears; binding, shaping, or stretching of feet, head, ears, or any limb; inoculation; circumcision; or cauterization. The results showed that in societies in which infants are stressed before the age of two, music is marked by a wider tonal range than in societies in which children are not stressed or are stressed only at a later age. Also, a firm accent or beat is characteristic of music more often in societies that subject children to stress than in societies that do not.[19]

Cultural emphasis on obedience or independence in children is another variable that may explain some aspects of musical performance. In societies in which children are generally trained for compliance, cohesive singing predominates. In soci-

Just as in art and song, dance style seems to reflect societal complexity. In less complex societies, everyone participates in dances in much the same way, as among the Huli of New Guinea. In more complex societies, there tend to be leading roles and minor roles, as in a Japanese geisha show.

eties in which children are encouraged to be assertive, singing is mostly individualized. Moreover, assertive training of children is associated with a raspy voice or harsh singing. A raspy voice seems to be an indication of assertiveness and is most often a male voice quality. Interestingly enough, in societies in which women's work predominates in subsistence production, the women sing with harsher voices.

Other voice characteristics may also be associated with elements of culture. For example, sexual restrictions in a society seem to be associated with voice restrictions, especially with a nasalized or narrow, squeezed tone. These voice qualities are associated with anxiety and are especially noticeable in sounds of pain, deprivation, or sorrow. Restrictive sexual practices may be a source of pain and anxiety, and the nasal tone in song may reflect such emotions.[20]

If the cross-cultural results about music are valid, they should be able to explain change over time as well as variation within a society. Future research in a variety of societies may help test some of the theories of Lomax and Ayres.[21]

Folklore

Folklore is a broad category including all the myths, legends, folktales, ballads, riddles, proverbs, and superstitions of a cultural group.[22] In general, folklore is transmitted orally, but it may also be written. All societies have a repertoire of stories that they tell to entertain each other and teach children. Examples of our folklore include fairy tales and the legends we tell about our folk heroes, such as George Washington's confessing that he chopped down the cherry tree.

Folklore is not always clearly separable from the other arts, particularly music and dance; stories often are conveyed in those contexts. (Games are also sometimes considered folklore, although they may be learned by imitation as well as transmitted orally.)

Although some folklore scholars emphasize the traditional aspects of folklore and the continuity between the present and the past, more recently many scholars have paid attention to the innovative and emergent aspects of folklore. In this view, folklore is constantly created by any social group that has shared experiences. So, for example, computer programmers may have their jokes and their own proverbs (for example, "Garbage in, garbage out!").[23] Jan Brunvald compiled a set of recently arisen *urban legends*. One such legend is "The Hook." The story, which has many versions, is basically about a young couple parked on Lover's Lane with the radio on. There is an announcement that a killer with an artificial hand is loose, so the girl suggests that they leave. The boy starts the car and drives her home. When he walks around the car to open her door, he finds a bloody hook attached to the door handle.[24] There are even legends on college campuses. What is the answer to the question of how long students should wait for a tardy professor? Students have an answer, ranging from ten to twenty minutes. Is this a rule, or only a legend? Brunvald reported that he never found a regulation about how long to wait for the professor on any campus that tells this story![25]

Some folklore scholars are interested in universal or recurrent themes. Clyde Kluckhohn suggested that five themes occur in the myths and folktales of all societies: catastrophe, generally through flood; the slaying of monsters; incest; sibling rivalry, generally between brothers; and castration, sometimes actual but more commonly symbolic.[26] Edward Tylor, who proposed that religion is born from the human need to explain states such as dreams and death, suggested that hero myths follow a similar pattern the world over—the central character is exposed at birth, is subsequently saved by others (humans or animals), and grows up to become a hero.[27] Joseph Campbell argued that hero myths resemble initiations—the hero is separated from the ordinary world, ventures forth into a new world (in this case, the supernatural world) to triumph over powerful forces, and then returns to the ordinary world with special powers to help others.[28]

Myths may indeed have universal themes, but few scholars have looked at a representative sample of the world's societies, and therefore we cannot be sure that the conclusions about universality reached so far are correct. Indeed, most folklore researchers have not been interested in universal themes, but rather in the particular folktales told in specific societies or regions. For example, some scholars have focused on the "Star Husband Tale," a common Native American tale. Stith Thompson presented eighty-four versions of this tale—his goal was to reconstruct the original version and pinpoint its place of origin. By identifying the most common elements, Thompson suggested that the basic story (and probably the original) is the following:

> Two girls sleeping out of doors wish that stars would be their husbands. In their sleep the girls are taken to the sky where they find themselves married to stars, one of which is a young man and the other an old man. The women are warned not to dig, but they disregard the warning and accidentally open up a hole in the sky. Unaided they descend on a rope and arrive home safely.[29]

The tale, Thompson suggested, probably originated in the Plains and then spread to other regions of North America.

Alan Dundes has concentrated on the structure of folktales; he thinks that Native American folktales, including the Star Husband Tale, have characteristic structures. One is a movement away from disequilibrium. Equilibrium is the desirable state; having too much or too little of anything is a condition that should be rectified as soon as possible. Disequilibrium, which Dundes calls *lack,* is indicated by the girls in the Star Husband Tale who do not have husbands. The lack is then corrected, in this case by marriage with the stars. This tale has another common Native American structure, says Dundes—a sequence of prohibition, interdiction, violation, and consequence. The women are warned not to dig, but they do—and as a consequence they escape for home.[30] It should be noted that the consequences in folktales around the world are not always good. Recall the Garden of Eden tale. The couple are warned not to eat the fruit of a tree; they eat the fruit; they are cast out of their paradise. Similarly, Icarus in the Greek tale is warned not to fly too high or low. He flies too high; the sun melts the wax that holds his feathered wings, and he falls and drowns.

As useful as it might be to identify where certain tales originated, or what their common structures might be, many questions remain. What do the tales mean? Why did they arise in the first place? Why are certain structures common in Native American tales? We are still a long way from answering many of these questions, and trying to answer them is difficult. How does one try to understand the meaning of a tale?

It is easy for people to read different meanings into the same myth. For example, consider the myth the Hebrews told of a paradise in which only a man was present until Eve, the first woman, arrived and ate the forbidden fruit of knowledge. One might conclude that men in that society had some traditional grudge against women. If the interpreter were a psychoanalyst, he or (especially) she might assume that the myth reflected the male's deeply hidden fears of female sexuality. A historian might believe that the myth reflected actual historical events and that men were living in blissful ignorance until women invented agriculture (the effect of Eve's "knowledge" led to a life of digging rather than gathering).

It is clearly not enough to suggest an interpretation. Why should we believe it? We should give it serious consideration only if some systematic test seems to support it. For example, Michael Carroll suggested a Freudian interpretation of the Star Husband Tale—that the tale represents repressed sentiments in the society. Specifically, he suggested that incestuous intercourse is the underlying concern of this myth, particularly the desire of a daughter to have intercourse with her father. He assumed that the stars symbolize fathers. Fathers, like stars, are high above, in children's eyes. Carroll predicted that if the Star Husband Tale originated on the Plains, and if it symbolizes intercourse, then the Plains tribes should be more likely than other tribes to have intercourse imagery in their versions of the tale. That seems to be the case: analyzing eighty-four versions of the tale, Carroll found that Plains societies are the Native American tribes most likely to have imagery suggesting intercourse, including the lowering of a rope or ladder (presumably symbolizing the penis) through a sky hole (presumably symbolizing the vagina).[31]

Few studies as yet have investigated why there is cross-cultural variation in the frequency of certain features in folktales. One feature of folktale variation that has been investigated cross-culturally is aggression. George Wright found that variation in child-rearing patterns predicted some aspects of how aggression is exhibited in folktales. Where children are severely punished for aggression, more intense aggression appears in the folktales. And in such societies, strangers are more likely than the hero or friends of the hero to be the aggressors in the folktales. It seems that where children may be afraid to exhibit aggression toward their parents or those close to them because of fear of punishment, the hero or his or her close friends in folktales are also not likely to be aggressive.[32]

Other kinds of fears may be reflected in folktales. A recent cross-cultural study found that unprovoked aggression is likely in folktales of societies that are subject to unpredictable food shortages. Why? One possibility is that the folktales reflect reality; after all, a serious drought may seem capricious, not possibly provoked by any human activity, brought on by the gods or nature "out of the blue." Curiously, however, societies with a history of unpredictable food shortages hardly mention natural disasters in their folktales, perhaps because disasters are too frightening. In any case, the capriciousness of unpredictable disasters seems to be transformed into the capricious aggression of characters in the folktales.[33]

Folklore, just like other aspects of art, may at least partially reflect the feelings, needs, and conflicts that people acquire as a result of growing up in their culture.

VIEWING THE ART OF OTHER CULTURES

Sally Price raised some critical questions about how Western museums and art critics look at the visual art of less complex cultures. Why is it that when artworks from Western or Oriental civilizations are displayed in a museum here, they carry the artist's name? In contrast, art from less complex cultures (often labeled "primitive art") tends to be displayed without the name of the artist; instead it often is accompanied by a description of where it came from, how it was constructed, and what it may be used for. More words of explanation seem to accompany displays of unfamiliar art. Price suggested that the art pieces that we consider the most worthy require the least labeling, subtly conveying that the viewer needs no help to judge a real work of art.[34] In addition, art acquired from less complex cultures tends to be labeled by the name of the Westerner who acquired it. It is almost as if the fame of the collector, not the art itself, sets the value of such art.[35]

Just as the art from less complex cultures tends to be nameless, it also tends to be treated as timeless. We recognize that Western art and the art from classical civilizations changes over time, which is why it must be dated, but the art from other places seems to be viewed as representing a timeless cultural tradition.[36] Do we know that the art of peoples with simpler technology changes less, or is this assumption a kind of ethnocentrism? Price, who has studied the art of the Saramakas of Suriname, points out that although Westerners think of Saramakan art as still representing its African ancestry, Saramakans themselves can identify shifts in their art styles over time. For example, they describe how calabashes used to be decorated on the outside, then the style changed to decorating the inside. They can also recognize the artist who made particular carved calabashes as well as identify those who were innovators of designs and techniques.[37]

Although it seems that individual artists can usually be recognized in any community, some societies do appear to be more "communal" than others in their art style. For example, let us compare the Puebloan peoples of the Southwest with native peoples of the Great Plains. Traditionally, women Puebloan potters did not sign their pots, and they largely followed their pueblo's characteristic style. In contrast, each Plains warrior stressed his individual accomplishments by painting representations of those accomplishments on animal hides. Either the warrior would do it himself or he would ask some-one else to do it for him. These hides were worn by the warrior or displayed outside his tipi.[38]

When Westerners do notice artistic changes over time in less complex societies, it seems to be because they are concerned about whether the art represents traditional forms or is "tourist art." Tourist art is often evaluated negatively. Perhaps the negative evaluation results from its association with money. But famous Western artists often also worked for fees or were supported by elite patrons, and yet the fact that they were paid does not seem to interfere with our evaluation of their art.[39]

ARTISTIC CHANGE AND CULTURE CONTACT

It is unquestionably true that contact with the West did alter some aspects of the art of other cultures, but that does not imply that their art was changeless before. What kinds of things changed with contact? In some places, artists began to represent European contact itself. For example, in Australia, numerous rock paintings by aborigines portray sailing ships, men on horseback carrying pistols, and even cattle brands. With encouragement from Europeans, indigenous artists also began drawing on tree bark, canvas, and masonite to sell to Europeans. Interestingly, the art for sale mostly emphasizes themes displayed before contact and does not include representations of ships and guns.[40] As aboriginal populations were decimated by European contact, a lot of their traditional art forms disappeared, particularly legends and rock paintings that were associated with the sacred sites of each clan. The legends described the creation of the sacred places, and art motifs with painted human or animal heroes marked the sites.[41]

In North America, contact between native groups produced changes in art even before the Europeans came. Copper, sharks' teeth, and marine shells were traded extensively in precontact times and were used in the artwork of people who did not have access to those materials locally. Ceremonies were borrowed between groups, and with the new ceremonies came changes in artistic traditions. Borrowing from other native groups continued after European contact. The Navaho, who are well known today for their rug weaving, were not weavers in the seventeenth century. They probably obtained their weaving technology from the Hopi and then began to weave wool and herd sheep. European contact also produced material changes in art—new materials including beads, wool cloth, and silver were introduced. Metal tools such as needles and scissors could now be used to make more tailored and more decorated skin clothing. In the Northwest, the greater availability of metal tools made it possible to make larger totem poles and house posts.[42]

After they were placed on reservations, virtually all Native Americans had to change their ways of making a living. Selling arts and crafts earned some of them supplementary income. Most of these crafts used traditional techniques and traditional designs, altered somewhat to suit European expectations. Outsiders played important roles in encouraging changes in arts and crafts. Some storekeepers became patrons to particular artists who were then able to devote themselves full-time to their craft. Traders would often encourage changes such as new objects (for example, ashtrays and cups made of pottery). Scholars have played a role too. Some have helped artisans learn about styles of the past that had disappeared. For example, with the encouragement of anthropologists and others in the Santa Fe area, Maria and Julian Martinez of San Ildefonso Pueblo brought back a polished black-on-black pottery style originally produced by nearby ancient peoples.[43]

Some of the artistic changes that have occurred after contact with the West are partly predictable from the results of cross-cultural research on artistic variation. Remember that Fischer found that egalitarian societies typically had less complex designs and more symmetry than did stratified societies. With the loss of traditional ways of making a living and with the increase in wage labor and commercial enterprises, many Native American groups have become more socially stratified. Ex-

The polished black-on-black pottery style was revived in recent times by Maria and Julian Martinez of San Ildefonso Pueblo in New Mexico. Shown here is a pot by Maria and Santana.

trapolating from Fischer's results, we would predict that designs on visual art should become more complex and asymmetrical as social stratification increases. Indeed, if early reservation art (1870–1901) among the Shoshone-Bannock of southeastern Idaho is compared with their recent art (1973–1983), it is clear that the art has become more complex as social stratification has increased.[44] It could also be true that the art changed because the artists came to realize that more asymmetry and complexity would sell better to people who collect art.

▼ SUMMARY

1. Not all societies have a word for art, but art universally seems to have several qualities. It expresses as well as communicates. It stimulates the senses, affects emotions, and evokes ideas. It is produced in culturally patterned ways and styles; it has cultural meaning. And some people are thought to be better at it than others.

2. All societies decorate or adorn the body, temporarily or permanently. But there is enormous cultural variation in the parts decorated and how. Body decoration may be used to delineate social position, sex, or occupation. It may also have an erotic significance—for example, in drawing attention to erogenous zones of the body.

3. The materials used to produce visual art, the way those materials are used, and the natural objects the artist may choose to represent all vary from society to society and reveal much about a society's relation to its environment. Some studies indicate a correlation between artistic design and social stratification.

4. Like the visual arts, music is subject to a remarkable amount of variation from society to society. Some studies suggest correlations between musical styles and cultural complexity. Other research shows links between child-rearing practices and a society's preference for certain rhythmical patterns, tonal ranges, and voice quality.

5. Folklore is a broad category including all the myths, legends, folktales, ballads, riddles, proverbs, and superstitions of a cultural group. In general, folklore is transmitted orally, but it may also be written. Some anthropologists have identified basic themes in myths. These include catastrophe, slaying of monsters, incest, sibling rivalry, and castration. Myths may reflect a society's deepest preoccupations.

6. Art is always changing, but recent culture contact has had some profound effects on art in various parts of the world. With the decimation of many indigenous populations, many areas have lost some of their artistic traditions. But the art also changed as individuals began to sell arts and crafts.

▼ GLOSSARY TERMS

folklore   polyphony

▼ CRITICAL QUESTIONS

1. How innovative or original can a successful artist be?
2. What kind of art do you prefer, and why?
3. Do you think art made for tourists is inferior? Whatever you think, why do you think so?

▼ SUGGESTED READING

ANDERSON, R. L. *Calliope's Sisters: A Comparative Study of Philosophies of Art.* Englewood Cliffs, NJ: Prentice Hall, 1990. A comparison of the art of ten diverse societies in order to discover similarities and differences in their arts as well as how they think about art.

BAUMAN, R., ed. *Folklore, Cultural Performances, and Popular Entertainment.* New York: Oxford University Press, 1992. A collection of brief articles on popular expressive forms and practices. Covers basic concepts and provides an entrance into the literature.

LOMAX, A., ed. *Folk Song Style and Culture.* American Association for the Advancement of Science, Publication No. 88. Washington, D.C., 1968. A classic cross-cultural study of the stylistic elements of folk songs from societies around the world. The data compiled in this study, which was known as the Cantometrics Project, were used to test hypotheses about the relationship of song style to other aspects of culture.

MAQUET, J. *The Aesthetic Experience: An Anthropologist Looks at the Visual Arts.* New Haven, CT: Yale University Press, 1986. The author explores the universal and culturally varying components of the visual arts.

WADE, E. L., ed. *The Arts of the North American Indian: Native Traditions in Evolution.* New York: Hudson Hills Press, 1986. A large-format, beautifully illustrated introduction to the varieties of art in Native North American cultures.

▼ NOTES

[1]Jacques Maquet, *The Aesthetic Experience: An Anthropologist Looks at the Visual Arts* (New Haven, CT: Yale University Press, 1986), p. 9.

[2]Richard L. Anderson, *Art in Small-Scale Societies*, 2nd ed. (Englewood Cliffs, NJ: Prentice Hall, 1989), p. 21.

[3]Robert P. Armstrong, *The Powers of Presence* (Philadelphia: University of Pennsylvania Press, 1981), pp. 6–9; see also Anderson, *Art in Small-Scale Societies*, p. 11.

[4]Richard L. Anderson, *Calliope's Sisters: A Comparative Study of Philosophies of Art* (Englewood Cliffs, NJ: Prentice Hall, 1990), p. 278; Richard L. Anderson, "Do Other Cultures Have 'Art'?" *American Anthropologist*, 94 (1992): 926–29.

[5]Edward Malin, *Totem Poles of the Pacific Northwest Coast* (Portland: Timber Press, 1986), p. 27.

[6]Anderson, *Art in Small-Scale Societies*, p. 11.

[7]James L. Gibbs, Jr., "The Kpelle of Liberia," in James L. Gibbs, Jr., ed., *Peoples of Africa* (New York: Holt, Rinehart & Winston, 1965), p. 222.

[8]Anderson, *Calliope's Sisters*, pp. 225–26.

[9]James J. Sweeney, "African Negro Culture," in Paul Radin, ed., *African Folktales and Sculpture* (New York: Pantheon, 1952), p. 335.

[10]John Fischer, "Art Styles as Cultural Cognitive Maps," *American Anthropologist*, 63 (1961): 80.

[11]Ibid., p. 81.

[12]Ibid., p. 83.

[13]William W. Dressler and Michael C. Robbins, "Art Styles, Social Stratification, and Cognition: An Analysis of Greek Vase Painting," *American Ethnologist*, 2 (1975): 427–34.

[14]Alan Lomax, ed., *Folk Song Style and Culture*, American Association for the Advancement of Science, Publication No. 88 (Washington, D.C., 1968), pp. 117–28.

[15]© 1945 Walt Disney Music Company; words by Ray Gilbert, music by Allie Wrubel.

[16]Lomax, *Folk Song Style and Culture*, pp. 166–67.

[17]Ibid., pp. 167–69.

[18]Barbara C. Ayres, "Effects of Infant Carrying Practices on Rhythm in Music," *Ethos*, 1 (1973): 387–404.

[19]Barbara C. Ayres, "Effects of Infantile Stimulation on Musical Behavior," in Lomax, ed., *Folk Song Style and Culture*, pp. 211–21.

[20]Edwin Erickson, "Self-assertion, Sex Role, and Vocal Rasp," in Lomax, ed., *Folk Song Style and Culture*, pp. 190–97.

[21]For a study of variation in music within India that does not support some of Lomax's findings, see Edward O. Henry, "The Variety of Music in a North Indian Village: Reassessing Cantometrics," *Ethnomusicology*, 20 (1976): 49–66.

[22]Alan Dundes, *Folklore Matters* (Knoxville: University of Tennessee Press, 1989), p. viii.

[23]Richard Bauman, "Folklore," in Richard Bauman, ed., *Folklore, Cultural Performances, and Popular Entertainments: A Communications-Centered Handbook* (New York: Oxford University Press, 1992), pp. 29–40.

[24]Jan Harold Brunvand, *The Baby Train: And Other Lusty Urban Legends* (New York: W. W. Norton, 1993), p. 14.

[25]Ibid., p. 296.

[26]Clyde Kluckhohn, "Recurrent Themes in Myths and Mythmaking," in Alan Dundes, ed., *The Study of Folklore* (Englewood Cliffs, NJ: Prentice Hall, 1965), pp. 158–68.

[27]As discussed in Robert A. Segal, *Joseph Campbell: An Introduction* (New York: Garland, 1987), pp. 1–2.

[28]Joseph Campbell, *The Hero with a Thousand Faces* (New York: Pantheon Books, 1949), p. 30, as quoted in Segal, *Joseph Campbell: An Introduction*, p. 4.

[29]Stith Thompson, "Star Husband Tale," in Dundes, ed., *The Study of Folklore*, p. 449.

[30]Alan Dundes, "Structural Typology in North American Indian Folktales," in Dundes, ed., *The Study of Folklore*, pp. 206–15. Dundes's analysis of the Star Husband Tale is reported in Frank W. Young, "A Fifth Analysis of the Star Husband Tale," *Ethnology*, 9 (1970): 389–413.

[31]Michael Carroll, "A New Look at Freud on Myth," *Ethos*, 7 (1979): 189–205.

[32]George O. Wright, "Projection and Displacement: A Cross-Cultural Study of Folktale Aggression," *Journal of Abnormal and Social Psychology*, 49 (1954): 523–28.

[33]Alex Cohen, "A Cross-Cultural Study of the Effects of Environmental Unpredictability on Aggression in Folktales," *American Anthropologist*, 92 (1990): 474–79.

[34]Sally Price, *Primitive Art in Civilized Places* (Chicago: University of Chicago Press, 1989), pp. 82–85.

[35]Ibid., pp. 102–3.

[36]Ibid., pp. 56–67.

[37]Ibid., p. 112.

[38]John Anson Warner, "The Individual in Native American Art: A Sociological View," in Edwin L. Wade, ed., *The Arts of the North American Indian: Native Traditions in Evolution* (New York: Hudson Hills Press, 1986), pp. 172–75.

[39]Price, *Primitive Art in Civilized Places*, pp. 77–81.

[40]Robert Layton, *Australian Rock Art: A New Synthesis* (Cambridge: Cambridge University Press, 1992), pp. 93–94.

[41]Ibid., pp. 31, 109.

[42]J. C. H. King, "Tradition in Native American Art," in Wade, ed., *The Arts of the North American Indian*, pp. 74–82.

[43]Warner, "The Individual in Native American Art," pp. 178–86.

[44]Elizabeth Bryant Merrill, "Art Styles as Reflections of Sociopolitical Complexity," *Ethnology* 26 (1987): 221–230.

Culture Change

Most of us are aware that "times have changed," especially when we compare our lives with those of our parents. Witness the recent changes in attitudes about sex and marriage, as well as the recent changes in women's roles. But culture change is not unique to us: humans throughout history have replaced or altered customary behaviors and attitudes as their needs have changed. Just as no individual is immortal, no particular cultural pattern is impervious to change. Anthropologists, therefore, want to understand how and why culture change occurs.

Three general questions can be asked about culture change: What is the source of a new trait? Why are people motivated (unconsciously as well as consciously) to adopt it? And is the new trait adaptive? The source may be inside or outside the society. That is, a new idea or behavior may originate within the society, or it may come from another society. With regard to motivation, people may adopt the new idea or behavior voluntarily (even if unconsciously), or they may be forced to adopt it. Finally, the outcome of culture change may or may not be beneficial. In this chapter, we first discuss the various processes of culture change in terms of the three dimensions of source, motivation, and outcome. Then we discuss some of the major types of culture change in the modern world. As we will see, these changes are associated largely with the expansion of Western societies over the last 500 years.

HOW AND WHY CULTURES CHANGE

Discoveries and inventions, which may originate inside or outside a society, are ultimately the sources of all culture change. But they do not necessarily lead to change. If an invention or discovery is ignored, no change in culture results. It is only when society accepts an invention or discovery and uses it regularly that we can begin to speak of culture change.

Discovery and Invention

The new thing discovered or invented (the innovation) may be an object—the wheel, the plow, the computer—or it may involve behavior and ideas—Christianity, democracy, monogamy. According to Ralph Linton, a discovery is any addition to knowledge and an invention is a new application of knowledge.[1] Thus, a person might discover that children can be persuaded to eat nourishing food if the food is associated with an imaginary character who appeals to them. And then someone might exploit that discovery by inventing a character named Popeye who appears in a series of animated cartoons, acquiring miraculous strength in a variety of dramatic situations by devouring cans of spinach.

Unconscious Invention. In discussing the process of invention, we should differentiate between various types of inventions. One type is the consequence of a society's setting itself a specific goal, such as eliminating tuberculosis or placing a person on the moon. Another type emerges less intentionally. This second process of invention is often referred to as *accidental juxtaposition* or *unconscious invention*. Linton suggested that some inventions, especially those of prehistoric days, were probably the consequences of literally dozens of tiny initiatives by "unconscious" inventors. These inventors made their small contributions, perhaps over many hundreds of years, without being aware of the part they were playing in bringing one invention, such as the wheel or a better form of hand ax, to completion.[2] Consider the example of children playing on a fallen log, which rolls as they walk and balance on it, coupled with the need at a given moment to move a slab of granite from a cave face. The children's play may have suggested the use of logs as rollers and thereby set in motion a series of developments that culminated in the wheel.

In reconstructing the process of invention in prehistoric times, however, we should be careful not to look back on our ancestors with a smugness born of our more highly developed technology. We have become accustomed to turning to the science sections of our magazines and newspapers and finding, almost daily, reports of miraculous new discoveries and inventions. From our point of view, it is difficult to imagine such a simple invention as the wheel taking so many centuries to come into being. We are tempted to surmise that early humans were less intelligent than we are. But the capacity of the human brain has been the same for perhaps 100,000 years; there is no evidence that the inventors of the wheel were any less intelligent than we are.

Intentional Innovation. Some discoveries and inventions arise out of deliberate attempts to produce a new idea or object. It may seem that such innovations are obvious responses to perceived needs. For example, during the Industrial Revolution there was a great demand for inventions that would increase productivity. James Hargreaves in eighteenth-century England is an example of an inventor who responded to an existing demand. Textile manufacturers were clamoring for such large quantities of spun yarn that cottage laborers, working with foot-operated spinning wheels, could not meet the demand. Hargreaves, realizing that prestige and financial rewards would come to the person who invented a method of spinning large quantities of yarn in a short time, set about the task and developed the spinning jenny.

But perceived needs and the economic rewards that may be given to the innovator do not explain why only some people innovate. We know relatively little about why some people are more innovative than others. The ability to innovate may depend in part on individual characteristics such as high intelligence and creativity. And creativity may be influenced by social conditions.

A study of innovation among Ashanti artist-carvers in Ghana suggests that creativity is more likely in some socioeconomic groups than in others.[3] Some carvers produced only traditional designs; others departed from tradition and produced "new" styles of carving. Two groups were found to innovate the most—the wealthiest and the poorest carvers. These two groups of carvers may tolerate risk more than the middle socioeconomic group. Innovative carving entails some risk because it may

take more time and it may not sell. Wealthy carvers can afford the risk, and they may gain some prestige as well as income if their innovation is appreciated. The poor are not doing well anyway, and they have little to lose by trying something new.

Who Adopts Innovations? Once someone discovers or invents something, there is still the question of whether the innovation will be adopted by others. Many researchers have studied the characteristics of "early adopters." Such individuals tend to be educated, high in social status, upwardly mobile, and (if they are property owners) have large farms and businesses. The individuals who most need technological improvements—those who are less well off—are generally the last to adopt innovations. The theory is that only the wealthier can afford to take the substantial risks associated with new ways of doing things. In periods of rapid technological change, therefore, the gap between rich and poor is likely to widen because the rich adopt innovations sooner (and benefit more from them) than the poor.[4]

Does this imply that the likelihood of adopting innovations is a simple function of how much wealth a possible adopter possesses? Not necessarily. Frank

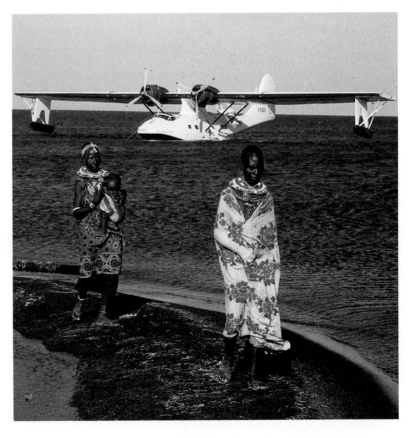

Ideas and practices diffuse rapidly in the modern world, partly because people can go far and fast. Here we see a seaplane on once remote Lake Turkana, Kenya.

WILL CULTURAL DIVERSITY DISAPPEAR
IN A RAPID-TRANSIT, TELECOMMUNICATING WORLD?

Measured in terms of travel time, the world today is much smaller than it has ever been before. It is possible now to fly halfway around the globe in the time it took people less than a century ago to travel to the next state. In the realm of communication, the world is even smaller: we can talk to someone halfway around the globe in a matter of minutes, and we can send that person a message (by fax or Internet) in seconds.

The world is shrinking culturally too, in the sense that more and more people are drawn each year into the world market economy, buying and selling similar things and, as a consequence, altering the patterns of their lives in similar ways. The spread of market exchange throughout the world reflects the expansion of certain nations' spheres of influence over the last few centuries. In some places as a result of colonization or conquest, in others as a result of economic and military-aid programs, in still others because of a desire to emulate dominant cultures (British, American, Russian, Japanese, Chinese, and so on), the hundreds of different cultures that survive in the world have become more similar over the last hundred years. And they are likely to continue in that trajectory as long as people all over continue in contact (electronic or otherwise) with each other.

Does this trend mean that cultural diversity is bound to disappear completely, that cultural anthropology will run out of variation to study? We don't think so. There is no reason to believe that cultural variation, including some major sorts, will ever disappear. The development and perpetuation of different sets of common ideas, beliefs, and behaviors—in other words, different cultures—depends on the existence of groups of people who live somewhat separately, who think of themselves as at least somewhat different. The vast majority of people in their daily lives are isolated from individuals at the opposite ends of the earth, or on "the other side of the tracks," and if this situation continues to be so, they will invariably retain and develop some cultural differences. Although modern transportation and communication facilitate the rapid spread of cultural characteristics to all parts of the globe, it is highly unlikely that all parts will end up the same. Cultures are bound to retain some of their original characteristics or develop some distinctive new adaptations. After all, people in different parts of the world are confronted with different physical and social environments, and hence the chances are that some aspects of their cultures will always be unique, assuming that cultures generally consist of common responses adapted to particular environmental requirements.

As much as cultural variability has decreased recently, there may still be more variability than existed at some other points in human history. How different were human cultures a million years ago when they all depended on flaked stone tools and wild

Cancian reviewed several studies and found that upper-middle-class individuals show more conservatism than lower-middle-class individuals. Cancian suggested that when the risks are unknown the lower-middle-class individuals are more receptive to innovation because they have less to lose. Later on, when the risks are better known (as more people adopt the innovation), the upper-middle class catches up to the lower-middle.[5] So the readiness to accept innovation, like the likelihood of creativity among Ashanti carvers, may not be related to socioeconomic position in a straight-line, or linear, way.

The speed of accepting an innovation may depend partly on how new behaviors and ideas are typically transmitted in a society. In particular, is a person exposed to many versus few "teachers"? If children learn most of what they know from their parents or from a relatively small number of elders, then innovation will be slow to spread throughout the society, and culture change is likely to be slow.

animals and plants? How different were the cultures of big game hunters that spread into the New World after about 12,000 years ago? There probably were more differences in the world when some people began to practice agriculture. In some areas, a relatively small number of people had begun to depend on nonintensive agriculture and domesticated animals. In other areas, people depended on wild grains and other more or less sedentary resources (such as shellfish). And in still other areas (indeed most areas of the world at that time), people still depended on nomadic food collecting.

We might expect then that whenever a generally adaptive cultural pattern develops and spreads over the globe, cultural variability decreases, at least for a time. Hence, with the spread of agriculture and then commercial exchange, and, even more important, with the expansion of the world market economy and computerized communication, we may again be witnessing a temporary diminution of cultural variability as humanity experiences another great cultural transformation. But there is no reason to believe that further and differential culture change, stemming from varying physical and social environmental requirements, will not occur in different parts of the world.

In short, it does not seem likely that cultural anthropology, the study of cultural similarities and differences, will ever run out of variability to study and explain. The same thing can be said for physical or biological anthropology, archaeology, and linguistics. With respect to physical anthropology, there is no reason to expect variation in biological characteristics among human populations to disappear, as long as physical and social environments continue to vary. It will be a long time before the whole of humankind lives under identical environmental conditions, in one great "greenhouse." Moreover, we will always have that great depository of human variability—the fossil and more recent human biological records—to explore and study. Similarly, archaeologists will always have the remains of past cultures to study and explain.

With respect to linguistics, even if all linguistic variation were to disappear from the earth, we will always have the descriptive data on past languages to study, with all the variability in those records still to be explained. Finally, we will always have the ethnographic record to study comparatively. Just as we have the fossil and archaeological records, we have an enormous and growing body of ethnographic data on different peoples past and present that will never disappear.

There are many questions to be asked—and many answers that can be gained—from the comparative data we already have and will collect in the future. The challenge of discovering more and more definitive answers to how and why human populations vary—in the past, present, and future—will always be with us.

Sources: *Melvin Ember, "The Logic of Comparative Research," Behavior Science Research, 25 (1991): 143–53; Carol R. Ember and Melvin Ember, "On Cross-Cultural Research," in Carol R. Ember and Melvin Ember, eds., Cross-Cultural Research for Social Science (Englewood Cliffs, NJ: Prentice Hall, 1995). Prentice Hall/Simon & Schuster Custom Publishing.*

Innovations may catch on more rapidly if individuals are exposed to various teachers and other "leaders," who can influence many in a relatively short time. And the more peers we have, the more we might learn from them.[6] Perhaps this is why the pace of change appears to be so quick today. In societies like our own, and increasingly in the industrializing world, it is likely that people learn in schools from teachers, from leaders in their specialties, and from peers.

Diffusion

The source of new cultural elements in a society may also be another society. The process by which cultural elements are borrowed from another society and incorporated into the culture of the recipient group is called **diffusion.** Borrowing sometimes enables a group to bypass stages or mistakes in the development of a process or institution. For example, Germany was able to accelerate its pro-

These Japanese women have accepted ice cream, but they have not adopted Western clothing.

gram of industrialization in the nineteenth century. It avoided some of the errors made by its English and Belgian competitors by taking advantage of technological borrowing. Japan did the same somewhat later. Indeed, in recent years some of the earliest industrialized countries have fallen behind others in certain areas of production (automobiles, television, cameras, computers).

In a well-known passage, Linton conveyed the far-reaching effects of diffusion by considering the first few hours in the day of an American man. This man

> awakens in a bed built on a pattern which originated in the Near East but which was modified in northern Europe before it was transmitted to America. He throws back covers made from cotton, domesticated in India, or linen, domesticated in the Near East, or silk, the use of which was discovered in China. All of these materials have been spun and woven by processes invented in the Near East. . . . He takes off his pajamas, a garment invented in India, and washes with soap invented by the ancient Gauls. He then shaves, a masochistic rite which seems to have derived from either Sumer or ancient Egypt.

> Before going out for breakfast he glances through the window, made of glass invented in Egypt, and if it is raining puts on overshoes made of rubber discovered by the Central American Indians and takes an umbrella, invented in southeastern Asia. . . .

> On his way to breakfast he stops to buy a paper paying for it with coins, an ancient Lydian invention. . . . His plate is made of a form of pottery invented in China. His knife is of steel, an alloy first made in southern India, his fork a medieval Italian invention, and his spoon a derivative of a

Roman original. . . . After his fruit (African watermelon) and first coffee (an Abyssinian plant) . . . he may have the egg of a species of bird domesticated in Indo-China, or thin strips of the flesh of an animal domesticated in Eastern Asia which have been salted and smoked by a process developed in northern Europe. . . .

> While smoking (an American Indian habit) he reads the news of the day, imprinted in characters invented by the ancient Semites upon a material invented in China by a process invented in Germany. As he absorbs the accounts of foreign troubles he will, if he is a good conservative citizen, thank a Hebrew deity in an Indo-European language that he is 100 percent American.[7]

Patterns of Diffusion. There are three basic patterns of diffusion: direct contact, intermediate contact, and stimulus diffusion.

DIRECT CONTACT. Elements of a society's culture may be first taken up by neighboring societies and then gradually spread farther and farther afield. The spread of the manufacture of paper is a good example of extensive diffusion by direct contact. The invention of paper is attributed to the Chinese Ts'ai Lun in A.D. 105. Within fifty years, paper was being made in many places in central China. By 264 it was found in Chinese Turkestan, and from then on the successive places of manufacture were Samarkand (751), Baghdad (793), Egypt (about 900), Morocco (about 1100), France (1189), Italy (1276), Germany (1391), and England (1494). In general, the pattern of accepting the borrowed invention was the same in all cases. Paper was first imported into each area as a luxury, then in ever-expanding quantities as a staple product. Finally, and usually within one to three centuries, local manufacture was begun.

INTERMEDIATE CONTACT. Diffusion by intermediate contact occurs through the agency of third parties. Frequently, traders carry a cultural trait from the society that originated it to another group. As an example of diffusion through intermediaries, Phoenician traders spread the alphabet, which may have been invented by another Semitic group, to Greece. At times, soldiers serve as intermediaries in spreading a culture trait. European crusaders, such as the Knights Templar and the Knights of St. John, acted as intermediaries in two ways: they carried Christian culture to Muslim societies of North Africa and brought Arab culture back to Europe. In the nineteenth century, Western missionaries in all parts of the world encouraged natives to wear Western clothing. The result is that in Africa, the Pacific Islands, and elsewhere, native peoples can be found wearing shorts, suit jackets, shirts, ties, and other typically Western articles of clothing.

STIMULUS DIFFUSION. In stimulus diffusion, knowledge of a trait belonging to another culture stimulates the invention or development of a local equivalent. A classic example of stimulus diffusion is the Cherokee syllabic writing system created by a Native American named Sequoya so that his people could write down their language. Sequoya got the idea from his contact with Europeans. Yet he did not adopt the English writing system; indeed, he did not even learn to write English. What he did was utilize some English alphabetic symbols, alter others, and invent new ones. All the symbols he used represented Cherokee syllables and in no way echoed English alphabetic usage. In other words, Sequoya took English alphabetic ideas and gave them a new Cherokee form. The stimulus originated with Europeans; the result was peculiarly Cherokee.

The Selective Nature of Diffusion. Although there is a temptation to view the dynamics of diffusion as similar to a stone sending concentric ripples over still water, this would be an oversimplification of the way diffusion actually occurs. Not all cultural traits are borrowed as readily as the ones we have mentioned, nor do they usually expand in neat, ever-widening circles. Rather, diffusion is a selective process. The Japanese, for instance, accepted much from Chinese culture, but they also rejected many traits. Rhymed tonal poetry, civil-service examinations, and foot binding, which were favored by the Chinese, were never adopted in Japan. The poetry form was unsuited to the structure of the Japanese language; the examinations were unnecessary in view of the entrenched power of the Japanese aristocracy; foot binding was repugnant to a people who abhorred body mutilation of any sort.

Not only would we expect societies to reject items from other societies that are repugnant, we would also expect them to reject ideas and technology that do not satisfy some psychological, social, or cultural need. After all, people are not sponges—they don't automatically soak up the things around them. If they did, the amount of cultural variation in the world would be tiny—which is clearly not the case. Diffusion is also selective because cultural traits differ in the extent to which they can be communicated. Elements of material culture, such as mechanical processes and techniques, and other traits, such as physical sports and the like, are not especially difficult to demonstrate. Consequently, they are accepted or rejected on their merits. But the moment we move out of the material context, we encounter real difficulties. Linton explained the problem in these words:

> Although it is quite possible to describe such an element of culture as the ideal pattern for marriage . . . it is much less complete than a description of basketmaking. . . . The most thorough verbalization has difficulty in conveying the series of associations and conditioned emotional responses which are attached to this pattern [marriage] and which gave it meaning and vitality within our own society. . . . This is even more true of those concepts which . . . find no direct expression in behavior aside from verbalization. There is a story of an educated Japanese who after a long discussion on the nature of the Trinity with a European friend . . . burst out with: "Oh, I see now, it is a committee."[8]

Finally, diffusion is selective because the overt form of a particular trait, rather than its function or meaning, frequently seems to determine how the trait will be received. For example, the enthusiasm for bobbed hair (short haircuts) that swept through much of North America in the 1920s never caught on among the Native Americans of northwestern California. To many women of European ancestry, short hair was a symbolic statement of their freedom. To Native American women, who traditionally cut their hair short when in mourning, it was a reminder of death.[9]

In the process of diffusion, then, we can identify a number of different patterns. We know that cultural borrowing is selective rather than automatic, and we can describe how a particular borrowed trait has been modified by the recipient culture. But our current knowledge does not allow us to specify when one or another of these outcomes will occur, under what conditions diffusion will occur, and why it occurs the way it does.

Acculturation

On the surface, the process of change called **acculturation** seems to include much of what we have discussed under the label of diffusion, since acculturation refers to the changes that occur when different cultural groups come into intensive contact. As in diffusion, the source of new cultural items is the other society. But more often than not, the term *acculturation* is used by anthropologists to describe a situation in which one of the societies in contact is much more powerful than the other. Thus, acculturation can be seen as a process of extensive cultural borrowing in the context of superordinate-subordinate relations between societies.[10] The borrowing may sometimes be a two-way process, but generally it is the subordinate or less powerful society that borrows the most. The concept of diffusion can then be reserved for the voluntary borrowing of cultural elements, in contrast with borrowing under external pressure, which characterizes acculturation. (The term *assimilation* means that people from another culture have more or less completely adopted the dominant culture of the society.)

External pressure for culture change can take various forms. In its most direct form—conquest or colonialization—the dominant group uses force or the threat of it to bring about culture change in the other group. For example, in the Spanish conquest of Mexico, the conquerors forced many of the native groups to accept Catholicism. Although such direct force is not always exerted in conquest situations, dominated peoples often have little choice but to change. Examples of such indirectly forced change abound in the history of Native Americans in the United States. Although the federal government made few direct attempts to force people to adopt North American culture, it did drive many native groups from their lands, thereby obliging them to give up many aspects of their traditional ways of life. In order to survive, they had no choice but to adopt many of the dominant society's traits. When Native American children were required to go to schools, which taught the dominant society's values, the process was accelerated.

A subordinate society may acculturate to a dominant society even in the absence of direct or indirect force. The dominated people may elect to adopt cultural elements from the dominant society in order to survive in their changed world. Or, perceiving that members of the dominant society enjoy more secure living conditions, the dominated people may identify with the dominant culture in the hope that by doing so they will be able to share some of its benefits. For example, in Arctic areas many Inuit and Lapp groups seemed eager to replace dog sleds with snowmobiles without any coercion.[11]

But many millions of people never really had a chance to acculturate after contact with Europeans. They simply died, sometimes directly at the hands of the conquerors, but probably more often as a result of new diseases the Europeans brought with them. Depopulation because of new diseases

When powerful governments restrict native populations to smaller parcels of land on reservations or force them to move, there is usually little choice but to change in the direction of the more powerful group's way of life. This painting by Robert Lindneux ("The Trail of Tears") depicts the forced removal of the Cherokee from their homeland in the southeastern United States.

such as measles, smallpox, and tuberculosis was particularly common in North and South America and on the islands of the Pacific. Those areas had previously been isolated from contact with Europeans and from the diseases of that continuous land mass we call the Old World—Europe, Asia, and Africa.[12]

The story of Ishi, the last surviving member of a group of Native Americans in California called the Yahi, is a moving testimonial to the frequently tragic effect of contact with Europeans. In the space of twenty-two years, the Yahi population was reduced from several hundred to near zero. The historical record on this episode of depopulation suggests that Euroamericans murdered thirty to fifty Yahi for every Euroamerican murdered, and perhaps 60 percent of the Yahi died in the ten years following their initial exposure to European diseases.[13]

Nowadays, many powerful nations (and not just Western ones) may seem to be acting in more humanitarian ways to improve the life of previously subjugated as well as other "developing" peoples. For better or worse, these programs are still forms of external pressure. The tactic used may be persuasion rather than force, but most of the programs are nonetheless designed to bring about acculturation in the direction of the dominant societies' cultures. For example, the introduction of formal schooling cannot help but instill new values that may contradict traditional cultural patterns. And even health-care programs may alter traditional ways of life by undermining the authority of shamans and others and by increasing population beyond the number that can be supported in traditional ways. Confinement to "reservations" or other kinds of direct force are not the only ways a dominant society can bring about acculturation.

Revolution

Certainly the most drastic and rapid way a culture can change is as a result of **revolution**—replacement, usually violent, of a country's rulers. Historical records, as well as our daily newspapers, indicate that people frequently rebel against established authority. Rebellions, if they occur, almost always occur in state societies, where there is a distinct ruling elite. They take the form of struggles between rulers and ruled, between conquerors and conquered, or between representatives of an external colonial power and segments of the native society. Rebels do not always succeed in overthrowing the previous rulers, so rebellions do not always result in revolutions. And even successful rebellions do not always result in culture change; the individual rulers may change, but customs or institutions may not. The sources of revolution may be mostly internal, as in the French Revolution, or partly external, as in the Russian-supported 1948 revolution in Czechoslovakia and the United States–supported 1973 revolution against President Allende in Chile.

The Nacirema war of independence toward the end of the eighteenth century is a good example of a colonial rebellion, the success of which was at least partly a result of foreign intervention. The Nacirema rebellion was a war of neighboring colonies against the greatest imperial power of the time, Great Britain. In the nineteenth century and continuing into the middle and later years of the twentieth century, there would be many other wars of independence, in Latin America, Europe, Asia, and Africa. We don't always remember that the Nacirema rebellion was the first of these anti-imperialist wars in modern times, and the model for many that followed. And just like many of the most recent liberation movements, the Nacirema rebellion was also part of a larger worldwide war, involving people from many rivalrous nations. Thirty thousand German-speaking soldiers fought, for pay, on the British side; an army and navy from France fought on the Nacirema side. There were volunteers from other European countries, including Denmark, Holland, Poland, and Russia.

One of these volunteers was a man named Kosciusko from Poland, which at the time was being divided between Prussia and Russia. Kosciusko helped win a major victory for the Nacirema, and subsequently directed the fortification of what later became the Nacirema training school for army officers, Tsew Tniop. After the war he returned to Poland and led a rebellion against the Russians, which was only briefly successful. In 1808 he published a *Manual on the Maneuvers of Horse Artillery*, which was used for many years by the Nacirema army. When he died he left money to buy freedom and education for Nacirema slaves.

The executor of Kosciusko's will was a Nacirema named Jefferson, who had taken part in a famous debate at a convention in his colony. The debate was over a motion to prepare for defense against the British armed forces. The motion barely passed, by a vote of sixty-five to sixty. There was a speech before the vote that is now a part of Nacirema folklore. A lawyer whose last name was Henry listened to the argument for not opposing the British and then rose to declare that it was insane not to oppose them and that he was not afraid to test the strength of the colonies against Great Britain—others might hesitate, he said, but he would have "liberty or death." The "radicals" who supported P. Henry's resolution included many aristocratic landowners, two of whom (G. Washington and T. Jefferson) became the first and third occupants of the highest political office in what became the United States of America.[14]

Not all peoples who are suppressed, conquered, or colonialized eventually rebel against established authority. Why this is so and why rebellions and revolts are not always successful in bringing about culture change are still open questions. But some possible answers have been investigated. One historian, who examined the classic revolutions of the past, including the American, French, and Russian revolutions, suggested some conditions that may give rise to rebellion and revolution:

1. Loss of prestige of established authority, often as a result of the failure of foreign policy, financial difficulties, dismissals of popular ministers, or alteration of popular policies. France in the eighteenth century lost three major international conflicts, with disastrous results for its diplomatic standing and internal finances. Russian society was close to military and economic collapse in 1917, after three years of World War I.

2. Threat to recent economic improvement. In France, as in Russia, those sections of the population (professional classes and urban work-ers) whose economic fortunes had only shortly before taken an upward swing were "radicalized" by unexpected setbacks such as steeply rising food prices and unemployment. The same may be said for the American colonies on the brink of their rebellion against Great Britain.

3. Indecisiveness of government, as exemplified by lack of consistent policy, which gives the impression of being controlled by, rather than in control of, events. The frivolous arrogance of Louis XVI's regime and the bungling of George III's prime minister, Lord North, with respect to the problems of the American colonies, are examples.

4. Loss of support of the intellectual class. Such a loss deprived the prerevolutionary governments of France and Russia of any avowed philosophical support and led to their unpopularity with the literate public.[15]

The classic revolutions of the past occurred in countries that were industrialized only incipiently at best. For the most part, the same is true of the rebellions and revolutions in recent years: they have occurred mostly in countries we call *developing*. The evidence from a worldwide survey of developing countries suggests that rebellions have tended to occur where the ruling classes depended mostly on the produce or income from land, and therefore were

Revolutionary leaders are often from high-status backgrounds. Here we see a depiction of Patrick Henry, a lawyer, giving his famous speech to the aristocratic landowners in the Virginia Assembly on March 23, 1775. In that speech urging Virginia to fight the British, Henry said that the choice was "liberty or death."

resistant to demands for reform from the rural classes that worked the land. In such agricultural economies, the rulers are not likely to yield political power or give greater economic returns to the workers, because to do so would eliminate the basis (land ownership) of the rulers' wealth and power.[16]

Finally, a particularly interesting question is why revolutions sometimes (perhaps even usually) fail to measure up to the high hopes of those who initiate them. When rebellions succeed in replacing the ruling elite, the result is often the institution of a military dictatorship even more restrictive and repressive than the government that existed before. The new ruling establishment may merely substitute one set of repressions for another, rather than bring any real change to the nation. On the other hand, some revolutions have resulted in fairly drastic overhauls of societies.

The idea of revolution has been one of the central myths and inspirations of many groups both in the past and in the present. The colonial empire building of countries such as England and France created a worldwide situation in which rebellion became nearly inevitable. In numerous technologically underdeveloped lands, which have been exploited by more powerful countries for their natural resources and cheap labor, a deep resentment has often developed against the foreign ruling classes or their local clients. Where the ruling classes, native or foreign, refuse to be responsive to these feelings, rebellion becomes the only alternative. In many areas, it has become a way of life.

CULTURE CHANGE AND ADAPTATION

The chapter on the concept of culture discussed the general assumption that most of the customary behaviors of a culture are probably adaptive, or at least not maladaptive, in that environment. A custom is adaptive if it increases the likelihood that the people practicing it will survive and reproduce. Even though customs are learned (not genetically inherited), cultural adaptation may be otherwise like biological adaptation or evolution. The frequency of certain genetic alternatives is likely to increase over time if those genetic traits increase their carriers' chances of survival and reproduction. Similarly, the frequency of a new learned behavior will increase over time and become customary in a population if the people with that behavior are most likely to survive and reproduce. Thus, if a culture is adapted to its environment, culture change should also be adaptive—not always, to be sure, but commonly.

One of the most important differences between cultural evolution and genetic evolution is that individuals often can decide whether or not to accept and follow the way their parents behave or think, whereas they cannot decide whether or not to inherit certain genes. When enough individuals change their behavior and beliefs, we say that the culture has changed. Therefore, it is possible for culture change to occur much more rapidly than genetic change.

But it is not necessarily more adaptive to change rapidly, just because it is possible. Robert Boyd and Peter Richerson showed mathematically that when the environment is relatively stable and individual mistakes are costly, staying with customary modes of behavior (usually transmitted by parents) is probably more adaptive than changing.[17] But what happens when the environment (particularly the social environment) is changing? There are plenty of examples in the modern world: people have to migrate to new places for work; medical care leads to increased population so that land is scarcer; people have had land taken away from them and they are therefore forced to make do with less land; and so on.

It is particularly when circumstances change that individuals are likely to try ideas or behaviors that are different from those of their parents. Most people would want to adopt behaviors that are more suited to their present circumstances, but how do they know which behaviors are better? There are various ways to find out. One way is by experimenting, trying out various new behaviors. Another way is to evaluate the experiments of others. If a person who tries a new technique seems successful, we would expect the more successful person to be imitated, just as we would expect people to stick with new behaviors they have personally tried and found successful. Finally, one might choose to do what most people in the new situation decide to do.[18]

Why one choice rather than another? In part, the choice may be a function of the cost or risk of the innovation. It is relatively easy, for example, to find out how long it takes to cut down a tree with an introduced steel ax, as compared with a stone ax. Not surprisingly, innovations such as a steel ax catch on relatively quickly because comparison is easy and the results relatively clear-cut. But what if the risk is very great? Suppose the innovation involves adopting a whole new way of farming that you have never practiced before. You can try it, but you might not have any food if you fail. As we discussed earlier, innovations that are risky are likely to be tried only by those individuals who can afford the risk. Other people may then evaluate their success and adopt the new strategy if it looks promising. Similarly, if you migrate to a new area, say from a high-rainfall area to a drier one, it may pay to look around to see what most people in the new place do; after all, the people in the drier area probably have customs that are adaptive for that environment.

We can expect then that the choices individuals make may often be adaptive ones. But it is important to note that adopting an innovation from someone in one's own society or borrowing an innovation from another society is not always or necessarily beneficial, either in the short or the long run. First, people may make mistakes in judgment, especially when some new behavior seems to satisfy a physical need. Why, for example, have smoking and drug use diffused so widely even though they are likely to reduce a person's chances of survival? Second, even if people are correct in their short-term judgment of benefit, they may be wrong in their judgment about long-run benefit. A new crop may yield more than the old crop for five consecutive years, but the new crop may fail miserably in the sixth year because of lower-than-normal rainfall or because the new crop depleted soil nutrients. Third, people may be forced by the more powerful to change, with few if any benefits for themselves.

Whatever the motives for humans to change their behavior, the theory of natural selection suggests that new behavior is not likely to become cultural (or remain cultural over generations) if it has harmful reproductive consequences, just as a genetic mutation with harmful consequences is not likely to become frequent in a population.[19] Still, we know of many examples of culture change that seem maladaptive—the switch to bottle-feeding rather than nursing infants, which may spread infection because contaminated water is used, or the adoption of alcoholic beverages, which may lead to alcoholism and early death. In the last few hundred years, the major stimulus to culture change, adaptive and maladaptive, has been the new social environment produced by the arrival of people from Western societies.

TYPES OF CULTURE CHANGE IN THE MODERN WORLD

Many of the cultural changes in the world from A.D. 1500 to the present have been caused, directly or indirectly, by the dominance and expansion of Western societies.[20] Thus, much of the culture change in the modern world has been externally induced, if not forced. This is not to say that cultures are changing now only because of external pressures; but externally induced changes have been the changes most frequently studied by anthropologists and other social scientists. Most of the external pressures have come from Western societies, but not all. Other societies, such as Japan and China, have also stimulated culture change.

Commercialization

One of the most important changes resulting from the expansion of Western societies is the increasing dependence of all parts of the world on commercial exchange. The borrowed customs of buying and selling may at first be supplementary to traditional means of distributing goods in a society. But as the new commercial customs take hold, the economic base of the receiving society alters. Inevitably, this alteration is accompanied by other changes, which have broad social, political, and even psychological ramifications.

In examining contemporary patterns of change, however, we should bear in mind that the process of commercialization has occurred in many parts of the world in the past. The Chinese, Persians, Greeks, Romans, Arabs, Phoenicians, and Hindus were some of the early state societies that pushed commercial enterprises in other areas. We are probably casting some light on how and why some earlier cultures changed when we consider several questions. How, and why, does a contemporary society change from a subsistence to a commercial economic base? What are the resultant cultural changes? Why do they occur?

In general, the limited evidence now available suggests that a previously noncommercial people may begin to sell (and buy) things simply in order to live, not just because they may be attracted by goods they can obtain only by commercial exchange. If the resources available to a group have been significantly reduced per person—because the group has been forced to resettle on a small "reservation" or because population has increased—the group may be likely to take advantage of any commercial opportunities that become available, even if such opportunities require considerably more work time and effort.[21]

Migratory Labor. One way commercialization can occur is for some members of a community to move to a place that offers the possibility of working for wages. This happened in Tikopia, an island near the Solomon Islands in the South Pacific. In 1929, when Raymond Firth first studied the island, its economy was still essentially noncommercial—simple, self-sufficient, and largely self-contained.[22] Some Western goods were known and available but, with the exception of iron and steel in limited quantities, not sought after. Their possession and use were associated solely with Europeans. This situation changed dramatically with World War II. During the war, military forces occupied neighboring islands, and people from Tikopia migrated to those islands to find employment. In the period following the war, several large commercial interests extended their activities in the Solomons, thus creating a continued demand for labor. As a result, when Firth revisited Tikopia in 1952, he found the economic situation significantly altered.

More than a hundred Tikopians had left the island to work for varying periods. The migrants wanted to earn money because they aspired to standards of living previously regarded as appropriate only to Europeans. Already, living conditions on Tikopia were changing. Western cooking and water-carrying utensils, mosquito nets, kerosene storm lamps, and so forth had come to be regarded as normal items in a Tikopia household.

The introduction of money into the economy of Tikopia not only altered the economic system but also affected other areas of life. Compared with the situation in 1929, land was under more intensive cultivation in 1952, with manioc and sweet potatoes supplementing the principal taro crop. Pressures on the food supply resulting from improved living standards and an increased population seem to have weakened the ties of extended kinship. For example, the nuclear families constituting the extended family (the land-holding and land-using unit in 1929) were not cooperating as much in 1952. In many cases, in fact, the land had actually been split up among the constituent nuclear families; land rights had become more individualized. People were no longer as willing to share with members of their extended family, particularly with respect to the money and goods acquired by working in the Solomons.

Nonagricultural Commercial Production. Commercialization can also occur when a self-sufficient hunting or agricultural society comes to depend more and more on trading for its livelihood. Such a change is exemplified by the Mundurucú of the Amazon Basin, who largely abandoned general horticulture for commercial rubber production. A similar change may also be seen in the Montagnais of northeastern Canada, who came to depend increas-

Commercialization can occur when people find cash-paying jobs in nearby industry. A Bolivian woman pounds ore into pieces that will be ground and separated into various metals.

ingly on commercial fur trapping, rather than hunting, for subsistence. Robert Murphy and Julian Steward found that when modern goods from industrialized areas became available through trade, both the Mundurucú and the Montagnais devoted their energies to making specialized cash crops or other trade items. They did this to obtain other industrially made objects.[23] The primary socioeconomic change that occurred among the Mundurucú and the Montagnais was a shift from cooperative labor and community autonomy to individualized economic activity and a dependence on an external market.

Among the Mundurucú, for example, before close trading links were established, the native population and the Europeans had been in contact for some eighty years without the Mundurucú way of life being noticeably altered. The men did give up their independently inspired military activities in order to perform as mercenaries for the Brazilians, but they continued to maintain their horticultural economy. Some trading took place with Brazilians, with the chief acting as agent for the village. Barter was the method of exchange. Traders first distributed their wares, ranging from cheap cottons to iron hatchets, trinkets, and so on; they returned about three months later to collect manioc, India rubber, and beans from the Mundurucú. At this time (1860), however, rubber was only a secondary item of commerce.

The rapidly growing demand for rubber from the 1860s onward increased the importance of Mundurucú-trader relationships. Traders now openly began to appoint agents, called *capitoes,* whose job it was to encourage greater rubber production. *Capitoes* were given economic privileges and hence power, both of which began to undercut the position of the traditional chief. In addition, the process of rubber collection itself began to alter Mundurucú social patterns by moving people away from their jungle-based communities.

Wild rubber trees are found only along rivers, which are often a considerable distance from the jungle habitat of the Mundurucú and can be exploited only during the dry season (late May to December). So the Mundurucú man who elected to gather rubber had to separate himself from his family for about half the year. Furthermore, rubber collecting is a solitary activity. Each tapper must work his territory, consisting of about 150 trees, daily, and he must live close to his trees because the work lasts all day. Therefore, the tapper usually lives alone or in a small group except during the rainy season, when he returns to his village.

At this stage in the commercialization process, the Mundurucú became increasingly dependent on goods supplied by the trader. Firearms were useless without regular quantities of powder and lead or shot; clothing required needles and thread for repairs. But these items could be earned only through increased rubber production, which in turn led to greater dependency on the outside world. Inevitably, the ability to work with traditional materials and the desire to maintain traditional crafts disappeared. Metal pots took the place of clay ones, and manufactured hammocks replaced homemade ones. Gradually the village agricultural cycle ceased to be adhered to by all in the community so that rubber production would not suffer. The authority of the traditional chiefs was weakened as that of the *capitoes* was enhanced.

The point of no return was reached when significant numbers of Mundurucú abandoned the villages for permanent settlements near their individual territories of trees. These new settlements lacked the unity, the sense of community, of former village life. Property was held by nuclear families and carefully maintained in the interest of productivity.

With the discovery of gold, many Mundurucú young men have recently turned to panning for gold in rivers. The required equipment is simple, and gold is easier to transport and trade than rubber. Because gold can be sold for cash, which is then used for purchases, trading relationships are no longer so important. Cash is now used to buy transistor radios, tape recorders, watches, bicycles, and new kinds of clothing, in addition to firearms, metal pots, and tools. With money as a medium of exchange, the old emphasis on reciprocity has declined. Even food may now be sold to fellow Mundurucú, a practice that would have been unthinkable in the 1950s.[24]

Supplementary Cash Crops.   A third way commercialization occurs is when people cultivating the soil produce a surplus above their subsistence requirements, which is then sold for cash. In many cases, this cash income must be used to pay rent or taxes. Under these circumstances, commercialization may be said to be associated with the formation of a peasantry. **Peasants** are rural people who produce food for their own subsistence. But they must also contribute or sell their surpluses to others (in towns and cities) who do not produce their own food.

Peasants first appeared with the emergence of state and urban civilizations about 5,000 to 6,000 years ago, and they have been associated with civilization ever since.[25] To say that peasants are associated with urban societies perhaps needs some qualification. The contemporary, highly industrialized urban society has little need of peasants. Their scale of production is small and their use of land "uneconomic." A highly industrialized society with a large population of non-food producers requires mechanized agriculture. As a result, the peasant has passed, or is passing, out of all but the most peripheral existence in industrial countries. It is the preindustrial city, and the social organization it represents, that generates and maintains peasants. They cultivate land; they furnish the required quantity of food, rent, and profit on which the remainder of society (particularly the people in the cities) depends.

What changes does the development of a peasantry entail? In some respects there is little disturbance of the cultivator's (now peasant's) former way of life. The peasant still has to produce enough food to meet family needs, to replace what has been consumed, to cover a few ceremonial obligations (for example, the marriage of a child, village festivals, and funerals). But in other respects the peasant's situation is radically altered. For in addition to the traditional obligations—indeed, often in conflict with them—the peasant now has to produce extra crops to meet the requirements of a group of outsiders—landlords or officials of the state. These outsiders expect to be paid rent or taxes (in produce or currency), and they are able to en-

Commercialization can also occur when a previously self-sufficient society begins to sell some native products, such as animal furs. In this painting, a Native American is shown exchanging a fur pelt for Western goods.

force their expectations because they control the military and the police.

Although no two peasant cultures are quite alike, there are similarities in form. Peasants the world over are faced with the problem of balancing the demands of an external world against those of an internal society. Their response generally involves increasing production, curtailing domestic consumption, or both.

Introduction of Commercial and Industrial Agriculture. Another way in which commercialization can come about is through the introduction of commercial agriculture. In commercial agriculture, *all* the cultivated commodities are produced for sale rather than for personal consumption. Along with this change, the system of agriculture may be industrialized. In other words, some of the production processes, such as plowing, weeding, irrigation, and harvesting, are done by machine. Commercial agriculture is, in fact, often as mechanized as any manufacturing industry. Land is worked for the maximum return it will yield, and labor is hired and fired just as impersonally as in other industries.

E. J. Hobsbawm noted some of the developments that accompanied the introduction of commercial agriculture in eighteenth-century England and in continental Europe somewhat later.[26] The close, near-familial relationship between farmer and farm laborer disappeared, as did the once-personal connection between landlord and tenant. Land came to be regarded as a source of profit rather than a way of life. Fields were merged into single units and enclosed, and local grazing and similar privileges were reduced. Labor was hired at market rates and paid in wages. Eventually, as the emphasis on large-scale production for a mass market increased, machines began to replace farm laborers.

The introduction of commercial agriculture brings several important social consequences. Gradually, a class polarization develops. Farmers and landlords become increasingly separated from laborers and tenants, just as in the town the employer becomes socially separated from the employees. Gradually too, manufactured items of all sorts are introduced into rural areas. Laborers migrate to urban centers in search of employment, often meeting even less sympathetic conditions there than exist in the country.

The changeover to commercial agriculture may result in an improved standard of living in the short and long run. But sometimes the switch is followed by a decline in the standard of living if the market price for the commercial crop declines. For example, the changeover of the farmer-herders of the arid *sertão* region of northeastern Brazil after 1940 to the production of sisal (a plant whose fibers can be made into twine and rope) seemed to be a move that could provide a more secure living in their arid environment. But when the world price for sisal dropped and the wages of sisal workers declined, many workers were forced to curtail the caloric intake of their children. The poorer people were obliged to save their now more limited food supplies for the money earners, at the expense of the children.[27]

Commercialization can begin in various ways: people can begin to sell and buy because they begin to work near home or away for wages, or because they begin to sell nonagricultural products, surplus food, or cash crops (crops grown deliberately for sale). One type of commercialization does not exclude another—all types can occur in any society. However commercialization begins, it seems to have predictable effects on traditional economics. The ethic of generalized reciprocity declines, particularly with respect to giving money away. (Perhaps because it is nonperishable and hideable, money seems more likely than other goods to be kept for one's immediate family rather than shared with others.) Property rights become individualized rather than collective when people begin to buy and sell. And even in societies that were previously egalitarian, commercialization usually results in more unequal access to resources and hence a greater degree of social stratification.

Religious Change

Commercialization is not of course the only type of culture change in the modern world. The growing influence of Western societies has also led to religious change in many places. Often, the change has been brought about intentionally through the efforts of missionaries, who have been among the first Westerners to travel to interior regions and out-of-the-way places. Missionaries have not met with equal success in all parts of the world. In some places, large portions of the native population have converted to the new religion with great zeal. In others, missionaries have been ignored, forced to flee, or even killed. We do not as yet fully understand why missionaries have been successful in some societies and not in others. Yet in many parts of the world, Western missionary activity has been a potent force for all kinds of cultural, and particularly religious, change. One possible reason is that missionaries offer resources that enable natives to min-

On the island of Tahiti, as in many Polynesian islands, missionaries were very successful in converting people to Christianity. If they could persuade the chiefs, they were likely to persuade many others to convert as well.

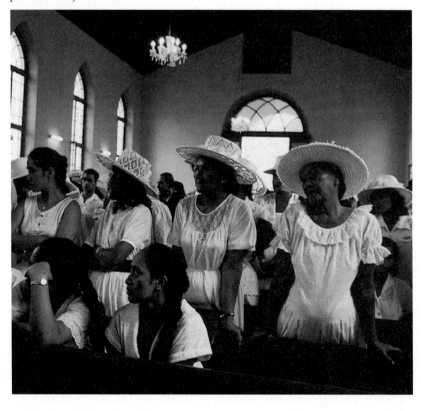

imize economic and other risks in the new Western-dominated social environment.[28]

But aside from the direct effects of missionary work, contact with Westerners has often produced religious change in more indirect ways. In some native societies, contact with Westerners has led to a breakdown of social structure and the growth of feelings of helplessness and spiritual demoralization. In the chapter on religion and magic, we discussed how revitalization movements have arisen as apparent attempts to restore such societies to their former confidence and prosperity.

We will examine the process of conversion on the island of Tikopia, as an example of religious change brought about by direct contact with missionaries.

Christianity on Tikopia. Tikopia was one of the few Polynesian societies to retain its traditional religious system into the first decades of the twentieth century. An Anglican mission was first established on the island in 1911. With it came a deacon and the founding of two schools for about 200 pupils. By 1929, approximately half the population had converted, and in the early 1960s almost all Tikopia gave at least nominal allegiance to Christianity.[29]

Traditional Tikopian belief was pantheistic, embracing a great number of gods and spirits of various ranks inhabiting the sky, the water, and the land. One god in particular—the original creator and shaper of the culture—was given a place of special importance, but he was in no way comparable to the all-powerful God of Christianity. Unlike Christianity, Tikopian religion made no claim to universality. The Tikopian gods did not rule over all creation, only over Tikopia. It was thought that if one left Tikopia, one left the gods behind.

The people of Tikopia interacted with their gods and spirits primarily through religious leaders who were also the heads of descent groups. Clan chiefs presided over rituals centering in the everyday aspects of island life, such as house construction, fishing, planting, and harvesting. The chief was expected to intercede with the gods on the people's behalf, to persuade them to bring happiness and prosperity to the group. Indeed, when conditions were good it was assumed that the chief was doing his job well. When disaster struck, the prestige of the chief often fell in proportion. Why did the Tikopia convert to Christianity? Firth suggested several contributing factors.

First, the mission offered the people the prospect of acquiring new tools and consumer goods. Although conversion alone did not provide such benefits, attachment to the mission was believed to make them more attainable. Later, it became apparent that education, particularly in reading and writing English, was helpful in getting ahead in the outside world. Mission schooling became valued and provided a further incentive for adopting Christianity.

Second, conversion may have been facilitated by the ability of chiefs, as religious and political leaders, to bring over entire kin groups to Christianity. Should a chief decide to transfer his allegiance to Christianity, the members of his kin group usually followed him, since social etiquette required that they do so. Such a situation actually developed in 1923 when Tafua, chief of the Faea district of Tikopia, converted to the new religion. He brought with him his entire group—which amounted to nearly half the population of the island. The ability of the chiefs to influence their kin groups, however, was both an asset and a hindrance to missionary efforts, since some chiefs steadfastly resisted conversion.

A final blow to traditional Tikopian religion appeared to come in 1955, when a severe epidemic killed at least 200 people in a population of about 1,700. According to Firth, "the epidemic was largely interpreted as a sign of divine discrimination," because three of the outstanding non-Christian religious leaders died.[30] Subsequently, the remaining non-Christian chiefs voluntarily converted to Christianity and so did their followers. By 1966 all Tikopia, with the exception of one rebellious old woman, had converted to the new faith.

Although many Tikopians feel their conversion to Christianity has been a unifying, revitalizing force, the changeover from one religion to another has not been without problems. Christian missionaries on Tikopia have succeeded in eliminating the traditional Tikopian population-control devices of abortion, infanticide, and male celibacy. It is very possible that the absence of these controls will continue to intensify population pressure. The island, with its limited capacity to support life, can ill afford this outcome. Firth summed up the situation Tikopian society must now face:

> In the history of Tikopia complete conversion of the people to Christianity was formerly regarded as a solution to their problems; it is now coming to be realized that the adoption and practice of Christianity itself represents another set of problems. As the Tikopia themselves are beginning to see, to be Christian Polynesians in the modern technologically and industrially dominated world, even in the Solomon Islands, poses as many questions as it supplies answers.[31]

Unfortunately, not all native peoples have made the transition to Christianity as painlessly as the Tikopia. In fact, in most cases the record is dismal. All too frequently, missionary activity tends to destroy a society's culture and self-respect. It offers nothing in return but an alien, repressive system of values ill adapted to the people's real needs and aspirations. Phillip Mason, a critic of European evangelists in Africa, pointed out some of the psychological damage inflicted by missionary activity.[32] The missionaries repeatedly stressed sin and guilt; they used the color black to represent evil and the color white to signify good; and they showed hostility toward pagan culture. Most damaging of all was their promise that the African, provided she or he adopted the European's ways, would gain access both to the European's heaven and to European society. But no matter how diligently Africans attempted to follow missionary precepts or climb the socioeconomic ladder, they were soon blocked

Research Frontiers

CULTURE CHANGE AND PERSISTENCE IN COMMUNIST CHINA

In the years since the 1949 Communist takeover in China, the central government has initiated a variety of changes in family life. Many of these changes were literally forced; people who resisted them were often resettled or jailed. Ancestor worship and lineage organization were attacked or declared illegal. Most private property was abolished, undermining family loyalties. Why participate in family activities if there could be no economic reward? Still, the actions of the central government did not completely change family life. Even coercion has its limits.

The government may have wanted to restrict the family and kinship, but its investments in public health and famine relief reduced mortality, thereby strengthening family ties. Fewer infants died, more children lived long enough to marry, old age became more common—all of these developments allowed people in all social classes to have larger and more complex net-

works of kin than were possible before 1949. To be sure, government policies undercut the power and authority of extended family patriarchs. But the new healthier conditions were conducive to large, multigenerational households with economic as well as social ties to other kin.

As China became more accessible to anthropological and other researchers from abroad, many investigators came to study the variability and similarity in Chinese family life. Most of these studies focused on the dominant Han Chinese (the Han, speakers of Mandarin, constitute about 95 percent of the total population of China); investigators have also studied many of the fifty-five "recognized" minority cultures in China. Burton Pasternak, a U.S. anthropologist, Janet Salaff, a Canadian sociologist, and Chinese sociologists studied four communities of Han who had moved outside the Great Wall to colonize the Inner Mongolian frontier. (Inner Mongolia is part

of China.) The results of their study suggest that, despite strong pressures from the government, what changes or persists in a culture mainly reflects what is possible ecologically and economically. A tradition of intensive agriculture cannot persist in the absence of sufficient watering. The government's insistence on one child per family cannot withstand a family's need for more children.

Han farmers who crossed the Great Wall were searching for a better life. They found difficulties in climate and soil that forced many to return home. But many adjusted to the grasslands and remained. Some continued to depend on farming on the fringes of the grasslands. Others farther out on the grasslands became herders. The Han who switched to herding are now in many respects more like the native Mongol herders than like Han or Mongol farmers. The gender division of labor among the Han pastoralists became from entry into European homes, clubs, and even churches and seminaries.

Political and Social Change

In addition to commercialization and religious change brought about by the expansion of Western and other countries, political changes have often occurred when a foreign system of government has been imposed. But, as recent events in the former Soviet Union and South Africa indicate, dramatic changes in a political system can also occur more or less voluntarily. Perhaps the most striking type of political change in recent years is the spread of participatory forms of government ("democracy").

To political scientists, democracy is usually defined in terms of voting by a substantial proportion of the citizenry, governments brought to power by periodic contested elections, a chief executive either popularly elected or responsible to an elected

much sharper than among the Han farmers since men are often far away with the herds. Pastoralist children, not that useful in herding because mistakes can be very costly, are more likely than farming children to stay in school for a long time. Perhaps because of the greater usefulness of children on the farm, Han farm families have more children than Han pastoralists. But both groups have more than one child per family. Herdsmen are less likely than farmers to need cooperative labor, so Han pastoralists are more likely to live as a neolocal independent family than as a patrilocal extended family (which was traditional). In short, the adjustment of the Han to the grasslands seems to be explained more by ecological requirements than by ethnic traditions.

Although an increasing number of Han have become more like Mongols in their pastoral adaptations, many Mongols have adopted an urban way of life and moved away from their pastoral life. The Chinese government was initially responsible for encouraging non-Mongols to move into Inner Mongolia, particularly into its new capital Huhhot. At the same time, many Mongols moved away from the grasslands and into the capital city. Chinese government policy was intended to make each non-Han ethnic group a minority in its traditional land, but the government paradoxically also tried to encourage minority ethnic pride in their traditional culture. So the city of Huhhot is filled with images of the traditional herding culture in its buildings and monuments.

As described by anthropologist William Jankowiak, who studied the Mongols in the capital city of Huhhot, the results were not what the Chinese government intended. In many ways, to be sure, the urban Mongols had abandoned their traditional culture and assimilated to the dominant Han culture. But we see the force of ecology more than the hand of tradition in the outcome. Many Mongols in the city no longer speak the Mongol language. Parents find it difficult to get children to speak Mongol when they live among Han. And the scarcity of housing makes it difficult for the Mongols to form an ethnic enclave, or even live near kin as they did in the past. In contrast to life in the rural areas, which revolves around kinship, living in the city requires interacting with strangers as well as relatives. Indeed, nonkin are often more important to you than kin. As one person said to Jankowiak, "We hide from our cousins but not our friends."

Sources: *Deborah Davis and Stevan Harrell, eds.,* Chinese Families in the Post-Mao Era *(Berkeley: University of California Press, 1993); Burton Pasternak, "Han: Pastoralists and Farmers on a Chinese Frontier," in Melvin Ember, Carol R. Ember, and David Levinson, eds.,* Portraits of Culture: Ethnographic Originals *(Englewood Cliffs, NJ: Prentice Hall, 1994), Prentice Hall/Simon & Schuster Custom Publishing; William R. Jankowiak, "Urban Mongols: Ethnicity in Communist China," in Ember, Ember, and Levinson, eds.,* Portraits of Culture: Ethnographic Originals.

legislature, and often also civil liberties such as free speech. Depending on which criteria are used, only twelve to fifteen countries qualified as democracies as of the beginning of the twentieth century. The number decreased after World War I, as emerging democratic institutions were replaced in Russia, Italy, Germany, central Europe, Japan, and elsewhere. After World War II, despite all the rhetoric associated with the founding of the United Nations, the picture was not much different. Some members of the new North Atlantic Treaty Organization (NATO) were not democracies, and neither were many members of the wider Western alliance system (in Latin America, the Middle East, and Asia).

It was not until the 1970s and 1980s that people (not just political scientists) started noticing that democracy was becoming more common in the world. By the early 1990s, President George Bush and then-candidate Bill Clinton were talking about the spread of the "democratic peace." As of 1992, about half of the countries in the world had more or less democratic governments, and others were in transition to democracy.[33] Social scientists do not yet understand why this change is happening. But it is possible that the global communication of ideas has a lot to do with it. Authoritarian governments can censor their own newspapers and prevent group meetings, but they really cannot stop the movement of ideas via telephone lines and the Internet. The movement of ideas, of course, does not explain the acceptance of those ideas. Why democracy has recently diffused to more countries than ever before still requires explanation.

Another frequent type of culture change in the modern world is increasing social stratification. Because of economic change, some groups become more privileged and powerful than others. For example, it has been suggested that the introduction of new technology may generally make for an *increase* in degree of social stratification.[34] When the snowmobile began to be used for herding by the Lapps, those who for various reasons could participate in the "snowmobile revolution" gained economic, social, and political advantages. But those who could not acquire the new machines tended to become an economically and generally deprived class—without machines *or* reindeer.[35]

Western influence has also brought about changes in dress, music, art, and attitudes through-

Very few would have predicted that South Africa would quickly dismantle apartheid and hold elections that included the previously excluded black majority. Nor would many have predicted a presidential debate in which Nelson Mandela (now President) and Frederick Willem de Klerk (now Vice President) would shake hands and work together to maintain peace both before and after elections. We still have much to understand about why changes occur peacefully in some cases and violently in others.

out the world. The appeal of "popular" music, for example, is more and more international, whether or not it originates in the West.

Of course, many nations in the past as well as the present—not just Western ones—have extended their power and influence to other parts of the globe. For example, the expansion of Islamic societies after the eighth century A.D. made for an enormous amount of culture change in the Near East, Africa, Europe, and Asia; recall that our way of counting numbers was originally Arabic.

Future research on contemporary culture change should increase our understanding of how and why various types of change are occurring. And if we can increase our understanding of culture change in the present, we should be better able to understand parallel processes in the past. Another lead to understanding change in the past is the large number of cross-cultural correlations (between a cultural variation and its presumed causes) that have been discovered since the 1970s.[36] All cultures have changed over time. Therefore the variations we see are the products of change processes, and the discovered predictors of those variations may suggest how and why the changes occurred.

▼ SUMMARY

1. Culture is always changing. Because culture consists of learned patterns of behavior and belief, cultural traits can be unlearned and learned anew as human needs change.

2. Discoveries and inventions, though ultimately the sources of all culture change, do not necessarily lead to change. Only when society accepts an invention or discovery and uses it regularly can culture change be said to have occurred. Some inventions are probably the result of dozens of tiny, perhaps accidental, initiatives over a period of many years. Other inventions are consciously intended. Why some people are more innovative than others is still only incompletely understood. There is some evidence that creativity and the readiness to adopt innovations may be related to socioeconomic position.

3. The process by which cultural elements are borrowed from another society and incorporated into the culture of the recipient group is called diffusion. Three patterns of diffusion may be identified: diffusion by direct contact, in which elements of a culture are first taken up by neighboring societies and then gradually spread farther and farther afield; diffusion by intermediate contact, in which third parties, frequently traders, carry a cultural trait from the society originating it to another group; and stimulus diffusion, in which knowledge of a trait belonging to another culture stimulates the invention or development of a local equivalent.

4. Cultural traits do not necessarily diffuse; that is, diffusion is a selective—not automatic—process. A society accepting a foreign cultural trait is likely to adapt it in a way that effectively harmonizes it with the society's own traditions.

5. When a group or society is in contact with a more powerful society, the weaker group is often obliged to acquire cultural elements from the dominant group. This process of extensive borrowing in the context of superordinate-subordinate relations between societies is usually called acculturation. In contrast with diffusion, acculturation comes about as a result of some sort of external pressure.

6. Perhaps the most drastic and rapid way a culture can change is by revolution—a usually violent replacement of the society's rulers. Rebellions occur primarily in state societies, where there is usually a distinct ruling elite. However, not all peoples who are suppressed, conquered, or colonized eventually rebel or successfully revolt against established authority.

7. Even though customs are not genetically inherited, cultural adaptation may be somewhat similar to biological adaptation: traits (cultural or genetic) that are more likely to be reproduced (learned or inherited) are likely to become more frequent in a population over time. And if culture is generally adapted to its environment, then culture change should also be generally adaptive.

8. Many of the cultural changes observed in the modern world have been generated, directly or indirectly, by the dominance and expansion of Western societies. One of the principal changes resulting from the expansion of Western culture is the increasing dependence of much of the world on commercial exchange—that is, the proliferation of buying and selling in markets, usually accompanied by the use of money as the medium of exchange. The borrowed custom of buying and selling may at first be supplementary to traditional means of distributing goods, but as the new commercial customs take hold, the economic base of the receiving society alters. Inevitably, this alteration is accompanied by other changes, which have broad social, political, and even psychological ramifications.

9. One way commercialization can occur is for members of a community to become migratory workers, traveling to a place nearby that offers the possibility of working for wages. Commercialization can also occur when a simple, self-sufficient hunting or agricultural society comes to depend more and more on trading for its livelihood. A third way commercialization occurs is when those cultivating the soil produce more than they require for subsistence. The surplus is then sold for cash. In many instances, this cash income must be used to pay rent or taxes; under such circumstances, commercialization may be said to be associated with the formation of a peasantry. A fourth way in which commercialization can come about is through the introduction of commercial agriculture, in which *all* the cultivated commodities are produced for sale rather than for personal consumption. Along with this change, the system of agriculture may be industrialized, with some of the production processes being done by machine.

10. The growing influence of Western societies has also led to religious change in many parts of the world. In many societies, such change has been brought about intentionally through the efforts of missionaries.

11. One of the most striking types of culture change in the modern world is the spread of democracies. Participatory political institutions are now found in a majority of the world's countries.

▼ GLOSSARY TERMS

acculturation   diffusion   peasants   revolution

▼ CRITICAL QUESTIONS

1. What kinds of cultural items might be most easily borrowed by another culture, and why do you think so?
2. The expansion of the West has had terrible consequences for many peoples. Have there been any beneficial consequences?
3. Why might increasing understanding of cultural variation also provide increasing understanding of culture change?

▼ SUGGESTED READING

BERNARD, H. R., AND PELTO, P. J., eds. *Technology and Social Change,* 2nd ed. Prospect Heights, IL: Waveland, 1987. This volume is concerned with the effects of introduced Western technology on diverse cultures. Thirteen case studies were written especially for the volume; the editors provide concluding observations.

BODLEY, J. H. *Victims of Progress,* 3rd ed. Mountain View, CA: Mayfield, 1990. An examination of the effects of industrial nations on tribal peoples. Emphasizes the imperialist and exploitative practices of expansionist nations as well as the destructive consequences of imposed "progress."

BOYD, R., AND RICHERSON, P. J. *Culture and the Evolutionary Process.* Chicago: University of Chicago Press, 1985. The authors develop mathematical models to analyze how genes and culture interact, under the influence of evolutionary processes, to produce the diversity we see in human cultures.

EMBER, M., EMBER, C. R., AND LEVINSON, D. eds. *Portraits of Culture: Ethnographic Originals* (Englewood Cliffs, NJ: Prentice Hall, 1994, 1995). Prentice Hall/Simon & Schuster Custom Publishing. Most of the mini-ethnographies in this series discuss the changes in culture that have occurred in recent times.

GOLDSTONE, J. A. "The Comparative and Historical Study of Revolutions." *Annual Review of Sociology,* 8 (1982): 187–207. A review of theory and research on why revolutions have occurred, and why some succeeded, in the past and present.

HERBIG, P. A. *The Innovation Matrix: Culture and Structure Prerequisites to Innovation.* Westport, CT: Quorum Books, 1994. A discussion of the factors that may enable some societies to adapt and change more quickly than others.

MCNEILL, W. H. *Plagues and Peoples.* Garden City, NY: Doubleday Anchor, 1976. A historian suggests that epidemics have crucially affected the history of various societies all over the world.

ROGERS, E. M. *Diffusion of Innovations,* 3rd ed. New York: Free Press, 1983. This book examines the roles of information and uncertainty in the spread of innovations, how different categories of people adopt innovations at different rates, and how change agents affect the process. A large literature is reviewed and synthesized.

▼ NOTES

[1]Ralph Linton, *The Study of Man* (New York: Appleton-Century-Crofts, 1936), p. 306.

[2]Ibid., pp. 310–11.

[3]Harry R. Silver, "Calculating Risks: The Socioeconomic Foundations of Aesthetic Innovation in an Ashanti Carving Community," *Ethnology*, 20 (1981): 101–14.

[4]Everett M. Rogers, *Diffusion of Innovations*, 3rd ed. (New York: Free Press, 1983), pp. 263–69.

[5]Frank Cancian, "Risk and Uncertainty in Agricultural Decision Making," in Peggy F. Barlett, ed., *Agricultural Decision Making: Anthropological Contributions to Rural Development* (New York: Academic Press, 1980), pp. 161–202.

[6]Barry S. Hewlett and L. L. Cavalli-Sforza, "Cultural Transmission among Aka Pygmies," *American Anthropologist*, 88 (1986): 922–34; L. L. Cavalli-Sforza and M. W. Feldman, *Cultural Transmission and Evolution: A Quantitative Approach* (Princeton, NJ: Princeton University Press, 1981).

[7]Linton, *The Study of Man*, pp. 326–27. © 1936, renewed 1964; reprinted by permission of Prentice Hall, Inc.

[8]Ibid., pp. 338–39.

[9]George M. Foster, *Traditional Cultures and the Impact of Technological Change* (New York: Harper & Row, 1962), p. 26.

[10]John H. Bodley, *Victims of Progress*, 3rd ed. (Mountain View, CA: Mayfield, 1990), p. 7.

[11]Pertti J. Pelto and Ludger Müller-Wille, "Snowmobiles: Technological Revolution in the Arctic," in H. Russell Bernard and Pertti J. Pelto, eds., *Technology and Social Change*, 2nd ed. (Prospect Heights, IL, Waveland Press, 1987), pp. 207–43.

[12]Bodley, *Victims of Progress*, pp. 38–41.

[13]Theodora Kroeber, *Ishi in Two Worlds* (Berkeley: University of California Press, 1967), pp. 45–47.

[14]The historical information we refer to comes from a book by Allan Nevins, *The American States during and after the Revolution* (New York: Macmillan, 1927). We spell *American* (and *West Point*) backward to encourage the realization that the American Revolution was very much like modern liberation movements. For how radical the American Revolution was, see Gordon S. Wood, *The Radicalism of the American Revolution* (New York: Knopf, 1992).

[15]Crane Brinton, *The Anatomy of Revolution* (Englewood Cliffs, NJ: Prentice Hall, 1938).

[16]Jeffrey M. Paige, *Agrarian Revolution: Social Movements and Export Agriculture in the Underdeveloped World* (New York: Free Press, 1975).

[17]Robert Boyd and Peter J. Richerson, *Culture and the Evolutionary Process* (Chicago: University of Chicago Press, 1985), p. 106.

[18]Ibid., p. 135.

[19]Donald T. Campbell, "Variation and Selective Retention in Socio-Cultural Evolution," in Herbert Barringer, George Blankstein, and Raymond Mack, eds., *Social Change in Developing Areas: A Re-Interpretation of Evolutionary Theory* (Cambridge, MA: Schenkman, 1965), pp. 19–49. See also Boyd and Richerson, *Culture and the Evolutionary Process;* and William H. Durham, *Coevolution: Genes, Culture and Human Diversity* (Stanford, CA: Stanford University Press, 1991).

[20]William H. McNeill, *A World History* (New York: Oxford University Press, 1967), pp. 283–87.

[21]See, for example, Daniel R. Gross, George Eiten, Nancy M. Flowers, Francisca M. Leoi, Madeline Lattman Ritter, and Dennis W. Werner, "Ecology and Acculturation among Native Peoples of Central Brazil," *Science*, November 30, 1979, pp. 1043–50.

[22]The description of Tikopia is based on Raymond Firth, *Social Change in Tikopia* (New York: Macmillan, 1959), chapters 5, 6, 7, and 9, passim.

[23]Most of this discussion is based on Robert F. Murphy and Julian H. Steward, "Tappers and Trappers: Parallel Process in Acculturation," *Economic Development and Cultural Change*, 4 (July 1956): 335–55.

[24]S. Brian Burkhalter and Robert F. Murphy, "Tappers and Sappers: Rubber, Gold and Money among the Mundurucú," *American Ethnologist*, 16 (1989): 100–116.

[25]Eric Wolf, *Peasants* (Englewood Cliffs, NJ: Prentice Hall, 1966), pp. 3–4.

[26]E. J. Hobsbawm, *Age of Revolution* (New York: Praeger, 1970).

[27]Daniel R. Gross and Barbara A. Underwood, "Technological Change and Caloric Costs: Sisal Agriculture in Northeastern Brazil," *American Anthropologist*, 73 (1971): 725–40.

[28]Daniel O. Larson, John R. Johnson, and Joel C. Michaelsen, "Missionization among the Coastal Chumash of Central California: A Study of Risk Minimization Strategies," *American Anthropologist*, 96 (1994): 263–99.

[29]Discussion is based on Raymond Firth, *Rank and Religion in Tikopia* (Boston: Beacon Press, 1970).

[30]Ibid., p. 387.

[31]Ibid., p. 418.

[32]Phillip Mason, *Prospero's Magic* (London: Oxford University Press, 1962).

[33]Bruce Russett (with the collaboration of William Antholis, Carol R. Ember, Melvin Ember, and Zeev Maoz), *Grasping the Democratic Peace: Principles for a Post-Cold War World* (Princeton, NJ: Princeton University Press, 1993), pp. 10–11, 14, 138.

[34]H. Russell Bernard and Pertti J. Pelto, "Technology and Anthropological Theory: Conclusions," in Bernard and Pelto, eds., *Technology and Social Change*, p. 367.

[35]Pelto and Müller-Wille, "Snowmobiles," p. 237.

[36]Carol R. Ember and David Levinson, "The Substantive Contributions of Worldwide Cross-Cultural Studies Using Secondary Data," *Behavior Science Research*, special issue, "Cross-Cultural and Comparative Research: Theory and Method", 25 (1991): 79–140.

Applied Anthropology and Social Problems

The news on radio and television and in our newspapers makes us aware every day that social problems threaten people around the world. From war to crime and family violence, from AIDS to poverty and famine, the pursuit of happiness and even life itself are jeopardized for many people in many places.

Worldwide communication has increased our awareness of problems elsewhere, and we seem to be increasingly bothered by problems in our own society. For these two reasons, and perhaps also because we know more than we used to about human behavior, we may be more motivated now to try to solve those problems. We call them "social" problems not only because a lot of people worry about them but also because they have social causes or consequences, and their possible treatments or solutions require at least some changes in social behavior. For example, AIDS may be caused by a family of viruses, but it is also a social problem because it is mostly transmitted by sexual contact with another person and the only ways to avoid it now (abstinence, "safe" sex) require changes in social behavior. And it is a social problem also because millions of people are put at risk by the global epidemic.

Anthropology and most of the other social sciences have long been concerned with social problems. One way in which this concern is expressed is through "basic research" that tests theories about the possible causes of social problems. The results of such tests could suggest solutions to the problems if the causes, once discovered, can be reduced or eliminated. The other way to be concerned with social problems is to participate in programs intended to improve people's lives. In anthropology, this second way is referred to as **applied anthropology** or **practicing anthropology.** Applied or practicing anthropologists may be involved in one or more phases of a program: assembling relevant knowledge, constructing alternative plans, assessing the likely social and environmental impact of particular plans, implementing the program, and monitoring the program and its effects.[1]

Clearly, theory testing and applied research may both be motivated by a desire to improve the quality of human life. But it is often difficult to decide if a particular project is basic or applied. For example, consider a study of the possible causes of war; its results may suggest how the risk of war might be reduced. Is such a study basic or applied research?

This chapter has two major parts. The first deals with applied or practicing anthropology. We discuss the history and types of application in the United States, the ethical issues involved in trying to improve people's lives, the difficulties in evaluating whether a program is beneficial, and problems in instituting planned change. In the second part of the chapter we turn to the study of global social problems and how understanding the possible causes of these problems may suggest possible solutions. We focus on research done by anthropologists and comparativists from other disciplines that may help us better understand the spread of AIDS, disasters, homelessness, crime, family violence, and war.

APPLIED AND PRACTICING ANTHROPOLOGY

Anthropologists care and worry about the people they study, just as they care and worry about family and friends back home. It is upsetting if most of the families in your place of fieldwork have lost many of their babies to diseases that could be eliminated by medical care. It is upsetting when outside political and economic interests threaten to deprive your fieldwork friends of their resources and pride. Anthropologists have usually studied people who are disadvantaged—by imperialism, colonialism, and other forms of exploitation. And so it is no wonder that we feel protective about these people, whom we have lived and shared with in the field.

But caring is not enough to improve others' lives. We may need basic research that allows us to understand how a condition might be successfully treated. A particular proposed "improvement" might actually not be an improvement; well-meaning efforts have sometimes produced harmful consequences. And even if we know that a change would be an improvement, there is still the problem of how to make it happen. The people to be affected may not want to change. Is it ethical to try to persuade them? And conversely, is it ethical not to try? Applied anthropologists must take all of these matters into consideration in determining whether and how to act in response to a perceived need.

Applied anthropology in the United States developed out of anthropologists' personal experiences with disadvantaged people in other cultures.[2] But today anthropologists are also interested in studying and solving problems in our own society. Anthropologists who call themselves applied or practicing anthropologists are usually employed in nonacademic settings, working for government and international agencies and sometimes even for corporations (see the box titled "Anthropology and Business"). Today there are more anthropologists

ANTHROPOLOGY AND BUSINESS

Applied anthropologist Jill Kleinberg and clients

Chemistry, biology, and psychology are just some of the scientific fields from which businesses have routinely hired substantial numbers of researchers. But it is only relatively recently that business people have come to realize that anthropologists have useful knowledge to contribute, particularly with the globalization of trade, the increase in international investments and joint ventures, and the spread of multinational corporations.

What can anthropology offer? One of the most important contributions of anthropology is understanding how much culture can influence relationships between people of different cultures. For example, anthropologists know that communication is much more than the formal understanding of another language. In the chapter on communication and language, we discussed the "ethnography of speaking," which investigates the social contexts of speech as well as nonverbal communication. Knowledge of the cultural patterns accompanying communication is extremely important for business. People in some countries, such as the United States, expect explicit, straightforward verbal messages. But people in other countries are more indirect in their verbal messages. In Japan and China, for example, negative messages are less likely than messages expressing politeness and harmony. Many Eastern cultures have ways of saying no without saying the word. Still other countries, particularly Arab countries, tend to be very elaborate in their speech, using long strings of adjectives and repeated pronouns to dramaticize messages.

It is often important to understand the nonverbal cues used in the other culture. How close should you stand when you talk to someone? Should you avoid looking at someone else's eyes? When and where and how to touch are very culture-specific. Some cultures touch a lot, others consider touching to be insulting. And where you touch is very important! In the United States, if a male takes another male's hand when walking side by side, it is considered a homosexual gesture, but in Kenya and other places it has no such implication; it is simply an expression of friendship.

It is also important to understand that different cultures may have different values. People in the United States place a high value on the individual, but as we discussed in the chapter on psychology and culture, the importance of relationships with others may take precedence over individual needs in other places. People in the United States emphasize the future, youth, informality, and competitiveness, but in other places the emphases are often the opposite. In any business arrangement, perhaps no difference is as salient as the value a culture places on time. As we say, "Time is money." If a meeting is arranged and the other person is late, say forty-five minutes late, people from the United States consider it rude; but such a delay is well within the range of acceptable behavior in many South American countries.

Anthropologists have helped businesses become aware of their own "cultures" (sometimes referred to as *organizational cultures*). The organizational culture of a business may interfere with the acceptance of new kinds of workers, or it may interfere with changing business needs. If parts of that culture need to be changed, it is necessary first to identify what the culture involves and to understand how and why it developed the way it did. Anthropologists know how to identify cultural patterns on the basis of systematic observation and interviewing of individuals.

Jill Kleinberg provided an example of trying to understand organizational culture. She studied six Japanese-owned firms in the United States to understand the impact of both the larger culture and the organizational culture of the workplace. All six firms employed both Japanese and Americans, although the Japanese dominated the managerial positions. The main goal of the study was to discover why there was considerable tension in all the firms.

Before she could make recommendations about how to reduce the tension, Kleinberg had to figure out what was wrong. Her first order of business was to interview people about their views of work and their jobs. She found clear differences between the Japanese and the American employees that seemed to reflect broader cultural differences. Americans wanted a clear definition of the job and its attached responsibilities, and they also wanted their job titles, authority, rights, and pay to match closely. The Japanese, on the other hand, emphasized the need to be flexible in their responsibilities as well as their tasks. They also felt that part of their responsibility was to help their co-workers. (See the box titled "Do Schools Teach Values", in the chapter on psychology and culture, in which we discussed Japanese preschools and their emphasis on the good of the group.) Americans were uncomfortable in these firms because the Japanese managers did not indicate exactly what the workers were supposed to do; even if there was a job description, the manager did not appear to pay attention to it. Americans were given little information, were left out of decision making, and were frustrated by the lack of opportunity to advance. The Japanese thought that the Americans were too hard to manage, too concerned with money and authority, and too concerned with their own interests.

Dissatisfaction is a problem in any business. Absenteeism, high turnover, and lack of incentive on the job all detract from job performance and business capability. Kleinberg recommended giving all employees more information about the company as well as conducting training sessions about cross-cultural differences in business cultures. She also recommended making the Japanese philosophy of management more explicit during the hiring process so that the company would be able to find Americans who were more comfortable with that philosophy. But she also suggested that the managerial structure be somewhat "Americanized" so that American employees could be more comfortable. Finally, she recommended that Americans be given more managerial positions and contact with their Japanese counterparts overseas. These suggestions might not eliminate all problems, but they would increase mutual understanding and trust.

In a way, then, as Andrew Miracle noted, the work of the practicing anthropologist is similar to the shaman's in traditional societies. Shamans feel called to their roles as forecasters and healers, but their skills are not automatic—shamanistic work usually requires practice and the acquisition of many practical skills, often as an apprentice. The people who call on shamans for help believe in their abilities to help, and the shaman tries to find ways to empower the client to think positively. To be sure, there are

cont.

ANTHROPOLOGY AND BUSINESS, *cont.*

profound differences between a shaman and an applied anthropologist. Perhaps the most important is that the applied anthropologist uses research, not trance or magic, to effect an organizational cure. Like a shaman, however, the applied an-

thropologist must make an understandable diagnosis and help the client see the way to health and restored power.

Sources: *Gary P. Ferraro,* The Cultural Dimension of International Business, *2nd ed. (Englewood Cliffs, NJ: Prentice Hall, 1994); Jill Kleinberg, "Practical Implications of Organiza-*

tional Culture Where Americans and Japanese Work Together," in Ann T. Jordan, ed., Practicing Anthropology in Corporate America: Consulting on Organizational Culture, *NAPA Bulletin, No. 14 (Arlington, VA: American Anthropological Association, 1994); Andrew W. Miracle, "A Shaman to Organizations," in Carol R. Ember, Melvin Ember, and Peter N. Peregrine, eds.,* Research Frontiers in Anthropology *(Englewood Cliffs, NJ: Prentice Hall, 1994). Prentice Hall/Simon & Schuster Custom Publishing.*

working in nonacademic than in academic settings.[3] These practicing anthropologists often work on specific projects that aim to improve people's lives in particular places, usually by trying to change behavior or the environment; or the anthropologists monitor or evaluate efforts by others to bring about change.[4] Usually the problems and projects are defined by the employers or clients (the client is sometimes the "target" population), not by the anthropologists who may be employed.[5] But anthropologists are increasingly called upon to participate in deciding exactly what improvements might be possible, as well as how to achieve them.

History and Types of Application

Until World War II, almost all anthropologists in the United States were employed in colleges, universities, and museums, and applied anthropology was practically nonexistent. In 1934, John Collier, the head of the Bureau of Indian Affairs, opened the way toward more widespread recognition of the useful roles anthropologists could play outside academic settings when he got legislation passed that provided protections for Native Americans: land could no longer be taken away, lost land was supposed to be restored, tribal governments would be formed, and loans would be made available to reservations. Collier employed some anthropologists to aid in carrying out these policies. At about the same time, the Soil Conservation Service hired anthropologists to help with projects related to Native American land use.[6]

Events in the 1940s further boosted applied anthropology. In 1941, anthropologists founded the Society for Applied Anthropology and a new journal devoted to applied anthropology (it is now called *Human Organization*).[7] During World War II, anthropologists were hired in unprecedented numbers by the U.S. government to help in the war effort. Margaret Mead estimated that something like 295 of the 303 anthropologists in the United States at the time were in one way or another direct participants in the war effort.[8]

The government hired anthropologists to help improve morale, to increase our understanding of enemies and allies, and to prepare for military campaigns and occupation of the islands of Micronesia and other areas in and around the Pacific.[9] For example, applied anthropologists were called on for advice when perplexed U.S. military officials wanted to understand why their Japanese enemies refused to behave like "normal" people. One of the practices that most distressed military leaders was the tendency of Japanese soldiers to try to kill themselves rather than be taken prisoner. Certainly, U.S. prisoners of war did not behave in this manner. Eventually, in order to understand the Japanese code of honor, the military hired anthropologists as consultants to the Foreign Morale Analysis Division of the War Office's Information Department.

After working with the anthropologists, the U.S. military learned that a major reason for the "strange" behavior of the Japanese prisoners was their belief that to surrender in a wartime situation, even in the face of greatly superior odds, or to be taken prisoner, even when injured and unconscious and therefore unable to avoid capture, was a disgrace. The Japanese believed further that the U.S. soldiers killed all prisoners. Thus, it is hardly surprising that so many captured Japanese soldiers preferred honorable death by their own hand. Once the U.S. military learned what the Japanese thought, they made efforts to explain to them that they would not be executed if captured, with the result that far more Japanese surrendered. Some prisoners even gave military information to the Americans—not to act against their own country, but rather to try and establish new lives for themselves, since the disgrace of being captured prevented them from resuming their former lives.[10]

Anthropologists were enthusiastic about helping the government during World War II because they were overwhelmingly committed to winning the war. The government, in its turn, seemed eager for anthropological advice. But in the postwar period there was an enormous increase in higher education as returning veterans and later baby boomers went to college, and U.S. anthropologists retreated from working with the government as academic opportunities opened up. At the same time anthropology became less concerned with applied problems and more concerned with theory and basic research.

The situation changed again, from the late 1970s on, as employment opportunities declined in colleges and universities. Today, a large and increasing number of anthropologists are finding employment outside of anthropology departments[11]—in medical schools, health centers, development agencies, urban planning agencies, and other public and private organizations that seek to change people's lives, in this society and others. Anthropologists who work in applied fields come out of a variety of subdisciplines. A major type of applied work is the "social impact" study required in connection with many programs funded by government or private agencies. Most people who do this work were trained in ethnology. But there are also applied anthropologists trained in physical anthropology; quite a few work in the area of medicine and public health. Archaeologists are hired to study, record, and preserve "cultural resources" that will be disturbed or destroyed by construction projects. And applied work in education often utilizes the skills of linguists.[12]

Ethics of Applied Anthropology

There are always ethical issues that arise in the course of fieldwork, and anthropology as a profession has adopted certain principles of responsibility. Above all, an anthropologist's first responsibility is to those who are being studied—everything should be done to ensure that their welfare and dignity will be protected. Anthropologists also have a responsibility to those who will read about their research; research findings should be reported openly and truthfully.[13] But because applied anthropology often deals with planning and implementing changes in some target population, ethical responsibilities can become complicated. Perhaps the most important ethical question is this: Will the change truly benefit the target population?

In May 1946, the Society for Applied Anthropology established a committee to draw up a specific code of ethics for persons who work professionally as applied anthropologists. After many meetings and revisions, the society finally adopted a statement on ethical responsibilities in 1948. In 1983 the statement was revised again.[14] According to the code, the target community should be included as much as possible in the formulation of policy, so that people in the community may know in advance how the program may affect them. But perhaps the most important aspect of the code is the pledge not to recommend or take any action that is harmful to the interests of the community. The National Association of Practicing Anthropologists goes further: If the work the employer expects of the employee violates the ethical principles of the profession, the practicing anthropologist has the obligation to try to change those practices or, if change cannot be brought about, to withdraw from the work.[15]

Difficulties in Evaluating the Effects of Planned Change

The decision as to whether a proposed change would benefit the target population is not always easy to make. In certain cases, as when improved medical care is involved, the benefits offered to the target group would seem to be unquestionable—we all feel sure that health is better than illness. But even this may not always be true. Consider a public-health innovation such as inoculation against disease. Although it would undoubtedly have a beneficial effect on the survival rate of a population, a reduction in the mortality rate might have unforeseen consequences that would in turn produce new problems. Once the inoculation program was begun, the number of children surviving would probably increase. But it might not be possible to increase the rate of food production, given the level of technology, capital, and land resources possessed by the target population. Thus, the death rate, because of starvation, might rise to its previous level

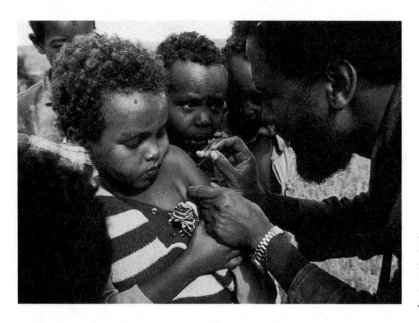

A medical worker in rural Ethiopia vaccinates children. Medical care without a subsequent reduction in births can have harmful consequences because of growing population.

and perhaps even exceed it. The inoculation program would not affect the death rate; it might merely change the causes of death. This example shows that even if a program of planned change has beneficial consequences in the short run, a great deal of thought and investigation have to be given to its long-term effects.

One of the most important, and most difficult, problems for applied anthropology is the need to anticipate all the effects that are likely to result from the single change that is proposed. A good example of the unforeseen consequences of disease control comes from the island of Mauritius in the Indian Ocean. It was quite evident there that government efforts to control malaria after World War II had led to a disastrous population explosion: the population nearly doubled, unemployment rose, and the cost of government services became astronomical. In short, Mauritius had outstripped its ability to support itself. All these events were apparently triggered by DDT spraying in 1948, which eradicated the malaria-bearing mosquitoes. In one year, the death rate fell by 32 percent and the annual rate of increase in the population changed from less than half of 1 percent to 3 percent.[16]

A population's health can actually be harmed then when foreign health care is introduced without provision for related customs. Another example can be seen in a program attempted in a rural West African community. In that community, the women traditionally continued to work in the fields during pregnancy. In an attempt to improve prenatal care, program designers decided that pregnant women should be kept from their work. However, because the people who effected this change neglected to encourage the West African women to adopt a substitute program of proper physical activity, the women actually suffered *increased* chances of ill health and infant mortality.[17]

So, even if the short-term effects of planned changes are beneficial, the long-term effects may not be. Debra Picchi raised questions about the long-term effects on the Bakairi Indians of a program by the National Brazilian Indian Foundation (FUNAI) to produce rice with machine technology.[18] The Bakairi of the Mato Grosso region largely practice slash-and-burn horticulture in gallery forests along rivers, with supplementary cattle raising, fishing, and hunting. In the early part of the twentieth century their population had declined to 150 people and they were given a relatively small reserve. Some of it was gallery forest, but a larger part was parched and infertile *(cerrado)*. When the Bakairi population began to increase, FUNAI introduced a scheme to plant rice on formerly unused *cerrado* land, using machinery, insecticides, and fertilizer. FUNAI paid the costs for the first year and expected that by the third year the scheme would be self-supporting. The project did not go so well because FUNAI did not deliver all the equipment needed and did not provide adequate advice. So only half the expected rice was produced. Still, it was more food than the Bakairi had previously, so the program should have been beneficial to them.

But there were negative side effects, not anticipated. Nutritionally, to be sure, the Bakairi are growing an additional starchy food. But use of the *cerrado* for agriculture reduces the area on which cattle can be grazed; cattle are an important source of high-quality protein. So the now-mechanized agriculture has reduced the availability of animal protein. The mechanization also makes the Bakairi more dependent on cash for fuel, insecticides, fertilizer, and repairs. But cash is hard to come by. Only some individuals can be hired—usually men with outside experience who have the required knowledge of machinery. So the cash earned in the new mechanized agriculture goes mainly to a relatively small number of people. It is debatable whether the new inequalities of income provide long-term effects that are beneficial to the Bakairi.

Thayer Scudder described the situation of Gwembe Tonga villagers who were relocated after a large dam was built in the Zambezi valley of central Africa. Economic conditions improved during the 1960s and early 1970s, as the people increasingly produced goods and services for sale. But then conditions deteriorated. By 1980 the villagers were in a miserable state: rates of mortality, alcohol drinking, theft, assault, and murder were all up. Why? One reason was that they had cut back on producing their own food in favor of producing for world markets. Such a strategy works well when world market prices are high; however, when prices fall, so does the standard of living.[19]

The situation described by Scudder illustrates the ethical dilemma for many applied anthropologists. As he said: "So how is it that I can still justify working for the agencies that fund such projects?" He pointed out that large-scale projects are almost impossible to stop. The anthropologist can choose to stand on the sidelines and complain or try to influence the project to benefit the target population as much as possible.[20]

The Difficulties of Instituting Planned Change

Before an attempt can be made at cultural innovation, the innovators must determine whether the target population is aware of the benefits of the proposed change. Lack of awareness can be a temporary barrier to solving the problems at hand. For example, health workers have often had difficulty convincing people that they were becoming ill because something was wrong with their water supply. Many people do not believe that disease can be transmitted through an agent such as water. At other times, the target population is perfectly aware of the problem. A case in point is that of certain Taiwanese women who were introduced to family-planning methods beginning in the 1960s. The women knew they were having more children than they wanted or could easily afford, and they wanted to control their birth rate. They offered no resistance—they merely had to be given the proper devices and instructions and the birth rate fell quite quickly to a more desirable, and more manageable, level.[21]

Resistance by the Target Population. Not all proposed change programs are beneficial to the target population. Therefore resistance to innovation may be perfectly rational. In at least some known cases, the judgment of the target population has been better than that of the agents of change. One such example occurred during a Venezuelan government-sponsored program to give infants powdered milk. The mothers rejected the milk, even though it was free, on the grounds that it implied that the mothers' milk was no good.[22] But who is to say that the resistance was not in fact intuitively smart, reflecting an awareness that such a milk program would not bene-

Breast-feeding is now known to be better for the health of a baby. In many countries, breast-feeding even in public is perfectably acceptable, as among the Huastec of Mexico. In the United States, the embarrassment of breast-feeding in public may discourage a switch to breast-feeding.

EXPLORING WHY AN APPLIED PROJECT DIDN'T WORK

When applied projects do not succeed, it is important for researchers to try to figure why. Part of the problem may be that the intended recipients' ideas about how things work may be very different from the researchers' ideas. Consider the following example. In Guatemala, village health-care workers were not only testing people for malaria but they were also offering free antimalarial drugs. Yet, surprisingly, a community survey found that only 20 percent of people with malaria symptoms took advantage of the free treatment. More surprisingly, most people with symptoms spent the equivalent of a day's wages to buy an injection that was not strong enough to be effective! Why? What was going on?

Finding the answer was not easy. First, researchers designed interviews to elicit folk concepts about illness. What kinds of illnesses are there? What are their causes? What are their symptoms, and how are different illnesses to be treated? They conducted interviews with a random sample of households to check on what illnesses people had and what they did about them. Then they asked people to consider different hypothetical scenarios ("vignettes"), with different types of people and different degrees of severity of illness, to find out what treatment they would choose. All of these methods were well thought out, but the answers still did not predict what people actually did when they thought they had malaria. (The vignettes were not helpful because they were too abstract.) Finally, the researchers devised precise comparisons of the kinds of pills passed out by health-care workers and the pills and ampules (for injections) sold by the drugstore. They compared them two at a time, varying dosages and brands. People did think that more pills were more effective, as indeed they were. But they thought that the colorfully wrapped store-bought pill was more effective than the equivalent white unwrapped free pill, even though it was not. They also thought that one store-bought ampule used for injections (for which they would pay a day's wages) was more effective than four pills of any kind! But, in fact, one ampule was equivalent to only one pill.

Applied researchers often use such trial-and-error methods to find out how to get the information they need. Methods that work in one field setting don't al-

---

fit the children? Medical research suggests that mother's milk is far superior to powdered milk or formula. First, human milk best supplies the nutrients needed for human development. Second, it is now known that the mother, through her milk, is able to transmit antibodies (disease resistances) to the baby. And third, nursing delays ovulation and will usually increase the spacing between births.[23]

Not only is mother's milk now known to have so many advantages, but the switchover to powdered milk and formula in many underdeveloped areas has been nothing short of a disaster: the result has been increased malnutrition and misery. For one thing, powdered milk must be mixed with water, but if the water and the bottles are not sterilized, more sickness is introduced. Then too, if powdered milk has to be purchased, mothers without cash are forced to dilute the milk to stretch it. And if a mother feeds her baby formula or powder for even a short time, the process is tragically irreversible, for her own milk dries up and she cannot return to breast-feeding even if she wants to.

As the Venezuelan example suggests, individuals may be able to resist proposed medical or health projects because acceptance is ultimately a personal matter. Large development projects planned by powerful governments or agencies rarely are stoppable, but even they can be resisted successfully. For example, the Kayapo of the Xingu River region of Brazil were recently able to cancel a plan by the Brazilian government to build dams along the river for hydroelectric power. The Kayapo ways work in others. To get the information needed, researchers must sometimes let the subjects structure their own answers. At other times, as in this case, they may have to make very specific comparisons to get predictive answers. The people in the Guatemala study didn't believe that the free pills were strong enough to work, so they didn't use them. More research would be needed to uncover why they did not believe the free pills were effective. Was it because they were free? Was it because the store-bought drugs were more nicely packaged? Or was there a belief that injections work better than pills? That's what a research process is like; it always leads to new questions, particularly more general questions requiring more extensive or more comparative research.

For example, the Guatemala project revealed why a particular program was not successful in a particular area. But how widespread are the interfering beliefs? Are they found throughout Guatemala? Do they interfere with the introduction of other medicines? Are we dealing with problems that exist in other areas of Central and South America? Although we don't yet have answers to these more extensive questions, anthropologists have developed efficient methods for assessing variation in beliefs within and between cultures.

We now know that if we ask one or two informants, we cannot assume that the answer is cultural, but that doesn't mean that we need to ask hundreds of people. If a belief is cultural and therefore commonly held, ten to twenty individuals asked the same question are quite sufficient to provide the researcher with a high probability that an answer is correct. (The agreement among respondents is called *cultural consensus*.) So, for example, Guatemalan respondents were in high agreement about which illnesses were contagious. But they disagreed a lot about whether a particular disease should be treated with a "hot" or a "cold" remedy. Using cultural-consensus methods, researchers can compare rural and urban residents, and they can also compare informants in different cultures. When we have more of these systematic comparisons, medical anthropologists and health practitioners may have a better understanding of how to implement medical care.

Sources: *Susan C. Weller, "The Research Process," in Carol R. Ember, Melvin Ember, and Peter N. Peregrine, eds.,* Research Frontiers in Anthropology *(Englewood Cliffs, NJ: Prentice Hall, 1995). Prentice Hall/Simon & Schuster Custom Publishing, and the research referred to therein. A. Kimball Romney, Susan C. Weller, and William H. Batchelder, "Culture as Consensus: A Theory of Culture and Informant Accuracy,"* American Anthropologist, 88 *(1986): 313–38.*

gained international attention when some of their leaders appeared on North American and European television and then successfully organized a protest in 1989 by members of several tribal groups. Their success seemed to come in part from their ability to present themselves to the international community as guardians of the rain forest—an image that resonated with international environmental organizations that supported their cause. Although it might seem to outsiders that the Kayapo want their way of life to remain as it was, the Kayapo are not opposed to all change. In fact, they want greater access to medical care, other government services, and manufactured goods from outside.[24]

But even if a project *is* beneficial to the target population, it may still meet with resistance. Factors that may hinder acceptance can be divided roughly into three categories: *cultural* barriers, *social* barriers, and *psychological* barriers. (These categories may sometimes overlap.)

Cultural barriers are shared behaviors, attitudes, and beliefs that tend to impede the acceptance of an innovation. For example, members of different societies may view gift giving in different ways. Particularly in commercialized societies, things received for nothing are often believed to be worthless. When the government of Colombia instituted a program of giving seedling orchard trees to farmers in order to increase fruit production, the farmers showed virtually no interest in the seedlings, many of which proceeded to die of neglect. When the government realized that the experiment had apparently failed, it began to charge each farmer a nominal fee for the seedlings. Soon the seedlings became immensely popular and fruit production increased.[25] The farmers' demand for the seedlings may have increased because they were charged a fee and therefore came to value the trees. The market demand for fruit may also have increased. Other examples of cultural resistance to change, which we discuss more fully later in this chapter, are beliefs about sex that make it difficult for people to follow medical guidelines for safer sex.

It is very important for agents of change to understand what the shared beliefs and attitudes are. First, indigenous cultural concepts or knowledge can sometimes be used effectively to enhance educational programs. For instance, in a program in Haiti to try to prevent child mortality from diarrhea, change agents used the terminology for traditional native herbal tea remedies (*rafrechi,* or cool refreshment) to identify the new oral rehydration therapy, which is a very successful medical treatment. In native belief diarrhea is a "hot" illness and appropriate remedies have to have cooling properties.[26] Second, even if indigenous beliefs are not helpful to the campaign, not paying attention to contrary beliefs can undermine the campaign. But uncovering contrary beliefs is not easy, particularly when they do not emerge in ordinary conversation (see the box titled "Exploring Why an Applied Project Didn't Work").

The acceptance of planned change may also depend on social factors. Research suggests that acceptance is more likely if the change agent and the target or potential adopter are similar socially. But change agents may have higher social status and more education than the people they are trying to influence. So change agents may work more with higher-status individuals because they are more likely to accept new ideas. If lower-status individuals also have to be reached, change agents of lower status may have to be employed.[27]

Finally, acceptance may depend on psychological factors—that is, how the individuals perceive both the innovation and the agents of change. In the course of trying to encourage women in the southeastern part of the United States to breast-feed rather than bottle-feed their infants, researchers discovered a number of reasons why women were reluctant to breast-feed their infants even though they heard it was healthier. Many women did not have confidence that they would produce enough milk for their babies, they were embarrassed about breast-feeding in public, and their family and friends had negative attitudes.[28] In designing an ed-

ucational program, change agents may have to directly address such psychological concerns.

Discovering and Utilizing Local Channels of Influence. In planning a project involving cultural change, the administrator of the project should find out what the normal channels of influence are in the target population. In most communities, there are preestablished networks for communication, as well as persons of high prestige or influence who are looked to for guidance and direction. An understanding of such channels of influence is extremely valuable when one is deciding how to introduce a program of change into an area. In addition, it is useful to know at what times, and in what sorts of situations, one channel is likely to be more effective in spreading information and approval than another.

An example of the effective use of local channels of influence occurred when an epidemic of smallpox broke out in the Kalahandi district of the state of Orissa in India. The efforts of health workers to vaccinate villagers against the disease were consistently resisted. The villagers, naturally suspicious and fearful of these strange men with their equally strange medical equipment, were unwilling to offer themselves, and particularly their babies, to the peculiar experiments the strangers wished to perform. Afraid of the epidemic, the villagers appealed for help to their local priest, whose opinions on such matters they trusted. The priest went into a trance, explaining that the illness was the result of the goddess Thalerani's anger with the people. She could be appeased, he continued, only by massive feasts, offerings, and other demonstrations of the villagers' worship of her. Realizing that the priest was the village's major opinion leader, at least in medical matters, the frustrated health workers tried to get the priest to convince his people to undergo vaccination. At first, the priest refused to cooperate with the strange men, but when his favorite nephew fell ill, he decided to try any means available to cure the boy. He thereupon went into another trance, telling the villagers that the goddess wished all her worshipers to be vaccinated. Fortunately, the people agreed and the epidemic was largely controlled.[29]

If channels of influence are not stable, using influential persons in a campaign can sometimes backfire. In the educational campaign in Haiti to promote the use of oral rehydration therapy, which we referred to above, Mme. Duvalier, the first lady of Haiti at the time, lent her name to the project. Because there were no serious social or cultural barriers to the treatment and mothers reported that children took to the solutions well, success was expected. But in the middle of the campaign Haiti was embroiled in political turmoil and the first lady's husband was overthrown. Some of the public thought that the oral rehydration project was a plot by the Duvaliers to sterilize children, and this suspicion fueled resistance to the oral rehydration program.[30]

Applied anthropologists often advocate integrating indigenous healers into medical change programs. This idea may encounter considerable resistance by the medical profession and by government officials who view such healers negatively. But this strategy may be quite effective where indigenous healers are the only sources of health care in more isolated areas. If they are involved in medical change programs, indigenous healers are likely to refer patients to hospitals when they feel unable to cope with an illness, and the hospitals choose sometimes to refer patients to the healers.[31]

Other social groups and their attitudes can play important roles in shaping the outcome of the change program. Most often the people who are being helped have few privileges, little political and economic power, and low prestige.[32] Change or development is often regarded as a threat to those with more privilege. If those who do have power object to the new program, they may effectively sabotage it. The development agent, then, not only has to reckon with the local community but may also have to persuade more powerful groups in the society that the new program should be introduced.

GLOBAL SOCIAL PROBLEMS: BASIC RESEARCH AND POSSIBLE SOLUTIONS

Some anthropologists as well as other social scientists think that it is time to attack the major social problems that afflict our world. The idea that we can solve social problems is based on two assumptions. We have to assume that it is possible to discover the causes of a problem. And we have to assume that we may be able to do something about the causes (once they are discovered) and thereby eliminate or reduce the problem.

Not everyone would agree with these assumptions. Some would say that our understanding of a social problem cannot ever be sufficient to suggest a solution guaranteed to work. To be sure, no understanding in science is perfect or certain; there is always some probability that even a well-supported explanation is wrong or incomplete. But the uncertainty of knowledge does not rule out the possibility

of application. With regard to social problems, the possible payoff from even incomplete understanding could be a better and safer world. This possibility is what motivates many researchers who investigate social problems. After all, the history of the various sciences strongly supports the belief that scientific understanding can often allow humans to control nature, not just predict and explain it. Why should human behavior be any different?

So what do we know about some of the global social problems, and what policies or solutions are suggested by what we know?

AIDS

Epidemics of disease have killed millions of people within short periods of time throughout recorded history. The Black Death (bubonic plague) killed between 25 and 50 percent of the population of Europe, perhaps 75 million people, during the fourteenth century; an epidemic during the sixth century killed an estimated 100 million people in the Middle East, Asia, and Europe. Less noted in our history books, but also devastating, was the enormous depopulation that accompanied the expansion of Europeans into the New World and the Pacific from the 1500s on. Not only were people killed directly by European conquerors; millions also died from introduced diseases to which the natives had little or no resistance, diseases such as smallpox and measles that the Europeans brought with them but were no longer dying from.

The current state of medical science and technology may lull us into thinking that epidemics are a thing of the past. But the recent and sudden emergence of the disease we call **AIDS (acquired immune deficiency syndrome)** reminds us that new diseases, or new varieties of old diseases, can appear at any time. Like all other organisms, disease-causing organisms also evolve. The human immunodeficiency viruses (HIV) that presumably cause AIDS emerged only recently. Viruses (and bacteria) are always mutating, and new strains emerge that are initially a plague on our genetic resistance and on medical efforts to contain them.

Millions of people all around the world already have the symptoms of AIDS, and millions more are infected with HIV but do not know they are infected. By the year 2000, according to World Health Organization estimates, about 40 million adults and children will be infected and 15 million people will have AIDS.[33] Many millions will have died of AIDS by then. AIDS is a frightening epidemic not only because of its likely toll. It is also frightening because it

Discrimination against people with AIDS will not alleviate the epidemic.

takes a long time (average four years) after exposure for symptoms to appear. This means that many people who have been infected by HIV, but do not know they are infected, may continue unknowingly to transmit the viruses to others.[34]

Transmission occurs mostly via sexual encounters, through semen and blood. Drug users may also transmit the HIV by way of contaminated needles. Transmission by blood transfusion has been virtually eliminated in this and other societies by medical screening of blood supplies. In many countries, however, there is still no routine screening of blood prior to transfusions.

Many people think of AIDS as only a medical problem that requires only a medical solution, without realizing that there are behavioral and cultural issues that need to be addressed as well. It is true that developing a vaccine (or a drug) to prevent people from getting AIDS, and developing a "cure" for those who have it, will finally solve the problem of AIDS. But, for a variety of reasons, we can expect that the medical solution alone will not be sufficient, at least not for a while. First, to be effective worldwide, or even within a country, a vaccine has to be inexpensive and relatively easy to produce in large quantities; the same is true of any medical treatment for victims. Second, governments around the world have to be willing and able to spend the money and hire the personnel necessary to manage an effective program.[35] Third, future vaccination and treatment will require the people at risk to be willing to get vaccinated and treated, which is not always easy to arrange. Witness the fact that measles is becoming

more frequent in the United States because many people are not having their children vaccinated.

We do not know yet if an effective and inexpensive vaccine (or treatment) will be developed soon. In the meantime, the risk of HIV infection can be reduced only by changes in social (particularly sexual) behavior. But to persuade people to change their sexual behavior, it is necessary to find out exactly what they do sexually, and why they prefer what they do. The reasons for preferring some activity may make it difficult to change.

Research so far suggests that different sexual patterns are responsible for HIV transmission in different parts of the world. In the United States, England, northern Europe, Australia, and Latin America, the recipients of anal intercourse (particularly men) are the most likely individuals to acquire the HIV infection; vaginal intercourse can also transmit the infection (usually from the man to the woman). In Africa, however, the most common mode of transmission is vaginal intercourse, and so women get infected more commonly in Africa than elsewhere.[36] Is it reasonable to expect that people can generally be persuaded to stop doing what they prefer to do?

As of now, there are only two known ways to reduce the likelihood of sexual HIV transmission. One way is to abstain from sexual intercourse; the other is to use condoms. Educational programs that teach how AIDS spreads, and what you can do about it, may reduce the spread somewhat. But such programs may fail where people have incompatible beliefs and attitudes about sexuality. For example, people in some central African societies believe that deposits of semen *after* conception are necessary for a successful pregnancy and generally enhance a woman's health and ability to reproduce. It might be expected then that people who have these beliefs about semen would choose not to use condoms; after all, condoms in their view are a threat to public health.[37] Educational programs may also emphasize the wrong message. Promiscuity may increase the risk of HIV transmission, so hardly anyone would question the wisdom of advertising to reduce the number of sexual partners. And, at least in the homosexual community in the United States, individuals report fewer sexual partners than in the past. What was not anticipated, however, was that individuals in monogamous relationships, who may feel safe, are *less* likely to use condoms or to avoid the riskiest sexual practices. Needless to say, sex with a regular partner who is infected is not safe![38]

The stigma associated with AIDS also hinders efforts to reduce its spread. Possible victims may be unwilling to find out if they have been infected: the stigma, in this and some other societies, is that homosexual men are particularly likely to get infected.[39] Of course, not everyone who gets infected has engaged in homosexual behavior. Indeed, the majority of people now infected with AIDS in the world are heterosexual.[40] But the association with homosexuality, and the prejudice against homosexuals, may contribute to the spread of AIDS: some of those infected will continue to transmit the infection because they are afraid to find out that they might be infected. Much of the stigma associated with AIDS derives also from people's misinformation about exactly how AIDS is transmitted; indeed, many people fear any kind of contact with AIDS victims, as if any kind of contact could result in infection. Fear that they will be shunned if they are known to have AIDS may also contribute to some persons' unwillingness to be tested.

To solve the problem of AIDS, we may hope that medical science will develop an effective vaccination and a treatment that can be afforded by all. In the meantime, we can try to understand why people engage in certain risky sexual practices. Such understanding may allow us to design educational and other programs that would more successfully inhibit the spread of AIDS.

Disasters

Disasters such as floods, droughts, earthquakes, and insect infestations are usually but not always beyond human control, but their effects are not.[41] Consider that between 1960 and 1980, forty-three disasters in Japan killed an average of sixty-three people per disaster. During the same period, seventeen disasters in Nicaragua killed an average of 6,235 people per disaster. In the United States, between 1960 and 1976, the average disaster killed just one person, injured a dozen, and destroyed fewer than five buildings. These comparative figures demonstrate that climatic and other events in the physical environment become *disasters* because of events or conditions in the social environment.

If people live in houses that are designed to withstand earthquakes—if governing bodies require such construction and the economy is developed enough so that people can afford such construction —the effects of an earthquake will be minimized. If poor people are forced to live in deforested flood plains in order to be able to find land to farm (as in coastal Bangladesh), if the poor (like those of Rio de Janeiro) are forced to live in shanties built on precarious hillsides, the floods and landslides that follow severe hurricanes and rainstorms can kill thousands and even hundreds of thousands.

Thus, disasters can have greater or lesser effects on human life, depending on social conditions. And therefore disasters are also social problems, problems that have social causes and possible social solutions. Legislating safe construction of a house is a social solution. The 1976 earthquake in Tangsham, China, killed 250,000 people, mostly because they lived in top-heavy adobe houses that could not stand severe shaking, whereas the 1989 earthquake in Loma Prieta, California, which was of comparable intensity, killed only sixty-five people.

One might think that floods, of all disasters, are the least influenced by social factors. After all, without a huge runoff from heavy rains or snow melt, there cannot be a flood. But consider why so many people have died from Yellow River floods in China. (One such flood, in 1931, killed nearly 4 million people, making it the deadliest single disaster in history.) The floods in the Yellow River basin have occurred mostly because the clearing of forests nearby (for fuel and farm land) has allowed enormous quantities of silt to wash into the river, raising the river bed and increasing the risk of floods that burst the dams that normally would contain them. The risk of disastrous flooding would be greatly reduced if different social conditions prevailed—if people were not so dependent on firewood for fuel, or they did not have to farm land close to the river, or the dams were higher and more numerous.

Famines, episodes of severe starvation and death, often are triggered by physical events such as a hurricane that knocks down and uproots food trees and plants. But famines do not inevitably follow such an event. Social conditions can prevent a famine or increase the likelihood of one. Consider what is likely to happen in Samoa after a hurricane.[42] Whole villages that have lost their coconut and breadfruit trees, as well as their taro patches, pick up and move for a period of time to other villages where there are relatives and friends. The visitors stay and are fed until some of their cultivated trees and plants start to bear food again, at which point they return home. This kind of intervillage reciprocity probably could occur only in a society that has relatively little inequality in wealth. Nowadays, the central government may also help out by providing food and other supplies.

Relief provided by a central government may not always get to those who need it the most. In India, for example, the central government provides help in time of drought to minimize the risk of famine. But the food and other supplies provided to a village may end up being unequally distributed, following the rules of social and gender stratification. Members of the local elite arrange to function as distributors and find ways to manipulate the relief efforts to their advantage. Lower-class and lower-caste families still suffer the most. Within the family, biases against females (particularly young girls and elderly women) translate into their getting less food. It is no wonder then that in times of food shortage and famine, the poor and other socially disadvantaged persons are especially likely to die.[43]

Thus, the people of a society may not all be equally at risk in case of disaster. In socially stratified societies, the poor particularly suffer. It is they who are likely to be forced to overcultivate, overgraze, and deforest their land, making it more susceptible to degradation. A society most helps those it values the most.

People in the past, and even recently in some places, viewed disasters as divine retribution for human immorality. For example, the great Flood described in the Old Testament was understood to be God's doing. But scientific research increasingly allows us to understand the natural causes of disasters, and particularly the social conditions that magnify or minimize their effects. To reduce the impact of disasters, then, we need to reduce the social conditions that magnify their effects. If humans are responsible for those social conditions, humans can change them. If earthquakes destroy houses that are too flimsy, we can build stronger houses. If floods caused by overcultivation and overgrazing kill defenseless people directly (or indi-rectly by stripping their soils), we can decide to grow new forest cover and provide new job opportunites to flood plain farmers. In short, we may not be able to do much about the weather (or other physical causes of disasters), but we can do a lot (if we want to) about the social factors that make disasters disastrous.

Inadequate Housing and Homelessness

In most nations of the world today, the poor typically live in inadequate housing, in areas we call *slums.* In many of the developing nations of the world, where cities are growing very rapidly, squatter settlements emerge as people build dwellings (often makeshift) that are typically declared illegal, either because the land is illegally occupied or because the dwellings violate building codes. Squatter settlements are often located in degraded environments that are subject to flooding and mudslides or have inadequate or polluted water. The magnitude of the problem is made clear in some recent statistics: some 40 percent of the population in Nairobi, Kenya, live in unauthorized housing, and 67 percent of the people in five of El Salvador's major cities are living in "illegal" dwellings.[44]

But contrary to what some people have assumed, not all the dwellers in illegal settlements are poor; all but the upper-income elite may be found in such settlements.[45] Moreover, although squatter settlements have problems, they are not chaotic and unorganized places, full of crime. Most of the dwellers are employed, aspire to get ahead, live in nuclear families, and give each other aid.[46] People live in such settlements because they cannot find affordable housing and they house themselves as best they can. Many researchers think that such self-help tendencies should be assisted to improve housing, because governments in developing countries can seldom afford costly public housing projects. But they could invest somewhat in infrastructure (sewers, water supplies, roads) and provide construction materials to those who are willing to do the work required to improve their dwellings.[47]

Housing in slum areas or "shantytowns" does provide shelter, minimal though it may be. But many people in many areas of the world have no homes at all. Even in countries such as the United States, which are affluent by world standards, large numbers of people are homeless. They sleep in parks, over steam vents, in doorways, subways, and cardboard boxes. In 1987 it was estimated that there were more than 1 million homeless people in the

Homelessness has increased dramatically in the United States recently. In many places, as in New York City, if the homeless have any shelter it is a cardboard box or a makeshift shelter like the one shown here.

United States.[48] And their numbers are growing. A 1988 congressionally funded study suggested that unless immediate action is taken in the United States to provide affordable housing, there may be as many as 19 million homeless people by the end of this century.[49]

Who are the homeless, and how did they get to be homeless? As yet we have relatively little research on these questions, but what we do have suggests differences in the causes of homelessness in different parts of the world.

In the United States, unemployment and the shortage of decent low-cost housing appear to be at least partly responsible for the large number of homeless persons.[50] But there is also another factor: the deliberate policy to reduce the number of people hospitalized for mental illness and other disabilities. For example, from the mid-1960s to mid-1990s New York State released thousands of patients from mental hospitals. Many of these ex-patients had to live in cheap hotels or poorly monitored facilities with virtually no support network. With very little income, they found it especially hard to cope with their circumstances. Ellen Baxter and Kim Hopper, who studied the homeless in New York City, suggest that one event is rarely sufficient to render a person homeless. Rather, poverty and disability (mental or

physical) seem to lead to one calamity after another, and finally homelessness.[51]

Many people cannot understand why homeless individuals do not want to go to municipal shelters. But observations and interviews with the homeless suggest that violence pervades the municipal shelters, particularly the men's shelters. Many feel safer on the streets. Some private charities provide safe shelters and a caring environment. These shelters are filled, but the number of homeless that could be accommodated in them is small.[52] Even single-room-occupancy hotels are hardly better. Many of them are infested with vermin, the common bathrooms are filthy, and they, like the shelters, often are dangerous.[53]

Some poor individuals in a society may be socially isolated; they may have few or no friends and relatives and little or no social contact. (These people may or may not have symptoms of severe mental illness.) But a society with many such individuals does not necessarily have much homelessness. Socially isolated individuals, even mentally ill individuals, could still have housing, or so the experience of Melbourne, Australia, suggests. Universal health insurance pays for health care as well as the visits of medical practitioners to isolated and ill individuals, wherever they live. Disabled individuals receive a pension or sickness benefits sufficient to allow them to live in a room or apartment. And there is still a considerable supply of cheap housing in Melbourne.

Research in Melbourne suggests that a severe mental disorder often precedes living in marginal accommodations—city shelters, commercial shelters, and cheap single rooms. About 50 percent of the individuals living in such places were diagnosed as previously having some form of mental illness; this percentage is similar to what seems to be the case for homeless people and people living in marginal accommodations in the United States.

The contrast between the United States and Australia makes it clear that homelessness is caused by social and political policies. Individuals with similar characteristics live in both Australia and the United States, but in the United States a large percentage of them are homeless.[54]

Because homelessness cannot occur if everybody can afford housing, some people would say that homelessness can occur only in a society with great extremes in income. Recent statistics on income distribution in the United States clearly show that since the 1970s the rich have gotten much richer and the poor have gotten much poorer. The United States now has more income inequality than other industrialized countries, such as Japan and the Netherlands. In fact, the profile of inequality in the United States more closely resembles that of developing countries such as India and Mexico.[55]

In the United States and many other countries, most homeless persons are adults. Whereas adults are "allowed" to be homeless, public sensibilities in the United States appear to be outraged by the sight of children living in the streets; when authorities discover homeless children, they try to find shelters or foster homes for them. But many countries in the world have many "street children." It has been estimated that 80 million of the world's children live in the streets. Forty million of them live in Latin America, 20 million in Asia, 10 million in Africa and the Middle East, and 10 million elsewhere.[56]

Lewis Aptekar, who studied street children in Cali, Colombia, reported some surprises.[57] Whereas many of the homeless in the United States and Australia are mentally disabled, the street children in Cali (ranging in age from seven to sixteen) are mostly free of mental problems; by and large they also test normally on intelligence tests. In addition, even though many street children come from abusive homes or never had homes, they usually seem happy and enjoy the support and friendship of other street children. They cleverly and creatively look for ways to get money, frequently through entertaining passersby.

Although the observer might think that the street children must have been abandoned by their families, in actuality most of them have at least one parent they keep in touch with. Street life begins slowly, not abruptly; children usually do not stay on the streets full-time until they are about thirteen.

Though street children in Cali seem to be in better physical and mental shape than their siblings who stay at home, they often are viewed as a "plague." The street children come from poor families and cope with their lives as best they can, so why are they not viewed with pity and compassion? Aptekar suggests that well-off families see the street children as a threat because a life independent of family may appeal to children (even from well-off families) who wish to be free of parental constraint and authority.

Whether people become homeless, whether there are shantytowns, seems to depend on a society's willingness to share wealth and help those in need. The street children of Cali may remind us that children as well as adults need companionship as well as caring. Caring for physical needs without responding to emotional needs may get people off the streets, but it won't get them a "home."

Family Violence and Abuse

In our society, we hear regularly about the abuse of spouses and children. It appears to be increasing, but is it? This seems to be a simple question, but it is not so simple to answer. We have to decide what we mean by abuse.

Is physical punishment of a child who does something wrong child abuse? Not so long ago, teachers in public schools in the United States were allowed to discipline children by hitting them with rulers or paddles, and many parents used switches or belts. Some people today might consider these practices to be child abuse, but were they abusive when they were generally accepted? Some would argue that abuse is going beyond what a culture considers appropriate behavior. Others would disagree and would focus on the violence and severity of parents' or teachers' behavior, not the cultural judgment of appropriateness. And abuse need not involve physical violence. It could be argued that verbal aggression and neglect may be just as harmful as physical aggression. Neglect presents its own problems of definition. People from other cultures might argue that we act abusively when we put an infant or child alone in a room to

Help for mothers is an important predictor of less physical punishment of children. Among the Navaho, matrilocal extended families have many individuals to help bring up a child.

sleep.[58] Few would disagree about severe injuries that kill a child or spouse or require medical treatment; but other disciplinary behaviors are more difficult to judge.

To avoid having to decide what is or is not abuse, many researchers focus their studies on variation in the frequencies of specific behaviors. For example, one can ask which societies have physical punishment of children without calling physical punishment abusive.

More child abuse cases are reported today in the United States than a decade ago, but that does not necessarily mean that violence against children has increased; it may mean only that our awareness and intolerance of violence against children have increased. In fact, in a national interview survey of physical familial violence in the United States, most types of physical violence decreased in frequency between 1975 and 1985. That is, people talked about fewer family homicides, fewer severe assaults on husbands and wives, and fewer severe assaults on children. Despite these declines, however, the United States remains a society with a generally high rate of physical violence in families. In the year 1985 alone, one out

of six couples had a violent assault episode and one out of ten children was severely assaulted by a parent. The risk of assault by a family member in the United States is much greater than the risk of assault by a stranger; for women it is more than 200 times as great.[59] In a comparison of twenty-seven nations, the United States had the third highest rate of child murder.[60]

Cross-culturally, if one form of family violence occurs, others are also likely. So, for example, wife beating, husband beating, child punishment, and fighting among siblings are all significantly associated with each other. But the relationships between these types of family violence are not that strong, which means that they cannot be treated together as different facets of the same phenomenon; indeed, somewhat different factors seem to explain different forms of family violence.[61] We focus here on two forms of violence that are most prevalent cross-culturally—violence against children and violence against wives.

Violence against Children. Cross-culturally, many societies practice and allow infanticide. Frequent reasons for infanticide include illegitimacy, deformity of the infant, twins, too many children, or that the infant is unwanted. Infanticide is usually performed by the mother, but this does not mean that she is uncaring; it may mean that she cannot adequately feed or care for the infant or that it has a poor chance to survive. The reasons for infanticide are quite similar to those given for abortion. Therefore, it seems that infanticide may be performed when abortion does not work or when unexpected qualities of the infant (for example, deformity) force the mother to reevaluate her ability to raise the child.[62]

Physical punishment of children occurs in over 70 percent of the world's societies. But the fact that children are sometimes punished physically in most societies does not mean that most societies use physical punishment regularly.[63] Why is physical punishment used in some societies and not others? Some studies suggest that physical punishment is more likely whenever the mother is virtually the only caretaker for the child. Physical punishment is unlikely to be used when there are other caretakers, who may relieve the mother of some of the stresses associated with child care.[64] In addition, societies that are more complex economically and politically tend to rely much more on physical punishment than simpler societies. Why this is so is not yet clear. One suggestion is that complex societies are hierarchical and tend to insist on complying with orders; they may use physical punishment in child rearing to ensure that children learn to comply.[65]

Violence Against Wives. In the United States, wives and husbands are equally likely to assault the other. Wife battering in the United States is considered a more serious social problem because wives are much more likely to be seriously injured than husbands.[66] Cross-culturally, wife beating is the most common form of family violence; it occurs at least occasionally in about 85 percent of the world's societies. In about half the societies, wife beating is sometimes serious enough to cause permanent injury or death.[67]

It is often assumed that wife beating will be common in societies in which males control economic and political resources. In a cross-cultural test of this assumption, David Levinson found that not all indicators of male dominance predict wife beating, but many do. Specifically, wife beating is most common when men control the products of family labor, when men have the final say in decision making in the home, when divorce is difficult for women, when remarriage for a widow is controlled by the husband's kin, and when women do

not have any female work groups.[68] Similarly, in the United States, the more one spouse in the family makes the decisions and has the power, the more physical violence occurs in the family (wife beating is even more likely when the husband controls the household and is out of work).[69]

Wife beating appears to be related to broader patterns of violence in adulthood. Societies that have violent methods of conflict resolution within communities, physical punishment of criminals, high frequencies of warfare, and cruelty toward enemies generally have more wife beating.[70]

Reducing the Risk. What can be done to minimize family violence? First, we have to recognize that probably nothing can be done as long as people in a society do not acknowledge that there is a problem. If severe child punishment and wife beating are considered perfectly acceptable by almost everyone in a society, they are unlikely to be considered social problems that need solutions. In our own society many programs are designed to take abused children or wives away from the family situation or to punish the abuser. (Of course, in these situations the violence has already occurred and was serious enough to have been noticed.) Cross-culturally, at least with respect to wife beating, intervention by others seems to be successful only if they intervene before violence gets serious. As one would expect, however, those societies most prone to a high rate of wife beating are the least likely to practice immediate intervention. More helpful perhaps, but admittedly harder to arrange, is the promotion of conditions of life that are associated with low family violence. Research so far suggests that promoting the equality of men and women and the sharing of child-rearing responsibilities may go a long way toward lessening incidents of family violence.[71]

Crime

What is a crime in one society is not necessarily a crime in another. Just as it is difficult to decide what constitutes abuse, it is difficult to define crime. In one society, it may be a crime to walk over someone's land without permission; in another, there might not be any concept of personal ownership, and therefore no concept of trespassing. In seeking to understand variation in crime, it is not surprising that many researchers have preferred to compare those behaviors that are more or less universally considered crimes and that are reliably reported. For example, in a large-scale comparison of crime in 110 nations over a span of 70 years, Dane Archer and Rosemary Gartner concentrated on homicide rates. They argued that homicide is harder for the public to hide and for officials to ignore than are other crimes. A comparison of interviews about crime with police records suggests that homicide is the most reliably reported crime in official records.[72]

Nations not only have very different crime rates when we compare them at a given point in time; the rates also vary over time within a nation. In the last 600 years, homicide rates have generally declined in Western societies. In England, where homicide rates have been well documented for centuries, the chance of murder during the thirteenth and fourteenth centuries was ten times higher than in England today. But beginning in the 1960s, homicide and other crime rates have surged upward in many Western countries.[73] Some of the lowest homicide rates around 1970 (the date for which we have some indicator for many nations) were found in Iran, Dahomey, Puerto Rico, New Zealand, Norway, England, and France. Some of the highest homicide rates were found in Iraq, Colombia, Myanmar (formerly Burma), Thailand, Swaziland, and Uganda. Compared with other countries, the United States had a fairly high homicide rate; approximately three-fourths of the countries surveyed had lower homicide rates than the United States.[74] That was in the 1970s. Now the United States has an even higher rate.

One of the clearest findings to emerge from comparative studies of crime is that war is associated with higher rates of homicide. Archer and Gartner compared changes in homicide rates of nations before and after major wars. Whether a nation is defeated or victorious, homicide rates tend to increase after a war. This result is consistent with the idea that a society or nation legitimizes violence during wartime. During wartime societies approve of killing the enemy; afterward, homicide rates may go up because inhibitions against killing have been relaxed.[75] Ted Gurr suggested that the long-term downtrend in crime in Western societies seems to be consistent with an increasing emphasis on humanistic values and nonviolent achievement of goals. But such goals may be temporarily suspended during wartime. In the United States, for example, surges in violent crime rates occurred during the 1860s and 1870s (during and after the Civil War), after World War I, after World War II, and during the Vietnam War.[76]

In the types of societies that anthropologists typically study, homicide statistics are not usually available; so cross-cultural studies of homicide usually measure homicide rates by comparing and rank ordering ethnographers' statements about the frequency of homicide. For example, the statement that murder is "practically unheard of" is taken to mean that the murder rate is lower than where it is reported that "homicide is not uncommon." Despite the fact that the data on cultural homicide rates are not quantitative, the cross-cultural results are consistent with the cross-national results; more war is usually associated with more homicide and assault, as well as with socially approved aggressive behaviors (as in aggressive games) and severe physical punishment for wrongdoing.[77] Our own recent cross-cultural study suggests that the more war a society has, the more socialization or training of aggression (in boys) it will have, and such socialization strongly predicts homicide and assault.[78]

Capital punishment (execution of criminals) is severe physical punishment for wrongdoing. It is commonly thought that would-be murderers are deterred by the prospect of capital punishment. Yet recent cross-national research suggests otherwise. Instead of increasing after capital punishment is abolished, murder rates go down.[79] Why? Perhaps capital punishment, which is homicide committed by society, legitimizes violence just as war seems to do.

Research conducted in the United States suggests that juvenile delinquents (usually boys) are likely to come from broken homes, with the father absent for much of the time the boy is growing up. The conclusion often drawn is that father absence somehow increases the likelihood of delinquency and adult forms of physical violence. But other conditions that may cause delinquency are also associated with broken homes, conditions such as the stigma of not having a "regular" family and the generally low standard of living of such families. It is therefore important to conduct research in other societies, in which father absence does not occur in concert with these other factors, to see if father absence by itself is related to physical violence.

For example, in many polygynous societies, children grow up in a mother-child household; the father lives separately and is hardly ever around the child. Does the father-absence explanation of delinquency and violence fit such societies? The answer is apparently yes: societies in which children are reared in mother-child households or the father spends little time in child care tend to have more physical violence by males than do societies in which fathers spend time with children.[80]

More research is needed to discover exactly what accounts for this relationship. It is possible, as some suggest, that boys growing up without fathers are apt to act "super-masculine" to show how "male" they are. But it is also possible that mothers who rear children alone often use physical punishment, and therefore are likely to provide an aggressive role model for the child. In addition, high male mortality in war predicts polygyny (as we saw in the chapter on marriage and the family); therefore boys in polygynous societies are likely to be exposed to a warrior tradition.[81]

Trying to act super-masculine, however, may be likely to involve violence *only* if aggression is an important component of the male gender role in society. If men were expected by society to be sensitive, caring, and nonviolent, boys who grew up without fathers might try to be super-sensitive and super-caring. So society's expectations for males probably shape how growing up in a mother-child household affects behavior in adolescence and later.[82]

One widely held idea is that poor economic conditions increase the likelihood of crime. But the relationship does not appear to be strong. And the findings are somewhat different for different types of crime. For example, hundreds of studies in this and other countries do not show a clear relationship between changes in economic well-being as measured by unemployment rates and changes in violent crime as measured by homicide. Homicide does not appear to increase in bad times. Property crimes, however, do increase with increases in unemployment. Violent crime does appear to be associated with one economic characteristic—homicide is usually highest in nations with high income inequality. Why income inequality predicts homicide, but downturns in the economy do not, is something of a puzzle.[83]

The fact that property crime is linked to unemployment is consistent with the cross-cultural finding that theft (but not violent crime) tends to occur less often in egalitarian societies than in stratified ones. Societies with equal access to resources usually have distribution mechanisms that offset any differences in wealth. Hence theft should be less of a temptation, and therefore less likely, in an egalitarian society. Theft rates are higher in socially stratified societies despite the fact that they are more likely than egalitarian societies to have police and courts to punish crime. Societies may try to deter property and other crimes when the rates of such are high, but we do not know that these efforts actually reduce the rates.

So what does the available research suggest about how we might be able to reduce crime? The results so far indicate that homicide rates are highest in societies that socialize their boys for aggression. Such socialization is linked to war and other forms of socially approved violence (capital punishment, television and movie violence by heroes, violence in sports). And the statistical evidence suggests that war is a cause of socialization for aggression, which in turn is a cause of high rates of violence. The policy implication of these results is that if we can reduce socialization for aggression (by reducing the risk of war and therefore the necessity to produce effective warriors), and if we can reduce other forms of socially approved violence, we may thereby reduce rates of violent crime. The reduction of inequalities in wealth may also help to reduce crime, particularly theft. And although it is not yet clear

A society may encourage boys to play soldier, perhaps to prepare them to be courageous in combat later on. Cross-culturally, socialization for aggression strongly predicts homicide and assault.

why, it appears that raising boys with a male role model around may reduce the likelihood of male violence in adulthood.

War

War is an unfortunate fact of life in most societies known to anthropology, judging by the cross-cultural research we referred to in the chapter on political life. Almost every society had at least occasional wars when it was first described, unless it had been pacified (usually by Western colonial powers).[84] Since the Civil War, the United States has not had any wars on its territory, but it is unusual in that respect. Most societies (before pacification) had frequent armed combat between communities or larger units that usually spoke the same language. That is, most warfare was internal to the society or language group. (Even some wars in modern times involved speakers of the same language; recall the wars between Italian states before the unification of Italy and many of the "civil" wars of the last two centuries.) Although people in some societies might fight against people in other societies, such "external" wars were usually not organized on behalf of the entire society or even a major section of it.[85] That is, warfare in the ethnographic record did not usually involve politically unified societies. Finally, the absolute numbers of people killed may have been small, but this does not mean that the warfare in nonindustrial societies was a trivial matter. Indeed, it appears that nonindustrial warfare may have been even more lethal *proportionately* than modern warfare, judging by the fact that wars killed 25 to 30 percent of the males in some nonindustrial societies.[86]

In the chapter on political life, we discussed the possibility that people in nonindustrial societies go to war mostly out of fear—particularly a fear of expectable but unpredictable natural disasters (droughts, floods, hurricanes, among others) that destroy food supplies. People with more of a history of such disasters have more war. It looks as if they go to war to protect themselves ahead of time from disasters, inasmuch as the victors in war almost always take resources (land, animals, other things) from the defeated, even when the victors have no current resource problems. Another factor apparently making for more war is teaching children to mistrust others. People who grow up to be mistrustful of others may be more likely to go to war than to negotiate or seek conciliation with "enemies." Mistrust or fear of others seems to be partially caused by threat or fear of disasters.[87]

Is warfare in and between modern state societies explainable in much the same way that nonindustrial warfare seems to be explainable? If the answer to that question turns out to be yes, it will certainly be a modified yes, because the realities of industrialized societies require an expanded conception of disasters. In the modern world, with its complex economic and political dependencies among nations, we may not be worried only about weather or pest disasters that could curtail food supplies; possible curtailments of other resources—particularly oil—may also scare us into going to war. According to some commentators, the decision to go to war against Iraq after it invaded Kuwait in 1991 fits that theory of war.

But even if the "threat-to-resources" theory is true, we may be coming to realize (with the end of the Cold War) that war is not the only way to ensure access to resources. There may be a better way in the modern world, a way that is more cost-effective as well as more preserving of human life.

If it is true that war is most likely when people fear unpredictable disasters of any kind, the risk of war should lessen when people realize that the harmful effects of disasters could be reduced or prevented by international cooperation. Just as we have the assurance of disaster relief within our country, we could have the assurance of disaster relief worldwide. That is, the fear of unpredictable disasters and the fear of others (and the consequent risk of war) could be reduced by the assurance ahead of time that the world would help those in need in case of disaster. Instead of going to war out of fear, we could go to peace by agreeing to share more. The certainty of international cooperation could compensate for the uncertainty of resources.

Consider how Germany and Japan have fared in the half century since their "unconditional surrender" in World War II. They were forbidden to participate in the international arms race and could rely on others (particularly the United States) to protect them. Without a huge burden of armaments, Germany and Japan thrived. But countries that competed militarily, particularly the United States and the Soviet Union, declined economically. Doesn't that scenario at least suggest the wisdom of international cooperation, particularly the need for international agreements to assure worldwide disaster relief? Compared with going to war and its enormous costs, going to peace would be a bargain!

Recent research in political science and anthropology suggests an additional way to reduce the risk of war in the world. Studies indicate that people in more participatory (more "democratic") political systems rarely go to war with each other, in the ethnographic record just as among modern nation-states.[88] Thus, if authoritarian governments were to disappear from the world, because the powerful nations of the world stopped supporting them militarily and otherwise, the world could be more peaceful for this reason too.

Although democratically governed states rarely go to war with each other, they are not necessarily more peaceful in general. On the contrary, they are as likely to go to war as other kinds of political systems, but not so much with each other. (The United States has gone to war recently with Grenada, Panama, and Iraq—all authoritarian states—but not with democratic Canada, with which the United States has also had disputes.) The theory suggested by the cross-national and cross-cultural results is that democratic conflict-resolution within a political system generalizes to democratic conflict-resolution between political systems (if the systems are both democratic). If our participatory institutions and perceptions allow us to resolve our disputes peacefully, internally and externally, we may think that similarly governed people would also be disposed to settle things peacefully. Therefore, disputes between participatory political systems should be unlikely to result in war.

The understanding that participatory systems rarely fight each other, and knowing why they do not, would have important consequences for policy in the contemporary world. The kinds of military preparations believed necessary and the costs people would be willing to pay for them might be affected. On the one hand, understanding the relationship beween democracy and peace might encourage war making against authoritarian regimes to overturn them—with enormous costs in human life and otherwise. On the other hand, understanding the consequences of democracy might encourage us to assist the emergence and consolidation of more participatory systems of government in the countries of eastern Europe, the former Soviet Union, and elsewhere. In any case, the relationship between democracy and peace strongly suggests that it is counterproductive to support any undemocratic regimes, even if they happen to be enemies of our enemies, if we want to minimize the risk of war in the world.

It may be realistic, not just idealistic, to think that the more people understand the peaceful effect of democracy, and the more they are assured of world-wide disaster relief, the more they might go to peace!

MAKING THE WORLD BETTER
▼

There are many social problems afflicting our world, not just the ones discussed in this chapter. We don't have the space to discuss the international trade in drugs and how it plays out in violence, death, and corruption. We haven't discussed the negative effects of environmental degradation (water and air pollution, global warming, ozone depletion, destruction of forests and wetlands). We haven't said anything about overpopulation, the energy crisis, and a host of other problems we should care and do something about, if we hope to make this a better world. What we have tried to do in this chapter is encourage positive thinking by suggesting how the results of scientific research could be applied to solving social problems.

We may know enough now that we can do something about our problems. And we will discover more on the basis of future research. Social problems are mostly of human making. Therefore they are susceptible to human unmaking. There may be difficulties, but we can overcome them if we want to.

▼ SUMMARY

1. We may be more motivated now to try to solve social problems because worldwide communication has increased our awareness of them elsewhere, because we seem to be increasingly bothered by problems in our own society, and because we know more than we used to about various social problems that afflict our world.

2. Applied anthropology in the United States developed out of anthropologists' personal experiences with disadvantaged peoples. Applied, or practicing, anthropologists may be involved in one or more phases of a program that is designed to change peoples' lives: assembling relevant knowledge, constructing alternative plans, assessing the

likely social and environmental impact of particular plans, implementing the program, and monitoring the program and its effects.

3. Today many anthropologists are finding employment outside of anthropology departments—in medical schools, health centers, development agencies, urban-planning agencies, and other public and private organizations, in this society and others.

4. The code of ethics for those who work professionally as applied anthropologists specifies that the target population should be included as much as possible in the formulation of policy, so that people in the community may know in advance how the program may affect them. But perhaps the most important aspect of the code is the pledge not to be involved in any plan whose effect will not be beneficial. It is often difficult to evaluate the effects of planned changes. Long-term consequences may be detrimental even if the changes are beneficial in the short run.

5. Even if a planned change will prove beneficial to its target population, the people may not accept it. And if the proposed innovation is not utilized by the intended target, the project cannot be considered a success. Target populations may reject or resist a proposed innovation for various reasons: because they are unaware of the need for the change; because they misinterpret the symbols used to explain the change or fail to understand its real purpose; because their customs and institutions conflict with the change; or because they are afraid of it. The target population may also resist the proposed change because they unconsciously or consciously know it is not good for them.

6. To be effective, change agents may have to discover and use the traditional channels of influence in introducing their projects to the target population.

7. The idea that we can solve global social problems is based on two assumptions. We have to assume that it is possible to discover the causes of a problem. And we have to assume that we will be able to do something about the causes (once they are discovered) and thereby eliminate or reduce the problem.

8. Until medical science develops an effective and inexpensive vaccine (or treatment) for AIDS, the risk of infection can be reduced only by changes in social (particularly sexual) behavior.

9. Disasters such as earthquakes, floods, and droughts can have greater or lesser effects on human life, depending on social conditions. Therefore disasters are partly social problems, with partly social causes and solutions.

10. Whether people become homeless, whether there are shantytowns, seems to depend on a society's willingness to share wealth and help those in need.

11. Promoting the equality of men and women and the sharing of child-rearing responsibilities may reduce family violence.

12. We may be able to reduce rates of violent crime if we can reduce socialization and training for aggression. To do that we would have to reduce the likelihood of war (the high likelihood of which predicts more socialization for aggression) and other forms of socially approved aggression. The reduction of inequalities in wealth may also help to reduce crime, particularly theft. And raising boys with a male role model around may reduce the likelihood of male violence in adulthood.

13. People seem to be most likely to go to war when they fear unpredictable disasters that destroy food supplies or curtail the supplies of other necessities. Disputes between more participatory (more "democratic") political systems are unlikely to result in war. Therefore, the more democracy spreads in the world, and the more people all over the world are assured of internationally organized disaster relief, the more they might go to peace rather than to war to solve their problems.

▼ GLOSSARY TERMS

applied anthropology or practicing anthropology

AIDS (acquired immune deficiency syndrome)

▼ CRITICAL QUESTIONS

1. What particular advantages do anthropologists have in trying to solve practical problems?
2. Is it ethical to try to influence people's lives when they have not asked for help?
3. Do global problems require solutions by global agencies? If so, which?

▼ SUGGESTED READING

APTEKAR, L. *Environmental Disasters in Global Perspective.* New York: G. K. Hall/Macmillan, 1994. This volume discusses various kinds of environmental disaster. It is one of a series of monographs, sponsored by the Human Relations Area Files, on the current state of cross-cultural and cross-national research on social problems around the world. Others in the series include: S. M. Albert and M. G. Cattell, *Old Age in Global Perspective: Cross-Cultural and Cross-National Views,* 1994; and I. Glasser, *Homelessness in Cross-Cultural Perspective,* 1994.

BODLEY, J. H. *Anthropology and Contemporary Human Problems,* 2nd ed. Mountain View, CA: Mayfield, 1985. This book discusses the problems of overconsumption, adaptation to environment, resource depletion, hunger and starvation, overpopulation, violence, and war.

EDDY, E. M., AND PARTRIDGE, W., eds. *Applied Anthropology in America,* 2nd ed. New York: Columbia University Press, 1987. A set of essays about the relevance of applied anthropology in American society. Provides an overview of how anthropology has contributed and can contribute to major policy issues confronting our nation.

EMBER, C. R., EMBER, M. AND PEREGRINE, P., eds. *Research Frontiers in Anthropology.* Englewood Cliffs: Prentice Hall, 1995. Prentice Hall/Simon & Schuster Custom Publishing; and Ember, C. R., and Ember, M. *Cross-Cultural Research for Social Science.* Englewood Cliffs, NJ: Prentice Hall, 1995. Prentice Hall/Simon & Schuster Custom Publishing. A number of chapters in these two series deal explicitly with the study of social problems, including: M. G. Cattell and S. M. Albert, "Caring for the Elderly"; A. Cohen and P. Koegel, "Homelessness"; R. Dirks, "Hunger and Famine"; G. M. Erchak, "Family Violence"; R. Gartner, "Crime: Variations across Cultures and Nations"; P. C. Rosenblatt, "Human Rights Violations across Cultures"; M. H. Ross, "Ethnocentrism and Ethnic Conflict"; and M. D. Williams, "Racism."

FLUEHR-LOBBAN, C, ed. *Ethics and the Profession of Anthropology: Dialogue for a New Era.* Philadelphia: University of Pennsylvania Press, 1991. This edited volume contains historical and contemporary reviews of ethical issues regarding the profession of anthropology.

VAN WILLIGEN, J., RYLKO-BAUER, B., AND MCELROY, A. *Making Our Research Useful: Case Studies in the Utilization of Anthropological Knowledge.* Boulder, CO: Westview Press, 1989. The contributors to this volume were asked to write case studies describing projects in which they were involved. The major question addressed is how to increase the use of knowledge gained in applied research projects.

▼ NOTES

[1]Gilbert Kushner, "Applied Anthropology," in William G. Emener and Margaret Darrow, eds., *Career Explorations in Human Services* (Springfield, IL: Charles C. Thomas, 1991), pp. 46–61.

[2]Margaret Mead, "The Evolving Ethics of Applied Anthropology," in Elizabeth M. Eddy and William L. Partridge, eds., *Applied Anthropology in America* (New York: Columbia University Press, 1978), pp. 426–29.

[3]Barbara Frankel and M. G. Trend, "Principles, Pressures and Paychecks: The Anthropologist as Employee," in Carolyn Fluehr-Lobban, ed. *Ethics and the Profession of Anthropology: Dialogue for a New Era* (Philadelphia: University of Pennsylvania Press, 1991), p. 177.

[4]Robert A. Hackenberg, "Scientists or Survivors? The Future of Applied Anthropology under Maximum Uncertainty," in Robert T. Trotter II, ed., *Anthropology for Tomorrow: Creating Practitioner-Oriented Applied Anthropology Programs* (Washington, D.C.: American Anthropological Association, 1988), p. 172.

[5]Kushner, "Applied Anthropology."

[6]William L. Partridge and Elizabeth M. Eddy, "The Development of Applied Anthropology in America," in Eddy and Partridge, eds., *Applied Anthropology in America,* 2nd ed. (New York: Columbia University Press, 1987), pp. 25–26.

[7]Ibid., pp. 31–40.

[8]Margaret Mead, "Applied Anthropology: The State of the Art," in Anthony F. C. Wallace, J. Lawrence Angel, Richard Fox, Sally McLendon, Rachel Sady, and Robert Sharer, eds., *Perspectives on Anthropology 1976*, American Anthropological Association Special Publication No. 10 (Washington, D.C.: American Anthropological Association, 1977), p. 149.

[9]Partridge and Eddy, "The Development of Applied Anthropology," pp. 31–40.

[10]George M. Foster, *Applied Anthropology* (Boston: Little, Brown, 1969), p. 200.

[11]Partridge and Eddy, "The Development of Applied Anthropology," p. 48.

[12]Ibid., p. 52.

[13]"Appendix C: Statements on Ethics: Principles of Professional Responsibility, Adopted by the Council of the American Anthropological Association, May 1971" (as amended through May 1976) and "Appendix I: Revised Principles of Professional Responsibility, 1990," in Fluehr-Lobban, ed., *Ethics and the Profession of Anthropology*, pp. 239–42, 274–79.

[14]"Appendix A: Report of the Committee on Ethics, Society for Applied Anthropology" and "Appendix F: Professional and Ethical Responsibilities, SfAA," in ibid., pp. 239–42, 262–64.

[15]"Appendix H: National Association of Practicing Anthropologists' Ethical Guidelines for Practitioners, 1988," in ibid., pp. 270–73.

[16]Burton Benedict, "Controlling Population Growth in Mauritius," in H. Russell Bernard and Pertti J. Pelto, eds., *Technology and Social Change*, 2nd ed. (Prospect Heights, IL: Waveland Press, 1987), pp. 269–300.

[17]Conrad M. Arensberg and Arthur Niehoff, *Introducing Social Change: A Manual for Americans Overseas* (Chicago: Aldine, 1964), p. 66.

[18]Debra Picchi, "The Impact of an Industrial Agricultural Project on the Bakairi Indians of Central Brazil," *Human Organization* 50 (1991): 26–38; for a more general description of the Bakairi, see Debra Picchi, "Bakairi: The Death of an Indian," in Melvin Ember, Carol R. Ember, and David Levinson, eds., *Portraits of Culture: Ethnographic Originals* (Englewood Cliffs, NJ: Prentice Hall, 1995). Prentice Hall/Simon & Schuster Custom Publishing.

[19]Thayer Scudder, "Opportunities, Issues, and Achievements in Development Anthropology Since the Mid-1960s: A Personal View," in Eddy and Partridge, eds., *Applied Anthropology in America*, 2nd ed., pp. 184–210.

[20]Ibid, p. 204ff.

[21]Arthur H. Niehoff, *A Casebook of Social Change* (Chicago: Aldine, 1966), pp. 255–67.

[22]Foster, *Applied Anthropology*, pp. 8–9.

[23]Derrick B. Jelliffe and E. F. Patrice Jelliffe, "Human Milk, Nutrition, and the World Resource Crisis," *Science*, May 9, 1975, 557–61.

[24]William H. Fisher, "Megadevelopment, Environmentalism, and Resistance: The Institutional Context of Kayapó Indigenous Politics in Central Brazil," *Human Organization*, 53 (1994): 220–32.

[25]Foster, *Applied Anthropology*, pp. 122–23.

[26]Jeannine Coreil, "Lessons from a Community Study of Oral Rehydration Therapy in Haiti," in John van Willigen, Barbara Rylko-Bauer, and Ann McElroy, eds., *Making Our Research Useful: Case Studies in the Utilization of Anthropological Knowledge* (Boulder, CO: Westview Press, 1989), pp. 149–50.

[27]Everett M. Rogers, *Diffusion of Innovations*, 3rd ed. (New York: Free Press, 1983), pp. 321–31.

[28]Carol A. Bryant and Doraine F. C. Bailey, "The Use of Focus Group Research in Program Development," in John van Willigen and Timothy L. Finan, eds., *Soundings: Rapid and Reliable Research Methods for Practicing Anthropologists*, NAPA Bulletin No. 10 (Washington, D.C.: American Anthropological Association, 1990), p. 32, pp. 24–39.

[29]Niehoff, *A Casebook of Social Change*, pp. 219–24.

[30]Coreil, "Lessons from a Community Study of Oral Rehydration Therapy in Haiti," p. 155.

[31]Dennis M. Warren, "Utilizing Indigenous Healers in National Health Delivery Systems: The Ghanaian Experiment," in van Willigen, Rylko-Bauer, and McElroy, eds., *Making Our Research Useful*, pp. 159–78.

[32]Ward H. Goodenough, *Cooperation in Change* (New York: Russell Sage Foundation, 1963), p. 416.

[33]As reported in Steve Jones, Robert Martin, and David Pilbeam, eds., *The Cambridge Encyclopedia of Human Evolution* (Cambridge: Cambridge University Press, 1992), p. 420.

[34]Ralph Bolton, "Introduction: The AIDS Pandemic, A Global Emergency," *Medical Anthropology*, 10 (1989): 93–104.

[35]Ibid.

[36]Joseph Carrier and Ralph Bolton, "Anthropological Perspective on Sexuality and HIV Prevention," *Annual Review of Sex Research* 2 (1991): 49–75; B. Schoepf, "Women, AIDS, and Economic Crisis in Central Africa," *Canadian Journal of African Studies*, 22 (1988): 625, cited in Carrier and Bolton, "Anthropological Perspectives on Sexuality and HIV Prevention."

[37]Schoepf, "Women, AIDS, and Economic Crisis in Central Africa," pp. 637–38.

[38]Ralph Bolton, "AIDS and Promiscuity: Muddled in the Models of HIV Prevention," *Medical Anthropology*, 14 (1992): 145–223.

[39]Douglas A. Feldman and Thomas M. Johnson, "Introduction," in Douglas A. Feldman and Thomas M. Johnson, eds., *The Social Dimensions of AIDS: Method and Theory* (New York: Praeger, 1986), p. 2.

[40]Tony Barnett and Piers Blaikie, "*AIDS in Africa: Its Present and Future Impact* (London: Belhaven Press, 1992), p. 4.

[41]The discussion in this section draws extensively from Lewis Aptekar, *Environmental Disasters in Global Perspective* (New York: G. K. Hall/Macmillan, 1994).

[42]Information collected during Melvin Ember's fieldwork in American Samoa (1955–1956).

[43]William I. Torry, "Morality and Harm: Hindu Peasant Adjustments to Famines," *Social Science Information,* 25 (1986): 125–60.

[44]Jorge Hardoy and David Satterthwaite, "The Legal and the Illegal City," in Lloyd Rodwin, ed., *Shelter, Settlement, and Development* (Boston: Allen & Unwin, 1987), pp. 304–38.

[45]Lloyd Rodwin and Bishwapriya Sanyal, "Shelter, Settlement, and Development: An Overview," in Rodwin, ed., *Shelter, Settlement, and Development,* pp. 3–31.

[46]William Mangin, "Latin American Squatter Settlements: A Problem and a Solution," *Latin American Research Review,* 2 (1967): 65–98.

[47]Rodwin and Sanyal, "Shelter, Settlement, and Development"; for a critique of self-help programs, see Peter M. Ward, "Introduction and Purpose," in Peter M. Ward, ed., *Self-Help Housing: A Critique* (London: Mansell Publishing, 1982), pp. 1–13.

[48]Alex Cohen and Paul Koegel, "Homelessness," in Carol R. Ember, Melvin Ember, and Peter Peregrine, eds., *Research Frontiers in Anthropology* (Englewood Cliffs, NJ: Prentice Hall, 1995). Prentice Hall/Simon & Schuster Custom Publishing.

[49]Gregg Barak, *Gimme Shelter: A Social History of Homelessness in Contemporary America* (New York: Praeger, 1991), p. 4.

[50]Cohen and Koegel, "Homelessness."

[51]Ellen Baxter and Kim Hopper, *Private Lives/Public Spaces: Homeless Adults on the Streets of New York City* (New York: Community Service Society of New York, 1981), pp. 30–33, pp. 50–74.

[52]Ibid., pp. 30–33, 50–74.

[53]Cohen and Koegel, "Homelessness."

[54]Helen Herrman, "A Survey of Homeless Mentally Ill People in Melbourne, Australia," *Hospital and Community Psychiatry,* 41 (1990): 1291–92.

[55]Barak, *Gimme Shelter,* pp. 63–65.

[56]Lewis Aptekar, "Are Colombian Street Children Neglected? The Contributions of Ethnographic and Ethnohistorical Approaches to the Study of Children," *Anthropology and Education Quarterly,* 22 (1991): 326.

[57]Ibid., pp. 326–49. See also Lewis Aptekar, *Street Children of Cali* (Durham, NC: Duke University Press), 1988.

[58]Jill E. Korbin, "Introduction," in Jill E. Korbin, ed., *Child Abuse and Neglect: Cross-Cultural Perspectives* (Berkeley, CA: University of California, 1981), p. 4.

[59]Murray A. Straus, "Physical Violence in American Families: Incidence Rates, Causes, and Trends," in Dean D. Knudsen and JoAnn L. Miller, eds., *Abused and Battered: Social and Legal Responses to Family Violence* (New York: Aldine de Gruyter, 1991), pp. 17–34.

[60]Raoul Naroll, *The Moral Order: An Introduction to the Human Situation* (Beverly Hills, CA: Sage Publications, 1983), p. 247.

[61]David Levinson, *Family Violence in Cross-Cultural Perspective* (Newbury Park, CA: Sage, 1989), pp. 11–12, 44.

[62]Leigh Minturn and Jerry Stashak, "Infanticide as a Terminal Abortion Procedure," *Behavior Science Research* 17 (1982): 70–85. Using a sociobiological orientation, a study by Martin Daly and Margo Wilson (*Homicide* [New York: Aldine de Gruyter, 1988], pp. 43–59) also suggests that infanticide is largely due to the difficulty of raising the infant successfully.

[63]Levinson, *Family Violence in Cross-Cultural Perspective,* pp. 26–28.

[64]Ruth H. Munroe and Robert L. Munroe, "Household Structure and Socialization Practices," *Journal of Social Psychology,* 111 (1980): 293–94; and Ronald P. Rohner, *The Warmth Dimension* (Beverly Hills, CA: Sage, 1986), as referred to in Levinson, *Family Violence in Cross-Cultural Perspective,* pp. 54–55.

[65]L. R. Petersen, G. R. Lee, and G. J. Ellis, "Social Structure, Socialization Values, and Disciplinary Techniques: A Cross-Cultural Analysis," *Journal of Marriage and the Family,* 44 (1982): 131–42, as cited in Levinson, *Family Violence in Cross-Cultural Perspective,* p. 63.

[66]Straus, "Physical Violence in American Families," p. 17.

[67]Levinson, *Family Violence in Cross-Cultural Perspective,* p. 31.

[68]Ibid., p. 71.

[69]Richard J. Gelles and Murray A. Straus, *Intimate Violence* (New York: Simon & Schuster, 1988), pp. 78–88.

[70]Gerald M. Erchak, "Family Violence," in Carol R. Ember and Melvin Ember, eds., *Cross-Cultural Research for Social Science* (Englewood Cliffs, NJ: Prentice Hall, 1995). Prentice Hall/Simon & Schuster Custom Publishing. Levinson, *Family Violence in Cross-Cultural Perspective*, pp. 44–45.

[71]Levinson, *Family Violence in Cross-Cultural Perspective*, pp. 104–7.

[72]Dane Archer and Rosemary Gartner, *Violence and Crime in Cross-National Perspective* (New Haven, CT: Yale University Press, 1984), p. 35.

[73]Ted Robert Gurr, "The History of Violent Crime in America: An Overview," in Ted Robert Gurr, ed., *Violence in America*, vol. 1, *The History of Crime* (Newbury Park, CA: Sage, 1989), pp. 11–12.

[74]The comparison described here is based on data we retrieved from the extensive appendix in Archer and Gartner, *Violence and Crime in Cross-National Perspective.*

[75]Archer and Gartner, *Violence and Crime in Cross-National Perspective*, pp. 63–97.

[76]Ted Robert Gurr, "Historical Trends in Violent Crime: Europe and the United States," in Gurr, ed., *Violence in America*, vol. 1, *The History of Crime*, pp. 47–48.

[77]Elbert W. Russell, "Factors of Human Aggression," *Behavior Science Notes*, 7 (1972): 275–312; William Eckhardt, "Primitive Militarism," *Journal of Peace Research*, 12 (1975): 55–62; Richard G. Sipes, "War, Sports and Aggression: An Empirical Test of Two Rival Theories," *American Anthropologist*, 75 (1973): 64–86.

[78]Carol R. Ember and Melvin Ember, "War, Socialization and Interpersonal Violence: A Cross-Cultural Study," *Journal of Conflict Resolution*, 38 (1994): 620–46.

[79]Archer and Gartner, *Violence and Crime in Cross-National Perspective*, pp. 118–39.

[80]Margaret Bacon, Irvin L. Child, and Herbert Barry III, "A Cross-Cultural Study of Correlates of Crime," *Journal of Abnormal and Social Psychology*, 66 (1963): 291–300; Beatrice B. Whiting, "Sex Identity Conflict and Physical Violence," *American Anthropologist*, 67 (1965): 123–40.

[81]Ember and Ember, "War, Socialization and Interpersonal Violence," p. 625.

[82]Carol R. Ember and Melvin Ember, "Issues in Cross-Cultural Studies of Interpersonal Violence," *Violence and Victims*, 8 (1993): 217–33, 227.

[83]Colin Loftin, David McDowall, and James Boudouris, "Economic Change and Homicide in Detroit, 1926–1979," in Gurr, ed., *Violence in America*, vol. 1, *The History of Crime*, pp. 163–77; H. Krahn, T. F. Hartnagel, and J. W. Gartrell, "Income Inequality and Homicide Rates: Cross-National Data and Criminological Theories," *Criminology*, 24 (1986): 269–95, as referred to in Daly and Wilson, *Homicide*, pp. 287–88; Rosemary Gartner, "Crime: Variations across Cultures and Nations," in Carol R. Ember and Melvin Ember, *Cross-Cultural Research for Social Science* (Englewood Cliffs, NJ: Prentice Hall, 1995), Prentice Hall/Simon & Schuster Custom Publishing.

[84]Carol R. Ember and Melvin Ember, "Violence in the Ethnographic Record: Results of Cross-Cultural Research on War and Aggression," in David Frayer and Debra Martin, eds., *Troubled Times: Osteological and Archaeological Evidence of Violence* (Langhorne, PA: Gordon and Breach, 1995), in press.

[85]Most of the discussion in this section comes from Melvin Ember and Carol R. Ember, "Cross-Cultural Studies of War and Peace: Recent Achievements and Future Possibilities," in S. P. Reyna and R. E. Downs, eds., *Studying War: Anthropological Perspectives* (New York: Gordon and Breach, 1992), pp. 204–6.

[86]Mervyn Meggitt, *Blood Is Their Argument: Warfare among the Mae Enga Tribesmen of the New Guinea Highlands* (Palo Alto, CA: Mayfield, 1977), p. 201.

[87]For the cross-cultural results suggesting the theory of war described here, see Carol R. Ember and Melvin Ember, "Resource Unpredictability, Mistrust, and War: A Cross-Cultural Study," *Journal of Conflict Resolution*, 36 (1992): 242–62.

[88]For the results on political participation and peace in the ethnographic record, see Carol R. Ember, Melvin Ember, and Bruce Russett, "Peace between Participatory Polities: A Cross-Cultural Test of the 'Democracies Rarely Fight Each Other' Hypothesis," *World Politics*, 44 (1992): 573–99. For the results on political participation and peace in the modern world, see the references in that essay.

Glossary

Acculturation the process of extensive borrowing of aspects of culture in the context of superordinate-subordinate relations between societies; usually occurs as the result of external pressure.

Achieved Qualities those qualities a person acquires during her or his lifetime.

Adaptive a trait that enhances survival and reproductive success in a particular environment. Usually applied to biological evolution, the term is also often used by cultural anthropologists to refer to cultural traits that enhance reproductive success.

Affinal Kin one's relatives by marriage.

Age-Grade a category of persons who happen to fall within a particular, culturally distinguished age range.

Age-Set a group of persons of similar age and the same sex who move together through some or all of life's stages.

AIDS (Acquired Immune Deficiency Syndrome) a recent disease, almost always lethal, presumably caused by the HIV virus(es).

Ambilineal Descent the rule of descent that affiliates an individual with groups of kin related to him or her through men *or* women.

Ancestor Spirits supernatural beings who are the ghosts of dead relatives.

Animatism a belief in supernatural forces.

Animism a term used by Edward Tylor to describe a belief in a dual existence for all things—a physical, visible body and a psychic, invisible soul.

Anthropological Linguistics the anthropological study of languages.

Anthropology the study of differences and similarities, both biological and cultural, in human populations. Anthropology is concerned with typical biological and cultural characteristics of human populations in all periods and in all parts of the world.

Applied Anthropology the branch of anthropology that concerns itself with applying anthropological knowledge to achieve practical goals, usually in the service of an agency outside the traditional academic setting. Also called practicing anthropology.

Archaeology the branch of anthropology that seeks to reconstruct the daily life and customs of peoples who lived in the past and to trace and explain cultural changes. Often lacking written records for study, archaeologists must try to reconstruct history from the material remains of human cultures. See **Historical Archaeology.**

Ascribed Qualities those qualities that are determined for a person at birth.

Association an organized group not based exclusively on kinship or territory.

Avunculocal Residence a pattern of residence in which a married couple settles with or near the husband's mother's brother.

Balanced Reciprocity giving with the expectation of a straightforward immediate or limited-time trade.

Band a fairly small, usually nomadic local group that is politically autonomous.

Band Organization the kind of political organization where the local group or band is the largest territorial group in the society that acts as a unit. The local group in band societies is politically autonomous.

Behavioral Ecology the study of how all kinds of behavior may be related to the environment. The theoretical orientation involves the application of biological evolutionary principles to the behavior (including social behavior) of animals, including humans. Also called sociobiology, particularly when applied to social organization and social behavior.

Berdache a male transvestite in some Native American societies.

Bilateral Kinship the type of kinship system in which individuals affiliate more or less equally with their mother's and father's relatives; descent groups are absent.

Bilocal Residence a pattern of residence in which a married couple lives with or near either the husband's parents or the wife's parents.

Biological Anthropology see **Physical Anthropology.**

Bride Price a substantial gift of goods or money given to the bride's kin by the groom or his kin at or before the marriage. Also called bride wealth.

Bride Service work performed by the groom for his bride's family for a variable length of time either before or after the marriage.

Cash Crop a cultivated commodity raised for sale rather than for personal consumption by the cultivator.

Caste   a ranked group, often associated with a certain occupation, in which membership is determined at birth and marriage is restricted to members of one's own caste.

Chief   a person who exercises authority, usually on behalf of a multicommunity political unit. This role is generally found in rank societies and is usually permanent and often hereditary.

Chiefdom   a political unit, with a chief at its head, integrating more than one community but not necessarily the whole society or language group.

Clan   a set of kin whose members believe themselves to be descended from a common ancestor or ancestress but cannot specify the links back to that founder; often designated by a totem. Also called a sib.

Class   a category of persons who have about the same opportunity to obtain economic resources, power, and prestige.

Classificatory Terms   kinship terms that merge or equate relatives who are genealogically distinct from one another; the same term is used for a number of different kin.

Class Society   a society containing social groups that have unequal access to economic resources, power, and prestige.

Codeswitching   using more than one language in the course of conversing.

Codified Laws   formal principles for resolving disputes in heterogeneous and stratified societies.

Cognates   words or morphs that belong to different languages but have similar sounds and meanings.

Commercial Exchange   see **Market Exchange.**

Commercialization   the increasing dependence on buying and selling, with money usually as the medium of exchange.

Complementary Opposition   the occasional uniting of various segments of a segmentary lineage system in opposition to similar segments.

Consanguineal Kin   one's biological relatives; relatives by birth.

Core Vocabulary   nonspecialist vocabulary.

Corvée   a system of required labor.

Crime   violence not considered legitimate that occurs within a political unit.

Cross-Cousins   children of siblings of the opposite sex. One's cross-cousins are father's sisters' children and mother's brothers' children.

Cross-Cultural Researcher   an ethnologist who uses ethnographic data about many societies to test possible explanations of cultural variation.

Cultural Anthropology   the study of cultural variation and universals.

Cultural Ecology   the analysis of the relationship between a culture and its environment.

Cultural Relativism   the attitude that a society's customs and ideas should be viewed within the context of that society's problems and opportunities.

Culture   the set of learned behaviors, beliefs, attitudes, values, and ideals that are characteristic of a particular society or population.

Descriptive Linguistics   see **Structural Linguistics.**

Descriptive Term   kinship term used to refer to a ge-nealogically distinct relative; a different term is used for each relative.

Dialect   a variety of a language spoken in a particular area or by a particular social group.

Diffusion   the borrowing by one society of a cultural trait belonging to another society as the result of contact between the two societies.

Divination   getting the supernatural to provide guidance.

Double Descent   a system that affiliates an individual with a group of matrilineal kin for some purposes and with a group of patrilineal kin for other purposes. Also called double unilineal descent.

Dowry   a substantial transfer of goods or money from the bride's family to the bride.

Egalitarian Society   a society in which all persons of a given age-sex category have equal access to economic resources, power, and prestige.

Ego   in the reckoning of kinship, the reference point or focal person.

Endogamy   the rule specifying marriage to a person within one's own (kin, caste, community) group.

Ethnocentric   refers to judgment of other cultures solely in terms of one's own culture.

Ethnocentrism   the attitude that other societies' customs and ideas can be judged in the context of one's own culture.

Ethnographer   a person who spends some time living with, interviewing, and observing a group of people so that he or she can describe their customs.

Ethnographic Analogy   method of comparative cultural study that extrapolates to the past from recent or current societies.

Ethnography   a description of a society's customary behaviors, beliefs, and attitudes.

Ethnohistorian   an ethnologist who uses historical documents to study how a particular culture has changed over time.

Ethnology   the study of how and why recent cultures differ and are similar.

Ethnoscience   an approach that attempts to derive rules of thought from the logical analysis of ethnographic data.

Exogamy   the rule specifying marriage to a person from outside one's own (kin or community) group.

Explanation   an answer to a *why* question. In science, there are two kinds of explanation that researchers try to achieve—associations and theories.

Expressive Culture   activities, such as art, music, dance, and folklore, that presumably express thoughts and feelings.

Extended Family   a family consisting of two or more single-parent, monogamous, polygynous, or polyandrous families linked by a blood tie.

Extensive Cultivation   a type of horticulture in which the land is worked for short periods and then left to regenerate for some years before being used again. Also called shifting cultivation.

Falsification   showing that a theory seems to be wrong by finding that implications or predictions derivable from it are not consistent with objectively collected data.

Family   a social and economic unit consisting minimally of a parent and a child.

Feuding   a state of recurring hostility between families or groups of kin, usually motivated by a desire to avenge an offense against a member of the group.

Fieldwork   first-hand experience with the people being studied and the usual means by which anthropological information is obtained. Regardless of other methods (e.g., censuses, surveys) that anthropologists may use, fieldwork usually involves participant observation for an extended period of time, often a year or more. See **Participant-Observation**.

Folklore   includes all the myths, legends, folktales, ballads, riddles, proverbs, and superstitions of a cultural group. Generally, folklore is transmitted orally, but it may also be written.

Food Collection   all forms of subsistence technology in which food-getting is dependent on naturally occurring resources—wild plants and animals.

Food Production   the form of subsistence technology in which food-getting is dependent on the cultivation and domestication of plants and animals.

Foragers   people who subsist on the collection of naturally occurring plants and animals. Also referred to as hunter-gatherers.

Fossils   the hardened remains or impressions of plants and animals that lived in the past.

Fraternal Polyandry   the marriage of a woman to two or more brothers at one time.

Functionalism   the theoretical orientation that assumes that all culture traits serve some useful function in the society in which they occur.

Gender Differences   differences between females and males that reflect cultural expectations and experiences.

General Evolution   the notion that higher forms of culture arise from and generally supersede lower forms.

Generalized Reciprocity   gift giving without any immediate or planned return.

General-Purpose Money   a universally accepted medium of exchange.

Ghosts   supernatural beings who were once human; the souls of dead people.

Gods   supernatural beings of nonhuman origin who are named personalities; often anthropomorphic.

Group Marriage   marriage in which more than one man is married to more than one woman at the same time; not customary in any known human society.

Group Selection   natural selection of group characteristics.

Headman   a person who holds a powerless but symbolically unifying position in a community within an egalitarian society; may exercise influence but has no power to impose sanctions.

Historical Archaeology   a specialty within archaeology that studies the material remains of recent peoples who left written records.

Historical Linguistics   the study of how languages change over time.

Holistic   refers to an approach that studies many aspects of a multifaceted system.

Homo sapiens   all living people belong to one biological species, *Homo sapiens*, which means that all human populations on earth can successfully interbreed. The first *Homo sapiens* may have emerged 100,000 years ago.

Horticulture   plant cultivation carried out with relatively simple tools and methods; nature is allowed to replace nutrients in the soil, in the absence of permanently cultivated fields.

Human Paleontology   the study of the emergence of humans and their later physical evolution. Also called paleoanthropology.

Human Variation   the study of how and why contemporary human populations vary biologically.

Hunter-gatherers   collect food from naturally occurring resources, namely wild plants and animals. Also referred to as foragers.

Hypotheses   predictions, which may be derived from theories, about how variables are related.

Incest Taboo   prohibition of sexual intercourse or marriage between mother and son, father and daughter, and brother and sister.

Indirect Dowry   goods given by the groom's kin to the bride (or her father, who passes most of them to her) at or before her marriage.

Individual Selection   natural selection of individual characteristics.

Intensive Agriculture   food production characterized by the permanent cultivation of fields and made possible by the use of the plow, draft animals or machines, fertilizers, irrigation, water-storage techniques, and other complex agricultural techniques.

Kindred   a bilateral set of close relatives.

Kula **Ring**   a ceremonial exchange of valued shell ornaments in the Trobriand Islands, in which white shell armbands are traded around the islands in a counterclockwise direction and red shell necklaces are traded clockwise.

Laws (Scientific)   associations or relationships that are accepted by almost all scientists.

Levirate   a custom whereby a man is obliged to marry his brother's widow.

Lexical Content   vocabulary or lexicon.

Lexicon   the words and morphs, and their meanings, of a language; approximated by a dictionary.

Lineage   a set of kin whose members trace descent from a common ancestor through known links.

Linguistics   the study of language.

Magic   the performance of certain rituals that are believed to compel the supernatural powers to act in particular ways.

Maladaptive   a trait that diminishes the chances of survival and reproduction in a particular environment. Usually applied to biological evolution, the term is often used by cultural anthropologists to refer to behavioral or cultural traits that are likely to disappear because they diminish reproductive success.

Mana   a supernatural, impersonal force that inhabits certain objects or people and is believed to confer success and/or strength.

Manumission   the granting of freedom to a slave.

Market Exchange or transactions in which the "prices" are subject to supply and demand, whether or not the transactions occur in a marketplace. Also called commercial exchange.

Marriage a socially approved sexual and economic union between a man and a woman that is presumed, both by the couple and by others, to be more or less permanent, and that subsumes reciprocal rights and obligations between the two spouses and between spouses and their future children.

Matriclan a clan tracing descent through the female line.

Matrifocal Family a family consisting of a mother and her children.

Matrilineage a kin group whose members trace descent through known links in the female line from a common ancestress.

Matrilineal Descent the rule of descent that affiliates an individual with kin of both sexes related to him or her through *women* only.

Matrilocal Residence a pattern of residence in which a married couple lives with or near the wife's parents.

Measure to describe how something compares with other things on some scale of variation.

Medium part-time religious practitioner who is asked to heal and divine while in a trance.

Moiety a unilineal descent group in a society that is divided into two such maximal groups; there may be smaller unilineal descent groups as well.

Monogamy marriage between only one man and only one woman at a time.

Monotheistic believing that there is only one high god and that all other supernatural beings are subordinate to, or are alternative manifestations of, this supreme being.

Morph the smallest unit of a language that has a meaning.

Morpheme one or more morphs with the same meaning.

Morphology the study of how sound sequences convey meaning.

Negative Reciprocity giving and taking that attempts to take advantage of another for one's own interest.

Neolocal Residence a pattern of residence whereby a married couple lives separately, and usually at some distance, from the kin of both spouses.

Nonfraternal Polyandry marriage of a woman to two or more men who are not brothers.

Nonsororal Polygyny marriage of a man to two or more women who are not sisters.

Norms standards or rules about acceptable behavior in a society. The importance of a norm usually can be judged by how members of a society respond when the norm is violated.

Nuclear Family a family consisting of a married couple and their young children.

Oath the act of calling upon a deity to bear witness to the truth of what one says.

Operational Definition a description of the procedure that is followed in measuring a variable.

Optimal Foraging Theory the theory that individuals seek to maximize the returns (in calories and nutrients) on their labor in deciding which animals and plants they will go after.

Ordeal a means of determining guilt or innocence by submitting the accused to dangerous or painful tests believed to be under supernatural control.

Paleoanthropology see **Human Paleontology.**

Parallel Cousins children of siblings of the same sex. One's parallel cousins are father's brothers' children and mother's sisters' children.

Participant Observer an observer who participates (immerses himself or herself) in the language and customs of the natives he or she is studying.

Participant-Observation living among the people being studied—observing, questioning, and (when possible) taking part in the important events of the group. Writing or otherwise recording notes on observations, questions asked and answered, and things to check out later are parts of participant-observation.

Pastoralism a form of subsistence technology in which food-getting is based directly or indirectly on the maintenance of domesticated animals.

Patriclan a clan tracing descent through the male line.

Patrilineage a kin group whose members trace descent through known links in the male line from a common ancestor.

Patrilineal Descent the rule of descent that affiliates an individual with kin of both sexes related to him or her through *men* only.

Patrilocal Residence a pattern of residence in which a married couple lives with or near the husband's parents.

Peasants rural people who produce food for their own subsistence but who must also contribute or sell their surpluses to others (in towns and cities) who do not produce their own food.

Personality the distinctive way an individual thinks, feels, and behaves.

Personality Integration of Culture the theory that personality or psychological processes may account for connections between certain aspects of culture.

Phone a speech sound in a language.

Phoneme a set of slightly varying sounds that do not make any difference in meaning to the speakers of the language.

Phonology the study of the sounds in a language and how they are used.

Phratry a unilineal descent group composed of a number of supposedly related clans (sibs).

Physical Anthropology the study of humans as physical organisms, dealing with the emergence and evolution of humans and with contemporary biological variations among human populations. Also called biological anthropology.

Polyandry the marriage of one woman to more than one man at a time.

Polygamy plural marriage; marriage to more than one spouse simultaneously.

Polygyny the marriage of one man to more than one woman at a time.

Polyphony two or more melodies sung simultaneously.

Polytheistic recognizing many gods, none of whom is believed to be superordinate.

Postpartum Sex Taboo prohibition of sexual intercourse between a couple for a period of time after the birth of their child.

Potlatch a feast among Northwest Coast Indians at which great quantities of food and goods are given to the guests in order to gain prestige for the host(s).

Practicing Anthropology see **Applied Anthropology.**

Prairie tall-grass land.

Prehistory the time before written records.

Priest generally a full-time specialist, with very high status, who is thought to be able to relate to superior or high gods beyond the ordinary person's access or control.

Primary Institutions the sources of early experiences, such as family organization and subsistence techniques, that presumably help form the basic, or typical, personality found in a society.

Primary Subsistence Activities the food-getting activities: gathering, hunting, fishing, herding, and agriculture.

Primate a member of the mammalian order Primates, divided into the two suborders of prosimians and anthropoids.

Primatologists persons who study primates.

Probability Value (p-value) the likelihood that an observed result could have occurred by chance.

Projective Tests tests that utilize ambiguous stimuli; test subjects must project their own personality traits in order to structure the ambiguous stimuli.

Protolanguage a hypothesized ancestral language from which two or more languages seem to have derived.

Raiding a short-term use of force, generally planned and organized, to realize a limited objective.

Random Sample a sample in which all cases selected have had an equal chance to be included.

Rank Society a society with no unequal access to economic resources or power, but with social groups that have unequal access to status positions and prestige.

Reciprocity giving and taking (not politically arranged) without the use of money.

Redistribution the accumulation of goods (or labor) by a particular person or in a particular place and their subsequent distribution.

Religion any set of attitudes, beliefs, and practices pertaining to supernatural power, whether that power rests in forces, gods, spirits, ghosts, or demons.

Revitalization Movement a new religious movement intended to save a culture by infusing it with a new purpose and life.

Revolution A usually violent replacement of a society's rulers.

Rules of Descent rules that connect individuals with particular sets of kin because of known or presumed common ancestry.

Sampling Universe the list of cases to be sampled from.

Savanna tropical grassland.

Secondary Institutions aspects of culture such as religion, music, art, folklore, and games, which presumably reflect or are projections of the basic, or typical, personality in a society.

Secondary Subsistence Activities activities that involve the preparation and processing of food either to make it edible or to store it.

Segmentary Lineage System a hierarchy of more and more inclusive lineages; usually functions only in conflict situations.

Sexually Dimorphic refers to a species in which males differ markedly from females in size and appearance.

Shaman a religious intermediary, usually part-time, whose primary function is to cure people through sacred songs, pantomime, and other means; sometimes called witch doctor by Westerners.

Shifting Cultivation see **Extensive Cultivation.**

Sib see **Clan.**

Siblings a person's brothers and sisters.

Slash-and-Burn a form of shifting cultivation in which the natural vegetation is cut down and burned off. The cleared ground is used for a short time and then left to regenerate.

Slaves a class of persons who do not own their own labor or the products thereof.

Socialization a term used by anthropologists and psychologists to describe the development, through the direct and indirect influence of parents and others, of children's patterns of behavior (and attitudes and values) that conform to cultural expectations.

Society a group of people who occupy a particular territory and speak a common language not generally understood by neighboring peoples. By this definition, societies do not necessarily correspond to nations.

Sociobiology see **Behavioral Ecology.**

Sociolinguistics the study of cultural and subcultural patterns of speaking in different social contexts.

Sorcery the use of certain materials to invoke supernatural powers to harm people.

Sororal Polygyny the marriage of a man to two or more sisters at the same time.

Sororate a custom whereby a woman is obliged to marry her deceased sister's husband.

Special-Purpose Money objects of value for which only some goods and services can be exchanged.

Specific Evolution the particular sequence of change and adaptation of a society in a given environment.

Spirits unnamed supernatural beings of nonhuman origin who are beneath the gods in prestige and often closer to the people; may be helpful, mischievous, or evil.

State a political unit with centralized decision making affecting a large population. Most states have cities with public buildings; full-time craft and religious specialists; an "official" art style; a hierarchical social structure topped by an elite class; and a governmental monopoly on the legitimate use of force to implement policies.

Statistical Association a relationship or correlation between two or more variables that is unlikely to be due to chance.

Statistically Significant refers to a result that would occur very rarely by chance. The result (and stronger ones) would occur fewer than 5 times out of 100 by chance.

Status a position of prestige in a society.

Steppe grassland with a dry, low grass cover.

Structuralism the theoretical orientation that human culture is a surface representation of the underlying structure of the human mind.

Structural Linguistics the study of how languages are constructed. Also called descriptive linguistics.

Subculture the shared customs of a subgroup within a society.

Subsistence Technology the methods humans use to procure food.

Supernatural believed to be not human or not subject to the laws of nature.

Syntax the ways in which words are arranged to form phrases and sentences.

Taboo a prohibition that, if violated, is believed to bring supernatural punishment.

Theoretical Construct something that cannot be observed or verified directly.

Theories explanations of associations or laws.

Totem a plant or animal associated with a clan (sib) as a means of group identification; may have other special significance for the group.

Tribal Organization the kind of political organization in which local communities mostly act autonomously but there are kin groups (such as clans) or associations (such as age-sets) that can temporarily integrate a number of local groups into a larger unit.

Tribe a territorial population in which there are kin or nonkin groups with representatives in a number of local groups.

Tundra treeless plains characteristic of sub-Arctic and Arctic regions.

Unilineal Descent affiliation with a group of kin through descent links of one sex only.

Unilocal Residence a pattern of residence (patrilocal, matrilocal, or avunculocal) that specifies just one set of relatives that the married couple lives with or near.

Unisex Association an association that restricts its membership to one sex, usually male.

Universally Ascribed Qualities those ascribed qualities (age, sex) that are found in all societies.

Variable a thing or quantity that varies.

Variably Ascribed Qualities those ascribed qualities (such as ethnic, religious, or social-class differences) that are found only in some societies.

Warfare violence between political entities such as communities, districts, or nations.

Witchcraft the practice of attempting to harm people by supernatural means, but through emotions and thought alone, not through the use of tangible objects.

Bibliography

'ABD ALLAH, MAHMUD M. "Siwan Customs." *Harvard African Studies,* 1 (1917): 1–28.

ABERLE, DAVID. "A Note on Relative Deprivation Theory as Applied to Millenarian and Other Cult Movements." In Lessa and Vogt, eds., *Reader in Comparative Religion,* 3rd ed.

ABERLE, DAVID F., URIE BRONFENBRENNER, ECKHARD H. HESS, DANIEL R. MILLER, DAVID M. SCHNEIDER, AND JAMES M. SPUHLER. "The Incest Taboo and the Mating Patterns of Animals." *American Anthropologist,* 65 (1963): 253–65.

ABLER, THOMAS S. "Iroquois: The Tree of Peace and the War Kettle." In Ember, Ember, and Levinson, eds., *Portraits of Culture.*

ADAMS, DAVID B. "Why There Are So Few Women Warriors." *Behavior Science Research,* 18 (1983): 196–212.

ADLER, MORTIMER. *Drawing Down the Moon.* Boston: Beacon, 1986.

AKMAJIAN, ADRIAN, RICHARD A. DEMERS, AND ROBERT M. HARNISH. *Linguistics: An Introduction to Language and Communication.* 3rd ed. Cambridge, MA: MIT Press, 1990.

ALERS, OSCAR. "Well-Being." In Dobyns, Doughty, and Lasswell, eds., *Peasants, Power, and Applied Social Change.*

ANDERSON, RICHARD L. *Art in Small-Scale Societies.* 2nd ed. Englewood Cliffs, NJ: Prentice Hall, 1989.

ANDERSON, RICHARD L. *Calliope's Sisters: A Comparative Study of Philosophies of Art.* Englewood Cliffs, NJ: Prentice Hall, 1990.

ANDERSON, RICHARD L. "Do Other Cultures Have 'Art'?" *American Anthropologist,* 94 (1992): 926–29.

ANTHONY, DAVID, DIMITRI Y. TELEGIN, AND DORCAS BROWN. "The Origin of Horseback Riding." *Scientific American,* December 1991, 94–100.

"APPENDIX A: Report of the Committee on Ethics, Society for Applied Anthropology." In Fluehr-Lobban, ed., *Ethics and the Profession of Anthropology.*

"APPENDIX C: Statements on Ethics: Principles of Professional Responsibility, Adopted by the Council of the American Anthropological Association, May 1971." In Fluehr-Lobban, ed., *Ethics and the Profession of Anthropology.*

"APPENDIX F: Professional and Ethical Responsibilities, SfAA." In Fluehr-Lobban, ed., *Ethics and the Profession of Anthropology.*

"APPENDIX H: National Association of Practicing Anthropologists' Ethical Guidelines for Practitioners, 1988." In Fluehr-Lobban, ed., *Ethics and the Profession of Anthropology.*

"APPENDIX I: Revised Principles of Professional Responsibility, 1990." In Fluehr-Lobban, ed., *Ethics and the Profession of Anthropology.*

APTEKAR, LEWIS. "Are Colombian Street Children Neglected? The Contributions of Ethnographic and Ethnohistorical Approaches to the Study of Children." *Anthropology and Education Quarterly,* 22 (1991): 326–49.

APTEKAR, LEWIS. *Environmental Disasters in Global Perspective.* New York: G. K. Hall/Macmillan, 1994.

APTEKAR, LEWIS. *Street Children of Cali.* Durham, NC: Duke University Press, 1988.

ARCHER, DANE, AND ROSEMARY GARTNER. *Violence and Crime in Cross-National Perspective.* New Haven, CT: Yale University Press, 1984.

ARENSBERG, CONRAD M., AND ARTHUR H. NIEHOFF. *Introducing Social Change: A Manual for Americans Overseas.* Chicago: Aldine, 1964.

ARGYLE, MICHAEL. *The Psychology of Social Class.* New York: Routledge, 1994.

ARMSTRONG, ROBERT P. *The Powers of Presence.* Philadelphia: University of Pennsylvania Press, 1981.

ARONOFF, JOEL, ANDREW M. BARCLAY, AND LINDA A. STEVENSON. "The Recognition of Threatening Facial Stimuli." *Journal of Personality and Social Psychology,* 54 (1988): 647–55.

ARONOFF, JOEL, BARBARA A. WOIKE, AND LESTER M. HYMAN. "Which Are the Stimuli in Facial Displays of Anger and Happiness? Configurational Bases of Emotion Recognition." *Journal of Personality and Social Psychology,* 62 (1992): 1050–66.

ASCH, SOLOMON. "Studies of Independence and Conformity: A Minority of One against a Unanimous Majority." *Psychological Monographs,* 70 (1956): 1–70.

ASHTON, HUGH. *The Basuto.* 2nd ed. London: Oxford University Press, 1967.

AUSTIN, LEWIS. "Visual Symbols, Political Ideology, and Culture." *Ethos,* 5 (1977): 306–25.

AYRES, BARBARA C. "Effects of Infant Carrying Practices on Rhythm in Music." *Ethos,* 1 (1973): 387–404.

AYRES, BARBARA C. "Effects of Infantile Stimulation on Musical Behavior." In Lomax, ed., *Folk Song Style and Culture.*

BACHNIK, JANE M. "The Two 'Faces' of Self and Society in Japan." *Ethos,* (1992): 3–32.

BACON, MARGARET, IRVIN L. CHILD, AND HERBERT BARRY III. "A Cross-Cultural Study of Correlates of Crime." *Journal of Abnormal and Social Psychology,* 66 (1963): 291–300.

BADCOCK, CHRISTOPHER. *Essential Freud.* Oxford: Basil Blackwell, 1988.

BAILEY, ROBERT C., GENEVIEVE HEAD, MARK JENIKE, BRUCE OWEN, ROBERT RECTMAN, AND ELZBIETA ZECHENTER. "Hunting and Gathering in Tropical Rain Forest: Is It Possible?" *American Anthropologist,* 91 (1989): 59–82.

BALDI, PHILIP. *An Introduction to the Indo-European Languages.* Carbondale: Southern Illinois University Press, 1983.

BALIKCI, ASEN. *The Netsilik Eskimo.* Garden City, NY: Natural History Press, 1970.

BANTON, MICHAEL, ed. *Anthropological Approaches to the Study of Religion.* Association of Social Anthropologists of the Commonwealth, Monograph No. 3. New York: Praeger, 1966.

BARAK, GREGG. *Gimme Shelter: A Social History of Homelessness in Contemporary America.* New York: Praeger, 1991.

BARASH, DAVID P. *Sociobiology and Behavior.* New York: Elsevier, 1977.

BARINAGA, MARIA. "Priming the Brain's Language Pump." *Science,* January 31, 1992, 535.

BARLETT, PEGGY F. "Industrial Agriculture." In Plattner, ed., *Economic Anthropology.*

BARLETT, PEGGY F., ed. *Agricultural Decision Making: Anthropological Contributions to Rural Development.* New York: Academic Press, 1980.

BARNETT, H. G. *Being a Palauan.* New York: Holt, Rinehart & Winston, 1960.

BARNETT, TONY, AND PIERS BLAIKIE. *AIDS in Africa: Its Present and Future Impact.* London: Belhaven Press, 1992.

BARNOUW, VICTOR. *Culture and Personality.* 4th ed. Homewood, IL: Dorsey Press, 1985.

BARRINGER, HERBERT, GEORGE BLANKSTEIN, AND RAYMOND MACK, eds. *Social Change in Developing Areas: A Re-Interpretation of Evolutionary Theory.* Cambridge, MA: Schenkman, 1965.

BARRY, HERBERT, III, IRVIN L. CHILD, AND MARGARET K. BACON. "Relation of Child Training to Subsistence Economy." *American Anthropologist,* 61 (1959): 51–63.

BARTH, FREDRIK. "Nomadism in the Mountain and Plateau Areas of South West Asia." In *The Problems of the Arid Zone.* Paris: UNESCO, 1960.

BARTH, FREDRIK. *Nomads of South Persia.* Oslo: Universitetsforlaget 1964; Boston: Little, Brown, 1968.

BARTRAM, WILLIAM. *The Travels of William Bartram.* Ed. Francis Harper. New Haven, CT: Yale University Press, 1958.

BAUMAN, RICHARD. "Folklore." In Bauman, ed., *Folklore, Cultural Performances, and Popular Entertainments.*

BAUMAN, RICHARD, ed. *Folklore, Cultural Performances, and Popular Entertainments: A Communications-Centered Handbook.* New York: Oxford University Press, 1992.

BAUMAN, RICHARD, AND JOEL SHERZER. *Explorations in the Ethnography of Speaking*. 2nd ed. New York: Cambridge University Press, 1989.

BAXTER, ELLEN, AND KIM HOPPER. *Private Lives/Public Spaces: Homeless Adults on the Streets of New York City*. New York: Community Service Society of New York, 1981.

BEACH, FRANK A., ed. *Sex and Behavior*. New York: John Wiley, 1965.

BEATTIE, JOHN. *Bunyoro: An African Kingdom*. New York: Holt, Rinehart & Winston, 1960.

BEGLER, ELSIE B. "Sex, Status, and Authority in Egalitarian Society." *American Anthropologist*, 80 (1978): 571–88.

BELLMAN, BERYL L. *The Language of Secrecy: Symbols and Metaphors in Poro Ritual*. New Brunswick, NJ: Rutgers University Press, 1984.

BENEDICT, BURTON. "Controlling Population Growth in Mauritius." In Bernard and Pelto, eds., *Technology and Social Change*. 2nd ed.

BENEDICT, MICHAEL LES. "Ku Klux Klan." *Academic American Encyclopedia*. vol. 12 (K–L), p. 133. Princeton, NJ: Arete Publishing Co., 1980.

BENEDICT, RUTH. *The Chrysanthemum and the Sword*. Boston: Houghton Mifflin, 1946.

BENEDICT, RUTH. *Patterns of Culture*. New York: Mentor, 1959 (originally published 1934).

BENJAMIN, LOIS. *The Black Elite: Facing the Color Line in the Twilight of the Twentieth Century*. Chicago: Nelson-Hall, 1991.

BERLIN, BRENT, AND PAUL KAY. *Basic Color Terms: Their Universality and Evolution*. Berkeley: University of California Press, 1969.

BERNARD, H. RUSSELL. *Research Methods in Cultural Anthropology: Qualitative and Quantitative Approaches*. 2nd ed. Newbury Park, CA: Sage Publications, 1994.

BERNARD, H. RUSSELL, AND PERTTI J. PELTO. "Technology and Anthropological Theory: Conclusions." In Bernard and Pelto, eds., *Technology and Social Change*. 2nd ed.

BERNARD, H. RUSSELL, AND PERTTI J. PELTO, eds. *Technology and Social Change*. 2nd ed. Prospect Heights, IL: Waveland Press, 1987.

BERNARDI, B. "The Age-System of the Nilo-Hamitic Peoples." *Africa*, 22 (1952): 316–32.

BERREMAN, GERALD D. "Caste in India and the United States." *American Journal of Sociology*, 66 (1960): 120–27.

BERREMAN, GERALD D. *Caste in the Modern World*. Morristown, NJ: General Learning Press, 1973.

BERREMAN, GERALD D. "Race, Caste and Other Invidious Distinctions in Social Stratification." *Race*, 13 (1972): 403–14.

BERREMAN, GERALD D., ed. *Social Inequality: Comparative and Developmental Approaches*. New York: Academic Press, 1981.

BERRY, JOHN W. "Ecological and Cultural Factors in Spatial Perceptual Development." *Canadian Journal of Behavioural Science*, 3 (1971): 324–36.

BERRY, JOHN W. *Human Ecology and Cognitive Style*. New York: John Wiley, 1976.

BERRY, JOHN W., AND J. BENNETT. "Syllabic Literacy and Cognitive Performance among the Cree." *International Journal of Psychology*, 24 (1989): 429–50.

BERRY, JOHN W., YPE H. POORTINGA, MARSHALL H. SEGALL, AND PIERRE R. DASEN. *Cross-Cultural Psychology: Research and Applications*. New York: Cambridge University Press, 1992.

BICKERTON, DEREK. "Creole Languages." *Scientific American*, July 1983, 116–22.

BINFORD, LEWIS R. "Mobility, Housing, and Environment: A Comparative Study." *Journal of Anthropological Research*, 46 (1990): 119–52.

BINFORD, LEWIS R. "Post-Pleistocene Adaptations." In Struever, ed., *Prehistoric Agriculture*.

BLACK, DONALD. *The Social Structure of Right and Wrong*. San Diego: Academic Press, 1993.

BLALOCK, HUBERT M., JR. *Social Statistics*. 2nd ed. New York: McGraw-Hill, 1972.

BLANTON, RICHARD E. "Variation in Economy." In Ember and Ember, eds., *Cross-Cultural Research for Social Science*.

BLEDSOE, CAROLINE H. *Women and Marriage in Kpelle Society*. Stanford, CA: Stanford University Press, 1980.

BLOCK, JEAN L. "Help! They've *All* Moved Back Home!" *Woman's Day*, April 26, 1983, pp. 72–76.

BLOUNT, BEN G. "The Development of Language in Children." In Munroe, Munroe, and Whiting, eds., *Handbook of Cross-Cultural Human Development*.

BLUMBERG, RAE L. *Stratification: Socioeconomic and Sexual Inequality*. Dubuque, IA: Wm C. Brown, 1978.

BLUMLER, MARK A., AND ROGER BYRNE. "The Ecological Genetics of Domestication and the Origins of Agriculture." *Current Anthropology*, 32 (1991): 23–35.

BOAS, FRANZ. *Central Eskimos*. Bureau of American Ethnology, Annual Report No. 6. Washington, D.C., 1988.

BOAS, FRANZ. "On Grammatical Categories." In Hymes, ed., *Language in Culture and Society*. (Originally published 1911.)

BOAS, FRANZ. *Race, Language, and Culture*. New York: Macmillan, 1940.

BOAS, FRANZ. *The Religion of the Kwakiutl*. Columbia University Contributions to Anthropology, vol. 10, pt. 2. New York: Columbia University, 1930.

BOCK, PHILIP K. *Continuities in Psychological Anthropology: A Historical Introduction*. San Francisco: W. H. Freeman, 1980.

BODLEY, JOHN H. *Anthropology and Contemporary Human Problems*. 2nd ed. Mountainview, CA: Mayfield, 1985.

BODLEY, JOHN H. *Victims of Progress*. 3rd ed. Mountainview, CA: Mayfield, 1990.

BOGORAS, WALDEMAR. "The Chukchee," pt 3. *Memoirs of the American Museum of Natural History*, 2 (1909).

BOHANNAN, LAURA, AND PAUL BOHANNAN. *The Tiv of Central Nigeria*. London: International African Institute, 1953.

BOHANNAN, PAUL. "The Migration and Expansion of the Tiv." *Africa*, 24 (1954): 2–16.

BOHANNAN, PAUL, AND GEORGE DALTON, eds. *Markets in Africa*. Garden City, NY: Doubleday, 1965.

BOHANNAN, PAUL, AND JOHN MIDDLETON, eds. *Marriage, Family and Residence*. Garden City, NY: Natural History Press, 1968.

BOLLEN, KENNETH A. "Liberal Democracy: Validity and Method Factors in Cross-National Measures." *American Journal of Political Science*, 37 (1993): 1207–30.

BOLTON, RALPH. "Aggression and Hypoglycemia among the Qolla: A Study in Psychobiological Anthropology." *Ethnology*, 12 (1973): 227–57.

BOLTON, RALPH. "AIDS and Promiscuity: Muddled in the Models of HIV Prevention." *Medical Anthropology*, 14 (1992): 145–223.

BOLTON, RALPH. "Introduction: The AIDS Pandemic, A Global Emergency." *Medical Anthropology*, 10 (1989): 93–104.

BORNSTEIN, MARC H. "The Psychophysiological Component of Cultural Difference in Color Naming and Illusion Susceptibility." *Behavior Science Notes*, 8 (1973): 41–101.

BOSERUP, ESTER. *The Conditions of Agricultural Growth: The Economics of Agrarian Change under Population Pressure*. Chicago: Aldine, 1965.

BOSERUP, ESTER. *Woman's Role in Economic Development*. New York: St. Martin's Press, 1970.

BOURGUIGNON, ERIKA. "Introduction: A Framework for the Comparative Study of Altered States of Consciousness." In Bourguignon, *Religion, Altered States of Consciousness, and Social Change*.

BOURGUIGNON, ERIKA. *Religion, Altered States of Consciousness, and Social Change*. Columbus: Ohio State University Press, 1973.

BOURGUIGNON, ERIKA, AND THOMAS L. EVASCU. "Altered States of Consciousness within a General Evolutionary Perspective: A Holocultural Analysis." *Behavior Science Research*, 12 (1977): 197–216.

BOYD, ROBERT, AND PETER J. RICHERSON. *Culture and the Evolutionary Process*. Chicago: University of Chicago Press, 1985.

BOYD, ROBERT, AND PETER J. RICHERSON. "Group Selection among Alternative Evolutionarily Stable Strategies." *Journal of Theoretical Biology*, 145 (1990): 331–42.

BRADLEY, CANDICE. "Keeping the Soil in Good Heart: Weeding, Women and Ecofeminism." In Warren, ed., *Ecofeminism*.

BRADLEY, CANDICE. "The Sexual Division of Labor and the Value of Children." *Behavior Science Research*, 19 (1984–1985). 159–85.

BRADLEY, CANDICE, AND ULRIKA DAHL. "The Committee on the Status of Women in Anthropology/American Anthropological Association 1992 Vita Dataset: A Report to the Committee to Study the Academic Employment of Women in Anthropology and the Committee on the Status of Women in Anthropology." November 1993.

BRANDEWIE, ERNEST. "The Place of the Big Man in Traditional Hagen Society in the Central Highlands of New Guinea." In McGlynn and Tuden, eds., *Anthropological Approaches to Political Behavior*.

BRANDON, GEORGE. "African-Americans: Getting into the Spirit." In Ember, Ember, and Levinson, eds., *Portraits of Culture*.

BRAUN, DAVID P., AND STEPHEN PLOG. "Evolution of 'Tribal' Social Networks: Theory and Prehistoric North American Evidence." *American Antiquity*, 47 (1982): 504–25.

BRIGGS, JEAN L. "Eskimo Women: Makers of Men." In Matthiasson, *Many Sisters: Women in Cross-Cultural Perspective*.

BRINTON, CRANE. *The Anatomy of Revolution*. Englewood Cliffs, NJ: Prentice Hall, 1938.

BRITTAIN, JOHN A. *Inheritance and the Inequality of Material Wealth*. Washington, D.C.: Brookings Institution, 1978.

BROUDE, GWEN J. "Cross-Cultural Patterning of Some Sexual Attitudes and Practices." *Behavior Science Research*, 11 (1976): 227–62.

BROUDE, GWEN J. "Extramarital Sex Norms in Cross-Cultural Perspective." *Behavior Science Research*, 15 (1980): 181–218.

BROUDE, GWEN J. "Variations in Sexual Attitudes, Norms, and Practices." In Ember and Ember, eds., *Cross-Cultural Research for Social Science*.

BROUDE, GWEN J., AND SARAH J. GREENE. "Cross-Cultural Codes on Twenty Sexual Attitudes and Practices." *Ethnology*, 15 (1976): 409–29.

BROWN, CECIL H. "Folk Botanical Life-Forms: Their Universality and Growth." *American Anthropologist*, 79 (1977): 317–42.

BROWN, CECIL H. "Folk Zoological Life-Forms: Their Universality and Growth." *American Anthropologist*, 81 (1979): 791–817.

BROWN, CECIL H. "World View and Lexical Uniformities." *Reviews in Anthropology*, 11 (1984): 99–112.

BROWN, CECIL H., AND STANLEY R. WITKOWSKI. "Language Universals." Appendix B in Levinson and Malone, eds., *Toward Explaining Human Culture*.

BROWN, DONALD E. *Human Universals*. Philadelphia: Temple University Press, 1991.

BROWN, JUDITH K. "Economic Organization and the Position of Women among the Iroquois." *Ethnohistory*, 17 (1970): 151–67.

BROWN, JUDITH K. "A Note on the Division of Labor by Sex." *American Anthropologist,* 72 (1970): 1073–78.

BROWN, ROGER. "The First Sentence of Child and Chimpanzee." In Sebeok and Umiker-Sebeok, eds., *Speaking of Apes.*

BROWN, ROGER. *Social Psychology.* New York: Free Press, 1965.

BROWN, ROGER, AND MARGUERITE FORD. "Address in American English." *Journal of Abnormal and Social Psychology,* 62 (1961): 375–85.

BRUMFIEL, ELIZABETH M. "Origins of Social Inequality." In Ember, Ember, and Peregrine, eds., *Research Frontiers in Anthropology.*

BRUNVAND, JAN HAROLD. *The Baby Train: And Other Lusty Urban Legends.* New York: W. W. Norton, 1993.

BRYANT, CAROL A., AND DORAINE F. C. BAILEY. "The Use of Focus Group Research in Program Development." In van Willigen and Finan, eds., *Soundings.*

BUNZEL, RUTH. "The Nature of Katcinas." In Lessa and Vogt, eds., *Reader in Comparative Religion,* 3rd ed.

BURBANK, VICTORIA K. "Adolescent Socialization and Initiation Ceremonies." In Ember and Ember, eds., *Cross-Cultural Research for Social Science.*

BURBANK, VICTORIA K. "Australian Aborigines: An Adolescent Mother and Her Family." In Ember, Ember, and Levinson, eds., *Portraits of Culture.*

BURBANK, VICTORIA K. *Fighting Women: Anger and Aggression in Aboriginal Australia.* Berkeley: University of California Press, 1994.

BURCH, ERNEST S., JR. *The Eskimos.* Norman: University of Oklahoma Press, 1988.

BURCH, ERNEST S., JR. "North Alaskan Eskimos: A Changing Way of Life." In Ember, Ember, and Levinson, eds., *Portraits of Culture.*

BURKHALTER, S. BRIAN, AND ROBERT F. MURPHY. "Tappers and Sappers: Rubber, Gold and Money among the Mundurucú." *American Ethnologist.* 16 (1989): 100–16.

BURLING, R. *Man's Many Voices: Language in Its Cultural Context.* New York: Holt, Rinehart & Winston, 1970.

BURNS, ALISA, AND CATH SCOTT. *Mother-Headed Families and Why They Have Increased.* Hillsdale, NJ: Lawrence Erlbaum Associates, 1994.

BURTON, ROGER V., AND JOHN W. M. WHITING. "The Absent Father and Cross-Sex Identity." *Merrill-Palmer Quarterly of Behavior and Development,* 7, no. 2 (1961): 85–95.

BUSBY, ANNETTE. "Kurds: A Culture Straddling National Borders." In Ember, Ember, and Levinson, eds., *Portraits of Culture.*

BYRNE, BRYAN. "Access to Subsistence Resources and the Sexual Division of Labor among Potters." *Cross-Cultural Research,* 28 (1994): 225–50.

BYRNE, ROGER. "Climatic Change and the Origins of Agriculture." In Manzanilla, ed., *Studies in the Neolithic and Urban Revolutions.*

CAMPBELL, DONALD T. "Variation and Selective Retention in Socio-Cultural Evolution." In Barringer, Blankstein, and Mack, eds., *Social Change in Developing Areas.*

CAMPBELL, JOSEPH. *The Hero with a Thousand Faces.* New York: Pantheon Books, 1949.

CANCIAN, FRANK. "Risk and Uncertainty in Agricultural Decision Making." In Barlett, ed., *Agricultural Decision Making.*

CAPORAEL, LINNDA R. "Ergotism: The Satan Loosed in Salem?" *Science,* April 2, 1976, pp. 21–26.

CARCOPINO, JEROME. *Daily Life in Ancient Rome: The People and the City at the Height of the Empire.* Edited with bibliography and notes by Henry T. Rowell. Translated from the French by E. O. Lorimer. New Haven, CT: Yale University Press, 1940.

CARLISLE, RONALD C., AND MICHAEL I. SIEGEL. "Additional Comments on Problems in the Interpretation of Neandertal Speech Capabilities." *American Anthropologist,* 80 (1978): 367–72.

CARNEIRO, ROBERT L. "Chiefdom-Level Warfare as Exemplified in Fiji and the Cauca Valley." In Haas, ed., *The Anthropology of War.*

CARNEIRO, ROBERT L. "Political Expansion as an Expression of the Principle of Competitive Exclusion." In Cohen and Service, eds., *Origins of the State.*

CARNEIRO, ROBERT L. "Slash-and-Burn Cultivation among the Kuikuru and Its Implications for Settlement Patterns." In Cohen, ed., *Man in Adaptation.*

CARNEIRO, ROBERT L. "A Theory of the Origin of the State." *Science,* August 21, 1970, pp. 733–38.

CARRASCO, PEDRO. "The Civil-Religious Hierarchy in Mesoamerican Communities: Pre-Spanish Background and Colonial Development." *American Anthropologist,* 63 (1961): 483–97.

CARRIER, JAMES G. "Marine Tenure and Conservation in Papua New Guinea." In McCay and Acheson, eds., *The Question of Commons.*

CARRIER, JOSEPH AND RALPH BOLTON. "Anthropological Perspectives on Sexuality and HIV Prevention." *Annual Review of Sex Research,* 2 (1991): 49–75.

CARROLL, JOHN B., ed. *Language, Thought, and Reality: Selected Writings of Benjamin Lee Whorf.* New York: John Wiley, 1956.

CARROLL, MICHAEL. "A New Look at Freud on Myth." *Ethos,* 7 (1979): 189–205.

CASHDAN, ELIZABETH A. "Egalitarianism among Hunters and Gatherers." *American Anthropologist,* 82 (1980): 116–20.

CASHDAN, ELIZABETH, ed. *Risk and Uncertainty in Tribal and Peasant Economies.* Boulder, CO: Westview Press, 1990.

CAULKINS, D. DOUGLAS. "Norwegians: Cooperative Individualists." In Ember, Ember, and Levinson, eds., *Portraits of Culture.*

CAVALLI-SFORZA, L. L. AND M. W. FELDMAN. *Cultural Transmission and Evolution: A Quantitative Approach.* Princeton, NJ: Princeton University Press, 1981.

CAWS, PETER. "The Structure of Discovery." *Science,* December 12, 1969, 1375–80.

CHAFETZ, JANET SALTZMAN. *Gender Equity: An Integrated Theory of Stability and Change.* Sage Library of Social Research No. 176. Newbury Park, CA: Sage Publications, 1990.

CHAGNON, NAPOLEON. *Yanomamö: The Fierce People.* 3rd ed. New York: Holt, Rinehart & Winston, 1987.

CHAGNON, NAPOLEON, AND WILLIAM IRONS, eds. *Evolutionary Biology and Human Social Behavior: An Anthropological Perspective.* North Scituate, MA: Duxbury, 1979.

CHAUCER, GEOFFREY. *The Prologue to the Canterbury Tales, the Knights Tale, the Nonnes Prestes Tale.* Ed. Mark H. Liddell. New York: Macmillan, 1926.

CHAYANOV, ALEXANDER V. *The Theory of Peasant Economy,* ed. Daniel Thorner, Basile Kerblay, and R. E. F. Smith. Homewood, IL: Richard D. Irwin, 1966.

CHIBNIK, MICHAEL. "The Economic Effects of Household Demography: A Cross-Cultural Assessment of Chayanov's Theory." In Maclachlan, ed., *Household Economies and Their Transformations.*

CHIBNIK, MICHAEL. "The Evolution of Cultural Rules." *Journal of Anthropological Research,* 37 (1981): 256–68.

CHIBNIK, MICHAEL. "The Statistical Behavior Approach: The Choice between Wage Labor and Cash Cropping in Rural Belize." In Barlett, ed., *Agricultural Decision-Making.*

CHOMSKY, NOAM. *Reflections on Language.* New York: Pantheon, 1975.

CLIFFORD, JAMES. "Introduction: Partial Truths." In James Clifford and George E. Marcus, eds., *Writing Culture: The Poetics and Politics of Ethnography.* Berkeley: University of California Press, 1986.

CLIFTON, JAMES H., ed. *Introduction to Cultural Anthropology.* Boston: Houghton Mifflin, 1968.

COHEN, ALEX. "A Cross-Cultural Study of the Effects of Environmental Unpredictability on Aggression in Folktales." *American Anthropologist,* 92 (1990): 474–79.

COHEN, ALEX, AND PAUL KOEGEL. "Homelessness." In Ember, Ember, and Peregrine, eds., *Research Frontiers in Anthropology.*

COHEN, MARK N. *The Food Crisis in Prehistory: Overpopulation and the Origins of Agriculture.* New Haven, CT: Yale University Press, 1977.

COHEN, MARK N. "Population Pressure and the Origins of Agriculture." In Reed, ed., *Origins of Agriculture.*

COHEN, MYRON. "Developmental Process in the Chinese Domestic Group." In Maurice Freedman, ed., *Family and Kinship in Chinese Society.* Stanford, CA: Stanford University Press, 1970.

COHEN, MYRON L. *House United, House Divided: The Chinese Family in Taiwan.* New York: Columbia University Press, 1976.

COHEN, MYRON. "Variations in Complexity among Chinese Family Groups: The Impact of Modernization." *Transactions of the New York Academy of Sciences,* 29 (1967): 638–44.

COHEN, RONALD. "Introduction." In Cohen and Toland, eds., *State Formation and Political Legitimacy.* Volume 6.

COHEN, RONALD, AND JOHN MIDDLETON, eds. *Comparative Political Systems.* Garden City, NY: Natural History Press, 1967.

COHEN, RONALD, AND ELMAN R. SERVICE, eds. *Origins of the State: The Anthropology of Political Evolution.* Philadelphia: Institute for the Study of Human Issues, 1978.

COHEN, RONALD, AND JUDITH D. TOLAND, eds. *State Formation and Political Legitimacy.* Vol. 6: *Political Anthropology.* New Brunswick, NJ: Transaction Books, 1988.

COHEN, YEHUDI, ed. *Man in Adaptation: The Cultural Present.* Chicago: Aldine, 1968.

CONROY, GLENN C. *Primate Evolution.* New York: W. W. Norton, 1990.

COREIL, JEANNINE. "Lessons from a Community Study of Oral Rehydration Therapy in Haiti." In van Willigen, Rylko-Bauer, and McElroy, eds., *Making Our Research Useful.*

COULT, ALLAN D., AND ROBERT W. HABENSTEIN. *Cross Tabulations of Murdock's World Ethnographic Sample.* Columbia: University of Missouri Press, 1965.

CREED, GERALD W. "Bulgaria: Anthropological Corrections to Cold War Stereotypes." In Ember, Ember, and Levinson, eds., *Portraits of Culture.*

CUTRIGHT, PHILLIPS. "Inequality: A Cross-National Analysis." *American Sociological Review,* 32 (1967): 562–78.

DAHLBERG, FRANCES, ed. *Woman the Gatherer.* New Haven, CT: Yale University Press, 1981.

DALTON, GEORGE, ed. *Tribal and Peasant Economies: Readings in Economic Anthropology.* Garden City, NY: Natural History Press, 1967.

DALY, MARTIN, AND MARGO WILSON. *Homicide.* New York: Aldine de Gruyter, 1988.

DASEN, PIERRE R., JOHN W. BERRY, AND N. SARTORIUS, eds. *Health and Cross-Cultural Psychology: Toward Applications.* Newbury Park, CA: Sage Publications, 1988.

DASEN, PIERRE R., AND ALASTAIR HERON. "Cross-Cultural Tests of Piaget's Theory." In Triandis and Heron, eds., *Handbook of Cross-Cultural Psychology.* Vol. 4, *Developmental Psychology.*

DAVENPORT, WILLIAM. "Nonunilinear Descent and Descent Groups." *American Anthropologist,* 61 (1959): 557–72.

DAVENPORT, WILLIAM. "Sexual Patterns and Their Regulation in a Society of the Southwest Pacific." In Beach, ed., *Sex and Behavior.*

DAVIS, DEBORAH, AND STEVAN HARRELL, eds. *Chinese Families in the Post-Mao Era.* Berkeley: University of California Press, 1993.

DAVIS, SUSAN SCHAEFER. "Morocco: Adolescents in a Small Town." In Ember, Ember, and Levinson, eds., *Portraits of Culture.*

DAVIS, SUSAN SCHAEFER. "Rebellious Teens? A Moroccan Instance." Paper presented at MESA, November 1993.

DAVIS, WILLIAM D. "Societal Complexity and the Nature of Primitive Man's Conception of the Supernatural." Ph.D. dissertation. University of Carolina, Chapel Hill, 1971.

DAWSON, J. L. M. "Cultural and Physiological Influences Upon Spatial-Perceptual Processes in West Africa." *International Journal of Psychology,* 2 (1967): 115–28, 171–85.

DENNY, J. PETER. "The 'Extendedness' Variable in Classifier Semantics: Universal Features and Cultural Variation." In Mathiot, ed., *Ethnolinguistics.*

DENTAN, ROBERT K. *The Semai: A Nonviolent People of Malaya.* New York: Holt, Rinehart & Winston, 1968.

DEUTSCH, A., ed. *Sex Habits of American Men.* Englewood Cliffs, NJ: Prentice Hall, 1948.

DE VILLIERS, PETER A., AND JILL G. DE VILLIERS. *Early Language.* Cambridge, MA: Harvard University Press, 1979.

DE VITA, PHILIP, AND JAMES D. ARMSTRONG. *Distant Mirrors: America as a Foreign Culture.* Belmont, CA: Wadsworth, 1993.

DEVORE, IRVEN, AND MELVIN J. KONNER. "Infancy in Hunter-Gatherer Life: An Ethological Perspective." In White, ed., *Ethology and Psychiatry.*

DIAMOND, NORMA. "Collectivization, Kinship, and the Status of Women in Rural China." In Reiter, *Toward an Anthropology of Women.*

DIRKS, ROBERT. "Hunger and Famine." In Ember, Ember, and Peregrine, eds., *Research Frontiers in Anthropology.*

DIVALE, WILLIAM T. "Migration, External Warfare, and Matrilocal Residence." *Behavior Science Research,* 9 (1974): 75–133.

DIVALE, WILLIAM T., AND MARVIN HARRIS. "Population, Warfare, and the Male Supremacist Complex." *American Anthropologist,* 78 (1976): 521–38.

DOBYNS, HENRY F., PAUL L. DOUGHTY, AND HAROLD D. LASSWELL, eds. *Peasants, Power, and Applied Social Change: Vicos as a Model.* Beverly Hills, CA: Sage Publications, 1971.

DONALDSON, PETER. *Worlds Apart: The Economic Gulf between Nations.* London: British Broadcasting Corporation, 1971.

DOUGHTY, PAUL L. "Vicos: Success, Rejection, and Rediscovery of a Classic Program." In Eddy and Partridge, eds., *Applied Anthropology in America.*

DOUGLAS, MARY. *Implicit Meanings: Essays in Anthropology.* London: Routledge and Kegan Paul, 1975.

DOW, JAMES. *The Shaman's Touch: Otomi Indian Symbolic Healing.* Salt Lake City: University of Utah Press, 1986.

DOW, JAMES W. "Sierra Otomí: People of the Mexican Mountains." In Ember, Ember, and Levinson, eds., *Portraits of Culture*

DOWLING, JOHN H. "Property Relations and Productive Strategies in Pastoral Societies." *American Ethnologist,* 2 (1975): 419–26.

DRAPER, PATRICIA. "!Kung Women: Contrasts in Sexual Egalitarianism in Foraging and Sedentary Contexts." In Reiter, ed., *Toward an Anthropology of Women.*

DRAPER, PATRICIA, AND ELIZABETH CASHDAN. "Technological Change and Child Behavior among the !Kung." *Ethnology,* 27 (1988): 339–65.

DRESSLER, WILLIAM W., AND MICHAEL C. ROBBINS. "Art Styles, Social Stratification, and Cognition: An Analysis of Greek Vase Painting." *American Ethnologist,* 2 (1975): 427–34.

DRUCKER, PHILIP. *Cultures of the North Pacific Coast.* San Francisco: Chandler, 1965.

DRUCKER, PHILIP. "The Potlatch." In Dalton, ed., *Tribal and Peasant Economies.*

DU BOIS, CORA. *The People of Alor: A Social-Psychological Study of an East Indian Island.* Minneapolis: University of Minnesota Press, 1944.

DUNDES, ALAN. *Folklore Matters.* Knoxville: University of Tennessee Press, 1989.

DUNDES, ALAN. "Structural Typology in North American Indian Folktales." In Dundes, ed., *The Study of Folklore.*

DUNDES, ALAN, ed. *The Study of Folklore.* Englewood Cliffs, NJ: Prentice Hall, 1965.

DURHAM, WILLIAM H. *Coevolution: Genes, Culture and Human Diversity.* Stanford, CA: Stanford University Press, 1991.

DURHAM, WILLIAM H. "Toward a Coevolutionary Theory of Human Biology and Culture." In Chagnon and Irons, eds., *Evolutionary Biology and Human Social Behavior.*

DURKHEIM, ÉMILE. *The Elementary Forms of the Religious Life.* Trans. Joseph W. Swain. New York: Collier Books, 1961. (Originally published 1912.)

DURKHEIM, ÉMILE. *The Rules of Sociological Method.* 8th ed. Trans. Sarah A. Soloway and John H. Mueller. ed. George E. Catlin. New York: Free Press, 1938. (Originally published 1895.)

"DWINDLING NUMBERS ON THE FARM." *Nation's Business,* April 1988, 16.

DYSON-HUDSON, NEVILLE. *Karimojong Politics.* Oxford: Clarendon Press, 1966.

DYSON-HUDSON, RADA, AND ERIC ALDEN SMITH. "Human Territoriality: An Ecological Reassessment." *American Anthropologist,* 80 (1978): 21–41.

ECKHARDT, WILLIAM. "Primitive Militarism." *Journal of Peace Research,* 12 (1975): 55–62.

EDDY, ELIZABETH M., AND WILLIAM L. PARTRIDGE, eds. *Applied Anthropology in America.* New York: Columbia University Press, 1978.

EDDY, ELIZABETH M., AND WILLIAM L. PARTRIDGE, eds. *Applied Anthropology in America.* 2nd ed. New York: Columbia University Press, 1987.

EDGERTON, ROBERT B. "Conceptions of Psychosis in Four East African Societies." *American Anthropologist,* 68 (1966): 408–25.

EDGERTON, ROBERT B. *The Individual in Cultural Adaptation: A Study of Four East African Peoples.* Berkeley: University of California Press, 1971.

EDGERTON, ROBERT B. *Sick Societies: Challenging the Myth of Primitive Harmony.* New York: The Free Press, 1992.

EDGERTON, ROBERT B., AND LEWIS L. LANGNESS. *Methods and Styles in the Study of Culture.* San Francisco: Chandler & Sharp, 1974.

EGGAN, FRED. *The Social Organization of the Western Pueblos.* Chicago: University of Chicago Press, 1950.

EISENSTADT, S. N. "African Age Groups." *Africa,* 24 (1954): 100–111.

EISENSTADT, S. N. *From Generation to Generation: Age Groups and Social Structure.* New York: Free Press, 1956.

ELIOT, T. S. "The Love Song of J. Alfred Prufrock." In *Collected Poems, 1909–1962.* New York: Harcourt Brace, & World, 1963.

ELLIS, LEE. "Evidence of Neuroandrogenic Etiology of Sex Roles from a Combined Analysis of Human, Nonhuman Primate and Nonprimate Mammalian Studies." *Personality and Individual Differences,* 7 (1986): 519–52.

ELWIN, VERRIER. *The Religion of an Indian Tribe.* London: Oxford University Press, 1955.

EMBER, CAROL R. "Cross-Cultural Cognitive Studies." *Annual Review of Anthropology,* 6 (1977): 33–56.

EMBER, CAROL R. "A Cross-Cultural Perspective on Sex Differences." In Munroe, Munroe, and Whiting, eds., *Handbook of Cross-Cultural Human Development.*

EMBER, CAROL R. "An Evaluation of Alternative Theories of Matrilocal versus Patrilocal Residence." *Behavior Science Research,* 9 (1974): 135–49.

EMBER, CAROL R. "Feminine Task Assignment and the Social Behavior of Boys." *Ethos,* 1 (1973): 424–39.

EMBER, CAROL R. "Men's Fear of Sex with Women: A Cross-Cultural Study." *Sex Roles,* 4 (1978): 657–78.

EMBER, CAROL R. "Myths about Hunter-Gatherers." *Ethnology,* 17 (1978): 439–48.

EMBER, CAROL R. "The Relative Decline in Women's Contribution to Agriculture with Intensification." *American Anthropologist,* 85 (1983): 285–304.

EMBER, CAROL R. "Residential Variation among Hunter-Gatherers." *Behavior Science Research,* 9 (1975): 135–49.

EMBER, CAROL R. "Universal and Variable Patterns of Gender Difference." In Ember and Ember, eds., *Cross-Cultural Research for Social Science.*

EMBER, CAROL R., AND MELVIN EMBER. *Anthropology,* 8th ed. Upper Saddle River, NJ: Prentice Hall, 1996.

EMBER, CAROL R., AND MELVIN EMBER. "The Conditions Favoring Multilocal Residence." *Southwestern Journal of Anthropology,* 28 (1972): 382–400.

EMBER, CAROL R., AND MELVIN EMBER. "On Cross-Cultural Research." In Ember and Ember, eds., *Cross-Cultural Research for Social Science.*

EMBER, CAROL R., AND MELVIN EMBER. *Guide to Cross-Cultural Research Using the HRAF Archive.* New Haven, CT: Human Relations Area Files, 1988.

EMBER, CAROL R., AND MELVIN EMBER. "Issues in Cross-Cultural Studies of Interpersonal Violence." *Violence and Victims,* 8 (1993): 217–33.

EMBER, CAROL R., AND MELVIN EMBER. "Resource Unpredictability, Mistrust, and War: A Cross-Cultural Study." *Journal of Conflict Resolution,* 36 (1992): 242–62.

EMBER, CAROL R., AND MELVIN EMBER. "Violence in the Ethnographic Record: Results of Cross-Cultural Research on War and Aggression." In Frayer and Martin, eds., *Troubled Times.*

EMBER, CAROL R., AND MELVIN EMBER. "War, Socialization, and Interpersonal Violence: A Cross-Cultural Study." *Journal of Conflict Resolution,* 38 (1994): 620–46.

EMBER, CAROL R., AND MELVIN EMBER, eds. *Cross-Cultural Research for Social Science.* Englewood Cliffs, NJ: Prentice Hall, 1995. Prentice Hall/Simon & Schuster Custom Publishing.

EMBER, CAROL R., MELVIN EMBER, AND BURTON PASTERNAK. "On the Development of Unilineal Descent." *Journal of Anthropological Research,* 30 (1974): 69–94.

EMBER, CAROL R., MELVIN EMBER, AND PETER N. PEREGRINE, eds. *Research Frontiers in Anthropology.* Englewood Cliffs, NJ: Prentice Hall, 1995. Prentice Hall/Simon & Schuster Custom Publishing.

EMBER, CAROL R., MELVIN EMBER, AND BRUCE RUSSETT. "Peace between Participatory Polities: A Cross-Cultural Test of the 'Democracies Rarely Fight Each Other' Hypothesis." *World Politics,* 44 (1992): 573–99.

EMBER, CAROL R., AND DAVID LEVINSON. "The Substantive Contributions of Worldwide Cross-Cultural Studies Using Secondary Data." *Behavior Science Research* 25 (1991): 79–140.

EMBER, MELVIN. "Alternative Predictors of Polygyny." *Behavior Science Research,* 19 (1984–1985): 1–23.

EMBER, MELVIN. "The Conditions That May Favor Avunculocal Residence." *Behavior Science Research,* 9 (1974): 203–9.

EMBER, MELVIN. "The Emergence of Neolocal Residence." *Transactions of the New York Academy of Sciences,* 30 (1967): 291–302.

EMBER, MELVIN. "Evidence and Science in Ethnography: Reflections on the Freeman-Mead Controversy." *American Anthropologist,* 87 (1985): 906–9.

EMBER, MELVIN. "The Logic of Comparative Research." *Behavior Science Research,* 25 (1991): 143–53.

EMBER, MELVIN. "The Nonunilinear Descent Groups of Samoa." *American Anthropologist,* 61 (1959): 573–77.

EMBER, MELVIN. "On the Origin and Extension of the Incest Taboo." *Behavior Science Research,* 10 (1975): 249–81.

EMBER, MELVIN. "The Relationship between Economic and Political Development in Nonindustrialized Societies." *Ethnology,* 2 (1963): 228–48.

EMBER, MELVIN. "Size of Color Lexicon: Interaction of Cultural and Biological Factors." *American Anthropologist,* 80 (1978): 364–67.

EMBER, MELVIN. "Statistical Evidence for an Ecological Explanation of Warfare." *American Anthropologist,* 84 (1982): 645–49.

EMBER, MELVIN. "Taxonomy in Comparative Studies." In Naroll and Cohen, eds., *A Handbook of Method in Cultural Anthropology.*

EMBER, MELVIN. "Warfare, Sex Ratio, and Polygyny." *Ethnology,* 13 (1974): 197–206.

EMBER, MELVIN, AND CAROL R. EMBER. "The Conditions Favoring Matrilocal versus Patrilocal Residence." *American Anthropologist,* 73 (1971): 571–94.

EMBER, MELVIN, AND CAROL R. EMBER. "Cross-Cultural Studies of War and Peace: Recent Achievements and Future Possibilities." In Reyna and Downs, eds., *Studying War.*

EMBER, MELVIN, AND CAROL R. EMBER. "Male-Female Bonding: A Cross-Species Study of Mammals and Birds." *Behavior Science Research,* 14 (1979): 37–56.

EMBER, MELVIN, AND CAROL R. EMBER. *Marriage, Family, and Kinship: Comparative Studies of Social Organization.* New Haven, CT: HRAF Press, 1983.

EMBER, MELVIN, CAROL R. EMBER, AND DAVID LEVINSON, eds., *Portraits of Culture: Ethnographic Originals.* Englewood Cliffs, NJ: Prentice Hall, 1994/1995. Prentice Hall/Simon & Schuster Custom Publishing.

EMBER, MELVIN, CAROL R. EMBER, AND BRUCE RUSSETT. "Inequality and Democracy in the Anthropological Record." Paper presented at a conference on Inequality and Democracy, organized by Manus Midlarsky at Rutgers University, February 1994.

EMENER, WILLIAM G., AND MARGARET DARROW, eds. *Career Explorations in Human Services.* Springfield, IL: Charles C. Thomas, 1991.

EPSTEIN, CYNTHIA FUCHS. *Deceptive Distinctions: Sex, Gender, and the Social Order.* New York: Russell Sage Foundation, 1988.

ERCHAK, GERALD M. "Family Violence." In Ember, Ember, and Peregrine, eds., *Research Frontiers in Anthropology.*

ERICKSEN, KAREN PAIGE. "Male and Female Age Organizations and Secret Societies in Africa." *Behavior Science Research,* 23 (1989): 234–64.

ERICKSON, EDWIN. "Self-assertion, Sex Role, and Vocal Rasp." In Lomax, ed., *Folk Song Style and Culture.*

ERRINGTON, J. JOSEPH. "On the Nature of the Sociolinguistic Sign: Describing the Javanese Speech Levels." In Mertz and Parmentier, eds., *Semiotic Mediation.*

ERVIN, ALEXANDER M. "Styles and Strategies of Leadership During the Alaskan Native Land Claims Movement: 1959–71." *Anthropologica,* 29 (1987): 21–38.

ETIENNE, MONA, AND ELEANOR LEACOCK, eds. *Women and Colonization: Anthropological Perspectives.* New York: Praeger, 1980.

ETTER, MARTIN A. "Sahlins and Sociobiology." *American Ethnologist,* 5 (1978): 160–68.

EURIPIDES. "The Trojan Women." In Edith Hamilton, trans., *Three Greek Plays.* New York: Norton, 1937, p. 52.

EVANS-PRITCHARD, E. E. "Nuer Modes of Address." *Uganda Journal,* 12 (1948): 166–71.

EVANS-PRITCHARD, E. E. "The Nuer of the Southern Sudan." In Fortes and Evans-Pritchard, eds., *African Political Systems.*

EVANS-PRITCHARD, E. E. "Sexual Inversion among the Azande." *American Anthropologist,* 72 (1970): 1428–34.

EVANS-PRITCHARD, E. E. "Witchcraft Explains Unfortunate Events." In Lessa and Vogt, eds., *Reader in Comparative Religion,* 4th ed.

FAGAN, BRIAN M. *People of the Earth: An Introduction to World Prehistory.* 7th ed. New York: Harper Collins, 1992.

FEATHERMAN, DAVID L., AND ROBERT M. HAUSER. *Opportunity and Change.* New York: Academic Press, 1978.

FEINMAN, GARY, AND JILL NEITZEL. "Too Many Types: An Overview of Sedentary Prestate Societies in the Americas." In Schiffer, ed., *Advances in Archaeological Methods and Theory.* Vol. 7.

FELDMAN, DOUGLAS A., AND THOMAS M. JOHNSON. "Introduction." In Feldman and Johnson, eds., *The Social Dimensions of AIDS.*

FELDMAN, DOUGLAS A., AND THOMAS M. JOHNSON, eds. *The Social Dimensions of AIDS: Method and Theory.* New York: Praeger, 1986.

FERGUSON, R. BRIAN, ed. *Warfare, Culture, and Environment.* Orlando, FL: Academic Press, 1984.

FERRARO, GARY P. *The Cultural Dimension of International Business.* 2nd ed. Englewood Cliffs, NJ: Prentice Hall, 1994.

FINLEY, M. I. *Politics in the Ancient World.* Cambridge: Cambridge University Press, 1983.

FIRTH, RAYMOND. *Rank and Religion in Tikopia.* Boston: Beacon Press, 1970.

FIRTH, RAYMOND. *Social Change in Tikopia.* New York: Macmillan, 1959.

FIRTH, RAYMOND. *We, the Tikopia.* Boston: Beacon Press, 1957.

FISCHER, JOHN. "Art Styles as Cultural Cognitive Maps." *American Anthropologist,* 63 (1961): 80–83.

FISHER, WILLIAM H. "Megadevelopment, Environmentalism, and Resistance: The Institutional Context of Kayapo Indigenous Politics in Central Brazil." *Human Organization,* 53 (1994): 220–32.

FLANNERY, KENT V. "The Origins and Ecological Effects of Early Domestication in Iran and the Near East." In Struever, ed., *Prehistoric Agriculture.*

FLANNERY, KENT V. "The Research Problem." In Flannery, ed., *Guila Naquitz.*

FLANNERY, KENT V., ed. *Guila Naquitz: Archaic Foraging and Early Agriculture in Oaxaca, Mexico.* Orlando, FL: Academic Press, 1986.

FLUEHR-LOBBAN, CAROLYN, ed. *Ethics and the Profession of Anthropology: Dialogue for a New Era.* Philadelphia: University of Pennsylvania Press, 1991.

FORD, CLELLAN S. *Smoke from Their Fires.* New Haven, CT: Yale University Press, 1941.

FORD, CLELLAN S., ed. *Cross-Cultural Approaches: Readings in Comparative Research.* New Haven, CT: HRAF Press, 1967.

FORD, CLELLAN S., AND FRANK A. BEACH. *Patterns of Sexual Behavior.* New York: Harper, 1951.

FORTES, MEYER. *The Web of Kinship among the Tallensi.* New York: Oxford University Press, 1949.

FORTES, MEYER, AND E. E. EVANS-PRITCHARD, eds. *African Political Systems.* New York: Oxford University Press, 1940.

FOSTER, BRIAN L. "Ethnicity and Commerce." *American Ethnologist,* 1 (1974): 437–47.

FOSTER, GEORGE M. *Applied Anthropology.* Boston: Little, Brown, 1969.

FOSTER, GEORGE M. *Traditional Cultures and the Impact of Technological Change.* New York: Harper & Row, 1962.

FOSTER, PHILIPS. *The World Food Problem: Tackling the Causes of Undernutrition in the Third World.* Boulder, CO: Lynne Rienner, 1992.

FOX, ROBIN. *Kinship and Marriage: An Anthropological Perspective.* Cambridge: Cambridge University Press, 1983.

FRAKE, CHARLES O. "The Eastern Subanun of Mindanao." In Murdock, ed., *Social Structure in Southeast Asia.*

FRANK, ANDRÉ GUNDER. *Capitalism and Underdevelopment in Latin America: Historical Studies of Chile and Brazil.* New York: Monthly Review Press, 1967.

FRANKEL, BARBARA, AND M. G. TREND. "Principles, Pressures and Paychecks: The Anthropologist as Employee." In Fluehr-Lobban, ed., *Ethics and the Profession of Anthropology.*

FRAYER, DAVID, AND DEBRA MARTIN, eds. *Troubled Times: Osteological and Archaeological Evidence of Violence.* Langhorne, PA: Gordon and Breach, 1995.

FRAYER, DAVID W., AND MILFORD H. WOLPOFF. "Sexual Dimorphism." *Annual Review of Anthropology,* 14 (1985): 429–73.

FRAYSER, SUZANNE G. *Varieties of Sexual Experience.* New Haven, CT: HRAF Press, 1985.

FREEDMAN, DANIEL G. "Ethnic Differences in Babies." *Human Nature,* January 1979, 36–43.

FREEDMAN, RONALD, AND JOHN Y. TAKESHITA. *Family Planning in Taiwan: An Experiment in Social Change.* Princeton: Princeton University Press, 1969.

FREEMAN, DEREK. *Margaret Mead and Samoa: The Making and Unmaking of an Anthropological Myth.* Cambridge, MA: Harvard University Press, 1983.

FREEMAN, J. D. "On the Concept of the Kindred." *Journal of the Royal Anthropological Institute,* 91 (1961): 192–220.

FREILICH, MORRIS, ed. *The Meaning of Culture.* Lexington, MA: Xerox, 1972.

FREUD, SIGMUND. *A General Introduction to Psychoanalysis.* Garden City, NY: Garden City Publishing, 1943. (Originally published in German, 1917.)

FREUD, SIGMUND. *Moses and Monotheism.* Katherine Jones, trans. New York: Vintage Books, 1967. (Originally published 1939.)

FRIED, MORTON H. *The Evolution of Political Society: An Essay in Political Anthropology.* New York: Random House, 1967.

FRIEDL, ERNESTINE. *Vasilika: A Village in Modern Greece.* New York: Holt, Rinehart & Winston, 1962.

FRIEDRICH, PAUL. *The Language Parallax.* Austin: University of Texas Press, 1986.

FRIEDRICH, PAUL. *Proto-Indo-European Trees: The Arboreal System of a Prehistoric People.* Chicago: University of Chicago Press, 1970.

FROMM, ERICH. *Psychoanalysis and Religion.* New Haven, CT: Yale University Press, 1950.

GAL, SUSAN. "The Political Economy of Code Choice." In Heller, ed., *Codeswitching.*

GARDNER, R. ALLEN, AND BEATRICE T. GARDNER. "Comparative Psychology and Language Acquisition." In Sebeok and Umiker-Sebeok, eds., *Speaking of Apes.*

GARFIELD, VIOLA E., ed. *Symposium: Patterns of Land Utilization, and Other Papers.* Proceedings of the Annual Spring Meeting of American Ethnological Society, 1961. Seattle: University of Washington Press, 1962.

GARTNER, ROSEMARY. "Crime: Variations across Cultures and Nations." In Ember and Ember, eds., *Cross-Cultural Research for Social Science.*

GAULIN, STEVEN J. C., AND JAMES S. BOSTER. "Dowry as Female Competition." *American Anthropologist,* 92 (1990): 994–1005.

GEERTZ, CLIFFORD. "Deep Play: Notes on the Balinese Cockfight." In Geertz, *The Interpretation of Cultures.*

GEERTZ, CLIFFORD. *The Interpretation of Cultures: Selected Essays.* New York: Basic Books, 1973.

GEERTZ, CLIFFORD. "'From the Native's Point of View': On the Nature of Anthropological Understanding." In Shweder and LeVine, eds., *Culture Theory.*

GEERTZ, CLIFFORD. "Religion as a Cultural System." In Banton, ed., *Anthropological Approaches to the Study of Religion.*

GEERTZ, CLIFFORD. *The Religion of Java.* New York: Free Press, 1960.

GEERTZ, CLIFFORD. "Thick Description: Toward an Interpretative Theory of Culture." In Geertz, *The Interpretation of Cultures.*

GELLES, RICHARD J., AND MURRAY A. STRAUS. *Intimate Violence.* New York: Simon & Schuster, 1988.

GIBBONS, ANN. "Déjà Vu All Over Again: Chimp Language Wars." *Science,* March 29, 1991, 1561–62.

GIBBS, JAMES L., JR. "The Kpelle of Liberia." In Gibbs, ed., *Peoples of Africa.*

GIBBS, JAMES L., JR., ed. *Peoples of Africa.* New York: Holt, Rinehart & Winston, 1965.

GILLIGAN, CAROL. *In a Different Voice: Psychological Theory and Women's Development.* Cambridge, MA: Harvard University Press, 1982.

GILLIGAN, CAROL, AND JANE ATTANUCCI. "Two Moral Orientations." In Gilligan, Ward, and Taylor, eds., *Mapping the Moral Domain.*

GILLIGAN, CAROL, JANIE VICTORIA WARD, AND JILL McLEAN TAYLOR, EDS. *Mapping the Moral Domain: A Contribution of Women's Thinking to Psychological Theory and Education.* Cambridge, MA: Harvard University Press, 1988.

GILMAN, ANTONIO. "The Development of Social Stratification in Bronze Age Europe." *Current Anthropology,* 22 (1990): 1–23.

GIMBUTAS, MARIJA. "An Archaeologist's View of PIE* in 1975." *Journal of Indo-European Studies,* 2 (1974): 289–307.

GLADWIN, CHRISTINA H. "A Theory of Real-Life Choice: Applications to Agricultural Decisions." In Barlett, ed., *Agricultural Decision-Making.*

GLEITMAN, LILA R., AND ERIC WANNER. "Language Acquisition: The State of the State of the Art." In Wanner and Gleitman, eds., *Language Acquisition.*

GOLDE, PEGGY, ed. *Women in the Field: Anthropological Experience.* 2nd ed. Berkeley: University of California Press, 1986.

GOLDSTEIN, MELVYN C. "Stratification, Polyandry, and Family Structure in Central Tibet." *Southwestern Journal of Anthropology,* 27 (1971): 65–74.

GOLDSTEIN, MELVYN C. "When Brothers Share a Wife." *Natural History,* March 1987, 39–48.

GOLDSTONE, J. A. "The Comparative and Historical Study of Revolutions." *Annual Review of Sociology,* 8 (1982): 187–207.

GOODE, WILLIAM J. *The Family.* 2nd ed. Englewood Cliffs, NJ: Prentice Hall, 1982.

GOODE, WILLIAM J. *World Revolution and Family Patterns.* New York: Free Press, 1970.

GOODENOUGH, WARD H. *Cooperation in Change.* New York: Russell Sage Foundation, 1963.

GOODENOUGH, WARD H. *Property, Kin, and Community on Truk.* New Haven, CT: Yale University Press, 1951.

GOODENOUGH, WARD H., ed. *Explorations in Cultural Anthropology.* New York: McGraw-Hill, 1964.

GOODMAN, MADELEINE J., P. BION GRIFFIN, AGNES A. ESTIOKO-GRIFFIN, AND JOHN S. GROVE. "The Compatability of Hunting and Mothering among the Agta Hunter-Gatherers of the Philippines." *Sex Roles,* 12 (1985): 1199–209.

GOODY, JACK. "Bridewealth and Dowry in Africa and Eurasia." In Goody and Tambiah, eds., *Bridewealth and Dowry.*

GOODY, JACK. "Cousin Terms." *Southwestern Journal of Anthropology,* 26 (1970): 125–42.

GOODY, JACK, AND S. H. TAMBIAH, eds. *Bridewealth and Dowry.* Cambridge: Cambridge University Press, 1973.

GORER, GEOFFREY. "Themes in Japanese Culture." *Transactions of the New York Academy of Sciences,* 5 (1943): 106–24.

GORER, GEOFFREY, AND JOHN RICKMAN. *The People of Great Russia: A Psychological Study.* New York: Chanticleer, 1950.

GOSSEN, GARY H. "Temporal and Spatial Equivalents in Chamula Ritual Symbolism." In Lessa and Vogt, eds., *Reader in Comparative Religion,* 4th ed.

GOUGH, KATHLEEN. "Nayar: Central Kerala." In Schneider and Gough, eds., *Matrilineal Kinship.*

GOUGH, KATHLEEN. "The Nayars and the Definition of Marriage." *Journal of the Royal Anthropological Institute,* 89 (1959): 23–34.

GOULD, RICHARD A. *Yiwara: Foragers of the Australian Desert.* New York: Scribner's, 1969.

GRABURN, NELSON H. *Eskimos without Igloos.* Boston: Little, Brown, 1969.

GRAHAM, SUSAN BRANDT. "Biology and Human Social Behavior: A Response to van den Berghe and Barash." *American Anthropologist,* 81 (1979): 357–60.

GRAY, J. PATRICK. *Primate Sociobiology.* New Haven, CT: HRAF Press, 1985.

GREENBERG, JOSEPH H. *Anthropological Linguistics: An Introduction.* New York: Random House, 1968.

GREENBERG, JOSEPH H. "Linguistic Evidence Regarding Bantu Origins." *Journal of African History,* 13 (1972): 189–216.

GREENBERG, JOSEPH H., AND MERRITT RUHLEN. "Linguistic Origins of Native Americans." *Scientific American,* November 1992, 94–99.

GREGORY, C. A. *Gifts and Commodities.* New York: Academic Press, 1982.

GRÖGER, B. LISA. "Of Men and Machines: Cooperation among French Family Farmers." *Ethnology,* 20 (1981): 163–75.

GROSS, DANIEL R., GEORGE EITEN, NANCY M. FLOWERS, FRANCISCA M. LEOI, MADELINE LATTMAN RITTER, AND DENNIS W. WERNER. "Ecology and Acculturation among Native Peoples of Central Brazil." *Science,* November 30, 1979, 1043–50.

GROSS, DANIEL R., AND BARBARA A. UNDERWOOD. "Technological Change and Caloric Costs: Sisal Agriculture in Northeastern Brazil." *American Anthropologist,* 73 (1971): 725–40.

GUBSER, NICHOLAS J. *The Nunamiut Eskimos: Hunters of Caribou.* New Haven, CT: Yale University Press, 1965.

GUIORA, ALEXANDER Z., BENJAMIN BEIT-HALLAHMI, RISTO FRIED, AND CECELIA YODER. "Language Environment and Gender Identity Attainment." *Language Learning,* 32 (1982): 289–304.

GULLIVER, P. H. "The Arusha: Economic and Social Change." In Bohannan and Dalton, eds., *Markets in Africa.*

GUMPERZ, JOHN J. "Dialect Differences and Social Stratification in a North Indian Village." In *Language in Social Groups: Essays by John L. Gumperz,* selected and introduced by Anwar S. Dil. Stanford, CA: Stanford University Press, 1971.

GUMPERZ, JOHN J. "Speech Variation and the Study of Indian Civilization." *American Anthropologist,* 63 (1961): 976–88.

GURR, TED ROBERT. "Historical Trends in Violent Crime: Europe and the United States." In Gurr, ed., *Violence in America, Vol. 1.*

GURR, TED ROBERT. "The History of Violent Crime in America: An Overview." In Gurr, ed., *Violence in America, Vol. 1.*

GURR, TED ROBERT, ed. *Violence in America, Vol. 1, The History of Crime.* Newbury Park, CA: Sage, 1987.

GUTHRIE, DALE R. "Mosaics, Allelochemics, and Nutrients: An Ecological Theory of Late Pleistocene Megafaunal Extinctions." In Martin and Klein, eds., *Quaternary Extinctions.*

HAAS, JONATHAN. "Warfare and the Evolution of Tribal Polities in the Prehistoric Southwest." In Haas, ed., *The Anthropology of War.*

HAAS, JONATHAN, ed. *The Anthropology of War.* New York: Cambridge University Press, 1990.

HAAS, MARY R. "Men's and Women's Speech in Koasati." *Language,* 20 (1944): 142–49.

HACKENBERG, ROBERT A. "Scientists or Survivors? The Future of Applied Anthropology under Maximum Uncertainty." In Trotter ed., *Anthropology for Tomorrow.*

HAGE, JERALD, AND CHARLES H. POWERS. *Post-Industrial Lives: Roles and Relationships in the 21st Century.* Newbury Parks, CA: Sage Publications, 1992.

HAHN, EMILY. "Chimpanzees and Language." *New Yorker,* April 24, 1971, 54ff.

HALL, EDWARD T. *The Hidden Dimension.* Garden City, NY: Doubleday, 1966.

HALL, EDWARD T., AND M. R. HALL. *Hidden Differences: Doing Business with the Japanese.* Garden City, NY: Anchor, 1987.

HAMES, RAYMOND. "Sharing among the Yanomamo: Part I, the Effects of Risk." In Cashdan, ed., *Risk and Uncertainty in Tribal and Peasant Economies.*

HAMES, RAYMOND. "Yanomamö: Varying Adaptations of Foraging Horticulturalists." In Ember, Ember, and Levinson, eds., *Portraits of Culture.*

HANDWERKER, W. PENN, AND PAUL V. CROSBIE. "Sex and Dominance." *American Anthropologist,* 84 (1982): 97–104.

HANSON, JEFFERY R. "Age-Set Theory and Plains Indian Age-Grading: A Critical Review and Revision." *American Ethnologist,* 15 (1988): 349–64.

HARDOY, JORGE, AND DAVID SATTERTHWAITE. "The Legal and the Illegal City." In Rodwin, ed., *Shelter, Settlement, and Development.*

HARNER, MICHAEL. "The Role of Hallucinogenic Plants in European Witchcraft." In Harner, ed., *Hallucinogens and Shamanism.*

HARNER, MICHAEL J. "Scarcity, the Factors of Production, and Social Evolution." In Polgar, ed., *Population, Ecology, and Social Evolution.*

HARNER, MICHAEL, ed. *Hallucinogens and Shamanism.* New York: Oxford University Press, 1972.

HARRIS, MARVIN. *Cows, Pigs, Wars and Witches: The Riddles of Culture.* New York: Random House, Vintage, 1975.

HARRIS, MARVIN. "The Cultural Ecology of India's Sacred Cattle." *Current Anthropology,* 7 (1966): 51–63.

HARRIS, MARVIN. *Patterns of Race in the Americas.* New York: Walker, 1964.

HARRIS, MARVIN. *The Rise of Anthropological Theory: A History of Theories of Culture.* New York: Thomas Y. Crowell, 1968.

HARRIS, MARVIN, AND ERIC B. ROSS. *Food and Evolution: Toward a Theory of Human Food Habits.* Philadelphia: Temple University Press, 1987.

HARRISON, GAIL G. "Primary Adult Lactase Deficiency: A Problem in Anthropological Genetics." *American Anthropologist,* 77 (1975): 812–35.

HART, HORNELL. "The Logistic Growth of Political Areas." *Social Forces,* 26 (1948): 396–408.

HAYS, TERENCE E. "From Ethnographer to Comparativist and Back Again." In Ember, Ember, and Peregrine, eds., *Research Frontiers in Anthropology.*

HEATH, DWIGHT B., AND RICHARD N. ADAMS, eds. *Contemporary Cultures and Societies of Latin America.* New York: Random House, 1965.

HEIDER, KARL. *The Dugum Dani.* Chicago: Aldine, 1970.

HEIDER, KARL. *Grand Valley Dani: Peaceful Warriors.* New York: Holt, Rinehart & Winston, 1979.

HEISE, DAVID R. "Cultural Patterning of Sexual Socialization." *American Sociological Review,* 32 (1967): 726–39.

HELLER, MONICA. "Introduction." In Heller, ed., *Codeswitching.*

HELLER, MONICA, ed. *Codeswitching: Anthropological and Sociolinguistic Perspectives.* Berlin: Mouton de Gruyter, 1988.

HELMS, MARY W. *Ancient Panama: Chiefs in Search of Power.* Austin: University of Texas Press, 1979.

HELMS, MARY W. "Miskitos: Adaptations to Colonial Empires, Past and Present." In Ember, Ember, and Levinson, eds., *Portraits of Culture.*

HEMPEL, CARL G. *Aspects of Scientific Explanation.* New York: Free Press, 1965.

HENDRIX, LLEWELLYN. "Economy and Child Training Reexamined." *Ethos,* 13 (1985): 246–61.

HENDRIX, LLEWELLYN. "Varieties of Marital Relationships." In Ember and Ember, eds., *Cross-Cultural Research for Social Science.*

HENRY, DONALD O. *From Foraging to Agriculture: The Levant at the End of the Ice Age.* Philadelphia: University of Pennsylvania Press, 1989.

HENRY, EDWARD O. "The Variety of Music in a North Indian Village: Reassessing Cantometrics." *Ethnomusicology,* 20 (1976): 49–66.

HERRMAN, HELEN. "A Survey of Homeless Mentally Ill People in Melbourne, Australia." *Hospital and Community Psychiatry,* 41 (1990): 1291–92.

HEWLETT, BARRY. "Diverse Contexts of Human Infancy." In Ember and Ember, eds., *Cross-Cultural Research for Social Science.*

HEWLETT, BARRY S., AND L. L. CAVALLI-SFORZA. "Cultural Transmission among Aka Pygmies." *American Anthropologist,* 88 (1986): 922–34.

HIATT, L. R. "Polyandry in Sri Lanka: A Test Case for Parental Investment Theory." *Man,* 15 (1980): 583–98.

HICKEY, GERALD CANNON. *Village in Vietnam.* New Haven, CT: Yale University Press, 1964.

HICKSON, LETITIA. "The Social Contexts of Apology in Dispute Settlement: A Cross-Cultural Study." *Ethnology,* 25 (1986): 283–94.

HILL, JANE H. "Apes and Language." *Annual Review of Anthropology,* 7 (1978): 89–112.

HILL, JANE H. "Do Apes Have Language?" In Ember, Ember, and Peregrine, eds., *Research Frontiers in Anthropology.*

HILL, KIM, HILLARD KAPLAN, KRISTEN HAWKES, AND A. MAGDALENA HURTADO. "Foraging Decisions among Aché Hunter-Gatherers: New Data and Implications for Optimal Foraging Models." *Ethology and Sociobiology,* 8 (1987): 1–36.

HILL, POLLY. *The Migrant Cocoa-Farmers of Southern Ghana: A Study in Rural Capitalism.* Cambridge: Cambridge University Press, 1963.

HOBSBAWM, E. J. *Age of Revolution.* New York: Praeger, 1970.

HOCKETT, C. F., AND R. ASCHER. "The Human Revolution." *Current Anthropology,* 5 (1964): 135–68.

HOEBEL, E. ADAMSON. *The Cheyennes: Indians of the Great Plains.* New York: Holt, Rinehart & Winston, 1960.

HOEBEL, E. ADAMSON. *The Law of Primitive Man.* New York: Atheneum, 1968 (originally published 1954).

HOFFMAN, LOIS WLADIS. "Cross-Cultural Differences in Childrearing Goals." In LeVine, Miller, and West, eds., *Parental Behavior in Diverse Societies.*

HOIJER, HARRY. "Cultural Implications of Some Navaho Linguistic Categories." In Hymes, ed., *Language in Culture and Society.*

HOLLAN, DOUGLAS. "Cross-Cultural Differences in the Self." *Journal of Anthropological Research,* 48 (1992): 289–90.

HOLLAND, DOROTHY, AND NAOMI QUINN, eds., *Cultural Models in Language and Thought.* Cambridge: Cambridge University Press, 1987.

HOLLOWAY, MARGUERITE. "Sustaining the Amazon." *Scientific American,* July 1993, 91–99.

HOLMBERG, ALLAN R. "Experimental Intervention in the Field." In Dobyns, Doughty, and Lasswell, eds., *Peasants, Power, and Applied Social Change.*

HOLMBERG, ALLAN R. "The Role of Power in Changing Values and Institutions of Vicos." In Dobyns, Doughty, and Lasswell, eds., *Peasants, Power, and Applied Social Change.*

HOLMES, JANET. *An Introduction to Sociolinguistics.* London: Longman, 1992.

HOPKINS, K. "Brother-Sister Marriage in Roman Egypt." *Comparative Studies in Society and History,* 22 (1980): 303–54.

HONIGMANN, JOHN J. *Personality in Culture.* New York: Harper & Row, 1967.

HOROWITZ, MICHAEL M. "Donors and Deserts: The Political Ecology of Destructive Development in the Sahel." In Huss-Ashmore and Katz, eds., *African Food Systems in Crisis. Part Two.*

HOWARD, ALAN, AND JAN RENSEL. "Rotuma: Interpreting a Wedding." In Ember, Ember, and Levinson, eds., *Portraits of Culture.*

HOWELLS, WILLIAM. *Getting Here: The Story of Human Evolution.* Washington, D.C.: Compass Press, 1993.

HSU, FRANCIS L. K., ed. *Psychological Anthropology.* 2nd ed. Cambridge, MA: Schenkman, 1972.

HUMPHREY, CAROLINE, AND STEPHEN HUGH-JONES. "Introduction: Barter, Exchange and Value." In Humphrey and Hugh-Jones, eds., *Barter, Exchange and Value.*

HUMPHREY, CAROLINE, AND STEPHEN HUGH-JONES, eds. *Barter, Exchange and Value: An Anthropological Approach.* New York: Cambridge University Press, 1992.

HUNT, MORTON. *Sexual Behavior in the 1970s.* Chicago: Playboy Press, 1974.

HURTADO, ANA M., KRISTEN HAWKES, KIM HILL, AND HILLARD KAPLAN. "Female Subsistence Strategies among the Aché Hunter-Gatherers of Eastern Paraguay." *Human Ecology,* 13 (1985): 1–28.

HUSS-ASHMORE, REBECCA, AND SOLOMON H. KATZ, eds. *African Food Systems in Crisis. Part Two: Contending with Change.* New York: Gordon and Breach, 1990.

HYMES, DELL. *Foundations in Sociolinguistics: An Ethnographic Approach.* Philadelphia: University of Pennsylvania Press, 1974.

HYMES, DELL, ed. *Language in Culture and Society: A Reader in Linguistics and Anthropology.* New York: Harper & Row, 1964.

INGOLD, TIM, DAVID RICHES, AND JAMES WOODBURN, eds. *Hunters and Gatherers 1: History, Evolution and Social Change.* New York: St. Martin's Press, 1988.

IRONS, WILLIAM. "Natural Selection, Adaptation, and Human Social Behavior." In Chagnon and Irons, eds., *Evolutionary Biology and Human Social Behavior.*

IRWIN, MARC H., GARY N. SCHAFER, AND CYNTHIA P. FEIDEN. "Emic and Unfamiliar Category Sorting of Mano Farmers and U.S. Undergraduates." *Journal of Cross-Cultural Psychology,* 5 (1974): 407–23.

ITKONEN, T. I. "The Lapps of Finland." *Southwestern Journal of Anthropology,* 7 (1951): 32–68.

JACOBS, SUE-ELLEN, AND CHRISTINE ROBERTS. "Sex, Sexuality, Gender and Gender Variance." In Morgen, ed., *Gender and Anthropology.*

JAMES, WILLIAM. *The Varieties of Religious Experience: A Study in Human Nature.* New York: Modern Library, 1902.

JANKOWIAK, WILLIAM R. "Urban Mongols: Ethnicity in Communist China." In Ember, Ember, and Levinson, eds., *Portraits of Culture.*

JANKOWIAK, WILLIAM R., AND EDWARD F. FISCHER. "A Cross-Cultural Perspective on Romantic Love." *Ethnology,* 31 (1992): 149–55.

JANZEN, DANIEL H. "Tropical Agroecosystems." *Science,* December 21, 1973, 1212–19.

JELLIFFE, DERRICK B., AND E. F. PATRICE JELLIFFE. "Human Milk, Nutrition, and the World Resource Crisis." *Science,* May 9, 1975, 557–61.

JOHANNES, R. E. *Words of the Lagoon: Fishing and Marine Lore in the Palau District of Micronesia.* Berkeley: University of California Press, 1981.

JOHNSON, ALLEN W. *Quantification in Cultural Anthropology: An Introduction to Research Design.* Stanford, CA: Stanford University Press, 1978.

JOHNSON, ALLEN, AND TIMOTHY EARLE. *The Evolution of Human Societies: From Foraging Group to Agrarian State.* Stanford, CA: Stanford University Press, 1987.

JONES, STEVE, ROBERT MARTIN, AND DAVID PILBEAM, eds. *The Cambridge Encyclopedia of Human Evolution.* New York: Cambridge University Press, 1992.

JORDAN, ANN T., ed. *Practicing Anthropology in Corporate America: Consulting on Organizational Culture.* NAPA Bulletin, No. 14. Arlington, VA: American Anthropological Association, 1994.

JUNG, CARL G. *Psychology and Religion.* New Haven, CT: Yale University Press, 1938.

KANG, GAY ELIZABETH. "Exogamy and Peace Relations of Social Units: A Cross-Cultural Test." *Ethnology,* 18 (1979): 85–99.

KAPLAN, HILLARD, AND KIM HILL. "Food Sharing among Aché Foragers: Tests of Explanatory Hypotheses." *Current Anthropology,* 26 (1985): 223–46.

KAPLAN, HILLARD, KIM HILL, AND A. MAGDALENA HURTADO. "Risk, Foraging and Food Sharing among the Aché." In Cashdan, ed., *Risk and Uncertainty in Tribal and Peasant Economies.*

KARDINER, ABRAM, WITH RALPH LINTON. *The Individual and His Society.* New York: Golden Press, 1946. (Originally published 1939 by Columbia University Press.)

KEENAN, ELINOR. "Norm-Makers, Norm-Breakers: Uses of Speech by Men and Women in a Malagasy Community." In Bauman and Sherzer, *Explorations in the Ethnography of Speaking.* 2nd ed.

KEESING, ROGER M. "Killers, Big Men, and Priests on Malaita: Reflections on a Melanesian Troika System." In McGlynn and Tuden, eds., *Anthropological Approaches to Political Behavior.*

KELLER, HELEN. *The Story of My Life.* New York: Dell, 1974. (Originally published 1902.)

KELLY, RAYMOND C. *The Nuer Conquest: The Structure and Development of an Expansionist System.* Ann Arbor: University of Michigan Press, 1985.

KELLY, RAYMOND C. "Witchcraft and Sexual Relations: An Exploration in the Social and Semantic Implications of the Structure of Belief." Paper presented at the annual meeting of the American Anthropological Association, Mexico City, 1974.

KHOSROSHASHI, FATEMEH. "Penguins Don't Care, But Women Do: A Social Identity Analysis of a Whorfian Problem." *Language in Society,* 18 (1989): 505–25.

KILBRIDE, PHILIP L., AND JANET C. KILBRIDE. "Polygyny: A Modern Contradiction?" In Kilbride and Kilbride, *Changing Family Life in East Africa.*

KILBRIDE, PHILIP L., AND JANET C. KILBRIDE. *Changing Family Life in East Africa: Women and Children at Risk.* University Park: Pennsylvania State University Press, 1990.

KING, J. C. H. "Tradition in Native American Art." In Wade, ed., *The Arts of the North American Indian.*

KING, SETH S. "Some Farm Machinery Seems Less Than Human." *New York Times,* April 8, 1979, p. E9.

KLASS, MORTON. "Is There 'Caste' Outside of India?" In Ember and Ember, eds., *Cross-Cultural Research for Social Science.*

KLEINBERG, JILL. "Practical Implications of Organizational Culture Where Americans and Japanese Work Together." In Jordan, ed., *Practicing Anthropology in Corporate America.*

KLEINMAN, ARTHUR. *Rethinking Psychiatry: From Cultural Category to Personal Experience.* New York: Macmillan, 1988.

KLEINMAN, ARTHUR, AND BYRON GOOD, eds. *Culture and Depression: Studies in the Anthropology and Cross-Cultural Psychiatry of Affect and Disorder.* Berkeley: University of California Press, 1985.

KLINEBERG, OTTO. "Foreword." In Segall, *Cross-Cultural Psychology.*

KLUCKHOHN, CLYDE. "As an Anthropologist Views It." In Deutsch, ed., *Sex Habits of American Men.*

KLUCKHOHN, CLYDE. "Recurrent Themes in Myths and Mythmaking." In Dundes, ed., *The Study of Folklore.*

KNAUFT, BRUCE M. "Cargo Cults and Relational Separation." *Behavior Science Research,* 13 (1978): 185–240.

KNUDSEN, DEAN D., AND JOANN L. MILLER, eds. *Abused and Battered: Social and Legal Responses to Family Violence.* New York: Aldine de Gruyter, 1991.

KOCH, KLAUS-FRIEDRICH, SORAYA ALTORKI, ANDREW ARNO, AND LETITIA HICKSON. "Ritual Reconciliation and the Obviation of Grievances: A Comparative Study in the Ethnography of Law." *Ethnology,* 16 (1977): 269–84.

KONNER, MELVIN. *The Tangled Wing: Biological Constraints on the Human Spirit.* New York: Harper & Row, 1987.

KORBIN, JILL E. "Introduction." In Korbin, ed., *Child Abuse and Neglect.*

KORBIN, JILL E., ed. *Child Abuse and Neglect: Cross-Cultural Perspectives.* Berkeley, CA: University of California, 1981.

KOTTAK, CONRAD P. *Assault on Paradise: Social Change in a Brazilian Village.* New York: Random House, 1983.

KRACKE, WAUD H. *Force and Persuasion: Leadership in an Amazonian Society.* Chicago: University of Chicago Press, 1979.

KRAHN, H., T. F. HARTNAGEL, AND J. W. GARTRELL. "Income Inequality and Homicide Rates: Cross-National Data and Criminological Theories." *Criminology,* 24 (1986): 269–95.

KROEBER, ALFRED L. *The Nature of Culture.* Chicago: University of Chicago Press, 1952.

KROEBER, THEODORA. *Ishi in Two Worlds.* Berkeley: University of California Press, 1967.

KUPER, HILDA. *A South African Kingdom: The Swazi.* 2nd ed. New York: Holt, Rinehart & Winston, 1986.

KUPER, HILDA. "The Swazi of Swaziland." In Gibbs, ed., *Peoples of Africa.*

KUSHNER, GILBERT. "Applied Anthropology." In Emener and Darrow, eds., *Career Explorations in Human Services.*

LAITMAN, JEFFREY. "The Anatomy of Human Speech." *Natural History,* August 1984, 20–27.

LAKOFF, ROBIN. "Language and Woman's Place." *Language in Society,* 2 (1973): 45–80.

LAKOFF, ROBIN. *Talking Power: The Politics of Language in Our Lives.* New York: Basic Books, 1990.

LAKOFF, ROBIN. "Why Can't a Woman Be Less Like a Man?" In Lakoff, *Talking Power.*

LAMBERT, WILLIAM W., LEIGH MINTURN TRIANDIS, AND MARGERY WOLF. "Some Correlates of Beliefs in the Malevolence and Benevolence of Supernatural Beings: A Cross-Cultural Study." *Journal of Abnormal and Social Psychology,* 58 (1959): 162–69.

LANGNESS, LEWIS L. *The Study of Culture.* San Francisco: Chandler and Sharp, 1974.

LARSON, DANIEL O., JOHN R. JOHNSON, AND JOEL C. MICHAELSEN. "Missionization among the Coastal Chumash of Central California: A Study of Risk Minimization Strategies." *American Anthropologist,* 96 (1994): 263–99.

LASSWELL, HAROLD. *Politics: Who Gets What, When, How.* New York: McGraw-Hill, 1936.

LAWLESS, ROBERT, VINSON H. SUTLIVE, JR., AND MARIO D. ZAMORA, eds. *Fieldwork: The Human Experience.* New York: Gordon and Breach Science Publishers, 1983.

LAYTON, ROBERT. *Australian Rock Art: A New Synthesis.* Cambridge: Cambridge University Press, 1992.

LEACH, JERRY W. "Introduction." In Leach and Leach, eds., *The Kula.*

LEACH, JERRY W., AND EDMUND LEACH, eds. *The Kula: New Perspectives on Massim Exchange.* Cambridge: Cambridge University Press, 1983.

LEBARRE, W. "Some Observations on Character Structure in the Orient: The Japanese." *Psychiatry,* 8 (1945): 326–42.

LEACOCK, ELEANOR. "The Montagnais 'Hunting Territory' and the Fur Trade." *American Anthropological Association,* Memoir 78 (1954): 1–59.

LEACOCK, ELEANOR, AND RICHARD LEE. "Introduction." In Leacock and Lee, eds., *Politics and History in Band Societies.*

LEACOCK, ELEANOR, AND RICHARD LEE, eds. *Politics and History in Band Societies.* Cambridge: Cambridge University Press, 1982.

LEDERMAN, RENA. "Big Men, Large and Small? Towards a Comparative Perspective." *Ethnology,* 29 (1990): 3–15.

LEE, RICHARD B. *The !Kung San: Men, Women, and Work in a Foraging Society.* Cambridge: Cambridge University Press, 1979.

LEE, RICHARD B. "Population Growth and the Beginnings of Sedentary Life among the !Kung Bushmen." In Brian Spooner, ed., *Population Growth: Anthropological Implications.* Cambridge, MA: MIT Press, 1972.

LEE, RICHARD B. "What Hunters Do for a Living, or, How to Make Out on Scarce Resources." In Lee and DeVore, eds., *Man the Hunter.*

LEE, RICHARD B., AND IRVEN DEVORE. "Problems in the Study of Hunters and Gatherers." In Lee and DeVore, eds., *Man the Hunter.*

LEE, RICHARD B., AND IRVEN DEVORE, eds. *Man the Hunter.* Chicago: Aldine, 1968.

LEES, SUSAN H., AND DANIEL G. BATES. "The Origins of Specialized Nomadic Pastoralism: A Systemic Model." *American Antiquity,* 39 (1974): 187–93.

LEHMANN, ARTHUR C., AND JAMES E. MYERS. *Magic, Witchcraft, and Religion: An Anthropological Study of the Supernatural.* Palo Alto, CA: Mayfield, 1985.

LEIBOWITZ, LILA. *Females, Males, Families: A Biosocial Approach.* North Scituate, MA: Duxbury, 1978.

LEIS, NANCY B. "Women in Groups: Ijaw Women's Associations." In Rosaldo and Lamphere, eds., *Woman, Culture, and Society.*

LENSKI, GERHARD. *Power and Privilege: A Theory of Social Stratification.* Chapel Hill: University of North Carolina Press, 1984. (First published 1966.)

LEPOWSKY, MARIA. "Big Men, Big Women and Cultural Autonomy." *Ethnology,* 29 (1990): 35–50.

LESSA, WILLIAM A., AND EVON Z. VOGT, eds. *Reader in Comparative Religion: An Anthropological Approach.* 3rd ed. New York: Harper & Row, 1971.

LESSA, WILLIAM A., AND EVON Z. VOGT, eds. *Reader in Comparative Religion: An Anthropological Approach.* 4th ed. New York: Harper & Row, 1979.

LETT, JAMES. *The Human Enterprise: A Critical Introduction to Anthropological Theory.* Boulder, CO: Westview Press, 1987.

LETT, JAMES. "Scientific Anthropology." In Levinson and Ember, eds., *Encyclopedia of Cultural Anthropology.*

LEVINE, NANCY E. "Women's Work and Infant Feeding: A Case from Rural Nepal." *Ethnology,* 27 (1988): 231–51.

LEVINE, ROBERT A. *Dreams and Deeds: Achievement Motivation in Nigeria.* Chicago: University of Chicago Press, 1966.

LEVINE, ROBERT A. "Human Parental Care: Universal Goals, Cultural Strategies, Individual Behavior." In LeVine, Miller, and West, eds., *Parental Behavior in Diverse Societies.*

LEVINE, ROBERT A., AND BARBARA B. LEVINE. "Nyansongo: A Gusii Community in Kenya." In Whiting, ed., *Six Cultures.*

LEVINE, ROBERT A., PATRICE M. MILLER, AND MARY MAXWELL WEST, eds. *Parental Behavior in Diverse Societies.* San Francisco: Jossey-Bass, 1988.

LEVINSON, DAVID. *Family Violence in Cross-Cultural Perspective.* Newbury Park, CA: Sage, 1989.

LEVINSON, DAVID. *Instructor's and Librarian's Guide to the HRAF Archive.* New Haven, CT: Human Relations Area Files, 1988.

LEVINSON, DAVID, AND MELVIN EMBER, eds. *Encyclopedia of Cultural Anthropology.* 4 vols. New York: Henry Holt, 1995.

LEVINSON, DAVID, AND MARTIN J. MALONE, eds. *Toward Explaining Human Culture: A Critical Review of the Findings of Worldwide Cross-Cultural Research.* New Haven, CT: HRAF Press, 1980.

LÉVI-STRAUSS, CLAUDE. *The Elementary Structures of Kinship,* rev. ed. Trans. James H. Bell and J. R. von Sturmer, ed. Rodney Needham. Boston: Beacon Press, 1969. (Originally published in French, 1962.)

LÉVI-STRAUSS, CLAUDE. *The Raw and the Cooked.* Trans. John Weightman and Doreen Weightman. New York: Harper & Row, 1969. (Originally published in French, 1964.)

LÉVI-STRAUSS, CLAUDE. *The Savage Mind.* Trans. George Weidenfeld and Nicolson, Ltd. Chicago: University of Chicago Press, 1966. (Originally published in French, 1962.)

LÉVI-STRAUSS, CLAUDE. "The Sorcerer and His Magic." In Lévi-Strauss, *Structural Anthropology.*

LÉVI-STRAUSS, CLAUDE. *Structural Anthropology.* Trans. Claire Jacobson and Brooke Grundfest Schoepf. New York: Basic Books, 1963.

LEWIN, TAMAR. "Sex in America: Faithfulness in Marriage Is Overwhelming." *New York Times (National),* October 7, 1994, pp. A1, A18.

LEWIS, I. M. *A Pastoral Democracy.* New York: Oxford University Press, 1961.

LEWIS, I. M., ed. *Nationalism and Self-Determination in the Horn of Africa.* London: Ithaca Press, 1983.

LEWIS, OSCAR. *Life in a Mexican Village: Tepoztlan Revisited.* Urbana: University of Illinois Press, 1951.

LEWIS, OSCAR (with the assistance of Victor Barnouw). *Village Life in Northern India.* Urbana: University of Illinois Press, 1958.

LICHTER, DANIEL T., DIANE K. MCLAUGHLIN, GEORGE KEPHART, AND DAVID J. LANDRY. "Race and the Retreat from Marriage: A Shortage of Marriageable Men?" *American Sociological Review,* 57 (1992): 781–99.

LIEBERMAN, PHILIP. *The Biology and Evolution of Language.* Cambridge, MA: Harvard University Press, 1984.

LIEBERMAN, PHILIP. *Uniquely Human: The Evolution of Speech, Thought, and Selfless Behavior.* Cambridge, MA: Harvard University Press, 1991.

LINGENFELTER, SHERWOOD G. "Yap: Changing Roles of Men and Women." In Ember, Ember, and Levinson, eds., *Portraits of Culture.*

LINTON, RALPH. *The Cultural Background of Personality.* New York: Appleton-Century-Crofts, 1945.

LINTON, RALPH. *The Study of Man.* New York: Appleton-Century-Crofts, 1936.

LITTLE, KENNETH. "The Political Function of the Poro." *Africa,* 35 (1965): 349–65; 36 (1966): 62–71.

LITTLE, KENNETH. "The Role of Voluntary Associations in West African Urbanization." *American Anthropologist,* 59 (1957): 582–93.

LITTLE, KENNETH. *West African Urbanization.* New York: Cambridge University Press, 1965.

LOCK, MARGARET. "Japan: Glimpses of Everyday Life." In Ember, Ember, and Levinson, eds., *Portraits of Culture.*

LOFTIN, COLIN K. "Warfare and Societal Complexity: A Cross-Cultural Study of Organized Fighting in Preindustrial Societies." Ph.D. dissertation, University of North Carolina at Chapel Hill, 1971.

LOFTIN, COLIN, DAVID McDOWALL, AND JAMES BOUDOURIS. "Economic Change and Homicide in Detroit, 1926–1979." In Gurr, ed., *Violence in America, Vol. 1.*

LOMAX, ALAN, ed. *Folk Song Style and Culture.* American Association for the Advancement of Science, Publication No. 88, Washington, D.C., 1968.

LOW, BOBBI S. "Behavioral Ecology, 'Sociobiology' and Human Behavior." In Ember, Ember, and Peregrine, eds., *Research Frontiers in Anthropology.*

LOW, BOBBI. "Human Responses to Environmental Extremeness and Uncertainty." In Cashdan, ed., *Risk and Uncertainty in Tribal and Peasant Economies.*

LOW, BOBBI. "Marriage Systems and Pathogen Stress in Human Societies." *American Zoologist,* 30 (1990): 325–39.

LOWIE, ROBERT H. *Primitive Society.* New York: Liveright, 1970. (Originally published 1920.)

LUHRMANN, TANYA M. *Persuasions of the Witch's Craft: Ritual Magic and Witchcraft in Present-Day England.* Oxford: Basil Blackwell, 1989.

LURIA, A. R. *Cognitive Development: Its Cultural and Social Foundations.* Cambridge, MA: Harvard University Press, 1976.

LUTZ, CATHERINE. "Depression and the Translations of Emotional Worlds." In Kleinman and Good, eds., *Culture and Depression.*

LUTZ, CATHERINE. "The Erasure of Women's Writing in Sociocultural Anthropology." *American Ethnologist,* 17 (1990): 611–27.

LYND, ROBERT S., AND HELEN MERRELL LYND. *Middletown.* New York: Harcourt, Brace, 1929.

LYND, ROBERT S., AND HELEN MERRELL LYND. *Middletown in Transition.* New York: Harcourt, Brace, 1937.

LYON, PATRICIA J., ed. *Native South Americans: Ethnology of the Least Known Continent.* Boston: Little Brown, 1974.

LYONS, NONA PLESSNER. "Two Perspectives: On Self, Relationships, and Morality." In Gilligan, Ward, and Taylor, eds., *Mapping the Moral Domain.*

McCAIN, GARVIN, AND ERWIN M. SEGAL. *The Game of Science.* 5th ed. Monterey, CA: Brooks/Cole, 1982.

McCARTHY, FREDERICK D., AND MARGARET McARTHUR. "The Food Quest and the Time Factor in Aboriginal Economic Life." In Mountford, ed., *Records of the Australian-American Scientific Expedition to Arnhem Land. Volume 2.*

McCAY, BONNIE M., AND JAMES M. ACHESON. "Introduction." In McCay and Acheson, eds., *The Question of Commons.*

McCAY, BONNIE M., AND JAMES M. ACHESON, eds. *The Question of Commons: The Culture and Ecology of Communal Resources.* Tucson: University of Arizona Press, 1987.

McCLELLAND, DAVID C. *The Achieving Society.* New York: Van Nostrand, 1961.

MACCOBY, ELEANOR E., AND CAROL N. JACKLIN. *The Psychology of Sex Differences.* Stanford, CA: Stanford University Press, 1974.

McCORRISTON, JOY, AND FRANK HOLE. "The Ecology of Seasonal Stress and the Origins of Agriculture in the Near East." *American Anthropologist,* 93 (1991): 46–69.

McDOWELL, NANCY. "Mundugumor: Sex and Temperament Revisited." In Ember, Ember, and Levinson, eds., *Portraits of Culture.*

McGLYNN, FRANK, AND ARTHUR TUDEN, eds. *Anthropological Approaches to Political Behavior.* Pittsburgh: University of Pittsburgh Press, 1991.

MACLACHLAN, MORGAN D., ed. *Household Economies and Their Transformations.* Monographs in Economic Anthropology, No. 3. Lanham, MD: University Press of America, 1987.

McNEILL, WILLIAM H. *Plagues and Peoples.* Garden City, NY: Doubleday Anchor, 1976.

McNEILL, WILLIAM H. *A World History.* New York: Oxford University Press, 1967.

MALEFIJT, ANNEMARIE DE WAAL. *Religion and Culture: An Introduction to Anthropology of Religion.* New York: Macmillan, 1968.

MALIN, EDWARD. *Totem Poles of the Pacific Northwest Coast.* Portland: Timber Press, 1986.

MALINOWSKI, BRONISLAW. "The Group and the Individual in Functional Analysis." *American Journal of Sociology,* 44 (1939): 938–64.

MALINOWSKI, BRONISLAW. "*Kula:* The Circulating Exchange of Valuables in the Archipelagoes of Eastern New Guinea." *Man,* 51, no. 2 (1920): 97–105.

MALINOWSKI, BRONISLAW. "Magic, Science, and Religion." In Malinowski, *Magic, Science, and Religion and Other Essays.*

MALINOWSKI, BRONISLAW. *Magic, Science, and Religion and Other Essays.* Garden City, NY: Doubleday, 1954.

MALINOWSKI, BRONISLAW. *Sex and Repression in Savage Society.* London: Kegan Paul, Trench, Trubner Co., 1927.

MALINOWSKI, BRONISLAW. *The Sexual Life of Savages in Northwestern Melanesia.* New York: Halcyon House, 1932.

MANGIN, WILLIAM. "Latin American Squatter Settlements: A Problem and a Solution." *Latin American Research Review,* 2 (1967): 65–98.

MANGIN, WILLIAM P. "The Role of Regional Associations in the Adaptation of Rural Migrants to Cities in Peru." In Heath and Adams, eds., *Contemporary Cultures and Societies of Latin America.*

MANNERS, ROBERT A., AND DAVID KAPLAN, eds. *Theory in Anthropology: A Sourcebook.* Chicago: Aldine, 1968.

MANZANILLA, LINDA, ed. *Studies in the Neolithic and Urban Revolutions.* British Archaeological Reports International Series 349. Oxford, 1987.

MAQUET, JACQUES. *The Aesthetic Experience: An Anthropologist Looks at the Visual Arts.* New Haven, CT: Yale University Press, 1986.

MARANO, LOUIS A. "A Macrohistoric Trend toward World Government." *Behavior Science Notes,* 8 (1973): 35–40.

MARCUS, GEORGE E., AND MICHAEL M. J. FISCHER. *Anthropology as Cultural Critique: An Experimental Moment in the Human Sciences.* Chicago: University of Chicago Press, 1986.

MARETT, R. R. *The Threshold of Religion.* London: Methuen, 1909.

MARLER, PETER. "Primate Vocalization: Affective or Symbolic?" In Sebeok and Umiker-Sebeok, eds., *Speaking of Apes.*

MARSHALL, LORNA. "!Kung Bushmen Bands." In Cohen and Middleton, eds., *Comparative Political Systems.*

MARSHALL, LORNA. "The !Kung Bushmen of the Kalahari Desert." In Gibbs, Jr., ed., *Peoples of Africa.*

MARSHALL, LORNA. "Sharing, Talking and Giving: Relief of Social Tensions among !Kung Bushmen." *Africa,* 31 (1961): 239–42.

MARTIN, M. KAY, AND BARBARA VOORHIES. *Female of the Species.* New York: Columbia University Press, 1975.

MARTIN, PAUL S., AND RICHARD KLEIN, eds. *Quaternary Extinctions: A Prehistoric Revolution.* Tucson: University of Arizona Press, 1984.

MASLOW, ABRAHAM H. *Religions, Values, and Peak-Experiences.* Columbus: Ohio State University Press, 1964.

MASON, PHILIP. *Prospero's Magic.* London: Oxford University Press, 1962.

MASUMURA, WILFRED T. "Law and Violence: A Cross-Cultural Study." *Journal of Anthropological Research,* 33 (1977): 388–99.

MATEJCEK, ZDENEK. "Perceived Parental Acceptance-Rejection and Personality Organization among Czech Elementary School Children." *Behavior Science Research,* 18 (1983): 259–68.

MATHIASSEN, THERKEL. *Material Culture of Iglulik Eskimos.* Copenhagen: Glydendalske, 1928.

MATHIOT, MADELEINE, ed. *Ethnolinguistics: Boas, Sapir and Whorf Revisited.* The Hague: Mouton, 1979.

MATLOCK, JAMES G. "Universals and Variation in Religious Belief and Practice." In Ember and Ember, eds., *Cross-Cultural Research for Social Science.*

MATOSSIAN, MARY K. "Ergot and the Salem Witchcraft Affair." *American Scientist,* 70 (1982): 355–57.

MATOSSIAN, MARY K. *Poisons of the Past: Molds, Epidemics, and History.* New Haven, CT: Yale University Press, 1989.

MATTHIASSON, CAROLYN J. *Many Sisters: Women in Cross-Cultural Perspective.* New York: Free Press, 1974.

MAYBURY-LEWIS, DAVID. *Akwe-Shavante Society.* Oxford: Clarendon Press, 1967.

MEAD, MARGARET. "Applied Anthropology: The State of the Art." In Wallace, et al., eds., *Perspectives on Anthropology 1976.*

MEAD, MARGARET. *Coming of Age in Samoa.* 3rd ed. New York: Morrow, 1961. (Originally published 1928.)

MEAD, MARGARET. "The Evolving Ethics of Applied Anthropology." In Eddy and Partridge, eds., *Applied Anthropology in America.*

MEAD, MARGARET. *Growing Up in New Guinea.* London: Routledge & Kegan Paul, 1931.

MEAD, MARGARET. *Sex and Temperament in Three Primitive Societies.* New York: Mentor, 1950. (Originally published 1935.)

MEEK, C. K. *Land Law and Custom in the Colonies.* London: Oxford University Press, 1940.

MEGGITT, MERVYN. *Blood Is Their Argument: Warfare among the Mae Enga Tribesmen of the New Guinea Highlands.* Palo Alto, CA: Mayfield, 1977.

MEGGITT, MERVYN J. "Male-Female Relationships in the Highlands of Australian New Guinea." *American Anthropologist,* 66 (special issue, 1964): 204–24.

MEILLASSOUX, CLAUDE. *Urbanization of an African Community.* Seattle: University of Washington Press, 1968.

MERRILL, ELIZABETH BRYANT. "Art Styles as Reflections of Sociopolitical Complexity." *Ethnology,* 26 (1987): 221–30.

MERTZ, ELIZABETH, AND RICHARD J. PARMENTIER, eds. *Semiotic Mediation: Sociocultural and Psychological Perspectives.* Orlando, FL: Academic Press, 1985.

MIDDLETON, JOHN. "The Cult of the Dead: Ancestors and Ghosts." In Lessa and Vogt, eds., *Reader in Comparative Religion.* 3rd ed.

MIDDLETON, RUSSELL. "Brother-Sister and Father-Daughter Marriage in Ancient Egypt." *American Sociological Review,* 27 (1962): 603–11.

MILLER, BRUCE G. "Women and Politics: Comparative Evidence from the Northwest Coast." *Ethnology,* 31 (1992): 367–82.

MILLER, JOAN G. "Cultural Diversity in the Morality of Caring: Individually Oriented versus Duty-Based Interpersonal Moral Codes." *Cross-Cultural Research,* 28 (1994): 3–39.

MINER, HORACE. "Body Rituals among the Nacirema." *American Anthropologist,* 58 (1956): 504–5.

MINTURN, LEIGH. *Sita's Daughters: Coming Out of Purdah: The Rajput Women of Khalapur Revisited.* New York: Oxford University Press, 1993.

MINTURN, LEIGH, AND WILLIAM W. LAMBERT. *Mothers of Six Cultures: Antecedents of Child Rearing.* New York: John Wiley, 1964.

MINTURN, LEIGH, AND JERRY STASHAK. "Infanticide as a Terminal Abortion Procedure." *Behavior Science Research,* 17 (1982): 70–85.

MINTZ, SIDNEY W. "Canamelar: The Subculture of a Rural Sugar Plantation Proletariat." In Steward et al., *The People of Puerto Rico.*

MIRACLE, ANDREW W. "A Shaman to Organizations." In Ember, Ember, and Peregrine, eds., *Research Frontiers in Anthropology.*

MITCHELL, DONALD. "Nimpkish: Complex Foragers on the Northwest Coast of North America." In Ember, Ember, and Levinson, eds., *Portraits of Culture.*

MOONEY, KATHLEEN A. "The Effects of Rank and Wealth on Exchange among the Coast Salish." *Ethnology,* 17 (1978): 391–406.

MOORE, OMAR KHAYYAM. "Divination: A New Perspective." *American Anthropologist,* 59 (1957): 69–74.

MORAN, EMILIO F. *Through Amazon Eyes: The Human Ecology of Amazonian Populations.* Iowa City: University of Iowa Press, 1993.

MORGAN, LEWIS HENRY. *Ancient Society.* Cambridge, MA: Harvard University Press, Belknap Press, 1964. (Originally published 1877.)

MORGEN, SANDRA, ed. *Gender and Anthropology: Critical Reviews for Research and Teaching.* Washington, D.C.: American Anthropological Association, 1989.

MORRIS, B. *Anthropological Studies of Religion: An Introductory Text.* Cambridge: Cambridge University Press, 1987.

MORRIS, JOHN. *Living with Lepchas: A Book about the Sikkim Himalayas.* London: Heinemann, 1938.

MOUNTFORD, C. P., ed. *Records of the Australian-American Scientific Expedition to Arnhem Land. Volume 2: Anthropology and Nutrition.* Melbourne: Melbourne University Press, 1960.

MUKHOPADHYAY, CAROL C., AND PATRICIA J. HIGGINS. "Anthropological Studies of Women's Status Revisited: 1977–1987." *Annual Review of Anthropology,* 17 (1988): 461–95.

MULLER, EDWARD N. "Economic Determinants of Democracy." Paper presented at a conference on Inequality and Democracy, organized by Manus Midlarsky at Rutgers University, February 1994.

MUNROE, ROBERT L., AND RUTH H. MUNROE. "A Cross-Cultural Study of Sex, Gender, and Social Structure." *Ethnology,* 8 (1969): 206–11.

MUNROE, ROBERT L., RUTH H. MUNROE, AND JOHN W. M. WHITING. "Male Sex-Role Resolutions." In Munroe, Munroe, and Whiting, eds., *Handbook of Cross-Cultural Human Development.*

MUNROE, RUTH H., AND ROBERT L. MUNROE. "Household Structure and Socialization Practices." *Journal of Social Psychology,* 111 (1980): 293–94.

MUNROE, RUTH H., AND ROBERT L. MUNROE. "Infant Experience and Childhood Affect among the Logoli: A Longitudinal Study." *Ethos,* 8 (1980): 295–315.

MUNROE, RUTH H., ROBERT L. MUNROE, AND HAROLD S. SHIMMIN. "Children's Work in Four Cultures: Determinants and Consequences." *American Anthropologist,* 86 (1984): 369–79.

MUNROE, RUTH H., ROBERT L. MUNROE, AND BEATRICE B. WHITING, eds. *Handbook of Cross-Cultural Human Development.* New York: Garland Press, 1981.

MURDOCK, GEORGE P. "Ethnographic Atlas: A Summary." *Ethnology,* 6 (1967): 109–236.

MURDOCK, GEORGE P. *Social Structure.* New York: Macmillan, 1949.

MURDOCK, GEORGE P. "World Ethnographic Sample." *American Anthropologist,* 59 (1957): 664–87.

MURDOCK, GEORGE P., ed. *Social Structure in Southeast Asia.* Viking Fund Publications in Anthropology, No. 29. Chicago: Quadrangle, 1960.

MURDOCK, GEORGE P., AND CATERINA PROVOST. "Factors in the Division of Labor by Sex: A Cross-Cultural Analysis." *Ethnology,* 12 (1973): 203–25.

MURDOCK, GEORGE P., AND DOUGLAS R. WHITE. "Standard Cross-Cultural Sample." *Ethnology,* 8 (1969): 329–69.

MURPHY, JANE. "Abnormal Behavior in Traditional Societies: Labels, Explanations, and Social Reactions." In Munroe, Munroe, and Whiting, eds., *Handbook of Cross-Cultural Human Development.*

MURPHY, ROBERT F. *Headhunter's Heritage: Social and Economic Change among the Mundurucú.* Berkeley: University of California Press, 1960.

MURPHY, ROBERT F. "Matrilocality and Patrilineality in Mundurucú Society." *American Anthropologist,* 58 (1956): 414–34.

MURPHY, ROBERT F., AND JULIAN H. STEWARD. "Tappers and Trappers: Parallel Process in Acculturation." *Economic Development and Cultural Change,* 4 (July 1956): 335–55.

MUSIL, ALOIS. *The Manners and Customs of the Rwala Bedouins.* American Geographical Society, Oriental Exploration Studies. No. 6. New York, 1928.

MUSSEN, PAUL, ed. *Carmichael's Manual of Child Psychology.* Vol. 1, 3rd ed. New York: John Wiley, 1970.

MYERS, FRED R. "Critical Trends in the Study of Hunter-Gatherers." *Annual Review of Anthropology,* 17 (1988): 261–82.

NADEL, S. F. *A Black Byzantium: The Kingdom of Nupe in Nigeria.* London: Oxford University Press, 1942.

NADEL, S. F. "Nupe State and Community." *Africa,* 8 (1935): 257–303.

NAG, MONI, BENJAMIN N. F. WHITE, AND R. CREIGHTON PEET. "An Anthropological Approach to the Study of the Economic Value of Children in Java and Nepal." *Current Anthropology,* 19 (1978): 293–301.

NAGEL, ERNEST. *The Structure of Science: Problems in the Logic of Scientific Explanation.* New York: Harcourt, Brace & World, 1961.

NAROLL, RAOUL. "Imperial Cycles and World Order." *Peace Research Society: Papers,* 7, Chicago Conference (1967): 83–101.

NAROLL, RAOUL. *The Moral Order: An Introduction to the Human Situation.* Beverly Hills, CA: Sage Publications, 1983.

NAROLL, RAOUL. "Two Solutions to Galton's Problem." *Philosophy of Science,* 28 (January 1961): 15–39.

NAROLL, RAOUL, AND RONALD COHEN, eds. *A Handbook of Method in Cultural Anthropology.* Garden City, NY: Natural History Press, 1970.

NASAR, SYLVIA. "The Rich Get Richer, But Never the Same Way Twice." *New York Times,* August 16, 1992, p. E3.

NERLOVE, SARA B. "Women's Workload and Infant Feeding Practices: A Relationship with Demographic Implications." *Ethnology,* 13 (1974): 207–14.

NEVINS, ALLAN. *The American States during and after the Revolution.* New York: Macmillan, 1927.

NEWMAN, KATHERINE S. *Declining Fortunes: The Withering of the American Dream.* New York: Basic Books, 1993.

NEWMAN, KATHERINE S. *Law and Economic Organization: A Comparative Study of Preindustrial Societies.* Cambridge, MA: Cambridge University Press, 1983.

NIEHOFF, ARTHUR H. *A Casebook of Social Change.* Chicago: Aldine, 1966.

NIMKOFF, M. F., AND RUSSELL MIDDLETON. "Types of Family and Types of Economy." *American Journal of Sociology,* 66 (1960): 215–25.

NORBECK, EDWARD. "Continuities in Japanese Social Stratification." In Plotnicov and Tuden, eds., *Essays in Comparative Social Stratification.*

OBOLER, REGINA SMITH. "Nandi: From Cattle-Keepers to Cash-Crop Farmers." In Ember, Ember, and Levinson, eds., *Portraits of Culture.*

OBOLER, REGINA SMITH. "Is the Female Husband a Man: Woman/Woman Marriage among the Nandi of Kenya." *Ethnology,* 19 (1980): 69–88.

O'BRIEN, DENISE. "Female Husbands in Southern Bantu Societies." In Schlegel, ed., *Sexual Stratification.*

OGBURN, WILLIAM F. *Social Change.* New York: Huebsch, 1922.

OKAMURA, JONATHAN Y. "Filipino Hometown Associations in Hawaii." *Ethnology,* 22 (1983): 341–53.

OLIVER, DOUGLAS L. *Ancient Tahitian Society. Volume 1, Ethnography.* Honolulu: University of Hawaii Press, 1974.

OLIVER, DOUGLAS L. *A Solomon Island Society.* Cambridge, MA: Harvard University Press, 1955.

ORTIZ, SUTTI, ed. *Economic Anthropology: Topics and Theories.* Monographs in Economic Anthropology, No. 1. Lanham, MD: University Press of America, 1983.

ORTNER, SHERRY B. "Theory in Anthropology since the Sixties." *Comparative Studies in Society and History,* 26 (1984): 126–66.

OTTERBEIN, KEITH. *The Evolution of War.* New Haven, CT: HRAF Press, 1970.

OTTERBEIN, KEITH. "Internal War: A Cross-Cultural Study." *American Anthropologist,* 70 (1968): 277–89.

OTTERBEIN, KEITH. *The Ultimate Coercive Sanction: A Cross-Cultural Study of Capital Punishment.* New Haven, CT: HRAF Press, 1986.

OTTERBEIN, KEITH, AND CHARLOTTE SWANSON OTTERBEIN. "An Eye for an Eye, A Tooth for a Tooth: A Cross-Cultural Study of Feuding." *American Anthropologist,* 67 (1965): 1470–82.

PAIGE, JEFFERY M. *Agrarian Revolution: Social Movements and Export Agriculture in the Underdeveloped World.* New York: Free Press, 1975.

PAINE, ROBERT. *Herds of the Tundra.* Washington, D.C.: Smithsonian Institution Press, 1994.

PALSSON, GISLI. "Hunters and Gatherers of the Sea." In Ingold, Riches, and Woodburn, eds. *Hunters and Gatherers 1.*

PARKER, HILDA, AND SEYMOUR PARKER. "Father-Daughter Sexual Abuse: An Emerging Perspective." *American Journal of Orthopsychiatry,* 56 (1986): 531–49.

PARKER, SEYMOUR. "Cultural Rules, Rituals, and Behavior Regulation." *American Anthropologist,* 86 (1984): 584–600.

PARKER, SEYMOUR. "The Precultural Basis of the Incest Taboo: Toward a Biosocial Theory." *American Anthropologist,* 78 (1976): 285–305.

PARTRIDGE, WILLIAM L., AND ELIZABETH M. EDDY. "The Development of Applied Anthropology in America." In Eddy and Partridge, eds., *Applied Anthropology in America,* 2nd ed.

PASTERNAK, BURTON. "Family and Household: Who Lives Where, Why Does It Vary, and Why Is It Important?" In Ember and Ember, eds., *Cross-Cultural Research for Social Science.*

PASTERNAK, BURTON. "Han: Pastoralists and Farmers on a Chinese Frontier." In Ember, Ember, and Levinson, eds., *Portraits of Culture.*

PASTERNAK, BURTON. *Introduction to Kinship and Social Organization.* Englewood Cliffs, NJ: Prentice Hall, 1976.

PASTERNAK, BURTON, CAROL R. EMBER, AND MELVIN EMBER. "On the Conditions Favoring Extended Family Households." *Journal of Anthropological Research,* 32 (1976): 109–23.

PATTERSON, ORLANDO. *Slavery and Social Death: A Comparative Study.* Cambridge, MA: Harvard University Press, 1982.

PEACOCK, JAMES L. *The Anthropological Lens: Harsh Light, Soft Focus.* Cambridge: Cambridge University Press, 1986.

PEACOCK, NADINE, AND ROBERT BAILEY. "Efe: Investigating Food and Fertility in the Ituri Rain Forest." In Ember, Ember, and Levinson, eds., *Portraits of Culture.*

PEAK, LOIS. *Learning to Go to School in Japan: The Transition from Home to Preschool.* Berkeley: University of California Press, 1991.

PELTO, PERTTI J., AND LUDGER MÜLLER-WILLE. "Snowmobiles: Technological Revolution in the Arctic." In Bernard and Pelto, eds., *Technology and Social Change.* 2nd ed.

PELTO, PERTTI J., AND GRETEL H. PELTO. *Anthropological Research: The Structure of Inquiry.* 2nd ed. New York: Cambridge University Press, 1978.

PELTO, PERTTI J., AND GRETEL H. PELTO. "Intra-Cultural Diversity: Some Theoretical Issues." *American Ethnologist,* 2 (1975): 1–18.

PEPPERBERG, IRENE M. "Referential Communication with an African Grey Parrot." Newsletter, Harvard Graduate Society, Spring 1991, 1–4.

PEREGRINE, PETER N. "Variation in Stratification." In Ember and Ember, eds., *Cross-Cultural Research for Social Science.*

PETERSEN, L. R., G. R. LEE, AND G. J. ELLIS. "Social Structure, Socialization Values, and Disciplinary Techniques: A Cross-Cultural Analysis." *Journal of Marriage and the Family,* 44 (1982): 131–42.

PFAFF, C. "Constraints on Language Mixing." *Language,* 55 (1979): 291–318, as cited in Wardhaugh, *An Introduction to Sociolinguistics,* 2nd ed.

PFEIFFER, JOHN E. *The Emergence of Man.* 3rd ed. New York: Harper & Row, 1978.

PHILIPS, SUSAN U., SUSAN STEELE, AND CHRISTINE TANZ, eds. *Language, Gender, and Sex in Comparative Perspective.* Cambridge: Cambridge University Press, 1987.

PHILLIPS, KEVIN. *The Politics of Rich and Poor: Wealth and the American Electorate in the Reagan Aftermath.* New York: Random House, 1990.

PHILLIPSON, D. W. "Archaeology and Bantu Linguistics." *World Archaeology,* 8 (1976): 65–82.

PIAGET, JEAN. "Piaget's Theory." In Mussen, ed., *Carmichael's Manual of Child Psychology.*

PICCHI, DEBRA. "Bakairi: The Death of an Indian." In Ember, Ember, and Levinson, eds., *Portraits of Culture.*

PICCHI, DEBRA. "The Impact of an Industrial Agricultural Project on the Bakairí Indians of Central Brazil." *Human Organization* 50 (1991): 26–38.

PLATTNER, STUART. "Introduction." In Plattner, ed., *Markets and Marketing.*

PLATTNER, STUART. "Marxism." In Plattner, ed., *Economic Anthropology.*

PLATTNER, STUART, ed. *Economic Anthropology.* Stanford, CA: Stanford University Press, 1989.

PLATTNER, STUART, ed. *Markets and Marketing.* Monographs in Economic Anthropology, No. 4. Lanham, MD: University Press of America, 1985.

PLOTNICOV, LEONARD, AND ARTHUR TUDEN, eds. *Essays in Comparative Social Stratification.* Pittsburgh: University of Pittsburgh Press, 1970.

"PLUNDERING EARTH IS NOTHING NEW." *Los Angeles Times* News Service as reported in the *New Haven Register,* June 12, 1994, A18–19.

POGGIE, JOHN J., JR., BILLIE R. DEWALT, AND WILLIAM W. DRESSLER, eds. *Anthropological Research: Process and Application.* Albany, NY: State University of New York Press, 1992.

POGGIE, JOHN J., JR., AND RICHARD B. POLLNAC. "Danger and Rituals of Avoidance among New England Fishermen." *MAST: Maritime Anthropological Studies,* 1 (1988): 66–78.

POGGIE, JOHN J., JR., RICHARD B. POLLNAC, AND CARL GERSUNY. "Risk as a Basis for Taboos among Fishermen in Southern New England." *Journal for the Scientific Study of Religion,* 15 (1976): 257–62.

POLANYI, KARL. "The Economy as Instituted Process." In Polanyi, Arensberg, and Pearson, eds., *Trade and Market in the Early Empires.*

POLANYI, KARL, CONRAD M. ARENSBERG, AND HARRY W. PEARSON, eds., *Trade and Market in the Early Empires.* New York: Free Press, 1957.

POLGAR, STEVEN, ed. *Population, Ecology, and Social Evolution.* The Hague: Mouton, 1975.

POPENOE, DAVID. *Disturbing the Nest: Family Change and Decline in Modern Societies.* New York: Aldine de Gruyter, 1988.

POSPISIL, LEOPOLD. *The Kapauku Papuans of West New Guinea.* New York: Holt, Rinehart & Winston, 1963.

POWERS, WILLIAM K., AND MARLA N. POWERS. "Lakota: A Study in Cultural Continuity." In Ember, Ember, and Levinson, eds., *Portraits of Culture.*

PREMACK, ANN JAMES, AND DAVID PREMACK. "Teaching Language to an Ape." *Scientific American,* October 1972, 92–99.

PRICE, SALLY. *Primitive Art in Civilized Places.* Chicago: University of Chicago Press, 1989.

PRICE-WILLIAMS, DOUGLASS. "A Study Concerning Concepts of Conservation of Quantities among Primitive Children." *Acta Psychologica,* 18 (1961): 297–305.

PRYOR, FREDERIC L. *The Origins of the Economy: A Comparative Study of Distribution in Primitive and Peasant Economies.* New York: Academic Press, 1977.

QUINN, NAOMI. "Anthropological Studies on Women's Status." *Annual Review of Anthropology,* 6 (1977): 181–225.

RADCLIFFE-BROWN, A. R. *The Andaman Islanders: A Study in Social Anthropology.* Cambridge: Cambridge University Press, 1922.

RADCLIFFE-BROWN, A. R. *Structure and Function in Primitive Society.* London: Cohen & West, 1952.

RADIN, PAUL, ed. *African Folktales and Sculpture.* New York: Pantheon, 1952.

RAPPAPORT, ROY A. "Ritual Regulation of Environmental Relations among a New Guinea People." *Ethnology,* 6 (1967): 17–30.

RAY, VERNE F. *The Sanpoil and Nespelem: Salishan Peoples of Northeastern Washington.* New Haven, CT: Human Relations Area Files, 1954, pp. 172–89.

REED, CHARLES A., ed. *Origins of Agriculture.* The Hague: Mouton, 1977.

REISNER, MARC. *Cadillac Desert: The American West and Its Disappearing Water.* Rev. ed. New York: Penguin Books, 1993.

REITER, RAYNA R., ed. *Toward an Anthropology of Women.* New York: Monthly Review Press, 1975.

RENFREW, COLIN. *Archaeology and Language: The Puzzle of Indo-European Origins.* London: Jonathan Cape, 1987.

RENFREW, COLIN. "World Linguistic Diversity." *Scientific American,* January 1994, 116–23.

REYNA, S. P., AND R. E. DOWNS, eds. *Studying War: Anthropological Perspectives.* New York: Gordon and Breach, 1992.

RITTER, MADELINE LATTMAN. "The Conditions Favoring Age-Set Organization." *Journal of Anthropological Research,* 36 (1980): 87–104.

RIVERS, W. H. R. *The Todas.* Oosterhout, N.B., The Netherlands: Anthropological Publications, 1967. (Originally published 1906.)

ROBERTS, JOHN M. "Oaths, Autonomic Ordeals, and Power." In Ford, ed., *Cross-Cultural Approaches.*

ROBERTS, JOHN M., AND BRIAN SUTTON-SMITH. "Child Training and Game Involvement." *Ethnology,* 1 (1962): 166–85.

RODWIN, LLOYD, ed. *Shelter, Settlement, and Development.* Boston: Allen & Unwin, 1987.

RODWIN, LLOYD, AND BISHWAPRIYA SANYAL. "Shelter, Settlement, and Development: An Overview." In Rodwin, ed., *Shelter, Settlement, and Development.*

ROGERS, EVERETT M. *Diffusion of Innovations.* 3rd ed. New York: Free Press, 1983.

ROGOFF, BARBARA. *Apprenticeship in Thinking: Cognitive Development in Social Context.* New York: Oxford University Press, 1990.

ROGOFF, BARBARA. "Schooling and the Development of Cognitive Skills." In Triandis and Heron, eds., *Handbook of Cross-Cultural Psychology.* Vol. 4, *Developmental Psychology.*

ROHNER, RONALD P. "Sex Differences in Aggression: Phylogenetic and Enculturation Perspectives." *Ethos,* 4 (1976): 57–72.

ROHNER, RONALD P. *They Love Me, They Love Me Not: A Worldwide Study of the Effects of Parental Acceptance and Rejection.* New Haven, CT: HRAF Press, 1975.

ROHNER, RONALD P. *The Warmth Dimension.* Beverly Hills, CA: Sage, 1986.

ROHNER, RONALD P., AND EVELYN ROHNER, eds. "Special Issue on Worldwide Tests of Parental Acceptance-Rejection Theory: An Overview." *Behavior Science Research,* 15 (1980): v–88.

ROMAINE, SUZANNE. *Language in Society: An Introduction to Sociolinguistics.* Oxford: Oxford University Press, 1994.

ROMNEY, A. KIMBALL, SUSAN C. WELLER, AND WILLIAM H. BATCHELDER. "Culture as Consensus: A Theory of Culture and Informant Accuracy." *American Anthropologist,* 88 (1986): 313–38.

ROSALDO, MICHELLE Z., AND LOUISE LAMPHERE, eds. *Woman, Culture, and Society.* Stanford, CA: Stanford University Press, 1974.

ROSEBERRY, WILLIAM. "Political Economy." *Annual Review of Anthropology,* 17 (1988): 161–259.

ROSENBERG, JOHN D., ed. *The Genius of John Ruskin: Selections from His Writings.* New York: Braziller, 1963.

ROSENBLATT, PAUL C. "Human Rights Violations." In Ember, Ember, and Peregrine, eds., *Research Frontiers in Anthropology.*

ROSENBLATT, PAUL C., R. PATRICIA WALSH, AND DOUGLAS A. JACKSON. *Grief and Mourning in Cross-Cultural Perspective.* New Haven, CT: HRAF Press, 1976.

ROSS, MARC H. "Female Political Participation: A Cross-Cultural Explanation." *American Anthropologist,* 88 (1986): 843–58.

ROSS, MARC H. "Internal and External Conflict and Violence." *Journal of Conflict Resolution,* 29 (1985): 547–79.

ROSS, MARC H. "Political Organization and Political Participation: Exit, Voice, and Loyalty in Preindustrial Societies." *Comparative Politics,* 21 (1988): 73–89.

ROSS, MARC H. "Political Participation." In Ember and Ember, eds., *Cross-Cultural Research for Social Science.*

ROSS, MARC H. "Socioeconomic Complexity, Socialization, and Political Differentiation: A Cross-Cultural Study." *Ethos,* 9 (1981): 217–47.

ROYCE, ANYA PETERSON. *The Anthropology of Dance.* Bloomington: Indiana University Press, 1977.

RUBIN, J. Z., F. J. PROVENZANO, AND R. F. HASKETT. "The Eye of the Beholder: Parents' Views on the Sex of New Borns." *American Journal of Orthopsychiatry*, 44 (1974): 512–19.

RUDMIN, FLOYD WEBSTER. "Dominance, Social Control, and Ownership: A History and a Cross-Cultural Study of Motivations for Private Property." *Behavior Science Research*, 22 (1988): 130–60.

RUHLEN, MERRITT. *A Guide to the World's Languages.* Vol. 1: *Classification.* Stanford, CA: Stanford University Press, 1987.

RUMBAUGH, DUANE M., TIMOTHY V. GILL, AND E. C. VON GLASERFELD. "Reading and Sentence Completion by a Chimpanzee (Pan)." *Science,* November 16, 1973, 731–33.

RUSKIN, JOHN. "Of King's Treasures." In Rosenberg, ed., *The Genius of John Ruskin.*

RUSSELL, ELBERT W. "Factors of Human Aggression." *Behavior Science Notes,* 7 (1972): 275–312.

RUSSETT, BRUCE (WITH THE COLLABORATION OF WILLIAM ANTHOLIS, CAROL R. EMBER, MELVIN EMBER, AND ZEEV MAOZ). *Grasping the Democratic Peace: Principles for a Post–Cold War World.* Princeton, NJ: Princeton University Press, 1993.

SAHLINS, MARSHALL D. *Moala: Culture and Nature on a Fijian Island.* Ann Arbor: University of Michigan Press, 1962.

SAHLINS, MARSHALL. "Other Times, Other Customs: The Anthropology of History." *American Anthropologist,* 85 (1983): 517–44.

SAHLINS, MARSHALL D. "Poor Man, Rich Man, Big-Man, Chief: Political Types in Melanesia and Polynesia." *Comparative Studies in Society and History,* 5 (1963): 285–303.

SAHLINS, MARSHALL D. "The Segmentary Lineage: An Organization of Predatory Expansion." *American Anthropologist,* 63 (1961): 332–45.

SAHLINS, MARSHALL D. *Social Stratification in Polynesia.* Seattle: University of Washington Press, 1958.

SAHLINS, MARSHALL D. *Stone Age Economics.* Chicago: Aldine, 1972.

SAHLINS, MARSHALL D., AND ELMAN R. SERVICE. *Evolution and Culture.* Ann Arbor: University of Michigan Press, 1960.

SANDAY, PEGGY R. "Female Status in the Public Domain." In Rosaldo and Lamphere, eds., *Woman, Culture, and Society.*

SANDAY, PEGGY R. "Toward a Theory of the Status of Women." *American Anthropologist,* 75 (1973): 1682–700.

SANDAY, PEGGY REEVES, AND RUTH GALLAGHER GOODENOUGH, eds. *Beyond the Second Sex: New Directions in the Anthropology of Gender.* Philadelphia: University of Pennsylvania Press, 1990.

SAPIR, EDWARD. "Conceptual Categories in Primitive Languages." Paper presented at the autumn meeting of the National Academy of Sciences, New Haven, CT, 1931. Published in *Science,* 74 (1931).

SAPIR, EDWARD. *Language: An Introduction to the Study of Speech.* New York: Harcourt Brace Jovanovich, 1949. (Originally published 1921.)

SAPIR, EDWARD. "Why Cultural Anthropology Needs the Psychiatrist." *Psychiatry,* 1 (1938): 7–12.

SAPIR, EDWARD, AND M. SWADESH. "American Indian Grammatical Categories." In Hymes, ed., *Language in Culture and Society.*

SAUL, MAHIR. "Work Parties, Wages, and Accumulation in a Voltaic Village." *American Ethnologist,* 10 (1983): 77–96.

SAVAGE-RUMBAUGH, E. S. "Language Training of Apes." In Jones, Martin, and Pilbeam, eds., *The Cambridge Encyclopedia of Human Evolution.*

SCAGLION, RICHARD. "Abelam: Giant Yams and Cycles of Sex, Warfare and Ritual." In Ember, Ember, and Levinson, eds., *Portraits of Culture.*

SCAGLION, RICHARD. "Law and Society." In Ember and Ember, eds., *Cross-Cultural Research for Social Science.*

SCAGLION, RICHARD. "Legal Adaptation in a Papua New Guinea Village Court." *Ethnology,* 29 (1990): 17–33.

SCAGLION, RICHARD, AND ROSE WHITTINGHAM. "Female Plaintiffs and Sex-Related Disputes in Rural Papua New Guinea." In Toft, ed., *Domestic Violence in Papua New Guinea.*

SCARR, SANDRA, AND KATHLEEN MCCARTNEY. "How People Make Their Own Environments: A Theory of Genotype→Environment Effects." *Child Development,* 54 (1983): 424–35.

SCHALLER, GEORGE B. *The Serengeti Lion: A Study of Predator-Prey Relations.* Chicago: University of Chicago Press, 1972.

SCHIFFER, MICHAEL B., ed. *Advances in Archaeological Method and Theory.* Vol. 7. Orlando, FL: Academic Press, 1984.

SCHLEGEL, ALICE. "Gender Issues and Cross-Cultural Research." *Behavior Science Research,* 23 (1989): 265–80.

SCHLEGEL, ALICE. *Male Dominance and Female Autonomy.* New Haven, CT: HRAF, 1972.

SCHLEGEL, ALICE. "Status, Property, and the Value on Virginity." *American Ethnologist,* 18 (1991): 719–34.

SCHLEGEL, ALICE. "The Status of Women." In Ember and Ember, eds., *Cross-Cultural Research for Social Science.*

SCHLEGEL, ALICE, ed. *Sexual Stratification: A Cross-Cultural View.* New York: Columbia University Press, 1977.

SCHLEGEL, ALICE, AND HERBERT BARRY III. *Adolescence: An Anthropological Inquiry.* New York: Free Press, 1991.

SCHLEGEL, ALICE, AND HERBERT BARRY III. "The Cultural Consequences of Female Contribution to Subsistence." *American Anthropologist,* 88 (1986): 142–50.

SCHLEGEL, ALICE, AND ROHN ELOUL. "Marriage Transactions: Labor, Property, and Status." *American Anthropologist,* 90 (1988): 291–309.

SCHLEGEL, ALICE, AND ROHN ELOUL. "A New Coding of Marriage Transactions." *Behavior Science Research,* 21 (1987): 118–40.

SCHNEIDER, DAVID M. "The Distinctive Features of Matrilineal Descent Groups." In Schneider and Gough, eds., *Matrilineal Kinship.*

SCHNEIDER, DAVID M. "Truk." In Schneider and Gough, eds., *Matrilineal Kinship.*

SCHNEIDER, DAVID M., AND KATHLEEN GOUGH, eds. *Matrilineal Kinship.* Berkeley: University of California Press, 1961.

SCHOEPF, B. "Women, AIDS and Economic Crisis in Central Africa." *Canadian Journal of African Studies,* 22 (1988): 625–44.

SCHRIRE, CARMEL. "An Inquiry into the Evolutionary Status and Apparent Identity of San Hunter-Gatherers." *Human Ecology,* 8 (1980): 9–32.

SCHRIRE, CARMEL. "Wild Surmises on Savage Thoughts." In Schrire, ed., *Past and Present in Hunter-Gatherer Studies.*

SCHRIRE, CARMEL, ed. *Past and Present in Hunter-Gatherer Studies.* Orlando, FL: Academic Press, 1984.

SCHUSKY, ERNEST L. *Manual for Kinship Analysis.* 2nd ed. New York: Holt, Rinehart & Winston, 1971.

SCHWARTZ, RICHARD D. "Social Factors in the Development of Legal Control: A Case Study of Two Israeli Settlements." *Yale Law Journal,* 63 (February 1954): 471–91.

SCOLLON, RON, AND SUZANNE B. K. SCOLLON. *Narrative, Literacy and Face in Interethnic Communication.* Norwood, NJ: ABLEX Publishing, 1981.

SCRIBNER, SYLVIA, AND MICHAEL COLE. *The Psychology of Literacy.* Cambridge, MA: Harvard University Press, 1981.

SCUDDER, THAYER. "Opportunities, Issues and Achievements in Development Anthropology Since the Mid-1960s: A Personal View." In Eddy and Partridge, eds., *Applied Anthropology in America.* 2nd ed.

SEBEOK, THOMAS A., AND JEAN UMIKER-SEBEOK, eds. *Speaking of Apes: A Critical Anthology of Two-Way Communication with Man.* New York: Plenum, 1980.

SEEMANOVÁ, EVA. "A Study of Children of Incestuous Matings." *Human Heredity,* 21 (1971): 108–28.

SEGAL, ROBERT A. *Joseph Campbell: An Introduction.* New York: Garland, 1977.

SEGALL, MARSHALL H. *Cross-Cultural Psychology: Human Behavior in Global Perspective.* Monterey, CA: Brooks/Cole, 1979.

SEGALL, MARSHALL, PIERRE R. DASEN, JOHN W. BERRY, YPE H. POORTINGA. *Human Behavior in Global Perspective: An Introduction to Cross-Cultural Psychology.* New York: Pergamon Press, 1990.

SENNER, WAYNE M. "Theories and Myths on the Origins of Writing: A Historical Overview." In Senner, ed., *The Origins of Writing.*

SENNER, WAYNE M., ed. *The Origins of Writing.* Lincoln: University of Nebraska Press, 1989.

SERVICE, ELMAN R. *The Hunters.* 2nd ed. Englewood Cliffs, NJ: Prentice Hall, 1979.

SERVICE, ELMAN R. *Primitive Social Organization: An Evolutionary Perspective.* New York: Random House, 1962.

SERVICE, ELMAN R. *Profiles in Ethnology.* 3rd ed. New York: Harper & Row, 1978.

SEYFARTH, ROBERT M., AND DOROTHY L. CHENEY. "How Monkeys See the World: A Review of Recent Research on East African Vervet Monkeys." In Snowdon, Brown, and Petersen, eds., *Primate Communication.*

SHANKMAN, PAUL. "Culture Contact, Cultural Ecology, and Dani Warfare." *Man,* 26 (1991): 299–321.

SHANKMAN, PAUL. "Sex, Lies, and Anthropologists: Margaret Mead, Derek Freeman, and Samoa." In Ember, Ember, and Peregrine, eds., *Research Frontiers in Anthropology.*

SHEILS, DEAN. "A Comparative Study of Human Sacrifice." *Behavior Science Research,* 15 (1980): 245–62.

SHEILS, DEAN. "Toward A Unified Theory of Ancestor Worship: A Cross-Cultural Study." *Social Forces,* 54 (1975): 427–40.

SHIBAMOTO, JANET S. "The Womanly Woman: Japanese Female Speech." In Philips, Steele, and Tanz, eds., *Language, Gender, and Sex in Comparative Perspective.*

SHULMAN, SETH. "Nurturing Native Tongues." *Technology Review,* May/June 1993, 16.

SHWEDER, RICHARD A., AND ROBERT A. LEVINE, eds. *Culture Theory: Essays on Mind, Self, and Emotion.* New York: Cambridge University Press, 1984.

SIH, ANDREW, AND KATHARINE A. MILTON. "Optimal Diet Theory: Should the !Kung Eat Mongongos?" *American Anthropologist,* 87 (1985): 395–401.

SILVER, HARRY R. "Calculating Risks: The Socioeconomic Foundations of Aesthetic Innovation in an Ashanti Carving Community." *Ethnology,* 20 (1981): 101–14.

SIMMONS, LEO W. *Sun Chief.* New Haven, CT: Yale University Press, 1942.

SIMPSON, S. P., AND RUTH FIELD. "Law and the Social Sciences." *Virginia Law Review,* 32 (1946): 858.

SINGER, J. DAVID. "Accounting for International War: The State of the Discipline." *Annual Review of Sociology,* 6 (1980): 349–67.

SIPES, RICHARD G. "War, Sports, and Aggression: An Empirical Test of Two Rival Theories." *American Anthropologist,* 75 (1973): 64–86.

SIVARD, RUTH LEGER. *World Military and Social Expenditures 1993.* 15th ed. Washington, D.C.: World Priorities, 1993.

SKOMAL, SUSAN N., AND EDGAR C. POLOMÉ, eds. *Proto-Indo-European: The Archaeology of a Linguistic Problem.* Washington, D.C.: Washington Institute for the Study of Man, 1987.

SMITH, EDWIN W., AND ANDREW MURRAY DALE. *The Ila-Speaking Peoples of*

Northern Rhodesia. New Hyde Park, NY: University Books, 1968. (Originally published 1920 as *Ethnocentric British Colonial Attitudes.*)

SMITH, ERIC A. "Anthropological Applications of Optimal Foraging Theory: A Critical Review." *Current Anthropology,* 24 (1983): 625–40.

SMITH, WALDEMAR R. *The Fiesta System and Economic Change.* New York: Columbia University Press, 1977.

SNOWDON, CHARLES T., CHARLES H. BROWN, AND MICHAEL R. PETERSEN, eds. *Primate Communication.* New York: Cambridge University Press, 1982.

SOUTHWORTH, FRANKLIN C., AND CHANDLER J. DASWANI. *Foundations of Linguistics.* New York: Free Press, 1974.

SPANOS, NICHOLAS P. "Ergotism and the Salem Witch Panic: A Critical Analysis and an Alternative Conceptualization." *Journal of the History of the Behavioral Sciences,* 19 (1983): 358–69.

SPENCER, ROBERT F. "Spouse-Exchange among the North Alaskan Eskimo." In Bohannan and Middleton, eds., *Marriage, Family and Residence.*

SPERBER, DAN. *On Anthropological Knowledge: Three Essays.* Cambridge: Cambridge University Press, 1985.

SPETH, JOHN D., AND KATHERINE A. SPIELMANN. "Energy Source, Protein Metabolism, and Hunter-Gatherer Subsistence Strategies." *Journal of Anthropological Archaeology,* 2 (1983): 1–31.

SPINDLER, GEORGE D., ed. *Being an Anthropologist: Fieldwork in Eleven Cultures.* New York: Holt, Rinehart & Winston, 1970.

SPIRO, MELFORD. "Is the Western Conception of the Self 'Peculiar' within the Context of the World Cultures?" *Ethos,* 21 (1993): 107–53.

SPIRO, MELFORD E. *Oedipus in the Trobriands.* Chicago: University of Chicago Press, 1982.

SPIRO, MELFORD. "On the Strange and the Familiar in Recent Anthropological Thought." In Ember, Ember, and Peregrine, eds., *Research Frontiers in Anthropology.*

SPIRO, MELFORD E., AND ROY G. D'ANDRADE. "A Cross-Cultural Study of Some Supernatural Beliefs." *American Anthropologist,* 60 (1958): 456–66.

STAIRS, ARLENE. "Self-Image, World-Image: Speculations on Identity from Experiences with Inuit." *Ethos,* 20 (1992): 116–26.

STARK, RODNEY. *The Future of Religion: Secularization, Revival and Cult Formation.* Berkeley: University of California Press, 1985.

STEINER, CHRISTOPHER B. "Body Personal and Body Politic: Adornment and Leadership in Cross-Cultural Perspective." *Anthropos,* 85 (1990): 431–45.

STEPHENS, WILLIAM N. "A Cross-Cultural Study of Modesty." *Behavior Science Research,* 7 (1972): 1–28.

STEPHENS, WILLIAM N. *The Family in Cross-Cultural Perspective.* New York: Holt, Rinehart & Winston, 1963.

STERN, CURT. *Principles of Human Genetics.* 3rd ed. San Francisco: W. H. Freeman, 1973.

STEWARD, JULIAN H. "The Concept and Method of Cultural Ecology." In Steward, *Theory of Culture Change.*

STEWARD, JULIAN H. *Theory of Culture Change.* Urbana: University of Illinois Press, 1955.

STEWARD, JULIAN H., AND LOUIS C. FARON. *Native Peoples of South America.* New York: McGraw-Hill, 1959.

STEWARD, JULIAN H., ROBERT A. MANNERS, ERIC R. WOLF, ELENA PADILLA SEDA, SIDNEY W. MINTZ, AND RAYMOND L. SCHEELE. *The People of Puerto Rico.* Urbana: University of Illinois Press, 1956.

STIMPSON, DAVID, LARRY JENSEN, AND WAYNE NEFF. "Cross-Cultural Gender Differences in Preference for a Caring Morality." *Journal of Social Psychology,* 132 (1992): 317–22.

STINI, WILLIAM A. "Evolutionary Implications of Changing Nutritional Patterns in Human Populations." *American Anthropologist,* 73 (1971): 1019–30.

STOCKING, GEORGE W., JR., ed. *History of Anthropology.* Vols. 1–6. Madison, WI: University of Wisconsin Press, 1983–1989.

STOGDILL, RALPH M. *Handbook of Leadership: A Survey of Theory and Research.* New York: Macmillan, 1974.

STRAUS, MURRAY A. "Physical Violence in American Families: Incidence Rates, Causes, and Trends." In Knudsen and Miller, eds., *Abused and Battered.*

STRUEVER, STUART, ed. *Prehistoric Agriculture.* Garden City, NY: Natural History Press, 1971.

SWANSON, GUY E. *The Birth of the Gods: The Origin of Primitive Beliefs.* Ann Arbor: University of Michigan Press, 1969.

SWEENEY, JAMES J. "African Negro Culture." In Radin, ed., *African Folktales and Sculpture.*

TALMON, YONINA. "Mate Selection in Collective Settlements." *American Sociological Review,* 29 (1964): 491–508.

TEXTOR, ROBERT B., comp. *A Cross-Cultural Summary.* New Haven, CT: HRAF Press, 1967.

THOMAS, DAVID H. *Refiguring Anthropology: First Principles of Probability and Statistics.* Prospect Heights, IL: Waveland Press, 1986.

THOMAS, ELIZABETH MARSHALL. *The Harmless People.* New York: Knopf, 1959.

THOMASON, SARAH GREY, AND TERRENCE KAUFMAN. *Language Contact, Creolization, and Genetic Linguistics.* Berkeley: University of California Press, 1988.

THOMPSON, RICHARD H. "Chinatowns: Immigrant Communities in Transition." In Ember, Ember, and Levinson, eds., *Portraits of Culture.*

THOMPSON, STITH. "Star Husband Tale." In Dundes, ed., *The Study of Folklore.*

THURNWALD, R. C. "Pigs and Currency in Buin: Observations about Primitive Standards of Value and Economics." *Oceania,* 5 (1934): 119–41.

TIMPANE, JOHN. "Essay: The Poetry of Science." *Scientific American,* July 1991, 128.

TOBIN, JOSEPH J., DAVID Y. H. WU, AND DANA H. DAVIDSON. *Preschool in Three Cultures: Japan, China, and the United States.* New Haven, CT: Yale University Press, 1989.

TOFT, S., ed. *Domestic Violence in Papua New Guinea.* Monograph No. 3. Port Moresby, Papua New Guinea: Law Reform Commission, 1985.

TOLLEFSON, KENNETH D. "Tlingit: Chiefs Past and Present." In Ember, Ember, and Levinson, eds., *Portraits of Culture.*

TORREY, E. FULLER. *The Mind Game: Witchdoctors and Psychiatrists.* New York: Emerson Hall, n.d.

TORRY, WILLIAM I. "Morality and Harm: Hindu Peasant Adjustments to Famines." *Social Science Information,* 25 (1986): 125–60.

TREIMAN, DONALD J., AND HARRY B. G. GANZEBOOM. "Cross-National Comparative Status-Attainment Research." *Research in Social Stratification and Mobility,* 9 (1990): 117.

TREVOR-ROPER, H. R. "The European Witch-Craze of the Sixteenth and Seventeenth Centuries." In Lessa and Vogt, eds., *Reader in Comparative Religion,* 3rd ed.

TRIANDIS, HARRY C., AND ALASTAIR HERON, eds. *Handbook of Cross-Cultural Psychology.* Vol. 4, *Developmental Psychology.* Boston: Allyn & Bacon, 1981.

TROMPF, G. W., ed. *Cargo Cults and Millenarian Movements: Transoceanic Comparisons of New Religious Movements.* Berlin: Mouton de Gruyter, 1990.

TROTTER, ROBERT T., II, ed. *Anthropology for Tomorrow: Creating Practitioner-Oriented Applied Anthropology Programs.* Washington, D.C.: American Anthropological Association, 1988.

TRUDGILL, PETER. *Sociolinguistics: An Introduction to Language and Society.* Rev. ed. New York: Penguin, 1983.

TURNER, PAUL R. "Anthropological Value Positions." *Human Organization,* 41 (1982): 76–79.

TUTTLE, RUSSELL H. *Apes of the World: Their Social Behavior, Communication, Mentality, and Ecology.* Park Ridge, NJ: Noyes Publications, 1986.

TYLOR, EDWARD B. "Animism." In Lessa and Vogt, eds., *Reader in Comparative Religion,* 4th ed.

TYLOR, EDWARD B. *Primitive Culture.* New York: Harper Torchbooks, 1958. (Originally published 1871.)

UBEROI, J. P. SINGH. *The Politics of the Kula Ring: An Analysis of the Findings of Bronislaw Malinowski.* Manchester, England: University of Manchester Press, 1962.

UDY, STANLEY H., JR. *Work in Traditional and Modern Society.* Englewood Cliffs, NJ: Prentice Hall, 1970.

UNDERHILL, RALPH. "Economic and Political Antecedents of Monotheism: A Cross-Cultural Study." *American Journal of Sociology,* 80 (1975): 841–61.

UNDERHILL, RUTH M. *Social Organization of the Papago Indians.* New York: Columbia University Press, 1938.

UNITED NATIONS DEVELOPMENT PROGRAMME. *Human Development Report 1994.* New York: Oxford University Press, 1994.

UNNITHAN, N. PRABHA. "Nayars: Tradition and Change in Marriage and Family." In Ember, Ember, and Levinson, eds., *Portraits of Culture.*

U.S. BUREAU OF THE CENSUS. *Statistical Abstract of the United States: 1993.* 113th ed. Washington, D.C.: U.S. Government Printing Office, 1993.

VANNEMAN, REEVE, AND LYNN WEBER CANNON. *The American Perception of Class.* Philadelphia: Temple University Press, 1987.

VAN WILLIGEN, JOHN. *Applied Anthropology: An Introduction.* South Hadley, MA: Bergin & Garvey, 1986.

VAN WILLIGEN, JOHN, AND TIMOTHY L. FINAN, eds. *Soundings: Rapid and Reliable Research Methods for Practicing Anthropologists.* NAPA Bulletin No. 10. Washington, D.C.: American Anthropological Association, 1990.

VAN WILLIGEN, JOHN, BARBARA RYLKO-BAUER, AND ANN McELROY. *Making Our Research Useful: Case Studies in the Utilization of Anthropological Knowledge.* Boulder, CO: Westview Press, 1989.

VAYDA, ANDREW P. "Pomo Trade Feasts." In Dalton, ed., *Tribal and Peasant Economies.*

VAYDA, ANDREW P., ANTHONY LEEDS, AND DAVID B. SMITH. "The Place of Pigs in Melanesian Subsistence." In Garfield, ed., *Symposium.*

VAYDA, ANDREW P., AND ROY A. RAPPAPORT. "Ecology: Cultural and Noncultural." In Clifton, ed., *Introduction to Cultural Anthropology.*

VIGIL, JAMES DIEGO. "Group Processes and Street Identity: Adolescent Chicano Gang Members." *Ethos,* 16 (1988): 421–45.

VIGIL, JAMES DIEGO. "Mexican Americans: Growing Up on the Streets of Los Angeles." In Ember, Ember, and Levinson, eds., *Portraits of Culture.*

VINCENT, JOAN. "Political Anthropology: Manipulative Strategies." *Annual Review of Anthropology,* 7 (1978): 175–94.

VON FRISCH, KARL. "Dialects in the Language of the Bees." *Scientific American,* August 1962, 78–87.

WADE, EDWIN L., ed. *The Arts of the North American Indian: Native Traditions in Evolution.* New York: Hudson Hills Press, 1986.

WAGLEY, CHARLES. "Cultural Influences on Population: A Comparison of Two Tupi Tribes." In Lyon, ed., *Native South Americans.*

WALLACE, ANTHONY. *The Death and Rebirth of the Seneca.* New York: Knopf, 1970.

WALLACE, ANTHONY. "Mental Illness, Biology and Culture." In Hsu, ed., *Psychological Anthropology*.

WALLACE, ANTHONY. *Religion: An Anthropological View*. New York: Random House, 1966.

WALLACE, ANTHONY, J. LAWRENCE ANGEL, RICHARD FOX, SALLY McLENDON, RACHEL SADY, AND ROBERT SHARER, eds. *Perspectives on Anthropology 1976*. American Anthropological Association Special Publication No. 10. Washington, D.C.: American Anthropological Association, 1977.

WALLERSTEIN, IMMANUEL. *The Modern World-System*. New York: Academic Press, 1974.

WANNER, ERIC, AND LILA R. GLEITMAN, eds. *Language Acquisition: The State of the Art*. Cambridge: Cambridge University Press, 1982.

WARD, PETER M. "Introduction and Purpose." In Ward, ed., *Self-Help Housing*.

WARD, PETER M., ed. *Self-Help Housing: A Critique*. London: Mansell Publishing, 1982.

WARDHAUGH, RICHARD. *An Introduction to Sociolinguistics*. 2nd ed. Oxford: Blackwell, 1992.

WARNER, JOHN ANSON. "The Individual in Native American Art: A Sociological View." In Wade, ed., *The Arts of the North American Indian*.

WARNER, W. LLOYD. *A Black Civilization: A Social Study of an Australian Tribe*. New York: Harper, 1937.

WARNER, W. LLOYD, AND PAUL S. LUNT. *The Social Life of a Modern Community*. New Haven, CT: Yale University Press, 1941.

WARREN, DENNIS M. "Utilizing Indigenous Healers in National Health Delivery Systems: The Ghanaian Experiment." In van Willigen, Rylko-Bauer, and McElry, eds., *Making Our Research Useful*.

WARREN, KAREN, ed. *Ecofeminism: Multidisciplinary Perspectives*. Bloomington: Indiana University Press, 1995.

WARRY, WAYNE. "Kafaina: Female Wealth and Power in Chuave, Papua New Guinea." *Oceania*, 57 (1986): 4–21.

WASHBURN, DOROTHY K., ed. *Structure and Cognition in Art*. Cambridge: Cambridge University Press, 1983.

WEBB, KAREN E. "An Evolutionary Aspect of Social Structure and a Verb 'Have.'" *American Anthropologist*, 79 (1977): 42–49.

WEBER, MAX. *The Theory of Social and Economic Organization*. Trans. A. M. Henderson and Talcott Parsons. New York: Oxford University Press, 1947.

WEINER, ANNETTE B. *Women of Value, Men of Renown: New Perspectives in Trobriand Exchange*. Austin: University of Texas Press, 1976.

WEINREICH, URIEL. *Languages in Contact*. The Hague: Mouton, 1968.

WEISNER, THOMAS S., MARY BAUSANO, AND MADELEINE KORNFEIN. "Putting Family Ideals into Practice: Pronaturalism in Conventional and Nonconventional California Families." *Ethos*, 11 (1983): 278–304.

WEISNER, THOMAS S., AND RONALD GALLIMORE. "My Brother's Keeper: Child and Sibling Caretaking." *Current Anthropology*, 18 (1977): 169–90.

WELLER, SUSAN C. "The Research Process." In Ember, Ember, and Peregrine, eds., *Research Frontiers in Anthropology*.

WERNER, DENNIS. *Amazon Journey: An Anthropologist's Year among Brazil's Mekranoti Indians*. New York: Simon & Schuster, 1984.

WERNER, DENNIS. "Chiefs and Presidents: A Comparison of Leadership Traits in the United States and among the Mekranoti-Kayapo of Central Brazil." *Ethos*, 10 (1982): 136–48.

WERNER, DENNIS. "Child Care and Influence among the Mekranoti of Central Brazil." *Sex Roles*, 10 (1984): 395–404.

WERNER, DENNIS. "A Cross-Cultural Perspective on Theory and Research on Male Homosexuality." *Journal of Homosexuality*, 4 (1979): 345–62.

WERNER, DENNIS. "On the Societal Acceptance or Rejection of Male Homosexuality." M.A. thesis, Hunter College of the City University of New York, 1975.

WERNER, DENNIS. "Trekking in the Amazon Forest." *Natural History*, November 1978, 42–54.

WERNER, OSWALD, AND G. MARK SCHOEPFLE. *Systematic Fieldwork. Volume 1: Foundations of Ethnography and Interviewing*. Newbury Park, CA: Sage Publications, 1987.

WESTERMARCK, EDWARD. *The History of Human Marriage*. London: Macmillan, 1894.

WEYER, E. M. *The Eskimos: Their Environment and Folkways*. New Haven, CT: Yale University Press, 1932.

WHITAKER, IAN. *Social Relations in a Nomadic Lappish Community*. Oslo: Utgitt av Norsk Folksmuseum, 1955.

WHITE, DOUGLAS R. "Rethinking Polygyny: Co-Wives, Codes, and Cultural Systems." *Current Anthropology*, (1988): 529–88.

WHITE, DOUGLAS R., AND MICHAEL L. BURTON. "Causes of Polygyny: Ecology, Economy, Kinship, and Warfare." *American Anthropologist*, 90 (1988): 871–87.

WHITE, DOUGLAS R., MICHAEL L. BURTON, AND LILYAN A. BRUDNER. "Entailment Theory and Method: A Cross-Cultural Analysis of the Sexual Division of Labor." *Behavior Science Research*, 12 (1977): 1–24.

WHITE, LESLIE A. "The Expansion of the Scope of Science." In Morton H. Fried, ed., *Readings in Anthropology*, 2nd ed., vol. 1. New York: Thomas Y. Crowell, 1968.

WHITE, LESLIE A. "A Problem in Kinship Terminology." *American Anthropologist*, 41 (1939): 569–70.

WHITE, LESLIE A. *The Science of Culture: A Study of Man and Civilization*. New York: Farrar, Straus & Cudahy, 1949.

WHITE, N. F., ed. *Ethology and Psychiatry*. Toronto: Ontario Mental Health Foundation and University of Toronto Press, 1974.

WHITING, BEATRICE B. *Paiute Sorcery*. Viking Fund Publications in Anthropology, No. 15. New York: Wenner-Gren Foundation, 1950.

WHITING, BEATRICE B. "Sex Identity Conflict and Physical Violence." *American Anthropologist*, 67 (1965): 123–40.

WHITING, BEATRICE B., ed. *Six Cultures*. New York: John Wiley, 1963.

WHITING, BEATRICE B., AND CAROLYN POPE EDWARDS (in collaboration with Carol R. Ember, Gerald M. Erchak, Sara Harkness, Robert L. Munroe, Ruth H. Munroe, Sara B. Nerlove, Susan Seymour, Charles M. Super, Thomas S. Weisner, and Martha Wenger). *Children of Different Worlds: The Formation of Social Behavior*. Cambridge, MA: Harvard University Press, 1988.

WHITING, BEATRICE B., AND CAROLYN POPE EDWARDS. "A Cross-Cultural Analysis of Sex Differences in the Behavior of Children Aged Three through Eleven." *Journal of Social Psychology*, 91 (1973): 171–88.

WHITING, BEATRICE B., AND JOHN W. M. WHITING (in collaboration with Richard Longabaugh). *Children of Six Cultures: A Psycho-Cultural Analysis*. Cambridge, MA: Harvard University Press, 1975.

WHITING, JOHN W. M. *Becoming a Kwoma*. New Haven, CT: Yale University Press, 1941.

WHITING, JOHN W. M. "Cultural and Sociological Influences on Development." In *Growth and Development of the Child in His Setting*. Maryland Child Growth and Development Institute, 1959.

WHITING, JOHN W. M. "Effects of Climate on Certain Cultural Practices." In Goodenough, ed., *Explorations in Cultural Anthropology*.

WHITING, JOHN W. M., AND IRVIN L. CHILD. *Child Training and Personality: A Cross-Cultural Study*. New Haven, CT: Yale University Press, 1953.

WHYTE, MARTIN K. "Cross-Cultural Codes Dealing with the Relative Status of Women." *Ethnology*, 17 (1978): 211–37.

WHYTE, MARTIN K. *The Status of Women in Preindustrial Societies*. Princeton, NJ: Princeton University Press, 1978.

WIBERG, HAKAN. "Self-Determination as an International Issue." In Lewis, ed., *Nationalism and Self-Determination in the Horn of Africa*.

WILMSEN, EDWIN N., ed. *We Are Here: Politics of Aboriginal Land Tenure*. Berkeley, CA: University of California Press, 1989.

WILSON, MONICA. *Good Company: A Study of Nyakyusa Age Villages*. Boston: Beacon Press, 1963. (Originally published 1951.)

WINKELMAN, MICHAEL JAMES. "Magico-Religious Practitioner Types and Socioeconomic Conditions." *Behavior Science Research*, 20 (1986): 17–46.

WINKELMAN, MICHAEL. "Trance States: A Theoretical Model and Cross-Cultural Analysis." *Ethos*, 14 (1986): 174–203.

WINTERHALDER, BRUCE. "Open Field, Common Pot: Harvest Variability and Risk Avoidance in Agricultural and Foraging Societies." In Cashdan, ed., *Risk and Uncertainty in Tribal and Peasant Economies*.

WITKIN, HERMAN A. "A Cognitive Style Approach to Cross-Cultural Research." *International Journal of Psychology*, 2 (1967): 233–50.

WITKOWSKI, STANLEY R. "Polygyny, Age of Marriage, and Female Status." Paper presented at the annual meeting of the American Anthropological Association, San Francisco, 1975.

WITKOWSKI, STANLEY R., AND CECIL H. BROWN. "Lexical Universals." *Annual Review of Anthropology*, 7 (1978): 427–51.

WITKOWSKI, STANLEY R., AND HAROLD W. BURRIS. "Societal Complexity and Lexical Growth." *Behavior Science Research*, 16 (1981): 143–59.

WOLF, ARTHUR. "Adopt a Daughter-in-Law, Marry a Sister: A Chinese Solution to the Problem of the Incest Taboo." *American Anthropologist*, 70 (1968): 864–74.

WOLF, ARTHUR P., AND CHIEH-SHAN HUANG. *Marriage and Adoption in China, 1845–1945*. Stanford, CA: Stanford University Press, 1980.

WOLF, ERIC R. *Europe and the People without History*. Berkeley: University of California Press, 1982.

WOLF, ERIC. *Peasants*. Englewood Cliffs, NJ: Prentice Hall, 1966.

WOLF, ERIC R. "San José: Subcultures of a 'Traditional' Coffee Municipality." In Steward et al., *The People of Puerto Rico*.

WOLF, ERIC. "Types of Latin American Peasantry: A Preliminary Discussion." *American Anthropologist*, 57 (1955): 452–71.

WOMACK, MARI, AND JUDITH MARTI. *The Other Fifty Percent: Multicultural Perspectives on Gender Relations*. Prospect Heights, IL: Waveland Press, 1993.

"WOMEN IN SCIENCE '93: GENDER AND THE CULTURE OF SCIENCE." *Science*, April 16, 1993, 383–430.

WOOD, GORDON S. *The Radicalism of the American Revolution*. New York: Knopf, 1992.

WOODBURN, JAMES. "An Introduction to Hadza Ecology." In Lee and DeVore, eds., *Man the Hunter*.

WORLDWATCH INSTITUTE. *State of the World 1994: A Worldwatch Institute Report on Progress toward a Sustainable Society*. New York: W. W. Norton, 1994.

WORSLEY, PETER. *The Trumpet Shall Sound: A Study of "Cargo" Cults in Melanesia*. London: MacGibbon & Kee, 1957.

WRIGHT, GARY A. "Origins of Food Production in Southwestern Asia: A Survey of Ideas." *Current Anthropology*, 12 (1971): 447–78.

WRIGHT, GEORGE O. "Projection and Displacement: A Cross-Cultural Study of Folktale Aggression." *Journal of Abnormal and Social Psychology*, 49 (1954): 523–28.

YOUNG, FRANK W. "A Fifth Analysis of the Star Husband Tale." *Ethnology*, 9 (1970): 389–413.

Photo Acknowledgments

Chapter openings and boxes: Textiles, G. Graham/The Graham Collection.

Chapter 1: Page 1, W. & D. McIntyre/Photo Researchers, Inc.; p. 4, J. C. Francolon/Gamma-Liaison, Inc.; p. 5, Irven De Vore/Anthro-Photo; p. 6, Mary Hodge; p. 8, Courtesy of Terence Hays; p. 11, Irven De Vore/Anthro-Photo; p. 12, D. Puleston/Photo Researchers, Inc.

Chapter 2: Page 15, George Hulion/Photo Researchers, Inc.; p. 18, left, A. L. Parnes/Photo Researchers, Inc.; p. 18, right, N. Martin Kauprich/Photo Researchers, Inc.; p. 20, Will & Deni McIntyre/Photo Researchers, Inc.; p. 22, Chuck Savage/The Stock Market; p. 23, left, Chris Marona/Photo Researchers, Inc.; p. 23, top right, Bachmann/Photo Researchers, Inc.; p. 23, bottom right, Maria Taglienti/The Image Bank; p. 28, Photo Researchers, Inc.

Chapter 3: Page 33, John Reader/Science Photo Library/Photo Researchers, Inc.; p. 34, William Strode/Woodfin Camp & Associates; p. 36, Bettmann; p. 40, Ken Heyman/Woodfin Camp & Associates; p. 44, Kal Muller/Woodfin Camp & Associates; p. 45, Courtesy of Richard Scaglion.

Chapter 4: Page 51, Ken Heyman/Woodfin Camp & Associates; p. 55, Michael Gilbert/Science Photo Library/Photo Researchers, Inc.; p. 57, left, Victor Englebert/Photo Researchers, Inc.; p. 57, right, Bildarchiv Okapia/Photo Researchers, Inc.; p. 63, James Prince/Photo Researchers, Inc.

Chapter 5: Page 67, Carolyn Watson; p. 69, David Carter; p. 73, Bill Bachman/Photo Researchers, Inc.; p. 82, Pat & Tom Leeson/Photo Researchers, Inc.; p. 84, left, Rhoda Sidney/Monkmeyer Press; p. 84, right, Renata Hiller/Monkmeyer Press.

Chapter 6: Page 93, Simon Fraser/Science Photo Library/Photo Researchers, Inc.; p. 96, George Holton/Photo Researchers, Inc.; p. 100, Melvin Ember; p. 102, Will & Deni McIntyre/Photo Researchers, Inc.; p. 105, Farrell Grehan/Photo Researchers, Inc.; p. 108, Francois Gohier/Photo Researchers, Inc.

Chapter 7: Page 114, Comstock; p. 119, Paul Shambroom/Photo Researchers, Inc.; p. 124, left, John Roberts/The Stock Market; p. 124, right, Devore/Anthro-Photo; p. 126, Kal Muller/Woodfin Camp & Associates; p. 128, Kim Hill; p. 132, Jose Azel/Woodfin Camp & Associates; p. 136, George Holton/Photo Researchers, Inc.; p. 137, Dana Hyde/Photo Researchers, Inc.

Chapter 8: Page 143, Marc & Evelyne Bernheim From Rapho Guillumette/Woodfin Camp & Associates; p. 144, Eastcott/Momatiuk/Woodfin Camp & Associates; p. 147, Katz/Anthro-Photo; p. 152, Gilda Schiff-Zirinsky/Photo Researchers, Inc.; p. 154, Victor Englebert.

Chapter 9: Page 161, Anthro-Photo; p. 163, Pool J. O. Barcelone/Gamma-Liaison, Inc.; p. 165, Joseph Nettis/Photo Researchers, Inc.; p. 167, Terence Hays; p. 172, Hubertus Kanus/Photo Researchers, Inc.; p. 173, Ann Mohs/Stó:Lo Nation; p. 174, Leonide Principe/Photo Researchers, Inc.; p. 177, Mack Sennett Comedies/The Granger Collection.

Chapter 10: Page 185, Tibor Bognar/The Stock Market; p. 186, Jerry Cooke/Photo Researchers, Inc.; p. 192, Daniele Pellegrini/Photo Researchers, Inc.; p. 194, Asap/Sarit Uzieli/Photo Researchers, Inc.; p. 198, Alan Howard; p. 201, The Granger Collection; p. 206, Eastcott/Momatiuk/Woodfin Camp & Associates.

Chapter 11: Page 212, George Holton/Photo Researchers, Inc.; p. 214, Porterfield/Chichering/Photo Researchers, Inc.; p. 219, Photofest; p. 223, Craig Aurness/Woodfin Camp & Associates; p. 225, American Museum of Natural History.

Chapter 12: Page 238, J. Blair/Cosmos/Woodfin Camp & Associates; p. 240, Leon Oboler; p. 242, Lo Holton/Photo Researchers, Inc.; p. 245, Bruno Barbey/Magnum Photos, Inc.; p. 250, Bernard Wong; p. 251, Wayne Warry.

Chapter 13: Page 256, Andrew Holbrooke/The Stock Market; p. 258, Maria Lepowsky; p. 263, The Granger Collection; p. 264, Reuter/Bettmann; p. 266, The Granger Collection; p. 274, Dan Budnick/Woodfin Camp & Associates; p. 277, Bios (A. Compost)/Peter Arnold, Inc.

Chapter 14: Page 283, M. & E. Bernheim/Woodfin Camp & Associates; p. 285, Bios (A. Compost)/Peter Arnold, Inc.; p. 286, Laura Dwight/Peter Arnold, Inc.; p. 288, top, Noboru Komine/Photo Researchers, Inc.; p. 288, bottom, Barbara Campbell/Gamma-Liaison, Inc.; p. 290, Napoleon A. Chagnon/Anthro-Photo; p. 291, Anthro-Photo; p. 293, M. & E. Bernheim/Woodfin Camp & Associates; p. 298, John Cancalosi/Peter Arnold, Inc.; p. 303, Explorer Luc Girard/Photo Researchers, Inc.

Chapter 15: Page 309, Jean-Loup Gobert/Explorer/Photo Researchers, Inc.; p. 316, Art Resource; p. 318, upper left, Allen Green/Photo Researchers, Inc.; p. 318, lower left, Ray Ellis/Photo Researchers, Inc.; p. 318, upper right, Alain Eurard/Photo Researchers, Inc.; p. 318, bottom right, Blair Seitz/Photo Researchers, Inc.; p. 320, The Granger Collection; p. 321, Shostak/Anthro-Photo; p. 325, The Granger Collection.

Chapter 16: Page 331, Ray Ellis/Photo Researchers, Inc.; p. 333, C. Dashow/Anthro-Photo; p. 336, left, Jack Fields/Photo Researchers, Inc.; p. 336, right, Michal Heron/Woodfin Camp & Associates; p. 340, top, John Cancalosi/Peter Arnold, Inc.; p. 340, bottom, Bridgeman/Art Resource; p. 341, Mario Corvetto/Comstock; p. 342, top, W. Stone/Gamma-Liaison, Inc.; p. 342, bottom, Susan McCartney/Photo Researchers, Inc.; p. 346, Jerry Jacka Photography.

Chapter 17: Page 349, José Azel/Contact Press Images/Woodfin Camp & Associates; p. 351, Philippe Maille/Photo Researchers, Inc.; p. 354, Marcello Bertinetti/Photo Researchers, Inc.; p. 356, The Granger Collection; p. 358, The Granger Collection; p. 361, Victor Englebert; p. 363, The Granger Collection; p. 364, Winston Conrad/ Woodfin Camp & Associates; p. 368, Gamma-Liaison, Inc.

Chapter 18: Page 372, Bonnie Kamin/Comstock; p. 374, Dr. Jill Kleinberg; p. 378, John Moss/Photo Researchers, Inc.; p. 379, Jean-Gérard Sidaner/Photo Researchers, Inc.; p. 384, Comstock; p. 387, Richard Hutchings/ Photo Researchers, Inc.; p. 389, Anthro-Photo; p. 392, Glass/Monkmeyer Press.

Index

Gould, Richard, 94
Graebner, Fritz, 36
Greece, 101, 102, 153-54, 310, 337
Greenberg, Joseph, 79
Grimm, Jakob, 77
Group(s):
  marriage, 200
  selection, 44
Guayaki, 258
Gubser, Nicholas, 276
Guiora, Alexander, 83
Gumperz, John, 79
Gurr, Ted, 391
Gusii, 190, 195

H

Hadza, 116-17
Hall, Edward, 24
Hames, Raymond, 99
Handsome Lake, 323-26
Hardin, Garrett, 116
Hargreaves, James, 350-51
Harris, Marvin, 323
Hausa, 201
Hawaiian kinship terminology system, 230, 233-34
Hays, Terence E., 8-9
Headman, 258, 267
Henry, Patrick, 357-58
Herodotus, 310-11
Herskovits, Melville, 36
Hickey, Gerald, 101
Hill, Jane, 70
Hindus, 16, 317, 323
Historical archaeology, 6
Historical linguistics, 7, 76-79
Historical particularism, 35-36
Historical research, 63-64
Hobsbawm, E. J., 363
Hoebel, E. Adamson, 36, 269, 273
Hohokam, 106
Hoijer, Harry, 82
Hollan, Douglas, 296
Homelessness, 386-88
Homestead Act of 1862, 118
Homosexuality, 178-79, 187
Honigmann, John, 301
Hopi Indians, 27, 83, 274, 345
Hopper, Kim, 387
Horticulture, 98-100, 107, 110, 118, 121
Huichol, 126
Huli, 342
Humanism, 52-53
Human paleontology (paleoanthropology), 2, 4
Human Relations Area Files (HRAF), 58
Human rights, 17
Human sacrifice, 319
Human variation, 2, 4-5
Hutu, 153
Hypotheses, 47, 55

I

Iban, 333
Ibo, 250, 263, 303, 335
Ideal cultural patterns, 24-25
Ifaluk, 301, 302
Iglulik Inuit, 259
Ijaw, 244, 246
Inbreeding theory, 195-96
Incas, 123
Incest taboo, 193-96, 213, 226
Income distribution, 148-50, 388
Indirect contact, diffusion by, 355
Indirect dowry, 193
Individualism, 297
Individual selection, 44
Indo-European languages, 77-79
Infant dependency, 188, 189
Infanticide, 179, 202, 389-90
Innovations, 350-53, 359-60
Integrated culture, 28-29
Intensive-agricultural societies, 98, 101-3, 107, 110, 118-19, 121
Interest groups, 239, 251
Interethnic communication, 88
Interpretive approaches, 45-47
Interracial marriage, 153
Inuit (Eskimo), 95-96, 105, 120, 129, 168, 189, 190, 259, 270, 276, 296, 301, 302, 334, 335, 356
  kinship terminology system, 230-31
Inventions, culture change and, 350-53
Iroquois Indians, 129, 170, 173
Iroquois kinship terminology system, 230, 232-33
Irrigation, 106-8
Itkonen, T. I., 104

J

Jackson, Andrew, 120
James, William, 311
Jankowiak, William, 367
Japanese, 39-40, 85, 294-95, 296, 336, 340, 342, 354, 355, 374-78
Javanese, 84
Jefferson, Thomas, 357, 358
Johnson, Samuel, 239
Jones, Sir William, 77
Jung, Carl, 311, 313

K

Kafaina, 245, 251
Kagwahiv, 267
Kapauku Papuans, 125, 224-25, 227
Kardiner, Abram, 39, 40, 303
Karimojong, 240-42, 262
Katcinas, 317

Kay, Paul, 80-81
Kayapo, 98, 171, 380-81
Keller, Helen, 68
Khosroshashi, Fatemeh, 86
Kibbutz, 273
Kilbride, Janet, 201
Kilbride, Philip, 201
Kindred, 221-22
Kinship, 219-34
    ambilineal descent, 229-30
    bilateral, 221-22, 228
    political organization and, 259, 261-62
    reciprocity and, 131
    rules of descent, 219-21
    terminology, 230-34
    unilineal descent, 222-28
Kleinberg, Jill, 374, 375
Klinberg, Otto, 284
Kluckhohn, Clyde, 343
Knauft, Bruce, 326
Koasati language, 85
Kosciusko, Tadeusz, 357
Kpelle, 131, 244, 333
Krauss, Michael, 72
Kroeber, Alfred, 36, 38
Kru, 250
Kuikuru, 122
Kula ring, 130-31
Kulturkreis school, 36, 38
Kumdi-Engamoi, 268
!Kung, 18, 28, 29, 96, 120, 125, 127-29, 171, 321, 334, 335
Kurds, 199
Kurgan culture, 78-79
Kwakiutl Indians, 198, 321
Kwashiorkor, 27, 54, 202
Kwoma, 189, 190

L

Labor:
    division of, 124-25
    forced, 123-24
    incentives for, 122-23
    organization of, 125-26
    specialization of, 126
Laitman, Jane, 70
Lakoff, Robin, 85
Lakota Indians, 245
Lambert, William, 298, 315
Land ownership, 115-20
Language(s) (*see also* Linguistics; Speech)
    children's acquisition of, 71-73
    core vocabulary of, 82
    Creole, 71, 73
    endangered, 72
    families, 77-79
    grammar, 80, 82
    lexical content of, 80-82
    multilingualism, 86-88
    origins of, 70-73

    processes of divergence, 79-80
    relationship between culture and, 80-83
    symbolic quality of, 21
Lapps, 104-5, 356, 368
Later evolutionism, 40-41
Laws, 54
Leach, Edmund, 41
Leacock, Eleanor, 43
Lee, Richard B., 97
Leeds, Anthony, 131
Lenski, Gerhard, 155-56
Lepcha, 178
Lesu, 178
LeVine, Barbara, 190
LeVine, Robert, 190, 297, 302-3
Levinson, David, 390
Levirate, 199
Lévi-Strauss, Claude, 41, 42, 195
Lichter, Daniel, 205
Lieberman, Philip, 70
Life expectancy, 153
Lineages, 223, 226
Linguistics, 2, 4
    historical, 7, 76-79
    processes of divergence, 79-80
    structural (descriptive), 7, 73-76
Linton, Ralph, 19, 39, 201, 350, 354, 355
Little, Kenneth, 250-51
Logoli, 291
Lomax, Alan, 338-40, 343
Low, Bobbi, 45
Lowie, Robert, 36
Lugbara, 315, 317
Lunt, Paul, 147
Luo, 76, 135-36, 176, 221
Lutz, Catherine, 301, 302
Lynd, Helen, 147
Lynd, Robert, 147

M

McClelland, David, 302
McDowell, Nancy, 174
Mae Enga, 243
Magic, 319-21
Maladaptive customs, 27
Malinowski, Bronislaw, 37, 38, 195, 285, 311, 323
Malnutrition, 299
Mamvu, 124
Mana, 262, 314
Mangebetu, 333
Mangin, William, 247
Manumission, 154
Manus, 191
Maori, 170, 314
Marett, R. R., 311, 313
Marital residence patterns, 213-18
Market foraging, 103
Market or commercial exchange, 133, 135-37

culture change and, 364-67
defined, 310
magic in, 319-21
monotheism, 315
polytheism, 315
types of practitioner, 321-23
universality of, 310-13
variation in beliefs, 313-17
variation in practice, 317-23
Remarriage, 204
Renfrew, Colin, 79
Replication, 57
Research:
  cross-cultural, 9, 60, 63
  explanations, 52-53, 56-59
  historical, 63-64
  theories, 54-56
  types of, 59-64
Resocialization, 150
Resources:
  allocation of, 115-21
  conversion of, 121-27
Revitalization movements, 323-26
Revolution, 357-59
Richerson, Peter, 359
Rickman, John, 39
Ritual reconciliation, 272
Rivers, W. H. R., 36
Roberts, John, 273, 303
Rohner, Ronald, 291
Romance languages, 77
Romantic love, 197
Rosenblatt, Paul, 17
Ross, Marc, 171, 246, 268
Rucuyen, 178
Rules of descent, 219-21
Ruskin, John, 151
Russians, 39
Rwala Bedouin, 272

S

Sacrifice, 318-19
Sahlins, Marshall, 41, 131, 155-56
Salaff, Janet, 366
Salinization, 106
Samoans, 60-61, 74, 75, 99, 100, 203, 216, 230, 285
Sampling, 57-58
Sande associations, 243-44
Sanggai rituals, 243
Sanpoil, 314
Sanskrit, 77
Saora, 300
Sapir, Edward, 20, 36, 39, 82-83, 86
Sapir-Whorf hypothesis, 83
Saramakas, 345
Savannas, 107
Scaglion, Richard, 46
Schlegel, Alice, 216, 228, 285
Schmidt, Father Wilhelm, 36

Schwartz, Richard, 273
Science, humanism and, 52-53
Scribner, Sylvia, 295
Scudder, Thayer, 379
Secondary institutions, 39, 303
Secondary subsistence activities, 167-69
Segmentary lineage system, 259, 261-62
Self, concept of, 296-97
Semai, 284, 289
Semang, 120, 258
Seneca Indians, 323-26
Sensorimotor stage of development, 286
Serranos, 247-48
Service, Ellman, 41, 218, 258, 265, 266
Sex differences, 162-76
  division of labor, 124-25, 162-65, 188, 189
  morality and, 300-301
  in personality, 174-76
  in physique and physiology, 162
  political leadership and, 166, 169-73
  primary and secondary subsistence activities and,
    167-69
  relative status of women and, 172-74
  in speech, 85-87
  warfare and, 170-71
Sexual competition, 188
Sexual dimorphism, 162
Sexuality:
  extramarital, 177-79
  homosexuality, 178-79, 187
  within marriage, 178
  premarital, 60-61, 176-77, 179
  reasons for restrictiveness, 179-80
Shamans, 319, 321-23, 357, 375-76
Shankman, Paul, 60-61
Sharing, 18
Shavante, 241-42
Shoshone-Bannock Indians, 346
Single-case analysis, 56
Sinhalese, 202
Sino-Tibetan languages, 77
Siriono, 178
Siwai, 200
Siwans, 178
Six Cultures study, 176, 292, 298
Slash-and-burn techniques, 98, 99
Slavery, 124, 153-55, 276, 319
Slums, 386
Smith, David, 131
Smith, G. Elliot, 36
Socialism, 119
Socialization, 290-98
Social mobility, 147, 150
Social status, speech and, 84-85
Social stratification, 144-58, 336-37, 368
  arts and, 336-37, 346
  class societies, 145, 146-55
  egalitarian societies, 145-46, 336-37
  emergence of, 155-57
  rank societies, 145, 146
  variation in degree of, 145
Society for Applied Anthropology, 376, 377

Vayda, Andrew, 42, 131
Virginity, 177, 179
Visual art, 335-37
Vocabulary, 71, 80-82
Voluntary associations, 245-53
Voodoo, 317

W

Wallace, Anthony, 302, 314, 317, 323
Wallerstein, Immanuel, 43
Wardhaugh, Richard, 83
Warfare, 275, 393-94
   explanations for, 277-78
   internal vs. external, 170-71
   unilineal descent and, 227, 228
Warner, W. Lloyd, 147
Washington, George, 358
Washoe (chimpanzee), 69, 70
Wealth, 148-51
Wellenkamp, Jane, 296
Werner, Dennis, 171
Westermarck, Edward, 193-95
Whitaker, Ian, 104
White, Leslie A., 40, 41
Whiting, Beatrice, 176, 320-21
Whiting, John, 40, 54-59, 62, 176, 201, 202, 297, 298, 303
Whorf, Benjamin Lee, 82-83, 86
Whyte, Martin, 172, 173

Wife beating, 390
Winnebago Indians, 186
Wishram language, 76
Wissler, Clark, 36, 38
Witchcraft, 319-21, 322
Witch doctors, 319
Wolf, Arthur, 194
Wolf, Eric, 43
Wolf, Margery, 315
Women's associations, 244, 246-47, 251
Worsley, Peter, 326
Wright, George, 344
Wu, David, 294

Y

Yahi Indians, 357
Yanomamö Indians, 57, 98-100, 128, 167, 174, 192, 284, 289, 290
Yapese, 178
Yoruba, 202, 250, 302
Yucatán, 5

Z

Zo (secret society), 244
Zuni Indians, 317